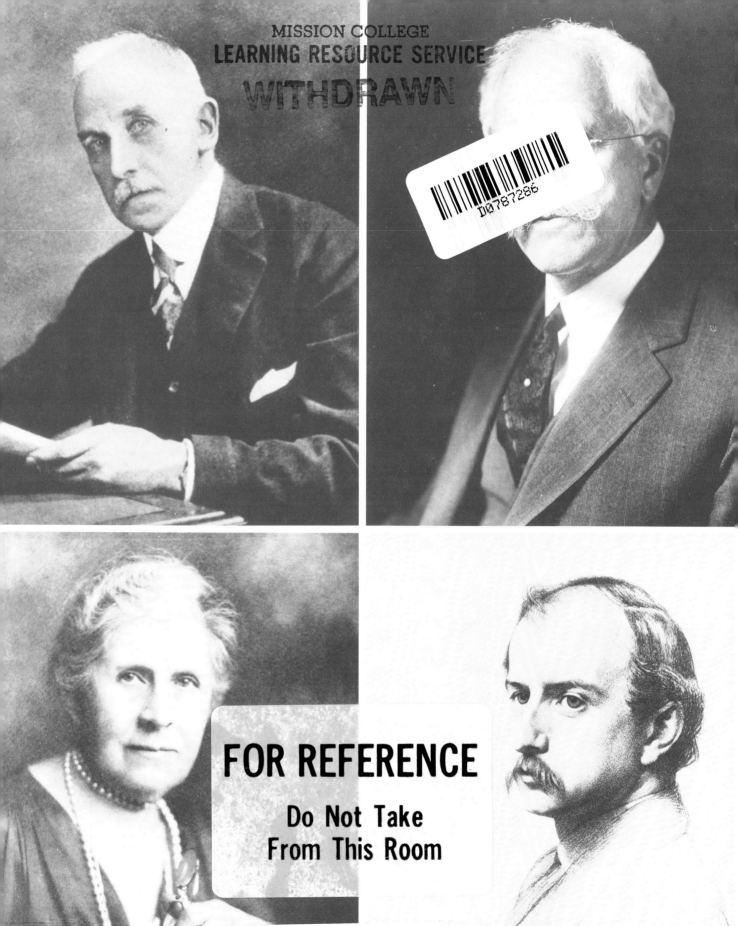

Dictionary of Literary Biography • Volume Forty-seven

American Historians, 1866-1912

Dictionary of Literary Biography

1: *The American Renaissance in New England,* edited by Joel Myerson (1978)

2: *American Novelists Since World War II,* edited by Jeffrey Helterman and Richard Layman (1978)

3: *Antebellum Writers in New York and the South,* edited by Joel Myerson (1979)

4: *American Writers in Paris, 1920-1939,* edited by Karen Lane Rood (1980)

5: *American Poets Since World War II,* 2 parts, edited by Donald J. Greiner (1980)

6: *American Novelists Since World War II,* Second Series, edited by James E. Kibler, Jr. (1980)

7: *Twentieth-Century American Dramatists,* 2 parts, edited by John Mac-Nicholas (1981)

8: *Twentieth-Century American Science-Fiction Writers,* 2 parts, edited by David Cowart and Thomas L. Wymer (1981)

9: *American Novelists, 1910-1945,* 3 parts, edited by James J. Martine (1981)

10: *Modern British Dramatists, 1900-1945,* 2 parts, edited by Stanley Weintraub (1982)

11: *American Humorists, 1800-1950,* 2 parts, edited by Stanley Trachtenberg (1982)

12: *American Realists and Naturalists,* edited by Donald Pizer and Earl N. Harbert (1982)

13: *British Dramatists Since World War II,* 2 parts, edited by Stanley Weintraub (1982)

14: *British Novelists Since 1960,* 2 parts, edited by Jay L. Halio (1983)

15: *British Novelists, 1930-1959,* 2 parts, edited by Bernard Oldsey (1983)

16: *The Beats: Literary Bohemians in Postwar America,* 2 parts, edited by Ann Charters (1983)

17: *Twentieth-Century American Historians,* edited by Clyde N. Wilson (1983)

18: *Victorian Novelists After 1885,* edited by Ira B. Nadel and William E. Fredeman (1983)

19: *British Poets, 1880-1914,* edited by Donald E. Stanford (1983)

20: *British Poets, 1914-1945,* edited by Donald E. Stanford (1983)

21: *Victorian Novelists Before 1885,* edited by Ira B. Nadel and William E. Fredeman (1983)

22: *American Writers for Children, 1900-1960,* edited by John Cech (1983)

23: *American Newspaper Journalists, 1873-1900,* edited by Perry J. Ashley (1983)

24: *American Colonial Writers, 1606-1734,* edited by Emory Elliott (1984)

25: *American Newspaper Journalists, 1901-1925,* edited by Perry J. Ashley (1984)

26: *American Screenwriters,* edited by Robert E. Morsberger, Stephen O. Lesser, and Randall Clark (1984)

27: *Poets of Great Britain and Ireland, 1945-1960,* edited by Vincent B. Sherry, Jr. (1984)

28: *Twentieth-Century American-Jewish Fiction Writers,* edited by Daniel Walden (1984)

29: *American Newspaper Journalists, 1926-1950,* edited by Perry J. Ashley (1984)

30: *American Historians, 1607-1865,* edited by Clyde N. Wilson (1984)

31: *American Colonial Writers, 1735-1781,* edited by Emory Elliott (1984)

32: *Victorian Poets Before 1850,* edited by William E. Fredeman and Ira B. Nadel (1984)

33: *Afro-American Fiction Writers After 1955,* edited by Thadious M. Davis and Trudier Harris (1984)

34: *British Novelists, 1890-1929: Traditionalists,* edited by Thomas F. Staley (1985)

35: *Victorian Poets After 1850,* edited by William E. Fredeman and Ira B. Nadel (1985)

36: *British Novelists, 1890-1929: Modernists,* edited by Thomas F. Staley (1985)

37: *American Writers of the Early Republic,* edited by Emory Elliott (1985)

38: *Afro-American Writers After 1955: Dramatists and Prose Writers,* edited by Thadious M. Davis and Trudier Harris (1985)

39: *British Novelists, 1660-1800,* 2 parts, edited by Martin C. Battestin (1985)

40: *Poets of Great Britain and Ireland Since 1960,* 2 parts, edited by Vincent B. Sherry, Jr. (1985)

41: *Afro-American Poets Since 1955,* 2 parts, edited by Trudier Harris and Thadious M. Davis (1985)

42: *American Writers for Children Before 1900,* edited by Glenn E. Estes (1985)

43: *American Newspaper Journalists, 1690-1872,* edited by Perry J. Ashley (1985)

44: *American Screenwriters,* Second Series, edited by Randall Clark (1986)

45: *American Poets, 1880-1945,* First Series, edited by Peter Quartermain (1986)

46: *American Literary Publishing Houses, 1900-1980,* edited by Peter Dzwonkoski (1986)

47: *American Historians, 1866-1912,* edited by Clyde N. Wilson (1986)

Documentary Series

1: *Sherwood Anderson, Willa Cather, John Dos Passos, Theodore Dreiser, F. Scott Fitzgerald, Ernest Hemingway, Sinclair Lewis,* edited by Margaret A. Van Antwerp (1982)

2: *James Gould Cozzens, James T. Farrell, William Faulkner, John O'Hara, John Steinbeck, Thomas Wolfe, Richard Wright,* edited by Margaret A. Van Antwerp (1982)

3: *Saul Bellow, Jack Kerouac, Norman Mailer, Vladimir Nabokov, John Updike, Kurt Vonnegut,* edited by Mary Bruccoli (1983)

4: *Tennessee Williams,* edited by Margaret A. Van Antwerp and Sally Johns (1984)

Yearbooks

1980, edited by Karen L. Rood, Jean W. Ross, and Richard Ziegfeld (1981)

1981, edited by Karen L. Rood, Jean W. Ross, and Richard Ziegfeld (1982)

1982, edited by Richard Ziegfeld; associate editors: Jean W. Ross and Lynne C. Zeigler (1983)

1983, edited by Mary Bruccoli and Jean W. Ross; associate editor: Richard Ziegfeld (1984)

1984, edited by Jean W. Ross (1985)

Dictionary of Literary Biography • Volume Forty-seven

American Historians, 1866-1912

Edited by
Clyde N. Wilson
University of South Carolina

A Bruccoli Clark Book
Gale Research Company • Book Tower • Detroit, Michigan 48226

Manufactured by Edwards Brothers, Inc.
Ann Arbor, Michigan
Printed in the United States of America

Library of Congress Cataloging-in-Publication Data
Main entry under title:

American historians, 1866-1912.

(Dictionary of literary biography; v. 47)
"A Bruccoli Clark book."
Includes index.
I. Histories—United States—Biography. I. Wilson.
Clyde Norman. II. Title. III. Series.
E175.45.A483 1986 973'.072022   85-29245
ISBN 0-8103-1725-7

For Anne and Lee

Contents

Plan of the Series

The advisory board, the editors, and the publisher of the *Dictionary of Literary Biography* are joined in endorsing Mark Twain's declaration. The literature of a nation provides an inexhaustible resource of permanent worth. It is our expectation that this endeavor will make literature and its creators better understood and more accessible to students and the literate public, while satisfying the standards of teachers and scholars.

To meet these requirements, *literary biography* has been construed in terms of the author's achievement. The most important thing about a writer is his writing. Accordingly, the entries in *DLB* are career biographies, tracing the development of the author's canon and the evolution of his reputation.

The publication plan for *DLB* resulted from two years of preparation. The project was proposed to Bruccoli Clark by Frederick G. Ruffner, president of the Gale Research Company, in November 1975. After specimen entries were prepared and typeset, an advisory board was formed to refine the entry format and develop the series rationale. In meetings held during 1976, the publisher, series editors, and advisory board approved the scheme for a comprehensive biographical dictionary of persons who contributed to North American literature. Editorial work on the first volume began in January 1977, and it was published in 1978.

In order to make *DLB* more than a reference tool and to compile volumes that individually have claim to status as literary history, it was decided to organize volumes by topic or period or genre. Each of these freestanding volumes provides a biographical-bibliographical guide and overview for a particular area of literature. We are convinced that this organization—as opposed to a single alphabet method—constitutes a valuable innovation in the presentation of reference material. The volume

plan necessarily requires many decisions for the placement and treatment of authors who might properly be included in two or three volumes. In some instances a major figure will be included in separate volumes, but with different entries emphasizing the aspect of his career appropriate to each volume. Ernest Hemingway, for example, is represented in *American Writers in Paris, 1920-1939* by an entry focusing on his expatriate apprenticeship; he is also in *American Novelists, 1910-1945* with an entry surveying his entire career. Each volume includes a cumulative index of subject authors. The final *DLB* volume will be a comprehensive index to the entire series.

With volume ten in 1982 it was decided to enlarge the scope of *DLB* beyond the literature of the United States. By the end of 1985 twenty-one volumes treating British literature had been published, and volumes for Commonwealth and Modern European literature were in progress. The series has been further augmented by the *DLB Year-books* (since 1981) which update published entries and add new entries to keep the *DLB* current with contemporary activity. There have also been occasional *DLB Documentary Series* volumes which provide biographical and critical background source materials for figures whose work is judged to have particular interest for students. One of these companion volumes is entirely devoted to Tennessee Williams.

The purpose of *DLB* is not only to provide reliable information in a convenient format but also to place the figures in the larger perspective of literary history and to offer appraisals of their accomplishments by qualified scholars.

We define literature as the *intellectual commerce of a nation:* not merely as belles lettres, but as that ample and complex process by which ideas are generated, shaped, and transmitted. *DLB* entries are not limited to "creative writers" but extend to other figures who in this time and in this way influenced the mind of a people. Thus the series encompasses historians, journalists, publishers, and screenwriters. By this means readers of *DLB* may be aided to perceive literature not as cult scripture in the keeping of cultural high priests, but as at the center of a nation's life.

DLB includes the major writers appropriate to each volume and those standing in the ranks immediately behind them. Scholarly and critical counsel has been sought in deciding which minor figures to include and how full their entries should be. Wherever possible, useful references will be made to figures who do not warrant separate entries.

Each *DLB* volume has a volume editor responsible for planning the volume, selecting the figures for inclusion, and assigning the entries. Volume editors are also responsible for preparing, where appropriate, appendices surveying the major periodicals and literary and intellectual movements for their volumes, as well as lists of further readings. Work on the series as a whole is coordinated at the Bruccoli Clark editorial center in Columbia, South Carolina, where the editorial staff is responsible for the accuracy of the published volumes.

One feature that distinguishes *DLB* is the illustration policy—its concern with the iconography of literature. Just as an author is influenced by his surroundings, so is the reader's understanding of the author enhanced by a knowledge of his environment. Therefore *DLB* volumes include not only drawings, paintings, and photographs of authors, often depicting them at various stages in their careers, but also illustrations of their families and places where they lived. Title pages are regularly reproduced in facsimile along with dust jackets for modern authors. The dust jackets are a special feature of *DLB* because they often document better than anything else the way in which an author's work was launched in its own time. Specimens of the writers' manuscripts are included when feasible.

A supplement to *DLB*—tentatively titled *A Guide, Chronology, and Glossary for American Literature*—will outline the history of literature in North America and trace the influences that shaped it. This volume will provide a framework for the study of American literature by means of chronological tables, literary affiliation charts, glossarial entries, and concise surveys of the major movements. It has been planned to stand on its own as a vade mecum, providing a ready-reference guide to the study of American literature as well as a companion to the *DLB* volumes for American literature.

Samuel Johnson rightly decreed that "The chief glory of every people arises from its authors." The purpose of the *Dictionary of Literary Biography* is to compile literary history in the surest way available to us—by accurate and comprehensive treatment of the lives and work of those who contributed to it.

The *DLB* Advisory Board

Foreword

American Historians, 1866-1912 is a companion to *DLB 17: Twentieth-Century American Historians* and *DLB 30: American Historians, 1607-1865.* This volume is designed to present permanently useful treatments of the more important American writers of history whose first works were published between the end of the Civil War and 1912. The year 1912 saw publication of James Harvey Robinson's *The New History: Essays Illustrating the Modern Historical Outlook* and is thus a convenient dividing point marking a shift in historical styles. However, like all dates used by historians to designate the beginnings and endings of eras, it is merely a useful benchmark and can be misleading if applied too literally to mean that historical writing was all of one sort one year and all of another sort the next.

Historians are notorious for their long careers, and the professional lives of some of the figures treated in this volume continued well into the twentieth century, the period covered by *DLB 17.* Only writers of United States history are discussed in *DLB 17.* Those who might be considered twentieth-century figures but who devoted their energies to fields other than U.S. history are included here. For example, of the five master essays herein, three concern giants from the first generation of American professional historical scholars who went abroad to find their subject matter. These are James Henry Breasted, Charles Homer Haskins, and James Harvey Robinson, pioneering Americans and masters, respectively, in ancient, medieval, and modern European history. The other two master entries are devoted to Henry Adams, whom some have claimed as the greatest of American historians and who is certainly sui generis and a major figure in any accounting; and John Bach McMaster, whose monumental work as a social historian marked a decisive broadening of the content of historical writings.

The late nineteenth century was preeminently the period of the professionalization of the historian in America. During that period young Americans, some trained in the research seminars of German universities, first established themselves as full-time historians associated with institutions of higher education and research. Beginning in the 1870s Johns Hopkins, Columbia, Harvard, and other schools began offering graduate training in history and soon after began regularly publishing scholarly monographs that were the products of research by their faculties and students in history. The American Historical Association was founded in 1884, and the *American Historical Review*, a scholarly journal, in 1895.

The emphasis of the new historical professionals was on training in research methods, on exhaustive use of primary sources, on detachment and objectivity, and on the study of the way in which institutions had evolved. This was in contrast to the traditional gentleman scholars and popular writers who had supposedly concentrated on literary polish, been deeply committed patriots and partisans, and portrayed great men and spectacular events at the expense of fundamental economic and social factors. At its theoretical extreme the new school appeared to postulate that sufficient accumulation of objective data would establish a historical knowledge that constituted permanent truth and even uncover scientific laws of causation and evolution in human affairs.

Few American historians, it is true, subscribed to the extreme ideal of "scientific history," at least in practice. Their national character was too pragmatic, and for the most part the Americans quietly shucked off the vaster claims (though not the prestige) of the new school as well as the Hegelianism that had accompanied it in its Continental origins. What was essentially different about the academic historians was their professional self-consciousness, their interest in underlying institutional evolution, and their disengagement from popular historical mythology and old controversies. Even so, they did not depart quite so sharply from what their predecessors in historical writing had done as they sometimes imagined.

The "New History," a broad movement for which Robinson's 1912 book serves as a convenient benchmark, was a conscious rejection of "scientific history," even though the "New History," too, was a movement chiefly of academic professionals. The "New History" accepted, even joyfully embraced, the principle that the historian's work was not and never could be conclusive, but was inescapably subjective. History was not a finished body of knowledge but an exercise in finding and interpreting what in the past was relevent to the present—a task that had to be repeated by each generation for itself. Though there was no necessary logical connection between reform and the realization that historical knowledge was subjective, the "New History" was usually "Progressive," that is, it was accompanied by social engagement of a melioristic cast. Thus, Robinson's collaborator Charles A. Beard believed that in describing (in his *An Economic Interpretation of the Constitution of the United States*, 1913) how the Constitution had been motivated at least in part by economic class interests, he was liberating Americans from a misguided piety that diverted them from solving their current problems.

As in *Twentieth-Century American Historians* and *American Historians, 1607-1865*, in this volume historical writing has been defined as a retrospective examination of the past. The definition excludes that body of literature composed of firsthand accounts of historical events. To include writers of such books would expand the material to be compassed to unmanageable dimensions. For the period 1866-1912 the literature based on firsthand observations of politics, of business, of exploration, and of other phases of American experience is voluminous. Participants in the Civil War who produced such literature after 1865 would fill several *DLB* volumes, even if only the most meritorious works were discussed. But because the recording of the Civil War loomed so large in the era covered by this volume, an appendix has been included that describes two of the period's major publications related to the nation's most sanguinary and memorable conflict.

That the period of historical writing surveyed by this volume was that of "scientific history" is necessary to state. But however necessary this categorization is by way of introduction, it does not subsume the whole of the American historical literature produced in that time. The gentleman scholar, the popular writer, and the literary entrepreneur did not disappear from the field of history. They remained numerous, were influenced by and in turn influenced the professionals, and were even joined by a new type of historian, the crusading muckraker. As with *DLB 17* and *DLB 30*, the net has been cast wide to include historical writers of many types.

Historians of the period 1866-1912 might be nationalists or regionalists or cosmopolitans; they might approach the past in a spirit that was romantic, scientific, or reformist; or they might belong to the familiar tradition of the antiquarian or cultural preservationist. No approach or orientation necessarily excluded another. A single historian often combined, knowingly or unknowingly, two or more. Whatever their styles and motivations, all the writers in this volume contributed to the "intellectual commerce of the nation," which it is the goal of the *Dictionary of Literary Biography* to record.

—Clyde N. Wilson

Acknowledgments

Special thanks are due from the editor to Professor John Braeman.

This book was produced by BC Research. Karen L. Rood is senior editor for the *Dictionary of Literary Biography* series. Margaret A. Van Antwerp was the in-house editor.

Art supervisor is Patricia M. Flanagan. Copyediting supervisor is Patricia Coate. Production coordinator is Kimberly Casey. Typesetting supervisor is Laura Ingram. The production staff includes Rowena Betts, Matt Brook, Deborah Cavanaugh, Kathleen M. Flanagan, Joyce Fowler, Pamela Haynes, Judith K. Ingle, Vickie Lowers, Beatrice McClain, Judith McCray, George Stone Saussy, Mary Scott Sims, Joycelyn R. Smith, and Lucia Tarbox. Jean W. Ross is permissions editor. Joseph Caldwell, photography editor, and James Adam Sutton did photographic copy work for the volume.

Walter W. Ross did the library research with the assistance of the staff at the Thomas Cooper Library of the University of South Carolina: Lynn Barron, Daniel Boice, Connie Crider, Kathy Eckman, Michael Freeman, Gary Geer, David L. Haggard, Jens Holley, Marcia Martin, Dana Rabon, Jean Rhyne, Jan Squire, Ellen Tillett, and Virginia Weathers.

Dictionary of Literary Biography • Volume Forty-seven

American Historians, 1866-1912

Dictionary of Literary Biography

Brooks Adams
(24 June 1848-13 February 1927)

Clyde N. Wilson
University of South Carolina

SELECTED BOOKS: *The Emancipation of Massa-chusetts* (Boston & New York: Houghton Mif-flin, 1887); revised and enlarged as *The Emancipation of Massachusetts; The Dream and the Reality* (Boston & New York: Houghton Mifflin, 1919);

The Gold Standard. An Historical Study (Boston: Printed by A. Mudge & Son, 1894; revised, Washington, D.C.: R. Beall, 1895; revised again, 1896);

The Law of Civilization and Decay. An Essay on History (London: Sonnenschein, 1895; revised, New York: Macmillan, 1896); revised again and translated as *La Loi de la civilisation et de la décadence* (Paris: Atlan, 1899);

America's Economic Supremacy (New York & London: Macmillan, 1900);

The New Empire (New York & London: Macmillan, 1902);

The Theory of Social Revolutions (New York: Macmillan, 1913).

OTHER: "Nature of Law: Methods and Aim of Legal Education" and "Law under Inequality; Monopoly," in *Centralization and the Law*, ed-ited by Melville M. Bigelow (Boston: Little, Brown, 1906), pp. 20-134;

"The Seizure of the Laird Rams," in *Proceedings of the Massachusetts Historical Society*, 45 (Decem-ber 1911): 243-333;

"The Revolt of Modern Democracy against Stan-dards of Duty," in *Proceedings of the American Academy of Arts and Letters*, 2 (November 1916): 8-12;

"The Heritage of Henry Adams," in *The Degrada-tion of the Democratic Dogma*, by Henry Adams

Brooks Adams

(New York: Macmillan, 1920), pp. 1-22.

Brooks Adams's books are no longer read as history (if indeed they ever were), but they remain in the judgment of divers authorities significant documents for the historical study of American thought in the late nineteenth and early twentieth centuries. Possibly no American historical writer is more difficult to characterize and evaluate than Brooks Adams. It is safe to say that he would have been amused and not at all surprised at the ambiguity of his reputation more than a half century after his death, for during his lifetime he took evident satisfaction in being considered complicated, eccentric, perverse, and misunderstood. He referred to himself more than once as "an unusable man" and "a crank" who very few people could bear to have about.

A partial account of favorable responses to his work indicates something about both its importance and the difficulty of evaluating it. Charles A. Beard, dean of Progressive historians, considered Adams's *The Law of Civilization and Decay* (1895) to be one of the "outstanding documents of intellectual history in the United States and . . . the Western World." Vernon L. Parrington devoted a complimentary chapter, entitled "Brooks Adams, Rebel," to him in *Main Currents in American Thought* (1930). According to Parrington, Brooks was a fit heir of John Adams, and he had pointed out "to a romantic generation the unpleasant realities that confuted its optimism." Both Beard and Parrington were doubtless attracted by Adams's economic determinism and distaste for finance capitalism. But, from an entirely different standpoint, Russell Kirk, dean of conservative writers, devoted a section of *The Conservative Mind* (1968) to Adams, finding him, in some respects, sympathetic. Perry Miller, who deplored Adams's debunking of the Puritans, considered him a writer possessing those "rare qualities" that should be "treasured wherever they appear" and declared in his introduction to a 1962 edition of Adams's *Emancipation of Massachusetts* that Adams had "read the lesson of modern civilization" profoundly.

Brooks Adams was the youngest of the six children of Charles Francis Adams and Abigail Brooks Adams. He was born in Quincy, Massachusetts, in the same year that his father was the Free Soil candidate for vice president of the United States and that his grandfather John Quincy Adams died. He was the younger brother of Henry and Charles Francis Adams, Jr.

During the Civil War, when his father was U.S. minister to Great Britain, Brooks Adams, like his brother Henry, spent time in Europe and attended English schools. He was graduated from Harvard in 1870 and then spent a year at the Harvard Law School, passing the bar examinations and

being admitted to practice without completing his law school studies. After a brief period of practice, he accompanied his father to Europe once more as a secretary during the Alabama Claims arbitration.

The Adams family fortunes fluctuated somewhat during the economic turbulence of the late nineteenth century—which was not without relevance to the content of Brooks Adams's historical writings—but he was always a man of means whose problem was not to find gainful employment but to occupy his time. Given the self-exile of his generation of Adams men from public life, indirect participation in public affairs through writing was a natural outlet. Even in the midst of a busy career his father had prepared editions of the works of John Adams and the diaries of John Quincy Adams. Brooks Adams's resources were such that he was able to make leisurely visits to most of Europe, the Mideast, and India and to pursue such studies as he wished.

Prior to the publication of his first book he had published more than twenty articles and reviews, mostly on public affairs. His first extended historical effort, *The Emancipation of Massachusetts* (1887), clearly revealed a man involved in the damaging love-hate relationship with his background that was to mark him all his life. The purpose of the book, on the face of it, was to show in convincing detail that Massachusetts, during the revered period of its seventeenth-century founders, was in fact "a petty state" ruled by an "autocratic priesthood"; that it was not "in reality the thing which its historians have described . . . not a society guided by men devoted to civil liberty, and as liberal in religion as was consistent with the temper of their age. . . ." The editor who had contracted for the book was shocked, as were several scholars whom Adams had contacted personally for material. The Protestant press, which outside the South was largely under New England dominance, condemned the author's irreligion. The scholarly establishment, then largely genteel and antiquarian, condemned, not without reason, the shallowness of the learning and the one-sidedness of the presentation. Almost alone, William Dean Howells, writing in *Harper's* (May 1887), found the work a refreshing breath of realism.

The response is not surprising when one considers that American historical writing, which was still largely New England-created or inspired, generally presented the Puritan Fathers of Massachusetts as the noblest people in history and as directly responsible for everything of political and cultural value in American society. In retrospect, Adams's work can be considered a healthy catalyst which stimulated a new era of Puritan scholarship that continues to the present. Coming from the source it did, it shook the self-image of the genteel center of American culture. Yet the iconoclasm is not too surprising, for all of Brooks Adams's forebears had, at times, taken pains to distance themselves from parts of New England orthodoxy.

Adams's reaction to his critics was characteristic. He claimed that he had been misunderstood; that his purpose was not the debunking of early Massachusetts history; rather, he was interested only in exhibiting "the action of the [human] mind" at a particular stage of development, a demonstration which might as well have been taken from India as from Massachusetts. It would seem that Adams was no more than half truthful at best. Whatever his privately expressed motives, readers were not to be blamed for treating the book for what it appeared to be. The disparity between his stated intentions and the actual content of his books was a recurrent problem, and the response it provoked led Adams to adopt the pose of a chronically misunderstood and misrepresented writer. He was perhaps correct in stating that his books, to him, were illustrations of theories designed to elicit laws of history and not examinations of particular historical situations. But the theories, which may have been very clearly worked out in his mind, never meshed systematically and comfortably with the content of his books, as his brother Henry was aware.

Very characteristically, in 1919, more than thirty years after *The Emancipation of Massachusetts* was first published, Adams brought out another edition. He declared he was more than ever convinced of the soundness of the book, and he added a 168-page "Preface" which, as Perry Miller observed, constituted an entirely disparate book that could be reconciled with the original by only the eccentric logic of the author.

The personal and intellectual relationship between Henry and Brooks Adams was close over many years and is extensively documented in letters, published and unpublished. Most observers have noted that Brooks Adams, throughout his life, was emotionally dependent on his brother's approval, while Henry seems to have regarded keeping company with Brooks largely as a duty. It might be incorrect to assume, however, that the older brother was always the tutor and the younger always the pupil. Brooks Adams's other important book, *The Law of Civilization and Decay* (1895), was

a direct outgrowth of studies prompted by the panic of 1893 and by extended conversations with Henry at that time. Charles Beard, who studied the origins of the book closely, points out that, while Henry Adams was already an established historian, his published works, before he read *The Law* in manuscript in 1893, had been unconcerned with the laws and philosophy of history and that perhaps Henry's *Mont-Saint-Michel and Chartres* (1904) owes something to Brooks. The question of influences cannot be definitely settled. The temperamental difference was nearly unbridgeable for Henry. He was, as Parrington pointed out, a prototypical detached intellectual, unable to empathize with Brooks Adams's earnestness.

An amazing centralization of economic power through the monetary system was observed with distress by many in the late nineteenth century. Brooks Adams was one of those, and *The Law of Civilization and Decay* was the result. Typically, Adams tinkered with the manuscript for several years until in 1895 he finally brought out a version in London at his own expense. This sold so well (including its distribution by Macmillan in the United States) that Macmillan brought out an American edition, but not before the author had tinkered again with the text. The 1899 French translation, thanks to more revision by the author, contained still further changes.

No single thesis emerges from *The Law of Civilization and Decay*. Adams, in fact, presents a number of different, vaguely related ideas, some of which he illustrated in the text and others which he merely asserted at the beginning or end. One notion in Adams's work was a pessimistic, deterministic idea of social energy. A given people had a certain amount of energy (varying among peoples) which was used up in the process of competition. When the energy was exhausted only an infusion of new blood could create forward movement again.

Another aspect of Adams's "law" of history was descriptive of the stages of civilization's movement. A civilization began in a dispersed state. In this stage the martial and agricultural type predominated (with all that implied in politics, culture, economics, and religion). The main motive force of competition was fear. Civilization proceeded inevitably toward centralization, particularly in economic power. It then reached a new stage in which the acquisitive, rational type predominated (with all that implied) and the main motive force was greed. The end result was a static, exhausted regime. Adams's theory was not so much systematically argued as it was randomly illustrated by discussions of Rome, the Middle Ages, and English history. The process of centralization was related to the concentration of trade and economic power. Historically, the center of economic power had moved from Rome, to Constantinople, to Venice, to Northern Europe, to London.

Evident to any reader was the implication that modern society was far advanced into the second stage and near the exhaustion of its energies. Evident also was a hostility to capitalist civilization and a pessimistic and determinist view of the future of culture, prosperity, and the relations of social classes. The treatment owed something to Karl Marx and to Herbert Spencer, and a little to the traditional agrarian mistrust of centralization and abstract finance. It was also anticipatory of the ideas later worked out much more systematically by Oswald Spengler in *The Decline of the West* (1918, 1922). The blending of elements was, however, idiosyncratic.

America was not discussed, but in Adams's later works, which were largely devoted to working out further aspects of the ideas presented in *The Law of Civilization and Decay*, the point of economic centralization was shifted to America. Though America did not figure directly in *The Law*, it was obvious to contemporary readers that much of the material in the book bore directly on the current political conflicts over the monetary system. In the conflict between proponents of the gold standard and those who supported the free and unlimited coinage of silver, Adams, very unfashionably for his class and region, sided with the latter. The monetary ideas were not particularly well meshed with other parts of Adams's philosophy of history, however.

The reception given *The Law of Civilization and Decay* was more favorable and more considered than that given *The Emancipation of Massachusetts*. It struck a responsive chord in many quarters. Though he disagreed with Adams, Theodore Roosevelt gave it a respectful review. Critics did not fail to note the unevenness of the scholarship and the unsystematic presentation of ideas. In the long view, the book remains readable and suggestive but is far from a convincing evocation of the "law" of history.

Adams's bibliography, including books, articles, reviews, published legal briefs, addresses, and translations and reprints of his works, contains well over one hundred items. From 1904 to 1911 he lectured at the Boston University School of Law. He worked out the legal ramifications of the cen-

tralization of power in a plutocratic class and made specific applications of his ideas in legal briefs opposing trusts and railroads. His later books, *America's Economic Supremacy* (1900), *The New Empire* (1902), and *The Theory of Social Revolutions* (1913), described the transfer of economic concentration to America and the unhappy effects of the power of capital and of a utilitarian and rationalist stage of civilization. As a member of the Massachusetts constitutional convention in 1917, Adams unsuccessfully advocated the liberal measures of popular initiative and referendum.

Adams's reputation was always dubious and has become more so. The reasons are many. One is the anti-Semitism which he shared with Henry Adams and others of the beleagured New England aristocracy. Another is the incompleteness and idiosyncrasy of his efforts to establish "laws" for the rise and fall of civilization. No one has ever succeeded in establishing an accepted philosophy of historical causation. But some writers, including Arnold Toynbee and Oswald Spengler, have remained of interest because of the thoroughness of their attempts. Brooks Adams was too irritable, unsystematic, and ambivalent to be in this company. Finally, the debunking, modern tone of his works, which was shocking in its day, has become so familiar that it no longer excites interest.

In the final analysis all that remains, in Perry Miller's terms, is Adams's style and the interest of witnessing the mind of a "capricious genius" at work. Though Adams's motive was, perhaps, the hope of giving guidance to a democracy that had gone astray and securing the restoration of an older and better public order, the means he chose were inappropriate. As Russell Kirk observed, his head was fatally divided from his heart. If his heart was fixed on old values, his head was inextricably caught up in the modernism he detested because he accepted the premise that man is foremost an economic being. A more clinical observer might well observe that Adams's genius was fatally flawed by an unintegrated personality. His life, according to Perry Miller, was one long spiritual crisis.

In his private life, especially in later years, Adams seems to have been bitter, rude, and self-indulgent. His marriage to Evelyn Davis, sister of Anna Davis (Mrs. Henry Cabot) Lodge, brought no great comfort to either. He was the last Adams to inhabit the family mansion at Quincy and, like his brother Henry, left no direct descendants.

Bibliography:

Thornton Anderson, *Brooks Adams, Constructive*

Conservative (Ithaca: Cornell University Press, 1951), pp. 229-243.

Biography:

Arthur F. Beringause, *Brooks Adams: a Biography* (New York: Knopf, 1955).

References:

Thornton Anderson, *Brooks Adams, Constructive Conservative* (Ithaca: Cornell University Press, 1951);

Charles A. Beard, Introduction to Brooks Adams's *The Law of Civilization and Decay. An Essay on History* (New York: Knopf, 1943);

Russell Kirk, *The Conservative Mind: From Burke to Eliot* (New York: Avon, 1968), pp. 348-354;

Perry Miller, Introduction to Brooks Adams's *The Emancipation of Massachusetts; The Dream and the Reality* (Boston: Houghton Mifflin, 1962);

Paul C. Nagel, *Descent from Glory: Four Generations of the John Adams Family* (New York & Oxford: Oxford University Press, 1983);

Vernon L. Parrington, *Main Currents in American Thought*, volume 3 (New York: Harcourt, Brace, 1930), pp. 212-236.

Papers:

Brooks Adams's papers are at the Massachusetts Historical Society and the Houghton Library, Harvard University.

Charles Francis Adams, Jr.

(27 May 1835-20 March 1915)

John C. Meleney
University of South Carolina

SELECTED BOOKS: *The Erie Railroad Row Considered as an Episode in Court* (Boston: Little, Brown, 1868);

Railroad Legislation (Boston: Little, Brown, 1868);

Chapters of Erie and Other Essays, by Adams and Henry Adams (Boston: Osgood, 1871);

Railroads: Their Origin and Problems (New York: Putnam's, 1878; revised and enlarged, 1878);

The New Departure in the Common Schools of Quincy and Other Papers on Educational Topics (Boston: Estes & Lauriat, 1879);

Notes on Railroad Accidents (New York: Putnam's, 1879);

Episodes in New England History (Cambridge: Privately printed, 1883);

Richard Henry Dana, a Biography, 2 volumes (Boston: Houghton Mifflin, 1890);

History of Braintree, Massachusetts (1639-1708), the North Precinct of Braintree (1708-1792) and the Town of Quincy (1792-1889) (Cambridge: Privately printed, 1891);

Three Episodes of Massachusetts History: The Settlement of Boston Bay; The Antinomian Controversy; A Study of Church and Town Government, 2 volumes (Boston: Houghton Mifflin, 1892; revised, 1894);

Massachusetts; Its Historians and Its History: An Object Lesson (Boston: Houghton Mifflin, 1893);

"Imperialism" and "The Tracks of Our Forefathers" (Boston: Estes, 1899);

Charles Francis Adams, by His Son, Charles Francis Adams (Boston & New York: Houghton Mifflin, 1900; London: Duckworth, 1900);

Lee at Appomattox, and Other Papers (Boston & New York: Houghton Mifflin, 1902; enlarged, 1902);

Three Phi Beta Kappa Addresses: A College Fetich, 1883; "Shall Cromwell Have a Statue?" 1902; Some Modern College Tendencies, 1906 (Boston & New York: Houghton Mifflin, 1907);

Studies Military and Diplomatic, 1775-1865 (New York: Macmillan, 1911);

" 'Tis Sixty Years Since." Address of Charles Francis Adams, Founders' Day, January 16, 1913, University of South Carolina (New York: Macmillan, 1913);

Trans-Atlantic Historical Solidarity: Lectures Delivered before the University of Oxford in Easter and Trin-

ity Terms, 1913 (Oxford: Clarendon Press, 1913);

Charles Francis Adams, 1835-1915: An Autobiography (Boston & New York: Houghton Mifflin, 1916).

OTHER: *The New English Canaan of Thomas Morton,* edited with introductory material and notes by Adams (Boston: Prince Society, 1883);

"Some Phases of Sexual Morality and Church Discipline in Colonial New England," in *Proceedings of the Massachusetts Historical Society,* second series, 6 (1890-1891), pp. 477-516;

Antinomianism in the Colony of Massachusetts Bay, 1636-1638. Including the Short Story and Other Documents, edited by Adams (Boston: Prince Society, 1894);

Life in a New England Town: 1787, 1788. Diary of John Quincy Adams, While a Student in the Office of Theophilus Parsons at Newburyport, edited by Adams (Boston: Little, Brown, 1903);

"The Trent Affair," in *Proceedings of the Massachusetts Historical Society,* 45 (1911-1912), pp. 35-148;

"The Negotiation of 1861 Relating to the Declaration of Paris of 1856," in *Proceedings of the Massachusetts Historical Society,* 46 (1912-1913), pp. 23-84;

Correspondence of John Quincy Adams, 1811-1814, edited by Adams (Worcester, Mass.: American Antiquarian Society, 1913);

"The Golgotha Year," in *Proceedings of the Massachusetts Historical Society,* 47 (1913-1914), pp. 334-340;

"A Crisis in Downing Street," in *Proceedings of the Massachusetts Historical Society,* 47 (1913-1914), pp. 372-424;

"The British Proclamation of May, 1861," in *Proceedings of the Massachusetts Historical Society,* 48 (1914-1915), pp. 190-242.

PERIODICAL PUBLICATIONS: [The Railroad System], *North American Review,* 104 (April 1867): 476-511;

"Boston," *North American Review,* 106 (January, April 1868): 1-25, 555-591;

"The Erie Railroad Row," *American Law Review,* 3 (October 1868): 41-86;

"Railroad Inflation," *North American Review,* 108 (January 1869): 130-164;

"A Chapter of Erie," *North American Review,* 109 (July 1869): 30-106;

"Railway Problems in 1869," *North American Review,* 110 (January 1870): 116-150;

"The Government and the Railroad Corporations," *North American Review,* 112 (January 1871): 31-61;

"An Erie Raid," *North American Review,* 112 (April 1871): 241-291;

"The Currency Debate of 1873-74," *North American Review,* 119 (July 1874): 111-165;

"The Granger Movement," *North American Review,* 120 (April 1875): 394-424;

"The State and the Railroads," *Atlantic Monthly,* 37 (March 1876): 360-371; 37 (June 1876): 691-699; 38 (July 1876): 72-85;

"The May-Pole of Merrymount," *Atlantic Monthly,* 39 (May 1877): 557-567; 39 (June 1877): 686-697;

"Albert Gallatin" (review of Henry Adams's *The Life of Albert Gallatin*), *Nation,* 28 (21 August 1879): 128-129; 28 (28 August 1879): 144-145;

"The Sifted Grain and the Grain Sifters," *American Historical Review,* 6 (January 1901): 197-234;

"An Undeveloped Function," *American Historical Review,* 7 (January 1902): 203-232.

Charles Francis Adams, Jr., was born in Boston on 27 May 1835, the third child and second son of Charles Francis and Abigail Brooks Adams. He was the great-grandson of John Adams, the second president of the United States, and the grandson of John Quincy Adams, the sixth. His father was minister to Great Britain during the Civil War and was instrumental in forestalling British recognition of the Confederacy.

Of the fourth generation in a distinguished line, Adams inherited the family tradition of public duty and civic responsibility, and the interaction between the received tradition and the dynamic materialism of the Gilded Age dramatically shaped his career and character. During his long life, he was variously Union cavalry officer, social reformer and bureaucrat, investor and sometime speculator in land and securities, businessman and corporate executive, civic leader, Harvard overseer, and historian.

Adams's work as historian was, in effect, a second career begun relatively late. But he wrote continually throughout his life, and the bibliography of his published books, pamphlets, articles, and addresses is extensive. Much of his work was not history in the traditional sense, and, when writing history, he used and reused his materials, working them over in the process. The major historical work to which he aspired, an extended biography of his father encompassing a diplomatic history of the Civil War, was never finished. None of his completed work has been accorded, or deserves, the eminence of his brother Henry's nine-volume *History of the United States of America During the Administrations of Thomas Jefferson and James Madison* (1884-1891), but his historical interests were more varied than Henry's and his commitment to historical study was as sustained. And his best work is of such quality as to suggest that his reputation as historian might have been higher had he turned sooner than he did to serious historical work or had he disciplined his efforts toward more limited and precisely defined goals. "I have continually attempted too much," he lamented in his *Autobiography* (1916), "always had too many irons in the fire."

Adams was educated first at small private schools in Boston, then at Boston Latin School, and finally at Harvard, from which he graduated in 1856. He completed his studies at Harvard "receiving no rank, but avoiding all difficulties." Nonetheless, he developed his literary skills to become, by his own estimation, "one of the recognized litterateurs of my time and class."

He graduated from Harvard with "no particular sense of a special vocation." As a matter of course, he turned to the law and was taken as a student into the office of Richard Henry Dana and Francis E. Parker in Boston. After twenty months of study, "and decently prepared for practice in my own eyes only," he was admitted to the bar in 1858.

By his own account, Adams had neither enthusiasm nor aptitude for a professional life in the law. The record confirms at least the first of these self-judgments. His father was elected to Congress in 1858 and again in 1860, and he spent much of his time in Washington during the years 1859 to 1861. His legal career was not advanced in those years, but his political education flourished. Given his family connections, he was on friendly terms with most of the important political leaders and was a privileged observer of the turmoil in Washington in late 1860 and early 1861.

With the appointment of his father as ambassador to Great Britain, Adams returned, without enthusiasm, to his law office in Boston. Before the year was out, however, he applied for a commission in the First Massachusetts Cavalry and was accepted with the rank of first lieutenant. He served first with the force occupying Port Royal, South Carolina, and thereafter with the Army of the Potomac. He saw action at Antietam and Gettysburg, in the Wilderness campaign, and before Petersburg. In 1864 he was assigned to the Fifth Massachusetts Cavalry, a Negro regiment, of which he assumed command in 1865. He was mustered out of the army in August 1865 a brevet brigadier general, the only member of his family in military service in the Civil War.

In November 1865 Adams married Mary Hone Ogden of New York and Newport and departed on an extended trip abroad. Returning to Quincy in October 1866 and still uninterested in the practice of law, his immediate problem was to set himself on a constructive course for the future. Between 1866 and 1870 he "caught the step," as he put it, proceeding with typically Adamsian single-mindedness. "Surveying the whole field," he observed, "I fixed on the railroad system as the most developing force and largest field of the day, and determined to attach myself to it."

In the inherited Adams family creed, education was the distinguishing requirement for positions of leadership. Adams accordingly believed that the country needed educated, philosophical leaders, whom he chose to call "sophists," and set about to educate himself and the public on the subject of railroads. Beginning in 1867, he completed a series of articles on various railroad topics and argued for the creation of a state railroad commission in Massachusetts. When such a commission was established in 1869, Adams, "making a strike for the position," succeeded in obtaining appointment to it.

The most dramatic product of Adams's early interest in railroads was a series of essays on the Erie Railroad written with his brother Henry. The collaboration was planned when Charles was in London on his wedding trip in 1866. Henry was then contemplating a career in journalism, "the last resort of the educated poor" he would later call it, and the brothers agreed on a division of labor in which Charles would focus on railroads and Henry would focus on public finance.

Adams began the series with two articles (1868 and 1869), later revised and combined into one, describing in detail the contest for control of the Erie in the period 1866 to 1868 between Daniel Drew, Jay Gould, and Jim Fisk on one side and Commodore Vanderbilt on the other and the attendant corporate, financial, and legal machinations in which both sides engaged. In 1869 Gould and Fisk, having forced Drew out of the Erie and beaten off Vanderbilt, launched a raid on the Albany and Susquehanna Railroad in an effort to obtain for the Erie a connection to Albany and access to New England in competition with Vanderbilt's New York Central. Then, in September

Adams (second from right) with officers of his regiment at Petersburg, 1864

1869, Gould made his famous attempt to corner the gold market.

This conjunction of events suggested to the Adams brothers a scandal so dramatic that, in Henry's words, they "jumped at it like a salmon to a fly." Henry's contribution was "The New York Gold Conspiracy," which first appeared in the *Westminster Review* in October 1870. Charles, already involved with the railroad commission in Massachusetts, contributed a study of the Erie raid on the Albany and Susquehanna.

These essays and others by Charles and Henry were collected in *Chapters of Erie and Other Essays* (1871). As indicated by the title, Charles's Erie essays were featured. Taken together, they illustrated the potential for damage to the public interest when power derived from the state by chartered corporations was beyond the power of state control. He called it "Caesarism." Of perhaps greater importance, these pieces were precursors of the best of the muckraking genre of the next generation. Historical detachment was not an objective; judicious impartiality was not intended.

They were savage attacks on observed depredations extreme even for a period in which speculative finance and corruption in legislatures and courts were common phenomena. But they did not exaggerate. Adams so carefully researched his topic and so thoroughly mastered its intricacies that his factual analysis has not been superseded in any material respect.

By 1870, the pattern of Adams's life for the next twenty years was in place. He served on the railroad commission in Massachusetts for ten years and was its chairman after 1872. In 1878 he joined the board of directors of the Union Pacific Railroad as chairman of the five public directors representing the interests of the United States government. He resigned the following year to begin five years of service with the major trunk line railroads arbitrating differences concerning rates and related matters. In 1883 he rejoined the board of the Union Pacific and in June 1894 became its president.

Adams's term as president of the Union Pacific was not a resounding success. Although he made significant progress in dealing with the company's immediate financial problems and in reducing its outstanding debt, resolution of long-term financial and operating problems escaped him. In 1890 he surrendered managerial control to Jay Gould and resigned his office. "Ejected by Jay Gould from the presidency of the Union Pacific, I at last, and instantly, fell back on my proper vocation," he wrote in the *Autobiography*. "I was then fifty-five; but it was not too late."

Committed as he was to his railroad career between 1870 and 1890, Adams nevertheless found time to accumulate a modest personal fortune, to participate actively in civic affairs in Quincy and Boston, to study, and to write. Toward the end of his term of service on the Massachusetts commission, he discussed the current state of affairs in the rapidly expanding railroad industry in *Railroads: Their Origin and Problems* (1878). Drawing on his experience as a member of the local school committee in Quincy, he described in *The New Departure in the Common Schools of Quincy* (1879) reforms anticipating what later came to be known as progressive education. In 1882 he was named to the Board of Overseers of Harvard University, on which he served actively and with distinction for twenty-four years. Characteristically, he began by delivering an address to the Phi Beta Kappa Society in 1883 severely criticizing Harvard's emphasis on the classics.

Adams's career in history had its early beginnings in the 1870s and 1880s. In 1874 he was invited to deliver an address commemorating the two hundred and fiftieth anniversary of the founding of Weymouth, a town adjacent to Quincy and sharing its early history. Continuing the study thus begun, he completed *Episodes in New England History*, privately printed in 1883, in which he announced his plan for a multivolume work on the history of Massachusetts "by periods and episodes of especial importance." He also completed in 1883 an annotated edition of Thomas Morton's *New English Canaan* (Amsterdam, 1637), describing life in pre-Puritan settlements established on Massachusetts Bay under the sponsorship of Sir Ferdinando Gorges. Similarly, he presented an impromptu obituary of Richard Henry Dana to the Massachusetts Historical Society in 1882, which ultimately led to a biography of Dana published in 1890, just as Adams was leaving the Union Pacific.

With the Union Pacific and the Dana biography behind him, Adams promptly turned to his Massachusetts project. An extended history of Braintree and Quincy, 1639-1889, was completed

in 1891 and privately published in a limited edition of fifty copies. The finished product, *Three Episodes of Massachusetts History*, appeared in two volumes in 1892.

The *Three Episodes of Massachusetts History* is essentially an extended history of Quincy which proceeds from the general to the particular, since the early history of Massachusetts and that of the Massachusetts Bay settlements were the same. It is divided into three sections entitled "The Settlement of Boston Bay," "The Antinomian Controversy," and "A Study of Church and Town Government." The first covers the early settlements in the Massachusetts Bay area, with special emphasis on the settlement established prior to arrival of the Puritan colony in 1630 in which Thomas Morton was one of the more colorful participants until banished by the Pilgrims of Plymouth. The second describes the Antinomian controversy in Massachusetts Bay under John Winthrop which resulted in the banishment of Anne Hutchinson in 1638. The third, and longest, is a history of Quincy and its predecessor towns from 1639 to 1890.

Critical response was generally enthusiastic. "We have here probably the most original and suggestive town history ever written in this country," Herbert L. Osgood wrote in the *Political Science Quarterly*. "The varied subjects are woven together with a unity which is both true and impressive." Nearly fifty years later, in 1940, Van Wyck Brooks called the third section "by all odds, the finest history of an American town that has ever been written."

The *Three Episodes* is much more than a chronological narrative of local events. Anticipating the "new history" of more recent time, it describes the community and its people, their strengths, weaknesses, concerns, and purposes, their relationships to one another and to the larger world beyond, and their institutions and how they worked. It is also a stern critique of the sentimental filiopietism of New England historians, a theme to which Adams shortly returned in *Massachusetts; Its Historians and Its History: An Object Lesson* (1893). Edward C. Kirkland, in his excellent 1965 biography of Adams, called the *Three Episodes* his "single most important historical work" and his critique of filiopietism in American history his "greatest contribution as a historian." Walter Muir Whitehill was more direct and more pungent. Reviewing Kirkland's biography in the *New England Quarterly* in 1966, he observed that Adams had not only enlarged the scope of Massachusetts history but had "killed filio-pietism deader than a smelt."

In 1893, distressed by the growth and commercialization of Quincy, Adams moved to Lincoln and resumed work on his planned magnum opus, a diplomatic history of the Civil War based on his father's papers. But he was too often diverted. "He lacked the will to prevent himself from dissipating his force," Kirkland says.

He was diverted first by his continuing engagement in civic affairs. He was diverted further when the economic collapse of 1893 forced him to focus on his personal affairs. Although modestly wealthy, he was somewhat overextended and, in relative terms, heavily in debt. Although his difficulties were surmounted during the years 1893 to 1898, the cost in time and energy was substantial. Finally, he was diverted by calls upon his time for lectures and articles. "Of work of this kind, I have done altogether too much," he wrote in the *Autobiography*, "and looking back on it, it seems to have been singularly useless and barren." But he enjoyed the center stage and could seldom resist the opportunity to occupy it.

Another diversion occurred when John T. Morse, Jr., prevailed upon him to write a biography of his father for the American Statesmen series. *Charles Francis Adams, by His Son* was first published in 1900. "The following sketch is . . . in part a preliminary study, and in part the condensed abstract of a larger and more detailed work already far advanced in preparation," Adams wrote in the preface with his magnum opus in mind. The book was well enough received but not with the acclaim accorded the *Three Episodes*. As a work of history, its most singular feature was the essential objectivity with which Adams managed to treat his subject, and one commentator called it "a model of the very delicate art of recounting the life of one with close personal ties with the author." A contrary view suggested that he so completely effaced himself as nearly to efface his father in an arid summary of depersonalized politics and diplomacy.

By 1900 Adams had achieved some eminence in his second career. In 1875, after the Weymouth address, he was elected to the Massachusetts Historical Society, membership in which was selective and by no means automatic, except perhaps for an Adams. He became vice-president in 1890, and was president from 1895 until his death in 1915. He was, in addition, president of the American Historical Association in 1901-1902. From these positions, he could speak generally on history and historians.

Adams represented the Massachusetts Historical Society at ceremonies in late 1900 dedicating the new building of the State Historical Society of Wisconsin. There he delivered a long address entitled "The Sifted Grain and the Grain Sifters," published in the *American Historical Review* in 1901 and constituting his single most comprehensive statement on history and the role of the historian. Explicitly taking his text in part from Darwin, he described "the modern conception of history" as "a unified whole—a vast scheme systematically developing to some result not yet understood." Thus, "history, ceasing to be a mere narrative, made up of disconnected episodes having little or no bearing on each other, became a connected whole." The function of the historian was to assign a proper place in the evolutionary process to "each development, each epoch, race and dynasty." Performance of this function by major English and American historians of the nineteenth century (the "grain sifters") was evaluated in terms of "learning, judgment and literary sense." Predictably, all fell short in some respect. "A perfect history, like a perfect poem," Adams said, "must have a beginning, a middle, and an end; and the well proportioned parts should be kept in strict subservience to the whole." Anticipating Samuel Eliot Morison's later criticism of the monographists, Adams emphasized the importance of communication between the historian and the public. "Not only is it possible for a writer to combine learning and accuracy with vivacity," he said, "but to be read and to be popular should not in the eyes of the judicious be a species of stigma." Further, reflecting his own approach in the *Three Episodes of Massachusetts History*, he urged that "however it may have been heretofore, what is known as politics will be but a part, and by no means the most important part, of the history of the future. The historian will look deeper." Finally, the historian should strive to know his own time so that he may sympathetically and correctly read "to the present the lessons to be derived from the experience of the past."

Adams returned to the theme of the historian as educator of the public from the experience of the past a year later in his presidential address to the American Historical Association. Reviewing the issues debated in past political campaigns, with special emphasis on those presented during the campaign of 1900, he found the level of discourse inadequate and suggested that "the time has now come when organizations such as this of ours, instead of, as heretofore, scrupulously standing aloof from the political debate, are under obligation to participate in it." He therefore proposed that the association's schedule of meetings be arranged to provide for a meeting during the summer preceding each presidential election at which the issues of the campaign could be analyzed and clarified in historical perspective. Although his historical analysis of the campaign issues was subsequently praised, particularly his discussion of American imperialism as debated in 1900, his proposal was regarded by his colleagues as wholly impractical and was never seriously considered.

The years after 1900 were full and sometimes frustrating. Adams was totally involved in the activities of the Massachusetts Historical Society. He continued his research and completed preliminary studies on various aspects of Civil War diplomatic history. He delivered papers on a variety of other topics. The *Autobiography* was completed and laid aside for publication after his death. He assisted in preparation of the Massachusetts Historical Society's edition of William Bradford's *History of Plymouth Plantation*. He was in constant demand as a speaker. Moreover, his energies were declining. In 1912 he would complain that he was "utterly unequal to the drudgery of historical investigation." And he had come to recognize that understanding of his father's English mission in order to finish the magnum opus would require extensive examination of British public and private records.

In 1913 he delivered a series of lectures at Oxford University on the invitation of the Rhodes Scholarship Foundation and took advantage of the occasion to begin examination of the pertinent English materials. He was in England again to continue that task later the same year. With a substantial amount of new material in hand, and planning further investigations in both England and France, he called on others to assist him, most notably E. D. Adams of Stanford University. Two long studies based on the British documents appeared in the *Proceedings of the Massachusetts Historical Society* in 1914 and early 1915; and two volumes were substantially finished, the first taking the life of the elder Adams to 1848, the second to 1860. But the crucial Civil War years had not been covered, and the project ended when Adams died in March 1915, just short of his eightieth birthday.

The *Autobiography* appeared in 1916. It is more interesting for what it discloses of the man, often inadvertently, than of his work. More than three-quarters of it deals with his early life and Civil War experience. Like his forbears, he was introspectively critical of his mistakes, often overdrawn and magnified, and complained of lost opportunities. He was uncompromisingly direct, and probably unduly harsh, in describing his shortcomings

as chief executive of the Union Pacific, observing that during the last eighteen months of his tenure he was "wholly demoralized." His most evident satisfaction was reserved for his civic achievements in Quincy and for the financial success of the Kansas City Stockyards Company, of which he had been president for a number of years. His history was also a source of pleasure and satisfaction, tinged with regret that more had not been achieved. "His remarkably sensitive and revealing autobiography stands out as the most important work of its type by a *fin de siècle* businessman—stylistically it is by far the best—and it reveals Adams the man in all his contradictory dimensions," Gabriel Kolko said in a review of Kirkland's biography. L. H. Butterfield called the *Autobiography* "perhaps the best critical commentary on America's Gilded Age written by anyone who played a large part in it." And Carl Becker found it "fascinating chiefly as an incomparable product of the Puritan mind and temperament, the self-revelation of a true child of New England" who wished to be emancipated "but could never quite bring it about."

Adams is perhaps more interesting as a historical figure in his own right than as a historian. His life spanned the Gilded Age, and he was in it if not entirely of it. He was ambivalent concerning the materialistic orientation of his time, clearly enjoying wealth and the good life, seeking and grasping opportunities to invest for profit, but critical of those whom he considered "mere money-getters and traders." In his view they were "essentially unattractive and uninteresting." He had known many. In an often-quoted passage from the *Autobiography* he said: "Not one that I have ever known would I care to meet again, either in this world or the next; nor is one of them associated in my mind with the idea of humor, thought or refinement." By implication, such men lacked the essential qualifications for leadership required by the Adams creed.

Adams was not a major figure of his time, but he was an important one. His sense of civic responsibility was traditional, and his civic contributions to Quincy and Boston were substantial. On the Massachusetts railroad commission he clearly understood that the primary interest to be served was the public interest, and he was somewhat ahead of his time in the balanced view he took of that interest. As railroad executive, he was a rational man of prudence seeking his way in a business and political environment in which the prevailing rules of the game were sometimes inconsistent with his own personal standards. He was essentially a bureaucrat in an entrepreneurial era before the bu-

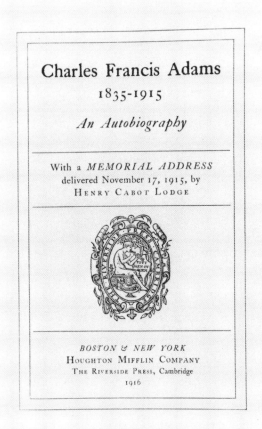

Frontispiece and title page for the work completed by Adams in March 1912 and set aside for posthumous publication

reaucrat was a respectable figure. He was right in 1866 when he identified the importance of railroad development, and he established himself as a significant actor in that development of whom historians have duly taken note.

Although not a prototypical mugwump, Adams shared mugwump social and political views, and his name appears and reappears in the historiography of mugwump culture and Gilded Age approaches to reform. He was on the fringe of the Liberal Republican movement of 1872 in opposition to Grant, when his father was a possible third party presidential candidate; he was critical of Radical Reconstruction in the South; and he was in the forefront of the independent Republican defection from Blaine in 1884. He favored civil service reform and tariff reduction. Although he actively sought involvement in the mainstream of modern American life, he was no egalitarian. He was consistent in the view that those of traditional moral values and educated intelligence were those who

should lead. He rejected the proposition that a superior people could or would assimilate successfully an inferior race. "I believe in the equality of men before the law; but social equality, whether for man or child, is altogether another thing," he said in the *Autobiography*.

Adams was also in the forefront of the anti-imperialist campaign of 1898-1900, which Geoffrey Blodgett has called the mugwumps' last hurrah. He joined the debate in December 1898 with an address to the Lexington Historical Society in Massachusetts entitled " 'Imperialism' and 'The Tracks of Our Forefathers' " (published in 1889). Taking his text from Edmund Burke, he posed the issue as one of choice between traditional and distinctly American principles and the principles and practices of European imperialism "which heretofore we have made it the basis of our faith to deny and repudiate." Attacking the historical validity of the arguments of the expansionists one by one, he urged that Americans adhere to their own historically validated precedent. But he turned away from the debate when it became apparent that the cause was hopeless and, to the annoyance of other anti-imperialists, lectured them on the need to be more constructive.

After the Boer War entered its final guerrilla phase in September 1900, Adams delivered an address to the American Antiquarian Society in 1901 in which he praised Lee's statesmanship at Appomattox and thereafter in rejecting a similar course for the Confederacy and "in deciding . . . in favor of a new national life, even if slowly and painfully to be built up by his own people under conditions arbitrarily and by force imposed on them." Originally entitled "The Confederacy and the Transvaal: A People's Obligation to Robert E. Lee," this address was later published as the title piece in *Lee at Appomattox, and Other Papers* (1902). The South African connection was dropped and the defense of Lee expanded in "Shall Cromwell Have a Statue?," delivered to the Phi Beta Kappa Society at the University of Chicago in 1902. The theme was developed further in "The Constitutional Ethics of Secession," delivered to the New England Society of Charleston, South Carolina, the same year, and achieved final form in "Lee's Centennial," an address delivered in 1907 at Washington and Lee University. "Shall Cromwell Have a Statue?" was included in an enlarged edition of *Lee at Appomattox, and Other Papers* and in *Three Phi Beta Kappa Addresses* (1907). "The Constitutional Ethics of Secession" and "Lee's Centennial" were included in *Studies Military and Diplomatic, 1775-1865* (1911).

The common theme of these addresses was conciliatory to the South. Lee was embraced as a national hero, and his decision to take the side of Virginia was explained and defended. The historical basis of Southern belief in the right to secede was acknowledged; the harshness of Radical Reconstruction was also acknowledged; and the propriety of Southern home rule was accepted. Social reform in the South was not, in Adams's view, a proper function of the federal government. These themes were consistent with political and historiographic views of the South and Reconstruction emerging in the decade after 1900, including a new image of Lee to which Adams was an important contributor.

The reputation of Adams as historian rests primarily on the *Three Episodes of Massachusetts History*, which stands as an early model for local history. Rejecting the sentimental filial piety of nineteenth-century New England historians, he significantly extended the range of New England

historical study. The *Autobiography* stands as a character study of a unique patrician personality thrust into the changing world of the Gilded Age. *Railroads: Their Origin and Problems* is a period piece which reflects a stage in the historical development of the nation's transportation system and offers a perspective on the early railroad era free of the pejorative implications common to many modern general descriptions of the late nineteenth century. The Dana biography is still useful, particularly for its description of the fugitive slave cases in which Dana was involved just prior to the Civil War. Finally, the Erie articles are still relevant and unsurpassed as vivid descriptions of the dark side of unrestrained entrepreneurial conduct in the early postbellum period.

Adams was more than a gifted amateur historian. He read widely and systematically in history and literature. He fully understood the importance of sources, and his own research was thorough, sometimes to the point of diminishing returns. He was a perceptive critic and sometimes sharp. "In writing history suppress the patriotic glow," he noted in the margin of a proof copy of Henry's *History*. His own narrative style was lucid, direct, and graceful, if occasionally ornate by modern standards and sometimes heavily laden with literary allusions. Trained early to military command and later to the marshaling and analysis of data as bureaucrat and businessman, his thought was secular and concrete. He also understood the value of ideas. He was familiar with the works of Charles Darwin and Herbert Spencer, and he observed in the *Autobiography* that John Stuart Mill's essay on Auguste Comte, which he read in 1865, "revolutionized in a single morning my whole mental attitude. I emerged from the theological state, in which I had been nurtured, and passed into the scientific." Like others of his time, he searched for form and pattern; but he was no determinist. Where ideas of Darwin and Comte are reflected in his work, they are not dominant themes which control the narrative presentation or his analytical frame of reference.

Adams sustained the literary tradition in history as the idea of scientific history emerged and spread. He was, in important respects, both traditional and modern, in his history as in his life; the quality of his best work supports the posthumous observation of J. Franklin Jameson to Lord Bryce that Adams's powers may have been greater than those he demonstrated in any of his completed historical works.

Letters:

A Cycle of Adams Letters, 1861-1865, edited by Worthington Chauncey Ford, 2 volumes (Boston: Houghton Mifflin, 1920).

Bibliography:

Mrs. Wendell Garrett, "The Published Writings of Charles Francis Adams, II (1835-1915): An Annotated Bibliography," in *Proceedings of the Massachusetts Historical Society*, 72 (1957-1960), pp. 237-293.

Biography:

Edward C. Kirkland, *Charles Francis Adams, Jr., 1835-1915: The Patrician at Bay* (Cambridge: Harvard University Press, 1965).

References:

James Truslow Adams, *The Adams Family* (Boston: Little, Brown, 1930);

Robert L. Beisner, "Brooks Adams and Charles Francis Adams, Jr.: Historians of Massachusetts," *New England Quarterly*, 35 (March 1962): 48-70;

Beisner, *Twelve Against Empire: The Anti-Imperialists, 1898-1900* (New York: McGraw-Hill, 1968);

Geoffrey Blodgett, "The Mugwump Reputation, 1870 to the Present," *Journal of American History*, 66 (March 1980): 867-887;

Martin Duberman, *Charles Francis Adams, 1870-1886* (Stanford: Stanford University Press, 1960);

Frederick C. Hicks, ed., *High Finance in the Sixties: Chapters from the Early History of the Erie Railway by Charles Francis Adams, Jr., Henry Adams, Albert Stickney, George Ticknor Curtis and Jeremiah S. Black* (New Haven: Yale University Press, 1929);

Edward C. Kirkland, *Business in the Gilded Age: The Conservatives' Balance Sheet* (Madison: University of Wisconsin Press, 1952);

Kirkland, "Charles Francis Adams, Jr.: The Making of an Historian," in *Proceedings of the Massachusetts Historical Society*, 75 (1963), pp. 39-51;

Thomas K. McCraw, *Prophets of Regulation: Charles Francis Adams, Lewis D. Brandeis, James M. Landis, Alfred E. Kahn* (Cambridge: Harvard University Press, 1984);

Paul C. Nagel, *Descent from Glory: Four Generations of the John Adams Family* (New York: Oxford University Press, 1983);

Stephen T. Riley, "Charles Francis Adams, Conservationist," in *Proceedings of the Massachusetts Historical Society*, 90 (1978), pp. 22-37;

Jack Shepherd, *The Adams Chronicles: Four Generations of Greatness* (Boston: Little, Brown, 1975);

Walter Muir Whitehill, "A Versatile Sophist," *New England Quarterly*, 39 (December 1966): 516-521;

Harvey Wish, *The American Historian: A Social-Intellectual History of the Writing of the American Past* (New York: Oxford University Press, 1960).

Papers:

Charles Francis Adams, Jr.'s papers are at the Massachusetts Historical Society.

Henry Adams

Michael O'Brien
University of Arkansas

See also the Adams entry in *DLB 12, American Realists and Naturalists.*

BIRTH: Boston, Massachusetts, 16 February 1838, to Charles Francis and Abigail Brooks Adams.

EDUCATION: B.A., Harvard University, 1858.

MARRIAGE: 27 June 1872 to Marian Hooper.

AWARDS AND HONORS: Loubat Prize for *History of the United States of America During the Administrations of Thomas Jefferson and James Madison,* 1894; installed as president of the American Historical Association, 1894; Pulitzer Prize for *The Education of Henry Adams,* 1919.

DEATH: Washington, D.C., 27 March 1918.

SELECTED BOOKS: *Chapters of Erie and Other Essays,* by Adams and Charles Francis Adams, Jr. (Boston: Osgood, 1871);
The Life of Albert Gallatin (Philadelphia & London: Lippincott, 1879);
Democracy: An American Novel, anonymous (New York: Holt, 1880; London: Macmillan, 1882);
John Randolph (Boston & New York: Houghton Mifflin, 1882; revised, 1883);
Esther: A Novel, as Frances Snow Compton (New York: Holt, 1884; London: Bentley, 1885);
History of the United States of America During the Administrations of Thomas Jefferson and James Madison:
History of the United States of America During the First Administration of Thomas Jefferson (Cambridge, Mass.: Privately printed, 1884; revised edition, 2 volumes, New York: Scribners, 1889); republished in *History of the United States of America,* 9 volumes (London: Putnam's, 1891-1892);
History of the United States of America During the Second Administration of Thomas Jefferson (Cambridge, Mass.: Privately printed, 1885; revised edition, 2 volumes, New York: Scribners, 1890);

Henry Adams as sketched in 1868 by Samuel Laurence

republished in *History of the United States of America;*
History of the United States of America During the First Administration of James Madison (Cambridge, Mass.: Privately printed, 1888; revised edition, 2 volumes, New York: Scribners, 1890); republished in *History of the United States of America;*
History of the United States of America During the Second Administration of James Madison, 3 volumes (New York: Scribners, 1891); republished in *History of the United States of America;*
Historical Essays (New York: Scribners, 1891; London: Unwin, 1891);

Memoirs of Marau Taaroa Last Queen of Tahiti (N.p.: Privately printed, 1893); revised as *Memoirs of Arii Taimai e Marama of Eimeo Teriirere of Tooarai Teriinui of Tahiti*, as Tauraatua I Amo (Paris: Privately printed, 1901);

Mont-Saint-Michel and Chartres (Washington, D.C.: Privately printed, 1904; revised and enlarged, 1912; Boston & New York: Houghton Mifflin, 1913; London: Constable, 1914);

The Education of Henry Adams (Washington, D.C.: Privately printed, 1907; Boston & New York: Houghton Mifflin, 1918; London: Constable, 1919);

A Letter to American Teachers of History (Washington: Privately printed, 1910);

The Life of George Cabot Lodge (Boston & New York: Houghton Mifflin, 1911);

The Degradation of the Democratic Dogma, edited by Brooks Adams (New York & London: Macmillan, 1919).

OTHER: *Essays in Anglo-Saxon Law*, edited with an essay by Adams (Boston: Little, Brown/London: Macmillan, 1876);

Documents Relating to New-England Federalism, 1800-1815, edited with a preface by Adams (Boston: Little, Brown, 1877);

The Writings of Albert Gallatin, edited with a preface by Adams, 3 volumes (Philadelphia & London: Lippincott, 1879);

"King," in *Clarence King Memoirs* (New York & London: Putnam's, 1904), pp. 157-185;

Letters of John Hay and Extracts from Diary, edited by Adams, 3 volumes (Washington, D.C.: Privately printed, 1908).

PERIODICAL PUBLICATIONS: "American Finance, 1865-1869," *Edinburgh Review*, 129 (April 1869): 504-533;

Review of Clarence King, *Systematic Geology*, in *Nation*, 28 (23 January 1879): 73-74;

"Napoleon Ier et Saint-Domingue," *Revue Historique*, 24 (January-April 1884): 92-130;

"Count Edward de Crillon," *American Historical Review*, 1 (October 1895): 51-69.

No American historian of the nineteenth century has so enchanted, irritated, and impressed his contemporaries and successors as Henry Brooks Adams. He was and is his country's greatest historian, and its most elusive. His achievement was various: he helped to fashion and define the school of "scientific" history, so that his *History of the United States of America During the Administrations of Thomas Jefferson and James Madison* (1884-1891) is a work of stamina and grace that may, with some indulgence, be mentioned in the same breath with Edward Gibbon's *History of the Decline and Fall of the Roman Empire;* he was among the first and best of American medievalists, and his *Mont-Saint-Michel and Chartres* (1904) is an unpretending and quirky combination of travel literature, intellectual history, and architectural celebration; his autobiography, philosophical dissertation, and memoir, *The Education of Henry Adams* (1907), is the most compelling and intractable of American fin-de-siècle writings. In addition, Adams was a minor novelist, an artful humorist, and an unsuccessful philosopher of history. He was, most consistently, an intellectual gamester who liked to play labyrinthine tricks upon posterity, with a cunning that has guaranteed his continuing appeal. He made of himself a puzzle, with books, letters, and essays as clues, and thereby defined a teasing quest that a legion of critics has been obliged to undertake.

Adams was born in 1838 in Boston, "distinctly branded," as he put it in *The Education of Henry Adams*, by being the great-grandson of John Adams, second president of a United States he had helped to found; the grandson of John Quincy Adams, sixth president, diplomat, major opponent of slavery, and minor Harvard rhetorician; and son of Charles Francis Adams, Massachusetts statesman and editor of ancestral papers. It was a wealthy, enveloping, and unsettling heritage, since the Adamses had combined political service, intellectual anxiety, and prickly vanity for several generations, all of which weighed heavily on "ten pounds of unconscious babyhood." He was educated at schools in Boston and at Harvard, by Unitarian services that led eventually to agnosticism, by summers at the family's country seat in Quincy, and by his father, to whom he became private secretary when Charles Francis Adams undertook between 1850 and 1858 an edition of the papers of John Adams. It was in the library of his father's house on Beacon Hill, in an alcove, that Henry Adams listened to Bostonians debating one another and the slave power, and he came into possession of a political creed, Unionist, Free Soil, suspicious of England and South Carolina, antislavery but not quite abolitionist, eventually Republican with a streak of wary independence. Harvard, when he attended between 1854 and 1858, was not yet at its best, but it constituted a necessary rite of passage, in Adams's words a matter of "custom, social ties, convenience." It offered gripping lectures on geology by Louis Agassiz, tedious ones by Henry W.

Adams as a student at Harvard, 1858

Torrey on history, several engaging undergraduate clubs and journals, and interesting contemporaries, including Phillips Brooks, Alexander Agassiz, H. H. Richardson, and Oliver Wendell Holmes. Afterwards, mulling over the choice of a career, Adams took the traditional pretext of seeking an answer in Berlin and in a Grand Tour that took him through Germany, Austria, Italy (including Sicily, where he met and interviewed Garibaldi), France, and England. Berlin failed to give Adams a taste for the civil law, though it did give him a respect for painstaking historical scholarship. For the moment, Adams's interests ran to journalism, marked by a sprightly irresponsibility natural to a third son of private means, newly free in a world beyond New England. He acquired a permanent taste for travel, which was to lead to dozens of Atlantic crossings and one circumnavigation of the globe, besides side trips to the Caribbean and the American West, an Adams "trait of restlessness" that was to express itself in the evasive mobility of his prose.

Adams returned to America in late 1860 and

resumed the position of his father's secretary. He traveled first to Washington to witness the "great secession winter," which he chronicled in letters to the *Boston Daily Advertiser;* and then to London upon his father's appointment by Lincoln as American minister, which he defined in letters to the *New York Times* in 1861 and 1862, before the stripping of his anonymity led to diplomatic embarrassment. London gave him political excitement, for he was involved intimately with the crucial struggle to prevent British recognition of the Confederacy; and a permanent taste for English society through a host of friends, notably Charles Milnes Gaskell, whose home on Wenlock Edge, with its ruined priory, exposed a predilection for the medieval to which New England had offered no opportunity. England also generated a growing excitement at the intellectual paradigm of Darwinism and a permanent suspicion, inherent in an Adams, of British imperial policy.

To practice his trade as a journalist Adams went to Washington in 1868, in time to be appalled by the new President Grant and his undistinguished cabinet, an administration that marked a defection from the Unionist idealism to which distance in London had lent color. Adams became a scathing opponent, in essays for the *North American Review* and the *Nation,* of political incompetence, corruption, and the stupendous pilferings of a newly ambitious American capitalism. He joined in organizing the civil service reform movement and the independent Republicans who bolted from Grant in 1872, though not—as he had hoped—to his father, but to Horace Greeley. Adams's indictment of Grant and Gilded Age politics in *The Education of Henry Adams* was to become justly famous: "The progress of evolution from President Washington to President Grant, was alone evidence enough to upset Darwin." But Adams's influence upon the opinion of posterity was to prove greater than his capacity to deflect the powers of 1870 into genteel reform; thus it was natural that he accepted an invitation to teach medieval history at Harvard. Adams's appointment was more convenient, however, than plausible, since his claim in 1870 to being a historian, let alone a medieval historian, was slim. He had written just three historical essays, one on Captain John Smith and Pocahontas, two on British monetary policy in the early nineteenth century. Harvard president Charles W. Eliot tendered the invitation, because he wished bright young men to help reform an intellectually dormant Cambridge, because Henry was an Adams, because the position carried with it the editorship of the *North American*

Review for which Adams was qualified, and because there were no American medievalists to invite.

Thus Adams became a historian by chance, though he had the perfect temperament of curiosity, skepticism, detachment, and stamina. In later life he pretended, as the literary fulcrum upon which *The Education of Henry Adams* was made to turn, that he had failed in politics and so became a student. "He never got to the point of playing the game at all; he lost himself in the study of it, watching the errors of the players." Yet there is little evidence that he ever aspired to hold political office, though much that he wanted influence, and abundant proof of a soaring intellectual ambition. Obliged to become a historian, a teacher and author, first in medieval history, later in American, he glimpsed the prospect of becoming the American Gibbon. It has been plausibly argued that the playful frustration of his memoirs stemmed, not as he claimed from a failure to become an occupant of the White House, that Adams family heirloom, but from an awareness that he had not quite rivaled the author of the *Decline and Fall of the Roman Empire*, whose moment of inspiration amid the ruins of the Capitol Adams in 1859 had wistfully mimicked, "more than once . . . at sunset on the steps of the Church of Santa Maria di Ara Coeli."

At Harvard Adams proved a talented, conscientious, informal, and eccentric teacher. He founded, without fuss, the first graduate seminar in history in the United States and advanced the emphasis on the history of the Middle Ages that was known as the "germ" theory of Anglo-Saxon consitutional development. In the *North American Review*, Adams wrote in his *Education*, "If copy fell short, he was obliged to scribble a book review on the virtues of the Anglo-Saxons or the vices of the Popes" and so came to grips with the richer European tradition of medievalism, expressed in the writings of Edward A. Freeman, Henry Sumner Maine, Fustel de Coulanges, Bishop Stubbs, John Richard Green, Henry Hallam, all of whom overlaid Adams's long-standing taste for Jules Michelet. In 1876 he published with his students *Essays in Anglo-Saxon Law*, in which the first piece, "Anglo-Saxon Courts of Law," was his own. But increasingly Adams drifted into modern topics and began to teach American history, quite natural for an Adams and logical for a Whiggish historian whose medievalism faced resolutely towards the future and who was impressed by a Romantic literature which saw the definition of national character as the historian's most severe and important task. In 1877 this drift was given a crucial impulse when

the Gallatin family asked him to write the official biography of Albert Gallatin, secretary of the treasury under Thomas Jefferson. This commission plunged Adams into the melee of the early republic, offered schooling in writing and documents, and kindled an ambition to follow the biography with a history of the United States under Jefferson and Madison. The history would be his bid for immortality as a scientific historian, mingling the patriotism of Bancroft, the literary accomplishment and spareness of Macaulay, and the thoroughness of Ranke. The production of the Gallatin biography, three volumes of Gallatin papers, a brief study of John Randolph, an abortive biography of Aaron Burr, nine volumes of *The History of the United States During the Administrations of Thomas Jefferson and James Madison*, a collection of *Historical Essays*, plus (by-the-bye) two short novels, was to engage Adams's energies from 1877 to 1891.

In 1872 Henry Adams had married Marian Hooper of Boston, known as "Clover." She was of unimpeachable social and financial standing, something of a bluestocking, plain of demeanor but sharp in wit, snobbish to all but those customary exceptions, those who rose by their intelligence or artistry. They went for a long marriage trip to Europe and Egypt, not returning to Cambridge until 1877, when Adams resigned his Harvard position so that they might move, inexplicably to his Massachusetts familiars, to Washington. There, happy with his wife, his library, and their salon, he settled into a productive repose that was unusual in being broken only once by foreign travel in 1879 and 1880. Marian Adams helped with his research, both in Washington and in Europe, where he scoured archives in Paris and Madrid. She joined in the amusements of mocking and studying Washington politics. She offered a model for the heroines of his two novels, *Democracy*, published anonymously in 1880, and *Esther*, which appeared under the pseudonym Frances Snow Compton in 1884. In the first Marian Adams appears as Madeleine Lee, a rich New York widow who comes to the national capital in search of answers to the riddle of American democracy. In Washington she finds only a debauched and amoral corruption, to which, despite temptation, she does not succumb. The novel was a succès de scandale, promoted by the gossip attendant on its anonymity, and is an amusingly cynical though slight study of manners and ideas. In *Esther* Marian Adams was cast more bleakly as a heroine whose coldness rejects the suit of a New England cleric, spurning after a struggle both marriage and religious faith, in both influenced by an

The only known photograph of Marian Hooper, taken about three years before she married Adams in 1872 (Massachusetts Historical Society)

overly strong love of her agnostic father. In both novels, ominously, the heroine is left unable to find a satisfactory love or a solution to the problem that increasingly fascinated Adams, the status of women in society. In each novel there is an undercurrent of dissatisfaction, an intimation that bonds of love are always unsatisfactory, since human nature and society require conflicting loyalties.

Marian Adams was devoted to her father, Dr. Robert William Hooper, and wrote to him every Sunday of her married life. In 1885 Dr. Hooper died. She went into a profound depression, which led that same year to her suicide. Adams found her corpse in their Washington home; she had swallowed photographic chemicals. This event marked the end of an epoch in Adams's life, for it undermined the even, confident rhythm of his early historical writing and precipitated a restless pessimism that found expression in his late works. He was, by his own admission, broken but philosophical, con-

scious of having failed to keep alive the woman he loved. Ten days after her death, he wrote to E. L. Godkin: "I have had happiness enough to carry me over some years of misery; and even in my worst prostration I have found myself strengthened by two thoughts. One was that life could have no other experience so crushing. The other was that at least I had got out of life all the pleasure it had to give. I admit that fate at last has smashed the life out of me; but for twelve years I had everything I most wanted on earth." The motives for her suicide have excited much speculation, stimulated by Adams's own silence in the *Education*, which omits all mention of his wife and marriage and tragedy. It has been conjectured that their childlessness bred unhappiness, that he was sterile, that she resented his chivalry toward the beautiful Elizabeth Cameron, wife of a Pennsylvania senator. It has been pointed out that the Hooper family was prone to suicide, that both Marian's aunt and brother (and perhaps even her sister) killed themselves and that Adams's brother Charles, surprised at the news of their betrothal, is said to have exclaimed unguardedly and prophetically, "Heavens!—no—they're all crazy as coots. She'll kill herself, just like her aunt!"

After the death, Adams, while he faithfully completed his *History of the United States* and moved into the house on Lafayette Square that he and she had planned together, became a wanderer who returned to Washington "as a horse goes back to his stable, because he knew nowhere else to go." After visits to Japan, to Cuba, to Polynesia and Ceylon, to Mexico, to Egypt and the Balkans, to Rússia, he settled into an oscillation that took him each year between Paris and Washington. These two cities, the one of aesthetic and intellectual excitement, the other of political interest to a man ambivalently fascinated and troubled by his native land, alone held attractions. Of a generation of Bostonians that produced many expatriates, notably his friend Henry James, Adams maintained a balance between the claims of nativity and foreign education and held on jocosely to the title of tourist, a standing James only acknowledged on the American scene. In later years Adams leaned on friends, notably John Hay, John La Farge, and Clarence King, and on his many nieces. These young women guarded him from the intrusions of strangers in exchange for readings from Swinburne and Tennyson, instruction in the fine arts (for he had a choice collection of paintings, sculpture, pottery, curios, and sketches of himself), the chance to play with the dolls he kept in a special cupboard, the opportunity to listen to the diminutive, bald,

Adams (at bottom) with friends at Wenlock Abbey, England, 1873

bearded, sad man who so often packed his bags or wandered in Rock Creek Cemetery and so often made them laugh. It was to this private audience that Adams addressed his last major works, *The Education of Henry Adams*, printed for his friends, and *Mont-Saint-Michel and Chartres*, cast as an address by an uncle to a niece. Although he contemplated with some cunning the inevitable posthumous publication of his writings, Adams put little before the general public in his later years. The exceptions were mostly duties, like a short biography of his friend, George Cabot Lodge (1911) and a required address upon accepting his election as president of the American Historical Association in 1894. As it was, Adams contrived to be out of the country and to send his address, "The Tendency of History" (later collected in *The Degradation of the Democratic Dogma*, 1919), to be read by another. As his grief ebbed, the solitude of his private world turned into a useful coyness which was to serve his reputation well. He suffered a serious stroke in 1912, but recovered. He died in Washington in 1918 and was buried next to his wife, beneath the inscrutable and melancholy statue that years before he had commissioned from Augustus Saint-Gaudens.

Adams's two early biographies, *The Life of Albert Gallatin* (1879) and *John Randolph* (1882), were apprentice pieces. The former was overlong and marred by an admiration for Gallatin which cut across the grain of Adams's talents as the devil's advocate of American history. The latter's sharp witty condemnation of the Virginian Randolph was a portrait that compounded Randolph's self-confessed and self-promoted bizarreness with Adams's own lack of sympathy for the South. Yet both were given energy as narratives by an implicit meditation on the potentialities of the young American republic: Gallatin was failed by a country grown insensitive to talent and honesty, while Randolph, being too odd, mad, and independent, failed the nation, save in elaborating a bitter assault upon Virginia's leaders Jefferson and Madison. This theme, the betrayal of the country's hopes by men and circumstance, came to dominate Adams's *History of the United States*. His narrative and aesthetic assumptions were best expressed in *The Education of Henry Adams*: "whether, by the severest process of stating, with the least possible comment, such facts as seemed sure, in such order as seemed rigorously consequent, he could fix for a familiar moment a necessary sequence of human movement." The *History of the United States* liberally gathered and quoted documents, and adhered to a strict chronology between 1800 and 1817.

It begins with six chapters that, echoing Macaulay's famous essay into cultural and social definition in the third chapter of *The History of England*, sought to establish the character of the American republic in 1800 by sketching its physical resources, its "popular characteristics," the intellects of New England, the Middle States, and the South, and "American ideals." Thereafter it proceeds through four volumes on Jefferson's administration and five on Madison's with an austere evenness of pace through a narrative, chiefly political, diplomatic, and military. Volume nine ends with four chapters that describe the economy in 1817, religious and political thought, literature and art, and the "American character," thus closing the circle. The *History's* standpoint is ironically bleak and severe in its judgment of Jefferson and Madison. This was not, as was understandably claimed, because Adams wished to settle an ancestral Federalist grudge against the victor of 1800, but, to the contrary, because he sympathized with the Jeffersonian experiment, thought those years to have been the best chance for the fulfillment of optimistic American ambitions for a simple, free, and prosperous democracy blessed with peace, and was disappointed to chronicle a different story. Part of that story, it seemed true to Adams, lay in the failure of individuals: Jefferson sacrificed principle to convenience in making the Louisiana Purchase and imposing the Embargo; Burr acted out the role of the conspiratorial adventurer; Madison drifted towards Federalist policy; the Essex Junto and the Hartford Convention verged on treason. But mostly the causes were blind circumstance and necessity. War between the United States and Britain was a case in point: "The workings of human development were never more strikingly shown than in the helplessness with which the strongest political and social forces in the world followed or resisted at haphazard the necessities of a movement they could not control or comprehend." That the United States could not embody the Jeffersonian dream was occasioned by stubborn facts of economy and preference: it was a huge country, poorly linked by a feeble transportation system, its culture balkanized by sectionalism and religion, its temperment hostile to scientific centralization and planning—all these traits conflicted with the advantages the U.S. possessed because the European inhibitions of monarchy, aristocracy, class struggle, trade barriers, war, and pessimism were absent. These early years showed that the United States shared the ordinary human condition, yet—the *History of the United States* ends with a curious and ambivalent optimism—the War of 1812 had deepened a sense of national unity and impelled a practical flexibility which, if a defection from idealism, was a recognition of wisdom. In short, the years of Jefferson and Madison exposed the terms of the American debate, but indicated no clear preference. The last paragraph of the *History* ends with, not a conclusion, but a series of questions: "The traits of American character were fixed; the rate of physical and economical growth was established; and history, certain that at a given distance of time the union would contain so many millions of people, became thenceforward chiefly concerned to know what kind of people these millions were to be. They were intelligent, but what paths would their intelligence select? They were quick, but what solution of insoluble problems would quickness hurry? . . . What interests were to vivify a society so vast and uniform? What ideals were to ennoble it? What object, besides physical content, must a democratic continent aspire to attain?"

Such questions mirrored Adams's uncertainty at the capacity of scientific history to define, let alone predict, reality. In an 1883 letter, he expressed a taste for determinism: "They [Jefferson, Madison, and Monroe] appear like mere grasshoppers kicking and gesticulating on the middle of the Mississippi River. . . . They were carried along on a stream which floated them, after a fashion, without much regard to themselves. This I take to be the result that students of history generally reach in regard to modern times. The element of individuality is the free-will dogma of the science, if it is a science. My own conclusion is that history is simply social development along the lines of weakest resistance, and that in most cases the line of weakest resistance is found as unconsciously by society as by water." This was written when Adams felt most strongly that a combination of Taine, Comte, Macaulay, and Darwin might yield a historical science. But the *History of the United States*, not finished until 1891, betrayed an uncertainty of which its closing questions were the emblem. Adams never abandoned a taste for historical speculation that might yield generalizations as firm as Darwin's in biology, and he conferred a benign patronage upon his brother Brooks Adams's *The Law of Civilization and Decay* (1895), yet his own ventures grew increasingly paradoxical and playful. He observed honestly to the American Historical Association in 1894, "You may be sure that four out of five serious students of history who are living to-day have, in the course of their work, felt that they stood on the brink of a great generalization that would reduce all history under a law as clear as the laws which govern the material world. . . . He has seemed to have it, as the Spanish say, in his inkstand." But his various later efforts at defining that generalization, in the later chapters of *The Education of Henry Adams*, in "The Rule of Phase Applied to History" (1909), and in *A Letter to American Teachers of History* (1910), started in confusion and ended in lampoon, by himself of himself.

Adams had discovered, by the hard discipline of a researched and sustained narrative, that history suggested facts but did not mandate meaning, which had to be asserted, not found. History became an image, dancing by the will and in the eye of the historian. The disappointed determinist became that rarity, the imagist historian, doing for the past what Baudelaire did for poetry. Adams became intoxicated with imagery. His two late masterpieces, *Mont-Saint-Michel and Chartres* and *The Education of Henry Adams*, were a conscious pair made to do service for an image, asserted more than believed, of the tendency of history since the Middle Ages. "Eight or ten years of study had led Adams to think," he explained in the *Education*, "he might use the century 1150-1250, expressed in Amiens Cathedral and the Works of Thomas Aquinas, as the unit from which he might measure motion down to his own time, without assuming anything as true or untrue, except relation. The movement might be studied at once in philosophy and mechanics. Setting himself to the task, he began a volume which he mentally knew as 'Mont-Saint-Michel and Chartres: A Study of Thirteenth-Century Unity.' From that point he proposed to fix a position for himself, which he could label: 'The Education of Henry Adams: A Study of Twentieth-Century Multiplicity.' " Thus, in the former, the image of unity would be concentrated by the portrait of a coherent and clarifying society, while, in the latter, the image of dissipation would be enhanced by showing how Adams himself had failed to comprehend and master the multiplying energies of a complicating world. Of medieval unity the symbol was the Virgin Mary, installed in the heart of Chartres Cathedral. Of modern disunity the symbol was the dynamo, celebrated at the Chicago Exposition of 1893.

Mont-Saint-Michel and Chartres is written as a tour, for nieces by an uncle, of the two cathedrals, by which the architecture, the art, the literature, and the theology of thirteenth-century northern France are explicated. Its tone is bantering, informal, conversational, "my talk," Adams called it, "for I deny that it is a book." Adams was an unsure guide. While with Ruskin's *Stones of Venice* (1851-1853) in hand one can tour the city and find one's way, the cathedrals in *Mont-Saint-Michel and Chartres* are unevenly, often inaccurately described. For architectural details Adams leaned heavily on Eugene Viollet-le-Duc's *Dictionnaire raisonné de l'architecture française* (1889), though he did not hesitate to alter details when it was convenient. His Old French was self-taught and wobbly, his interpretations of fabliaux and scholastic philosophy uncertain, yet his verve and insight were unquestionable and his translations were vigorous and free of Pre-Raphaelite sentimentality. Adams's Normans were energetic, imperial, and practical, which made their devotion to the Virgin Mary the more impressive. Her Court of Love was a business mediating earth and heaven with firm feminine wit and power which suggested that the ghost of Marian Adams still walked through her widower's imagination. As a connoisseur Adams was more sensitive to the stained glass than to the stones, and

most sensitive to the thought of the scholastics. In the glass moved figures from life, capable of and inviting interpretation. And the final three chapters are a remarkable recreation of the dialectics, and more of the personalities of Abelard, William of Clairvaux, Bernard, and Thomas Aquinas. The moral of the tour is indicated in the sweeping final pages: "Truth, indeed, may not exist; science avers it to be only a relation; but what men took for truth stares one everywhere in the eye and begs for sympathy. The architects of the twelfth and thirteenth centuries took the Church and the universe for truths, and tried to express them in a structure which should be final. Knowing by an enormous experience precisely where the strains were to come, they enlarged their scale to the utmost point of material endurance, lightening the load and distributing the burden until the gutters and gargoyles that seem mere ornament, and the grotesques that seem rude absurdities, all do work either for the arch or for the eye; and every inch of material, up and down, from crypt to vault, from man to God, from the universe to the atom, had its task, giving support where support was needed, or weight where concentration was felt, but always with the condition of showing conspicuously to the eye the great lines which led to unity and the curves which controlled divergence; so that, from the cross on the fleche and the keystone of the vault, down through the ribbed nervures, the columns, the windows, to the foundation of the flying buttresses far beyond the walls, one idea controlled every line; and this is true of Saint Thomas's Church as it is of Amiens Cathedral." This unity depended on faith, on assertion, on not truth absolute but "what men took for truth." The personal moral is clear. Adams's books were his cathedrals. Of one cathedral he wrote: "The delight of its aspirations is flung up to the sky. The pathos of its self-distrust and anguish of doubt is buried in the earth as its last secret. You can read out of it whatever else pleases your youth and confidence; to me, this is all."

For Adams history could enact a jester's role or a death masque, but it had to move. His Middle Ages were no moment of harmonious repose, but a triumph of will over strain for which the ordered restlessness of Gothic architecture was a symbol. Yet, it was important for Adams to stress even of the thirteenth century, "danger lurks in every stone," disaster was always but a half-step away. A taste for catastrophe had grown on Adams during the 1890s, fed by the social and financial upheavals of his own country which, briefly, threatened to ruin him, and by a steady diet of international crises that a traveler and the close friend of Secretary of State John Hay was obliged to notice and delighted to plot. "During this last decade every one talked, and seemed to feel *fin-de-siècle*," he wrote in *The Education of Henry Adams*. Like Graham Greene later, his jaded curiosity needed and welcomed excitement and novelty, the bleaker the better. Adams was never gayer than when he thought the world was imminently going to smash. In this spirit he studied science, with its laws of entropy and thermodynamics and its rule of phase, partly because he conventionally believed it might offer a science of society, and much more devoutly because he guessed it might end society, certainly as he knew it, perhaps utterly. "My belief," he told Brooks Adams in 1902, "is that science is to wreck us, and that we are like monkeys monkeying with a loaded shell; we don't in the least know or care where our practically infinite energies come from or will bring us to." Thus when he addressed American teachers

of history in 1910, he made a sly joke by mimicking the scholastic dialogue between Abelard and William in *Mont-Saint-Michel and Chartres* in another dialogue involving a host of modern scientists whose tumble of contradictory theories provided no settled act of will by which history and society might be ordered. Understanding had fragmented, but energy and power had increased, and scientists, when honest, saw the future as "a toss-up between anarchy and order." With this insight, Adams prefaced the bleak modernists of the 1920s for whom Eliot's *The Waste Land* became a talisman of intelligent hopelessness along with *The Education of Henry Adams*. The center could not hold, or rather, it was ensconced in a hurtling locomotive upon which shifts of scientific engineers, indifferent to one another, maniacally stoked the fire, and the astounded passenger, jarred beyond comfort, was left to decide if the final catastrophe would be occasioned by an exploding boiler, a derailment, or the brick wall of the terminus.

The Education of Henry Adams is, as Sir Denis Brogan once observed, "a great work of art and in its first half, at any rate, a nearly perfect work of art." It would have to be judged a failure as an autobiography, especially where it projected upon Adams's youth the despairing sensibility of his age. Adams, however, never intended it to be an autobiography. It is partly a modernist version of the old Puritan form, the jeremiad, urging lessons but not solutions "to fit young men, in universities or elsewhere, to be men of the world, equipped for any emergency; and the garment offered to them is meant to show the faults of the patchwork fitted on their fathers." It is partly an exposition of Adams's philosophy of history, but it is mostly, and triumphantly, a memoir, though Adams was so used to and fond of dissimulation and so wary of accusations of vanity that he felt obliged to write his memoirs apologetically in the third person.

In the richness and genius of memory the *Education* enchants, while its philosophy and jeremiad irritate. It is packed with vignettes, the *pointillisme* of character. Adams liked to think he knew everyone worth knowing, which was silly, but he had known many and portrayed them: John Quincy Adams, bald in the family pew; Lincoln, fretting over white kid gloves at his inaugural ball; Thackeray, half-blind, crying at the news of an old love's death; Swinburne, launched into poetic monologue far into the night; Grant, the anthropoid president. As vividly, the *Education* is an evocation of place: the "intense blue of the sea, as he saw it a mile or two away, from the Quincy hills";

Adams in Washington, circa 1900

Washington in 1850, with its "want of barriers, of pavements, of forms; the looseness, the laziness; the indolent Southern drawl; the pigs in the street; the negro babies and their mothers with bandanas"; London in the 1860s, its footmen still periwigged, the air smelling of coal; Paris in 1901, where "the pale-faced student of the Latin Quarter in the haunts of Montparnasse or Monmartre . . . must feel no fatigue at two o'clock in the morning in a beer-garden even after four hours of Mounet Sully at the Théâtre Française." Almost above all, the *Education* is a testament of friendship, to John Hay, to Clarence King, to John La Farge, to Augustus Saint-Gaudens and a few, very few, others. The book ends with the death of John Hay, as though history should keep time by the anniversaries of friendship. Of such people and places, the *Education* is a masterly and tantalizingly allusive portrait. Of institutions it is an unsatisfactory account. Adams claimed whimsically to be a "conservative Christian anarchist," and there was truth in his joke. To people and objects, he was usually just, even indulgent. With institutions and nations, he preferred the stance of opposition. Universities, governments, chancelleries, banks (especially Jewish banks, for he was a violent anti-Semite) fascinated but appalled him. Thus it was fitting that at Harvard, though President Eliot had charged Adams with helping in his great reform, the historian used to write letters to friends during faculty meetings—a neat expression of his priorities.

The idiosyncrasy of his style is so marked and his own claim to have been an intellectual fossil of the eighteenth century so insistently argued that it would be easy to miss how much of Adams was conventional to his times. His taste for German scholarship, for Darwinism, for genteel reform, for economic and racial theory, for expanding American influence in the world, for medieval art, all these were ordinary, even Bostonian—a truth he would have hated. Quite intentionally, his style kicked up much dust around his thought, which he feared was unoriginal, in the hope that the dust would only settle after his death. Were it not that style transmutes thought, his fear might be thought correct. No American historian has laid so many traps for his readers, scattered so many clues, camouflaged so many truths. Adams's propensity for mystification arose not from indecisiveness of standpoint, but from an unwillingness to appear decisive. In youth his reticence came from insecurity. In age it became a more subtle evasiveness. He did not fear failure, the red herring of *The Education of Henry Adams*, but rather a success that

would set a limit to achievement, define it, close it down, deaden curiosity. He wanted the prerogative to slip away, to catch the night boat-train for Calais.

Adams's influence has been great, though inferior to the interest generated by his life and writings. At Harvard he produced a small crop of historians who, when they did not go on to political power as did Henry Cabot Lodge and Theodore Roosevelt, merged into the new cohorts of American professional history. His *History of the United States During the Administrations of Thomas Jefferson and James Madison* sold only moderately, yet for a long work that few historians to this day bother to read, was his most influential work of interpretation; students of the Jeffersonian period still refer to it, while the works of George Bancroft, Francis Parkman, and John Lothrop Motley are studied primarily as literature. The paradoxical result is that the stylistic accomplishment of the *History* has been overshadowed by its content, by Adams's own later mature style, and by the prejudice that scientific history must be tedious. His novels survive, though *Esther* is the least read and *Democracy* is most often used as a primer for the political manners of the Gilded Age. Adams's historical philosophy has influenced almost no one, though it is much studied as a tract for his times. *Mont-Saint-Michel and Chartres* was pirated in his lifetime, and Adams consented to its general publication in 1913. But, eccentric in form and motive, uneven as medieval history and uncertain as a guide, it has had a twilight existence; often mentioned, it is less frequently read. But *The Education of Henry Adams*, published posthumously in 1918, immediately attained celebrity and was influential in the 1920s the way that Byron was influential in the 1820s, for the pose and the tone. That fashion having gone, the *Education* has remained securely an American classic. Interest in Adams himself has been steady, even rising. His life has been written in three volumes, his works are republished, his relationship to his times is weighed by intellectual historians, social historians, and literary critics, and a second edition of his letters is in preparation. Historians love a puzzle, as they respect genius.

Letters:

Letters to a Niece and Prayer to the Virgin of Chartres, edited by Mabel La Farge (Boston & New York: Houghton Mifflin, 1920; London: Constable, 1920);

A Cycle of Adams Letters, 1861-1865, edited by Worthington C. Ford, 2 volumes (Boston & New York: Houghton Mifflin, 1920);

Letters of Henry Adams (1858-1891), edited by Ford (Boston & New York: Houghton Mifflin, 1930);

Letters of Henry Adams (1892-1918), edited by Ford (Boston & New York: Houghton Mifflin, 1938);

Henry Adams and His Friends, edited by Harold Dean Cater (Boston: Houghton Mifflin, 1947);

The Letters of Henry Adams, 1858-1892, edited by J. C. Levenson, Ernest Samuels, and others, 3 volumes to date (Cambridge, Mass.: Harvard University Press, 1982-   ).

Bibliography:

Earl N. Harbert, *Henry Adams: A Reference Guide* (Boston: G. K. Hall, 1978).

Biographies:

James Truslow Adams, *Henry Adams* (New York: A. & C. Boni, 1933);

Ernest Samuels, *The Young Henry Adams* (Cambridge: Harvard University Press, 1948);

Elizabeth Stevenson, *Henry Adams: A Biography* (New York: Macmillan, 1955);

Samuels, *Henry Adams: The Middle Years* (Cambridge: Harvard University Press, 1958);

Samuels, *Henry Adams: The Major Phase* (Cambridge: Harvard University Press, 1964).

References:

Max I. Baym, *The French Education of Henry Adams* (New York: Columbia University Press, 1951);

Sacvan Bercovitch, *The American Jeremiad* (Madison: University of Wisconsin Press, 1978);

Richard P. Blackmur, *Henry Adams* (New York & London: Harcourt Brace Jovanovich, 1980);

D. W. Brogan, "The Importance of Being Adams," in his *American Aspects* (London: Hamilton, 1964), pp. 129-139;

Joseph F. Byrnes, *The Virgin of Chartres: An Intellectual and Psychological History of the Work of Henry Adams* (Rutherford, N.J.: Fairleigh Dickinson University Press, 1981);

John J. Conder, *A Formula of His Own: Henry Adams's Literary Experiment* (Chicago & London: University of Chicago Press, 1970);

David R. Contosta, *Henry Adams and the American Experiment* (Boston: Little, Brown, 1980);

Timothy P. Donovan, *Henry Adams and Brooks Adams: The Education of Two American Historians* (Norman: University of Oklahoma Press, 1961);

William Dusinberre, *Henry Adams: The Myth of Failure* (Charlottesville: University Press of Virginia, 1980);

Earl N. Harbert, *The Force So Much Closer Home: Henry Adams and the Adams Family* (New York: New York University Press, 1977);

Harbert, ed., *Critical Essays on Henry Adams* (Boston: G. K. Hall, 1981);

George Hochfield, *Henry Adams: An Introduction and Interpretation* (New York: Barnes & Noble, 1962);

Robert A. Hume, *Runaway Star: An Appreciation of Henry Adams* (Ithaca: Cornell University Press, 1951);

William H. Jordy, *Henry Adams: Scientific Historian* (New Haven & London: Yale University Press, 1952);

J. C. Levenson, *The Mind and Art of Henry Adams* (Boston: Houghton Mifflin, 1957);

Melvin Lyon, *Symbol and Idea in Henry Adams* (Lincoln: University of Nebraska Press, 1970);

Robert Mane, *Henry Adams on the Road to Chartres* (Cambridge: Harvard University Press, 1971);

John Carlos Rowe, *Henry Adams and Henry James: The Emergence of a Modern Consciousness* (Ithaca: Cornell University Press, 1976);

Robert F. Sayre, *The Examined Self: Benjamin Franklin, Henry Adams, Henry James* (Princeton: Princeton University Press, 1969);

Ernst Scheyer, *The Circle of Henry Adams: Art and Artists* (Detroit: Wayne State University Press, 1970);

Richard C. Vitzthum, *The American Compromise: Theme and Method in the Histories of Bancroft, Parkman, and Adams* (Norman: University of Oklahoma Press, 1974);

Vern Wagner, *The Suspension of Henry Adams: A Study of Manner and Matter* (Detroit: Wayne State University Press, 1969).

Papers:

Most of Henry Adams's papers are at the Massachusetts Historical Society.

Herbert Baxter Adams

(16 April 1850-30 July 1901)

Raymond J. Cunningham
Fordham University

BOOKS: *Maryland's Influence in Founding a National Commonwealth; or the History of the Accession of Public Lands by the Old Confederation* (Baltimore: Johns Hopkins University, 1877);
History of the Thomas Adams and Thomas Hastings Families of Amherst, Massachusetts (Amherst: Privately printed, 1880);
The Germanic Origin of New England Towns (Baltimore: Johns Hopkins University, 1882);
Saxon Tithing-Men in America (Baltimore: Johns Hopkins University, 1883);
Norman Constables in America (Baltimore: Johns Hopkins University, 1883);
Village Communities of Cape Anne and Salem (Baltimore: Johns Hopkins University, 1883);
Bluntschli's Life-Work (Baltimore: Privately printed, 1884);
Methods of Historical Study (Baltimore: N. Murray, Publication agent, Johns Hopkins University, 1884);
Maryland's Influence upon Land Cessions to the United States. With Minor Papers on George Washington's Interest in Western Lands, the Potomac Company, and a National University (Baltimore: N. Murray, Publication agent, Johns Hopkins University, 1885);
Seminary Libraries and University Extension (Baltimore: N. Murray, Publication agent, Johns Hopkins University, 1887);
The College of William and Mary: A Contribution to the History of Higher Education, With Suggestions for Its National Promotion (Washington, D.C.: Government Printing Office, 1887);
The Study of History in American Colleges and Universities (Washington, D.C.: Government Printing Office, 1887);
Notes on the Literature of Charities (Baltimore: N. Murray, Publication agent, Johns Hopkins University, 1887);
Higher Education of the People: The Work of Chautauqua (Buffalo: Chautauqua Press?, 1888?);
Thomas Jefferson and the University of Virginia: With Authorized Sketches of Hampden-Sidney, Randolph-Macon, Emory-Henry, Roanoke, and Rich-

Herbert Baxter Adams

mond Colleges, Washington and Lee University, and Virginia Military Institute (Washington, D.C.: Government Printing Office, 1888);
The Encouragement of Higher Education: An Address by Herbert B. Adams, Ph.D., Associate Professor of History in the Johns Hopkins University, on Commemoration Day, February 22, 1889 (Baltimore: Johns Hopkins University Press, 1889);
In Memoriam: Charles Dickinson Adams, 1839-1889 (Baltimore: Privately printed, 1889);
Work Among Working Women in Baltimore: A Social Study (Baltimore: Printed by John Murray, 1889);

28

The Life and Writings of Jared Sparks: Comprising Selections from His Journal and Correspondence, 2 volumes (Boston & New York: Houghton Mifflin, 1893);

Is History Past Politics? (Baltimore: Johns Hopkins Press, !895);

The Study and Teaching of History: Phi Beta Kappa Address at William and Mary College, Williamsburg, Va., February 18, 1898 (Richmond: Whittet & Shepperson, 1898);

Jared Sparks and Alexis de Tocqueville (Baltimore: Johns Hopkins Press, 1898);

Public Educational Work in Baltimore (Baltimore: Johns Hopkins Press, 1899);

The Church and Popular Education (Baltimore: Johns Hopkins Press, 1900);

Public Libraries and Popular Education (Albany: University of the State of New York, 1900);

Summer Schools and University Extension (Albany: J. B. Lyon, 1900);

Educational Extension in the United States (Washington, D.C.: Government Printing Office, 1901).

OTHER: "The State and Higher Education," in *Annual Report of the Board of Regents of the Smithsonian Institution, Showing the Operations, Expenditures, and Condition of the Institution to July 1889* (Washington, D.C.: Government Printing Office, 1890), pp. 695-710;

"The Teaching of History," in *Annual Report of the American Historical Association for the Year 1896* (Washington, D.C.: Government Printing Office, 1897), pp. 245-263;

"The Study of History in Schools, being the Report to the American Historical Association by the Committee of Seven," by Adams and others, in *Annual Report of the American Historical Association for the Year 1898* (Washington, D.C.: Government Printing Office, 1899), pp. 427-564.

PERIODICAL PUBLICATIONS: "A New Historical Movement," *Nation*, 39 (18 September 1884): 240;

"Defence of a Civil Academy," *Science: An Illustrated Journal*, 9 (20 May 1887): 484-485;

"Leopold von Ranke," *Papers of the American Historical Association*, 3 (1888): 101-120;

"Arnold Toynbee," *Chautauqua Assembly-Herald*, 4 August 1888, p. 5;

"University Extension in America," *Forum*, 11 (July 1891): 510-523.

The name of Herbert Baxter Adams, historian and teacher, has more than that of any other individual been rightly associated with the creation of the modern American historical profession. During his twenty-five years in the combined department of history, politics, and economics at the Johns Hopkins University (1876-1901), Adams came to be identified as the chief voice of the "New Historical School" which had as its aim the systematic application to American historical sources of the so-called scientific or critical approach which was the hallmark of nineteenth-century German historiography. In his famous seminar, Adams, a gifted teacher, trained a generation of professional historical scholars and authors which included such men as J. Franklin Jameson, Woodrow Wilson, Frederick Jackson Turner, Charles M. Andrews, and John Spencer Bassett. The implications of such professionalization for historical writing in the United States were enormous, for by 1900 historical learning was no longer generally regarded as a branch of literature but as an academic discipline closely allied to the social sciences. Its most characteristic literary form had become the scholarly monograph. Adams placed himself in the vanguard of this transformation in yet another way, when in 1883 and 1884 he assumed the lead in founding the American Historical Association, which immediately became the principal national organization created to foster a sense of identity and purpose within the new profession. During the next fifteen years he remained a pivotal figure among fellow historians through his position as secretary of the association.

Herbert Adams, the youngest of three sons, was born on 16 April 1850 to Nathaniel Dickinson and Harriet Hastings Adams in Shutesbury, a small town in western Massachusetts where his father was a partner in the family lumber business. Both parents, who came of old New England Congregationalist stock, traced their American roots back to the early seventeenth century—a heritage which significantly influenced Adams's historical interests. Neither father nor mother had more than elementary schooling, but they were determined that their children (all of whom became professional men) should have greater educational advantages. After Nathaniel Adams's death, the family moved to the neighboring college town of Amherst. Here Herbert Adams attended public schools and experienced the excitement of the Civil War years. Although Adams lived most of his adult life in Baltimore, he considered Amherst his home and returned there every summer.

After graduating from Phillips Exeter Academy in July 1868, Adams entered Amherst College with the class of 1872. The curriculum, typical of mid-nineteenth-century liberal arts colleges, was based on the ancient classics, supplemented by mathematics, modern languages, and some natural science; history was not taught as a distinct field. Adams, who was active in the literary society and on the student paper, contemplated a career in journalism. During his senior year, however, a lecture by Amherst's moral philosopher Julius Seelye on the philosophy of history was credited by Adams with steering him toward postgraduate historical training. In the 1870s this necessarily meant study at one or more of the German universities, and Adams joined the swelling numbers of young Americans bent upon advanced work abroad.

Adams spent six months in European travel before beginning his studies in history and political science at Heidelberg University in January 1874. With the exception of one semester (winter 1874-1875) at Berlin University, he remained at Heidelberg from 1874 to May 1876, when he was awarded his doctorate of philosophy summa cum laude. Adams's historical perspective was permanently fixed in several crucial respects by his association with German scholarship. Of primary importance here was the conservative political philosophy undergirding nineteenth-century German social science which taught that the state is a living organism grounded on the relationship of a people to their land, not a mere contractual arrangement to preserve individual rights. Another central theme interacting with this organicism was the racialism that manifested itself in a variety of contexts. Adams's mentor, Johann Bluntschli, an eminent political scientist, held that the Aryan race was destined to lead mankind to the ultimate stage in its political evolution, as the Semites had been destined to shape its highest religious aspirations. In Bluntschli's benevolent view this goal would be a world-state governed by international law. A different expression of race chauvinism which prevailed among German (and English) historians also affected Adams profoundly. This was the so-called Teutonist thesis, according to which the towns and municipal governments of medieval Europe (with their early institutions of popular representation) were thought to have developed from a largely hypothetical, primitive form of free village-community (*Markgenossenschaft*) introduced by the barbarian, Germanic invaders. All these assumptions were later incorporated in Adams's own teaching and writing.

In 1876 Adams returned to the United States

to take up a postdoctoral fellowship that fall at the recently opened Johns Hopkins University in Baltimore, the first American institution dedicated principally to graduate education and advanced research. Here he produced his first published monograph, *Maryland's Influence in Founding a National Commonwealth* (1877), which was characteristic of the new academic historical literature. Adams took as his premise the familiar organic principle that a nation is founded "upon that community of material interests which arises from the *permanent* relation of a people to some fixed territory." He then went on to marshal an array of primary source material in support of his argument that Maryland, by refusing to ratify the Articles of Confederation until Virginia, New York, Massachusetts, and Connecticut had agreed to surrender their western land claims to the central government, deserved the credit for the establishment of a national domain, always the prerequisite for the development of a national state. Though long since superseded, the study was well received by contemporary scholars, with Henry Adams acknowledging it as a "very excellent monograph."

In June 1878 Johns Hopkins appointed Adams to the rank of associate, while agreeing that he might also accept a teaching post at Smith College during the spring semester. This arrangement, which lasted four years, proved him to be an imaginative and effective undergraduate instructor. By 1883 Adams's own research and that of his graduate students were beginning to win recognition, and in June he was named associate professor in full charge of the department of history, politics, and economics, to which he gave decisive administrative leadership for the next eighteen years. The centerpiece of the department was Adams's graduate seminar, an innovation of German origin, for which he chose the words of the English historian Edward A. Freeman as the motto: "History is past Politics and Politics present History." Although this dictum, which became famous, was never a truly accurate indicator either of Adams's concept of history or of the scope of historical studies pursued at Johns Hopkins, it did serve to emphasize the social-scientific orientation of the new professionals as opposed to the belletristic orientation of their predecessors.

The most distinctive work of the seminar, especially during its formative period, consisted of what Adams and others called "institutional history." In line with Adams's recent German training, this approach initially entailed research into both the immediate and remote origins of American local government and institutions as these took shape during the seventeenth century. Such studies were of intense historical and contemporary significance to Adams, who believed that this earliest phase of colonial development was the touchstone of the entire American experience.

In order to publicize the results of the new research, Adams established in 1882 the Johns Hopkins University Studies in Historical and Political Science which was the prototype of similar scholarly publications elsewhere. As part of the Studies Adams published the work for which he is most often remembered, a series of monographs which together comprised the findings and conjectures of several years' investigation into New England town origins. In *The Germanic Origin of New England Towns* (1882), the best-known of these, Adams revealed his debt to his German professors by attempting to bring early American history within the explanatory structure of Teutonism. While there was precedent for this in the work of others (whom Adams acknowledged), it was he who became the chief academic proponent of the so-called

"germ theory." According to this hypothesis, comparative historical studies were uncovering such remarkable similarities among the local political, economic, and social institutions of ancient Teutons, medieval Anglo-Saxons, and seventeenth-century New Englanders that the only satisfactory explanation had to be racial kinship. As Adams put it, "The town and village life of New England is as truly the reproduction of Old English types as these again are reproductions of the village community system of the ancient Germans."

Adams's other monographs were intended to provide additional evidence for Teutonism: *Saxon Tithing-Men in America* (1883); *Norman Constables in America* (1883); *Village Communities of Cape Anne and Salem* (1883). At the same time students were exploring the early institutional history of Virginia, Maryland, New York, and other colonies from this same perspective. But the "germ theory," which owed much of its appeal to its apparent congruence to current Darwinian evolutionary thought, did not go unchallenged even among Adams's own students, as is evident in the work of Charles M. An-

Adams's seminar room at Johns Hopkins University. Displayed on the wall is Edward A. Freeman's dictum "History is past Politics and Politics present History," chosen by Adams as the motto of the seminar.

drews and Frederick Jackson Turner. Adams himself was never obsessed by his Teutonist view of colonial origins; on the contrary, he encouraged the greatest latitude in historical study and interpretation. Within a few years his students had enlarged the scope of American institutional history to include such topics as church-state relations, utopian socialist communities, public land law and policy, tariff and monetary history, and mining camps and trading posts. Some broke away from the institutional framework to engage in intellectual and diplomatic history. Adams particularly urged students on to regional studies of the South and West with important consequences for the development of American historiography. Theses on slavery and race relations in the South made Johns Hopkins a center for the study of Southern history. In February 1891 Adams's highly successful efforts to build his department into one of the most prestigious in the country were acknowledged when he was appointed full professor.

One of Adams's purposes from the outset, in which he was supported by the university administration, was that graduate education in his department should train not only professional scholars but an elite cadre of public servants, journalists, and social workers as well. His own involvement in public affairs took many forms which sooner or later showed their influence on his teaching and writing. One such commitment was to good government reform and civil service which was reflected academically in student theses and monographs on urban government. In this connection Adams also became a champion of the idea of a national university or "civil academy," to be located in Washington, D.C., which would train public administrators much as West Point and Annapolis trained military and naval officers. Although he was essentially conservative in his economic and social opinions, Adams interested himself and his students in a wide range of socioeconomic issues, including charity organization, settlement work, land and labor questions, and tariff and currency problems. Experts on these and related matters were frequent guests at the seminar meetings. Adams's popular course on international law, which echoed Bluntschli's optimistic Aryan internationalism, was given for many years, and he deeply believed in the cause of international arbitration.

It was, however, to the advancement of education that Adams instinctively turned as the most promising route to long-term social improvement, and he participated in various experiments which aimed at the diffusion of higher education among the people. He harbored great expectations for the Chautauqua adult education movement, and he held the post of lecturer in history at the Chautauqua summer College of Liberal Arts in western New York for six years in the late 1880s and 1890s. During this same period Adams was one of the first American educators to introduce the university extension idea into the United States from Great Britain, and he became one of its best-known publicists. Some of Adams's finest students were initiated into the art of teaching as extension lecturers. In the summer of 1896 Adams, on behalf of the federal Bureau of Education, undertook a trip abroad to study university extension in England and Scotland. Not surprisingly, his interest in contemporary education carried over into his history courses, in which educational institutions and ideas received increasing attention. From 1887 to 1901 Adams edited the Contributions to American Educational History, a multivolume series produced by the Bureau of Education, the purpose of which was to provide historical understanding of the present conditions and needs of higher education in each of the states. Adams introduced the project with two monographs on the educational history of Virginia.

In *The College of William and Mary: A Contribution to the History of Higher Education, With Suggestions for Its National Promotion* (1887), Adams did not attempt to disguise the practical aim of the series. By recounting the proud but unfortunate history of the South's oldest college from its late-seventeenth-century beginnings onward, Adams was able to stimulate concern among Virginia legislators about its current lamentable state, thereby contributing importantly to the revival of the school. He also contrived to find in the curriculum offered at William and Mary in its heyday evidence to support his commitment to a trained civil service. "Indeed," he observed, "the conspicuous merit of southern leaders . . . was due to their superior political education which early ranged over topics that were not prominent in northern colleges until after the [Civil] War, notably history, political economy, and the science of government and administration."

Adams's second study in this vein, entitled *Thomas Jefferson and the University of Virginia* (1888), was a more substantial piece of scholarship. As the first analysis and appraisal of the educational ideals and accomplishments of Jefferson by a modern historian, it occupies an important place in the historiography of American intellectual history. The work is a judicious treatment of the genesis and development of Jefferson's educational thought, his political maneuvers in behalf of the nascent university, and his tenure as its first rector. Adams argued convincingly for the influence of Jefferson's ideas, not only in the South, but upon early-nineteenth-century collegiate reform in the North as well, specifically at Harvard. Adams was especially interested in Jefferson's views on the study of history and government and in the important place which he allotted to it in his curriculum. He, of course, seized upon Jefferson's emphasis on the need to teach American youth Anglo-Saxon language, history, and law, since this revealed Jefferson's appreciation of "the Saxon sources of the great modern stream of liberty and self-government then flowing through Virginia. . . ." Moreover, this focus also showed that Jefferson's political philosophy was no mere frothy derivative from French rationalism but rather was fundamentally historical and organic in character, rooted as it was in the English Whig tradition. On one point, however, Adams unequivocally rejected the Jeffersonian position: he branded as "intolerable" Jefferson's attempt to secure "party control" over the University of Virginia by dictating the texts to be used in political science instruction. In sum, during a period when the tendency of the Southern states was to retreat from their postwar commitment to popular education on all levels, Adams's monographs attempted to recall them to their better heritage.

A year before he undertook his assignment with the Bureau of Education, Adams had agreed to perform a different sort of editorial task. In 1886 he signed a contract with the heirs of Jared Sparks, the originator of the *Library of American Biography* and an early-nineteenth-century publisher of primary source materials for American history, to bring out an authorized two-volume memorial to this historical pioneer. The result, entitled *The Life and Writings of Jared Sparks* (1893), was a monumental life-and-letters biography which received mixed reviews. Much of the adverse criticism had to do with Adams's defense of Sparks's rather freewheeling editorial procedures, particularly in connection with his editions of the American diplomatic papers of the Revolutionary era and of the George Washington papers. While many of Adams's points could be well taken (such as the more permissive editorial standards of Sparks's day and the multiple forms of Washington's correspondence the best of which was not always available to the editor), Adams was justly reproached for displaying too little of the critical historical spirit which

he fostered in his students. There is an irony in the fact that Adams, a paragon of the scientific historian, should have come under fire for his extenuation of the editorial emendations made by Jared Sparks in the interest of then-accepted literary norms. In fact, however, Adams never disputed the literary dimension of historical writing, though he did consider it secondary. While upholding German historiography as the pacesetter in critical method, he warned students against the turgidity of German historical style. Adams admired and recommended the literary qualities of such historians as François Guizot and Thomas Carlyle, Francis Parkman and John Lothrop Motley, even when he cautioned against some of their scholarly tendencies. His own lecture notes show a strong penchant for historical color and dramatic detail. The problem of style was repeatedly addressed in seminar meetings, at one of which Adams called for "more of the old, Herodotus storytelling spirit."

During the 1890s Adams received calls to over a half-dozen university presidencies or other high administrative posts. In each instance, however, he chose to remain as director of his department in Baltimore with which he was now thoroughly identified. In 1900 he was among those under consideration to succeed Daniel Coit Gilman as president of Johns Hopkins. Whatever the likelihood of this contingency, it was precluded by the fatal illness which forced his resignation in February 1901. Adams died in Amherst, Massachusetts, on 30 July 1901. The outflow of tributes, public and private, occasioned by Adams's premature retirement and death testified to the central place which he held in the profession. The view of Woodrow Wilson expressed the general consensus: "If I were to sum up my impression of Dr. Adams, I should call him a great Captain of Industry, a captain in the field of systematic and organized scholarship. . . . The thesis work done under him may fairly be said to have set the pace for university work in history throughout the United States."

References:

Raymond J. Cunningham, "The German Historical World of Herbert Baxter Adams: 1874-1876," *Journal of American History*, 68 (September 1981): 261-275;

Cunningham, "Is History Past Politics? Herbert Baxter Adams as Precursor of the 'New History,'" *History Teacher*, 9 (February 1976): 244-257;

Herbert B. Adams: Tributes of Friends; with a Bibliog-

raphy of the Department of History, Politics and Economics of the Johns Hopkins University (Baltimore: Johns Hopkins Press, 1902);

W. Stull Holt, ed., *Historical Scholarship in the United States, 1876-1901: As Revealed in the Correspondence of Herbert B. Adams* (Baltimore: Johns Hopkins Press, 1938);

Bert James Loewenberg, *American History in American Thought: Christopher Columbus to Henry Adams* (New York: Simon & Schuster, 1972), pp. 363-379.

Papers:
Adams's personal and professional correspondence, lecture notes, and scrapbooks are in Special Collections, Milton S. Eisenhower Library, Johns Hopkins University. Diaries, notebooks, and minutes of Adams's seminar, 1877-1901, are at the same library in the Ferdinand Hamberger, Jr., Archives. Adams's correspondence as secretary of the American Historical Association, 1884-1900, is in the American Historical Association Papers, Manuscript Division, Library of Congress.

Hubert Howe Bancroft
(5 May 1832-2 March 1918)

Donald E. Green
Central Oklahoma State University

BOOKS: *The Native Races of the Pacific States of North America*, 5 volumes (San Francisco: A. L. Bancroft, 1874-1875);

Central America, 3 volumes (San Francisco: A. L. Bancroft, 1882-1887);

History of Mexico, 6 volumes (volumes 1-5, San Francisco: A. L. Bancroft, 1883; volume 6, San Francisco: History Company, 1888);

The Early American Chronicler, (San Francisco: A. L. Bancroft, 1883);

History of the Northwest Coast, 2 volumes (San Francisco: A. L. Bancroft, 1884);

California, 7 volumes (San Francisco: A. L. Bancroft, 1884-1890);

Life of Porfirio Díaz, 2 volumes (San Francisco: A. L. Bancroft, 1885);

Alaska, 1730-1885 (San Francisco: A. L. Bancroft, 1886);

History of Oregon, 2 volumes (San Francisco: History Company, 1886-1888);

British Columbia, 1792-1887 (San Francisco: History Company, 1887);

Popular Tribunals, 2 volumes (San Francisco: History Company, 1887);

Arizona and New Mexico, 1530-1880 (San Francisco: History Company, 1888);

California inter pocula (San Francisco: History Company, 1888);

California Pastoral, 1769-1848 (San Francisco: History Company, 1888);

History of Utah, 1540-1886 (San Francisco: History Company, 1889);

History of Nevada, Colorado, and Wyoming, 1540-1888 (San Francisco: History Company, 1890);

History of Texas and the North Mexican States, 2 volumes (San Francisco: History Company, 1890);

History of Washington, Idaho and Montana, 1845-1889 (San Francisco: History Company, 1890);

Essays and Miscellany (San Francisco: History Company, 1890);

Literary Industries (San Francisco: History Company, 1890);

The Book of the Fair; An Historical and Descriptive Presentation of the World's Science, Art, and Industry, As Viewed Through the Columbian Exposition at Chicago in 1893, 2 volumes (Chicago & San Francisco: Bancroft Company, 1893);

Resources and Development of Mexico (San Francisco: Bancroft Company, 1893);

Achievements of Civilization; The Book of Wealth, 10 volumes (New York: Bancroft Company, 1896-1908);

The New Pacific (New York: Bancroft Company, 1900; revised, 1912);

Some Cities and San Francisco (New York: Bancroft Company, 1907);

Hubert Howe Bancroft

Retrospection, Political and Personal (New York: Bancroft Company, 1912; revised, 1913);

Why a World Centre of Industry at San Francisco Bay? (New York: Bancroft Company, 1916);

In These Latter Days (Chicago: Blakely-Oswald, 1917);

History of the Life of Leland Stanford; A Character Study (Oakland: Biobooks, 1952).

OTHER: *Chronicles of the Builders of the Commonwealth,* 7 volumes, edited by Bancroft (San Francisco: History Company, 1891-1892).

Hubert Howe Bancroft was the first historian to produce a comprehensive account of the history of the American Far West. Anticipating the twentieth-century historical school of the "Spanish Borderlands," he included Mexico and Central America in his definition of the American West. Prior to his work as a historian, Bancroft was a successful West Coast book and stationery dealer as well as a publisher. His sixty-thousand-volume

library, which furnished the sources for his history, was later sold to the University of California at Berkeley, where it served as the basis for the University's priceless collection of Western Americana, the Bancroft Collection.

Descended from New England stock, Bancroft was born 5 May 1832 at Granville, Ohio, the son of Azariah Ashley and Lucy Howe Bancroft. The Bancroft and Howe families had migrated from Massachusetts and Vermont prior to 1815. The first American Bancroft, John, had arrived in the Massachusetts Bay Colony from London in 1632. Hubert Bancroft's father, known as Ashley, was a farmer and his mother was a schoolmarm in a family of teachers which included her father and brother. In late 1840 Ashley Bancroft sold his Licking County, Ohio, farm and moved his family to a farm near New Madrid, Missouri. The rich Missouri soil produced an abundance, but low farm prices ruined the elder Bancroft. Within a few years, the landless family was back in Granville, Ohio.

Ashley Bancroft was a political activist. By 1836 he was a vocal member of the abolitionist crusade. His barn was the setting for meetings and speeches for the cause, and he became one of the links in the Underground Railway. He was also a staunch Whig. During the campaign of 1840 young Hubert Howe Bancroft witnessed a Whig rally for William Henry Harrison in the county seat of Newark. In later years he vividly recalled many scenes from that day including log cabins mounted on wheels pulled through the streets by oxen, a tall liberty pole, and fights between Whigs and Democrats.

Hubert Howe Bancroft's childhood was not a happy one. He could read by the age of three but was shy and withdrawn. When he had difficulty in his uncle's grammar class, his mother took him out of school and taught him grammar at home. Bancroft did not care for the drudgery of farm work. And his avid reading took him farther and farther from his Puritan roots. As he approached his sixteenth birthday he began preparing himself to enter college but subsequently abandoned the idea because of his family's financial hardships.

At this time in Bancroft's youth, chance saved the day when on the muddy streets of Granville his sister met a stranger who in a gentlemanly gesture stepped from a plank to let her pass. From this encounter, which blossomed into a courtship, George H. Derby became the brother-in-law of Hubert Bancroft. Derby owned a bookstore in Buffalo, and in the late summer of 1848 young Bancroft left home, working his way to Buffalo by riding a canal tow horse to Cleveland before boarding a steamer on Lake Erie. Shortly after his arrival he went to work for Derby, first in the store's bindery, then in the bookkeeping department. The time which Bancroft spent in the lower echelons of the book business was, like his childhood, a miserable experience. After six months the head of the bookkeeping department fired him.

Feeling sympathy for the boy, Derby loaned him the money to return to Ohio and also provided him with a consignment of books. Back home Bancroft blossomed as a book salesman, hawking his wholesale wares around the countryside to rural storekeepers. After selling a number of shipments from Derby, Bancroft returned to Buffalo, where his brother-in-law once more employed him, this time as a clerk. For the first few months of his new "successful" life, Bancroft became something of a dandy. He bought himself a stylish broadcloth suit and high hat. A silver watch, cane, cigar, brightly colored cravat, and a ring completed his ensemble. For the next few years the young man spent many of his nights carousing with the youths of the city while his days were consumed with bookselling.

The California gold rush brought an even more significant change to the young salesman's life. His father and other relatives joined the bonanza movement to the West Coast. Derby sent an order of books to one of the Bancrofts in Oregon, followed by a few other shipments to California. Profits from those consignments prompted Derby to send his young brother-in-law to California with books and stationery valued at $5,000. With a fellow clerk, George L. Kenny, nineteen-year-old Hubert Bancroft stepped on board a steamer headed for the Isthmus of Panama by way of Cuba and Jamaica in February 1852. On the Pacific coast of Panama, Bancroft boarded another ship and, after stops at Acapulco, San Diego, and Monterey, entered San Francisco Bay on 1 April 1852.

Bancroft traveled to Sacramento to deliver the shipment of books to a partnership of merchants, then proceeded farther west into the Sierras, where he joined his father in a mining camp. The elder Bancroft had managed to accumulate a little money, enough to attract his son to help work the claim. After six months of a relatively fruitless search for the elusive yellow metal, Bancroft returned to Sacramento only to learn that George Derby had died. That shock was followed by the realization that no other book dealer in the East would entrust such valuable shipments to such a young wholesaler.

The young salesman spent the next few months in San Francisco in a futile attempt to find work. Hard times had descended on the Golden Gate city. Unemployed miners roamed the streets in droves. When Bancroft learned of new diggings in northwestern California, he journeyed up the coast to Crescent City with some books and stationery acquired in San Francisco on credit. There he found an opportunity to work as a bookkeeper in the general store of Crowell and Fairfield and to market his books and stationery through that firm. Within two years he had assets of $6,000 to $8,000, enough to buy a brick building which he rented to a hardware concern for $250 per month. Crowell and Fairfield ultimately went into bankruptcy and Bancroft lost his bookkeeping job, but he returned to San Francisco, where he continued to deal in books and stationery.

In late 1855 Bancroft returned East to visit his family. On that occasion his sister, the widow Derby, insisted that he take $5,500, most of her savings, as a loan to be invested in his new California enterprise, a book-stationery-printing business. He offered to make her an equal partner, but she declined, content to let her money earn twelve percent per annum.

On his return Bancroft stopped in New York, where he established a line of long-term credit through a business associate of the late George Derby, John C. Barnes, of the prestigious stationery house of Ames, Herrick, Barnes, and Rhoades. Using the credit, the book salesman purchased some $10,000 worth of paper supplies and books and dispatched the goods to California by way of Cape Horn while choosing the shorter Isthmus for his own itinerary.

In a rented building on Montgomery Street, the firm of H. H. Bancroft and Company opened its doors for business in December of 1856. Over the next several years, though the United States suffered an economic depression, Bancroft's business continued to grow until he had the lion's share of the trade in San Francisco. In 1857 he went back to New York and ordered $60,000 to $70,000 in supplies.

During that visit he met Emily Ketchum, whom he married and later brought to California. Although they were happily married and the parents of a daughter, it was a relationship between opposites. Emily was as devoutly religious in her Christian fundamentalist faith as Bancroft was an agnostic and freethinker. But during the decade they were married, he dutifully attended church with her. After her death in 1869, however, Bancroft dropped all pretense and ended his connection with organized religion. In 1876 Bancroft married Matilda Coley Griffing, a younger woman whom he had met in New Haven, and with whom he had four children.

During the late 1850s and early 1860s the business expanded rapidly. The Civil War offered opportunities for increasing profits as California merchants continued to accept payment for goods in gold while they paid their eastern creditors in depreciated greenback dollars. Bancroft enlarged his quarters until he occupied the entire three stories of the Montgomery Street building and rented another building on Merchant Street.

As a result of his new wealth Bancroft traveled to Europe, where he spent a year touring Great Britain and the Continent. During the tour Bancroft took mental note of the leisurely life of Europe's upper classes and toyed with the idea of retirement. Upon his return, however, he faced the problem of expansion once more. He decided to purchase property and build a structure on the west edge of the business district on Market Street. Work began on the five-story brick and wood building in 1869. When its doors were opened for business the next year Bancroft could boast of owning the largest book and stationery firm west of Chicago.

Financial success was not enough for H. H. Bancroft. While in Europe he had decided that he wanted to do something other than make money for the rest of his life. Financially, he was quite comfortable and his business was in the hands of competent managers. Moreover, he had a hobby which was consuming more and more of his time and which held the promise of a new vocation.

As John W. Caughey states in his biography of Bancroft, "Anyone who deals in books runs the risk of becoming a collector." The book dealer began collecting books in 1859, after assembling copies of all books and pamphlets on California he had in stock for the convenience of William H. Knight, an employee who was working on a handbook of California and the Pacific Coast for publication. The fifty to seventy-five books gathered for Knight's work constituted the beginning of a collection that would ultimately include some 60,000 volumes. Bancroft browsed through every bookshop he encountered in the United States and Europe. He broadened the search to include not only books on the Pacific Coast but the trans-Missouri West, Mexico, and Central America as well. He frequented estate auctions, employed agents, salvaged records, newspapers, and correspondence

files of notable individuals, and even interviewed older inhabitants of California. Through an auction in Leipzig he purchased a priceless collection of Mexican materials from the estate of an exiled follower of the late emperor Maximilian.

As the collection grew, so did Bancroft's determination to embark upon a literary career utilizing his volumes. In early 1871 he made an effort to participate both as a writer and as the manager for a cooperative encyclopedia of the Pacific states but suffered what may have been a nervous breakdown and abandoned the project.

Upon his recovery the collector began to envision a much larger project—a massive, multivolume history of western North America. Such a project, beyond the life span of a single historian, posed many obstacles. For one thing, the history of the region had not yet been defined; indeed, no history to furnish the researcher with basic guidelines and hypotheses for western expansion had yet been written. And Bancroft's collection, which now numbered between 18,000 and 20,000 volumes, had no guide or classification system to increase its usefulness. Determined to embark upon the project, Bancroft employed a staff of assistants headed by his librarian, Henry L. Oak, to index the materials and then to assist him in writing the volumes. No standard library cataloguing system existed. (Melvil Dewey's *A Classification and Subject Index for Cataloguing and Arranging the Books and Pamphlets of a Library* was not published until 1876 and did not gain acceptance until later in the nineteenth century.) After some experimentation Bancroft settled on his own system and put his staff to work on a subject index. As many as twenty men worked for several years. Bancroft spent $35,000 in putting the index together before a single line of the history could be written.

During the two decades in which Bancroft wrote, edited, and supervised the project, he employed more than 600 assistants, but not a single person remained for the duration. In his analysis of the organizational structure, John Caughey has pointed out that "at least twenty . . . were wheelhorses . . . and five or six proved so competent and valuable that they seemed indispensable." The indispensable ones included: Henry L. Oak, a native New Englander, schoolteacher, and sometime editor who was proficient in Spanish and French; William Nemos, an intellectual from the Swedish aristocracy who had worked as a clerk on three continents, dug for gold in Australia, and served before the mast; Thomas Savage, another New Englander, born in Cuba and experienced in the

American consular service; and Frances Fuller Victor of Ohio, who had come to San Francisco because she was married to a naval engineer. Victor had also contributed articles to the *Overland Monthly* and had already written books about the West Coast.

As the project grew, so did the quarters for the library. At first the volumes cluttered some shelves near the desk of William Knight. Then they were moved to a part of the second floor of the building on Merchant Street. Upon completion of the new five-story structure on Market Street to house all of Bancroft's business activities, library and staff took over the entire fifth floor, some 8,500 square feet.

In devising a method of work, Bancroft decided against apportioning volumes among the staff members. Instead he established a kind of assembly-line method. Assistants were put to work on various parts of a single volume with Bancroft as the final editor. In addition, the master himself worked on parts of the volumes. But when the books were published, between 1874 and 1890, only Hubert Howe Bancroft was named author on the title pages.

Much of the later criticism of Bancroft's work was the result of his failure to give credit to his collaborators as coauthors. In 1890 Bancroft published the autobiographical *Literary Industries*, which, among other things, gave the rationale for his production method. Three years later Henry L. Oak, who had left his former employer due to ill health, published his own account of the project, disagreeing with Bancroft on several important points, particularly with regard to the importance of the "assistants." Oak stated that the employees were true collaborators and should have been recognized as such. Oak did come to Bancroft's defense against various charges of his critics, including accusations of inaccuracy and the criticism that Bancroft himself was a poor writer. Later Frances Fuller Victor insisted that she should have been named coauthor of four of the volumes.

Bancroft's sole defense was to insist that the assistants were "employees" rather than collaborators, leading his biographer to conclude that Bancroft's lack of academic training was the cause of his ignorance about such matters. Whatever the reason for the omission, the matter became more than an in-house dispute in 1903 when William A. Morris published a scholarly treatment of the problem entitled "The Origin and Authorship of the Bancroft Pacific States Publications: A History of a History."

Bancroft began the series with a study of the Indians of western North America. The result was the five-volume *Native Races of the Pacific States of North America*, published in 1874 and 1875, with three volumes devoted primarily to the Indians of Mexico and Central America. A period of seven years elapsed before the next book in the series appeared, but the remaining twenty-eight volumes were published between 1882 and 1890: *Central America* (3 volumes, 1882-1887), *History of Mexico* (6 volumes, 1883-1888), *History of the Northwest Coast* (2 volumes, 1884), *California* (7 volumes, 1884-1890), *Alaska, 1730-1885* (1886), *History of Oregon* (2 volumes, 1886-1888), *British Columbia, 1792-1887* (1887), *Arizona and New Mexico, 1530-1880* (1888), *History of Utah, 1540-1886* (1889), *History of Nevada, Colorado, and Wyoming, 1540-1888* (1890), *History of Texas and the North Mexican States* (2 volumes, 1890), and *History of Washington, Idaho and Montana, 1845-1889* (1890). In addition to these thirty-three volumes of history, Bancroft published five volumes of essays and miscellaneous pieces: *Popular Tribunals* (2 volumes, 1887), *California inter pocula* (1888), *California Pastoral, 1769-1848* (1888), and *Essays and Miscellany* (1890). He also produced the autobiographical *Literary Industries* (1890), a two-volume biography of the Mexican president Porfirio Díaz (1885) from personal interviews, and other works.

About 1870 the name of H. H. Bancroft and Company was changed to A. L. Bancroft and Company, after Albert L. Bancroft, a younger brother who had taken over part of the business management. Hubert Bancroft's earlier works were published and vigorously marketed by A. L. Bancroft and Company. In 1886 the History Company was formed, probably to protect the assets of the historical business from the creditors of A. L. Bancroft and Company in the wake of a fire which destroyed the Market Street building. Fortunately, the Bancroft historical collection had been moved to the specially constructed Bancroft Library on Valencia Street prior to the fire. The History Company carried on after the disaster, erecting a new building on Market Street which became known as the History Building.

It is significant that more than one-fourth of the thirty-three volumes of history were devoted to Latin America. Moreover if the volumes on the Amerindians are considered with the works on Mexico and Central America, it is apparent that Bancroft devoted more than two-fifths of the books to the non-Anglo West and Southwest. In other words, before the "Spanish Borderlands" had be-

*The History Building, erected in the mid-1880s to house
Bancroft's business enterprises*

come a recognized academic field at the hands of such twentieth-century scholars as Herbert E. Bolton, Bancroft recognized the significance of the Spanish influence on the American West and the basic unity of North America. Even at a cursory glance, it is apparent that the work on the states and territories of the Anglo-West is uneven, with California receiving the lion's share of the attention (seven volumes). But this lack of balance was simply a reflection of California's bulky place in Bancroft's collection.

Most important, Bancroft's history was the first effort to treat the history of the American West as a whole. When Theodore Roosevelt wrote his four-volume *Winning of the West* (1889-1896), he treated the West as the frontier stretching from the colonial East Coast to Texas and stopped his narrative with the fall of the Alamo in 1836. By contrast, Bancroft's treatment concentrated on the West as a region.

Working prior to Frederick Jackson Turner's famous address "The Significance of the Frontier in American History," delivered in 1893, Bancroft

wrote history to present significant and interesting facts concerning the historical development of the West. In this effort he was necessarily influenced by common beliefs of his time, and the work certainly contains a pro-Anglo-civilization bias. But in his attempt to be objective, Bancroft demonstrates an understanding and sympathy for Spanish and Indian institutions which was not then characteristic of American scholarship. Although there are heroes in the work, Bancroft resisted the pull of ancestor adulation. His critical account of the Bear Flag Revolt and of John C. Fremont's place in that action brought the wrath of the Society of California Pioneers down upon him.

As Bancroft entered the sunset of his years, he became concerned about the final disposition of his library. Under the leadership of President Benjamin Ide Wheeler, the University of California purchased the entire collection in late 1905 for $250,000, of which $100,000 was contributed by Bancroft himself. Before the collection could be moved across the Bay to Berkeley, San Francisco was shaken by the earthquake of 1906, but the library was not damaged. On the Berkeley campus the Bancroft Collection has grown to become the most important repository of Western Americana in the nation.

After the sale of the library, Bancroft occupied himself largely with travel, books, his grandchildren, and his ranch filled with fruit trees across the Berkeley Hills at Walnut Creek. It seems odd that no university in the West, not even the University of California, ever awarded Bancroft an honorary degree, although early in his career as a publisher Yale gave him an honorary master's degree. He was recognized, however, by the Pacific Coast Branch of the American Historical Association, which elected him president in 1911.

At the age of eighty-five, a few days after he was bumped by a streetcar, Hubert Howe Bancroft died on 2 March 1918, ending an active life which began when Andrew Jackson was president and ended with Woodrow Wilson's leadership in World War I. Perhaps no greater tribute can be made to the memory of Bancroft than that by Henry Morse Stephens in the *San Francisco Examiner* the day after Bancroft's death: "No one seeking to know anything about the West can do anything without consulting the Bancroft histories and the Bancroft collection."

Biography:
John W. Caughey, *Hubert Howe Bancroft: Historian*

of the West (Berkeley & Los Angeles: University of California Press, 1946).

References:

John W. Caughey, "Hubert Howe Bancroft: Historian of Western History," *American Historical Review*, 50 (April 1945): 461-470;

Harry Clark, *A Venture in History: The Production, Publication and Sale of the Works of Hubert Howe Bancroft* (Berkeley: University of California Press, 1973);

Benjamin Draper, "Hubert Howe Bancroft in Colorado," *Colorado Magazine*, 48 (Spring 1971): 93-107;

S. George Ellsworth, "Hubert Howe Bancroft and

the History of Utah," *Utah Historical Quarterly*, 22 (Summer 1954): 99-124;

Frank A. Knapp, Jr., "Two Contemporary Historians: José María Iglesias and Hubert Howe Bancroft," *Pacific Historical Review*, 20 (February 1951): 25-29;

William A. Morris, "The Origin and Authorship of the Bancroft Pacific States Publications: A History of a History," *Oregon Historical Quarterly*, 4 (March-December 1903): 287-364.

Papers:

Some of Bancroft's manuscript writings, business records, and correspondence are at the Bancroft Library, University of California, Berkeley.

George L. Beer

(26 July 1872-15 March 1920)

Peter A. Coclanis
University of North Carolina at Chapel Hill

BOOKS: *The Commercial Policy of England Toward the American Colonies* (New York: Columbia College, 1893);

British Colonial Policy, 1754-1765 (New York: Macmillan, 1907);

The Origins of the British Colonial System, 1578-1660 (New York: Macmillan, 1908);

The Old Colonial System, 1660-1754. Part I: The Establishment of the System, 1660-1688, 2 volumes (New York: Macmillan, 1912);

The English-Speaking Peoples; Their Future Relations and Joint International Obligations (New York: Macmillan, 1917);

African Questions at the Paris Peace Conference, with Papers on Egypt, Mesopotamia, and the Colonial Settlement, edited by Louis Herbert Gray (New York: Macmillan, 1923).

PERIODICAL PUBLICATION: "Cromwell's Policy in its Economic Aspects," *Political Science Quarterly*, 16, no. 4 (1901): 582-611; 17, no. 1 (1902): 46-70.

Over the course of the twentieth century the careers of few American scholars have matched

that of George L. Beer in terms of versatility, much less importance. Before his premature death at the age of forty-seven, Beer—a diffident and unassuming man by nature—had proved his mettle in the demanding worlds of commerce, scholarship, journalism, and international relations. Today he is remembered above all else for his research and writings on the origins and evolution of the British Empire and as one of the founders of the influential "imperial school" of early American history.

George Louis Beer was born on Staten Island, New York, one of the early outposts of the empire to which he would later devote much of his scholarly life. He was the second son of Julius and Sophia Walter Beer, each of whom was from a family prominent in the German-Jewish community in New York City. Beer grew up in affluence as a result of the commercial success of the tobacco-importing business established by his father, who had immigrated to New York from Hamburg. Befitting his family's social class and status, Beer received a first-rate early education in various New York schools and in 1888 at the age of sixteen gained admittance into Columbia College.

Beer entered Columbia at a propitious time,

George L. Beer

for not only had the school's famed Faculty of Political Science recently been established but during the decade of the 1880s the school had brought into its embrace an impressive group of scholars, many of whom had survived the curricular rigors of German universities. Contact with three German-trained scholars in particular—John W. Burgess, E. R. A. Seligman, and Herbert L. Osgood—greatly influenced Beer both during his undergraduate years at Columbia and for the remainder of his life. Indeed, many of the characteristics found in Beer's later scholarly work—its institutional orientation, evolutionary bent, putative Rankean method, and self-conscious academism—can be seen in the work of one or another of his Columbia mentors as well.

After receiving his A.B. degree from Columbia in 1892, Beer continued his studies at that institution for another year and was awarded an A.M. degree in 1893. His master's thesis, entitled *The Commercial Policy of England Toward the American Col-*

onies, was written under the tutelage of Professor Osgood and published immediately in the Columbia University Studies in History, Economics and Public Law. In this work, completed before his twenty-first birthday, Beer staked out the basic interpretive position with which he generally is associated today. This early treatise was important for other reasons as well. At once a renunciation of the romantic, nationalistic, narrative history that had long captivated American audiences and an exemplar of what would come to pass for scientific history in the United States, *The Commercial Policy of England Toward the American Colonies* helped break new methodological ground.

That Osgood had made an indelible impression on his pupil is apparent throughout Beer's treatise. Indeed, the modern reader is struck immediately, but, upon a moment's reflection, not at all surprised by the close interpretive affinity between *The Commercial Policy of England Toward the American Colonies* and Osgood's pioneering article "England and the Colonies," which had appeared in 1887 in a journal newly established at Columbia, the *Political Science Quarterly*. In this article Osgood, anticipating if not initiating the imperial approach to early American history, urged his colleagues to study colonial history both with broader sympathies and within a broader interpretive frame. More specifically, Osgood argued in this piece for closer study of the structure and evolution of British imperial institutions, for he believed that the imperial administrative system established by the British and the problems inevitably created or exacerbated by this system constituted the "central thread" of early American history. This argument implied, of course, that the long-dominant patriotic, Whiggish fabric of early American history spun by George Bancroft among others was both raveled and frayed. Whereas idealists such as Bancroft had viewed early American history in teleological terms as a protracted struggle by the colonists against the British for freedom and liberty—a struggle resolved in favor of the colonists as a result of the American Revolution—Osgood offered a seemingly dispassionate, materialist approach, suggesting that constitutional disagreement and conflict between England and its colonies was not the result of British tyranny but was virtually foreordained, given the vast geographical, economic, and institutional differences between the metropolis and its North American dependencies. The Revolution, according to Osgood, brought independence to these colonists; liberty and freedom they possessed all along.

Beer's *Commercial Policy of England Toward the American Colonies* is best viewed, then, within the context of the interpretive schema set forth by Osgood in his 1887 article. Following Osgood's exhortation, Beer focuses in this treatise on one important aspect of the institutional relationship between England and her colonies: the structure and organization of imperial trade. In seven terse chapters—about one hundred and fifty pages in all—Beer not only discusses the origins and development of English commercial policy toward the colonies from the early seventeenth century to 1763 but also the mechanisms established to oversee and execute such policy, the mercantilist assumptions that informed it, and the extent to which such policy was obeyed. His main conclusions were that English policy, though perhaps somewhat harmful to colonial economic development, was certainly not rapacious either by design or in practice, and that such policy, as embodied in the Navigation System, inspired little political controversy in the colonies until after 1763. These conclusions were quite insightful and, with slight modification, are still tenable today. That such sound conclusions were based upon examination of printed sources only and arrived at by so young a scholar underscores the talent and ability with which Beer was blessed.

The continued viability of his conclusions today would not have surprised Beer, for he firmly believed that such conclusions followed logically and inexorably from his "scientific" method and were well nigh incontrovertible. Since Beer's treatise was one of the first fully realized "scientific" histories to be written in the United States, it merits consideration on methodological as well as interpretive grounds.

Beer's "scientific" method, which he later attributed to the influence of his mentor Osgood, bore only a limited resemblance to the German methodology upon which it ostensibly was based. Indeed, Beer's version of scientific history, like the versions of most of his contemporaries in the United States, differed from and in some ways was antithetical to the method actually employed by Ranke and his followers in Germany, as George G. Iggers has pointed out in an article entitled "The Image of Ranke in American and German Historical Thought" (*History and Theory*, 1962). In the hands of American scholars, the elaborate historicist assumptions underpinning German scientific history—the idealization of the state and the reification of its spiritual essence, the rejection of the idea that judgments about moral value can be de-

rived from normative thinking (*Antinormativität*), and, concomitantly, the rejection of the very ideas of conceptualization and conceptualized thinking (*Anti-Begrifflichkeit*)—were transformed, some would say reduced, to somewhat skimpy notions of induction and empiricism and a heightened concern for objectivity and impartiality. Thus, the origin of delicious ironies wherein we find, for example, materialist historians such as Beer, who had never studied in Germany, attacking the idealist Bancroft in the name of Ranke and scientific history, when, in fact, Ranke was an idealist who thought exceptionally well of the work of Bancroft, his former student.

Invocations of Ranke notwithstanding, the character of scientific history in the United States actually owed more to the broad movement away from romanticism and toward realism in American culture, the rise of the natural sciences, particularly evolutionary biology, and the desire of professional practitioners of history clearly to differentiate their discipline from philosophy, literature, and the social sciences by developing a discrete methodology. In retreating from "theory" and becoming the minions of "facts"—which they would critically examine, impartially describe, logically order, and, if necessary, follow to their inevitable conclusions—Beer and other historians in the United States in the late nineteenth century felt that they would create a method that was at once distinctive and almost unerringly severe. The method thus created, it should be noted, has been accepted more or less by historians in the United States ever since, despite occasional sniping and a few frontal attacks.

Upon publication Beer's *Commercial Policy of England Toward the American Colonies* was received very well. Reviewers commented favorably about the author's "exhaustive" research, broad vision, fresh interpretation, and evenhanded treatment of both England and the colonies. In retrospect, the book's reception is readily understandable. In a period of rapprochement with England and of virtually unrestrained Darwinism, the hallmarks of Beer's "imperial" approach—respect, if not overt sympathy toward England, a predisposition to study the American colonies within the context of the British Empire, and a tendency to trace the evolution of various institutions in quasi-biological terms—dovetailed nicely with trends in American intellectual culture as a whole. That the book was a self-conscious exercise in the science of history just as the discipline was sowing its professional oats did not hurt either, nor did the fact that despite a certain stylistic stiffness the treatise, when all is said and done, was remarkably good. The issuance of a reprint edition of this master's thesis in 1948, fifty-five years after its initial publication and twenty-eight years after its author's death, testifies to the importance and quality of the work.

After receiving his advanced degree from Columbia, Beer won a coveted appointment as lecturer at that institution. He accepted the appointment, teaching European history there from 1893 to 1897. At the same time, Beer embarked on a career in commerce as well, following in his father's footsteps as an importer of tobacco. He enjoyed much greater success as an importer than he did as a teacher and, as a result of his own and his family's earnings in commerce, Beer was able to quit the countinghouse by 1903 and devote himself more fully to scholarly pursuits. His abortive teaching career, one should note, had ended even earlier in 1897, the lectureship at Columbia having convinced Beer, and apparently his students, that teaching was not his forte.

Beer's commitments to students, scholarship, and tobacco did not occupy all of his attention during the decade of the 1890s, however, for he also found time for Edith Hellman, whom he married on 11 November 1896. She was the daughter of Theodore Hellman, a wealthy Jewish merchant, and the niece of E. R. A. Seligman, who had been one of Beer's early mentors at Columbia and, coincidently, was his brother-in-law, having married Beer's sister Caroline in 1888. Beer's marriage to Edith Hellman produced a daughter, Eleanor Frances, and lasted until Beer's death.

Upon his retirement from business in 1903 Beer embarked upon a research visit to London which lasted for fourteen months. Despite the various demands on his time since he had completed his master's thesis a decade earlier, Beer had never stopped thinking about the issues raised in that prescient study. He had, in fact, even found time to write a long two-part article which appeared in the *Political Science Quarterly* in 1901 and 1902 on Cromwell's key role in the creation of the first British Empire. Though most historians over the years have felt that in this article Beer overstated the importance of both Cromwell and economic factors in explaining the origins of the empire, recent work done by Marxist scholars and by non-Marxist scholars interested in early modern political economy suggests that Beer's bold interpretation is more feasible than previously believed. These recent studies notwithstanding, it is clear that Beer's early work was not without problems. Perhaps the most serious weakness in both Beer's article on Cromwell and

his earlier treatise was the author's lack of familiarity with the relevant manuscript sources in England. It was precisely this problem that Beer tried to solve by traveling to London and ensconcing himself in the Public Record Office for virtually his entire stay.

After months of painstaking archival research, Beer returned to New York in 1904 and began to formulate the monumental research project that was to claim his attention for the remainder of his active scholarly life: a multivolume study of the British Empire from its origins to the eve of the American Revolution, with special emphasis on its economic, political, and institutional development. Beer was unsure at first about the precise number of parts and volumes his project would entail, but later he envisioned a four-part, ten-volume format. As the project developed, it seems, Beer increasingly came to feel that the empire's early history fell naturally into distinct phases, each of which would make up a discrete part of his study. The gradual emergence of the empire in the years between the reign of Elizabeth and the end of the Protectorate would comprise one part of the study, for example, and the period between 1660 and 1688, during which many of the basic institutions of empire were created, would constitute another. The empire's development and maturation between the Glorious Revolution and the outbreak of the Seven Years War would be treated in the third part of the study, and the critical years between 1754 and 1765, during which the empire began to collapse, would be treated in the fourth. Though only three parts of the project, consisting of four volumes in all, were ever completed, it is upon this body of work, published from 1907 to 1912, along with his 1893 master's thesis, that Beer's scholarly reputation rests.

Since Beer had spent much of his research time in London examining manuscripts from the period of the Seven Years War, he decided, once back in the United States, to work on the last part of the project first, detailing not the empire's will to power but rather the beginnings of its dissolution. Thus, the appearance in 1907 of *British Colonial Policy, 1754-1765*, unquestionably Beer's greatest work. Obviously, Beer is concerned in this study, as the title suggests, with British colonial policy during and immediately after the Seven Years War. Less obvious, though no less important, is the author's concern with the way in which this war set into motion the forces that led ultimately to the American Revolution.

Beer's central argument in *British Colonial Pol-*

icy, 1754-1765 is simple but powerful. Moreover, against the twentieth century's increasingly esoteric idealist interpretations of Anglo-American relations in the colonial period, Beer's neat, materialist account stands out in bold relief. According to this account, British dissatisfaction with the colonists' conduct during the Seven Years War sparked a postwar attempt by the British government to restructure the imperial relationship in such a way as to reduce the possibility of similar conduct in the future. This attempt met with widespread and stubborn resistance in the colonies not only because the colonists felt the changes inimical to their interests and incompatible with their own, increasingly egalitarian conception of the empire, but also because the Peace of Paris had emboldened them to resist British policy initiatives with which they disagreed. In effectively eliminating the French from North America, the peace had weakened the cement of empire, enabling the colonists to act—and resist—with much greater impunity. Absent the French threat, acquiescence to Whitehall seemed to the colonists to be less advantageous than resistance. In this assessment, Beer implied, the colonists may well have been correct, at least in the short run. For the interests, ideology, and institutions of the English and the colonists had in fact gradually become distinct over time as a consequence of the vastly different material situations in which they found themselves in the seventeenth and eighteenth centuries. Thus, to Beer, the drift toward revolution and the dissolution of empire in the years after 1763 was understandable and, given the circumstances, probably inevitable. Whether or not this development redounded to the benefit of mankind and whether or not its consequences were irreversible, Beer could not yet say. It is quite clear, however, from the passage with which he concluded the work, that Beer viewed both the British and the imperial idea with the utmost sympathy.

That Beer's *British Colonial Policy, 1754-1765* is remembered today mainly because of the argument outlined above is both undeniable and justifiable. This said, it is important to note that the book's contribution to Anglo-American historical scholarship, as such scholarship stood in 1907, was much more substantial. Beer's discussions of the considerations involved in British policymaking and the actual manner in which policy was implemented, for example, represented notable contributions to the historiography on the eighteenth century. Moreover, his digression in chapter eight on early modern theories of colonization, which was based largely upon an examination of rare eco-

nomic tracts and pamphlets in E. R. A. Seligman's renowned collection, represented a significant contribution not just to history but to the other social sciences as well.

Beer's *British Colonial Policy, 1754-1765* won immediate, lavish, and virtually unanimous critical acclaim, with reviewers especially enthusiastic about the rigor and force of Beer's argument and, as Evarts B. Greene put it, the author's "unusual mastery of printed and manuscript sources." While a few of the early reviewers implied that Beer was perhaps a bit too pro-British in his analysis and others complained that the author's style was somewhat formal and academic—dull, if you will—none denied that Beer had produced an impressive and important study. Later generations of historians by and large have agreed with this assessment and, despite the changing winds of historiography, the study is still quite valuable. Few of Beer's findings in *British Colonial Policy, 1754-1765*, in fact, have been rendered obsolete by subsequent research; indeed, save for those with which economic historian Curtis Nettels took issue in a piece in the *New England Quarterly* in 1933, few have even been challenged.

With the completion of *British Colonial Policy, 1754-1765*, Beer shifted his attention back to the early history of the empire and in 1908 published the results of his research efforts in a volume entitled *The Origins of the British Colonial System, 1578-1660*. In this study, which constituted the first part of his four-part project, Beer is concerned with the process by which the empire was conceived and brought to life. Beer's commitment, even zeal, to trace the origins of the Old Empire in this study was consistent with the broader concern among many of his academic contemporaries, particularly those that could be classified as conservatives, with the social implications and potential applications of Darwin's theory of biological evolution. As one manifestation of this scholarly concern with evolution, in the late nineteenth and early twentieth centuries studies of "origins" came into vogue. Beer's 1908 book should be seen in this context, for it is nothing if not an account of "creation," tracing the empire from its tentative beginnings to the eve of the Restoration. Elaborating on and at times slightly revising the basic positions he already had set forth in his previous works, Beer once again treats of such matters as the empire's mercantilist ideology, the early attempts to settle colonies consistent with this ideology, the gradual and somewhat haphazard process through which imperial administrative systems evolved, and the residual problems of empire-building as of 1660.

The Origins of the British Colonial System, 1578-1660 is not as stimulating or original as Beer's book of the previous year, but it is a significant work nonetheless. Merely to bring together and make sensible the vast range of materials that bore upon the creation of the empire was an awesome task, which the critics applauded. A few reviewers, it is true, complained about Beer's arid prose, but otherwise *The Origins of the British Colonial System, 1578-1660* won unstinting praise. The volume, like everything else written by Beer, remains useful to scholars even now.

Pushing on with his project, Beer spent the next four years working on the history of the empire during the Restoration. In 1912, after a second research trip to England, he published his findings in two volumes under the forbidding title *The Old Colonial System, 1660-1754. Part I: The Establishment of the System, 1660-1688*. The period encompassed in the study was one of crucial importance in the history of the empire, for it was under the later Stuarts that the so-called Old Colonial System qua system really came into being. Beer examined this process of formalization in his usual thorough and clinical way, first discussing the economic imperatives of empire and the institutional mechanisms created to satisfy these imperatives, then treating of each royal colony or possession, Barbados to Newfoundland, individually. In these long, sober volumes Beer attempted nothing strikingly original, being content to extend and expand upon ideas, themes, and arguments from his earlier works. Clinging closely both to institutionalism and to his imperial point of view, he simply gives an additional twenty-eight years of the economic history of the British Empire in America, for which the scholarly community was thankful enough, judging by the reviews. Indeed, in recognition of this study, *The Origins of the British Colonial System, 1578-1660*, and *British Colonial Policy, 1754-1765*, Beer in 1913 was named the first recipient of the Loubat Prize, awarded by Columbia University for the "best work printed and published in the English language on the History, Geography, Archaeology, Ethnology, Philology, or numismatics of North America during the preceding five years." Thus, with four volumes completed and well received, things augured well for Beer's completion of his great project, or so it seemed.

World War I was to intervene, however, dashing the prospects that appeared so bright in 1913. This war would draw Beer away from his project for the rest of his life, making of Beer, who con-

sidered himself the most disinterested of scholars, a highly partisan figure in international affairs.

On the eve of war in the summer of 1914, Beer was busily at work on the history of the British Empire between 1688 and 1754. Having recently returned from a third research trip to England, he had hopes of treating this long period in six volumes, at the conclusion of which his life work would be complete. Soon after war was officially declared in August, though, Beer began to edge away from William and Mary and the Board of Trade, concentrating more and more instead on England's present plight. More specifically, for the duration of the war, Beer, the erstwhile scientific historian, became a passionate publicist for the English cause, writing frequently in both scholarly journals and mass-market magazines on the compelling need for the United States to join the Allied cause and on the mutual benefits that would accrue from a close strategic and political alliance between England and the United States, indeed, among English-speaking peoples throughout the world.

That the scholarly Beer would throw himself so vehemently behind the English cause seems in retrospect somewhat out of character, though one can point to several possible roots, if not the reasons for the urgency, of his wartime behavior. Anglophilia was common among upper-class groups in the United States in the late nineteenth and early twentieth centuries even penetrating New York City's Ashkenazic elite. Beer had grown up in this cultural milieu and had spent his life studying the history and institutions of England, at that time so endangered by the German threat. The fact that his father had fled Hamburg in part because of anti-Semitism could hardly have been missed by Beer either, though, in truth, the cause of Beer's departure from the scholarly life will never be precisely known. Perhaps, then, one should consider his actions as reflecting a strong belief that mankind would benefit from both an Allied victory and the survival of English civilization and leave it at that.

In any case, Beer spent the war years promoting the aforementioned ideas in such publications as *New Republic, Forum, Political Science Quarterly*, and the *Annals of the American Academy of Political and Social Science*. Some of these pieces were included in his 1917 book, *The English-Speaking Peoples; Their Future Relations and Joint International Obligations*, in which he argues his case for Anglo-American alliance in greater detail. If later judgments of the effects of his wartime efforts can be believed, Beer was every bit as skilled at Anglo-

American publicity and propaganda as he had been in the scholarly world.

In addition to his private efforts at advocacy during the war years, Beer put his varied talents to work for the United States government as well, first as a member of the Inquiry, the commission established by President Wilson and Colonel House in September 1917 to prepare the peace program that the U.S. would follow at the war's conclusion, then, as part of the American delegation at the Paris Peace Conference itself. Given Beer's scholarly reputation, linguistic ability—he had a good knowledge of French, German, and Italian—and his long years of research on problems relating to international relations, it is understandable that Wilson and House would find a place for him in these proceedings, Beer's openly acknowledged Republicanism notwithstanding.

Both as a member of the Inquiry and, afterward, with the American delegation in Paris, Beer specialized in colonial questions, particularly in the development of a postwar policy on the colonies and territories held by the Central Powers and Turkey in Africa, the Pacific, and the Middle East. He is, in fact, often seen as the father of the mandate system set up in Paris to administer these possessions, having strongly advocated and, according to some, devised this approach in his wartime reports for the Inquiry, some of which were collected and published in 1923 in a volume entitled *African Questions at the Paris Peace Conference, with Papers on Egypt, Mesopotamia, and the Colonial Settlement*. Whatever Beer's exact role in the origins of the mandate system—a system which was to prove so controversial in later years—he undoubtedly was influential in its establishment, for he was the chief of the American delegation's Colonial Division at the peace negotiations and later was appointed director of the Mandatory Section of the League of Nations, though because the United States failed to join the League, he was unable to serve. He was able to accept something for his peace efforts, however: a special decoration from the King of Belgium. In the area of international affairs, as in the worlds of journalism, scholarship, and commerce, Beer clearly had made a mark.

He returned home from Paris in late summer 1919 hopeful that at long last he might get back to his beloved study of the British Empire in the eighteenth century. This hope went unfulfilled, however, for Beer, who had been in ill health for a number of years prior to his feverish activity in Paris, died shortly after on 15 March 1920.

For someone who died so young, taught so briefly, and devoted so few years to full-time scholarly activity, George Louis Beer left a rich legacy both to the historical profession and to modern historiography. Along with his mentor, Herbert L. Osgood, and Charles M. Andrews, Beer helped to revolutionize the study of early American history, rejecting the narrow parochialism that then dominated the field in favor of a much broader interpretive frame, one that attempted both to place the colonies within the context of early modern European history and to treat the actors on that historical stage with greater dispassion and understanding, if not with total scientific objectivity as often was claimed. In his own deeply textured studies of the creation, development, and breakdown of the Old Colonial System, Beer, though he considered himself primarily a historian of the British Empire, helped to reshape thinking on the economic history of the American colonies and to retrace the road to revolution much more faithfully. While Beer's work was not without its problems— most notably his relative neglect of internal developments in the colonies—it still bears up well, more than seventy years after the publication of his last major study in 1912.

Despite the fact that he had no "students," he helped to found a "school" of history, the imperial school, which over the next generations would include among its adherents some of the greatest historians in the English-speaking world, Lawrence Henry Gipson, Lawrence A. Harper, Leonard W. Labaree, and Wesley Frank Craven, to name a few. Beer's legacy, furthermore, was not limited to scholarly contributions, for in his last will and testament he provided for a bequest of $5,000 to the American Historical Association to establish an annual book prize in his name. The prize, for the best book on any phase of European international history since 1895, is generally considered among the most prestigious in the historical world. For many reasons, then, all of them good ones, the work and memory of George Louis Beer remain alive today.

References:

Grace A. Cockroft, "George Louis Beer," in *Some Modern Historians of Britain: Essays in Honor of R. L. Schuyler*, edited by Herman Ausubel, J. Barlet Brebner, and Erling M. Hunt (New York: Dryen Press, 1951), pp. 269-285;

George Louis Beer: A Tribute to His Life and Work in the Making of History and the Moulding of Public Opinion (New York: Macmillan, 1924);

Lawrence Henry Gipson, "The Imperial Approach to Early American History," in *The Reinter-*

pretation of Early American History: Essays in Honor of John Edwin Pomfret, edited by Ray A. Billington (San Marino, Cal.: Huntington Library, 1966), pp. 185-199;

Jack P. Greene, "The Reappraisal of the American Revolution in Recent Historical Literature," in his *The Reinterpretation of the American Revolution, 1763-1789* (New York: Harper & Row, 1968), pp. 2-74;

Curtis Nettels, "The Place of Markets in the Old Colonial System," *New England Quarterly*, 6 (September 1933): 491-512;

Max Savelle, "The Imperial School of American Colonial Historians," *Indiana Magazine of History*, 45 (June 1949): 123-134;

Arthur P. Scott, "George Louis Beer," in *The Marcus W. Jernegan Essays in American Historiog-*

raphy, edited by William T. Hutchinson (Chicago: University of Chicago Press, 1937), pp. 313-322;

W. A. Speck, "The International and Imperial Context," in *Colonial British America: Essays in the New History of the Early Modern Era*, edited by Jack P. Greene and J. R. Pole (Baltimore: Johns Hopkins University Press, 1984), pp. 384-407.

Papers:

Beer's manuscript diary of his activities immediately before and during the Paris Peace Conference is located at the Rare Book and Manuscript Library of Columbia University. Papers relating to Beer can be found in other collections at this library as well.

Edward Gaylord Bourne

(24 June 1860-24 February 1908)

Charles J. Fleener
Saint Louis University

BOOKS: *The History of the Surplus Revenue of 1837; Being an Account of Its Origin, Its Distribution Among the States, and the Uses to Which It Was Applied* (New York & London: Putnam's, 1885);

Essays in Historical Criticism (New York: Scribners, 1901; London: Arnold, 1901);

Spain in America 1450-1580 (New York & London: Harper, 1904).

OTHER: "Prince Henry the Navigator," in *Annual Report of the American Historical Association for the Year 1893* (Washington, D.C.: Government Printing Office, 1895), pp. 111-121;

New England History Teachers' Association, *Historical Sources in Schools*, edited by Bourne and others (New York & London: Macmillan, 1902);

The Philippine Islands 1493-1803; Explorations by Early Navigators, Descriptions of the Islands and their Peoples, their History and Records of the Catholic missionaries, as related in contemporaneous

Books and Manuscripts, showing the Political, Economic, Commercial and Religious Conditions of those Islands from their earliest relations with European Nations to the beginning of the Nineteenth Century, 55 volumes, translated, edited, and annotated by Emma Helen Blair and James Alexander Robertson, historical introduction and additional notes by Bourne (Cleveland: Clark, 1903-1909);

Wilhelm Georg Friedrich Roscher, *The Spanish Colonial System*, translation edited by Bourne (New York: Holt, 1903);

Narratives of the Career of Hernando de Soto in the Conquest of Florida, as told by a Knight of Elvas, and in a Relation by Luys Hernandez de Biedma, Factor of the Expedition; translated by Buckingham Smith, together with An Account of de Soto's Expedition based on the Diary of Rodrigo Ranjel, His Private Secretary, translated from Oviedo's Historia general y natural de las Indias, 2 volumes, edited with an introduction by Bourne (New York: Barnes, 1904);

"The Voyages of Columbus and Cabot," edited by Bourne in *The Northmen, Columbus and Cabot, 985-1503* (New York: Scribners, 1906);

The Voyages and Explorations of Samuel de Champlain, 1604-1616, Narrated by Himself, edited by Bourne, 2 volumes (New York: Barnes, 1906).

PERIODICAL PUBLICATION: "The Naming of America," *American Historical Review,* 10 (October 1904): 41-51.

Edward Gaylord Bourne was a master of the art of historical criticism. He brought to his works great erudition and a talent for synthesis that enabled him to compress into a few pages the elements of a vast and complicated historical problem. The period in which he wrote saw the flowering of American scientific history. Bourne's essays, articles, reviews, introductions, and books are characterized by a strong emphasis on objectivity and the critical use of sources. Additionally, he demonstrated a clear and simple style which was ideal for his principal opus, *Spain in America 1450-1580,* written for the general reader.

Edward Gaylord Bourne was born in Strykersville, Wyoming County, New York, the son of the Reverend James Russell Bourne, a Congregational pastor, and Isabella Graham Staples Bourne. Both parents traced their ancestors back to the colonial period, Mrs. Bourne to Mayflower stock. Bourne's early life was spent mainly in rural New England. When he was ten years old he contracted a tubercular disease of the hip, and for a time his life was in danger. He recovered, but his left leg had outgrown the right and he was obliged to use crutches for three years. An appliance was developed to compensate for the different lengths of the legs. While obviously lame the rest of his life, he was quite mobile. Despite (or because of) his disability, he developed great physical strength in the chest and arms. The invention of the bicycle was a personal boon and he became expert in its use; on a visit to Colorado he rode one down Pike's Peak.

He prepared for college at the Norwich Free Academy in Connecticut, where he ranked first in his class. He graduated from Yale with a Bachelor of Arts degree in 1883. He had pursued the study of the classics until his senior year, when his interest in economics was aroused by William Graham Sumner. At commencement Bourne received the Cobden medal. He was offered a scholarship for classical study at the American School in Athens, but declined, preferring to remain at Yale to work with Sumner as a graduate student of economics

and history for the next five years. At Yale, he held a Foote fellowship and served as an instructor in medieval history (1885-1887) and as a lecturer in political science (1886-1888).

His first book, published in 1885, combined his work in the disciplines of history, economics, and political science. In *The History of the Surplus Revenue of 1837* Bourne's espousal of the scientific method of history was evident. In the preface he explained his intent: "To present a complete and impartial history of the origin and growth of the Surplus Revenue of 1837, and more especially of its disposition by the States among which it was divided. This work may seem to the general reader more like a collection of facts than the story of an important incident in our history. Of this defect, if it be a defect, I am as well aware as one can be; but if I am not mistaken this is the natural function of first works in a new field. Some one must clear the ground, loosen the soil, and raise a plain but useful crop before the finer growths can flourish."

This first crop, however, was fine enough to secure for Bourne a position, beginning in 1888, as instructor in history and economics at Adelbert College of Western Reserve University in Cleveland. An indication of the strength of Bourne's monograph is the fact that it was republished in 1968 as part of the Burt Franklin American Classics in History and Social Science series.

In 1890 Bourne was appointed the first professor of history at Western Reserve University. Though he held the position for only five years, he was long held in esteem by his colleagues. In an address delivered at a 1908 memorial service for Bourne at Adelbert College, Professor Francis H. Herrick evoked the spirit of Bourne's influence on his students and peers: "Professor Bourne was interested in all that pertains or that ever pertained to men, nations and things. He seemed to go about with living tentacles stretching in every direction, seizing, testing, weighing, questioning all things. His curiosity was without limit, and not of the idle sort. He was ready to exchange opinions and carry on an argument with anybody, at any time or place. . . . His mind was a ready reference-file on all kinds of subjects down to the current events of the day, and you could consult it with better confidence than the newspaper, because it mirrored both past and present alike."

In 1892 Bourne received a Ph.D. from Yale, and in 1895 he became professor of history at that institution, where he remained for the rest of his career. During the decade of the 1890s, Bourne came to prominence within the historical profession. He read papers at the annual meetings of the American Historical Association. In Washington in 1891 his topic was "The Demarcation Line of Pope Alexander VI." Conscious of the approaching Columbian anniversaries and the reawakened interest in all things pertaining to the discovery of the New World, Bourne chose a topic which brought him to the subject he would later study in his most successful work, the beginnings and early history of Spain's colonial ventures in America. The following year a brief essay on "Seneca and the Discovery of America" was published in London in the *Academy*. In this work Bourne demonstrated his classical training as well as his ability to read texts incisively and reinterpret them convincingly. In July of 1893 Bourne read a paper at the meeting of the American Historical Association held in Chicago in connection with the World's Historical Congress. His subject was "Prince Henry the Navigator" and his aim was "to try to determine as exactly as possible by a careful examination of contemporary sources just what his aims were, and what prompted his course of action." These and other papers were collected in *Essays in Historical Criticism* (1901).

For the first two years at Yale Bourne taught European history; thereafter mainly American subjects provided the topics of his courses. It is hard, however, to define his interests narrowly. Like his training, his teaching and writings reflected a scholar who combined different eras, areas, and disciplines. He sought, as he explained in his description of historical research, "the increase of positive historical knowledge, the elaboration of sound historical method, the enlargement of the range of historical evidence, and the development of the historical way of looking at things."

Also in 1895 Bourne married Annie Thomson Nettleton of Stockbridge, Massachusetts. Besides bearing him five children, Annie Bourne was a professional helpmate. She translated documents from the French, including those related to Champlain, the founder of Quebec, which appeared in *The Voyages and Explorations of Samuel de Champlain 1604-1616*, a 1906 publication of sources edited by Bourne.

Back in New Haven, Bourne joined the editorial board of the *Yale Review*, a post he held until his death. According to this periodical's editors, Bourne provided that "journal for the scientific discussion of economic, political and social questions" with his "wide knowledge of historical and economic literature and his unique acquaintance with writers, young and old, in these fields." He was also active in the American Historical Association. After

the turn of the century, he became the chairman of the association's historical manuscripts commission. As president of the New England History Teachers' Association, he directed the committee that prepared Macmillan's influential guide, *Historical Sources in Schools*, which appeared in print in 1902.

In 1901 Bourne's second volume, *Essays in Historical Criticism*, was published by Charles Scribner's Sons as part of the Yale Bicentennial Publications series. It contained thirteen essays, the most important of which was the first, "The Legend of Marcus Whitman." Marcus Whitman was a physician-missionary from New York who received an appointment to the Oregon territory. According to a late-nineteenth-century legend, he undertook a ride alone across the Rocky Mountains to the east in the winter of 1842-1843 to warn the United States of the imminent danger of the territory falling into the clutches of the British lion by annexation to Canada. Perhaps because Whitman was under consideration to become one of the fifty great Americans to be honored at the recently established Hall of Fame at New York University, Bourne decided to pursue and debunk Whitman's legend as an exercise in historical criticism.

The true story, as researched by Bourne, was that in 1842 Whitman, a worthy pioneer missionary in Oregon who later fell martyr to the cause of Christianity, did indeed journey east, but he was primarily on a trip related to the business of his mission. He traveled in a large party that included his wife, and he had no national/political motivations. Bourne, in his article, traced in some detail the literary history of the legend. His intent was to demonstrate "that this account of the genesis, diffusion, and wide acceptance in the latter half of the nineteenth century of a narrative about a momentous event in American history is as unhistorical as the legend of the Donation of Constantine." He hoped that his research would "prove to be a serviceable contribution to the literature of historical criticism." Although there were some heated responses to Bourne's conclusions, most scholars were convinced by his arguments.

Essays in Historical Criticism well demonstrates the diversity of Bourne's interests and his critical acumen. In addition to his papers on Prince Henry the Navigator, Seneca and the discovery of America, and the Demarcation Line of Pope Alexander VI, the collection included essays discussing the authorship of the Federalist Papers, the Mexican War, the historical seminar, and the historians Leopold von Ranke, James Anthony Froude, and Francis Parkman. In a later article, "The Naming of America," not in the collection but published in the *American Historical Review* in 1904, Bourne took on one of the most controversial questions in colonial history. A historian of American historical thought referred to this article when he wrote that Bourne's "study of the evidence is a splendid example of historical analysis."

That history could instruct and illuminate the way for statesmen and the populace as a whole was the belief of Bourne and most of his professional contemporaries. Acting on this conviction, he participated in a number of projects that were designed to shed light on the problems of the present. The one that perhaps best illustrates his conviction concerning the instructive role of history was the fifty-five-volume *Philippine Islands 1493-1803* (1903-1909), to which Bourne contributed an introduction and notes. The didactic enterprise of this venture was not hidden. In the introduction Bourne wrote:

> To govern [the Philippine people] or to train them to govern themselves are tasks almost equally perplexing, nor is the problem made easier or clearer by the clash of contradictory estimates of their culture and capacity which form the ammunition of party warfare.
>
> What is needed is as thorough and intelligent a knowledge of their political and social evolution as a people as can be gained from a study of their history. . . . To collect these sources, scattered and inaccessible as they are, to reproduce them and interpret them in the English language, and to make it possible for university and public libraries and the leaders in thought and policy to have at hand the complete and authentic records of the culture and life of the millions in the Far East whom we must understand in order to do them justice, is an enterprise large in its possibilities for the public good.

This massive work, edited by Emma Helen Blair and James Alexander Robertson, provided translations of "contemporaneous books and manuscripts showing the political, economic, commercial and religious conditions of those Islands from their earliest relations with European Nations to the beginning of the Nineteenth Century." On the title page, following the general editors but in the same size print, was the announcement that the series included a historical introduction provided by Edward Gaylord Bourne. In sixty-nine pages with 144

extended notations Bourne surveyed the history of the Philippines from 1493 to 1529.

In his introduction Bourne demonstrated the confidence of the turn-of-the-century scientific historian in the relevancy of his enterprise: "The aim of the Introduction is . . . to give the discovery and conquest of the Philippines their setting in the history of geographical discovery, to review the unparalleled achievements of the early conquerors and missionaries, to depict the government and commerce of the islands before the revolutionary changes of the last century, and to give such a survey, even though fragmentary, of Philippine life and culture under the old regime as will bring into relief their peculiar features and, if possible, to show that although the annals of the Philippines may be dry reading, the history of the Philippine people is a subject of deep and singular concern."

In 1904 at age forty-four, Bourne saw the publication of his *Spain in America 1450-1580*. This appeared as the third volume of *The American Nation: A History*, a twenty-seven-volume work designed to present to the general reader the best available scholarly historical knowledge of the time. Bourne's clear and simple style was ideally suited to a work designed for the general reader, and he demonstrated once again a talent for synthesis that enabled him to compress into a few pages complicated problems, such as the controversy surrounding the naming of America. In covering the long history of the early Spanish empire, Bourne had one of the more difficult tasks in the series, but according to a historian of American historical writing, *Spain in America* was "one of the best volumes in the series" that included as authors almost all of the leading lights of the first generation of professional American historians.

Charles Gibson, whose 1966 synthesis of the colonial period of Spanish America for the New American Nation series was designed to replace Bourne's study some sixty-two years after publication, made the following assessment of his predecessor: "[Bourne's merit] lay in the originality and acumen with which he interpreted sources, in the objectivity of his observations, and in the critical insights he applied to Spanish colonization prior to 1580. He did not pursue his subject in detail beyond the sixteenth century, but he did succeed, through an unequivocally scholarly presentation, in laying a positive assessment of early Hispanic colonization before the American public. He may justifiably be termed the first scientific historian of the United States to view the Spanish colonial process dispassionately and thereby to escape the con-

FERDINAND MAGELLAN

THE AMERICAN NATION : A HISTORY

VOLUME 3

SPAIN IN AMERICA

1450–1580

BY

EDWARD GAYLORD BOURNE, Ph.D.

PROFESSOR OF HISTORY, YALE UNIVERSITY

WITH MAPS

NEW YORK AND LONDON
HARPER & BROTHERS PUBLISHERS
1904

Frontispiece and title page for the work which, in the words of Charles Gibson, established Bourne as "the first scientific historian of the United States to view the Spanish colonial process dispassionately"

ventional Anglo-Protestant attitudes of outraged or tolerant disparagement."

Bourne's contemporaries were not all as impressed by his work. In a review of *Spain in America* in the January 1906 *American Historical Review*, Michael Oppenheim, a scholar of British maritime history, praised Bourne's scholarship and survey of the discovery and exploration of the New World but was aghast at his positive interpretation of Spanish colonial policy and administration. Oppenheim stated that the Spaniards' "motives were mean and sordid." He complained that Bourne provided only "incidental and general references to Spanish cruelties," charging that "the reader will hardly gather from them that the process of adaptation, as practised by the conquistadors, included burning, roasting, mutilating, whipping, starving to death, tearing to pieces with dogs, and every new form of torture, especially on the Indian women, that could be invented by the scum of the

Spanish gutters." In sum, for the reviewer "the story of Spanish conquest and legislation is a squalid one" which Bourne did not accurately present.

It has been argued that Bourne initiated the scholarly reaction in the United States against the *leyenda negra*, the "black legend" of Spanish cruelty and fanaticism that was the common inheritance of Anglo-Americans. Partly for this reason, Bourne's *Spain in America* was extremely popular and remained in print for more than sixty years. In 1962 it was published by Barnes and Noble with a new introduction and supplementary bibliography by Benjamin Keen.

Besides producing original work, Bourne continued to edit and translate histories he considered to be of importance to the discipline. In 1903 the English translation of Wilhelm Roscher's *The Spanish Colonial System* was published in an edition prepared by Bourne. In his preface the editor explained his intent: "The earlier and later absorption of Spanish possessions within our national boundaries make an intelligent appreciation of the work of Spain as a colonizing power an important object in the study of American history. Such a knowledge of the aims and work of Spain is no less necessary an adjunct to the understanding of the political problems of to-day in the West Indies and in the Philippines. The treatments of the subject in our ordinary textbooks and in the popular narrative histories are at best inadequate and too often misleading through the prejudices or lack of knowledge of their authors. What is needed is a broad historical and comparative treatment of the subject such as will be found in the chapter here presented in English. . . ."

In 1904 there appeared in two volumes *Narratives of the Career of Hernando de Soto in the Conquest of Florida*, edited with an introduction by Bourne. Two years later Bourne edited the original narratives of the voyages of Columbus and John Cabot for Charles Scribner's Sons. They appeared in a volume entitled *The Northmen, Columbus and Cabot, 985-1503*, which also included Julius E. Olson's edition of Norse documents. The same year, 1906, Bourne's *Voyages and Explorations of Samuel de Champlain*, for which his wife had done translations, was published.

From Havana, Cuba, in 1905, came the news that Bourne had been elected an honorary member of the Casino Español. That organization requested that they be allowed to translate and publish *Spain in America*. Bourne replied that he was honored by his membership and pleased to approve their editorial plans. "It was my hope," he wrote to the Cubans in Spanish regarding *España en América*, "that this historical work will promote a more cordial mutual appreciation between Hispanic-Americans and Anglo-Americans, as well as a more knowledgeable understanding on the part of the peoples of the United States of the great civilizing work accomplished by Spain in America." Prophetically he closed by stating: "I am convinced that this understanding will be greater in the future because the attractiveness of the study of the history of Spanish America is every day greater in our Universities."

Edward Gaylord Bourne, however, was not to develop directly a new generation of Latin American scholars. In 1906 he was felled, once again, by his boyhood tubercular disease. He was ill for many months, forced first to return to crutches, and then to his bed. He died on 24 February 1908, not yet forty-eight years of age. His historical career was relatively short, his scholarly production relatively slim. However, he produced work that can be and still is read with profit by scholar and layman alike.

References:

Francis H. Herrick, "Edward Gaylord Bourne," *Western Reserve University Bulletin*, 11, no. 3 (1906): 96-103;

James Ford Rhodes, Tribute to Bourne, in Rhodes's *Historical Essays* (New York: Macmillan, 1919; republished, Port Washington, N.Y.: Kennikat Press, 1966).

James Henry Breasted

William J. Murnane
University of Chicago

BIRTH: Rockford, Illinois, 27 August 1865 to Charles and Harriet Garrison Breasted.

EDUCATION: A.B., North-Western College, 1890; M.A., Yale University, 1892; Ph.D., University of Berlin, 1894.

MARRIAGES: 22 October 1894 to Frances Hart; children: Charles, James, Jr., Astrid. 7 June 1935 to Imogen Hart Richmond.

AWARDS AND HONORS: Prussian Royal Academy of Sciences, Berlin, corresponding life membership, 1907; American Oriental Society, president, 1918; LL.D., University of California, 1918; Society of Antiquaries, London, honorary membership, 1919; National Academy of Sciences, membership, 1920; D.Litt., *honoris causa*, Oxford University, 1922; Royal Asiatic Society of Great Britain and Ireland, honorary life membership, 1923; History of Science Society, president, 1926; American Historical Association, president, 1928; LL.D., Princeton University, 1929; University of Chicago, Ernest De Witt Burton Distinguished Service Professorship, 1930 (emeritus, 1933); Académie des Inscriptions et Belles-Lettres, Institut de France, foreign membership, 1930; American Council of Learned Societies, chairman, 1933-1935; Archaeologisches Institut des Deutschen Reiches, honorary membership, 1931; Bavarian Academy, honorary membership, 1931; Belgian Academy, corresponding fellow, 1931; British Academy, corresponding fellow, 1934; Danish Royal Academy, membership, 1935.

DEATH: New York, New York, 2 December 1935.

BOOKS: *The Battle of Kadesh* (Chicago: University of Chicago Press, 1903);
Egypt Through the Stereoscope (New York: Underwood & Underwood, 1905);
A History of Egypt from the Earliest Times down to the Persian Conquest (New York: Scribners, 1905; London: Hodder & Stoughton, 1906; revised, New York: Scribners, 1909); abridged as *A*

James Henry Breasted (courtesy of The Oriental Institute of The University of Chicago)

History of the Ancient Egyptians (New York: Scribners, 1908);
Ancient Records of Egypt; Historical Documents from the Earliest Times to the Persian Conquest, 5 volumes (Chicago: University of Chicago Press, 1906-1907);
Development of Religion and Thought in Ancient Egypt (New York: Scribners, 1912; London: Hodder & Stoughton, 1912);

Outlines of European History, 2 volumes, by Breasted, Charles A. Beard, and James Harvey Robinson (Boston: Ginn, 1914); volume one revised as *History of Europe, Ancient and Medieval,* by Breasted and Robinson (Boston: Ginn, 1920; revised again, 1929);

Ancient Times: A History of the Early World (Boston: Ginn, 1916; revised, 1935);

A General History of Europe, by Breasted, Robinson, and Emma Peters Smith (Boston: Ginn, 1921); republished as *Our World Today and Yesterday* (Boston: Ginn, 1924);

Oriental Forerunners of Byzantine Painting (Chicago: University of Chicago Press, 1924);

The Conquest of Civilization (New York & London: Harper, 1926; revised, 1938);

The Edwin Smith Surgical Papyrus, 2 volumes (Chicago: University of Chicago Press, 1930);

The Dawn of Conscience (New York & London: Scribners, 1933);

The Oriental Institute (Chicago: University of Chicago Press, 1933).

OTHER: Adolf Erman, *Egyptian Grammar; a Translation from the German of Erman's Aegyptische Grammatik* (London: Williams & Norgate, 1892);

"The Earliest Internationalism," in *Semicentenary Celebration of the Founding of the University of California* (Berkeley: University of California Press, 1919), pp. 192-214;

Chapter 3, "The Foundation and Expansion of the Egyptian Empire," chapter 4, "The Reign of Thutmose III," chapter 5, "The Zenith of Egyptian Power and the Reign of Amenhotep III," chapter 6, "Ikhnathon, the Religious Revolutionary," chapter 7, "The Age of Ramses II," and chapter 8, "The Decline and Fall of the Egyptian Empire," in volume 2, *The Cambridge Ancient History,* 12 volumes (Cambridge: Cambridge University Press, 1923-1939), pp. 40-195;

"The New Past," in *The New Past and Other Essays on the Development of Civilization,* edited by E. H. Carter (Oxford: Basil Blackwell, 1925), pp. 1-28;

"The Rise of Man and Modern Research," in *Smithsonian Institution Annual Report, 1932* (Washington, D.C., 1933), pp. 411-428.

PERIODICAL PUBLICATIONS: "Ramses II and the Princes in the Karnak Reliefs of Seti I," *Zeitschrift für ägyptische Sprache und Altertumskunde,* 37 (1899): 130-139;

"A New Chapter in the Life of Thutmose III," in *Untersuchungen zur Geschichte und Altertumskunde Ägyptens,* 12, no. 2 (1900);

"The Philosophy of a Memphite Priest," *Zeitschrift für ägyptische Sprache und Altertumskunde,* 39 (1901): 39-54;

"The Temples of Lower Nubia," *American Journal of Semitic Languages and Literatures,* 23 (October 1906): 1-64;

"The Monuments of Sudanese Nubia," *American Journal of Semitic Languages and Literatures,* 25 (October 1908): 1-110;

"The Place of the Near Orient in the Career of Man and the Task of the American Orientalist," *Journal of the American Oriental Society,* 39 (1919): 159-184;

"The Oriental Institute of the University of Chicago: A Beginning and a Program," *American Journal of Semitic Languages and Literatures,* 38 (July 1922): 233-328.

If one were asked to name a scholar who, above all others, stimulated the development of ancient historical studies in the United States during the earlier part of the twentieth century, that honor would have to fall to the colossal figure of James Henry Breasted. For nearly thirty years, until his death in 1935, he was generally acknowledged as America's leading Orientalist. Holding the first professorship in Egyptology at an American university, he became known initially as the author of a pioneering modern history of ancient Egypt and later for his widely read popular surveys of the ancient Mediterranean world. His contributions as a historian and in ancillary disciplines of Oriental studies were outstanding; but it is as a promoter of the study of the ancient past, and particularly the ancient Near East, that he made his most enduring mark. He presented what he called the "New Past" with unmatched fervor and persuasiveness, exemplifying himself the high standard of achievement he encouraged in others. In so doing he not only created an audience for the generations of scholars who followed in his footsteps, but also made possible the realization of a program of interdisciplinary research that is still in progress today.

Breasted's immense influence on his chosen field contrasts oddly with the comparatively slow start he made in it. He was born in Rockford, Illinois, in August 1865, the second son of Charles and Harriet Garrison Breasted. His father owned a small hardware business, and the family's economic position was modest. If it was not an uncultivated household, it was far removed from the academic and intellectual establishments of the day. Although Breasted entered North-Western (later North Central) College in 1880, he did not take his undergraduate degree until 1890. In the meantime he studied pharmacy and in 1886 was qualified as a registered druggist. Not content with a career so unsuited to his intellect and disposition, he pursued a course in divinity, a calling to which his family's deep religious faith inclined him, and in 1887 he entered the Congregational Institute (Chicago Theological Seminary). The doctrinal bent of this training did not harmonize with Breasted's awakening critical faculties, however, and he did not complete the program. Instead, encouraged by a sympathetic mentor at the seminary, he entered Yale University in 1890 to begin graduate study in Hebrew under William Rainey Harper.

By this time, plans for the new University of Chicago, with Harper as its first president, were well under way. The older man, impressed by his new student's ability and drive and already engaged in building a faculty, took Breasted aside shortly before the 1891 commencement and made him an offer that was as farsighted as it was generous. Of all the branches of ancient Near Eastern studies, Egyptian alone was a vacant field in America; let Breasted obtain a doctorate in Egyptology from Germany, and Harper would give him a professorship in Egyptology at his university. Characteristically, though he was penniless and without other prospects, Breasted refused to accept anything in writing. To go abroad for a prolonged course of study was beyond his personal means and would entail further sacrifices from his family. It is a measure of their confidence in him and of Breasted's own sense of his appointed calling that the material difficulties were overcome; and in the fall of 1891 Breasted entered the University of Berlin.

The training Breasted received in Germany over the next three years, as well as the intellectual ambience in which he found himself, had a profound effect on his development as a scholar. The study of ancient history at Berlin had been shaped by the rigorous source-critical methodology of Johann Gustav Droysen and, later, by the grounding in relevant languages demanded by Theodor Mommsen, who was still on the faculty when Breasted took his degree. Moreover, the professor of Egyptology was Adolf Erman, whose work had already gone far beyond the impressionistic, intuitive approach which had largely prevailed since the decipherment of the hieroglyphs, and who had placed the study of the ancient Egyptian language

on a scientific level that would provide the basis for all future advances in its understanding. Another important influence on the young American was Eduard Meyer, not yet at the University of Berlin but already renowned for his encyclopedic control over the primary sources for studying the entire ancient Mediterranean world and for his judicious approach to the writing of ancient history. The grounding Breasted received from his teachers and the approach he developed to the materials in his discipline remained continuing influences both on his own scholarship and on the school of Egyptology later associated with him. The emphasis on the Egyptian language as the primary key to understanding the ancient civilization of the Nile Valley, the concern for scrupulous accuracy in the copying of basic source materials (itself a reflection of the haphazard manner in which all too many documents had been recorded during the short history of a discipline less than a century old), and an insistence on interpreting these sources in the context of their ancient settings, all are the hallmarks of Breasted's scientific work and his enduring legacy to his students.

His studies concluded, the newly married Dr. Breasted and his bride Frances Hart set out for their honeymoon in Egypt in October of 1894. He had received his doctorate in June, and his appointment as instructor in Egyptology at the University of Chicago was officially confirmed later that summer. This first journey to the Nile Valley foreshadowed a number of later developments in Breasted's career. Already, at Erman's request, he had been asked to copy a number of inscriptions in Egypt for the Prussian Academy of Science's Egyptian Dictionary project. He was also involved in building a collection of Egyptian antiquities for a museum at his own university; and his first exposure to the monuments of Egypt in their natural setting fired Breasted's resolve to undertake a comprehensive survey of Egyptian historical documents as a necessary foundation to any further advances in this area. Returning to America the next year, he settled down to his teaching duties in Chicago. Although he soon established himself as a serious scholar and an extraordinarily fine lecturer, he acquired few pupils in America. Over the next few years, he found himself on the familiar treadmill of a young academic, his time taken up with routine teaching assignments at the university and with the popular University Extension lecturing by which he hoped not only to supplement his meager salary but also to build an audience for Egyptology in the United States. Thus, when the

Prussian Academy proposed that Breasted take an extended leave of absence to copy inscriptions in European museums for the dictionary project, it is not surprising that both he and the University of Chicago agreed.

The next nine years, from 1899 to 1908, may fairly be termed the "research period" of Breasted's career, during which his energies were devoted more intensively than at any other time to the furthering of his own scientific work. The collation of texts he performed between 1899 and 1904 for the Prussian Academy also laid the basis for his highly admired synthesis of Egyptian history, which he would bring to fruition soon thereafter in the interdependent *History of Egypt from the Earliest Times down to the Persian Conquest* (1905) and *Ancient Records of Egypt; Historical Documents from the Earliest Times to the Persian Conquest* (1906-1907). Each year yielded a rich harvest of new and firmly grounded interpretations, disseminated in articles and monographs as well as in the two works already named, which established Breasted's unquestioned authority as an Orientalist. His achievement did not go unacknowledged: despite his prolonged absences from the university, he rose steadily through the academic ranks and in 1905 attained a full professorship in Egyptology, the first at any American university.

Another enduring theme of Breasted's life's work was sounded for the first time in 1903, when he was instrumental in obtaining from the recently formed Rockefeller Foundation a fifty-thousand-dollar grant for an Oriental Exploration Fund at the University of Chicago. As a result, he was able to embark upon yet another long-deferred project and to begin in 1905 a survey of the inscribed monuments still standing in the Nile Valley. During the next two winters (1905-1906 and 1906-1907) his small expedition ranged through Lower Nubia and the Sudan, building up an archive of text copies, field notes, and photographs that remains of great value to this day. At this time, however, Breasted was not to complete his work. The death of President Harper and a subsequent policy of financial retrenchment at the University of Chicago brought this first survey to a sudden end. Discouraged by this reverse, Breasted returned to America in 1908. He would have to wait another twelve years before he could return to field work in the Near East.

It had been during those opening years of the twentieth century, filled with ceaseless travel and drudgery, that Breasted had established himself as America's leading historian of the ancient Near East and as a respected figure in international circles as well. Not only had he written an authoritative modern account of Egypt's ancient history, he had done so on the basis of original source materials for which he had been obliged to prepare reliable working editions. These arduous preliminaries were a practical necessity if there was to be any gain over previous works on Egyptian history. The gap between what was available and what was published, which still plagues modern scholarship today, was even more acute when Breasted wrote his *History of Egypt*. Existing copies had been made by many different hands over the previous three-quarters of a century. Their standard of reliability ranged from the adequate to the practically useless; and many vitally important documents were not published at all. Having worked over these sources for his own use, it was a logical step for Breasted to make them available both to his fellow historians and to interested members of the general public. This project he eventually realized with the publication of his path-breaking *Ancient Records of Egypt;* but he was well aware that even this enormous contribution was far from exhaustive. Although his work for the Prussian Academy had confirmed his early conviction that only lame research could result without the proper publication of relevant sources, the sheer bulk of all sorts of material from ancient Egypt ensured that one man would never be able to master it all. Uninscribed artifacts, in particular, required specialized skills possessed neither by Breasted nor by most of his contemporaries. Nor were all written records readily accessible even to the initiated: rigorous analysis of the Egyptian language which had been pioneered by German Egyptologists was only a quarter-century old; many classes of documents—literary, religious, administrative—would require prolonged study before they would yield coherent results. In choosing to concentrate on historical texts, Breasted was (for the time being) limiting his field to a relatively small area which, moreover, would not entail the conceptual or interpretive uncertainties of other genres that dealt with the more inward life of ancient man. Such thornier problems he would tackle at another time. The contents of the *Ancient Records of Egypt* are thus confined to documents which "bore directly on the events and conditions closely touching the career of the Egyptian state," having to do with the great personalities and with basic trends which were to be inferred from the extant material.

Although the *Ancient Records* is essentially a sourcebook rather than a history, it does have features that raise it above the level of a collection and

Breasted with his wife Frances Hart Breasted and their son Charles in Nubia, 1906, during Breasted's survey of inscribed monuments still standing in the Nile Valley (courtesy of The Oriental Institute of The University of Chicago)

bespeak the author's instructive purpose. Preliminary orientation is supplied by prefatory essays on the documentary sources for Egyptian history and on the evidence for its chronology. The material which follows is arranged in order, by dynasties and their component reigns, yet in a sequence that allows significant trends to emerge from the sources themselves. Each translation is preceded by a brief essay that describes the document's contents and its importance in the overall scheme of Pharaonic history. The texts are themselves extensively annotated, to provide the reader with enough background to evaluate the ambiguities of the original document in translation. If this appears unremarkable to historians for whom such collections are a common tool, it should be remembered that Breasted did his work at a time when basic reference books that scholars today take for granted, even dictionaries, were either unavailable or hopelessly inadequate. The *Ancient Records*, presenting

for the first time in any modern language a range of historical sources covering three millennia, was a major achievement that remains unduplicated to this day. Breasted's translations have been surpassed, predictably, in the course of later research into the language and into parts of the social background that Breasted himself described as needing further study. As an introduction to ancient Egyptian history, however, and a stimulus to further research, the *Ancient Records* still wears its years gracefully, and it continues to be a resource that is, at worst, convenient, but full of insight at its considerable best.

The sources printed in the *Ancient Records* are constantly cited in the pages of Breasted's *History of Egypt* to relieve the text (as its author put it) of the "workshop *debris*" of scholarship while, at the same time, maintaining "close contact with the sources for every fact adduced." Otherwise, however, there is little in the essentially interpretive *History of Egypt* that demonstrates the extent to which Breasted was forced to revise commonly held opinions, simply in matters of fact, before that work could be written. The process that Breasted followed is best illustrated in the articles and monographs produced during the "research period," such as *The Battle of Kadesh*. This slender work, described as a "study in the earliest known military strategy" at a critical battle during the thirteenth century B.C., is of interest for Breasted's approach to the sources and to the event itself. The historian and the philologist are in fine balance throughout. The object is to trace, for historians working in areas other than the ancient Near East, the main lines of a conflict that can be compared to similar clashes throughout ancient and modern history. Thus, although Breasted's marshaling of the sources set a new standard of thoroughness (and, indeed, anticipated the integral edition of the texts bearing on the battle which did not appear until 1928 under the auspices of Cairo's French Institute), his account is not overburdened with grammatical or lexicographical commentaries. Justice is done not only to the ancient written evidence, but also to the physical setting of the event: to Breasted falls the credit for having determined the correct site of the Battle of Kadesh, which had to be rediscovered by considering both the present-day terrain and a range of textual sources from ancient and modern writers. Modern readers may smile at the formulation of one of the author's conclusions, that "already in the fourteenth century B.C. the commanders of the time understood the value of placing troops advantageously before battle . . .

[and of] clever maneuvers masked from the enemy; and that they had therefore, even at this remote time, made contributions to that supposed science, which was brought to such perfection by Napoleon—the science of winning the victory before the battle." To insist on such a point may seem naive, but it is characteristic of Breasted the advocate. He always sought to show the human dimension of the ancient Egyptians and to give them their due, not merely as exponents of an exotic and faraway civilization, but as participants and pioneers in the adventure of man's progress toward enlightenment. Not the least of this little book's qualities has been its staying power as a minor classic in the literature of military history. Breasted's description of the conflict has been superseded in some details concerning movements of forces and the position of topographical features around the battlefield; but a modern account, appearing eighty years after *The Battle of Kadesh* was first published, still adheres to the shape of events which Breasted was the first in modern times to discern.

It was basic research of this sort, covering the more than three millennia of Pharaonic civilization, which gave Breasted's *History of Egypt* the authority it commanded virtually from the day it was published. Previously, indeed, history had not fared conspicuously well as a branch of Egyptology. Men such as Heinrich Brugsch, E. A. W. Budge, Flinders Petrie, and Ernst Wiedemann had made distinguished contributions in archaeology and other areas of research, but their histories were unworthy of the name: a heavy emphasis on documentation, natural in field work, turned these books into dry catalogues of data grouped mechanically under the reign of this or that king; and history suffocated under the weight of this ill-digested detail. More satisfactory had been the readable and stimulatingly interpretive histories of Gaston Maspero and (in German) Eduard Meyer—the latter being especially influential on Breasted's own *History*, as we shall see. By 1905, however, even works of this caliber had been overtaken by recent advances in methods and research: this was especially true of Maspero's widely read work *L'Histoire ancienne des peuples de l'Orient Classique*. In English translation, by 1900, there had appeared three volumes of this work which had courageously tackled the full span of ancient Near Eastern history, but which was undermined by an approach to sources that was often facile and uncritical. Between the dangers of over-documentation and glibness, Breasted steered a brilliantly judicious course. His use of the five volumes of *Ancient Records* as optional companions to

his *History* enabled him to avoid the factual clutter of earlier works; and his control over the source materials made his account of Egyptian history as reliable as it was possible to make it at that time. In Breasted's *History of Egypt* the English-speaking reader had, for the first time, not only an up-to-date guide to Pharaonic civilization, but also a definite sense of the career and achievements of the Egyptian people over the long course of their ancient history.

For Breasted, the fascination of Egypt's history lay in the interplay of creative energy with the political and spiritual conditions which might further or hamper its development. This theme first appears in his account of the Old Kingdom, circa 2980-2800 B.C.E. (all dates given in this discussion of the *History* are Breasted's), "a thousand years of inexhaustible fertility, when the youthful strength of a people . . . had for the first time found the organized form in which it could express itself best." We share his anxiousness as he ponders, "at the close of this remarkable age, whether the conflict of local with centralized authority [that is, the provincial nobility with the monarchy] shall exhaust the elemental strength of this ancient people." The flowering of civilization, in Breasted's view, was very much a hostage to the land's internal politics. Most of the remainder of his *History* is consequently devoted to the two great compromises that carried Pharaonic civilization forward after the collapse of the Old Kingdom: first, Egypt's "feudal age," when the kings of the Twelfth Dynasty (circa 2000-1788 B.C.E.) arrived at a stable balance of power with the provincial governors, or nomarchs; and second, with the rise of the military state during the Eighteenth Dynasty (circa 1580-1350 B.C.E.) and the establishment of the Empire. The latter period is graced by the appearance of the most attractive character in this history, Thutmose III, "a man of tireless energy, unknown in any Pharaoh before or since," yet also gifted with a versatility that has him "designing exquisite vases in a moment of leisure." In this monarch Breasted recognized a spirit that matched his own. More than a touch of German romanticism colors his summation of the king's achievements: "Never before in history had a single brain wielded the resources of so great a nation and wrought them into such a centralized, permanent and at the same time mobile efficiency. . . . The genius that arose . . . to accomplish this for the first time in history reminds us of an Alexander or a Napoleon. He built the first real empire and is thus the first character possessed of universal aspects, the first world hero."

Clearly, Breasted identified strongly with this energetic empire-builder, whose qualities as described here are similar to those Breasted himself brought to bear, many years later, on the creation of the Oriental Institute. Not surprisingly, we find Breasted less than enthusiastic when, with the Empire won, later Pharaohs abandoned the vigorous policies of their fathers. Such a retreat, he believed, could only erode the still-potent aura of divinity that hedged the king: when "consciously or not he [the king] had assumed a modern standpoint" in his regard for his office, he undermined his authority, "which must inevitably lead to sharp conflict with the almost irresistible inertia of tradition in an oriental country." The crisis came with the heretic Pharaoh Ikhnaton, a youthful dreamer who, though strong and courageous in some ways, could not avert the disaster that overtook his kingdom at home and abroad.

The debacle at the end of the Eighteenth Dynasty was, for Breasted, the turning point from which there was no recovery. Though the Empire lasted some centuries longer, it was now on the defensive. Foreign mercenaries replaced Egyptians in the ranks of the army; and the uncontrolled strength of the soldiery, alongside the bold assumptions of power by local authorities, precipitated a decline into anarchy at the end of the Empire period (circa 1090 B.C.E.). This fragmentation in turn left Egypt ripe for a succession of foreign conquerors against whom no lasting or effective defense could be found. Periods of relative vitality such as the Saite Twenty-sixth Dynasty (663-525 B.C.E.) were animated, not by a progressive, outward-looking spirit as in the past, but by the model of Egypt's former greatness: "the world was already growing old, and everywhere men were fondly dwelling on her faraway youth." Egypt's later assertions of independence were, for Breasted, no more than the convulsive final spasms of a corpse. The vitality of her people exhausted, "Egypt belonged to a new world, toward the development of which she had contributed much, but in which she could no longer play an active part. Her great work was done, and unable, like Nineveh and Babylon, to disappear from the scene, she lived on her artificial life, for a time under the Persians and the Ptolemies, ever sinking, till she became merely the granary of Rome. . . . But her unwarlike people, still making Egypt a garden of the world, show no signs of an awakening and the words of the Hebrew seer, 'There shall be no more a prince out of Egypt,' have been literally fulfilled."

As with politics and society, Breasted believed,

so it also went with morals, where ideas intrinsic to the development of the Egyptian people clashed with external conditions. The idea that one was personally accountable for one's actions before the gods was an ancient one, going back into the Old Kingdom. The deepening of this concept in later history and its extension from the upper classes to the generality of mankind were positive developments. They were undercut, however, by what Breasted called "the most baleful tendency of Egyptian life and religion"—the proliferation of cultic and mythological baggage imposed on the worshiper for no other reason than to provide "to an unscrupulous priesthood an opportunity for gain." Personal responsibility could be evaded by magic, thus introducing a casuistry that was "subversive of moral progress." The Empire, with its lavish subsidies to state-sponsored cults, lent the final corrupting blandishments to this process of moral retreat, and "the grotesque creations of a perverted priestly imagination finally gained the credence of the highest circles," including the king himself. Indeed, no less a figure than Thutmose III had been installed in office, Breasted believed, as the candidate of an ambitious priesthood. To this creeping sacerdotalism Ikhnaton's revolution was a violent but ultimately futile response: though he stressed the universal fatherhood of god to man, "the first time in history that a discerning eye has caught this universal truth," his concept could not prevail against the social forces ranged against it. It survived only in the domain of personal religion, while the official cults continued on the path that would lead them to the swollen, sterile state in which they would appear in the last days of paganism. The persistence of genuine spiritual values was an important phenomenon for Breasted. It was a theme to which he would return and to which he would devote his most original and stimulating thinking.

From the standpoint of today, Breasted's *History of Egypt* ranks as an acknowledged but dated classic. Not surprisingly, some of the factual data have been revised in the light of later research, and a number of Breasted's generalizations seem overly hasty: the religious literature he judged so harshly, for instance, is now taken more seriously; and modern writers insist less than Breasted did on the primacy of Egypt among the high civilizations of the ancient Near East. This is not to discount the importance of the *History of Egypt*, especially just after it appeared, but it calls attention to an inconsistency which is of some interest in evaluating Breasted the historian: that is, that while Breasted's research methods looked toward the twentieth century, his ideas about man, society, and the historical process were rooted firmly in the nineteenth. In this respect, Breasted's *History* owes a considerable debt to the *Aegyptische Geschichte* of Eduard Meyer (published in 1887), which it closely resembles in the shaping, interpretation, and relative importance given to events. These resemblances reflect Breasted's admitted debt to his German teachers and even more profoundly an outlook that arose from the intellectual tradition he shared with them. The organic metaphor applied to the course of Egyptian civilization was a common one in nineteenth-century historiography; so was the belief in moral progress that is implicit in Breasted's judgments on the spiritual life of the ancient Egyptians. His impatience with the ways of priestcraft similarly reflects attitudes common in his day, though leavened with a sympathetic humanism that compelled his admiration for an Ikhnaton. To acknowledge such influences on the *History of Egypt*, as well as its inevitable defects, does not at all imply that it lacked substance and originality: it would be wrong to dismiss it as a well-written popularization which owed its influence to a timely arrival in the marketplace. Breasted's personal contribution is seen not only in the research which gave his *History* its formidable authority, but also in the thought which, above all, went into his account of the spiritual and intellectual odyssey of the ancient Egyptians. Breasted's *History* rapidly established itself as the standard work on the subject; and his is the account against which all others have been measured.

In 1912 Breasted was invited to deliver a series of lectures at the Union Theological Seminary in New York. Published the same year in his *Development of Religion and Thought in Ancient Egypt*, these lectures represent the first systematic exposition of a theme Breasted would develop further in other presentations over the years—namely, the crucial role of ancient Egypt in the evolution of the moral tradition which the Western world inherited from the Hebrews. In time, Breasted developed his beliefs into a full-fledged humanist manifesto, celebrating the perception of moral values as a triumph of the human spirit which grew, not out of any exclusive revelation, but from man's experience in society. The development of this moral sense in man, the most precious of his possessions, was what Breasted set out to trace through the early history of the Near East. *The Dawn of Conscience* (1933) contains the author's fullest and most mature treatment of this material, embodying also his most intimate reflections on history and the human condition.

Breasted's inquiry into the historical origins of human morality sprang from his very contemporary sense that the values he saw underlying civilized life were eroding or under attack. From the vantage of the twentieth century, it seemed not so very long ago that "man began as an *unmoral* savage." Yet "the most fundamentally important thing in the developing life of man has been the rise of ideals of conduct and the emergence of character, a historical transformation of human life which can be historically demonstrated to have begun but yesterday." Faced with the disorienting pace of change in the modern world, it might be well for the emerging generation to consider the origins and historic role of "the crowning glory of [man's] life on earth, the discovery of character."

Ethics are, for many, religion's finest fruits; but this, Breasted believed, was not always so. Primitive religion in Egypt grew out of the two dominant natural phenomena, the sun and the verdant earth. Only later did the gods pass from the realm of nature into that of mankind to become arbiters of human conduct. Ethics arose separately and were grounded in the social experience of the Egyptian people—of individuals within the family and of wider groups interacting with the state. The earliest moral discernment, Breasted observed, was also a social judgment: doing what was "loved" and avoiding what was "hated," not yet any sense of right and wrong. Virtues during the Old Kingdom were mainly devices for social accommodation, but there already existed a concept that human conduct was liable to judgment before the gods. This concept was what made it possible, in the end, for religion to express the growing moral awareness that came about in later ages of Egyptian history.

For Breasted, the acceleration of this process came about in the wake of a catastrophe that, again, was social and political: the collapse of the Old Kingdom, with the apparent failure of the divinely ordained social order. Men reflected for the first time on the nature of human society, and out of the disorientation and deep pessimism of the age there arose two responses: one was a messianism which sought the means for implementing justice in the ideal government; the other was to look to the hereafter for the fulfillment of hopes that were not realized in this world. In this second response Breasted saw a significant extension of the old idea of a divine judgment in the next world: this was the acknowledgment of a moral sense, lodged in the "heart" (or conscience), to which all men were now accountable in the presence of the gods. Unfortunately, this ethical advance was undermined

Breasted at work (courtesy of The Oriental Institute of The University of Chicago)

by the influence of the priesthoods in Egyptian society and in particular by their encouragement of the belief that magic could divert the gods' attention from the sins committed in this life. Such devices, Breasted believed, could only detract from the healthy emphasis on personal responsibility toward which the mainstream of religious thinking was now leading.

The priestly stranglehold, in Breasted's view, doomed organized Egyptian religion to sterility: even reform at the highest level, as in Ikhnaton's religious revolution, could not prevail against the clergy. The interpenetration of ethics and religion, however, was already too deep-seated to be stopped. The fatherly solicitude of Ikhnaton's god for all his creatures was a new feature which anticipated the concept of God which ultimately passed into the modern world. A sense of personal communication with the deity, moreover, had led

Ikhnaton to effect his religious reforms on the basis of experience rather than mythological authority. This departure from tradition, which for Breasted made Ikhnaton the first individual in human history, was carried forward by the later concept of Egyptian gods as personal saviors for the individual. Ritual denials of guilt, fostered by priestly manipulations, gave way to a genuine acknowledgment of sin before the gods. The voice of conscience was now recognized as the voice of God, overriding the once all-important emphasis on social approbation. This emancipation of conscience was what Egypt passed directly to the Hebrews (completing a process which had begun 2,500 years before the national life of the Hebrews had even begun) and is what was transmitted through them to us today.

From this record of man's emergence as a moral being, Breasted believed his generation could take heart in what it revealed as "the unconquerable buoyancy of the human soul." No one could define what this was—but a historian could observe what it did. Looking at man's career in the widest possible perspective, it seemed evident that there was indeed a genealogy of human values which had arisen and developed through history. Such values were not transferred automatically from one age to the next: the history of character was no simple march of progress. In one way or another, however, enough was passed on so that nothing of essential value was lost. Through all the periods of retreat and stagnation, and especially with the horrors of World War I within memory, it was important to keep in mind both the persistence and the origins of this moral legacy. It was Breasted's belief that the facility with which modern man could now study the past might serve as a moral influence on the present.

The study of this "New Past"—the records of pre-Classical antiquity—demanded, as Breasted recognized, enormous scholarly versatility: to do this properly, the skills of the anthropologist, archaeologist, ethnologist, student of comparative religions and literatures, art historian, and linguist had to be combined in one man or at least incorporated into his thinking. For all that he was widely read, in the best traditions of nineteenth-century scholarship, Breasted's command of these disciplines was that of a well-informed generalist: modern specialists would find much that is dubious in the theoretical underpinnings of *The Dawn of Conscience*. Many of the written sources on which Breasted based his thinking were being studied in this fashion for the first time in Breasted's work: it is to be expected that deeper understanding would come only with further research. *The Dawn of Conscience* ranks now as a pioneering work, not a definitive one. In its day, however, it was a great advance over the primarily descriptive work of earlier writers. It was the first comprehensive account of the development of religion and thought in ancient Egypt which was based on an exhaustive examination of the original texts. The thesis which Breasted advanced in *The Dawn of Conscience* is essentially that which has entered the mainstream of modern thinking on Egypt's role in the ancient world. His perceptions of the Egyptians' awareness of the divine have been greatly altered by recent scholarship; but these later ideas were themselves developed from the basis of Breasted's classic synthesis, which (especially in its analysis of the social applications of Egypt's spiritual odyssey) still offers much that is of value today. Modern students may

question Breasted's emphases and interpretations, but none can accuse him of asking trivial questions or offering glib answers. For this honesty and seriousness, *The Dawn of Conscience* stands as a noble monument to its author's science and his humanity.

The second decade of the twentieth century, during which Breasted came into his own as the American spokesman on ancient Egypt, also saw his release from the grind to which his modest salary and circumstances had condemned him for so long. Authorship of a series of textbooks not only provided him with the income he needed to devote himself more thoroughly to serious pursuits, but also made him virtually into a household name, the recognized authority on ancient man. Indeed, in terms of its audience and its distribution, Breasted probably wrote no more influential book than *Ancient Times: A History of the Early World* (1916), a high-school survey covering the full span of civilization in the ancient Mediterranean world, beginning with prehistoric man and ending with the fall of Rome. So popular did this book become that its author was persuaded to prepare a special edition for adults, entitled *The Conquest of Civilization* (1926), which also achieved a wide circulation. Each of these books went through later editions which were updated to include recently discovered material. Both, however, remained essentially the same, particularly in emphasizing the influence of the ancient Near East on the shaping of the modern world. For Breasted, the Near East was in fact the cradle of civilization, its preserver until such time as it could take firm root in the West; and its influence remained potent, particularly over the countries of the Levant, long after these nations had ceased to play much of a role in world events. In contemplating this record, Breasted the optimist characteristically saw a message of hope. The monuments of the past "continue to reveal the age-long course along which the developing life of man has moved; and in thus following his conquest of civilization, we have been following a *rising path*." Breasted firmly believed this himself. During the dismal years of the Great War and in the heady recovery that followed, it was a belief many shared.

Even before World War I, Breasted had been trying to generate support for survey projects dealing with the standing monuments of the ancient Near East, first in Egypt, then in other parts of the Levant. With the war's conclusion, he was able to realize these plans on a scale which even he might not have dreamed. Alone among the great powers, America had emerged from the war confident, unravaged, and prosperous. American philanthropists were ready, indeed eager, to show the flag abroad, and in Breasted archaeology was blessed with an evangelical proponent. In 1919 he wrote to John D. Rockefeller, Jr., calling his attention to the favorable conditions for the University of Chicago's resumption of field work in the Near East. Rockefeller replied by agreeing to fund for five years what was to be called the Oriental Institute. An arduous survey trip in 1919-1920, which took Breasted and his team of associates to Egypt, then Iraq, and into Lebanon and Syria, helped set priorities for future research. For Breasted personally this journey brought a reward in the discovery at Salabiyah (Dura Europus), the easternmost outpost of the Roman Empire then known, of the late Roman paintings which Breasted would publish in his *Oriental Forerunners of Byzantine Painting* (1924). More important, he was now in a position to set in motion the greatest research undertaking ever conceived in the field of ancient studies, one which would study the course of early man in all the countries of the ancient Near East.

The next decade saw the fulfillment of all that Breasted had fought for since the beginning of his career. By 1930, the Oriental Institute, its funding now extended and enlarged, was sponsoring no fewer than six projects in Egypt, two each in Syria and Iraq, one in Turkey, and another in Iran—all the major centers of ancient civilization in the Near East. At home, its research enterprises embraced work on Egyptian, cuneiform, Syriac, and Arabic source materials. Some of these projects, such as the survey of epigraphs in Egypt and the Chicago-based Assyrian dictionary, were to turn into long-term operations that today, more than half a century after their inception, are still actively in progress. What is remarkable about all of these diverse activities, however, is not merely their scope, but their interrelations, as parts of a vast program of inquiry into the origins and development of human society. This was a subject central to Breasted's own scholarship; and in the work of the Oriental Institute his breadth and vision as a historian found their most lasting expression.

Despite the enormous strain placed on him by fund-raising and administration added to his professional work, Breasted always retained that buoyancy which marked for him man's best resource in adversity. He was undeterred by the recurrent illnesses which afflicted him in later life. "I cannot walk to my office," he wrote to his son in 1923, "but I am going to Egypt again, if I go on a stretcher!" His eminence in the field, no less than his ability to win the support of wealthy patrons,

made him much in demand as a lecturer, scientific consultant, and practical adviser to his colleagues. His international reputation, established during the "research period," would be fully acknowledged after World War I, as each year brought a new crop of academic honors and offices in professional associations. Yet other measures of his professional stature are that he was chosen to handle the historical aspects of the projected publication on the tomb of Tutankhamon soon after its discovery in 1922 and that he was asked to contribute the Egyptian chapters to the prestigious *Cambridge Ancient History*. Later, he would attempt to mediate the dispute which arose between the Egyptian authorities and the discoverers of Tutankhamon's tomb; and he acted as Rockefeller's personal representative during negotiations concerning the American millionaire's offer to underwrite the cost of a new museum of Egyptian antiquities in Cairo. The failure of both projects was not Breasted's fault, nor did these reverses impair his effectiveness in pursuing the goals of the Oriental Institute in Egypt. Throughout these many activities, and despite the demands they placed on his time and strength, he continued into his later years to work with students and younger colleagues. Those who still remember him from that time speak of him as an inspiring teacher, capable of presenting the driest grammatical form as an exciting achievement of the human mind. Nor did the administrator and the public figure eclipse the scholar. Breasted's last substantial work was his publication of a medical treatise dating to the middle of the second millennium B.C., *The Edwin Smith Surgical Papyrus* (1930). Worked on during odd hours and minutes left over between his rounds of teaching and other duties, it is not only first-rate from a philological standpoint, but also displays considerable sophistication in dealing with the historical and physiological aspects of a difficult text.

In 1934 Breasted's wife Frances died. He married her sister, Imogen Hart Richmond, the following year, shortly before his own sudden death of a hemolytic streptococcic infection contracted on his return journey from Europe near the end of 1935. Breasted's death came when the far-flung enterprises which were largely his own creation were at their height. He did not have to witness the pruning of the Oriental Institute's operations which the worldwide financial crises of the 1930s would eventually require. Death caught him at the peak of his powers. A distinguished Egyptologist, he had achieved wider recognition as spokesman for his generation on the development of ancient human society. His last fifteen years, it is true, had been spent less on his own original research than on creating the means for others to do their own. This achievement also ranks as an intellectual one, however, for Breasted was never merely a promoter, but always a designer and participant in the projects begun under his direction. These projects, as much as the writings of his maturity—*The Dawn of Conscience* and *The Conquest of Civilization*—reveal an intellect always attuned to both the absorbing of new information and the possibility of integrating it into a fresh synthesis. That this synthesis would change in the light of further study was something Breasted recognized and welcomed. In this sense, his books speak less eloquently of his stature than his legacy does. For both his own and the coming generations, Breasted had brought the "New Past" vibrantly to life. Perhaps more important, though, he had instilled a sense of "the inspiring task which confronts America in the Near East," a task which "cannot be achieved without the aid of a new generation of young Americans who are willing to spend the years necessary to gain the training and equipment

without which the work cannot be done." In the contributions he made to the practice of his profession and to the education of colleagues and students are to be found his best and most lasting achievements.

References:

Charles Breasted, *Pioneer to the Past: The Story of James Henry Breasted* (New York: Scribners, 1945);

John A. Wilson, "Biographical Memoir of James Henry Breasted, 1865-1935," *National Academy of Sciences of the United States of America, Biographical Memoirs*, 35, no. 5 (1937): 93-121;

Wilson, *Signs and Wonders upon Pharaoh* (Chicago: University of Chicago Press, 1964), pp. 124-143.

Papers:

Breasted's diaries, field notebooks, and other papers are at the Oriental Institute of the University of Chicago.

Philip Alexander Bruce

(7 March 1856-16 August 1933)

L. Moody Simms, Jr.
Illinois State University

SELECTED BOOKS: *The Social History of Virginia* (N.p., 1881);

The Plantation Negro as a Freeman; Observations on His Character, Condition, and Prospects in Virginia (New York & London: Putnam's, 1889);

Economic History of Virginia in the Seventeenth Century. An Inquiry into the Material Condition of the People, Based upon Original and Contemporaneous Records, 2 volumes (New York & London: Macmillan, 1895-1896);

A School History of the United States (New York: American Book Company, 1903);

The Rise of the New South (Philadelphia: Printed by G. Barrie, 1905; London: Cazenove, 1905);

Robert E. Lee (Philadelphia: Jacobs, 1907);

Social Life of Virginia in the Seventeenth Century. An Inquiry into the Origin of the Higher Planting

Class, Together With an Account of the Habits, Customs, and Diversions of the People (Richmond: Printed for the author by Whittet & Shepperson, 1907; revised and enlarged, Lynchburg, Va.: Bell, 1927);

Institutional History of Virginia in the Seventeenth Century. An Inquiry into the Religious, Moral, Educational, Legal, Military, and Political Condition of the People, Based on Original and Contemporaneous Records, 2 volumes (New York & London: Putnam's, 1910);

Pocahontas and Other Sonnets (Norfolk, Va., 1912);

Brave Deeds of Confederate Soldiers (Philadelphia: Jacobs, 1916);

History of the University of Virginia, 1819-1919: The Lengthened Shadow of One Man, 5 volumes (New York: Macmillan, 1920-1922);

Virginia Historical Society

Philip Alexander Bruce

History of Virginia: The Colonial Period (Chicago &
New York: American Historical Society,
1924);
The Virginia Plutarch, 2 volumes (Chapel Hill: University of North Carolina Press, 1929).

OTHER: "John Randolph," in *Library of Southern
Literature*, edited by E. A. Alderman and oth-
ers, 17 volumes (New Orleans & Atlanta:
Hoyt, 1907-1923), X: 4329-4356;
"The Economic and Social Life of Virginia in the
Seventeenth Century," "The Social Life of the
Upper South," "The South in the Economic
Policies of the United States," in *The South in
the Building of the Nation*, edited by J. A. C.
Chandler and others, 13 volumes (Richmond:
Southern Historical Publications Society,
1909-1913), I: 46-73; IV: 353-382; X: 1-16;
History of Virginia, edited by Bruce and Lyon Gar-
diner Tyler, 6 volumes (Chicago & New York:
American Historical Society, 1924);

Virginia: Rebirth of the Old Dominion, edited by
Bruce, 5 volumes (Chicago & New York:
Lewis, 1929).

PERIODICAL PUBLICATIONS: "The American
Negro of To-day," *Contemporary Review*, 77
(February 1900): 284-297;
"Social and Economic Revolution in the Southern
States," *Contemporary Review*, 78 (July 1900):
58-73;
"Plantation Memories of the Civil War," *South At-
lantic Quarterly*, 16 (January 1915): 28-46.

An experienced lawyer, businessman, and
newspaper editorial writer, Philip Alexander Bruce
eventually chose the life of the quiet scholar and
wrote over two million words dealing with the social
and economic history of the South. Today he is
primarily remembered for his five volumes on the
economic, institutional, and social history of seventeenth-century Virginia. These works are still
cited as standard references because Bruce was
painstaking in his research and a pioneer in the
use of colonial court records as a source of historical
interpretation. While it is true that errors of fact
and interpretation can be found in these volumes,
time has been kind to Bruce's history in general.
Even the aspects of the author's findings which
have been attacked most widely—his interpretation
of the origins of Virginia's higher planter class, for
example—have been partly revived by such subsequent scholars as Louis B. Wright.

A descendant of one of Virginia's important
older families, Bruce, the sixth child of Charles and
Sarah Seddon Bruce, was born at the Staunton Hill
plantation in Charlotte County, Virginia. Among
his earliest recollections, he wrote in 1911, were the
plantation, the plantation home, and slaves. Indeed, all of his first impressions of life were associated with plantation scenes, amusements, and
occupations. Although his antebellum years were
but five, he was eminently proud of that heritage
throughout his life. In later years he fondly recalled
the mansion at Staunton Hill. By 1861 this big
house—a crenellated, battlemented structure—
had become the center of one of the largest tobacco
plantations in Virginia, operated by over 500 slaves.

The Civil War began when Bruce was five and
firmly fixed its imprint upon him. At the age of
nine, he began his formal education at a neighboring old-field school. In 1871 Bruce left Staunton
Hill and entered Norwood Academy in Nelson
County, Virginia. Two years later he moved on to
the University of Virginia, where he studied history

and literature for several years. Believing that the law was to be his profession, he entered Harvard Law School, where he received a bachelor of laws degree in 1878.

Steeped in the glorious tradition of the Old South, Bruce was disillusioned as a young man by the mounting problems which faced the post-Civil War South. Convinced that industrialization was the only cure for the South's economic woes, he was genuinely interested in the New South philosophy of such men as Henry Grady and devoted much of his early work to the dissemination of the New South gospel. To Bruce, the free black seemed to be a major stumbling block for a region beginning the long climb back, and by 1884 he was determined to study this "obstacle" in detail.

Widely hailed in both the North and South, Bruce's first book, *The Plantation Negro as a Freeman*, was published in 1889 in G. P. Putnam's Questions of the Day series. Though it was an expansion of a series of articles he had written for the *New York Evening Post* in 1884, it was more pessimistic regarding the capacity of blacks to rise in society, more apprehensive as to the possibility of black domination by sheer weight of numbers, and more insistent on strict, perhaps permanent, white control. Bruce's disregard for the historical forces which had shaped the lives of Southern blacks contributed greatly to the book's pessimistic conclusions. Yet its detached, impersonal tone gave the impression that the book represented scientific fact, and its conclusions and pessimistic forebodings were shared by many, especially Southerners. *The Plantation Negro as a Freeman* evoked a national wave of comment and almost unanimous applause. It proved to be a seminal work for many writers who measured blacks on a scale of personality traits and found, when blacks fell short of the ideal, that they had serious character defects in comparison with whites.

By the mid-1880s Bruce found that he had no strong inclination toward the practice of law. In 1887 he became the secretary-treasurer of his brother's Vulcan Iron Works in Richmond. Though *The Plantation Negro* was not as successful in sales as its wide reception in the nation's press seemed to portend, the book did open doors for Bruce. In 1890 he moved on to the editorial staff of the *Richmond Times*, where his work ran the gamut from commentary against women in the pulpit to editorials on the "Negro problem."

All the while Bruce found himself slowly drifting further from the active life into academic pursuits. During the early 1890s he turned his mind to the antebellum South in an attempt to find the basis for the New South in the history of Virginia between the Revolution and the Civil War. Bruce left the *Times* in 1892 and became the corresponding secretary of the Virginia Historical Society. The following year he helped found the Society's *Virginia Magazine of History and Biography* and became its first editor. He held both positions until 1898. In his own historical research, he quickly concluded that antebellum Virginia was dependent on colonial foundations and that ultimately the basis of the society he had known in his youth lay in the seventeenth century.

The result of several years of intensive research and writing, Bruce's *Economic History of Virginia in the Seventeenth Century* was published in two volumes in 1895 and 1896. (He would deal later with the social, religious, intellectual, military, judicial, and political life.) In this work, Bruce described the reasons for colonization, the aboriginal economy, the methods of land acquisition, the use of indentured servants and slaves, and the development of the plantation economy. He stressed the decisive role of soil exhaustion, the wastefulness of a one-crop system, and the impact of material forces as clues to Southern life. Finally, Bruce argued that the management of large tobacco plantations and the supervision of numerous slaves created in the ruling class an aristocratic psychology which fostered habits of self-reliance and an intense love of liberty. A joining of seventeenth-century history and late-nineteenth-century New South optimism, the *Economic History* met a mixed reception from critics. Praise for its "censuslike fullness" (*Outlook*) was balanced by criticism citing the work as "encumbered by a great mass of detail" (*Bookman*). Yet Bruce was happy; in the course of his research for the work, he had developed a taste for history which was never to leave him.

In October 1896 Bruce married Elizabeth Tunstall Taylor Newton of Norfolk, Virginia. She brought to him more of that romantic view of the past which Bruce himself already had in excess. The couple had one daughter, Philippa Alexander. Bruce left his positions with the Virginia Historical Society in 1898 in order to visit England and explore various collections of colonial records. While there with his family, he contracted to write a history of the United States for young people, a volume on the New South, and a biography of Robert E. Lee. He also wrote articles explaining the New South and the "Negro problem" to British readers. Bruce's *A School History of the United States* was published in 1903. His only attempt at a general survey of American history, it lay undue emphasis on the part played by Virginia in the colonial period. Several critics castigated the work for the bias indicated by its strategic omissions.

Bruce's *The Rise of the New South* appeared in 1905. Marked by rampant optimism, it reads like an industrial gazetteer of the South, foretelling further Southern progress and prosperity based on the solid economic, social, and political accomplishments of the years since 1877. Even the difficult "Negro problem" seems to have lost much of its importance to Bruce. Blacks were now seen as proving their worth as industrial workers. The last of Bruce's major New South efforts, this work was well-received by the critics and achieved a two-fold distinction. As the first major work dealing with the subject, it established Bruce as a pioneer of the New South school of historians, and the book is still a capstone of the New South crusade.

In 1907 Bruce and his family returned to the United States and took up residence in Norfolk, Virginia. During his nine years abroad, he had traveled through all the countries of continental Europe except Russia, Spain, and the Balkan states. Bruce's mother, whom he later described as "a perfect representative of the noble pattern of the Southern matron of the Old Regime," had died early in 1907. Upon division of the Staunton Hill estate, he received 1,402 1/2 acres of hill and lowland and a modest personal income. Coupled with his earnings from writing, editing, and reviewing, this inheritance was to provide Bruce with his long-sought sense of financial security.

Bruce's *Robert E. Lee* was published in 1907. It is a straightforward study of Lee's life with two chapters in which Bruce evaluated his subject. The first of these chapters, entitled "Military Genius," in no way questions the place Lee held in Southern history as a military leader. The second, called "General Character," justifies Lee's adherence to the Southern cause and sums up the general attributes of Lee the citizen. Written for the series of American Crisis Biographies, Bruce's *Robert E. Lee* was truthfully labeled by critics an uncritical portrayal of a personal hero.

Social Life of Virginia in the Seventeenth Century, the second part of Bruce's history, was also published in 1907. It presents the thesis that there had been a distinct society in Virginia, one embodying both gentry and yeomanry; that this society was copied completely from the English social system; and that the homeland was a natural choice for the colonists' model. Bruce traced the origin of Virginia's planters to squirearchic and mercantile sources. Though partly based on Bruce's English research, the *Social Life of Virginia in the Seventeenth Century* does not measure up to the *Economic History* because it depends too heavily on secondary works.

In retrospect, the years 1903 through 1907 can be seen as marking a major change in Bruce's scholarly interests. More and more, a preoccupation with the glories of the Southern and Virginian past—with the myth of the Old South—took hold of him. Articles indicating an interest in the contemporary world would continue to come from his pen, but the bulk of his writings would be concerned with past history.

Work on the Virginia project continued. In 1910 the third part was completed and published as the two-volume *Institutional History of Virginia in the Seventeenth Century.* Based in part on materials found in England, this work deals with many facets of early Virginia life—religion and morals, education, legal administration, the military system, and political conditions. Bruce maintained that evidence gleaned from Virginia county records supported his conclusion that a deep religious spirit was universally present from the foundation of the colony. He conceded that the scattered planting of Virginia was not as favorable for popular education as was the compact settlement of New England, but he believed that this shortcoming was counterbalanced by the closer connection of Virginia with the mother country. Considering all five of Bruce's volumes on Virginia together, the *American Historical Review* cited the "flood of enlightenment" resulting from the author's "hard work and erudition," but some who reviewed the *Institutional History* criticized Bruce's "bias of local patriotism" and heavy emphasis on the Virginia aristocracy.

In 1913 Bruce again traveled to England, where he was to remain until the early part of 1916. The outbreak of World War I pulled him once again into the twentieth century, focusing his attention on contemporary affairs for several years. It was only natural that he would devote most of his time to observing the English people under the exigencies of wartime conditions. By 1917 Bruce appears to have accepted the necessity of United States military involvement in Europe. However, he immediately became an opponent of Wilson's Fourteen Points, especially attacking Wilson's concept of a League of Nations.

Upon his return to America in 1916, Bruce made his residence in Charlottesville, Virginia, having accepted the position as centennial historian of the University of Virginia. Soon after his arrival in Charlottesville (where he was to live for the last

Bruce in 1915 (Virginia Historical Society)

seventeen years of his life), Bruce's *Brave Deeds of Confederate Soldiers* (1916) was published. This work unmistakenly reflects his allegiance to the mythology and symbolism of the Old South and the Lost Cause. Bruce rejoiced in a population, untainted by immigrants, which clung to the traditions of the past and in that love of home which strengthened every Southern soldier. He reveled in the chivalric tournaments and the Code Duello which tempered the minds of Southern youth and made the Civil War—from the South's point of view—one vast field of honor. Facts were insignificant before a conglomeration of eulogia, omissions, and outright fables. Many of the journals and newspapers which had reviewed most of Bruce's previous works simply ignored *Brave Deeds of Confederate Soldiers.*

After four years of research and writing, Bruce published the first two volumes of his history of the University of Virginia, beginning in 1920. Three more volumes soon followed, the last appearing in January of 1922. Sold by subscription,

this work deals with the university as an institution of culture and learning about which centered much of Virginia's history. Bruce believed that the university projected its influence throughout the South and, in turn, reflected Southern cultural, social, and economic life. Tracing the university's development through nine chronological periods, he devoted particular attention to the institution's formative years. His subtitle for the work, "The Lengthened Shadow of One Man," summed up his belief that Thomas Jefferson's influence had been pervasive throughout the university's history.

The well-received *History of the University of Virginia* was followed quickly by the multivolume *History of Virginia* (1924), which Bruce (and Lyon Gardiner Tyler) edited and for which he wrote volume one, on the colonial period. Bruce's contribution relies heavily upon his earlier volumes on seventeenth-century Virginia. It is uneven in treatment and style, as is, in fact, the entire series which proved to be neither a critical nor financial success.

In 1927 a slightly revised and enlarged edition of the *Social Life of Virginia in the Seventeenth Century* appeared. Bruce edited a work entitled *Virginia: Rebirth of the Old Dominion* which appeared in five volumes in 1929. Consisting of contributions by a staff of writers, it is a survey of Virginia's history from Jamestown to 1876. The work as a whole contributed little that was new to existing knowledge of Virginia's past.

The Virginia Plutarch, Bruce's last major work, was published in two volumes in 1929. In sketching the lives of those whom he considered most important in Virginia's history, he created a series of warm and, for the most part, friendly portraits. Not surprisingly, only two individuals from the post-Civil War period—Woodrow Wilson and Walter Reed—were included. Bruce's love of Virginia caused him to claim as native sons some individuals who had at best only tenuous connections with the history of the Old Dominion. Most critics were taken with the charm of Bruce's portraits.

From 1930 until his death, Bruce was ill for extended periods. He died on 16 August 1933 at his home in Charlottesville and was buried in the cemetery of the University of Virginia. As Thomas Perkins Abernethy has remarked: "Few lives have been devoted so completely to the cause of historical research. . . ."

Though he tended steadily toward conservatism during his life, Bruce was basically a moderate. He alternately embraced the Old and New South, and throughout his life, these two sides of his thought were in conflict. However, he made sporadic efforts to reconcile this divided allegiance by compromise. For example, Bruce believed that blacks in the South posed a problem of large proportions, but he did not insist that the problem was a permanent one. He saw, too, that the day of a glorious antebellum society was gone forever, but he believed that "the simplicity of life, manliness of spirit, the love of house and family" inherited from the past could strengthen Southerners who were building a new society.

Throughout his long career as a historian and social commentator, Bruce stood alone. He remained aloof during the period when American historians became professionals, and he never held a position on a university faculty. He preferred to immerse himself in quiet scholarship, selecting his own topics for research and following wherever they led. As other historians turned increasingly to group efforts for expansive subjects, Bruce continued to undertake multivolume projects on his own. He continued to read widely, and though he occasionally overlooked recent findings on a subject, such oversights rarely led to fatal flaws in his work. Though much of his work was ephemeral, Bruce cannot be denied his place in the history of historical writing in the South and the United States. His work on seventeenth-century Virginia has endured, and this achievement has earned him the respect and admiration of his chosen profession.

References:

L. Moody Simms, Jr., "History as Inspiration: Philip Alexander Bruce and the Old South Mystique," *McNeese Review*, 18 (1967): 3-10;

Simms, "Philip Alexander Bruce and the Negro Problem, 1884-1930," *Virginia Magazine of History and Biography*, 75 (July 1967): 349-362;

Simms, "Philip Alexander Bruce and the New South," *Mississippi Quarterly*, 19 (Fall 1966): 171-183;

Simms, "Philip Alexander Bruce: His Life and Works," Ph.D. dissertation, University of Virginia, 1966;

Simms, "Philip Alexander Bruce: The Charlottesville Years," *Magazine of Albermarle County* (Virginia) *History*, 29 (1971): 69-79.

Papers:

Bruce's papers are at the Alderman Library, University of Virginia, Charlottesville, and the Virginia Historical Society, Richmond.

John W. Burgess

(26 August 1844-13 January 1931)

John Braeman
University of Nebraska at Lincoln

SELECTED BOOKS: *The American University. When Shall It Be? Where Shall It Be?* (Boston: Ginn, Heath, 1884);

Political Science and Comparative Constitutional Law, 2 volumes (Boston & London: Ginn, 1890, 1891); chapters on the nation and the state revised as *The Foundations of Political Science* (New York: Columbia University Press, 1933);

The Middle Period, 1817-1858 (New York: Scribners, 1897);

The Civil War and the Constitution, 1859-1865, 2 volumes (New York: Scribners, 1901);

Reconstruction and the Constitution, 1866-1876 (New York: Scribners, 1902);

The European War of 1914: Its Causes, Purposes, and Probable Results (Chicago: McClurg, 1915);

The Reconciliation of Government with Liberty (New York: Scribners, 1915);

The Administration of President Hayes (New York: Scribners, 1916);

America's Relations to the Great War (Chicago: McClurg, 1916);

Recent Changes in American Constitutional Theory (New York: Columbia University Press, 1923);

The Sanctity of Law, Wherein Does It Consist? (Boston: Ginn, 1927);

Reminiscences of an American Scholar: The Beginnings of Columbia University (New York: Columbia University Press, 1934).

OTHER: "The Methods of Historical Study and Research in Columbia College," in *Methods of Teaching History,* revised edition, edited by G. Stanley Hall (Boston: Ginn, 1885), pp. 215-221.

PERIODICAL PUBLICATIONS: "The Study of the Political Sciences at Columbia College," *International Review,* 12 (April 1882): 346-351; "Political Science and History," *American Historical Review,* 2 (April 1897): 401-408.

John William Burgess was one of the leaders in the professionalization of American social science. As an administrator, he was a pioneer in the establishment of graduate education in the United States. As a teacher, he counted among his former students many of the nation's academic elite. Other

John W. Burgess

students, the most famous being Theodore Roosevelt and Franklin D. Roosevelt, went on to gain prominence in the law, journalism, business, or public life. More than any other person, he laid the basis for the acceptance of political science as a scholarly discipline in the United States. He was regarded by contemporaries as the dean of comparative and American constitutional law studies. And he was a leading practitioner—though with his own distinctive neo-Hegelian twist—of "scientific history."

Burgess was born on 26 August 1844 in Giles County, in middle Tennessee adjacent to the Alabama border. He was of New England stock on his father's side, descended from a 1630s Puritan immigrant to Massachusetts. Successive generations of the Burgess family had lived in the Newport, Rhode Island, area, but his grandfather had moved to Baltimore, and his father, Thomas T. Burgess, crossed the mountains to Tennessee. His mother, the former Mary J. Edwards, was born the daughter of a Virginia-born physician. Although not belonging to the planter elite, his father was a successful farmer who owned some slaves. Politically, Thomas Burgess was a devoted admirer of Henry Clay, a staunch Whig, and an American nationalist who would remain loyal to the Union in the Civil War.

Burgess's father was financially capable to hire a private tutor for his son. The young Burgess then attended nearby Cumberland University until the institution closed its doors in early 1862 in face of the advancing Union Army. Finding himself harassed at home by pro-Confederate sympathizers, the not-yet-eighteen-year-old fled to join the Union forces. He was promoted to the rank of second lieutenant before being mustered out for health reasons in the summer of 1864. The bitter and fratricidal strife that raged in Tennessee left its lasting impress upon Burgess. In the first place, the experience reinforced his own strongly nationalist convictions. Second, as Burgess recalled in his autobiography, *Reminiscences of an American Scholar* (1934), the experience shattered any easy optimism about "the wisdom and goodness of the mass of men": except for the few "supermen" who "make the ideas and ideals of civilization," men were "ignorant, narrow, greedy, prejudiced, malicious, brutal, and vindictive." Simultaneously, however, Burgess was drawn—as he would later explain to a former student—"to do what I could for the development of political and legal education, for substituting the conservative methods of peace for the destructive effects of war."

In the fall of 1864, Burgess set out for Amherst College, where he had been admitted with sophomore standing. The next three years were probably the happiest time of his life. He was active in fraternity affairs; he met and fell in love with his future wife, Augusta Thayer Jones; and he was elected to Phi Beta Kappa. The esteem in which he was held by his fellow students was evidenced by his selection as class orator at graduation. His first two years at Amherst were devoted largely to study of the classics, mathematics, and natural science. During his last year he came under the influence of Julius H. Seelye—a future Amherst president—who taught the required senior-year course in moral philosophy. Seelye not only introduced Burgess to the Hegelian philosophy he had become acquainted with while studying theology in Germany, but he also played a catalytic role in inspiring Burgess to go on to study history, political science, and law. Although Burgess planned to attend Columbia Law School after graduating in June 1867, an attack of typhoid fever laid him up until it was too late for entry that fall. Instead, he obtained a clerkship with a Springfield, Massachusetts, law firm. In the early summer of 1869, he passed the state bar examination. At this juncture, however, he was offered a professorship of rhetoric by the president of Knox College in Galesburg, Illinois.

On 24 August 1869, Burgess married his college sweetheart and then went west to assume his new post. Along with rhetoric, he taught English literature and political economy; he organized a debate league; and he became involved in fundraising and public relations for the struggling institution. Dissatisfaction over being, as he put it, so "thinly spread out" led him the summer of 1871 to go to Germany for advanced work, first at Göttingen and then at Leipzig and Berlin. He studied under the most distinguished German scholars of the time: Johann Gustav Droysen, the dean of the Prussian nationalist school of history; Wilhelm Roscher, a leader of the historical school of economics; the eminent Roman historian Theodor Mommsen, whose linking history with law strongly influenced Burgess's own approach; and Rudolf von Gneist, the foremost authority on comparative constitutional law. Although he did not work toward a formal degree, the two years spent in Germany were pivotal in Burgess's development. The experience reinforced his Hegelianism. He acquired a lifelong admiration for things German. Most important, he was inspired to establish in the United States the opportunities for advanced study and research he had found there.

After Burgess's return to the United States in the summer of 1873, his patron Julius H. Seelye induced the Amherst authorities to establish a professorship in history and political science for him. Soon disappointed by the prevailing atmosphere of narrow evangelical piety, the petty academic politics, and the resistance to his plans for introducing graduate instruction, he eagerly accepted an invitation to deliver a series of lectures at Columbia Law School in January 1876. The lectures proved so successful that he was invited to fill the chair in public law that had been left vacant by the death of Francis Lieber. In addition to teaching at the law school, Burgess was given responsibility for instruction in history and political science in the undergraduate college. But he faced new frustrations. The faculty was largely unimpressive and conservative-minded; the physical facilities and library were inadequate. He found most of the undergraduates intellectually uninterested; and since his law school courses were optional, enrollment was disappointing. Worse, he came into increasing conflict with the dominant figure at the law school, Theodore W. Dwight, over Burgess's plan to add a third year to the two-year bachelor of laws course and make public law required for the degree.

Influenced partly by the blockage of his plans for the third-year law program, partly by the example of the recently found Ècole Libre des Sciences Politiques in Paris, and partly by his own interest in civil service reform, Burgess pushed for the establishment of a separate "department" that would provide a three-year course of study leading to the Ph.D., open to undergraduates who had completed their junior year, aimed at training students for public service. The program would include constitutional history and law, Roman law, international law and diplomacy, public administration, political economy, and statistics. He gained the support of Columbia president Frederick A. P. Barnard and of an influential faction among the trustees who shared his vision of making the institution a center for advanced study. In June 1880, the trustees voted to establish a School of Political Science with the first systematically organized curriculum in the political and social sciences in the United States. A decade later, Burgess was the moving force behind the reorganization that would transform Columbia into a real university in the modern sense, with an undergraduate college, separate professional schools, and the three graduate faculties of political science, philosophy, and pure science.

In May 1890, he was formally elected dean of

the Faculty of Political Science—a position he retained until his retirement in 1912. Burgess made the Faculty of Political Science the nation's preeminent center for social science research and advanced study. The Academy of Political Science was established in 1881; the *Political Science Quarterly* was launched in 1886; and the Studies in History, Economics, and Public Law was inaugurated in 1891 to publish doctoral dissertations. During the 1890s a tripartite departmental structure crystallized, consisting of Public Law and Comparative Jurisprudence, Economics and Social Science, and History and Political Philosophy. As of the academic year 1899-1900, the school had the largest enrollment of graduate students of any American institution in the field. A keen judge of talent, Burgess built—with the backing of presidents Seth Low and Nicholas Murray Butler—an unrivaled faculty: Munroe Smith in Roman law; Frank J. Goodnow in public administration; John Bassett Moore in international law; E. R. A. Seligman and John Bates Clark in economics; Herbert L. Osgood and William A. Dunning in American history; James Harvey Robinson in European history; and Franklin P. Giddings in sociology. After the turn of the century, a brilliant group of younger men—including Charles A. Beard, James T. Shotwell, and Carlton J. H. Hayes—were added.

Because of his involvement in building the university Burgess did not turn out any major scholarly contribution of his own until the appearance in 1890 and 1891 of the two-volume *Political Science and Comparative Constitutional Law*. Thereafter he produced a continuing flow of books and articles. He was by temperament not inclined to detailed research. His interest lay rather in expounding broad principles. The concept of the state was the key to, and the central theme in, his political theory. In sweeping terms in *Political Science and Comparative Constitutional Law*, Burgess defined as the essence of the state "sovereignty": "original, absolute, unlimited, universal power over the individual subject and over all associations of subjects." At first glance, this position appears to be a defense of absolutism. In fact, however, what Burgess meant when he used the term *state* might more accurately be described as *society*, or, as he put the matter, "a particular portion of mankind viewed as an organized unit." "I made," he explained in his autobiography, "the basis of the State the nation, and I defined the nation as a body of people, occupying a more or less definite geographical unity, who had developed through unity of language, custom, interest, and culture a substan-

tial consensus of opinion regarding the fundamental principles of right and wrong."

In contrast with the English social contract theorists, Burgess regarded the state—in the sense that he used the term—as divinely ordained because it was rooted in man's need for social controls. He directed his sharpest fire against the Lockean tradition of natural rights as existing independently of and anterior to society. "There never was, and there can never be," he laid down, "any liberty upon this earth and among human beings outside of state organization. . . . Mankind does not begin with liberty. Mankind acquires liberty through civilization." But he simultaneously affirmed that the "individual, both for his own highest development and the highest welfare of the society and state in which he lives, should act freely within a certain sphere; the impulse to such action is a universal quality of human nature." Burgess's point was simply that society defines the scope of the liberties enjoyed by the individual. Giving Hegelianism his own twist, he thus made a sharp distinction between the state and government. Government was the agent established by the state for carrying out limited purposes. The powers that the state—that is, society—granted government and the corollary, the protections afforded "the realm of Individual Immunity against governmental power," were spelled out in its constitutional, or what Burgess more broadly called public, law.

Looking at the evolution of the state historically, Burgess held that as men developed in civilization there was an accompanying expansion of the area of individual liberty. And he saw as the touchstone of that liberty the security that was guaranteed property. Men wanted property, he reasoned; ergo, property was a human right of the highest order. While acknowledging that cooperation—or what he loosely called socialism—was an indispensable adjunct of individualism, he distinguished between two types of socialism: voluntary and compulsory. Voluntary association played a vital role in advancing civilization, education, art, and culture. But he warned against the compulsory socialism involved in expanding governmental regulation of business. He was deeply suspicious of most politicians as motivated by partisan and personal advantage; he was even more fearful of the pressures coming from the unpropertied and ignorant majority "to crush the higher intelligence and the higher capacity by robbing them through legislation of their natural rewards." Hence, he apotheosized judicial review by the Supreme Court as the bulwark of American liberty: "law must rest upon justice and reason," he expostulated, and "the judiciary is a better interpreter of those fundamental principles than the legislature."

The intellectual stature that Burgess enjoyed among his contemporaries was due to the affinity between this outlook and the values held by the dominant elements of late-nineteenth-century America. But the long-range significance of his work in the development of American scholarship lay in his methodology. In the first place, he was a champion of the comparative approach—which he extolled as "the method, which has been found so productive in the domain of Natural Science"—to the study of political science and law. Second, he postulated that a nation's political and legal institutions were a reflection of its distinctive culture in the broad anthropological sense. The corollary was that changes in the form of government were products of—or more accurately, adaptations to—changes in social conditions. As he concluded in *Political Science and Comparative Constitutional Law* in his famous depiction of the adoption of the American Constitution as a revolutionary coup d'etat: "We must . . . give up the attempt altogether to find a legal basis for the adoption of the new constitution and have recourse to political science, to the natural and historical conditions of the society. . . ." Third, he saw political science and history as inextricably linked since "the state is *a* product, nay, *the* product, of history."

In his approach to history, Burgess started with the methodological premises of late-nineteenth-century scientific history. As he explained in "The Methods of Historical Study and Research in Columbia College" (1885), "we seek to teach the student, first, how to get hold of a historic fact, how to distinguish fact from fiction, how to divest it as far as possible of coloring or exaggeration. We send him, therefore, to the most original sources attainable. . . ." The next step was "to set the facts . . . thus attained in their chronological order." And the goal was to show change: "historical wisdom does not consist simply in knowing what has happened under given conditions, but also, and, I may say, chiefly, in correctly apprehending the variations, however slight, in the everchanging conditions and the accretions in the succeeding events produced thereby." Burgess went beyond the rigid factualism of contemporary American historical scholarship by warning against the trap of confusing "that which is mere antecedent and consequent as being cause and effect." The historian must apply a conceptual framework to order his data—or as Burgess strikingly put the matter, "must *construct*

history out of the chaos of original historic atoms."

Whereas the major thrust of orthodox scientific history was to free history from teleological assumptions, Burgess took as his touchstone Hegel's dictum: "Reason governs the world, and has consequently governed its history." As Burgess explained, "the substance of history is spirit. . . . History, in the making, is, therefore, the progressive realization of the ideals of the human spirit in all of the objective forms of their manifestation, in language, tradition, and literature, in customs, manners, laws, and institutions, and in opinion and belief. And history, in the writing, is the true and faithful record of these progressive revelations of the human reason. . . ." History was thus not simply accident; there was rather a purposeful pattern—or what he called "a plan of world civilization"—in the historical process. But Burgess was too much a moralist to accept an all-embracing determinism that denied men any choices. Man, he affirmed, "can and does, in large degree, at least, determine the nature of the means employed in the attainment of the predestined results." Thus, the historian's task was to reveal the direction in which history was moving, thereby enabling his readers to harmonize their activities with "the unseen but almighty power which conducts the development of man toward his ultimate destiny."

Burgess's most systematic effort to apply this approach to concrete historical events came in his contributions to Scribners' American History series: *The Middle Period, 1817-1858* (1897); the two-volume *Civil War and the Constitution, 1859-1865* (1901), and *Reconstruction and the Constitution, 1866-1876* (1902). He frankly acknowledged that his purpose was to illustrate the working of the Hegelian dialectic by showing how "in all the convulsions of political history, described as advance and reaction, the scientific student of history is able to discover that the zigzags of progress are ever bearing in the general direction which the combined impulses toward nationalism and humanism compel." And though running through the volumes were astute insights into the role of economic factors in the sectional conflict, he pictured as the central theme of American history from the War of 1812 to the Civil War the interwoven struggles of "particularism" (or "State sovereignty") versus "national sovereignty" and slavery versus "universal freedom." Nor did he disguise where his own sympathies lay: "secession as an abomination, and its chief cause, slavery, as a great evil." The time had come, he admonished, "when the men of the South should acknowledge that they were in error in their attempt to destroy the Union."

Yet Burgess departed in significant respects from the standard pro-Unionist treatments of the conflict. He consciously viewed his work as a contribution to sectional reconciliation. "The continued misunderstanding between the North and the South," he lamented, "is an ever present menace to the welfare of both sections and of the entire nation." Accordingly, he took pains to avoid personal attacks upon Southerners as individuals; even Jefferson Davis was portrayed as "noble, kind, generous in his feelings, if not in his intellect, brave, self-sacrificing, and grandly devoted to duty as he understood it." He similarly acknowledged the sincerity of Southerners in their outdated interpretation of the Constitution. By contrast, the villains of the story appear to be the Northern abolitionists. Most important, Burgess depicted the conflict as a tragic but necessary step in the progress of civilization. In "the plan of universal history," he explained, secession meant the "hastening of emancipation and nationalization. The United States were lagging in the march of modern civilization. Slavery and 'State sovereignty' were the fetters which held them back, and these fetters had to be screwed down tight in order to provoke the Nation to strike them off at one fell blow, and free itself, and assert its supremacy, forevermore."

Burgess's most influential contribution toward promoting "the re-establishment of a real national brotherhood between the North and the South" was his call for Northerners to acknowledge that Reconstruction had been "an error as well as a failure." He accepted the position of the Radical Republicans on the constitutional issue: the Southern states had committed suicide, thereby leaving to "the legislative department of the central Government exclusively . . . re-establishment of civil government." The Republicans' mistake lay in the failure to recognize "that there are vast differences in political capacity between the races, and that it is the white man's mission, his duty and his right, to hold the reins of political power in his own hands for the civilization of the world and the welfare of mankind." The result was that for a decade "the dark night of domination by the negro and adventurer had rested upon the unhappy section, until it had been reduced to the very abomination of desolation." And the counterpart of his attack upon Radical Reconstruction was his praise for Rutherford B. Hayes—as he explained more fully in his *The Administration of President Hayes* (1916)—for

"restoring all the States of the South to their full membership in the Union."

Burgess regarded the unification of Germany as part of the same divine plan that dictated the triumph of the Union in the Civil War. The national state was, he explained in his *Political Science and Comparative Constitutional Law,* "the most modern and the most complete solution of the whole problem of political organization which the world has as yet produced." Not all peoples had or could attain that level; not even all European peoples had the requisite qualities. Burgess differentiated three main races in Europe: the Slavonic, which had no political genius and always required autocracy to avert anarchy; the Romanic (the French, Spanish, and Italians), the leaders of the past who had lost their former pre-eminence; and the race that produced the great State builders of history, the Teutonic. The fact that the national state was "the creation of Teutonic political genius stamps the Teutonic nations as the political nations *par excellence,* and authorizes them, in the economy of the world, to assume the leadership in the establishment and administration of states." The Teutonic nations, therefore, had a duty to carry the blessings of their superior civilization to lesser breeds. "The political subjection or attachment of unpolitical nations to those possessing political endowment," he preached, "appears, if we may judge from history, to be as truly a part of the course of the world's civilization as is the national organization of states. I do not think that Asia and Africa can ever receive political organization in any other way."

Burgess was a vocal advocate of immigration restriction to save the United States from pollution by non-Teutonic elements. He similarly viewed with suspicion the political influence of the polyglot masses of America's cities. In a state whose population was composed of a variety of nationalities, he admonished, "the Teutonic element . . . should never surrender the balance of political power, either in general or local organization, to the other elements. Under certain circumstances it should not even permit participation of the other elements in political power." And though he would come to have second thoughts about the adverse effects of colonial rule upon American political institutions, he hailed at the time the overseas expansion resulting from the Spanish-American War as the fulfillment of this country's manifest destiny to bring order and civilization to backward peoples. But there was a pacifist, even utopian side, to Burgess. He viewed the national state as simultaneously the high point of historical development up to the present epoch and a stepping stone to the final stage in "the perfection of humanity": the "world-state" based upon universally shared principles.

Burgess saw United States-German friendship as the keystone of this hoped-for future of peace and harmony. In 1905 he succeeded in implementing his long-time dream of fostering closer German-American cultural relations through the exchange of professors between Columbia and the University of Berlin. Going over the following year as the first Theodore Roosevelt Visiting Professor, he made such a favorable impression in German official circles that Kaiser Wilhelm II conferred upon him the Order of the Prussian Crown. Although he planned to retire from active university service in 1909 upon reaching age sixty-five, President Butler prevailed upon him to stay on in the newly created position of dean of all three graduate faculties. Although ill health forced his retirement in the spring of 1912, he recovered and remained active for almost two more decades. During the winters, he practiced law in Brookline, Massachusetts; the summers he spent in Newport, Rhode Island. On the personal side, he had suffered a heavy blow when his wife died in 1884 after years of painful ill health. On 2 September 1885, he married Ruth Payne Jewett of Montpelier, Vermont. The couple had a son, Elisha Payne Jewett.

The outbreak of World War I dealt a shattering blow to Burgess's hopes for a new era of world peace. Unlike most American academics, he took the German side. He extolled the Empire as a peace-loving, democratic state in the vanguard of civilization; absolved Berlin of any responsibility for the conflict; and pictured Germany as the victim of Russian pan-Slavic ambitions, French dreams of revenge, and British commercial and industrial jealousy. He even warned that an Allied victory would directly menace this country's interests. He attacked the League of Nations as a would-be world government—as distinct from the future "world-state"—threatening America's independence and national existence. His pessimism regarding the future was heightened by what he saw as the growing trend toward state socialism within the United States. As a result, a mood of disillusionment, even despondency, suffused his post-1914 writings. At the age of eighty-six, Burgess made his last public appearance as guest of honor at the fiftieth anniversary celebration in 1930 of the founding of the School of Political Science. He died of a heart attack on 13 January 1931.

Burgess's place as a major figure in American scholarship does not rest upon his published work.

His historical studies are of interest only to students of historiography. Even as a political theorist he is largely forgotten. And his abler students went on to follow in their own intellectual development, in paths different from his. His major role was in the establishment in the United States of graduate education in the social sciences. His contributions lay not simply in the institutional structure he built, but in the animating spirit that he imparted. Despite his own personal conservatism, Burgess was committed to the ideal of the university as a center for free and untrammeled inquiry. The university student "must learn among his first lessons," he laid down, "that truth, as man knows it, is no ready-made article of certain and objective character, that it is a human interpretation, and subject therefore to the fallibility of human insight and reasoning." The function of the university, he reaffirmed in his final report as dean of the graduate faculties, "is the *advancement* of knowledge, the discovery of new truth and the readjustment of what has been regarded as truth already discovered." "It is to this spirit of free inquiry which he did so much to foster," his Faculty of Political Science colleagues eulogized upon his retirement, "that the School he founded chiefly owes whatever influence it has attained. . . ."

References:

Bernard E. Brown, *American Conservatives: The Political Thought of Francis Lieber and John W. Burgess* (New York: Columbia University Press, 1951);

Ralph G. Hoxie, "John W. Burgess, American Scholar. Book I: The Founding of the Faculty of Political Science," Ph. D. dissertation, Columbia University, 1950;

Hoxie and others, *A History of the Faculty of Political Science, Columbia University* (New York: Columbia University Press, 1955);

Bert J. Loewenberg, "John William Burgess, the Scientific Method, and the Hegelian Philosophy of History," *Mississippi Valley Historical Review*, 42 (December 1955): 490-509;

William R. Shepherd, "John William Burgess," in *American Masters of Social Science: An Approach to the Study of the Social Sciences Through a Neglected Field of Biography*, edited by Howard W. Odum (New York: Holt, 1927), pp. 23-57.

Papers:
The principal depositories of Burgess's papers are the Columbia University Libraries and the Jones Library in Amherst, Massachusetts.

Edward P. Cheyney
(17 January 1861-1 February 1947)

Daniel R. Gilbert
Moravian College

SELECTED BOOKS: *Early American Land Tenures* (Philadelphia: University of Pennsylvania, 1885);

The Anti-Rent Agitation in the State of New York, 1839-1846 (Philadelphia: University of Pennsylvania, 1887);

An Introduction to the Industrial and Social History of England (New York & London: Macmillan, 1901; revised, 1920);

European Background of American History, 1300-1600 (New York & London: Harper, 1904);

A Short History of England (Boston: Ginn, 1904; revised, 1927; revised again and enlarged, 1945);

A History of England, from the Defeat of the Armada to the Death of Elizabeth, with an Account of English Institutions During the Later Sixteenth and Early Seventeenth Centuries, 2 volumes (New York & London: Longmans, Green, 1914, 1926);

Law in History and Other Essays (New York: Knopf, 1927);

Modern English Reform, from Individualism to Socialism: A Course of Lowell Lectures (Philadelphia: University of Pennsylvania Press/London: Oxford University Press, 1931);

The Dawn of a New Era, 1250-1453 (New York & London: Harper, 1936);

History of the University of Pennsylvania, 1740-1940 (Philadelphia: University of Pennsylvania Press, 1940).

OTHER: "A Third Revolution," in *Annals of the American Academy of Political and Social Science*, 2 (1892), pp. 772-781;

"Recent Tendencies in the Reform of Land Tenure," in *Annals of the American Academy of Political and Social Science*, 2 (1892), pp. 309-323;

"The Medieval Manor," in *Annals of the American Academy of Political and Social Science*, 4 (1893), pp. 275-291;

English Constitutional Documents, edited by Cheyney (Philadelphia: University of Pennsylvania Department of History, 1894);

The Early Reformation Period in England, edited by

Edward P. Cheyney (University of Pennsylvania Archives)

Cheyney (Philadelphia: University of Pennsylvania Department of History, 1894);

Social Changes in England in the Sixteenth Century as Reflected in Contemporary Literature, edited by Cheyney (Boston: Ginn, 1895);

England in the Time of Wycliffe, edited by Cheyney (Philadelphia: University of Pennsylvania Department of History, 1895);

English Towns and Gilds, edited by Cheyney (Philadelphia: University of Pennsylvania Department of History, 1895);

English Manorial Documents, edited by Cheyney

(Philadelphia: University of Pennsylvania Department of History, 1896);

Documents Illustrative of Feudalism, edited by Cheyney (Philadelphia: University of Pennsylvania Department of History, 1898);

Readings in English History; Drawn from the Original Sources, Intended to Illustrate A Short History of England by Edward P. Cheyney, edited by Cheyney (Boston: Ginn, 1908; revised, 1922);

"The Trend Towards Industrial Democracy," in *Annals of the American Academy of Political and Social Science*, 90 (1920), pp. 1-9;

"How History Can Be Made a Science," in *Proceedings of the American Philosophical Society*, 66 (1927), pp. 581-591;

"Cardinal Wolsey," in *The Great Tudors*, edited by Katharine Garvin (London: Nicolson & Watson, 1935), pp. 69-84;

Freedom of Inquiry and Expression, edited with contributions by Cheyney, *Annals of the American Academy of Political and Social Sciences*, 200 (1938).

PERIODICAL PUBLICATIONS: "Recantations of the Early Lollards," *American Historical Review*, 4 (April 1899): 423-438;

"The Disappearance of English Serfdom," *English Historical Review*, 15 (January 1900): 20-37;

"Recent Writings on English History," *International Quarterly*, 1 (1900): 399-419;

"International Law Under Queen Elizabeth," *English Historical Review*, 20 (October 1905): 659-672;

"The Manor of East Greenwich in the County of Kent," *American Historical Review*, 11 (October 1905): 29-35;

"The England of our Forefathers," *American Historical Review*, 11 (July 1906): 769-778;

"Some English Conditions Surrounding the Settlement of Virginia," *American Historical Review*, 12 (April 1907): 507-528;

"The Court of Star Chamber," *American Historical Review*, 18 (July 1913): 727-750;

"England and Denmark in the Later Days of Queen Elizabeth," *Journal of Modern History*, 1 (March 1929): 9-39;

"A Century of War and Peace," *Barnwell Bulletin*, 7, no. 34 (1930).

Edward Potts Cheyney was one of a small group of American academicians who developed professional standards in historical scholarship and teaching in the late nineteenth and early twentieth centuries. While his main influence was perhaps as a teacher at his beloved University of Pennsylvania, he also found time to be an active leader in the development of the American Historical Association. He was elected the president of that organization in 1923 and served as the editor of the *American Historical Review* from 1912 to 1920. He was also a prolific author of books, articles, and other works on English history and on the history of early modern Europe.

Cheyney was born in Wallingford, Pennsylvania. His father, Waldron J. Cheyney, was of English ancestry, an Episcopalian, and a businessman with mining and chemical interests. His mother, Fannie Potts Cheyney, was a member of the Society of Friends who traced her ancestry back to the settlers of late-seventeenth-century Philadelphia. Cheyney himself was not active in any church but was regarded by his associates as a Christian with marked humanitarian concerns. Educated in country schools and at Penn Charter Academy in Philadelphia, he entered the University of Pennsylvania in 1879 after a brief sojourn as a minor functionary at the 1876 Philadelphia Centennial Exposition. He said later that he was poorly prepared for college, but he went on to achieve a number of honors including election to Phi Beta Kappa. He also served as class president and as editor of the *Pennsylvania Magazine*. He graduated in 1884 as a member of the first class of the university's new Wharton School of Finance. After a brief trip to Europe, he returned to the university, where he came under the influence of John Bach McMaster and received his M.A. in 1886. In June of that year he married Gertrude Levis Squires, with whom he eventually had three children. There is no evidence that Cheyney pursued a Ph.D. degree. After giving classes in math and classics at the university, he began his teaching and publishing career in history in the late 1880s. Before he retired he was a full professor and held the distinguished Lea Professorship in Medieval History. He retired from active teaching in 1934 but continued to write and be active in professional circles into the 1940s. A vigorous outdoorsman, Cheyney was an enthusiastic gardener and remained active until he was hospitalized in December 1946, after breaking his hip. He died of a heart attack on 1 February 1947 and was buried in the family cemetery in Cheyney, Pennsylvania.

Cheyney once defined the "simple but arduous task of the historian" as "to collect facts, view them objectively, and arrange them as the facts themselves demanded. . . ." This commitment to the prevailing "scientific history" and his rejection of approaching the past "with predetermined principles of classification and organization" permeated his early work in which he concentrated on translating and editing collections of medieval and early modern European historical documents. He, who also thought history should be useful in shaping public policy, frequently spoke out on major issues. He accepted, as did most of his contemporaries, the implications of evolution which he coupled with his faith in order and progress in human affairs and the ultimate triumph of democracy. While he was primarily a narrative and descriptive historian, he shared with the other "New Historians" a belief in the continuity of history, in the need to see the broad range of man's accomplishments in the past and to bring the insights and techniques of the developing social sciences into historical study. Throughout his career Cheyney also worked to improve instruction in the relatively new discipline of history.

Cheyney's first publications dealt with the broad issue of the distribution of land in America. After writing a short study of *Early American Land Tenures* (1885), he published *The Anti-Rent Agitation in the State of New York, 1839-1846* (1887), which was essentially a brief narrative account of the development of large land holdings in early New York, the outbreak of the anti-rent riots, and the legislative and court settlements of the issues. Although Cheyney carefully delineated the sequence of events, his analysis of the causes of the trouble was less satisfactory, and the documentation and bibliography were modest in the extreme.

By the early 1890s, Cheyney was an assistant professor at the University of Pennsylvania and active in the development of history curricula. With James Harvey Robinson and Dana C. Munro, he began editing a series of *Translations and Reprints from the Original Sources of European History,* to which he contributed six titles. These included *English Constitutional Documents* (1894), *The Early Reformation Period* (1894), *England in the Time of Wycliffe* (1895), *English Towns and Gilds* (1895), *English Manorial Documents* (1896), and *Documents Illustrative of Feudalism* (1898). These, and a similar collection, *Social Changes in England in the Sixteenth Century as Reflected in Contemporary Literature* (1895), point to his later work, *Readings in English History; Drawn from the Original Sources* (1908). These works reflect his growing preoccupation with English history and his desire to make available to students the basic primary materials upon which genuine historical study could be based. In the earlier series he provided little editorial comment beyond establishing,

in his familiar narrative style, the context of the document. Only the simplest of bibliographical entries were included to indicate sources. In his later *Readings in English History* he merged the documents into a textbook-style narration, though he continued to ignore the precise derivation of the chosen documents and to omit comment on the degree of his own editing and technical questions related to translation. These documentary collections were, in his words, to give students "further explanation and illustration of the principal points" discussed in text or classroom lectures. Thus he made clear that it was not his primary aim to publish this material for fellow scholars or for his graduate students.

While continuing to produce a variety of articles on early English history, Cheyney completed two books, *An Introduction to the Industrial and Social History of England* (1901) and *A Short History of England* (1904). Both were designed as textbooks for college and high school classes, and he prepared *Readings in English History* (1908) to accompany the latter book. Cheyney's texts suggest the author's genuine desire to improve the quality of teaching of history. In their integration of social and economic material into the narrative, they reflect his commitment to the "New History" of the times. Although the books were devoid of scholarly notes, they were clearly the product of Cheyney's broad reading and research and did include suggestions "for further reading."

During this most active period of his career Cheyney also wrote *European Background of American History, 1300-1600* (1904), the first volume in the American Nation series published by Harper. Beginning this work with the statement "The history of America is a branch of that of Europe," he went on to underscore the European origins of the population (that which "has counted in history") and the institutions of colonial America. Although he conceded that the "material conditions of America" did work to modify inherited patterns, he nonetheless saw a continuation of European influence throughout the formative period. The narrative, which began with developments in the thirteenth-century Mediterranean world and moved in traditional fashion through the emergence of the Atlantic powers to colonization, gave special attention to the political inheritance from Europe as well as to the colonizing roles of the chartered companies and the Reformation. The last third of the book was an intensive review of English local institutions to 1650. While Cheyney provided limited documentation in the chapters (and that basically to standard published sources), he added a critical evaluation of authorities on the European background of American history that still serves as a compendium of what was known of the subject at that time.

Much of Cheyney's early writing was aimed at a college audience, and it brought him considerable recognition. But his reputation as an American writing British history rested on his major work, *A History of England, from the Defeat of the Armada to the Death of Elizabeth, with an Account of English Institutions During the Later Sixteenth and Early Seventeenth Centuries.* The first volume was published in 1914; completion of the second, which did not appear until 1926, was delayed by World War I. With his work Cheyney apparently hoped to fill in a gap left by the two great nineteenth-century Victorian interpreters of Tudor England, Samuel Rawson Gardiner and James Anthony Froude, by giving a narrative account of the major events of the later years of Elizabeth's reign. He also provided a description of the political, religious, intellectual, and social institutions of the era, which, he noted in his preface, were of particular interest because many "were about to become the basis of a new form of society beyond the sea."

The first volume of the work was divided into four parts focusing in turn on royal administration, military affairs, exploration and commerce, and "violence on the sea." The second volume, in ten parts, was, except for five chapters on local government, a chronicle of the years 1596-1603. Cheyney's organization brought down the wrath of an English reviewer who said that the author had "reduced the Tudor period to chaos." American scholars were more charitable, noting that although he had found nothing new, the work was based on thorough scholarship and was "attractive to the general reader" even though Cheyney was not possessed of a dramatic style. In his introduction to the first volume Cheyney promised a general bibliography at the conclusion of the work. But in the end he referred readers to a general bibliography of Tudor history, not published until 1932 when it appeared under the title *Bibliography of British History: Tudor Period, 1485-1603.* One reviewer noted that the study would have been better served if Cheyney had done his own evaluation of the sources. This lack of an adequate bibliography plus his restraint in footnoting his conclusions made the work, in the eyes of some critics, more a series of interpretative essays than the definitive work Cheyney had hoped it would be. In its own time the two-volume study was regarded as a significant contri-

bution, but in recent years it has received less attention.

Cheyney is also remembered for his presidential address, "Law in History," given before the American Historical Association convention on 27 December 1923. This piece and other related writings were subsequently published in *Law in History and Other Essays* (1927), a collection which suggests the direction of Cheyney's mature thought. His belief in evolution, his progressive liberal's commitment to order and progress in human affairs, and his pioneering work with the developing social sciences came together here with his conviction, heightened by World War I, that the historian "must make his knowledge, such as it is, and his opportunities, whatever they may be, directly serviceable. He wishes to contribute, if he can, to the protection of civilization from the dangers that beset it, and help in the advancement of men to the possibilities that lie before them."

Law in History and Other Essays was an exploration of the possibilities of using history as a guide to man's progress. In the essays Cheyney described his view of the nature of history and the limited role man can play in shaping its course. In his presidential address he explained that there was "an independent trend of events, some inexorable necessity controlling the progress of human affairs." He postulated "six laws of history": the law of continuity, the law of democracy, the law of impermanence or mutability, the law of interdependence, the law of moral progress, and the law of necessity for free consent. These, he explained, had to be accepted and reckoned with "much as are the laws of gravitation, or of chemical affinity, or of organic evolution, or of human psychology." The understanding and application of these laws would allow historians to contribute toward improving the contemporary world, he suggested.

This effort to understand the vast changes taking place in the Victorian world of his youth was also evident in the lectures he gave in 1928 at the University of Pennsylvania's Lowell Institute and published as *Modern English Reform, from Individualism to Socialism* in 1931. Cheyney defined reform as the betterment of the condition of the people and he extolled the English genius for accomplishing changes by statute and without succumbing to the twentieth century's vice of revolution. The lectures traced the pattern from an England of contrasting wealth and poverty in 1800 through the efforts of the reformers of the nineteenth century, to the rise of the working classes by the twentieth century and the emergence of the modern concept of reform by means of "a gradual reorganization of society." He concluded that the orderly process of reform by traditional political means would continue in England, in contrast to what was then going on in Russia.

Late in his career Cheyney published *The Dawn of a New Era, 1250-1453* (1936), which was a volume in the Rise of Modern Europe series edited by William L. Langer. This basically interpretative work, well known to a generation of students of early modern Europe, demonstrated Cheyney at his best. At home with his sources, he ranged widely over church, literary, and intellectual history while describing the institutional developments of this important transitional era. He concluded the work with a "Recapitulation" in which he stressed his familiar themes of the unity and continuity of history and the importance of the "idea of nationality." He also continued to work on Tudor England and contributed a brief essay on Cardinal Wolsey to *The Great Tudors,* a volume edited by Katharine Garvin which was originally published in 1935 but not generally available until after World War II.

Upon his retirement from the University of Pennsylvania in 1934 Cheyney continued to be active in professional circles. He turned his attention to the political and ideological debates engendered by developments at home and abroad. This was not a new direction for him. He had been active earlier in the search for alternatives to the United States' entry into World War I. He had been preoccupied in the postwar era with the fate of America's form of government and gave a lecture in 1919 on "Historical Tests of Democracy," later included in *Law in History.* Similarly, he had made a defense of democracy and free institutions part of his famed "Law in History" address in 1923, and later in the decade he had spoken out in support of the Kellogg-Briand Pact of 1928 as a proper method of seeking peace among nations. By the 1930s he had turned to the problem of freedom of inquiry. This issue had great urgency to him because of the rise of radical ideologies abroad and restraint on informed discussion at home. Thus he published a brief pamphlet in 1936 on *Intellectual Freedom in a Democracy* and soon after accepted the assignment of the Social Science Research Council to edit a

study entitled *Freedom of Inquiry and Expression* (1938). To this collection of essays by leading scholars Cheyney contributed a brief history of the challenges to free speech in America and added a chapter of "Observations and Generalizations" as a conclusion. In his words: "An atmosphere of limitation, of restriction, is an atmosphere of sterility, of inertia." "Freedom of expression," Cheyney added, was an "essential condition of progress."

Cheyney's last important publication was a *History of the University of Pennsylvania, 1740-1940* (1940). His belief in the continuity of the university and his keen insights into the problems of internal administration of higher education and scholarship make this work one of the better university histories.

Cheyney was a prolific writer and no summary of his career is complete without reference to his lesser work. He was an editor of the *American Historical Review* in the early crucial years of that journal's growth and he was also a frequent reviewer of scholarly work for this and other publications. His concern for the improvement of the teaching of history is evident in his well-known textbooks on English history and in the curriculum guides he prepared for both colleges and high schools. He wrote scholarly articles for such journals as *American Historical Review* and the *Annals of the American Academy of Political and Social Science* as well as more popular material for other publications. His literary production, however, must be seen in the context of the other important parts of his career. A thoughtful editor and tireless adviser to the American Historical Association and other professional organizations and a beloved teacher, Cheyney was a consummate professional who helped to bring historical scholarship in America to full maturity.

Reference:

William Lingelbach, ed., *Portrait of an Historian: Edward Potts Cheyney* (Philadelphia: University of Pennsylvania Press, 1935).

Papers:

Cheyney's papers are in the University of Pennsylvania Archives.

Hiram Martin Chittenden

(25 October 1858-9 October 1917)

Gordon B. Dodds
Portland State University

SELECTED BOOKS: *The Yellowstone National Park: Historical and Descriptive* (Cincinnati: Clarke, 1895; revised, 1903; revised again, Cincinnati: Stewart & Kidd, 1915);
The American Fur Trade of the Far West, 3 volumes (New York: F. P. Harper, 1902);
History of Early Steamboat Navigation on the Missouri River; Life and Adventures of Joseph La Barge, 2 volumes (New York: F. P. Harper, 1903);
Life, Letters, and Travels of Father Pierre-Jean De Smet, S.J., 1801-1873, by Chittenden and Alfred T. Richardson, 4 volumes (New York: F. P. Harper, 1905);
War or Peace: A Present Duty and a Future Hope (Chicago: McClurg, 1911; London: Low, 1911);
Verse (Seattle: Holly Press, 1916).

Hiram Martin Chittenden, historian of the American West, wrote the definitive history of the American fur trade over eighty years ago. He produced less significant books concerning steamboat navigation on the Missouri River; the life and letters of Pierre-Jean De Smet, the eminent Jesuit missionary; and Yellowstone Park. Chittenden's works were transitional between romantic and scientific historiography and partook of both schools of historical writing.

Hiram Martin Chittenden, the son of William F. and Mary Jane Wheeler Chittenden, was born on a farm in Cattaraugus County in western New York State. He attended rural schools and a private academy in Franklinville ten miles from the family farm. At the academy he pursued classical studies and fixed on the profession of law. For a few months after graduation he taught in a rural school. During these early years Chittenden acquired a zeal for learning, a taste for hard work, and an ambition to improve his material and social lot.

Opportunity to escape the rural world came in 1878 when he won a tuition scholarship at Cornell University and an appointment to the United States Military Academy. He decided to attend Cornell for a few months to obtain the courses in lan-

Hiram Martin Chittenden

guages, literature, and history that were unavailable or slighted at West Point. Chittenden enjoyed his experiences at Ithaca, writing in his diary that "I left the school with a number of warm friends and quite an attachment to the University." Although the disciplined regimen at West Point was less pleasant than life at Cornell, Chittenden did well in his studies, graduating third in his class in 1884 and receiving his commission in the elite Corps of Engineers. After graduation he married Nettie M. Parker of Arcade, New York, with whom he eventually had three children, Eleanor, Hiram Martin, Jr., and Theodore. During his early career Chittenden served at various posts: New York City (where he took a law degree in his spare time), the Department of the Platte in Omaha, with the Missouri River Commission, and at Yellowstone Park.

In Yellowstone Chittenden began the road construction in the park during the years of 1891 to 1893. He also determined to write a book about the park, a task that he accomplished in his spare time during his next two assignments: at the Louisville and Portland Canal and in preparing an examination of canal routes in the state of Ohio. *The Yellowstone National Park: Historical and Descriptive* was published in 1895. Chittenden revised it in 1903 and 1915 and after his death editions appeared in 1924, 1927, 1933, 1940, 1949, and 1961. The book remains an authority. *The Yellowstone National Park* contains a history of the park from the era of the Indians; a description of its natural features; a sketch of the park administration; and a guided tour along the roads in the park.

Preparation of this thorough, interesting, and well-written book was important in Chittenden's development as a historian in two ways. Writing the work put him in touch with two men who were to become his intellectual mentors and companions: Elliott Coues, ornithologist and editor of the journals of Lewis and Clark, and George Bird Grinnell, conservationist, publisher of sportsman's magazines, ethnologist, and authority on the Cheyenne Indians. The Yellowstone book also demonstrated Chittenden's respect for accuracy, for he wrote to scores of people who had had experience in the park as well as consulting printed sources.

After completing the Ohio canal report, Chittenden received an assignment to survey prospective reservoir sites in Colorado and Wyoming and to investigate the general functions of reservoirs. His monumental report, published in 1897, was a milestone on the road to federal construction of irrigation works, a responsibility first authorized in the Newlands Act of 1902. Senator Thomas J. Walsh of Montana said that Chittenden's report was "probably the strongest single influence which turned the thought of our [western] people toward the policy of national construction of reservoirs."

After the reservoir report was completed, Chittenden worked at mundane river and harbor assignments on the Missouri River. Frustration with this tedious labor led to a turning point in his life and in Western historiography. As he remarked later in an autobiographical fragment: "I didn't care enough about the Missouri River to waste any unnecessary energy thereon, for I felt as certain then as I do now that it would all be labor lost. I therefore, had no compunction in directing as much of my time as I could to work which I believed would be of a great deal more use to my countrymen." His selected task was a history of the fur

trade, a project he pursued even after being returned to the congenial assignment of building roads in Yellowstone Park.

Chittenden was almost entirely self-taught as a scholarly historian. He had taken a historical seminar at Cornell from a professor who had research training in Germany. His legal training was of help. He had read widely in the classics for a self-study program going back to his days at Cornell, a regimen that brought him to the works of Francis Bacon, Victor Hugo, David Hume, John Milton, and Montesquieu. These authors surely helped form his style. He had learned to read French and Spanish at West Point, invaluable skills for one who would go through thousands of pages of manuscript materials in those languages. Work on the Yellowstone book had brought him the acquaintanceship of professional historians and introduced him to the lives of the fur men who had worked in the region of the park.

The heart of Chittenden's sources for *The American Fur Trade of the Far West* (1902) was the Chouteau papers in St. Louis. The descendants of this great fur trading family opened their records to him. Chittenden also consulted St. Louis newspapers, investigated local legal records, and interviewed the veteran river pilot Joseph La Barge. He corresponded with scholars and visited the libraries of midwestern and western historical societies. When Chittenden looked for guides among printed works, he could find few books on the subject of the fur trade and none approaching the scope of his work. There was Washington Irving's *Astoria* and *Adventures of Captain Bonneville*, the series by Francis Parkman, Theodore Roosevelt, and Hubert Howe Bancroft, and the documents edited by Reuben Gold Thwaites and Elliott Coues.

Chittenden determined, when the time came for composition, to work on a grand scale. The first edition was in three volumes, two of text, one of appendices. The text was divided into five sections which together combined narrative and thematic approaches. Part one (the shortest) dealt with the organization and financing of the fur trade. The second part, almost one half of the work, traced the origins of the North American fur trade and developed the histories of the major companies of the Trans-Mississippi West. Part three concerned "Contemporary Events Connected with the Fur Trade" and part four contained "Notable Incidents and Characters in the History of the Fur Trade." The last part of the text described the natural environment of the Plains and Rockies. Eight appendices followed, dealing with a variety of topics.

Chittenden labored for four years, 1896 to 1900, on *The American Fur Trade of the Far West*. It was finally published in 1902. Chittenden's friendship with Coues's publisher, Francis P. Harper, had opened the doors of the Harper house to him. *The American Fur Trade of the Far West* was well received by contemporary scholars. Frank H. Hodder of the University of Kansas and Frances Fuller Victor favored the work for the most part. Hodder, however, did criticize Chittenden's lack of bibliographic specificity. Frederick Jackson Turner described Chittenden's work as "excellent." Over the years this initial laudatory estimate has held up. Kenneth W. Porter considered Chittenden "shrewd and careful." Robert Glass Cleland labeled him as "one who among the hosts of students of the Western fur trade, towers like Saul head and shoulders above his brethren." The most distinguished modern historian of the fur trade, Dale L. Morgan, declared in 1966: "Very few, I suspect, would place Hiram Martin Chittenden in the same class with

Chittenden with his wife, Nettie Parker Chittenden, and two of their children, Eleanor and Hiram Martin, Jr., St. Louis, 1899

[Frederick Jackson] Turner and [Walter Prescott] Webb. . . . Yet anyone disposed to inquire into the historiography of the past sixty years will find that Chittenden's *The American Fur Trade of the Far West* has influenced nearly everything written about the history of the West in the first half of the nineteenth century . . . . The idea may affront the professional historians, but it can be seriously maintained that neither Turner nor Webb has had an impact on the writing of western history comparable to Chittenden's. . . . The point I more particularly wish to make is that Chittenden settled the ideas of two generations of historians who, directly or indirectly, have had to come to terms with the fur trade. His was a liberating influence originally, for he provided a rationale by which a diffuse and refractory history was made intelligible. Over the course of time, however, Chittenden has evolved into something of a tyrannical force, for he is still conditioning the thinking of students who should be pushing the frontiers of knowledge a good deal farther out. Pioneering is never easy, but it is time those interested in the trade should be stepping out on their own." Little has happened since Morgan wrote these words to diminish their validity.

Although monumental, Chittenden's achievement was not without flaws. His book was not documented with the precision that was required by professionally trained scholars of his time. As a general rule, Chittenden used notes only for quotations or for elaboration of material contained in the text. It is thus difficult to find exact sources for each passage of the book. The organization of *The American Fur Trade of the Far West* is also imperfect. The environmental section might better have appeared at the beginning of the book rather than at the end. Furthermore, the "Contemporary Events" and "Notable Characters" sections could have been integrated with the narrative text rather than left to stand as isolated entities. In sum, the reader is placed in the position of having to synthesize information from the two volumes more often than is desirable.

The content of the book has also drawn fire from scholarly critics in the matters of perspective and omissions. Chittenden focused on the fur trade as it developed in Trans-Mississippi regions that became part of the United States. In so doing, however, he largely omitted the area of the American Southwest where a beaver trade did flourish. When he did mention the Southwest, he sometimes made factual errors. Why Chittenden neglected this region is unclear, especially since he had spent a good deal of time there and had devoted a large section of his book to the Santa Fe trade. Another problem is that Chittenden chose to close his book in 1843 rather than carry on to the post-Civil War era; certainly the Missouri River beaver trade continued until the late nineteenth century. Other deficiencies include slighting the importance of liquor traffic, neglecting the political role of the fur-trading companies, and playing down the international context of the fur trade. It would be too much, however, to expect a historian of Chittenden's day to deal with the role of women, the class structure, and the ethnic configurations of the trade. In terms of factual errors, Chittenden committed surprisingly few. Some came from a faulty reading of the sources, others from neglect to scan certain records, and still others from unreliability of sources. In matters of interpretation he made some questionable judgments that might be expected in any innovative work. Chittenden was a modest man and recognized that future scholars would improve upon his work. Yet he also knew, as he recorded in an autobiographical fragment written two years before his death, that *The American Fur Trade of the Far West* was of enduring value: "It has often been referred to as a great work and has taken its place as a standard. On the whole, it is essentially accurate and it deals with broad outlines in such a way that the average reader follows it with ease and interest. I have never seen any cause to regret the course I have pursued. This work I put down as emphatically a thing well done and this view is confirmed as time goes on."

During the three years following the publication of *The American Fur Trade of the Far West*, Chittenden wrote two other histories while working on the Yellowstone roads and the Missouri River. The *History of Early Steamboat Navigation on the Missouri River* was published in 1903. Based on oral interviews with Joseph La Barge, a retired river pilot, captain, and ship owner, the book built upon this framework to produce a history of steamboat navigation. As Chittenden declared: "It is not the bare narration of events that gives history its true value, but those intimate pictures of human life in other times that show what people really did and the motives by which they were actuated. To this end, biography, and even fiction, possess distinct advantages over the ordinary method of historical writing."

The subtitle of the book, *Life and Adventures of Joseph La Barge,* is more accurate than the title, because La Barge's career dominates the analyses of topics such as the types of river craft employed in the fur trade that are interwoven with it. Anec-

dotes abound, for the style of the book is far more informal than that of *The American Fur Trade of the Far West.* Yet Chittenden did not fail to interpret. The *History of Early Steamboat Navigation on the Missouri River* discussed the effect of the events of the 1840s on the river. The Mormon settlements, troop movements, gold seekers, Indian-white relations, and government explorations all received attention. La Barge appears as a romantic, heroic figure, bluff and honest in personal and business relations. *The History of Steamboat Navigation* was never as popular with either scholars or public as *The American Fur Trade.* Chittenden blamed this reception upon an uninspiring title, but the book was not up to the quality of its predecessor. Its scholarly paraphernalia certainly was less elaborate. Yet the book remained the standard authority until 1962, when William E. Lass published his definitive *A History of Steamboating on the Upper Missouri River.*

Chittenden's final important historical work appeared in 1905. His *Life, Letters, and Travels of Father Pierre-Jean De Smet, S.J., 1801-1873* was prepared in collaboration with Alfred T. Richardson. Chittenden sought Richardson's aid because he believed the former newspaper editor and amateur student of the American West was a better linguist than he was. Chittenden found the De Smet work a "heavy task." He and Richardson translated and edited a selection of the correspondence and other literary memorabilia of the great missionary. Chittenden also provided a 144-page biography that was accurate in detail and served to introduce the material that followed. But this short biography was not a work of major interpretation, failing to locate De Smet's career in the context of Roman Catholic missionary efforts or, except superficially, in that of the policies of the United States Government towards the Indians. The last omission was the principal deficiency in an otherwise useful—if largely undocumented—account. Chittenden admired De Smet for his heroic qualities. Willingness to die for a cause and a life of marked utility were what Chittenden praised most about the missionary. He concluded that De Smet was more successful as a political leader than a religious figure, contributing most as a mediator between the Indians and the employees of the government.

The correspondence section of the work is less valuable than the biography. It contains only about thirty percent of De Smet's total extant correspondence and provides inadequate translations. It is further marred by the tendency of the editors to transpose or delete paragraphs in the letters without indicating these alterations to the reader.

Nevertheless, reviewers found *Life, Letters, and Travels of Father Pierre-Jean De Smet, 1801-1873* praiseworthy, a verdict still valid for amateur historians or general readers who want only an overview of De Smet's work or the flavor of his personality.

After the publication of De Smet's life and letters, Chittenden abandoned his historical pursuits. He was transferred to Seattle in 1906 where he served as district engineer until his retirement from the Corps of Engineers in 1910. He served as first president of the new Seattle Port Commission from 1911 to 1915. Until his death in 1917 Chittenden remained intellectually vigorous and active. Throughout his Seattle years he wrote numerous articles, which appeared in engineering journals and national magazines, on conservation (he became famous for criticizing the theory that tree planting would prevent erosion and regulate stream flow) and international affairs. In 1911 he published a book entitled *War or Peace: A Present Duty and a Future Hope* that assailed war and preparations for war ("The pathway of war is the trail of the serpent . . ."). In 1916 he added a slim volume of poems about nature and personal feelings to the list of his published works.

In his historical work Chittenden exemplified the bridge between the older romantic histories of John Lothrop Motley, Francis Parkman, William H. Prescott, and Theodore Roosevelt and the newer insights of the "scientific" historians such as Herbert Baxter Adams and Frederick Jackson Turner. Like the newer school, Chittenden relied on source materials, evaluated the validity of his sources, and provided at least some notations to them. Chittenden was also "scientific" in that he relied upon applied Darwinism to explain the successes of "Anglo-Saxon" peoples and the difficulties of the Native Americans.

Chittenden, however, was interested mainly in the romantic aspects of history. In any type of conflict he gave greater significance to heroic individualism than to evolutionary determinism. He praised the financial success of John Jacob Astor, the wilderness heroism of Jim Bridger, and the moral courage of Father De Smet. He also admired romantic institutions such as the Missouri River steamboat and romantic scenes such as the ruts of the Oregon Trail. In the end, Chittenden saw the frontier American West as a theater for the individuals to govern their own destinies in the struggle with the wilderness.

In any case, Chittenden certainly was not a profound student or practitioner of the philosophy of history. He never developed a school of followers as did Turner. He was more like Parkman, Hubert Howe Bancroft, or Webb in attempting a large subject on a monumental scale without ever bothering to state the purposes of history or its cosmic implications. What remains of Chittenden's historical efforts is not abstract speculation, but three solid histories of the West, one, *The American Fur Trade of the Far West*, a masterpiece. These books place him among the giants of frontier historiography.

References:

Gordon B. Dodds, *Hiram Martin Chittenden: His Public Career* (Lexington: University Press of Kentucky, 1973);

Bruce Le Roy, *H. M. Chittenden: A Western Epic* (Tacoma: Washington State Historical Society, 1961).

Papers:

Most of Chittenden's personal papers are at the Washington State Historical Society. His official correspondence is in Records of the Chief of Engineers (Record Group 77), the National Archives. There is a small collection of Chittenden papers at the University of Washington.

W. E. B. Du Bois

(23 February 1868-27 August 1963)

Murray Arndt

University of North Carolina at Greensboro

SELECTED BOOKS: *The Suppression of the African Slave-Trade to the United States of America, 1638-1870,* volume 1 of Harvard Historical Studies (New York & London: Longmans, Green, 1896);

The Conservation of Races (Washington, D.C.: American Negro Academy, 1897);

The Philadelphia Negro: A Social Study (Philadelphia: University of Pennsylvania, 1899);

The Souls of Black Folk: Essays and Sketches (Chicago: McClurg, 1903; London: Constable, 1905);

The Negro in the South, His Economic Progress in Relation to His Moral and Religious Development; Being the William Levi Bull Lectures for the Year 1907, by Du Bois and Booker T. Washington (Philadelphia: Jacobs, 1907);

John Brown (Philadelphia: Jacobs, 1909);

The Quest of the Silver Fleece (Chicago: McClurg, 1911);

The Negro (New York: Holt, 1915; London: Williams & Norgate, 1915);

Darkwater: Voices From Within the Veil (New York: Harcourt, Brace & Howe, 1920; London: Constable, 1920);

The Gift of Black Folk: The Negroes in the Making of America (Boston: Stratford, 1924);

Dark Princess: A Romance (New York: Harcourt, Brace, 1928);

Africa: Its Geography, People and Products (Girard, Kans.: Haldeman-Julius, 1930);

Africa: Its Place in Modern History (Girard, Kans.: Haldeman-Julius, 1930);

Black Reconstruction: An Essay Toward a History of the Part Which Black Folk Played in the Attempt to Reconstruct Democracy in America, 1860-1880 (New York: Harcourt, Brace, 1935);

Black Folk, Then and Now: An Essay in the History and Sociology of the Negro Race (New York: Holt, 1939);

Dusk of Dawn: An Essay Toward an Autobiography of a Race Concept (New York: Harcourt, Brace, 1940);

Color and Democracy: Colonies and Peace (New York: Harcourt, Brace, 1945);

The World and Africa: An Inquiry into the Part Which Africa Has Played in World History (New York: Viking, 1947);

In Battle for Peace: The Story of My 83rd Birthday (New York: Masses & Mainstream, 1952);

The Ordeal of Mansart (New York: Mainstream, 1957);

Mansart Builds a School (New York: Mainstream, 1959);

Worlds of Color (New York: Mainstream, 1961);

The Autobiography of W. E. B. Du Bois: A Soliloquy on Viewing My Life From the Last Decade of Its First

Century, edited by Herbert Aptheker (New York: International Publishers, 1968);

W. E. B. Du Bois Speaks: Speeches and Addresses, edited by Philip S. Foner (New York: Pathfinder Press, 1970);

W. E. B. Du Bois: The Crisis Writings, edited by Daniel Walden (Greenwich, Conn.: Fawcett, 1972);

The Emerging Thought of W. E. B. Du Bois: Essays and Editorials From "The Crisis," edited by Henry Lee Moon (New York: Simon & Schuster, 1972);

The Education of Black People: Ten Critiques, 1906-1960, edited by Aptheker (Amherst: University of Massachusetts Press, 1973).

OTHER: *Atlanta University Publications*, nos. 3-18, edited by Du Bois (Atlanta: Atlanta University Press, 1898-1914);

Haiti, in *Federal Theatre Plays*, edited by Pierre de Rohan (New York: Random House, 1938);

An Appeal to the World: A Statement on the Denial of Human Rights to Minorities in the Case of Citizens of Negro Descent in the United States of America and an Appeal to the United Nations for Redress, edited by Du Bois (New York: National Association for the Advancement of Colored People, 1947).

William Edward Burghardt Du Bois lived a life so full of conflictive action and reaction, so marked by radical gesture, so dramatically out of tune with the main thrusts of American life in the first half of the twentieth century that it is difficult to remember that by nature and training he was a scholar, a man driven to the encyclopedic recording of the social history of black folk. Born, in Thoreau's phrase, "in the very nick of time," Du Bois had thrust upon him the uncomfortable and often ill-fitting mantle of political activism, and the angry, untiring, original, and bitter ways that he bore "the black man's burden" in the political arena, in the courts, and in the marketplace overshadowed his private labors to redress history's judgment on the role of black folk in the making of America. What Du Bois did, at ninety-five, in one final radical gesture—renouncing American citizenship (becoming an "ornament of communism," as one biographer would have it)—has not only too often been an easy basis to demean or dismiss the achievements of his political and moral activism but it has also nearly obliterated the significance of his scholarly work as a sociologist, historian, and editor.

In characteristically grandiose but perceptive style Du Bois fixes his own birth "five years after

the Emancipation Proclamation, which began the freeing of the slaves," in the same year "that the Freedmen of the South were enfranchised and for the first time as a mass took part in the government," and five days after Thaddeus Stevens, "the clearest-headed leader of this attempt at industrial democracy made his last speech impeaching Andrew Johnson"; the date was 23 February 1868. Du Bois was the only child of Alfred and Mary Burghardt Du Bois (both of mixed blood) and grew up with his mother's family ("the black Burghardts") in Great Barrington, Massachusetts. Coming to manhood in a white, Puritan New England town full of high seriousness left indelible marks upon the character of the young son of one of the town's few black families. He remembered as early as adolescence a determination to "set his talents as a mediator between the two cultures."

Du Bois's real introduction to the "black problem" came with his matriculation in 1885 at Fisk University where for the first time he encountered strong segregation and ruthless discrimination. It was there that he developed the intense race consciousness that would determine the direction of his adult career. After his graduation from Fisk, Du Bois applied to Harvard University and was admitted as a junior classman in 1888. There he studied under George Santayana, Albert Bushnell Hart, and Barrett Wendell; most important, he became a favorite of William James, who, he said, "guided him out of the sterilities of scholastic philosophy to realist pragmatism." The pragmatic approach to truth would be the hallmark of Du Bois's thought throughout his career. He entered the university determined to follow a course in the sciences; in his senior year he shifted to a concentration in philosophy; but as a graduate student he majored in political economy and history.

Following completion of his M.A. degree at Harvard, in 1892 Du Bois went to study economics and sociology in Europe for two years, mostly at Berlin University. The reduced pressure of color prejudice, the enthusiastic interest, and the social camaraderie that he met in Europe encouraged him to adopt a broader vision of color and mankind. Under the tutelage of Max Weber and especially Gustav Schmoller, Du Bois turned away from history as a primary interest to a kind of political economics closely allied to sociology. In Germany, too, his interest in socialism and Marxism began.

Du Bois returned from Europe prepared with an education that few, if any, American Negroes before him had been afforded and with a sense of self and mission driving in its optimism and painful in its naiveté. He felt himself a person destined to redirect the history of his time and assumed that the accumulation of empirical knowledge would inevitably force the reform of social policy. He determined to set himself two tasks: to be a teacher who would dispel Negro ignorance and train other missionaries to carry the gospel back to their communities, and to do research that would convert white America to a just appraisal of the Negro.

In 1894 he began a frustrating and disillusioning two-year stint as professor of Latin and Greek at Wilberforce University, a small, strict, religious school in Ohio. In 1896 Du Bois not only completed his graduate work but also embarked upon his scholarly career with the publication of his dissertation, *The Suppression of the African Slave-Trade to the United States of America, 1638-1807*, in the prestigious Harvard Historical Studies. The book was a solid accomplishment, well received in periodical reviews, and led directly to his appointment as assistant instructor in sociology at the University of Pennsylvania where he made a year-long study of the conditions and circumstances of Negro life in Philadelphia. The book that resulted from this work, *The Philadelphia Negro: A Social Study* (1899), reflected the influence of his German exposure, concentrating on the collection and collation of sociological and economic facts about Negro life with the hope of dispelling ignorance, myth, and prejudice about and in that race.

In 1897 Du Bois, newly married to Nina Gomer and now a professor of economics and sociology at Atlanta University, settled down to a decade of truly secure and productive academic work. During his thirteen-year tenure Du Bois took charge of the annual Conference for the Study of Negro Problems and edited the proceedings which appeared under the series title Atlanta University Publications. The AUP was a typically ambitious and grand project: Du Bois conceived of it as a one hundred-year-long program that would produce annual studies of the Negro condition in America. He insisted that the collection and collation of the statistical, sociological truth about this condition would finally set the Negro free—from prejudice, from discrimination, and from his own inhibiting feelings of inferiority. If the grand vision was characteristic, so too was the work's limited success and its ultimate failure. The university produced twenty volumes of the publication between 1896 and 1917 (in itself a considerable achievement), and while the quality of the yearly reports is uneven, some of them are impressive monuments to Du

Bois's determined and pioneering energy. After he left Atlanta, however, the project disintegrated.

At Atlanta University Du Bois also produced (in 1903) what most critics agree is his best book, the minor American classic *The Souls of Black Folk: Essays and Sketches*. This volume signaled a dramatic turn in Du Bois's method and eventually his career. In and through the book Du Bois descends dramatically from the ivory tower of cool factual collection into the arena of passion, propaganda, and effective confrontation; the scientific statistician turns ardent activist. His first opponent was unfortunately, but importantly, Booker T. Washington.

Among the essays exploring the quality of black life at the beginning of the twentieth century, Du Bois included in *The Souls of Black Folk* a carefully stated and soft-pedaled criticism of Booker T. Washington's accommodationist tactics. To Washington's threefold position that the Negro bore the major responsibility for remedying his own problems, that this could only be done within the political system of the South and without disturbing it, and that in industrial education (like Tuskegee's, of course) lay the key to that improvement, Du Bois proposed some "supplementary truths." First of all, he pointed out that slavery and repression were the root causes of the Negro's plight and that their perpetrators bore much of the responsibility for alleviating the problems they had caused. He also suggested that complete political freedom for blacks was a sine qua non for economic improvement. But most strongly he argued the all-importance of developing leadership through the college education of those he called "the Talented Tenth" of the race, insisting that Washington's position that industrial education was the most or only important kind for the Negro could only lead to the perpetuation of the color caste system.

This dramatic and effective criticism of Washington, the undisputed leader of American Negroes, catapulted Du Bois into the public arena. It not only made him the sudden darling of black radicals (like William Monroe Trotter) and their white northern sympathizers, but it also precipitated the wrath of Washington and his powerful black and white supporters. Du Bois was vilified and intimidated in the press, his position at Atlanta University was threatened, and editors who had eagerly afforded him a forum in their magazines shied away from publishing his work. In his autobiography Du Bois said he chose to align himself against Washington not because their theories of racial uplift were contradictory, but because their methods were incompatible.

At this point in his life Du Bois clearly moved away from academic and scholarly work into power politics, agitation, and propaganda. It was by temperament or training a move he was ill-prepared to make, and the effectiveness of his work over the next several years suffered. The Niagara movement he had helped organize to fight segregation essentially failed; his sociological studies were apparently fruitless; the Negro community remained uninspired by his efforts; and the terrible Atlanta riots of 1906 demonstrated that racial peace was at best a distant dream. All this led him to believe that at the age of forty-two he was finished as an important contributor to Negro thought and action.

In 1910, however, a whole new career opened up for Du Bois when he was named to the board of directors of the fledgling National Association for the Advancement of Colored People and was appointed director of publications and research for the organization. The NAACP provided the basis for Du Bois's first alliance with white liberals, and it had the financial stability to support a national periodical, the *Crisis*, with enough liberal tolerance to allow Du Bois, its editor, freedom to express his views. He made the most of the opportunity and for the next twenty-five years produced a magazine that ranks among the most important organs of protest ever published in the United States.

Du Bois determined from the very beginning not only to make the *Crisis* the national Negro magazine he had always envisioned but also to make it *his* magazine in the bargain. Since the NAACP had originally underwritten the magazine as a house organ for its own publicity and not a vehicle for the opinions of its editor, confusion and friction attended its early years. In fact, debate between Oswald Garrison Villard, the chairman of the NAACP, and Du Bois over the magazine threatened to destroy the organization itself. Eventually Du Bois's uncompromising energy won out; Villard resigned his position, and his successor, Joel Spingarn, gave Du Bois control over the magazine so long as he reported organization business and refrained in his editorials from "petty irritations, insulting personalities, and vulgar recriminations."

The conflict between Du Bois and NAACP directors over the *Crisis* is an adequate yardstick for evaluating the relationship between him and the organization. Theirs was always a marriage of convenience. Each had something to gain from the other and something to offer in exchange, and within reason each was willing to ignore the embarrassments and frustrations the other caused. In the long run, the organization "gave in" more than Du Bois did, but that was, perhaps, because he contributed more to the "cause" than it could. What the NAACP offered Du Bois was a respectable and respected forum; what he offered was creative imagination, unbounded energy, perhaps the strongest voice an American protest organization ever had, and, equally important, an avenue into the Negro community.

The quality of the *Crisis* over the twenty-five years of Du Bois's editorship stands as sufficient justification for his self-assured stubbornness about it. During his tenure the magazine was an all-out, fire-eating, hammer-and-tongs indictment of everything that seemed simplistic, unjust, or repressive to Du Bois. It often exaggerated, it frequently lost its argument in invective or sentimentality, and it sometimes exhibited the grossest chauvinism, but unlike the pale product it evolved into after his departure, Du Bois's magazine was never dull. The intense excitement of the *Crisis* was reflected in its commercial success. Except for the first two years of its publication, the magazine throughout Du Bois's editorship was self-supporting, an extraordinary record for a protest organ of little mass appeal.

The effectiveness of the magazine catapulted Du Bois into national prominence. He became the most influential, respected, and feared Negro in the United States. Little escaped the scathing vitriol of his pen: he damned (seldom even with faint praise) such diverse institutions as lynching, the Southern caste system, labor unions, the convict lease system, white Christianity, Wall Street, militarism, colonialism, and sometimes the NAACP itself. On the other hand, he urged activism of every sort—voter registration, court tests, bloc voting, economic cooperation, pacifism, socialism, Pan-Africanism, vigilante protection, passive resistance, civil disobedience, and bloodless revolt. Moreover, he carried on the most extensive "Black is Beautiful" campaign the race had ever known, extolling the soft brown and creamy yellow Negro babies, the flashing dark eyes of quiet, brown women, the virile blackness of Jack Johnson, the power of Egyptian pharaohs and African chieftains. For twenty-five years the *Crisis* was a superbly unfettered and messianically dynamic organ of unified and effective racial propaganda.

Du Bois's work as editor of the *Crisis* falls into three clear periods, each characterized by a central energy and all evincing the pragmatic search for alternatives that is the real key to the unity of his life's work. The main thrust of the important first period of his editorship (1910-1918) was progressively political: in short, it was an extraordinary attempt to examine the ugliness and ignorance of racism and to confront the racists with every lawful expedient available. It is ridiculous to characterize the Du Bois of this period as a radical; he was operating as completely within the political system as Robert La Follette or Lincoln Steffens.

Several things stand out about Du Bois's efforts during this time. For one thing, his clear enemy was social racism. Lynching, discrimination, and disfranchisement—all were historic and real evils in the South and elsewhere, and his attacks on them were justified and heroic. For another thing, the methods with which he chose to fight these evils were traditionally democratic—publicity, legal tests, political maneuvering, and social pressure—and all his efforts were dedicated to the achievement of power within the American system. But it is true that finally all these efforts came to little: in Georgia and Alabama and Mississippi and Texas the lynching went on with impunity; the white primary and the poll tax continued to govern Southern politics; and the repeal of Jim Crow laws was decades away. Du Bois saw his people humiliated in second-class citizenship and held in thrall by less than second-class schooling. Not surprisingly, after the trauma of black experience in World War I, a thoroughly disillusioned Du Bois deserted the program of court tests, persuasion, and party politics to seek more immediately effective means of redeeming his race. In the May 1919 issue of the *Crisis* Du Bois printed materials he had uncovered that documented incredible discrimination within the army and the federal government; he sounded a call to the battle at home:

> By the God of Heaven, we are cowards and jackasses if now that the war is over, we do not marshal every ounce of our brain and brawn to fight a sterner, longer, more unbending battle against the forces of hell in our own land.
>> We *return.*
>> We *return from fighting.*
>> We *return fighting.*

The antagonistic note Du Bois struck at this beginning of the second stage of his editorship was prophetic of the whole period. He turned his back on white liberals and dismissed the possibility of achieving any significant gains through traditional politics; instead, Du Bois directed his search for solutions to the problem of color to extranational and international arenas.

In his quest for some kind of power fulcrum he turned to socialism and to Pan-Africanism. He called and organized several Pan-African congresses whose purposes were, in his words, "to demonstrate the solidarity of darker peoples of the world against the colonizing whites and to evolve methods of full emancipation." Du Bois's idea of color unity as a means of power within political states still clearly disavowed any separatist sentiments, so the enthusiasm stirred up by Marcus Garvey's back-to-Africa movement was of little value to Du Bois. Indeed, he actually had to spend the bulk of his energy arguing against Garvey's fantastic scheme of separatist repatriation rather than for his own cause.

As his hopes for Pan-African power dimmed, Du Bois began to explore the possibility of enlisting another potential and dispossessed ally—the great masses of the laboring class. For years he had been receptive to the socialist ideal, but in the 1920s he made his first important attempt to implement it as a means of achieving the old dream of racial redemption. A cursory acquaintance with postrevolutionary Russia convinced him that the problems of labor and of race made natural allies of the working class and black people. His romance with the Russian experiment and with socialist theory channeled his energies in two directions: he looked to the always chimerical possibility of a third political party and he dreamed of a power base rooted in labor unionism. But his hopes in these directions foundered on the same reefs that the Populist parties of 1890 and 1910 had—the incontinent and unreasonable color prejudice of the white laboring class. The American Federation of Labor remained one of the most segregated American institutions, and when even Negro leaders, like A. Philip Randolph, turned cold eyes on his dreams of wider union, Du Bois ceased hammering at the theme. His own political logic eventually led him to understand also that no third party had a real chance for victory in the American system, and when he finally concluded in 1929 that "national politics did not offer a way out for the Negro," it was clear that he had exhausted another set of alternatives; his dreams for broad-based power had the taste of ashes.

The last period of his editorship of the *Crisis* was marked by extremely conservative measures. When in 1929 the stock market crash plunged the nation into calamitous depression and Negroes into economic and social disaster, Du Bois turned to the only allies he felt he had left, his twelve million Negro fellow Americans. His advocacy during the early 1930s of the hitherto unacceptable separatism and segregation and his embrace of protorevolutionary tactics such as boycott, retaliatory ostracism, and pressuring threat not only reflected the desperateness of conditions but they were also clearly related to his insistence on the interrelations of politics and economics. In addition they foreshadowed the extreme positions and measures he would adopt in later years.

The quest for separate Negro ethos and culture began to dominate his thought. He became quixotically devoted to the idea of a Negro consumer-cooperative, turned away from extolling white universities as a redemptive possibility for young blacks and insisted instead (in ways that Booker T. Washington would have applauded) that *Negro* colleges, teaching *Negro* art and *Negro* history and *Negro* economics were the only reliable hope. He turned literary critic too, calling on all Negro writers to serve the cause, to use their talents as tools of uplift and genteel propaganda, roundly condemning the "garbage can" mentality of Harlem Renaissance writers.

To this economic, educational, and artistic separatism, Du Bois finally added political and social segregation. As always impatient with small battles within the large war and with the defense of positions won, he strove to implement another of his grand schemes—the creation of a self-sufficient Negro nation within white America. He called for Negroes everywhere to stop fighting segregation and instead raise it to the level of effective power. But rather than inspiring a new militancy within the race, Du Bois's movement backward toward Washingtonianism bewildered his friends and angered his rivals.

This last turn in Du Bois's editorial policies was unacceptable to the NAACP which, dedicated as it had always been to achieving total integration, could hardly countenance its own house organ espousing a contradictory position. Acrimony grew between Du Bois and Walter White, the NAACP's executive secretary; edicts came down silencing Du Bois. In 1934 Du Bois, bitter, angry, and essentially alone, resigned his position. An era ended.

During his *Crisis* years Du Bois wrote voluminously outside the pages of the magazine. He produced strangely gentle and genteel novels such as *The Quest of the Silver Fleece* (1911) and *Dark Princess* (1928) characterized by a sentimentalization of black beauty and an idealization of international movements. He wrote long thoughtful essays, including *Darkwater: Voices From Within the Veil* (1920) and *The Gift of Black Folk* (1924). But significantly the period is framed by two historical works, *John Brown* (1909) and *Black Reconstruction: An Essay Toward a History of the Part Black Folk Played in the Attempt to Reconstruct Democracy in America, 1860-1880* (1935). The two books tell a good deal about Du Bois as a historian: he was not so much interested in facts as he was in truth; he was a redresser, determined to set straight a record of black experience that had been grossly distorted by ignorant white historians or those with vested interests; and he saw the long course of black history in the only terms that seemed to allow optimistic resolution—the terms of the Marxist dialectic. *Black Reconstruction* remains an important and scholarly book, its principal merit lying in the impressive, patient, and original case it made in defense of the Reconstruction governments that had fared so badly at the hands of previous historians. *John Brown*, a late product of the Thoreauvian "John Brown Martyr" school, clearly reflects Du Bois's turn to Marxist economics, deriving its tension as much from class struggle as from racial conflict.

The last years of Du Bois's life were full of sound and fury, idea and event, triumphal tours and embittering disappointments, grand gestures and some foolishness, but in a sense the cause had passed him by. He was never a prophet without honor, but, much more frustrating to him, he became a prophet without power. He never again had a base from which to work and became a rootless wanderer ideologically as well as geographically.

Some events stand out; they form an ironic paradigm for the patternlessness of these years. In 1944 the NAACP rehired him as a kind of international ambassador, supporting African nationalism and opposing colonialism (especially American) at the United Nations. In 1950 he ran for the U.S. Senate as a peace and civil rights candidate from New York; his defeat was expectable and resounding. In 1951 he was indicted and tried as an unregistered agent of a foreign principal for his participation with Paul Robeson in the Peace Information Center. Though he was acquitted without even the need for defense, the trial alienated Du Bois finally from America. His wife and the mother of his two children had died in 1950; in February 1951 he married Shirley Lola Graham. For most of the rest of the decade he traveled in Asia and Africa, feted by world leaders, including Khrushchev, Mao Tse-tung, Chou En-lai, and African heroes such as Nkrumah and Mboya. In 1961 he applied for membership in the Communist party and accepted permanent exile in Ghana. He renounced his American citizenship in February 1963. This extreme and dramatic venture proved to be his last. He died in Accra on 27 August 1963; the news of his death was announced at the Washington Monument during the mammoth 1963 march on Washington; the announcement brought minutes of silent, bowed tribute.

W. E. B. Du Bois was, in almost every sense of the word, a great man—his vision was large, his dreams great, his influence extraordinary. Perhaps unfortunately, he was also a very sensitive man, easily chagrined by failure, ever enraged by frustration, and constantly injured by the narrowness of other men. Part of the tragedy of that combination is evident in his pathetic and tearful remark in Peking in 1959 to a massive celebration in honor of his ninety-first birthday: "In my own country for nearly a century I have never been nothing but a 'nigger.' "

The Autobiography of W. E. B. Du Bois, edited by Herbert Aptheker, was published posthumously in 1968. It is not an entirely reliable narrative, but it marvelously evokes the remarkable passion and energy with which one man confronted the conflicts inherent in being intelligent, black, and a twentieth-century American.

Letters:
The Correspondence of W. E. B. Du Bois, edited by Herbert Aptheker, 3 volumes (Amherst: University of Massachusetts Press, 1973-1978).

References:
Robert A. Bone, *The Negro Novel in America* (New Haven: Yale University Press, 1965);
Francis L. Broderick, *W. E. B. Du Bois, Negro Leader in a Time of Crisis* (Stanford, Cal.: Stanford University Press, 1959);
Shirley Graham Du Bois, *His Day Is Marching On: A Memoir of W. E. B. Du Bois* (Philadelphia: Lippincott, 1971);
August Meier, *Negro Thought in America, 1880-1915* (Ann Arbor: University of Michigan Press, 1963);
Arnold Rampersad, *The Art and Imagination of W. E. B. Du Bois* (Cambridge: Harvard University Press, 1976);
Elliott Rudwick, *W. E. B. Du Bois: Propagandist of the Negro Protest* (New York: Atheneum, 1968).

Papers:
Papers of W. E. B. Du Bois are at the University of Massachusetts, Amherst.

William Scott Ferguson

(11 November 1875-28 April 1954)

E. Christian Kopff
University of Colorado

BOOKS: *The Athenian Secretaries* (New York: Published for Cornell University by the Macmillan Company, 1898);
The Athenian Archons of the Third and Second Centuries before Christ (New York: Published for Cornell University by the Macmillan Company, 1899);
Hellenistic Athens, An Historical Essay (London: Macmillan, 1911);
Greek Imperialism (Boston & New York: Houghton Mifflin, 1913; London: Constable, 1913);
The Treasurers of Athena (Cambridge: Harvard University Press, 1932);
Athenian Tribal Cycles in the Hellenistic Age (Cambridge: Harvard University Press, 1932).

OTHER: "The Priests of Asklepios. A New Method of Dating Athenian Archons," in *University of California Publications, Classical Philology*, 1 (1906), pp. 131-173;

"Economic Causes of International Rivalries and Wars in Greece," in *Annual Report of the American Historical Association for 1915* (Washington, D.C.: Government Printing Office, 1917), pp. 113-121;

"The Zulus and the Spartans: A Comparison of Their Military Systems," in *Harvard African Studies*, 2 (1918), pp. 197-234;

Chapter 9, "Sparta and the Peloponnese," chapter

William Scott Ferguson

10, "The Athenian Expedition to Sicily,"
chapter 11, "The Oligarchical Movement in
Athens," and chapter 12, "The Fall of the
Athenian Empire," in volume 5, *The Cambridge Ancient History*, 12 volumes (Cambridge:
Cambridge University Press, 1923-1939), pp.
254-375;

Chapter 1, "The Leading Ideas of the New Period,"
in volume 7, *The Cambridge Ancient History*, 12
volumes (Cambridge: Cambridge University
Press, 1923-1939), pp. 1-40;

*Report on Some Problems of Personnel of the Faculty of
Arts and Sciences*, by Ferguson and others
(Cambridge: Harvard University Press,
1939);

"Orgeonika," in *Commemorative Studies in Honor of
Theodore Leslie Shear, Hesperia: Supplement VIII*
(Athens, 1949), pp. 130-163.

PERIODICAL PUBLICATIONS: "The Oligarchic
Revolution at Athens of the Year 103/2 B.C.,"
Klio, 4 (1904): 1-17;

"Athenian Politics in the Early Third Century,"
Klio, 5 (1905): 155-179;

"The Athenian Calendar," *Classical Philology*, 3 (October 1908): 386-398;

"Athens and Hellenism," *American Historical Review*,
16 (October 1910): 1-10;

"The Athenian Phratries," *Classical Philology*, 5
(July 1910): 257-284;

"Legalized Absolutism en route from Greece to
Rome," *American Historical Review*, 18 (October 1912): 29-47;

"Lachares and Demetrius Poliorcetes," *Classical
Philology*, 24 (January 1929): 1-31;

"The Salaminoi of Heptaphylai and Sounion," *Hesperia*, 7, no. 1 (1938): 1-74;

"*Polis* and *Idia* in Periclean Athens," *American Historical Review*, 45 (January 1940): 269-278;

"The Attic Orgeones and the Cult of Heroes," by
Ferguson and Arthur Darby Nock, *Harvard
Theological Review*, 37 (1944): 61-173.

In 1943 A. W. Gomme, who initiated the
standard commentary on the Greek historian Thucydides, called William Scott Ferguson "perhaps
the most distinguished living historian of Ancient
Greece." Ferguson, working with an insight that
first came to him as a graduate student, had a long
and productive career as author of scholarly monographs, historical narrative, and popular presentations of the Greek world from its emergence from
the Dark Ages about 800 B.C. until the domination
of the Mediterranean by Rome in the last two centuries B.C. As a teacher, he directed the dissertations and influenced the careers of some dozen of
the most distinguished American historians of the
ancient world. As an administrator, he helped
guide Harvard University into the tumultuous academic world that followed World War II. His
scholarly work still remains the foundation of research into the complicated world of the Mediterranean in the centuries after the death of
Alexander the Great at the end of the fourth century B.C.

William Scott Ferguson was born at Marsh-
field, Prince Edward Island, Canada, the son of
Donald and Elizabeth Scott Ferguson. Because his
father was senator and privy councillor of the Dominion of Canada, politics were a part of Ferguson's life from the beginning, politics seen from the
perspective of a proud minor power dominated by
the mighty nations of England and the United
States. He had a profound knowledge of both great
nations tempered by a Canadian's distance. This
distance perhaps helped form his understanding

of Athens in the Hellenistic age dominated by Rome. For example, of Athens's situation in the late Hellenistic period, when she was totally subject to Rome's wishes in foreign policy, he noted: "Probably her attitude toward Rome was much the same as that of the Dominion of Canada towards England to-day—one of affection for Rome and her political ideals, but of dislike for Romans individually."

Ferguson was graduated from McGill University with an A.B. in 1896 and earned his A.M. from Cornell University in 1897. His master's thesis, *The Athenian Secretaries,* was published in 1898. Cornell granted Ferguson his Ph.D. in classical philology in 1899. His mentor was Benjamin Ide Wheeler, the noted American classical scholar and linguist who later served as president of the University of California during its period of greatest growth as a research institution. In 1899 and 1900 Ferguson studied at the universities of Berlin and Athens. At a lecture in Berlin he heard the greatest classical philologist of the age, Ulrich von Wilamowitz-Moellendorff (1848-1931), mention "Ferguson's discovery" made in the master's thesis of 1898. It was one of the great moments in Ferguson's life, and he often talked of it and of the year he spent studying abroad.

On his return to the United States, Ferguson followed Wheeler to the University of California. He spent three years there as instructor of Greek and Roman history before being promoted to assistant professor in 1903 and to associate professor in 1906. In 1902 he married Mary Alena White, with whom he eventually had one daughter. Ferguson was research associate at the Carnegie Institute of Washington from 1906-1908. In 1908 he joined the faculty at Harvard, where he became professor of ancient history in 1912. He was visiting professor at the American School of Classical Studies in Athens, 1913-1914. In 1929 he was appointed McLean Professor of Ancient and Modern History at Harvard. After a successful term as chairman of the department of history, he served from 1939 to 1942 as dean of the faculty of arts and sciences, the office next in rank to the president at Harvard. In that office, he was one of the authors of an important *Report on Some Problems of Personnel of the Faculty of Arts and Sciences* (1939) and helped revise the tenure system.

Scholarly organizations to which he belonged included the American Philosophical Society, the British Academy of Arts and Sciences, Society for the Promotion of Hellenic Studies, American Academy of Arts and Sciences, and the Massachusetts Historical Society. He served as vice-president of the Archaeological Institute of America and as president of the American Historical Association. He received honorary LL.D. degrees from McGill (1921) and the University of Toronto (1934); the University of Louvain, Belgium, awarded him an honorary Litt.D. in 1927. In 1940 he was honored with a special issue of *Harvard Studies in Classical Philology,* containing a bibliography of his writings, essays from distinguished scholars, and essays by his students. In 1954 Ferguson died in Cambridge, Massachusetts, where he had lived without interruption since his return from Athens in 1914.

Ferguson had a dream career in scholarship. As a graduate student he made an observation which he was able to exploit and expand into a series of scholarly monographs, into a narrative history that would have been impossible before his discovery, and into several general essays. His initial observation was a crucial yet elementary one.

The Athenian democracy that prevailed in the Greek peninsula of Attica from the late sixth century B.C. until the fall of the Roman world in late antiquity recorded its decrees in stone. These inscriptions provide a potentially invaluable source with which to supplement and correct narrative historical sources on ancient Athens. The Athenians dated their inscriptions, however, by the names of their chief magistrates, or archons, and there is no complete and accurate list of the dates when each archon served. Where a substantial narrative history exists, such as that of Thucydides or Xenophon, this lack may be corrected. For the period of Alexander the Great and that following his death in 323 B.C., we have no narrative history until Polybius, who recounts the history of the Mediterranean world beginning in 218 B.C. German scholars had worked to correct and clarify many problems, especially the historian Julius Beloch and the philologist Wilamowitz-Moellendorff, but much remained to be done. Ferguson noted that, although the archons were listed in narrative accounts and other sources in no intelligible order, the secretaries of the Athenian Council (*boule*), whose names also appeared on the decrees to guarantee their accuracy, followed one another in a system of ordered rotation among the tribes of Athens. The tribal system had been introduced in the late sixth century B.C. by the democratic politician Cleisthenes to break down family and regional loyalties. It was totally artificial, but the order of the system was set and its very artificiality made it regular. The few official changes in this system were important and thus recorded. Ferguson first explained the discovery in his master's thesis and elaborated upon it in his dissertation, *The Athenian Archons of the Third and Second Centuries before Christ*, published in 1899. "During the thirty-one years of the fourth century, B.C.," Ferguson summarized, "from 352/1 till the end of the Lamnia War, the prytany secretaries at Athens followed one another in the official order of their tribes. The oligarchy introduced a new arrangement for the short period of its government. . . . After 307/6 B.C., however, the democracy returned to its earlier practice, and for every one of the following two hundred and eleven years we know which tribe furnished the secretary."

For the first time a viable and reliable chronology for the history of Athens from the time of Alexander to the domination of Rome was available, and this knowledge influenced the writing of the history of this entire era, known since the middle of the nineteenth century and the work of Johann Gustav Droysen as the Hellenistic Age. Ferguson followed the publication of his master's thesis and doctoral dissertation with a series of articles confirming the details of his idea. From 1904 until the culmination of his efforts in *Hellenistic Athens, An Historical Essay* (1911), he was writing articles on wider controversies in Hellenistic historiography, though the emphasis remained on Athens.

Hellenistic Athens gives a detailed, critical narrative history of the city of Athens from the time of Alexander the Great until the sack of Athens by the Roman general Sulla in 88 B.C. As a discussion of life in the ancient city, it remains unsurpassed. Chapter by chapter Ferguson divides the history of Athens into the eras of her struggles for renewed greatness and of her final political decline. Each chapter analyzes the political history of the city, with attention paid to constitutional development and change, and presents information on cultural and religious life as well. Ferguson evaluates literature, comments on philosophy and its cultural and political influences, and devotes pages to the round of Athenian festivals and the city's social life. For both depth and breadth *Hellenistic Athens* has had few rivals in ancient studies.

Ferguson's footnotes show mastery of an enormous bibliography. The Greek inscriptions, quoted on page after page, are sometimes used to clinch an argument, but just as often to show the Athenian way of thinking and talking. Ferguson's command of German scholarship is equally impressive. Although he was no Germanophile politically, on almost every page he shows his debt to

German scholars, major and minor. The names of three in particular appear again and again. Julius Beloch's work is used, with some corrections, for chronology. Wilamowitz-Moellendorff's work, especially his youthful *Antigonos von Karystos* (1881), provides chronological detail and insight into society and literature. Wilamowitz, though a great interpreter of classical Greek literature, was notorious for the attention and favor he bestowed on Hellenistic writers. His popular history of Greek literature (first published in 1905 and twice revised in the years before World War I) gave twice as much space to Hellenistic, Roman, and late ancient Greek literature as to the Classical Period. Although this earned the wrath of such American scholars as William Abbott Oldfather (1880-1945) of the University of Illinois, it naturally won Ferguson's attention. Most striking is Ferguson's admiration for the work of Eduard Meyer, whose *Geschichte des Altertums* (1884-1902) did not reach the Hellenistic era. Meyer, however, provided insights into Greek customs and traditions that were relevant to the historian of the Hellenistic Age. Ferguson's systematic use of Meyer's books and articles gives way to adulation at one point: "The genesis of deification has been recently sketched by 'the master of those who know' among living historians of antiquity, Ed. Meyer."

Hellenistic Athens continues to be held in high esteem because it combines mastery of detail with the ability to create a coherent total picture of an age and of a city, and because Ferguson's control of sources—literary, epigraphical, and narrative—is so impressive. Ferguson's total vision of Hellenistic Athens is based on an ideal of classical scholarship as an *Altertumswissenschaft*, a complete science of the ancient world in all its aspects, that was first formulated by Friedrich August Wolf, the great Homer scholar, at the end of the eighteenth century and reached its highest achievements in the work of Theodor Mommsen, Wilamowitz-Moellendorff, and Meyer. Ferguson deserves an honored place among their disciples.

Greek Imperialism (1913), the text of lectures given at Boston's Lowell Institute just before World War I, showed another side of Ferguson, his ability to generalize and popularize his enormous learning. Although Ferguson never gave up his commitment to precise and even pedantic scholarship, after *Hellenistic Athens* he devoted time to general essays on the ancient world and on the role of the historian. That Ferguson was still too close to his scholarly interests to be a perfect popularizer is indicated by his artless praise on one occasion of

Antigonus Doson, king of Macedon (227-221 B.C.), "whose name ought not to be unknown where Callicratidas, Agesilaus, Iphicrates, and Phocion are household words."

Greek Imperialism includes discussions of the empires of Athens and Sparta in the Classical era and of the empire of Alexander which led into the great Hellenistic monarchies of the Ptolemies (Egypt), Seleucids (Asia), and Antigonids (Macedon). The quality is uneven. The section on Athens is little more than an adulatory commentary on Thucydides' Periclean funeral oration. The sections on the Hellenistic era, on the other hand, are much more creative exercises, although there are notable pedantic intrusions. The work is now little used, although many passages are clearly and forcibly expressed, and Ferguson's wide reading of the English poets, especially the Romantics and late Victorians, is often reflected in his style.

In a century marked by two major wars between Germany and Great Britain, Ferguson and other American classical scholars (who were by personal heritage British but by professional heritage German) had necessarily complicated attitudes toward the culture and history of those two dominant European nations. Such tension is evident in *Greek Imperialism*. Ferguson's admiration for German scholarship remained constant. In *Greek Imperialism*, for example, German historical superiority to English archaeologists breaks out into satire as Ferguson touches on the great Spartan creative spring that preceded Sparta's retreat into philistinism in the sixth century B.C.: "All this, and much besides, was observed, and the proper inferences drawn, by Eduard Meyer twenty years ago; so that the amazement with which the English archaeologists, who have excavated in Laconia during the past five or six years, report their remarkable 'finds' is a source of no little amusement to the wary." Although he sided with the British politically, when he comes to discuss modern ideas of empire, Ferguson seems on the whole to prefer the German concept of 1913 to that of the British. And his detachment from the English-speaking world was sufficient for him to express some scorn for the imperial passion for spreading the American way of life far and wide. "Less exasperating, perhaps," he wrote, "than this assumption of moral and political superiority is the candid profession of the right of the stronger."

Ferguson's masterpiece of scholarly generalization is his introductory chapter to the seventh volume of *The Cambridge Ancient History* (1928), devoted to "The Leading Ideas of the New Period," that is, the Hellenistic Age. The essay surveys a wide area with a combination of scholarly accuracy and general knowledge that is still impressive. The second edition (1970) of *The Cambridge Ancient History*, volume seven, part one, *The Hellenistic World*, postpones a similar discussion until chapter eight, written by J. K. Davies, Rathbone professor of ancient history and classical archaeology, University of Liverpool, who broaches rather different topics. Whereas Ferguson dealt with such topics as "Religious Syncretism," "Science *versus* Religion," the Macedonian monarchy and Hellenistic kingship, the ruler-cult and deification, the decay of urban nationalism, and "Cosmopolitanism, Individualism, and Stoicism," Davies discusses "Sources and Approaches," "Demographic Problems," "The Degree of Economic Interplay," "Piracy and Its Ramifications," "Royal Policies and Regional Diversities," "The *Polis* Transformed and Revitalized," and "The Limits of the *Polis*." The chapter is entitled "Cultural, Social and Economic Features of the Hellenistic World." The emphasis on the role of the Greek city-state, or *polis*, is still there. Otherwise, the economic has overcome the political, intellectual, religious, and even the social. Trends in scholarship have changed, but it is not clear that Ferguson's emphases and insights have become outdated.

Ferguson by no means turned his back on scholarship. The year 1949 saw publication of a new version of an important inscription in "Orgeonika," which appeared in *Hesperia*, supplement eight, published by the American School at Athens, as well as a valuable discussion of "The Attic Orgeones and the Cult of Heroes," published in *Harvard Theological Review*. The latter Ferguson wrote with Arthur Darby Nock, the brilliant but eccentric expert on Greek religion who had left Cambridge for Harvard.

Ferguson influenced a generation by his training of graduate students, whose names are given in volume fifty-one of the *Harvard Studies in Classical Philology*, dedicated to Ferguson. Sterling Dow continued Ferguson's work in Greek epigraphy and directed many dissertations of Harvard. Jacob Larsen (Chicago) became the world's authority on representative government in the Greek world. Charles Edson (Madison, Wisconsin) became the only American to edit part of the Corpus of Greek Inscriptions. On the Latin side, Ralph Scramuzza (Fordham) published an early and valuable defense of the emperor Claudius I. It represents what is today the standard scholarly view, and Robert Graves's novels *I, Claudius* (1934) and *Claudius the God* (1935) helped to make it a popular one as well.

A. E. R. Boak (Michigan) argued forcibly that underpopulation was at the root of Rome's fall and though his view is no longer popular, his originality and his insights remain intriguing. Finally, Ferguson's student Nathan M. Pusey became president of Harvard.

To pass one's life without disgrace and with honors, to live to see one's offspring succeed, this was the essence of success for Herodotus and for the early Greeks in general. These were Ferguson's accomplishments. He moved from a single brilliant observation to develop a vision of an entire city and culture, and he was able to communicate his vision to both scholarly and popular audiences. He improved his institution by his administrative work and enriched his field by the students he trained. He died honored and respected, proof that service to the gods of ancient Greece may be rewarded even in the twentieth century.

Bibliography:

"Bibliography of William Scott Ferguson to July, 1940," *Harvard Studies in Classical Philology*, 51 (1940): pp. 1-9; supplemented by Sterling Dow, *Gnomon*, 27 (1955): 61.

Sydney George Fisher

(11 September 1856-22 February 1927)

Robert M. Weir
University of South Carolina

BOOKS: *The Cause of the Increase of Divorce* (Philadelphia, 1890);

Church Colleges: Their History, Position, and Importance ... (Philadelphia: Printed by G. H. Buchanan, 1895);

The Making of Pennsylvania; An Analysis of the Elements of the Population and the Formative Influences that Created One of the Greatest of the American States (Philadelphia: Lippincott, 1896);

Pennsylvania, Colony and Commonwealth (Philadelphia: Coates, 1897);

The Evolution of the Constitution of the United States, Showing that it is a Development of Progressive History and Not an Isolated Document Struck Off at a Given Time or an Imitation of English or Dutch Forms of Government (Philadelphia: Lippincott, 1897);

Men, Women & Manners in Colonial Times, 2 volumes (Philadelphia & London: Lippincott, 1897);

The True Benjamin Franklin (Philadelphia: Lippincott, 1899);

The True William Penn (Philadelphia: Lippincott, 1900);

The True History of the American Revolution (Philadelphia & London: Lippincott, 1902); revised and enlarged as *The Struggle for American Independence*, 2 volumes (Philadelphia & London: Lippincott, 1908);

The American Revolution and the Boer War: An Open Letter to Mr. Charles Francis Adams on his Pamphlet (Philadelphia: G. H. Buchanan, 1902);

The True Daniel Webster (Philadelphia & London: Lippincott, 1911);

American Education (Boston: Badger, 1917);

The Quaker Colonies; A Chronicle of the Proprietors of the Delaware (New Haven: Yale University Press, 1919).

OTHER: "The Legendary and Myth-making Process in Histories of the American Revolution," in *Proceedings of the American Philosophical Society*, 51 (April-June 1912), pp. 53-75.

PERIODICAL PUBLICATION: "The Twenty-eight Charges Against the King in the Declaration of Independence," *Pennsylvania Magazine of History and Biography*, 31 (July 1907): 257-303.

Sydney George Fisher was a prolific historian of the American colonial and Revolutionary eras, and, to a lesser extent, of the early national period. Generally more popular than scholarly in his ap-

Sydney George Fisher (Historical Society of Pennsylvania)

proach, he nevertheless made a substantial contribution to the historiography of the War for Independence.

Fisher, the son of lawyer Sidney George Fisher whose published diary has become something of a classic, was born in Philadelphia, where he attended private schools until the death of both his father and his mother, Elizabeth Ingersoll Fisher, in the early 1870s. The boy then went to St. Paul's School, Concord, New Hampshire, and, from 1876 to 1879, Trinity College, Hartford, Connecticut. While in college, Fisher served as president of the senior class and, as such, became embroiled in controversy over administrative control of student celebrations. His defiance of the authorities cost him a temporary suspension, but he still graduated with honors in three subjects, including English. From 1880 to 1882, Fisher attended Harvard Law School. Although he did not graduate, he became a member of the Philadelphia bar in 1883.

Fisher participated in the Bar Association but did not actively pursue a career in the law. Instead, he became a civic-minded man of letters, writing first on legal and governmental subjects and then on history. A brief letter to the editor of the *Nation* in September 1880 promoted national civil-service reform. An early article, published in 1895 as a pamphlet entitled *Church Colleges*, may have contributed to his election as a trustee of Trinity College. The work certainly extolled the role of small church-related (especially Episcopalian) schools while noting that "few places could be found better suited [than Hartford] to student life." Social attitudes implicit in these opinions became explicit in several essays on immigration. One published in the *Forum*, 1893, entitled "Alien Degradation of American Character," was typical; it and its counterparts were commonly believed to have contributed to the establishment of the Immigration Restriction League.

Beginning in 1896 with *The Making of Pennsylvania*, Fisher turned to history. This volume, subtitled "An Analysis of the Elements of the Population and the Formative Influences that Created One of the Greatest of the American States," and his next study, *Pennsylvania, Colony and Commonwealth* (1897), exhibited a bias in favor of the Quakers and an antipathy toward the later Penns that offended some readers. Skilled at clear exposition, Fisher was perhaps best in expounding issues with legal dimensions, such as the numerous boundary controversies involving the colony. On balance, however, the contemporary assessment of these volumes, especially of the latter, was mixed. One reviewer noted that while "Mr. Fisher has presented much that is old in a new and attractive garb, his close dependence upon secondary authorities, as well as the evident haste with which portions of the book have been written . . . detract somewhat from its value as a contribution to Pennsylvania history." In a more recent article, an authority on the history of the colony, Joseph E. Illick, lumped these works with others in a category of studies which "either do not fill the requirement of narrative history . . . or contribute little by way of new information or synthesis."

Fisher's next historical work was more successful. *The Evolution of the Constitution of the United States, Showing that it is a Development of Progressive History and Not an Isolated Document Struck Off at a Given Time or an Imitation of English or Dutch Forms of Government* (1897) provided the first relatively complete collation of similar provisions in the colonial charters, state constitutions, and the United States Constitution. Nevertheless, reviewers correctly noted that his ideas were not quite as new as Fisher seemed to think and that his language was "at times extravagant." The book, however, remains sufficiently useful to be cited in standard bibliographies of the Revolutionary era. Although Fisher doubtless worked on his books over a period of time, he continued to publish at breakneck speed. The two-volume *Men, Women & Manners in Colonial Times* (1897), treating the colonies in regional terms, revealed Fisher's considerable personal knowledge of South Carolina and not a little hostility to the Puritans. Cotton Mather's works, he observed, were "written with all the fulsomeness, unction and cant of his faith." Such judgments have not commended this work to modern scholars.

Two biographies followed. The first, of Benjamin Franklin, which appeared in 1899, was republished in 1927, though it is now considered badly dated. *The True William Penn* (1900), like the "true Benjamin Franklin," carried a series title for which Fisher was not responsible, but he approached his subject with something of the spirit of an investigative reporter writing an exposé. "William Penn," he noted, "is usually thought of as a pious, contemplative man, a peace-loving Quaker in a broad brim hat and plain drab clothes, who founded Pennsylvania in the most successful manner, on benevolent principles and kindness to the Indians." But, Fisher continued, "the real William Penn, though of a very religious turn of mind, was essentially a man of action, restless and enterprising, at times a courtier and a politician, who lived well, and although he undoubtedly kept faith with the red men, Pennsylvania was the torment of his life." The apparent paradoxes in Penn's life and character have long fascinated scholars, but recent biographers do not credit Fisher with throwing much new light on the subject.

After a brief pamphlet comparing the American Revolution and the Boer War (in which he supported the Boers), Fisher brought out *The True History of the American Revolution* in 1902. Tracing the Revolution from its causes to the end of the War for Independence, Fisher maintained that he had approached the subject more candidly than previous historians. The sources demonstrated, at least to his satisfaction, that British authorities were justified in trying to bring order and regularity to the empire in the 1760s and that Americans were bent upon independence ab initio. These views arose at least in part from an unusually conscientious reading of the pamphlet literature produced by the loyalists, and Fisher was among the first historians to attempt seriously to understand and categorize these individuals. Fisher's approach and sweeping condemnation of other historians' work were bound, as one reviewer predicted, to "create

violent discussion and startle a great many patriotic people out of long-cherished beliefs." They also offended Claude Van Tyne, who was to make a distinguished name for himself in part by also writing about the loyalists. Fisher's book, Van Tyne noted, was not a narrative of the American Revolution but "a series of special arguments to prove certain facts about the Revolution upon which the best historians and teachers of history have been agreed for twenty years." A revised version of Fisher's argument, published in two volumes as *The Struggle for American Independence* (1908) marshaled more evidence. Still "excessively 'otherwise-minded,'" in the apt words of one critic, Fisher failed to convince everyone of either the novelty or the accuracy of his point of view. Yet *The Struggle for American Independence* is considered to be his most important work. As a noted specialist in early American history, George Allan Billias, has recently noted, "Fisher's forthright and independent approach to the Revolution makes his work of considerable historical value to this day."

Fisher's work on the Revolution also produced two substantial essays. The first, "The Twenty-eight Charges Against the King in the Declaration of Independence," published in 1907, was a long, somewhat legalistic, and rather pedestrian—though useful—attempt to establish the origins and assess the validity to these famous indictments. More widely known, more stimulating, and more representative of Fisher's main ideas was a paper delivered before the American Philosophical Society in 1912 entitled, "The Legendary and Myth-making Process in Histories of the American Revolution." His contention was that prevailing interpretations of the American Revolution relied too heavily on the views of the (British) Whig opposition of the era. Sources for the Whig interpretation were readily accessible, and the notion that the actions of a misguided and corrupt ministry prompted virtually unanimous resistance on the part of patriotic America had obvious appeal in the United States where it served as the basis of a unifying national myth. Somewhat ironically, this analysis also proved useful to nineteenth-century Englishmen, for it made the American Revolution appear to be an isolated aberration rather than merely one more example of a phenomenon indigenous to empire. But, Fisher concluded, the time had come for Americans to immerse themselves in the "original evidence." After the "shock of the cold water is over, you will enjoy it. The real Revolution is more useful and interesting than the make-believe one. The actual factions, divisions, mistakes, atrocities, if you please, are far more useful to know about than the pretense that there were none. The real patriots who hated colonialism and alien rule in any form and who were determined to break from the empire no matter how well it governed them, are more worthy of admiration than those supposed 'affectionate colonists,' who, we are assured, if they had been a little more coddled by England, would have kept America in the empire to this day."

During the latter part of his career Fisher wrote a biography of Daniel Webster (1911), a critical study of American education (1917), and a volume entitled *The Quaker Colonies* (1919) for the Chronicles of America series. Although not widely noted at the time nor frequently cited since, *The True Daniel Webster* was termed as late as the 1960s "probably the best one-volume study which treats Webster's life as a whole." The small volume on the Quaker colonies was, somewhat surprisingly, rather thin in its discussion of Pennsylvania—perhaps because Fisher believed he had covered the subject adequately in his other volumes. Equally incomplete in its treatment of religious matters and imperial relations, it was one of the least successful works in the series.

Although not everything Fisher wrote has stood the test of time, he was and still is a figure of some significance. Essentially a popularizer rather than a scholar's scholar, he was—to judge by the number of printings and republications of his works—widely read during his lifetime. Moreover, his best work gave evidence, especially where the loyalists were concerned, that he had read fresh primary sources in original ways. But Van Tyne was correct. Fisher did not have graduate training as a historian, and he was not always aware of what his professional colleagues were doing; thus his condemnation of their myopia was too sweeping.

Fisher himself is difficult to categorize. He belongs neither to the imperial nor the Progressive "schools" of historical writing, both of which developed during his lifetime. Like the imperial historians, he demonstrated considerable Anglophilia and an understanding—if not total approval—of the British position on the eve of the Revolution; like the Progressives, he saw the Revolution as the result of "forces," often economic, that made colonial leaders actively seek independence. But Fisher was too much of the dapper Philadelphia aristocrat to share many of the popular sympathies of most Progressive historians. As such, he was something of a maverick whose "otherwise-mindness" still makes entertaining reading. More important, some of his insights have proved to be remarkably prescient about the direction of modern scholarship, and his implicit suggestions are by no means yet exhausted.

References:

Joseph E. Illick, "The Writing of Colonial Pennsylvania History," *Pennsylvania Magazine of History and Biography*, 94 (January 1970), 3-25;

Page Smith, "David Ramsay and the Causes of the American Revolution," *William and Mary Quarterly*, third series, 17 (January 1960): 51-77;

D. G. Brinton Thompson, "Sydney George Fisher, Son of the Diarist," *Pennsylvania Magazine of History and Biography*, 91 (April 1967): 181-192;

Nicholas B. Wainwright, ed., *A Philadelphia Perspective. The Diary of Sydney George Fisher Covering the Years 1834-1871* (Philadelphia: Historical Society of Pennsylvania, 1967).

John Fiske

(30 March 1842-4 July 1901)

William A. Link

University of North Carolina at Greensboro

SELECTED BOOKS: *Tobacco and Alcohol* (New York: Leypoldt & Holt, 1869);

Myths and Myth-Makers: Old Tales and Superstitions Interpreted by Comparative Mythology (Boston: Osgood, 1872);

Outlines of Cosmic Philosophy, Based on the Doctrine of Evolution, With Criticisms on the Positive Philosophy, 2 volumes (Boston: Osgood, 1874; London: Macmillan, 1874);

The Unseen World, and Other Essays (Boston: Osgood, 1876);

Darwinism and Other Essays (London & New York: Macmillan, 1879; revised and enlarged, Boston & New York: Houghton Mifflin, 1885);

Excursions of an Evolutionist (Boston: Houghton Mifflin, 1884; London: Macmillan, 1884);

The Destiny of Man Viewed in the Light of His Origin (Boston: Houghton Mifflin, 1884; London: Macmillan, 1884);

American Political Ideas Viewed from the Standpoint of Universal History: Three Lectures Delivered at the Royal Institution of Great Britain in May 1880 (New York: Harper, 1885; London: Macmillan, 1885);

The Idea of God as Affected by Modern Knowledge (Boston & New York: Houghton Mifflin, 1885; London: Macmillan, 1885);

The Critical Period of American History, 1783-1789 (Boston & New York: Houghton Mifflin, 1888; London: Macmillan, 1888; revised, Boston & New York: Houghton Mifflin, 1898);

The Beginnings of New England; or, The Puritan Theocracy in Its Relations to Civil and Religious Liberty (Boston & New York: Houghton Mifflin, 1889; London: Macmillan, 1889; revised, Boston & New York: Houghton Mifflin, 1898);

The War of Independence (Boston & New York: Houghton Mifflin, 1889);

Civil Government in the United States Considered with Some Reference to Its Origins (Boston & New York: Houghton Mifflin, 1890; London: Macmillan, 1890);

The American Revolution, 2 volumes (Boston & New York: Houghton Mifflin, 1891; London: Macmillan, 1891; revised, Boston & New York: Houghton Mifflin, 1896; London: Gay & Bird, 1897);

The Discovery of America, with Some Account of Ancient America and the Spanish Conquest, 2 volumes (Boston & New York: Houghton Mifflin, 1892; London: Macmillan, 1892);

Edward Livingston Youmans, Interpreter of Science for the People: A Sketch of His Life With Selections from His Published Writings and Extracts from His Correspondence with Spencer, Huxley, Tyndall and Others (New York: Appleton, 1894);

A History of the United States for Schools (Boston, New

York & Chicago: Houghton Mifflin, 1894;
London: Clarke, 1894);

Old Virginia and Her Neighbors, 2 volumes (Boston
& New York: Houghton Mifflin, 1897; London: Macmillan, 1897);

Through Nature to God (Boston & New York:
Houghton Mifflin, 1899; London: Macmillan,
1899);

The Dutch and Quaker Colonies in America, 2 volumes
(Boston & New York: Houghton Mifflin,
1899; London: Macmillan, 1899);

A Century of Science and Other Essays (Boston & New
York: Houghton Mifflin, 1899; London: Macmillan, 1900);

The Mississippi Valley in the Civil War (Boston & New
York: Houghton Mifflin, 1900);

Life Everlasting (Boston & New York: Houghton
Mifflin, 1901; London: Macmillan, 1902);

Colonization of the New World (Philadelphia & New
York: Lea, 1902);

Independence of the New World (Philadelphia & New
York: Lea, 1902);

Modern Development of the New World, completed by
John Bach McMaster (Philadelphia & New
York: Lea, 1902);

New France and New England (Boston: Houghton
Mifflin, 1902; London: Macmillan, 1902);

Essays Historical and Literary, 2 volumes (New York
& London: Macmillan, 1902);

*Unpublished Orations: "The Discovery of the Columbia
River, and the Whitman Controversy"; "The Cris-
pus Attucks Memorial"; and "Columbus Memorial"*
(Boston: Privately printed, 1909).

OTHER: *Appletons' Cyclopaedia of American Biography*, edited by Fiske and James Grant Wilson, 6 volumes (New York: Appleton, 1887-
1889).

John Fiske, essayist, philosopher, and lecturer, was the most popular historian of the late
nineteenth century. In an age before specialization
in the historical profession, the reading public regarded Fiske as an advocate of "scientific history,"
able to synthesize and communicate a large body
of knowledge. Fiske is not widely read today, and
little of his work was respected by contemporary
scholars. But, as a symbol of the values, as well as
the ambiguities, of his culture, the writings of John
Fiske are significant for modern historians.

John Fiske was born Edmund Fisk Green in
Hartford, Connecticut. His father, Edmund
Brewster Green, was a lawyer, politician, and news-
paper editor who died when Fiske was only ten

years old. The boy was then raised by his maternal
grandparents in Middletown, Connecticut, and, although Fiske's mother, Mary Fisk Bound Green,
remarried, he chose to stay in Middletown and to
take the name of his maternal grandmother in 1855
(to which he added an *e* five years later). Throughout childhood and adolescence, Fiske was confident
of his abilities and extremely ambitious. Indeed, he
was something of a prodigy. By age eight, he had
read most of Shakespeare, Milton, Bunyan, and
Pope; by thirteen, he had read all of Virgil, Horace,
Tacitus, and Sallust. Fiske was also an accomplished
child scholar in mathematics and philosophy. Most
prodigious of all was his linguistic ability; as a young
man he claimed to understand a total of eighteen
languages.

The precocious youth soon proved his mettle
in school. In 1855 he entered Betts Academy in
Stamford, Connecticut, where he followed a classical course of Latin, Greek, composition, and arith-
metic. Two years later, he was graduated from
Betts with the highest record of achievement in the
school's history. For the next three years, Fiske continued his studies under the direction of a private
tutor, the Reverend Henry M. Colleton, in preparation for entrance to Yale. But under Colleton's
influence Fiske grew eager to leave Connecticut
and avoid the religious orthodoxy of Yale, and, in
1860, he entered Harvard College. Even as a college freshman, Fiske's lifelong precepts had begun
to take shape. He soon earned a reputation as a
hard worker. Fiske had little time for socializing;
he maintained a strict schedule of reading for
twelve to sixteen hours a day. Even so, the youth
did not distinguish himself in the classroom. His
reading schedule frequently interfered with his academic responsibilities, and his grades, because of
excessive absences, were only mediocre.

At Harvard, Fiske was also known as a religious radical. As a youth, influenced by Colleton,
he had inclined toward religious unconventional-
ity. Young Fiske believed that advances in science,
and their application to society by such groups as
European positivists and English Social Darwinists,
necessitated a rethinking of the role of religion in
American culture. Even before entering Harvard—and as part of his general re-evaluation of
religious orthodoxy—Fiske had become an admirer of Auguste Comte's *Cours de philosophie positive*
(1830-1842), which, like the writings of English
positivist Henry Thomas Buckle, applied the laws
of natural science to philosophy. Fiske's preference
for positivism over religious orthodoxy earned him
few friends at Harvard, which, during the early

1860s, was under clerical domination and was the main forum for the anti-Darwinian biologist Asa Gray. In a notable incident during his second year at Harvard, Fiske was caught reading a volume of Comte during college chapel, an offense for which he was severely disciplined and nearly expelled.

Fiske became fascinated with the works of Charles Darwin and also with those of Herbert Spencer, an English philosopher who enjoyed wide popularity in the United States during the last half of the nineteenth century. As early as 1860, Fiske discovered the works of Spencer in a Boston bookstore, and he soon thereafter became a Spencerian. So converted was he that, when he was graduated from Harvard in 1863, he was determined to apply Spencer to a variety of scholarly enterprises. Yet his ambitions were in conflict with a more pressing need—to find a paying vocation, especially after his marriage to Abby Morgan Brooks on 6 September 1864. For a time, Fiske saw his future in the law, and, with the help of hard work and a photographic memory—according to some accounts, Fiske could remember verbatim entire chapters of Dickens—he passed the bar examination in July 1864. But it soon became apparent that the law held little interest for him, and, even more important, his law practice did not provide a living for his growing family which eventually numbered five children.

By the late 1860s, a failure as a lawyer, Fiske turned to writing. In 1869 Harvard, now under the presidency of Charles W. Eliot, hired him as lecturer; three years later, he was appointed assistant college librarian. These positions allowed him time to write, and soon he began to enjoy a reputation as a Spencerian, particularly after the publication of *Myths and Myth-Makers* (1872) and, especially, *Outlines of Cosmic Philosophy* (1874). Fiske offered few original ideas in these early writings. Instead, as was the case all through his life, he openly borrowed from other thinkers. Thus, in *Outlines of Cosmic Philosophy* Fiske presented a synthesis of the Spencerian universe and a theistic worldview. His philosophy, he wrote, involved a "stupendous" effort to apply evolutionary laws to a "cosmic" understanding of the world.

It was only after these early forays into philosophy that Fiske began a career as a popular historian, almost by accident. In 1879 he was offered the handsome fee of $1,000 to deliver a series of lectures on American history at the Old South Meeting House in Boston. These six lectures, entitled "America's Place in World History," traced American history from its aboriginal origins to the

"Professor John Fiske Flies the Evolution Kite in America," *cartoon inspired by Fiske's* Outlines of Cosmic Philosophy *and published in the* New York Daily Graphic, *12 September 1874*

nineteenth century. Fiske maintained that the history of the United States was visible proof of the role played by evolutionary processes. Columbus's voyage to the western hemisphere, he declared, was "in many respects the greatest event" since the birth of Christ, for it began the growth and maturation of Anglo-American political institutions. Fiske offered his audience an appealing combination of nationalism and popular Darwinism, and the response to his lectures was so strong that he was encouraged to embark on a new career as a lecturer-historian.

The following year, 1880, he began an active program of lecturing. In England he delivered a series of three lectures at the Royal Institution of Great Britain in London. Five years later, these lectures were published in his first full-length historical work, *American Political Ideas Viewed from the Standpoint of Universal History* (1885). In these lectures Fiske began to refine his conception of the special, universal role of Anglo-American political institutions in world history. Like most of his writings, *American Political Ideas* drew heavily on the work of others. Borrowing a "germ theory" of history from the English historians Edward A. Freeman, Sir Henry Maine, and William Stubbs, Fiske maintained that American self-government grew from a Teutonic source, spread to England, was carried to New England by freedom-loving Puritans, and reached fruition following the writing of the American Constitution in 1787. Fusing the "germ theory" with Spencerian principles and a strong dose of American nationalism, Fiske took matters a step further. For him history was a demonstration of the superiority of Anglo-American political institutions which had prevailed in a worldwide, Darwinian struggle.

Fiske's works of history after *American Political Ideas Viewed from the Standpoint of Universal History* largely elaborated on these ideas. In 1884 and 1885 he developed a series of lectures on the American Revolution, which were published in 1888 as *The Critical Period of American History, 1783-1789*, perhaps his best-known work of history. The 1780s were "critical," Fiske wrote, because it was then that the future of Anglo-American political institutions was determined; they would spread, through a federal constitution, from New England to the rest of the North American continent, and, ultimately, to the rest of the world. The themes of the role of evolution in history and of American exceptionalism were repeated in the flood of subsequent books. In his next work, *The Beginnings of New England; or, The Puritan Theocracy in Its Relations to Civil and Religious Liberty* (1889), Fiske dealt with the special role of New England, first in transmitting and then in helping to germinate democratic political institutions in the United States.

Thereafter, Fiske's writings repeated this message. In all of his subsequent works he relied heavily on the scholarship of others. Some of his books—which by the 1890s had attracted a considerable following—were simple narratives with emphasis on great men, battles, or diplomacy and with little attempt to examine political institutions, let alone the social and cultural environment of the past. Such was certainly the case in *The War of Independence* (1889) and *The American Revolution* (2 volumes, 1891). It was also the case in *Colonization of the New World, Independence of the New World*, and *Modern Development of the New World*, three posthumously published works by Fiske which appeared in 1902 as volumes twenty-one to twenty-three of *A History of All Nations*, edited by John Henry Wright. Other of his works examined dimensions of American history with a greater attempt at scholarship. Such, especially, was the case

in *The Discovery of America, with Some Account of Ancient America and the Spanish Conquest* (2 volumes, 1892), which was Fiske's most rigorously researched work. *Old Virginia and Her Neighbors* (2 volumes, 1897), *The Dutch and Quaker Colonies* (2 volumes, 1899), *The Mississippi Valley in the Civil War* (1900), and *New France and New England* (1902) were more intensive elaborations of Fiske's "germ theory."

By 1900 Fiske's reputation was so well established that it is no exaggeration to say that he had the highest income of any historian of his generation. His writings captured a large portion of the small nonfiction market at the turn of the century. Although none of his books was a best-seller, about ten thousand copies of Fiske's works were sold during the last ten years of his life. After 1889 Henry O. Houghton of Houghton Mifflin paid Fiske an annual salary of $5,000, a figure which, by 1899, had increased to $12,000. In return Fiske agreed to publish exclusively with Houghton's firm and to limit lecturing to three months of the year. Fiske did continue to address mainly urban, upper-middle-class audiences to supplement his income, which, although growing, remained insufficient to prevent periodic financial crises.

Fiske died at the height of his powers as a writer. At the time of his death on 4 July 1901, he was obese, weighing over three hundred pounds, and the strain of almost constant lecturing and overwork had finally taken its toll. Most contemporaries eulogized Fiske as a master historian. One, James Schouler, described him as the "chief of our native historians, living or dead" whose main contribution was to popularize the study of history. Fiske, wrote Schouler, could "enlist a hundred readers where ten had read before." Professional historians who were contemporaries of Fiske also noted his skills as a popularizer. As Albert Bushnell Hart put it, Fiske's main accomplishment was to synthesize the "dull and confused" and to communicate to the "average man wholesome truths about our ancestors."

Fiske's reputation as a historian did not, however, survive beyond his own time. Professional historians, though they admired his abilities as a popularizer, were suspicious of his scholarship and originality. Fiske, in fact, had little to do with professional historians or with universities. He never held a permanent position at any university, although he had temporary appointments at Harvard and at Washington University in St. Louis. Furthermore, Fiske was never entirely comfortable with professional historians. Although he was a member of several professional organizations, he took no active part in them and usually avoided attending meetings. Fiske had little contact with the American Historical Association, then the leading professional organization, and he even turned down an offer to serve on the *American Historical Review*'s editorial board. Yet, while he avoided contact with scholars, Fiske craved scholarly recognition.

Most academic historians have criticized Fiske's work for popularizing the ideas of others and for doing so in an unimaginative way. They have objected to his excessive attention to narrative detail, especially when writing about military history. George L. Beer, for example, concluded that although Fiske was "a man of brilliant talents, of vast learning," he would "never stand conspicuous in the list of American philosophers and historians." More recent historians have repeated this assessment. In 1931 James Truslow Adams's sketch in the *Dictionary of American Biography* criticized Fiske's work for similar reasons. As a historian, according to Adams, Fiske was "solely a popularizer," and his work was simply a narration of "conspicuous facts" which "never got below the surface." Jennings B. Sanders, writing six years later, provided a similar assessment of Fiske as a historian. For twentieth-century historians, he wrote, the career of John Fiske is "at once an inspiration and a warning." His learning was formidable, his power of literary expression impressive, and his productivity "well-nigh phenomenal." But, concluded Sanders, his work was "so prolific" that only rarely "may we detect the sure hand of a master."

Fiske's significance, in the final analysis, lies in his success as a popularizer. His version of history, although weak in scholarship and originality, was nonetheless attractive to the public and remains of significance to present-day cultural and intellectual historians. Reflecting the way in which Darwinism had diffused throughout American culture, Fiske's work is just as important for revealing how Darwinism became blended with a worldview distinctly ethnocentric and at the same time intensely concerned with the application of science to the study of society. If John Fiske mirrored the values of his culture, he was also a figure who stood in the midst of a transformation in the writing of history itself. He was one of the last of the literary giants who dominated American historical writing. When Fiske began his career as a historian, the discipline was made up of avocational writers whose main appeal was to the public rather than to a scholarly community. Yet during his generation a new, professional class of historians, increasingly estranged from the reading public, came into existence and began to dominate the writing of history.

Letters:

The Personal Letters of John Fiske (Cedar Rapids, Iowa: Printed for the Bibliophile Society by Torch Press, 1939);

Ethel F. Fisk, ed., *The Letters of John Fiske* (New York: Macmillan, 1940).

Biography:

John Spencer Clark, *The Life and Letters of John Fiske*, 2 volumes (Boston & New York: Houghton Mifflin, 1917).

References:

Milton Berman, *John Fiske: The Evolution of a Popularizer* (Cambridge: Harvard University Press, 1961);

Thomas S. Perry, *John Fiske* (Boston: Small, Maynard, 1906);

Jennings B. Sanders, "John Fiske," in *The Marcus W. Jernegan Essays in American Historiography*, edited by William T. Hutchinson (Chicago: University of Chicago Press, 1937), pp. 144-170.

Papers:

The most important collection of Fiske's papers is at the Huntington Library, San Marino, California. This collection includes most of his personal correspondence and a significant portion of his business and literary correspondence. The University of California, Los Angeles, which has Fiske's library, is the repository of some of Fiske's letters, scrapbooks, and journals. The Library of Congress has about sixty letters from Fiske to his wife and to his mother.

Worthington C. Ford

(16 February 1858-7 March 1941)

Michael E. Stevens
South Carolina Department of Archives and History

SELECTED BOOKS: *The American Citizen's Manual*, 2 volumes (New York: Putnam's, 1882-1883);

The Standard Silver Dollar and the Coinage Law of 1878 (New York: Society for Political Education, 1884);

George Washington, 2 volumes (Paris: Goupil/New York: Scribners, 1900);

The Boston Book Market, 1679-1700 (Boston: Club of Odd Volumes, 1917);

The Isle of Pines, 1668: An Essay in Bibliography (Boston: Club of Odd Volumes, 1920).

OTHER: David Ames Wells, *Wells's Natural Philosophy: For the Use of Schools, Academies, and Private Students*, edited by Ford (New York & Chicago: Ivison, Blakeman, Taylor, 1879);

Report of a Committee of the Lords of the Privy Council on the Trade of Great Britain with the United States, January 1791, edited by Ford (Washington, D.C.: Department of State, 1888);

Letters of Joseph Jones of Virginia, 1777-1787, edited by Ford (Washington, D.C.: Department of State, 1889);

The Spurious Letters Attributed to Washington, with a Bibliographical Note, edited by Ford (Brooklyn: Privately printed, 1889);

Washington as an Employer and Importer of Labor, edited by Ford (Brooklyn: Privately printed, 1889);

The Writings of George Washington, 14 volumes, edited by Ford (New York & London: Putnam's, 1889-1893);

General Orders Issued by Major-General William Heath when in Command of the Eastern Department, 23 May, 1777-3 October, 1777, With Some Fragmentary Orders of Major-General Putnam and Lt. Col. Wm. S. Smith, edited by Ford (Brooklyn: Historical Printing Club, 1890);

The United States and Spain in 1790: An Episode in Diplomacy Described from Hitherto Unpublished Sources, edited by Ford (Brooklyn: Historical Printing Club, 1890);

The Washington-Duché Letters, Now Printed, for the

Worthington C. Ford

First Time, from the Original Manuscripts, edited by Ford (Brooklyn: Privately printed, 1890);

Winnowings in American History, 15 volumes, edited by Ford and Paul L. Ford (Brooklyn: Historical Printing Club, 1890-1891);

The Controversy between Lieutenant-Governor Spotswood and His Council and the House of Burgesses, on the Appointment of Judges on Commissions of Oyer and Terminer, 1718, edited by Ford (Brooklyn: Historical Printing Club, 1891);

Letters of William Lee, Sheriff and Alderman of London; Commercial Agent of the Continental Congress in France; and Minister to the Courts of Vienna and Berlin, 1766-1783, 3 volumes, edited by Ford

(Brooklyn: Historical Printing Club, 1891);

Reply of William Lee to the Charges of Silas Deane, 1779, edited by Ford (Brooklyn: Historical Printing Club, 1891);

Wills of George Washington and His Immediate Ancestors, edited by Ford (Brooklyn: Historical Printing Club, 1891);

Boston in 1775: Letters from General Washington, Captain John Chester, Lieutenant Samuel B. Webb, and Joseph Barrell, edited by Ford (Brooklyn: Historical Printing Club, 1892);

Correspondence and Journals of Samuel Blachley Webb, edited by Ford (New York: Wickersham Press, 1893);

General Orders Issued by Major-General Israel Putnam, When in Command of the Highlands, in the Summer and Fall of 1777, edited by Ford (Brooklyn: Historical Printing Club, 1893);

General Orders of 1757: Issued by the Earl of Loudoun and Phineas Lyman in the Campaign against the French, edited by Ford (New York: Gilliss Press, 1899);

Letters of Jonathan Boucher to George Washington, edited by Ford (Brooklyn: Historical Printing Club, 1899);

Historical Manuscripts in the Public Library of the City of Boston, 5 volumes, edited by Ford (Boston: Privately printed, 1900-1904);

"The Governor and Council of the Province of Massachusetts Bay, August, 1647-March, 1715," edited by Ford, in *Proceedings of the Massachusetts Historical Society*, second series, 15 (1901-1902), pp. 327-362;

"Some Original Documents on the Genesis of the Monroe Doctrine," edited by Ford, in *Proceedings of the Massachusetts Historical Society*, second series, 15 (1901-1902), pp. 373-436;

Diary of George Washington, September-December 1785, edited by Ford (Boston: Privately printed, 1902);

"Letters from James Parker to Benjamin Franklin," edited by Ford, in *Proceedings of the Massachusetts Historical Society*, second series, 16 (1902), pp. 186-232;

"Cotton's 'Moses his Judicials,' " in *Proceedings of the Massachusetts Historical Society*, second series, 16 (1902), pp. 274-284;

"The Federal Constitution in Virginia, 1787-1788," in *Proceedings of the Massachusetts Historical Society*, second series, 17 (1903), pp. 450-510;

"Alexander Hamilton's Notes on the Federal Convention of 1787," edited by Ford, in *Proceedings of the Massachusetts Historical Society*, second series, 18 (1903-1904), pp. 348-362;

"Colonial America," in *Publications of the Colonial Society of Massachusetts*, 6 (1904), pp. 340-370;

Journals of the Continental Congress, 1774-1779, edited by Ford, 15 volumes (Washington, D.C.: Government Printing Office, 1904-1909);

"The Case of Samuel Shrimpton," in *Proceedings of the Massachusetts Historical Society*, second series, 19 (1905), pp. 37-51;

"Public Records in Our Dependencies," in *Annual Report of the American Historical Association for the Year 1904* (Washington, D.C.: Government Printing Office, 1905), pp. 129-147;

"Unpublished Letters of Edmund Pendleton," edited by Ford, in *Proceedings of the Massachusetts Historical Society*, second series, 19 (1905), pp. 107-167;

"Letters of William Duane," edited by Ford, in *Proceedings of the Massachusetts Historical Society*, second series, 20 (1906-1907), pp. 257-394;

"Use of Patronage in Elections," in *Proceedings of the Massachusetts Historical Society*, 41 (1907-1908), pp. 359-407;

"The Authorship of 'New Englands First Fruits,' " in *Proceedings of the Massachusetts Historical Society*, 42 (1908-1909), pp. 259-266;

"The Ensign Incident at Salem in 1634," edited by Ford, in *Proceedings of the Massachusetts Historical Society*, 42 (1908-1909), pp. 266-280;

"Letters of James Monroe, 1790-1827," edited by Ford, in *Proceedings of the Massachusetts Historical Society*, 42 (1908-1909), pp. 318-341;

"Quaker Protests, 1659-1675," edited by Ford, in *Proceedings of the Massachusetts Historical Society*, 42 (1908-1909), pp. 358-381;

"Van Buren-Bancroft Correspondence," edited by Ford, in *Proceedings of the Massachusetts Historical Society*, 42 (1908-1909), pp. 381-442;

"The Campaign of 1844," in *Proceedings of the American Antiquarian Society*, new series, 20 (1909), pp. 106-126;

"On Calendaring Manuscripts," in *Papers of the Bibliographical Society of America*, 4 (1909), pp. 45-56;

"Church Support in Virginia," edited by Ford, in *Proceedings of the Massachusetts Historical Society*, 42 (1908-1909), pp. 341-347;

"Davenport-Paget Controversy, 1634-1635," edited by Ford, in *Proceedings of the Massachusetts Historical Society*, 43 (1909-1910), pp. 45-68;

"Constitutionality of a National Bank, 1791, by Hamilton," edited by Ford, in *Proceedings of the Massachusetts Historical Society*, 43 (1909-1910), pp. 156-181;

"Letter of Francis Corbin, on Slavery in Virginia,

1819," edited by Ford, in *Proceedings of the Massachusetts Historical Society,* 43 (1909-1910), pp. 260-265;

"Charles Stuart and James Murray Letters, 1766-72," edited by Ford, in *Proceedings of the Massachusetts Historical Society,* 43 (1909-1910), pp. 449-458;

"Letter of William B. Lewis, 1839," edited by Ford, in *Proceedings of the Massachusetts Historical Society,* 43 (1909-1910), pp. 496-503;

"Bibliography of the Massachusetts House Journals, 1715-1776," in *Publications of the Colonial Society of Massachusetts,* 4 (1910), pp. 201-289;

"Bibliography of the Laws of the Massachusetts Bay, 1641-1776," by Ford and Albert Matthews, in *Publications of the Colonial Society of Massachusetts,* 4 (1910), pp. 291-480;

"Parliament and the Howes," in *Proceedings of the Massachusetts Historical Society,* 44 (1910-1911), pp. 120-143;

"The Mauduit Pamphlets," in *Proceedings of the Massachusetts Historical Society,* 44 (1910-1911), pp. 144-175;

"Diary of Cotton Mather," edited by Ford, in *Collections of the Massachusetts Historical Society,* Seventh Series, 7 (1911), 8 (1912);

Some Social Notes Addressed to Samuel Blachley Webb, 1776-1791, edited by Ford (Boston, 1911);

"Recall of John Quincy Adams, 1808," in *Proceedings of the Massachusetts Historical Society,* 45 (1911-1912), pp. 354-375;

William Bradford, *History of Plymouth Plantation, 1620-1647,* edited by Ford (Boston: Published for the Massachusetts Historical Society by Houghton Mifflin, 1912);

"Three Documents on the Early Years of the History of Massachusetts Bay Plantation," edited by Ford, in *Proceedings of the Massachusetts Historical Society,* 46 (1912-1913), pp. 275-302;

Writings of John Quincy Adams, edited by Ford, 7 volumes (New York: Macmillan, 1913-1917);

"John Wilkes and Boston," edited by Ford, in *Proceedings of the Massachusetts Historical Society,* 47 (1913-1914), pp. 190-215;

"Winthrop in the London Port Books," edited by Ford, in *Proceedings of the Massachusetts Historical Society,* 47 (1913-1914), pp. 178-190;

"Mather-Calef Papers on Witchcraft," edited by Ford, in *Proceedings of the Massachusetts Historical Society,* 47 (1913-1914), pp. 240-268;

"The Massachusetts Historical Society," in *Annual Report of the American Historical Association for the Year 1912* (Washington, D.C.: Government Printing Office, 1914), pp. 217-223;

"Letters of William Vans Murray to John Quincy Adams, 1797-1803," edited by Ford, in *Annual Report of the American Historical Association for the Year 1912* (Washington, D.C.: Government Printing Office, 1914), pp. 343-708;

Letters and Papers of John Singleton Copley and Henry Pelham, 1739-1776, edited by Ford, in *Collections of the Massachusetts Historical Society,* 71 (1914);

"Letters of William Pynchon, [1636-1644]," edited by Ford, in *Proceedings of the Massachusetts Historical Society,* 48 (1914-1915), pp. 35-56;

"The British Ghent Commission," edited by Ford, in *Proceedings of the Massachusetts Historical Society,* 48 (1914-1915), pp. 138-162;

"Extracts from the Diary of Benjamin Moran, 1860-1868," edited by Ford, in *Proceedings of the Massachusetts Historical Society,* 48 (1914-1915), pp. 431-492;

"Lydia Smith's Journal, 1805-1806," edited by Ford, in *Proceedings of the Massachusetts Historical Society,* 48 (1914-1915), pp. 508-534;

"The Treaty of Ghent, and After," in *Proceedings of the State Historical Society of Wisconsin for 1914* (Madison, 1915), pp. 77-106;

"Manuscripts and Historical Archives," in *Annual Report of the American Historical Association for the Year 1913,* 2 volumes (Washington, D.C.: Government Printing Office, 1915), I: 75-84;

"Smibert-Moffatt Letters," edited by Ford, in *Proceedings of the Massachusetts Historical Society,* 49 (1915-1916), pp. 23-41;

"Letters of Goldwin Smith, 1863-1872," edited by Ford, in *Proceedings of the Massachusetts Historical Society,* 49 (1915-1916), pp. 106-160;

"Letters to John Brazer Davis," edited by Ford, in *Proceedings of the Massachusetts Historical Society,* 49 (1915-1916), pp. 178-256;

"The Jefferson Papers," in *Thomas Jefferson, Architect: Original Designs in the Collection of Thomas Jefferson Coolidge, Junior, with an Essay and Notes by Fiske Kimball* (Cambridge: Privately printed, 1916), pp. 1-9;

Thomas Jefferson Correspondence, Printed from the Originals in the Collection of William K. Bixby, edited by Ford (Boston, 1916);

Warren-Adams Letters, Being Chiefly a Correspondence among John Adams, Samuel Adams, and James Warren . . . 1743-1814, edited by Ford, in *Collections of the Massachusetts Historical Society,* 72 (1917), 73 (1925);

"Captain Wollaston, Humphrey Rasdell and Thomas Weston," in *Proceedings of the Mas-*

sachusetts Historical Society, 51 (1917-1918), pp. 219-232;

"Journal of Jonathan Russell, 1818-1819," edited by Ford, in Proceedings of the Massachusetts Historical Society, 51 (1917-1918), pp. 369-498;

"Ezekiel Carré and the French Church in Boston," in Proceedings of the Massachusetts Historical Society, 52 (1918-1919), pp. 121-132;

"Some Papers of Aaron Burr," edited by Ford, in Proceedings of the American Antiquarian Society, new series, 29 (1919), pp. 43-128;

A Cycle of Adams Letters, 1861-1865, edited by Ford, 2 volumes (Boston & New York: Houghton Mifflin, 1920);

"Rev. Sampson Bond of the Bermudas," in Proceedings of the Massachusetts Historical Society, 54 (1920-1921), pp. 295-318;

Broadsides, Ballads, &c. Printed in Massachusetts, 1639-1800, in Collections of the Massachusetts Historical Society, 75 (1922);

"Letters of Thomas Coram," edited by Ford, in Proceedings of the Massachusetts Historical Society, 56 (1922-1923), pp. 15-56;

"Franklin's Accounts against Massachusetts," edited by Ford, in Proceedings of the Massachusetts Historical Society, 56 (1922-1923), pp. 94-120;

"The Isaiah Thomas Collection of Ballads," in Proceedings of the American Antiquarian Society, new series, 33 (1923), pp. 34-112;

"Benjamin Harris, Printer and Bookseller," in Proceedings of the Massachusetts Historical Society, 57 (1923-1924), pp. 34-68;

"The First Separate Map of Pennsylvania," in Proceedings of the Massachusetts Historical Society, 57 (1923-1924), pp. 172-184;

"Voting with Beans and Corn," in Proceedings of the Massachusetts Historical Society, 57 (1923-1924), pp. 230-239;

"Franklin's New England Courant," in Proceedings of the Massachusetts Historical Society, 57 (1923-1924), pp. 336-353;

"A Letter of Alexander Hamilton, 1779," in Proceedings of the Massachusetts Historical Society, 58 (1924-1925), pp. 219-236;

"Tyndall's Map of Virginia, 1608," in Proceedings of the Massachusetts Historical Society, 58 (1924-1925), pp. 244-247;

"Ten Years of the Photostat," in Proceedings of the Massachusetts Historical Society, 58 (1924-1925), pp. 288-316;

Winthrop Papers, volume 1, edited by Ford (Boston: Massachusetts Historical Society, 1925);

"A Seventeenth Century Letter of Marque," in Pro-

ceedings of the Massachusetts Historical Society, 59 (1925-1926), pp. 3-25;

"Some Letters of 1775," edited by Ford, in Proceedings of the Massachusetts Historical Society, 59 (1925-1926), pp. 106-138;

"Colonial Commerce in 1774-1776," edited by Ford, in Proceedings of the Massachusetts Historical Society, 59 (1925-1926), pp. 210-235;

"The Boston Gazette of March 12, 1770," in Proceedings of the Massachusetts Historical Society, 59 (1925-1926), pp. 253-259;

"Sumner's Letters to Governor Andrew," edited by Ford, in Proceedings of the Massachusetts Historical Society, 60 (1926-1927), pp. 222-235;

"French Royal Edicts etc., on America," in Proceedings of the Massachusetts Historical Society, 60 (1926-1927), pp. 250-304;

Statesman and Friend: Correspondence of John Adams with Benjamin Waterhouse, 1784-1822, edited by Ford (Boston: Little, Brown, 1927);

War Letters, 1862-1865, of John Chipman Gray . . . and John Codman Ropes . . . with Portraits, edited by Ford (Boston & New York: Houghton Mifflin, 1927);

"Washington's Map of the Ohio," in Proceedings of the Massachusetts Historical Society, 61 (1927-1928), pp. 71-79;

"A Pleading of William Leddra, 1659," edited by Ford, in Proceedings of the Massachusetts Historical Society, 61 (1927-1928), pp. 116-123;

"Forged Lincoln Letters," in Proceedings of the Massachusetts Historical Society, 61 (1927-1928), pp. 183-195;

"Henry Knox, Bookseller, 1771-1774," edited by Ford, in Proceedings of the Massachusetts Historical Society, 61 (1927-1928), pp. 227-303;

"Mrs. Warren's 'The Group,' " in Proceedings of the Massachusetts Historical Society, 62 (1928-1929), pp. 15-22;

"The Society's Photostat, 1925-1929," in Proceedings of the Massachusetts Historical Society, 62 (1928-1929), pp. 87-110;

"Mr. Emerson Was Present," in Proceedings of the Massachusetts Historical Society, 62 (1928-1929), pp. 130-138;

"A Division of Manuscripts," in Essays Offered to Herbert Putnam, edited by William Warner Bishop and Andrew Keogh (New Haven: Yale University Library, 1929), pp. 156-161;

Letters of Henry Adams, edited by Ford, 2 volumes (Boston & New York: Houghton Mifflin, 1930, 1938);

"Introduction: The John Quincy Adams Library," by Ford, and "Catalogue of the Deposit," by

Ford and Henry Adams, in *A Catalogue of the Books of John Quincy Adams Deposited in the Boston Athenaeum, with Notes on Books, Adams Seals and Book-Plates by Henry Adams* (Boston: Athenaeum, 1938), pp. 3-38, 79-132.

PERIODICAL PUBLICATIONS: "British and American Prisoners of War, 1778," *Pennsylvania Magazine of History and Biography*, 17, nos. 2, 3 (1893): 159-174, 316-324;

"British Officers Serving in America, 1754-1774," *New England Historical and Genealogical Register*, 48 (January, April, July, October 1894): 36-46, 157-168, 299-310, 424-436; 49 (January, April, July 1895): 47-58, 160-171, 292-296;

"Defences of Philadelphia in 1777," *Pennsylvania Magazine of History and Biography*, 18, nos. 1, 2, 3, 4 (1894): 1-19, 163-184, 329-353, 463-495; 19, nos. 1, 2, 3, 4 (1895): 72-86, 234-250, 359-373, 481-506; 20, nos. 1, 2, 3, 4 (1896): 87-115, 213-247, 391-404, 520-551; 21, no. 1 (1897): 51-71;

"Letters of Elbridge Gerry," edited by Ford, *New England Historical and Genealogical Register*, 49 (October 1895): 430-441; 50 (January 1896): 21-30;

"Thomas Jefferson and James Thomson Callender, 1798-1802," edited by Ford, *New England Historical and Genealogical Register*, 50 (July, October 1896): 321-333, 445-458; 51 (January, April, July 1897): 19-25, 153-158, 323-328;

"Washington and 'Centinel X,' " *Pennsylvania Magazine of History and Biography*, 22, no. 1 (1898): 436-451;

"Letters of Ralph Izard," edited by Ford, *South Carolina Historical and Genealogical Magazine*, 2 (July 1901): 194-204;

"Some Jefferson Correspondence," edited by Ford, *New England Historical and Genealogical Register*, 55 (July, October 1901): 272-276, 381-384;

"John Quincy Adams and the Monroe Doctrine," *American Historical Review*, 7 (July 1902): 676-696; 8 (October 1902): 28-52;

"Dr. S. Millington Miller and the Mecklenburg Declaration of Independence," *American Historical Review*, 11 (April 1906): 553-558;

"The Editorial Function in United States History," *American Historical Review*, 23 (January 1918): 273-286;

"Captain John Smith's Map of Virginia, 1612," *Geographical Review*, 14 (July 1924): 433-443;

"Early Maps of Carolina," *Geographical Review*, 16 (April 1926): 264-273;

"Historical Societies—Living and Dead," *Mississippi Valley Historical Review*, 16 (December 1929): 307-320.

Worthington Chauncey Ford helped bridge the gap between the amateur historical editors of the nineteenth century, such as Peter Force and Jared Sparks, and the professional historical editors of the twentieth century, such as Julian Boyd and Lyman Butterfield. Although he wrote several books and many articles, Ford made his mark as an editor of historical documents, especially those of the Adams family. He believed in making original sources available to researchers in a variety of forms, be it original manuscripts, published editions, or facsimile reproductions. Described as a "gentleman of the old school," he nonetheless eagerly adopted new technology when it meant that copies of rare documents could be made widely available. Furthermore, he believed that editors had a responsibility not to tamper with texts and that the federal government ought to support the editing and publishing of historical documents in its custody.

Ford was born into a prosperous Brooklyn, New York, family on 16 February 1858. His historical and literary interests seem to have been inherited from and cultivated by his parents. His father, Gordon Lester Ford, was a collector of books and manuscripts, while his mother, Emily Ellsworth Fowler Ford, was a published poet. Gordon Ford's collection contained over 100,000 books and 60,000 manuscripts, a family treasure that stimulated the interests of both Worthington and his younger brother, Paul Leicester Ford (1865-1902). Both of the boys suffered from handicaps—Paul was a hunchback and Worthington was partially deaf, a condition that became worse as he grew older. The desire to conquer these disabilities led them to pursue literary careers, unlike their brother, Malcolm Webster Ford (1862-1902), who showed little inclination for scholarship and instead became a prominent New York athlete.

Ford was educated at Brooklyn Polytechnic Institute and then at Columbia College, but his growing deafness forced him to drop out of college before acquiring a degree. After leaving Columbia, Ford worked for three years as a cashier for an insurance company and later as a writer for the *New York Evening Post* and the *New York Herald*. He developed an interest in economics and politics, and in 1879 he published a revised textbook edition of David Ames Wells's *Natural Philosophy.* In 1882 and 1883, he produced his own two-volume civics textbook entitled *The American Citizen's Manual,* which expressed views in accord with those of the Democratic Party.

With the installation of a Democratic administration under President Grover Cleveland in 1885, Ford was asked to head the Bureau of Statistics in the State Department. Here Ford discovered the vast historical resources held by that agency. Among them were the records of the Continental Congress as well as the papers of Washington, Jefferson, Madison, and other founding fathers, unarranged and difficult to use. Ford's proposal to publish these records was passed along to the president, but Congress rejected the plan when it was submitted to them. Despite this defeat, Ford edited and the State Department published a few small editions such as a 1791 report of the British Privy Council (1888) and the letters of Joseph Jones (1889), a Revolutionary War figure from Virginia.

When Cleveland was defeated in 1888, Ford lost his job and turned his full attention to documentary editing. He and his brother Paul published volumes under the imprint of their own Historical Printing Club. The works they issued ranged from short pamphlets to multivolume editions. Worthington Ford's contributions centered on manuscripts from the last third of the eighteenth century. These included the Revolutionary War orders of Generals William Heath (1890) and Israel Putnam (1893), documents dealing with diplomacy between Spain and the United States in 1790 (1890), and a three-volume edition of the letters of William Lee (1891), Revolutionary War diplomat and commercial agent.

During these years, Ford also prepared works for other publishers. He compiled and published in historical magazines lists of Revolutionary War prisoners of war (1893) and British officers in the colonial era (1894-1895). Of greater importance was the edition of Washington's papers that he prepared for G. P. Putnam's Sons. Worthington Ford produced his fourteen volumes of Washington's writings in four years (1889-1893); Paul took seven years to complete for Putnam's a similar ten-volume edition of Jefferson's works (1892-1899).

In all of his work Ford sought to give the documents "exactly as they were written." He was critical of the methods used by Washington's previous editor, Jared Sparks, who rewrote portions of documents to improve their style. Unfortunately, Ford's work did not always meet the standards he set for himself. Herbert Baxter Adams, a contemporary of Ford, reported that "literal exactness is not characteristic of all of Mr. Ford's editorial work." The flaw in his method was the rapid speed at which he worked. In more recent times, Lyman Butterfield found "errors in textual readings, transposed numerals in dates, and erroneous assignments of authorship." Contemporary critics attacked Ford's edition of Washington for its inaccuracies, its use of Sparks's annotation without acknowledgment, and its incompleteness. In his defense, Ford maintained that his edition was a temporary one, since only the federal government had the resources to publish a definitive edition.

Cleveland was re-elected in 1892, and Ford again obtained a federal job, this time as head of the Bureau of Statistics in the Treasury Department. He apparently had little time or inclination for history in these years. He tried to maintain his position after the Republicans returned to power in 1897 but was forced to resign in 1898. For the next four years he compiled statistical reports from his position as head of the Department of Documents and Statistics at the Boston Public Library.

In Boston his historical interests were revived. He published a series of five volumes based on historical manuscripts found in the library (1900-1904), edited some letters of Ralph Izard and Thomas Jefferson for historical journals in 1901, and wrote a two-volume life of Washington (1900) in which he attempted to make Washington "write his own biography, using his own phrases and words to illustrate his attitudes towards public questions." In Boston Ford cultivated a friendship with Charles Francis Adams, Jr., that initiated a lifelong interest in the Adams family. Adams permitted Ford to use the papers of John Quincy Adams in preparing a study of the Monroe Doctrine. In a piece that was published in the *American Historical Review* in 1902, Ford traced the development of a European issue into an American one and stressed that the Monroe Doctrine was the work of Secretary of State John Quincy Adams.

Ford's personal life underwent important changes while he was in Boston. In 1899 he married Bettina Fillmore Quin, and from this marriage were born two daughters, Crimora Chauncey and Emily Ellsworth. Three years after his marriage, his collaboration with Paul came to a tragic end. Their brother Malcolm, who had been disinherited by their father, came to Paul with a request for money. When his request was denied, Malcolm shot and killed Paul and then killed himself. Ford, always a reticent man, left few remarks about the impact of this incident on his life.

The year of Paul's death also marked an important turning point in Ford's life, for at the age of forty-four he embarked upon a full-time career devoted to history. He returned to Washington to head the newly established Division of Manuscripts at the Library of Congress. He proved to be a vigorous manuscript curator with broad interests. In 1903 he made a tour of the nation's new Pacific territories and inspected records in Guam, Hawaii, and the Philippines. With the support of President Theodore Roosevelt, many records were transferred to the Library from other federal agencies or were obtained from private owners. Among these documents were Revolutionary War records in the State Department as well as several collections of presidential papers. To make the manuscripts more accessible, Ford oversaw the preparation of lists and calendars. He still believed that the federal government ought to publish the papers in its custody, and in 1904 he launched the publication of the *Journals of the Continental Congress, 1774-1789*. He supplemented the bare, dry text of the journal by printing committee reports, yet he failed to include explanatory notes on the original manuscript sources. Ford had edited fifteen volumes by the time he left Washington in 1909, carrying the series to 1779. The series eventually ran to thirty-four volumes when it was completed in 1937.

Ford returned to Boston in 1909, lured there this time by Charles Francis Adams, Jr.'s request that he serve as editor for the Massachusetts Historical Society. Ford, who was fifty-one at the time, was entering the most prolific stage of his career. Over the next twenty years he edited more than fifty books for the Society, including twenty volumes of its *Proceedings*, ten volumes of the *Collections*, ten volumes of the journals of the state House of Representatives, as well as many other important materials. The volumes he prepared ranged over diverse fields and included an edition of Cotton Mather's *Diary* (1911-1912), a new edition of William Bradford's *History of Plymouth Plantation, 1620-1647* (1912), and a collection of Civil War letters (1927). He also edited, without title page credit, Senator Albert J. Beveridge's biography of Abraham Lincoln (1928).

In addition to editing, Ford served history in other ways. He compiled several bibliographies, the most important being his 1922 volume on seventeenth- and eighteenth-century *Broadsides, Ballads, &c. Printed in Massachusetts*. Ford was also active in

the historical profession, and his abilities were recognized nationally. He chaired the Committee on the Documentary Historical Publications of the United States Government, which recommended in 1908 that a national commission to promote documentary editions be established. It took nearly thirty years before this proposal became reality in the form of the National Historical Publications Commission. Ford also regularly delivered papers at the meetings of the American Historical Association, which honored him with its presidency in 1917. His presidential address was entitled "The Editorial Function in United States History." In it he criticized editors who falsified texts and attacked Jared Sparks for missing an opportunity to provide a reliable and accurate edition. According to Ford, the purpose of the historical editor was "to furnish the material in its full and unaltered shape."

Ford's interest in making the raw material of history widely available extended beyond editing. He called for the professional evaluation of public records and was aware of the problem of bulk created by modern records. He believed that related manuscript material should be brought together, and he arranged for some of the Massachusetts Historical Society's holdings to be transferred to more appropriate repositories. Ford was also quick to seize upon modern technological means for the dissemination of rare historical materials. The newly developed photostat machine permitted the making of facsimile copies of documents, and in 1914 he had one installed at the Society. Under Ford's direction, photostatic copies of rare books and newspapers in the Society's collections were sold to subscriber libraries in a series that he called Photostat Americana. As if his prodigious work at the Society were not enough, he somehow found time between 1919 and 1923 to supervise the preparation of a four-volume guide to the holdings of the John Carter Brown Library in Providence, Rhode Island, and wrote the library's annual reports between 1917 and 1923.

Ford's most significant historical work during his tenure at the Society was his editing of the Adams family's writings from four generations. Ford planned to publish a twelve-volume edition of the *Writings of John Quincy Adams*. Seven volumes appeared between 1913 and 1917 when World War I interrupted publication. As with his other works, annotation was sparse, and the series, which printed documents up to 1823, was never completed. An earlier generation was represented in the *Warren-Adams Letters* (1917-1925), which contained the correspondence of John Adams, Samuel

A Catalogue of the Books of

John Quincy Adams

Deposited in the Boston Athenæum

With Notes on
Books, Adams Seals and Book-Plates

By HENRY ADAMS

With an Introduction by
WORTHINGTON CHAUNCEY FORD

BOSTON
Printed for the Athenæum
1938

Frontispiece and title page for Ford's last published work. As the table of contents makes clear, Ford wrote the introduction and collaborated with Henry Adams on the "Catalogue of the Deposit"; Adams provided notes on "The Seals and Book-Plates of the Adams Family, 1783-1905."

Adams, and Revolutionary-era political leader James Warren. Under Ford's supervision, the Society had *Charles Francis Adams, Jr., 1835-1915; An Autobiography* published in 1916 and *The Education of Henry Adams* in 1918. Ford believed that these volumes distorted the characters of these two members of the fourth generation, and he hoped to correct the impression by editing *A Cycle of Adams Letters, 1861-1865.* Appearing in 1920, this two-volume edition contained the Civil War correspondence of Henry and Charles Francis Adams, Jr., and of their father, Charles Francis, Sr. Ford hoped that the letters would "develop other and deeper attributes natural to the writers, yet concealed almost to suppression in their self-accusing memoirs." Seven years later, Ford made available additional Adams material in *Statesman and Friend:*

Correspondence of John Adams with Benjamin Waterhouse (1927).

Unfortunately, Ford's career at the Society came to an unhappy end. In 1925, he published the first volume of the John Winthrop Papers, and, as with most of his work, it contained little in the way of annotation and showed signs of haste. Reviewers were critical; they noted transcription errors, mistakes in dating, problems with the index, and sparse annotation. After investigating the affair, the Society decided to recall the volume and appointed a committee to oversee Ford's work. Only with the committee's approval could new volumes be sent to the press. Ford, unwilling to work under these restrictions, submitted his resignation in 1928, and it was accepted, effective in 1929.

Although he was in his seventies, Ford remained active in historical work for another ten years. In 1930 he produced the first volume of his *Letters of Henry Adams* in which he again tried to counter the impression left by Adams's self-assessment. Ford hoped to use the volume to make Adams "better and more humanly known than he can be from the detached examination of himself in the 'Education'...." From 1929 to 1932, Ford served the Library of Congress in Europe as director of its project to obtain copies of foreign documents relating to America, a position in which he found great satisfaction. Ford's wife died in 1931, and when the European project ended, he made his permanent home in France. He returned to America only in 1937-1938 to finish the second volume of the Henry Adams letters, which appeared in 1938. His last published work fittingly was a catalogue of the John Quincy Adams library, prepared in collaboration with Henry Adams (1938). Ford also wrote the introduction for the volume. He returned to France in 1938 and remained there until early 1941 when he fled the Nazis through Spain and Portugal. He attempted to return to America once more but died at sea on 7 March 1941.

Described by his friends as "outwardly formal," Ford was "dapper in appearance, with a spry step, even in his old age." He enjoyed an occasional game of golf but generally was a quiet, retiring man, whose social life was minimal. When his wife objected to his refusal to go out at night, he told her "that she might just as well continue to be taken for a widow." Undoubtedly his deafness, which increased with age, contributed to his limited social life. By 1923 his hearing had so deteriorated that he could no longer converse on the telephone. This handicap limited Ford in some ways, but freed him from distractions and allowed him to immerse himself in his editing.

Ford had a remarkably productive career as an editor and manuscript curator. Although he wrote well, his own original work was minuscule compared to the amount of material that he edited. His editing, while superior to that of earlier generations in terms of fidelity to the text, too often showed the marks of haste. Ford's career straddled an important era of change in the historical profession. Before the turn of the century, Ford was a gentleman scholar—an amateur who dabbled in history in his spare time when not occupied by his career as a statistician. In the twentieth century, he took his place among the full-time paid professionals who were employed by cultural institutions. The changes in his career thus served as a paradigm of the events that transformed the historical profession.

References:

[Clarence S. Brigham], "Worthington Chauncey Ford," *Proceedings of the American Antiquarian Society,* new series, 51 (1941): 10-14;

L. H. Butterfield, "Worthington Chauncey Ford, Editor," *Proceedings of the Massachusetts Historical Society,* 83 (1971): 46-82;

Stewart Mitchell, "Worthington Chauncey Ford," *Proceedings of the Massachusetts Historical Society,* 69 (1947-1950): 407-411;

"Worthington Chauncey Ford," *American Historical Review,* 46 (June 1941): 1012-1014.

Papers:
The great bulk of Ford's papers are at the New York Public Library. Many additional papers are at the Massachusetts Historical Society.

Henry Harrisse

(24 March 1829-13 May 1910)

John J. Winberry
University of South Carolina

SELECTED BOOKS: *An Essay on the Literary Institution Best Adapted to the Present Wants and Interests of Our Country* (Columbia, S.C.: Gibbes, 1857);

Bibliotheca Barlowiana (New York, 1864);

Notes on Columbus (New York: Privately printed, 1865);

Bibliotheca Americana Vetustissima. A Description of Works Relating to America, Published Between the Years 1492 and 1551 (New York: Philes, 1866);

D. Fernando Cólon, historiador de su padre. Ensayo crítico (Sevilla: Tarasco, 1871);

Additions (Paris: Tross, 1872);

Fernand Colomb, sa vie, ses oeuvres; essai critique (Paris: Tross, 1872);

Notes pour servir à l'histoire, à la bibliographie et à la cartographie de la Nouvelle-France et des pays adjacents 1545-1700 (Paris: Tross, 1872);

Jean et Sébastien Cabot, leur origine et leurs voyages: Étude d'histoire critique (Paris: Leroux, 1882);

Les Corte-Real et leurs voyages au Nouveau-Monde (Paris: Leroux, 1883);

Christophe Colomb; Son origine, sa vie, ses voyages, sa famille et ses descendants, 2 volumes (Paris: Leroux, 1884, 1885);

The Discovery of North America: A Critical, Documentary, and Historic Investigation (London: Stevens, 1892);

Americus Vespuccius; A Critical and Documentary Review of Two Recent English Books Concerning That Navigator (London: Stevens, 1895);

John Cabot, the Discoverer of North America, and Sebastian, His Son; A Chapter of the Maritime History of England Under the Tudors, 1496-1557 (London: Stevens, 1896);

The Diplomatic History of America: Its First Chapter 1452-1493-1494 (London: Stevens, 1897);

Découverte et évolution cartographique de Terre-Neuve et des pays circonvoisins 1497-1501-1769; Essais de géographie historique et documentaire (London: Stevens, Son & Stiles/Paris: Welter, 1900).

PERIODICAL PUBLICATION: "Columbus in a

Nutshell," *New York Commercial Advertiser,* 9 July and 16 July 1864.

Henry Harrisse died on 13 May 1910; according to the dictates of his will, his body was cremated, and there were no obsequies, no death notices, and no mourning. He had requested that his ashes not be collected, but French law required their interment, and they were buried in an unmarked urn at Père-Lachaise in Paris. So ended the life of the historian-bibliographer of American exploration and discovery, a life that was devoted to intellectual debate and controversy but also characterized in the later years by a largely self-imposed loneliness and isolation. Almost five months after his death, a brief notice appeared in the *American Historical Review*. The anonymous author wrote for Harrisse a most fitting epitaph: "His fame was deserved by exactness of scholarship and unusual range in the search of materials, but was perhaps heightened by controversies to which his outspokenness and pungency of expression gave frequent rise, and in which he took evident delight." The Library of Congress bibliography of his works records ninety-four books, articles, monographs, and papers, of which eighty dealt with American history. His studies covered a range of topics related to early American discoveries but concentrated on John and Sebastian Cabot and Christopher Columbus. By the time of his death, Harrisse was recognized by historians on both sides of the Atlantic.

Harrisse (the original spelling was Herisse, but he Anglicized it about 1857) was born in Paris, on 24 March 1829, of a Jewish father, Abraham, from Russia and a Catholic mother, Annette Marcus Prague Herisse, from Paris. Little is known of his early years; he spoke very little of his parents or his childhood, perhaps because he was sensitive about his Semitic heritage. In 1847 he was in Charleston, South Carolina, undoubtedly having arrived in the United States some years before, and accepted a teaching position at Mount Zion Academy in Winnsboro, South Carolina. He taught there for several years and in September 1853 was appointed instructor of French at the University of North Carolina at Chapel Hill. South Carolina College in Columbia awarded him the A.M. degree in 1853. Although the college catalogue identified it as an honorary degree, President James H. Thornwell wrote later that Harrisse had "submitted exercises . . . which sufficiently evince[d] his fitness to be made a master."

Harrisse's tenure at North Carolina soon involved him in controversy and frenetic activity. Expected to attend chapel regularly, he rebelled against the narrow Presbyterianism that characterized the service. Outraged at one sermon in which the minister quoted Descartes's "Cogito ergo sum" ("I think, therefore I am") but showed no real understanding of its meaning, Harrisse sat down to translate Descartes's philosophical works. The result was a 3,200-page manuscript, which found no publisher because of fear it would not sell. During this time, however, Harrisse contributed several pieces dealing with philosophy and French writers to the *North American Review, Southern Quarterly Review*, and, under the nom de plume Gilbert, to the *North Carolina University Magazine*. In 1854 and 1855 he prepared *An Essay on the Literary Institution Best Adapted to the Present Wants and Interests of Our Country* (1857), outlining his idea of the structure of a collegiate institution, its general curriculum, and its disciplinary regulations. Besides such literary activities, he was involved in a number of disputes. He had little respect for the young Southern gentlemen who filled his classes but who had greater interest in a variety of nonacademic, extracurricular activities. His sentiments perhaps were best expressed in his essay on the literary institution when he discussed the students of his hypothetical college: "It is the collegian's nature to be prone to idleness, to consider study as a severe infliction and the college discipline as a tyranny, which he constantly and ingeniously strives to elude." The students mimicked his French accent and caused numerous disturbances, and his faculty colleagues gave little support to his attempts to reprimand or suspend them. He finally presented a lengthy and condemnatory memorial to the trustees of the university minutely detailing his criticisms regarding the poor quality of education and the total lack of discipline at Chapel Hill. As he later wrote, "I raised the devil generally on the board of trustees and faculty of the University by my strenuous efforts to improve the curriculum and pedagogical methods according to a system of my own." On other issues, he cast the sole dissenting vote against a resolution criticizing Professor Benjamin Hedrick for speaking in favor of John Frémont, the "Black Republican" candidate for president, in 1856 and directly opposed the university president on the appointment of two tutors in the department of foreign languages. His faculty support had eroded completely, and in October 1856 the university gladly accepted one of his often proffered resignations. "I had in the meanwhile graduated in the law school," Harrisse recalled, "and soon after left the d--d place, never to see it again!"

Harrisse went to Washington and took a temporary position as professor of French at Georgetown University during the academic year 1856-1857. He had become disenchanted with writings on philosophy after his experience with the Descartes translation and intended to pursue a career in the law. He consulted a range of well-known individuals in Washington, and Stephen Douglas convinced him of the opportunities in Illinois. He moved to Chicago and opened his law practice in September 1857. Douglas gave him no support, however, and Harrisse spent most of his time worrying about how to raise the four dollars to pay each week's board. He returned to writing and contributed pieces to local newspapers, an activity that certainly did not enhance his reputation as a lawyer. Finally, however, he received a case involving a city lot. He reviewed the entire body of law regarding property and prepared an erudite presentation. He argued it cogently but soon observed that the judge was not listening to him; instead he was reading a newspaper. In an autobiographical letter written to Samuel L. M. Barlow in 1884, Harrisse recalled how he "hurried the conclusions of [his] . . . argument, handed him the brief, bowed respectfully, withdrew,—and lost the case." It undoubtedly was a hard blow for the young attorney.

His luck soon turned, however, when he encountered the agent of a Spanish bank who had been sent to Chicago to dispose of some property that the bank had acquired in a legal settlement. The old gentleman spoke no English, and Harrisse took care of the entire matter with such efficiency that he was offered a position as North American correspondent for the bank's Havana branch. By 1861, he had moved to New York and begun a desultory practice of law. His day involved but a few hours devotion to business for which the bank paid him a monthly retainer; he had become a regular contributor to the *North American Review*, and he was writing also for the *Atlantic Monthly*. He described this period of his life in a letter of July 1861: "I don't think there ever was a man who enjoyed as much independence as I do at this moment."

Although Harrisse continued to write, he persistently had difficulty in finding publishers for his works on the philosophy of history and related studies. Many years later in his autobiography he wrote of a decision he made during this period: "The thought then struck me that history afforded yet a field of investigations, provided an attempt was made to ascertain the degree of precision which might be imparted to the narrative of events and the description of historical characters." He began writing about Christopher Columbus and published two articles in the *New York Commercial Advertiser* under the general title "Columbus in a Nutshell." His research had led him in 1863 to his first meeting with Samuel L. M. Barlow, a successful lawyer who was just beginning to develop a reputation as a collector of Americana. Harrisse wanted to consult Barlow's copy of Peter Martyr's writings and soon developed a close relationship with the older man, spending days on end poring over his collection. In 1864 he published *Bibliotheca Barlowiana*, a small volume cataloguing Barlow's collection; only four copies were printed. His research led eventually to the publication in 1865,

with Barlow's financial support, of *Notes on Columbus*. Harrisse later expressed his dissatisfaction with this early effort, but growing out of it was an important realization: "the character of Columbus, both as a man and a discoverer, could not be fully understood without first possessing an adequate knowledge of the main facts connected with the history of scientific thoughts and aspirations as well as political and economic necessities in the XV century." With the continued support and counsel of Barlow, Harrisse developed the historiographic approach that would characterize his work for the next four decades. Specifically, he committed himself to studying and evaluating the original documents with an almost legalistic objectivity to determine their actual meaning, exclusive of the published commentaries on them; Harrisse's method became a strict system of scholarship that later led him to libraries and archives throughout Europe. In New York he visited major private collections to make a record of all the volumes in them regarding America that were published from 1493 to 1551 and to take notes of references to other items of interest. The result of these labors was the monumental *Bibliotheca Americana Vetustissima* (1866). The title can be translated as "Bibliography of Ancient Americana," and Harrisse intended it as just that, a bibliographic review of all the publications about America during the decades just after the New World's discovery. It was a major contribution because it verified the existence of over 300 items, three times the number ever before recorded, and because Harrisse critically evaluated the authors, the various editions, and the importance of each citation, extensively documenting all of his comments. Acclaimed both in America and Europe, it evinced the thoroughness and scholarly accuracy that would characterize Harrisse's later publications, and it remains an important reference for Americanists even today. Despite such importance, it sold few copies, and the original printing (450 copies) was still in stock as late as 1899. This too was an experience that would repeat itself throughout Harrisse's career.

The publication of the *Bibliotheca Americana Vetustissima* involved some complications, and Harrisse even accused the publisher of a swindle. At the same time, he lost his position with the bank because an officer of the Havana branch absconded with its funds. As a result, with savings of $2,500, he decided to travel to Europe. When he arrived in Paris, he found himself to be something of a celebrity, as he put it in a letter to his close friend John Johnson in Charleston, "a very great man of wondrous learning and eloquence." He was caught up in the social scene, but his funds quickly dwindled. Still, he was able to tour the major libraries in Italy, Vienna, and Munich in search of documents and rare books. The result of this labor was the publication in 1872 of *Additions*. It included 186 entries, of which about two-thirds had not been included in the *Bibliotheca Americana Vetustissima*; the rest were fuller commentaries on items that originally had just been mentioned.

In September 1868 Harrisse returned to New York, but soon reported a sense of isolation, probably missing the limelight of Paris. He decided that to be successful in New York would require a tremendous effort, an effort that could make him successful anywhere he lived. Within a year he was again in Paris and soon ensconced at 30 Rue Cambacérès, his address for the remaining forty years of his life. His first six months in Paris were difficult, but he sought out books for Barlow and resumed his law practice. He was one of the few American lawyers in France and had a close friend, Henry Vignaud, who worked at the American embassy for many years. Vignaud had arrived in Paris some years before as a representative of the Confederate government and later joined the United States legation. Their mutual interest in early discoveries strengthened their relationship, and Vignaud directed many American businessmen to Harrisse. Harrisse's practice proved lucrative, and by 1877 he had saved over $40,000 in gold from his fees, even though he reported that his duties occupied only about two hours a day.

Within a few years of his return to Europe, France was at war with Germany and Paris was under siege. Unable to leave, Harrisse focused his research on early French exploration in Canada and prowled the French archives, finding a rich cache in the Depot des Cartes et Plans des Colonies (Depository of Colonial Maps and Surveys). This last activity led him into difficulties with the secret police who thought he was a Prussian spy making copies of the plans of French fortifications. That these forts had been surrendered over one hundred years earlier seemed not to impress the police, and the American ambassador had to intervene in Harrisse's behalf. Harrisse's volume on Canada, *Notes pour servir à l'histoire, à la bibliographie et à la cartographie de la Nouvelle-France et des pays adjacents 1545-1700*, his first written in French, was published in 1872. In the New World, he later wrote, it sold but thirty copies.

In the early 1870s, Harrisse began to show aspects of his character that had surfaced briefly while he was at North Carolina but would unfortunately haunt him the rest of his life. These were his egotism and acerbity. During his research at Archives de la Marine, he came into conflict with Pierre Margry, the archival director, who held back many important documents from American scholars while he completed his own six-volume work on early French exploration. Harrisse wrote of him, "This Margry was the personification of the French pen-pusher, of the narrowest and most intolerable sort. Without talent, without clarity of intellect, and of unparalleled vanity, his curatorship of the Archives was disastrous." It would not be his only criticism of European librarians and colleagues.

Harrisse, at this time, also began to move in the social and intellectual circles of Paris. During the Franco-Prussian War he had corresponded with George Sand. His opinion of himself apparently was considerable, an attitude that expressed itself frequently. Gustave Flaubert wrote in 1871, "I have met the unavoidable Harrisse, a man who knows everybody and knows everything, theatre, fiction, finances, politics, etc."

In May 1871, after the conclusion of the Franco-Prussian War, Harrisse was able to leave Paris. He wanted to continue his research on Spanish exploration of the New World and left for Seville to work in the Columbus Library. Soon, however, he was embroiled in another dispute, this time in regard to the poor administration of the library. Many of the volumes were being taken from it and sold in Paris bookstalls, and Harrisse argued that such a fate already had befallen at least half the collection. He published in 1871, in Spanish, his *D. Fernando Colón, historiador de su padre*. In it he argued that Fernando Columbus was not the author of *Historie*, a biography of his father. This volume apparently had been published first in Italian in 1571, some 32 years after Fernando Columbus's death, and there was no evidence of an earlier Spanish manuscript. Prevailing scholarly opinion, however, opposed Harrisse's argument, and he himself ultimately abandoned it. Between his criticism of the library and his calling attention to the deficiencies of Spanish historical scholarship, he alienated many Hispanic colleagues and strained relations with other friends as he vigorously supported his thesis of Fernando's doubtful authorship.

Harrisse had invested a good deal of money in researching his book on Columbus but realized virtually no return. He later wrote, "I imagine that the thickness of the paper on which the work is printed alone prevents the many copies I have presented to friends and amateurs from being put to a certain use, needless here to mention." In an 1874 letter he detailed his disillusionment with studying Americana: "Abuse, privations, money lost, time wasted and contempt have been my only rewards. . . . I don't care a d-d! and start anew, but in a new field of action. . . ."

Soon after the end of the Franco-Prussian War, Harrisse had made the acquaintance of the French Egyptologist Gaston Maspero. Long intrigued by the hieroglyphics on the Paris obelisk, he was determined to study ancient Egypt. His letters reflected his newfound excitement, and he avidly studied Egyptology for over three years. He translated inscriptions on obelisks and monuments, as well as texts, but found them of little historical interest. He did begin research on Amenhotep IV of the Eighteenth Dynasty and published announcements of a forthcoming book. Harrisse's boldness stunned many scholars in the field who had devoted their entire professional lives to the topic's study. By 1878, however, Harrisse had turned away from Egyptology, because, he claimed, of tremendous eyestrain from reading engravings. More probably, he had realized that the knowledge he could acquire within a few years would not allow him to add anything new to the field.

In 1878 a new controversy, involving the location of the remains of Christopher Columbus, drew his attention back to Americana. Buried originally in the cathedral of Santo Domingo, the body supposedly had been removed to Cuba in 1795 and later carried to the cathedral at Salamanca in Spain. The archbishop of Santo Domingo reviewed the records and concluded, however, that the Spaniards had taken the wrong body in 1795 and that Columbus still was buried at Santo Domingo. Harrisse with his characteristic thoroughness and pugnacity waded into the dispute and supported the archbishop, although he later expressed doubts about what definitely could be established about the location of the remains.

In 1884 and 1885 Harrisse's *Christophe Colomb; Son origine, sa vie, ses voyages, sa famille et ses descendants* appeared. This two-volume work on the life of Columbus was based on Harrisse's intensive archival research in Spain, and it brought many previously unknown documents to the attention of scholars. After publication of *Christophe Colomb*, Harrisse turned to the discovery of North America as a research topic. He gave no attention to the Norsemen, because their settlement had been short-lived and had left no cartographic record. In 1892 he produced *The Discovery of North America*,

noted by some critics as Harrisse's major work. In it, he again methodically reviewed cartographic and written documents to reach conclusions in support of John Cabot as the discoverer of North America, but once more his work reflected an intellectual contentiousness. As one scholar who interviewed him prior to the book's publication noted, "he professes that it will revolutionize the story of the discovery of North America, and prove Sebastian Cabot a humbug and a liar!"

In 1892 Harrisse was the recipient of two important honors. In December he was elected unanimously as honorary corresponding member to the Royal Society of Göttingen in Germany. In October, in honor of the four hundredth anniversary of Columbus's discovering the New World, the French Government bestowed on him the Cross of the Legion of Honor. Harrisse took umbrage over his not having been made an officer in the Legion and ascribed the affront to his Semitic parentage. He had been sensitive to anti-Semitism throughout his life and later wrote of his distress over the Dreyfus affair.

The celebration of the Columbian discovery involved Harrisse in several other ways. He had been selected by the Royal Italian Commission to prepare a lengthy text on various documents related to Columbus. He had worked on it for almost two years and put together 163 dossiers, but he had abruptly resigned, citing "the craft, narrow mindedness and ingratitude of that contemptible Italian race!" He also had been invited by the United States government to assist the 1893 Chicago World's Columbian Exposition in gathering information on such items as the house where Columbus was born, portraits, sailing charts, and other materials that could be included in the exhibition. Harrisse wrote of his reaction, "I am the last man on earth . . . whom they should ask for such claptrap." It reminded him of the publisher who offered him $100 for a history of Columbus as a youth, to whom Harrisse replied, "I would pay anyone five times that amount for the necessary data to pen such a work!" A great many books were published in anticipation of the anniversary, and many came under Harrisse's scrutiny. He was caustic in his criticism of various works and willingly became involved in controversies related to Columbus. One dispute involved which of two individuals had an authentic portrait of Columbus; Harrisse ended up attacking both contenders. One scholar who debated the birthplace of Columbus was dismissed as "an absolute idiot." In fact, Harrisse became increasingly acrimonious in talking and writing about others and contemptuously referred to several individuals as *mufles*, a French word meaning stupid persons. In 1894 he reviewed for the *London Atheneum* two books written about Amerigo Vespucci. The review was not published; "as I give fits to both of them, the editor dares not print my article now!" Perhaps Harrisse's most extreme reaction was to *La lettre et la carte de Toscanelli* (*Toscanelli and Columbus*), a book written by his close friend Henry Vignaud and published in 1901. Harrisse told a Canadian archivist, "It is not worth the paper it is printed on." It was a general attitude that won him no new friends and drove away many former colleagues. Vignaud, for instance, later severed his relations with Harrisse and spoke not one word to him over the last years of his life.

In 1890 Justin Winsor, the Boston librarian, visited Paris and interviewed Harrisse. He described him as "a short, stoutish man, with a rather pleasant countenance, gray-hair and with English side whiskers. He impresses you as his books do, somewhat over-confident, praising himself and his accomplishment in language not so much excessive, as fitted to be the testimony of others, rather than his own assertion." Harrisse chafed especially at the neglect that American historians had showed his works and commented to Winsor on how little he had earned for years of endeavor. A glass frame in his study held the $3.00 bill which he had received for his first article in the *North American Review*, and he noted that he had earned but 484 francs since. He showed Winsor the dedication for his new book, "To the five persons who have taken the trouble to read my writings." Harrisse seemed obsessed with this neglect and had written earlier of an instance in which he had sent free copies of a recent book to 20 individuals, postage paid, but not five had responded with a card of acknowledgment.

In 1896 Harrisse published the culmination of his study of the history of American discovery, *John Cabot, The Discoverer of North America, and Sebastian, His Son; A Chapter of the Maritime History of England Under the Tudors, 1496-1557*. George Parker Winship wrote this often quoted comment, "It is not a history; it is rather a laboratory manual, in which the student finds revealed each step in the process of thought, through which the material of history has been forced in order that it may be made to render up the truth contained in it." His last major volume, *Découverte et évolution cartographique de Terre-Neuve et des pays circonvoisins 1497-1501-1769*, was published in 1900. It dealt with the history of discovery along the Atlantic coast of Can-

ada through the analysis of Portuguese and French maps and the surveys of James Cook. Harrisse continued research, especially on Amerigo Vespucci, for the rest of his life and intended a volume on the Italian navigator to complete his triumvirate of early American explorers (Columbus, Cabot, Vespucci).

Harrisse became increasingly disconsolate after the turn of the century. He had suffered what was probably a stroke as early as 1880, but he had slowly recovered. Pulmonary congestion and bronchitis severely cut into his activities and were common complaints in his letters after 1900. He wrote in 1903 of his personal situation, "I have ceased to go into society, and scarcely know anybody at present." He had never married, which he regretted; but his lack of finances in his early years made him unable to support a wife and children. When he did have money, he believed himself too old. His loneliness was brought on by his own attitude more than by his illness. According to his former publisher H. Welter, he showed "a violent aggressive and vindictive character" even to friends and colleagues. Few visited or communicated with him in his last years, and his attacks on Margry and others closed the doors of his beloved archives to him. What was the cause of this behavior? In *Three Americanists* (1939) Randolph G. Adams ascribes it to Harrisse's failing health and attendant frustrations as he became weaker. Welter, however, believed that it was due to Harrisse's not having attained the recognition he envied and wanted and that he lashed out at others in brutish reprisal. In Welter's recollection he was especially savage toward "those who dared touch the subjects already treated by him and which he thought belonged exclusively to his domain." He wrote his will three times and, with no explanation, brusquely left out individuals to whom he had earlier promised bequests. The last years of his life were painfully lonely, and he died in 1910.

Harrisse published prodigiously in the field of exploration and discovery, and his works were well researched and solidly supported by documentary references. He fixed definitely the discoveries of the Cabots, exploded some myths about Columbus, made many contributions to other geographic questions, and brought order to the confusion of early maps. He was highly critical of other writings but readily backed down from his own ideas when proven wrong. Although his contribution to the history of discovery was considerable, Harrisse remains little known. One wonders whether his forty-year residence in Paris, his books

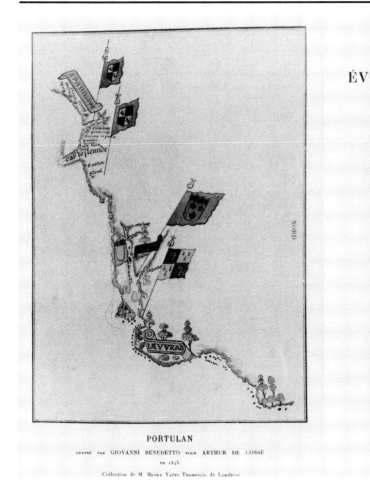

PORTULAN

DRESSÉ PAR GIOVANNI BENEDETTO POUR ARTHUR DE COSSÉ
en 1543

(Collection de M. Henry Yates Thompson, de Londres)

DÉCOUVERTE

ET

ÉVOLUTION CARTOGRAPHIQUE

DE

TERRE-NEUVE

ET DES

PAYS CIRCONVOISINS

1497—1501—1769

ESSAIS DE GÉOGRAPHIE HISTORIQUE ET DOCUMENTAIRE

PAR

HENRY HARRISSE

LONDON

HENRY STEVENS, SON & STILES

39, GREAT RUSSELL STREET, W.C.

PARIS

H. WELTER, ÉDITEUR

4, RUE BERNARD-PALISSY, 4

MDCCCC

Frontispiece and title page for Harrisse's last major work, based on maps by Portuguese and French cartographers and on the surveys of British explorer James Cook

in French, Italian, and Spanish which were published in Europe, and especially his irascibility diminished his impact on American historians. Nevertheless, Justin Winsor concluded his comments on his meeting with Harrisse with a most appropriate statement: "Despite all his faults or weaknesses, Harrisse deserves well of everybody interested in the earliest stages of American history, and no one else has done so much to illucidate it since the days of [Alexander von] Humboldt."

Bibliography and Biography:

A. Growoll, *Henry Harrisse, Biographical and Bibliographical Sketch* (New York: Dibdin Club, 1899);

Henry Vignaud, *Henry Harrisse; Étude biographique et morale* (Paris: Charles Chadenat, 1912)—includes bibliography, pp. 27-82.

References:

Randolph G. Adams, *Three Americanists* (Philadelphia: University of Pennsylvania Press, 1939), pp. 1-33;

Joseph A. Boromé, ed., "An Interview Between Justin Winsor and Henry Harrisse," *Hispanic-American Historical Review*, 32, no. 3 (1952): 376-379;

"Harrisse Bequest," *Report of the Librarian of Congress for 1915* (Washington, D.C.: Government Printing Office, 1915), pp. 31-35;

Edgar Knight, ed., "Henry Harrisse on Collegiate Education," *North Carolina Historical Review*, 24, no. 1 (1947): 55-111.

Papers:

Major collections of Harrisse's papers are located at the Library of Congress and in the Southern

Historical Collection, University of North Carolina at Chapel Hill. Additional materials are at the William L. Clements Library, University of Michigan, and in the John Johnson Papers at the Charleston, South Carolina, Library Society.

Charles Homer Haskins

Sally N. Vaughn
University of Houston

BIRTH: Meadville, Pennsylvania, 21 December 1870, to George Washington and Rachel A. McClintock Haskins.

EDUCATION: A.B., Johns Hopkins University, 1887; Ph.D., Johns Hopkins University, 1890.

MARRIAGE: 11 July 1912 to Clare Allen; children: George Lee, Charles Allen, Clare Elisabeth.

AWARDS AND HONORS: Chairman, American Council of Learned Societies, 1920-1926; Elected member of the American Philosophical Society, 1921; president, American Historical Association, 1922; president, Medieval Academy of America, 1926-1927; Honorary degrees, Harvard, 1908, 1924; University of Wisconsin, 1910; Allegheny College, 1915; University of Strasbourg, 1919; University of Padua, 1922; University of Manchester, 1922; University of Paris, 1926; University of Louvain, 1927; University of Caen, 1932; officer, French Legion of Honor; commander, Order of the Crown of Belgium.

DEATH: Cambridge, Massachusetts, 14 May 1937.

SELECTED BOOKS: *A History of Higher Education in Pennsylvania,* by Haskins and William I. Hull (Washington, D.C.: Government Printing Office, 1902);
The Historical Curriculum in Colleges (New York: Knickerbocker, 1904);
The Normans in European History (Boston & New York: Houghton Mifflin, 1915);
Norman Institutions (Cambridge: Harvard University Press, 1918);
Some Problems of the Peace Conference, by Haskins and Robert Howard Lord (Cambridge: Harvard University Press, 1920);
The Rise of Universities (New York: Holt, 1923);

Studies in the History of Mediaeval Science (Cambridge: Harvard University Press, 1924);
The Renaissance of the Twelfth Century (Cambridge: Harvard University Press, 1927);
Studies in Mediaevel Culture (Oxford: Clarendon Press, 1929).

OTHER: "The Yazoo Land Companies," in *Papers of the American Historical Association*, 5 (1891), pp. 59-103;

"The Study of History in Schools, being the Report to the American Historical Association by the Committee of Seven," by Haskins and others, in *Annual Report of the American Historical Association for the Year 1898* (Washington, D.C.: Government Printing Office, 1899), pp. 474-564;

"Report of the Conference on the First Year of College Work in History," in *Annual Report of the American Historical Association for the Year 1905* (Washington, D.C.: Government Printing Office, 1906), pp. 147-174;

"A List of Text-Books from the Close of the Twelfth Century," in *Harvard Studies in Classical Philology*, 20 (1909), pp. 75-94;

"The Study of History in Secondary Schools; Report of the Committee of Five," by Haskins and others, in *Annual Report of the American Historical Association for the Year 1910* (New York: Macmillan, 1911), pp. 209-242;

"Quelques problèmes de l'histoire des institutions anglo-normandes," in *Compte rendu des travaux du Congrès du Millénaire de la Normandie*, 1 (1912), pp. 562-570;

"History—As a College and University Study," in *A Cyclopedia of Education*, edited by Paul Monroe, 5 volumes (New York: Macmillan, 1911-1913), III: 282-288;

"The Manor of Portswood Under Henry I," in *Mélanges d'histoire offerts à M. Charles Bemont* (Paris: Alcan, 1913), pp. 78-83;

"Mediaeval Versions of the *Posterior Analytics*," in *Harvard Studies in Classical Philology*, 25 (1914), pp. 87-105;

"The Place of the Newer Humanities in the College Curriculum," in *The American College* (New York: Holt, 1915), pp. 41-57;

"Pascalis Romanus: Petrus Chrysolanus," in *Byzantion*, 2 (1925), pp. 231-236;

"Magister Gualterius Esculanus," in *Mélanges d'histoire du moyen age offerts à M. Ferdinand Lot* (Paris: Champion, 1925), pp. 245-257;

"Henry II as a Patron of Literature," in *Essays in Medieval History Presented to Thomas Frederick Tout*, edited by A. G. Little and F. M. Powicke (Manchester: Privately printed, 1925), pp. 71-77;

"An Early Bolognese Formulary," in *Mélanges d'histoire offerts à Henri Pirenne* (Brussels: Vromant, 1926), pp. 201-210;

"An Italian Master Bernard," in *Essays in History Presented to Reginald Lane Pool*, edited by

H. W. C. Davis (Oxford: Clarendon Press, 1926), pp. 221-226;

"Formularies of the Officialite of Rouen," in *Mélanges Paul Fournier* (Paris: Recueil Sirey, 1929), pp. 359-362;

"The Graduate School of Arts and Sciences," in *The Development of Harvard University Since the Inauguration of President Eliot, 1869-1929*, edited by Samuel Eliot Morison (Cambridge: Harvard University Press, 1930), pp. 451-462.

PERIODICAL PUBLICATIONS: "The Vatican Archives," *American Historical Review*, 2 (October 1896): 40-58;

"The Vatican Archives," *Catholic University Bulletin*, 3 (1897): 177-196;

"The Life of Medieval Students as Illustrated by Their Letters," *American Historical Review*, 3 (January 1898): 203-229;

"Opportunities for American Students of History at Paris," *American Historical Review*, 3 (April 1898): 418-430;

"Robert le Bougre and the Beginnings of the Inquisition in Northern France," *American Historical Review*, 7 (April and July 1902): 437-457, 631-652;

"The Early Norman Jury," *American Historical Review*, 8 (July 1903): 613-640;

"The University of Paris in the Sermons of the Thirteenth Century," *American Historical Review*, 10 (October 1904): 1-27;

"The Sources for the History of the Papal Penitentiary," *American Journal of Theology*, 9 (1905): 421-450;

"Knight-Service in Normandy in the Eleventh Century," *English Historical Review*, 22 (October 1907): 636-649;

"The Norman 'Consuetudines et Iusticie' of William the Conqueror," *English Historical Review*, 23 (July 1908): 502-508;

"Normandy under William the Conqueror," *American Historical Review*, 14 (April 1909): 453-476;

"The Administration of Normandy under Henry I," in *English Historical Review*, 24 (April 1909): 209-231;

"A Canterbury Monk at Constantinople, c. 1090," *English Historical Review*, 25 (April 1910): 293-295;

"Adelard of Bath," *English Historical Review*, 26 (July 1911): 491-498;

"England and Sicily in the Twelfth Century," *English Historical Review*, 26 (July 1911): 433-447; 26 (October 1911): 641-665;

"The Abacus and the King's Curia," *English Historical Review*, 27 (January 1912): 101-106;

"Normandy under Geoffrey Plantagenet," *English Historical Review*, 27 (July 1912): 417-444;

"Nimrod the Astronomer," *Romanic Review*, 5 (July-September 1914): 203-212;

"Moses of Bergamo," *Byzantinische Zeitschrift*, 23, no. 1 (1914): 133-142;

"The Government of Normandy under Henry II," *American Historical Review*, 20 (October 1914 and January 1915): 24-42 and 277-291;

"The Reception of Arabic Science in England," *English Historical Review*, 30 (January 1915): 56-69;

"The Materials for the Reign of Robert I of Normandy," *English Historical Review*, 31 (April 1916): 257-268;

"L'Histoire de France aux Etats-Unis," *Revue de Paris*, 27 (1 février 1920): 654-672;

"The Greek Element in the Renaissance of the Twelfth Century," *American Historical Review*, 25 (July 1920): 603-615;

"The 'De Arte Venandi cum Avibus' of Emperor Frederick II," *English Historical Review*, 36 (July 1921): 334-355;

"Michael Scot and Frederick II," *Isis*, 4 (October 1921): 250-275;

"Science at the Court of the Emperor Frederick II," *American Historical Review*, 27 (July 1922): 669-694;

"King Harald's Books," *English Historical Review*, 37 (July 1922): 398-400;

"Arabic Science in Western Europe," *Isis*, 7 (March 1925): 478-485;

"The Spread of Ideas in the Middle Ages," *Speculum*, 1 (January 1926): 19-30;

"The Latin Literature of Sport," *Speculum*, 2 (July 1927): 235-252;

"The *Alchemy* Ascribed to Michael Scot," *Isis*, 10 (January 1928): 350-359;

"Latin Literature under Frederick II," *Speculum*, 3 (April 1928): 129-151.

Charles Homer Haskins was one of a small group of American historians who initiated the study of medieval history at the professional level in the United States and one of the first American scholars of medieval history to win the high praise of nearly all his European contemporaries. The distinguished German classicist Theodor Mommsen, grandson of the great historian, judged that Haskins "represents the rare case of a man who combined the qualities of the efficient organizer, the original scholar, and the great teacher." The

eminent French medievalist F. Jonan des Longrais said "without exaggeration" that Charles Homer Haskins was "truly the soul of the renascence of mediaeval studies in the United States." Perhaps the greatest tribute to Haskins's "refined and balanced scholarship," his attractive writing—"neither light nor expansive"—and his "striking ideas, the far-reaching speculations which we expect in the great historian," came from Sir Frederick Maurice Powicke in his 1925 *English Historical Review* assessment of Haskins's *Studies in the History of Mediaeval Science* (1924): "As an American, he is free from our tradition of insularity; . . . yet his mind and outlook are English in the best sense of the word. . . ." In the early 1920s this was high praise indeed from a respected British scholar who was then operating within a one-hundred-year tradition of "scientific" history well established in Europe but just recently beginning to take root in the United States. George Burton Adams, Henry Adams, and Charles Gross had made the first tentative steps in planting the new doctrines and disciplines at Harvard; Henry Charles Lea, a respected private scholar in Philadelphia, had also helped to prepare the ground. But it was Haskins who rooted medieval history firmly in the curriculum of American universities and won the respect of the international community of scholars.

It is in this context that Powicke praised Haskins's thorough knowledge of the archives: "he knows his way about the manuscript collections, great and small, of Europe." "A pupil of [Charles Victor] Langlois," as Powicke described him, "[Haskins] would probably regard the French as his masters, but his best work is as massive as that of the great German scholars." For Powicke, Haskins was "a pioneer, yet a scrupulously tidy workman, . . . [whose *Studies in the History of Mediaeval Science*] will rank next to [R. L.] Poole's epoch-making volume as a study in method; in the use of new materials for the elucidation of old problems, it will be found . . . to have an importance comparable to that of [John Horace] Round's *Feudal England*." It was not the first time an American had gained respectability as a historian of European culture, for Gross and Lea were well regarded, but this praise was more effusive and Haskins's reputation was greater by several magnitudes than that of any American medieval historian before or since.

Haskins's writings not only became the foundation for general medieval studies in the United States; they also were formative influences for three important areas within medieval history—Normandy, science, and the "renaissance of the twelfth century." His *The Normans in European History* (1915) and *Norman Institutions* (1918) focused attention on eleventh- and twelfth-century Normandy as a rich area of study for sources of the institutions later developed in Norman England. One positive consequence of these books was to challenge British insularity and French exclusivity—to open the minds of each national group of scholars to a view of Normandy and England as a cross-channel empire, the parts of which could not be studied in isolation. These two books remain classics in Norman studies.

Haskins also gave impetus to the study of medieval science. For Europeans, he discovered new resources of unknown manuscripts in the archives of France, Italy, and Spain, as well as Germany. In America, he gave the new field vigor as a founder of the History of Science Society and its periodical *Isis*. In addition, Haskins almost single-handedly created a new historical concept and a fresh field for scholars with his interpretation of the High Middle Ages as the "Renaissance of the Twelfth Century." In 1928, one year after Haskins's book on the subject appeared, L. J. Paetow predicted that Haskins's interpretation would become "the standard . . . of a new intellectual movement, as was *Die Kultur der Renaissance in Italien*, by J [acob] Burckhardt, in 1860." He was partially right, for though Burckhardt's definition of Renaissance still persists in popular culture (and indeed among many Renaissance scholars) Haskins's views have largely prevailed, despite much debate and some revisionist thinking. Like Henri Pirenne's *Mohammed and Charlemagne* (1937), Haskins's book expounding his theory of medieval renaissance excited new inquiries, re-examinations of old materials, and searches for new evidence in many different areas. This work, too, is regarded as a classic.

Haskins was a man of boundless energy whose activities were by no means confined to the archives and the typewriter. Besides helping to establish the History of Science Society, he was a-founder of the Medieval Academy of America in 1925 and served as its president in 1926-1927. He became president of the American Historical Association in 1922, participated in the founding of the American Council of Learned Societies in 1920, and served as its chairman from 1920 to 1926. From 1908 to 1924 he was dean of the Harvard Graduate School of Arts and Sciences. In these positions he had a profound influence on the course of education in the United States. He served for many years on the selection committee for John Simon Guggenheim fellowships and was one of the prime architects in the remodeling of American secondary, undergraduate, and graduate education. As the intimate friend of three American presidents, Haskins became involved in government at the highest level, nationally and internationally. One of the aides to President Woodrow Wilson, he played an important role in the 1918-1919 Peace Conference at Versailles. In 1920, with Robert Howard Lord, Haskins wrote *Some Problems of the Peace Conference*, an eyewitness account that remains an important source for historians.

Charles Homer Haskins was born in Meadville, Pennsylvania, on 21 December 1870, to George Washington and Rachel A. McClintock Haskins. He was the oldest of three children. His father's family had come to Pennsylvania from England apparently in the eighteenth century. They settled first in Massachusetts or Connecticut, and then in Ticonderoga, New York, before moving to Meadville. His mother's family was Scotch-Irish. His father was a graduate of Allegheny College who moved from the position as superintendent of schools in Meadville to his alma mater, where he taught Greek and Latin from 1875 to 1886. Finally, he became a successful lawyer while continuing his teaching career.

George Washington Haskins was a conscientious father who spent a good deal of time and patience educating his son. He taught Latin to young Charles before the boy was five and Greek shortly thereafter. Haskins's intelligence, the classical education he had received from his father, and possibly also his father's position enabled him to enter Allegheny College at the age of thirteen in 1883. At this time American education was on the brink of a revolution.

Classical studies were a blend of literature, philology, and history, and history itself was dominated by a generation of romantics who saw its continuity as the unfolding of religious ideals and morals with freedom and democracy for all as the ultimate utopia to come. History in America was written with the emotions and intuition, and historical writing was regarded as an exercise in literary art. But in the early 1870s Henry Adams had been persuaded to come to Harvard as a professor of medieval history. Adams had only studied one year in Europe and claimed he knew nothing about its history, but he had been exposed to new beliefs and methods of objective historical inquiry just gaining their full vigor in Europe but largely unknown in the United States. These views were inspired by the scientific method and especially by the work of Charles Darwin. In Europe, history had come to be regarded as a social science, a discipline separate from literature, and emphasis was now given to two areas: the study of institutions (particularly political ones), and the use of the scientific method—accumulation of masses of data, objective observation, and the drawing of conclusions, unbiased by moral, religious, or political beliefs. Henry Adams brought these ideas to Harvard, where he initiated a new method of teaching: students were to meet strict qualifications for entry; they were to work primarily with original sources in narrow fields of inquiry; and they were to have free access to the Harvard library, which at that time was closely guarded by Harvard's librarians. Adams soon switched to American history, but was joined on the Harvard staff by Ephraim Emerton and Charles Gross, the former with a degree from the University of Leipzig and the latter with a degree from the University of Göttingen. Both taught European history on the European model.

The new scientific and institutional history was controversial in the United States. But to many eager young scholars it must have been exciting. To Haskins, weaned on the literature of the classics, it may well have appeared to be the key to many previously locked doors of understanding. At the end of his junior year at Allegheny in 1886, he tried to transfer to Harvard, but his application for admission was rejected because, at the age of fifteen, he was considered too young. Johns Hopkins University accepted him, and he received his A.B. there in 1887. Shortly thereafter, he traveled to Europe, where he studied in Berlin and Paris. His mentors at the École des Chartes in Paris included Charles Victor Langlois and Ferdinand Lot under whose guidance he seems to have begun his study in the history of medieval thought and institutions. The first fruits of his medieval work, an article entitled "The Vatican Archives," appeared in 1896 in the *American Historical Review*, and his first piece of historical research, "The Life of Medieval Students as Illustrated by Their Letters," appeared two years later in the same journal. It may well be significant that Haskins, still in his teens, should have chosen to investigate medieval student life. Whether his own inclinations or the guidance of his teachers led him in this direction, it seems singularly appropriate for Haskins to have begun his prodigious investigation of nearly every archive in Europe with a study of documents written by the youngest of his medieval subjects.

Haskins chose not to study in Europe for his Ph.D., electing to remain at Johns Hopkins instead.

He received his Ph.D. after only three years (1887-1890) at the age of nineteen. His work at Johns Hopkins centered around the famous seminar of Herbert Baxter Adams. Adams had been one of the many American students who had journeyed to Europe to study in the 1870s. He had received his Ph.D. with highest honors at the University of Heidelberg in 1876. That same year Johns Hopkins opened its doors, emphasizing graduate studies and hiring as instructors mainly European-trained scholars in an effort to emulate the Continental universities and their latest teaching and research methods. Adams's studies at the universities of Göttingen, Berlin, and Heidelberg eminently qualified him to teach the new scientific history at Johns Hopkins. It may well have been Adams who influenced young Haskins to study in Europe. When Haskins returned to Johns Hopkins to begin graduate studies, he found Adams's seminar modeled on the German example. The seminar, or as Adams and his contemporaries called it, "seminary," was a new concept in education in the United States. Prior to the influx of German-trained scholars, there had been no specially organized programs of education for American postgraduate students. The seminar stressed small, intimate classes conducted in a setting that promoted close contact with the instructor and face-to-face discussion among participants.

It was in Adams's seminar that Haskins met Woodrow Wilson, Charles M. Andrews, and Frederick Jackson Turner who became his lifelong friends and associates. And Adams himself certainly served as one of young Haskins's role models. Adams's interest in American history was reflected in Haskins's choice of a dissertation topic: the Yazoo land companies. Like Adams, Haskins devoted a significant part of his career to the advancement and improvement of American higher education— by numerous publications, service as dean of the Harvard Graduate School of Arts and Sciences, and organizational work. As early as 1898 Haskins contributed an article entitled "Opportunities for American Students of History at Paris" to the *American Historical Review*, and in the same year he was appointed to the American Historical Association's Committee of Seven to report on and recommend changes in the study of history in American schools. Haskins contributed an appendix, "History in the French Lycées," to the final report of the committee, which was published in 1899 under the title "The Study of History in Schools."

Like Adams, also, Haskins had a career marked by intense involvement in the development

Haskins (far left) as a student in the graduate seminar of Herbert Baxter Adams, Johns Hopkins University, late 1880s. Adams, who directed Haskins's dissertation on the Yazoo land companies, is seated third from left.

of professional organizations for specialists in history; in several he played a founding role and held administrative posts. The strenuous critical analysis of one another's work among Adams's students continued long after they had left Johns Hopkins and this professional dialogue had lasting effects on Haskins as well.

Haskins's own work, from the beginning, was characterized by thorough scholarship in the archives; a well-rounded knowledge of recent scholarship; careful and accurate reporting; and judicious, unbiased conclusions, firmly based on manuscript sources which are often quoted in the original language. Sir Frederick Maurice Powicke called his work a model of scholarship, praising him for avoiding those "faults" that had marred the works of the "old school" romantic American historians: religious and political bias and conclusions unsupported by evidence. His Ph.D. dissertation is a case in point. Thoroughly researched, well documented, and tightly reasoned, according to several experts it has never been surpassed as the definitive work on the Yazoo land companies and

the dispute which led to the Supreme Court case of *Fletcher v. Peck* decided by Chief Justice John Marshall in the early 1800s. Haskins's treatment is a legal one, and he handles the legal questions and problems superbly. Haskins, during the course of his early academic career at Johns Hopkins, studied law, on the model of his father. By the time he received his A.B., he had mastered all the materials but was too young to be admitted to the bar, although he had completed all the requirements. He never reapplied for admission to the bar because by the time he had attained the requisite age of twenty-one, he had begun to devote his time to the study of medieval history as his life's work.

Haskins's work on the Yazoo land companies, first published in 1891 in *Papers of the American Historical Association* and reprinted later that year in book form, is still regarded as a classic in American constitutional law and history, especially because of its bearing on the separation of powers. Haskins tended to downplay the Yazoo piece, probably because he discontinued his legal studies. But when Haskins's son George Lee Haskins, now professor of law at the University of Pennsylvania, wrote his contribution to *History of the Supreme Court of the United States* (1981), he expressed amazement at the legal perceptions of a man under twenty writing of the background of *Fletcher v. Peck.* "He understood not only the problem of constitutionally mandated separation of powers, but the force of the Contract Clause of the Constitution" as well. Others, including Paul A. Freund, an authority on Constitutional law at Harvard, have expressed agreement with this statement.

Haskins began his teaching career at Johns Hopkins in 1889, even before he received his Ph.D. degree. He remained there only a short time, however, for in 1892 the University of Wisconsin hired him as a full professor to teach European history. There, his former Johns Hopkins fellow student Frederick Jackson Turner was directing the study of American history. As Haskins later told his son George, he felt that American history was being preempted by Adams and Turner and thus welcomed the opportunity to turn to European history at this point. From that time on, Haskins's devotion to European history, and especially the Middle Ages, was assured.

It was largely because of Haskins's friendship with Turner and the terms of the offer he received, that he decided to go to Wisconsin. Turner and Haskins seem to have shared many traits and their close friendship resulted in a continuous interchange of ideas, both at Wisconsin and later, when Turner was persuaded by Haskins to join him at Harvard in 1910. As Haskins created a renascence in medieval studies in the United States, so Turner revolutionized the interpretation of American history with his Frontier Thesis. At Wisconsin Haskins and Turner were alike in the way that they departed from certain ways of looking at history shared by their elder mentors. For example, Herbert Baxter Adams belonged to that school of historical thought that looked for a kind of genetic progression of democratic institutions—with their origins in the forests of Germany, from which they were transplanted to England and thence to the New England villages of America. Thus American ideas of democracy were "inherited" almost genetically. Both Haskins and Turner looked more to environmental causes for institutions and ideas. And it is in this context that Turner discovered the importance of the American frontier as the environment shaping American democratic tendencies. In the same manner Haskins began to look at medieval environments, studying the conditions in intellectual centers, travel and interchanges of ideas,

interconnections of Byzantine, Muslim, and European cultures, and the Norman "environment" that produced, so Haskins later came to believe, many of England's fundamental political institutions. It is clear from a comparison of their work that Haskins and Turner were asking similar questions about their materials and sources at about the same time. And it was at this time, first in Baltimore and then in Wisconsin, that both began their work in separate fields. Their friendship would have afforded many opportunities to mull over and exchange ideas on "nature or nurture" as causes of historical change.

While he was at Wisconsin from 1892 to 1902, Haskins began publishing in earnest. It was there that he wrote his two-part article on opportunities for research in the Vatican Archives, his exposition of the life of medieval students based on their letters, his contributions to "The Study of History in Schools" and *A History of Higher Education in Pennsylvania.* He also wrote numerous book reviews, sometimes as many as three for a single issue of the *American Historical Review.* As a Wisconsin professor, too, he began his research in the archives of Normandy, Paris, the Vatican, and Spain that would ultimately lead to his great interpretive studies. In 1903 and 1904 two early articles on Norman institutions and medieval culture appeared in *American Historical Review.* In "The Early Norman Jury" Haskins delved into Norman charters to study instances of the appearance of juries, challenging English opinions that the jury was an Anglo-Saxon phenomenon. This study may well reflect the legal training Haskins had received at Johns Hopkins and developed in his dissertation. Less controversial and more exploratory in nature was "The University of Paris in the Sermons of the Thirteenth Century." Both studies were characteristically innovative and yielded impressive results.

Haskins began his work in Normandy in 1902, at Bayeux to look at the *Livre Noir*, a cartulary then receiving a great deal of attention from scholars interested in Norman institutions. David Bates, a later scholar in the field, has found the earliest reference to Haskins visiting Caen in 1905; the records thenceforth suggest that he returned to Normandy every year from 1905 to 1913, with the exception of 1909 and 1912 (the latter being the year of his marriage). While in Normandy he must have visited all the departmental archives and the numerous manuscript collections in public libraries; he must also have studied the large quantity of Norman archive material in the Bibliothèque Nationale. It is also clear that Haskins's almost yearly European trips were not limited to Normandy but ranged through many of the provincial and central archives of Europe. His labors included learning to read and to speak the languages of countries he visited—tasks at which he worked by himself both at home and on the long ocean voyages. He made many friends at Oxford's Bodleian Library, at the British Museum, at the British Public Record Office, at the Bibliothèque Nationale, and at archives throughout Western Europe.

Haskins himself describes the character of his work in the Norman archives in the preface to *Norman Institutions:* "If the book has been over-long in the making, this has not been without compensations for the author. He has had time to linger over the great Norman chroniclers with his students and to try his conclusions in the give and take of seminary discussion. He has made the personal acquaintance of a number of workers in the field of Norman history, and has enjoyed several summers of study and research in some of the pleasant places of the earth. And as the work comes to a close, the memories which it recalls are not so much of dusty *fonds d'archives* or weary journeys on the Ouest-État, as of quiet days of study in provincial collections, long evenings of reflection by the Orne or the Vire [rivers] or in the garden of some cathedral city, and rare afternoons at Chantilly with Leopold Delisle [a leading French scholar]. . . ."

After ten years at Wisconsin, Haskins was called to Harvard, where he became professor of history in 1902, Gurney Professor of History and Political Science in 1912, and the first Henry Charles Lea Professor of Medieval History in 1928. In 1912, four years after his appointment as Harvard's graduate dean of arts and sciences, he married Clare Allen. Haskins and Allen had much in common. Before attending college she had studied in France, and she had lived in France and Italy with members of her family after graduating from Vassar in 1903. She had studied voice and literature in Paris and had traveled widely in England as well as on the Continent. With her linguistic skills, she had taught—to support herself—at girls' schools in Wisconsin, New York, and finally Boston, where she met Haskins in about 1910. Her family on her father's side went back to William Bradford of Plymouth colony.

One can only speculate as to the reasons for Haskins's deferred marriage. Undoubtedly he was influenced by financial constraints. He felt obligated to help his brother through M.I.T., and he financed his sister's college education at Smith. His academic salary was small, as was his father's, so that a good portion of his pay went to his family. In Cambridge, he lived in a two-room apartment, which he shared with his brother. Travel abroad, even in the early 1900s, was not inexpensive, but it was a requirement of Haskins's scholarly career. On one occasion, Haskins used some of his savings to take his father, who had never traveled, abroad.

Clare Haskins was a woman of distinction when Haskins met her and developed her own career parallel to his. When they met, she was teaching French at the May School in Boston. Later, she was appointed to the Radcliffe faculty, and at the same time she headed a girls' school in Boston. Her field was Romance languages. She was fluent in French, and almost equally skilled in Italian and Spanish. Clare Haskins was a bastion of support for her husband throughout his life, and especially in his later years when he was stricken with Parkinson's disease.

Haskins's lifestyle changed dramatically after his marriage, yet he made the transition from bachelor to husband and father with ease. Although Haskins's three children—George Lee, Charles Allen, and Clare Elisabeth—were born late in his life, he relished his role as father and family man and devoted a good deal of time, thought, and effort to the task of child-rearing. Social life at the Haskins home had a European flavor; French was the second language of the household, the language used by the many eminent medievalists who gathered at the Haskins home. Leopold Delisle, Charles Victor Langlois, Sir Frederick Maurice Powicke, Henri Pirenne, Charles Bemont, E. K. Rand, R. P. Blake, G. R. Coffman, George Sarton, André Morize, G. M. Trevelyan (nephew of Lord Macaulay), and the Byzantine historian Charles Diehl were among the American and foreign visitors who paid regular visits to Haskins.

The regimen of the household was regulated, and George Haskins recalls that his father oversaw everything, including routine chores, to the last detail. He settled the minor family disputes peremptorily but justly; "Praise was given generously, when due," his son recalled, "but never lavishly, especially if one did only what was expected."

The intense pace of Haskins's earlier yearly research trips to Europe slowed somewhat after his marriage, and his wife sometimes accompanied him on these journeys. He was in Europe in 1912 for his honeymoon; in 1913 he attended the International Congress of Historical Sciences in London and continued his research. At this point his travels were interrupted, probably by the births of his children and also by the outbreak of hostilities in Europe in 1914, shortly before George's birth. Except to attend the Paris Peace Conference, he did not return to Europe until 1922. His final visit was in 1925, for research at Monte Cassino, the Vatican, Bologna, Paris, and London.

In 1922 the Haskinses vacationed in the Near East—a memorable trip which strengthened Haskins's belief in the importance of learning Arabic. Although the children were too young to be included in these journeys, Haskins often shared his experiences with them. He was fond of telling them the story of how before World War I he had climbed Mount Vesuvius and there met the Kaiser, to whom he complained of his worn-out shoes. He recounted how President Taft had, because of his weight, caused the bathtub to overflow when he was staying at a New York club; and how Harvard president Abbott Lawrence Lowell and he were caught by police while climbing the twelve-foot iron fence at the Harvard station because the gates were locked.

When he was at home, Haskins followed a set routine. He began the day with a large breakfast. He taught classes and worked until lunch and then napped for an hour at home in order to work late at night. He held one of his three graduate seminars from four to six and looked over his mail from six-thirty to seven. After dinner, he read to the children from Twain, Dickens, and contemporary authors. From eight-thirty to ten-thirty he returned to his work. In the summers, which the family spent in Maine, this routine was interrupted with excursions into the great outdoors, which Haskins had learned to love in the Crawford County, Pennsylvania, countryside of his childhood. Haskins and his friends—Frederick Jackson Turner and the classicists Francis G. Allinson and Moses S. Slaughter—often organized canoe expeditions for their families. They would assiduously plan the outings beforehand, laying out the trails and campgrounds. Then the "caravan" of canoes would streak to the prepared campsite and all, including children, would go tramping through the woods. The highlight of the excursion was always a grand picnic. In bad weather, the family often broke into two teams and played word charades in the evening.

As a member of the generation of Theodore Roosevelt, Haskins and his friends enjoyed "tramping," as he called it, for relaxation. This was one of the favorite activities at the Roosevelt home on Long Island, where he often visited. Until 1926 he regularly walked from home to meet his classes twice a day, a total of at least six miles. Every autumn until that year he tramped for a week in

southern New Hampshire, either alone or with the family and friends. Whether in Paris or at his summer home in Maine, Haskins continued this habit of tramping as long as he was able. In Paris, even at the time of the Versailles Peace Conference, he would take a train to Normandy and walk part of the way back. In Maine, he would often go by train to visit his friend Chief Justice Lucillus A. Emery, fourteen miles distant, and walk back. A man of enormous physical energy, he hiked or climbed in the Alps for two weeks each summer when he was single; his wife joined him for two such summers before World War I broke out.

Haskins was also active in city life in Cambridge, Boston, and New York. In New York, he enjoyed the Century Association, where, during long evenings of talk, he became a friend of William Howard Taft and Theodore Roosevelt. In Boston he was a member of the prestigious Saturday Club, and he belonged to two dining clubs in Cambridge. At the clubs he enjoyed conversations with the eminent Bostonians of his day, most of whom were not academicians. He also enjoyed the company of Harvard colleagues not in the history department—Roscoe Pound and Joseph Warren of the law school, Lawrence Henderson in biochemistry, and George F. Moore in theology.

Haskins read widely—four daily newspapers, at least five monthly periodicals including *Atlantic*, *Harpers*, *Saturday Review*, and contemporary literature—all in addition to the professional journals and books which came to his office in profusion. He often carried in his pocket an edition of Vergil or a play of Euripides.

He numbered his graduate students among his friends. *Anniversary Essays in Mediaeval History, by Students of Charles Homer Haskins, Presented on His Completion of Forty Years of Teaching* (1929) contains eighteen papers, each by one of the students he had taught by 1928. Nearly every graduate student in the history department at Harvard passed through at least one of his classes, and many went on to become prominent in their own right. On the average, in the 1920s Haskins supervised the work of about three or four Ph.D. students at a time. His students felt comfortable with him, and it is difficult to exaggerate the affection with which they remember him. His tall, blond, moustached good looks and his magnificent voice gave them the impression of what a Norman duke would have looked like, and among their own circles they called him the "Duke." Although Haskins knew about this appellation, his students seldom were bold enough to use it openly. Despite his extremely busy schedule as dean of the Graduate School, Haskins managed to spend a good deal of time with his students, whom he often entertained at his home.

Haskins spent much time in Harvard's Widener Library; he loved to work there and to linger in the stacks. Haskins had a room on the first floor of the library in the French literature and history section. He used to meet his students there for discussions of dissertations, but often students would run into him informally as he was, in the words of one, "charging up and down the aisles." He seldom lectured from notes but would bring to class great piles of books, to which he would refer as he talked. He particularly enjoyed his class History 25, "Historical Bibliography and Criticism." This class drew nearly all history graduate students, because Haskins admitted students in any field—ancient, medieval, European, or American history—and stayed thoroughly conversant with all of them. Students were required to submit a critical list of sources—original and secondary—and these Haskins would study and comment on. But he liked to say, with tongue in cheek, that "Bibliography is a very specious form of erudition."

Haskins's students recall the paleography and diplomatics class, which drew students from classics and the divinity school, as his most impressive. His knowledge of manuscripts and how to use them was monumental. Often he would aid his students with small, thoughtful gestures, sending copies of manuscripts he had found in Europe to students who he knew might find them useful. Powicke later remarked on Haskins's generosity and kindness to young men, his sometimes whimsical manner with them, and his "large capacity for affection. He endeared men to him. I have reason to remember how, when a young man, of whom he had never heard, began to wander into his chosen field of study, he . . . welcomed the beginner as a fellow-worker, and made of him a friend for life."

He handled his classes with benevolent good humor and was always ready with a joke. When one student, Gaines Post, nearly dozed during the famous paleography class, he was jolted into alertness when Haskins loudly answered the question of another student regarding a Latin abbreviation, which happened to be "post." "Yes, sir, what is it?" Post responded, as Haskins suspected he would. By evening, so Post reports, the story had spread throughout the Harvard community, and a young stranger seated next to Post at a concert that night reported the story to him with glee, not knowing who he was. This incident was typical of the stories

told by Haskins's graduates of their seminar experiences.

Haskins was equally in command when teaching large undergraduate classes. Harvard president Lowell, in a conversation with George Lee Haskins about 1940, described the undisciplined situation that prevailed in the first-year course in history, government, and economics. "Students were unruly and disruptive, as well as disrespectful in those classes, and their instructors could not control them. So we put your father in charge of the largest class. History 1, which soon included about 800 to 1,000 students, at nine in the morning. He would stride back and forth for an hour on the small platform, without notes, lecturing, telling an occasional anecdote in a sonorous voice that literally sounded like a Norman Duke going to battle. A student who was late might be greeted with an amused pause: 'I see, another late breakfast'—but no malice or scorn. Once he is said to have compared the principle of *cuis regio, eius religio* with the diversity of life even in modern France, where every village, every department, has its own cheese, compared with our one great American cheese, RAT CHEESE. He held his audience by his force of manner, his knowledge of broad movements as well as detail."

Haskins was adept at structuring his lectures so that they were attuned to his audience. His English colleague Powicke recalled in 1937 with admiration Haskins's 1924 address to the American Historical Association on the diffusion of ideas in the Middle Ages: "As I listened, the simile of the builder came into my mind. Each sentence was like a block of hewn stone, laid in its place by a skillful mason. The operation was directed by a clear and powerful mind, but every stone, so to speak, was left to make its own impression, without the aid of external graces. Anything wild and extravagant was unthinkable. . . . [This comparison] may give an impression of heaviness; but a finely proportioned building, honestly built, is massive rather than heavy in appearance. It speaks of purpose and achievement; its austere lines reveal unexpected lights and shadows. It excites interest and holds attention, and is neither dull nor wearisome. Haskins's work always seems to me to be like this."

An example of Haskins's lecturing style may be found in his book *The Rise of Universities* (1923), which includes the 1923 Colver lectures he delivered at Brown University. The volume contains three lectures—"The Earliest Universities," "The Mediaeval Professor," and "The Mediaeval Student," each superbly organized, and, in the words of one commentator, marked by "solid erudition . . . concealed from the casual eye by a touch of humor and a literary charm that are seldom met with in discussions of medieval learning." Omitting technical details found in his *Studies in Mediaeval Culture*, in the lectures Haskins compared the medieval university, students, and professors to the modern American university community. One can imagine Brown students entering the hall to hear a learned lecture on the "dark ages" only to be told that one of the first universities, Bologna, began as a guild of students, similar to guilds of barbers, carpenters, bakers, and so on, and that it was first formed to force the townspeople to stop charging outrageous prices for rooms and necessities. "Victorious over the townspeople, the students turned on 'their other enemies, the professors.' Here the threat was a collective boycott, and as the masters lived at first wholly from the fees of their pupils, this threat was equally effective. The professor was put under bond to live up to a minute set of regulations which guaranteed his students the worth of the money paid by each."

In the lectures as in his other works, Haskins masterfully used the primary sources to give his student audience an intimate knowledge of his topic. The vignettes that he culled from the massive amount of documents he had read (in *Studies in Mediaeval Culture* these sources and many others are quoted in Latin) must have brought the medieval university alive for the Brown students, as they do for students who read *The Rise of Universities* today. The Duke, with his tall, blond, mustachioed eminence, flashing smile and twinkling eyes, doubtless charmed his student audience no end. Masterful knowledge, a sure hand at selecting precisely the most appropriate and illustrative sources, and a ready wit combined to make him a remarkably effective teacher.

His American professional associates found him equally effective and admirable. As R. P. Blake, G. R. Coffman, and E. K. Rand, three of Haskins's closest colleagues, sketched Haskins's character in *Speculum* (1939): "Vigorous and progressive in his method of teaching history both as a liberal art and as a humane science, a sovereign influence on all advanced students of history, since all took one or more of his courses, powerful in Faculty debates, unravelling Gordian knots as quickly as others could cut them, marked out for a college president from the start, though not tempted by several important invitations to such an office, witty and gay in conversation, fond of long walks, a favorite at his clubs, best of friends, deeply reverential and

religious at heart, he made himself immediately one of the indispensables in the life of Harvard and left a name to be recorded among its greatest."

And one of his admirers in England, Powicke, describes Haskins: "Haskins was a well-built man, with broad shoulders on which his massive head was planted rather low down. He had a very straight look. He talked freely, with a touch of formality, in short incisive sentences. He listened as easily and naturally as he spoke, but conversation with him tended to take the form of question and answer and the interchange of opinions rather than of rapid give and take. . . . he was aware of his ability and was ready to shoulder responsibility. . . . He disliked pretentious and slovenly work, but his criticism was generally conveyed by inference rather than by definite words. . . . He welcomed good work and did not harp on trifles. It would be very hard to deduce his private opinions on political or spiritual matters from anything that he wrote. . . . he valued most the confidence of colleagues and pupils, and his friendship with other scholars in all parts of the world. As a scholar, he takes his place beside Lea and Gross; as a teacher and man of affairs he set an example. He did more than anyone in recent years to give a much-needed sense of the value of discipline and direction to the study of History in America."

It was as dean of the Graduate School of Arts and Sciences at Harvard that Haskins was in a position to wield such important influence. Haskins had arrived at Harvard in 1902 to find several medievalists already there: Giorgio Anacleto Corrado Bandelari, who specialized in the Early Middle Ages; Ephraim Emerton, who held the Winn chair in ecclesiastical history; Charles Gross, the pioneer investigator into the British Public Record Office and compiler of a monumental bibliography of sources in English history; and his student Charles McIlwain, who later became Haskins's colleague and one of the most distinguished American medievalists and political scientists. Although Emerton and Gross had been among many German-educated Ph.D.'s who came to the United States and eventually to Harvard, Emerton in 1876 and Gross in 1888, both were still active at Harvard when Haskins arrived. Emerton continued his career until 1925 and Gross until 1915. Bandelari, who was not known as a stimulating teacher, left Harvard to become a literary editor of the *New York Sun*, but Emerton, Gross, and Haskins remained as a talented trio to advance both the study of medieval history and the development of European methods of education. In the last quarter of the nineteenth century, institutional history was enjoying a tremendous vogue. A look at the Harvard history catalogue reveals that nearly all the courses taught in those years were concerned with the history of political institutions. Gross by himself taught three classes in English constitutional history, and Emerton alone emphasized the cultural aspects of history. But the future of American education was to be most influenced by a course initiated in 1879, History 1—a survey course in medieval and modern European history, intended as a general introduction to more detailed study. It was Haskins's experimentation with this class and later analyses of its function in the University education which contributed to the development of the teaching of Western civilization throughout the United States.

Haskins had arrived at Harvard in 1902 at a turning point in the history of that institution. Doctorates in history had been granted since 1873, but by 1902 Emerton and Gross and others had firmly entrenched the methods of scientific history and the techniques of training scholars which they had learned in Germany. The library collection had grown to rival the holdings at the finest European universities. The result, as Emerton and Samuel Eliot Morison so colorfully expressed it, was that "the former stream [of students] to Germany was dammed up in Cambridge." Now the tide was almost reversed, with a stream of English graduates seeking Harvard educations at Cambridge, Massachusetts. And this reversal was accompanied by a stream of European exchange professors and guest lecturers who came to Harvard from 1910 to 1930. Many of these professors were Haskins's personal friends and colleagues in medieval history or in some other field related to history such as art, philosophy, or literature. Their presence at Harvard can cer·ainly be attributed to his influence and initiative as dean of the Graduate School and as a scholar recognized widely abroad. It may well be significant that the number of Ph.D.'s in medieval and English history from 1901 to 1919—twenty-one—outnumbered the Ph.D.'s in American history in those years—fifteen. After Gross's death, the number of advanced degrees in English history remained about one per year—sixteen from 1901 to 1919, seven from 1920 to 1928—while the number of advanced degrees in medieval history grew from five for the period 1901 to 1919 to nine for the years 1920 to 1928. Since most of the degrees in English history were on medieval subjects, the majority of these students—a total of sixteen from 1920 to 1928—were Haskins's, as a look at the 1929 *Anniversary Essays* dedicated to Haskins reveals. It is instructive to note, for purposes of comparison, that in these years—1901 to 1928—only five students received degrees in ancient history, a number equal to those specializing in Latin American history.

Haskins began his contribution to the development of history at Harvard when he took up the teaching of History 1 in 1904. Emerton and Morison call Haskins one of Johns Hopkins's greatest sons. As Morison wrote: "Haskins laid out for himself a colossal programme of teaching and research, which he realized; and of all the Harvard historical scholars of the present generation, his name is best known abroad." Haskins made History 1 a course in medieval history. The limited scope permitted greater depth, but enrollments declined drastically in the more advanced medieval courses, so Haskins returned to the former practice of teaching a survey of medieval and modern history in History 1 and began bringing in guest lecturers from the Harvard history faculty and elsewhere, thereby creating a showcase in this enormous class for the most talented teachers in the department. Enrollments consequently soared in all fields of history. History 1, as finally organized by Haskins, set the pattern which nearly all colleges and universities in the United States adopted during World War I, when educators, led by Harvard, decided that the effort to make the world "safe for democracy" would not succeed unless American youth understood their Western heritage.

Haskins also regularly taught more advanced undergraduate classes, usually on French institutional history and medieval intellectual history; two of these he repeated in the afternoons at Radcliffe College for a small additional stipend. Often he taught at the Harvard summer school. In addition, he revived the abandoned graduate courses on diplomatics—the study of documents such as charters, legal writs, letters, and so on—and paleography—the art of reading holograph documents, recognizing and deciphering scribal hands and abbreviations, and dating manuscripts. According to Emerton and Morison, "these courses gave graduate students the sort of professional equipment and training that formerly they had to seek at the École des Chartes or a German university." With Haskins's teaching, the Harvard graduate school, at least in medieval history, at last met the standards of the finest European universities. As Emerton and Morison put it, "There is a certain massiveness about [Charles Homer] Haskins' character and intellect, combined with a sharpness of perception and a twinkling humor, that makes his personality the most pervasive in the department. His knowledge of history is equalled only by his acquaintance with historians and universities; and no one has so spent himself in the service of his adopted university."

In addition to developing History 1 into the model for Western civilization courses, Haskins was one of a small group of professors who devised a new plan of study at Harvard that would cut across departmental and course lines and allow interdisciplinary approaches to the study of particular subjects or eras. Harvard's appears to have been the first cross-disciplinary program in the United States. Haskins and his colleagues were concerned that the system of free electives at Harvard was permitting the students to become undisciplined and random in their selection of courses. They saw the lines between disciplines as becoming so rigid that students were not being encouraged to see any interconnections between them. Thus the "History and Literature" grouping was established in the 1906 catalogue as a "field" in the new regulations for the degree with distinction. The novel features of the grouping were that the candidate was required to study both the history and the literature of a country and of an era; that he had to pursue a course of independent reading in his subject under the supervision of one of the members of the committee; that he must enroll in at least six courses related to the history and literature of his subject; that he needed to complete with success an oral examination on his subject, not on his courses; and that he had to submit a thesis on his subject. Haskins and his colleagues had created interdisciplinary studies, a model which would later be adopted throughout the United States.

As dean of the Graduate School, Haskins also took great care to preserve the gains made in the past. Building on the work of Henry Adams in the use of the seminar, Haskins developed a program that would give students freedom to pursue their studies according to their own interests. There was no general curriculum for advanced students, and thus there were no rigid requirements to be met. Students were encouraged to enroll in classes in the "middle range," which included junior- and senior-level undergraduate courses, but for the most part they engaged in research at a very advanced and specialized level. Haskins set no limits on the time students took to complete their degrees, emphasizing only the ability to do independent research as determined by rigid examinations and superior work. Advanced students were selected according to the most rigorous standards.

Haskins himself regarded the Graduate School of Arts and Sciences as "a body of students rather than a body of instructors.... [It] derives its special character from the advancement and purpose of its students and the nature of their studies." His conception is reminiscent of his own descriptions of the medieval universities as guilds of students and teachers not affiliated with any specific buildings or facilities. His development of the graduate school may perhaps have been influenced by his own intense study of the development of universities and the nature of students and professors in the Middle Ages. Yet he was also concerned about attaining the most modern degree of professionalism in the school. He regarded the evolution of "resident graduates into graduate *students*," engaged in advanced instruction, as "one of the most significant developments in the entire history of the University." Tracing this development from the graduate department's foundation in 1872 to his own tenure as department head, Haskins credited Harvard president Charles W. Eliot with the motivating ideas of a graduate school but regarded the most important turning point to be in 1877-1878, when graduates were permitted to seek individual instruction from appropriate professors. In Haskins's words, "That is the sort of study for which a graduate school exists, and which marks it off from most other departments of the University." His own division of the Graduate School was created in 1905, only three years before he became its head. Thus Haskins himself must be regarded as the major architect of its policies and under his leadership the school grew by leaps and bounds. In 1903 the school had 325 students. By 1913 enrollment had grown to 504, and by 1928 to 946, a figure which included the 70 Ph.D.'s and 262 M.A.'s granted that year. During the years of Haskins's tenure degrees granted leaped from 159 to 332 per year.

As dean of the Graduate School he served as chairman of an administrative board of ten or twelve, chosen from the professors most closely connected with graduate study. An assistant dean and secretary, George W. Robinson, had charge of the routine office work, thus enabling Haskins to continue to devote most of his time to graduate instruction and consultation with individual students. Haskins's greatest emphasis in the administration of the school continued to be on close contact between students and their graduate directors, on independent study and research, and on careful individual attention to the course of each student's work. He left the primary direction of students' work in the hands of the professors they had chosen to guide them, rather than making such supervision a responsibility of the dean's office.

Haskins was very proud of the achievements of his students. He expected Harvard Ph.D.'s and M.A.'s to leave the university for important roles in America society or to join the Harvard faculty. Most of his graduate students—about seventy-five percent of Arts and Sciences Ph.D.'s—became teachers, as he expected them to. In 1929 one hundred members of the Faculty of Arts and Sciences were Harvard Ph.D.'s, and many more were teaching elsewhere. Other graduate students went on to become clergymen, presidents of universities (fifteen), editors, diplomats, librarians, physicians, and members of Congress (four); one became prime minister of Canada. Haskins took pride in the fact that most of the doctoral dissertations produced in his school were eventually published in whole or in part and usually in prestigious places. The quality of Harvard instruction was partly fostered by his enthusiastic support of a program by which graduate students and postdoctoral fellows could visit foreign libraries, museums, and archives for extended periods. The list of such "traveling fellows" includes a significantly large proportion of his own students in medieval or English history, indicating that Haskins especially encouraged his own students to travel to the sites associated with their research topics, as he had done throughout his career. At the same time he worked in close coordination with the Harvard University Library, whose directors Justin Winsor and later Archibald C. Coolidge and Robert P. Blake shared his conception of the function of a library in university life.

In the writings Haskins produced during his professional life, he was influenced by both his American and European training. It may appear at first glance that Haskins chose the scientific attitude toward history when he decided to study at Johns Hopkins and then in Europe, but in fact Haskins's writings incorporated the best of both the romantic and scientific schools. His works fall roughly into four groups: first, a group of "scientific" articles and books written for experts in the field of medieval history, heavily footnoted with extensive Latin and Greek quotations from manuscript sources; second, a group of books for general students of history, written with elegance and wit, setting forth general conclusions drawn from his close "scientific" studies, and containing few foreign quotations but enough documentation to satisfy his expert readers; third, books and articles on educational theories and practices and dealing with the practical problems which Haskins and his colleagues faced as the American higher educational system was taking shape; and, finally, several articles and one book on aspects of the Paris Peace Conference.

Haskins had a superb sense of his audience and a superb sense of style. He combined in all his works the skill of the storyteller with the precision and extreme accuracy and care of the scientific mind. Although the balance between these two might shift considerably according to the audience for which his work was intended, both elements were present in every one of his works. He avoided the romantic flights of fancy of some earlier American historians and never produced dull, dry catalogues of detail, as some scientific-minded historians did. Generally, his style was lively, lucid, and concise, and his instinct for choosing the appropriate quotation or anecdote to illustrate the line of his thought was unfailing. His erudition was evident in the scientific mode of writing he employed in his heavily documented, scholarly works as well as in his popular works, which were very well received by European and American scholars of medieval history.

Contemporary reviews of his books present an interesting mixture of reactions. Generally, American reviews guardedly praised his work, disputing a number of minor (sometimes very minor) points and omissions. Some of the English reviewers were more fulsome in their praise but at the same time they seemed perplexed by Haskins's approach and style. They seemed thoroughly impressed with his documentation and accuracy, but puzzled that he could write with such grace and charm on the model of the great romantic historians while exhibiting no religious, political, or social biases. Their ambivalent admiration is reflected as much in the faintly hostile, grudging praise of James Tait in a four-page microscopic critique of *Studies in the History of Mediaeval Science* in *English Historical Review* as in F. M. Powicke's assertion that the European-trained Haskins had an English mind. What Haskins had done was take the first pioneering steps toward new syntheses and methods of historical writing, transcending the century-long perception that in history, "art" and "science" are at opposite poles of the spectrum. He wrote scientific history with literary grace. As a pioneer in new theories of medieval history, he succeeded in gaining the respect of European historians for American medievalists who studied European history.

By any standard, whether European or American, Haskins broke new ground in a variety of areas. He began his publishing career in medieval history with a series of scholarly articles, which began with the piece on medieval students in 1898 and led to the appearance of his first book in 1915. Haskins ranged widely among broad and varied research topics, so that he seems to have been working simultaneously on his three areas of interest—the Normans and their institutions; intellectual history, particularly as it involved the medieval universities; and medieval science. These three topics eventually led him to a fourth—Norman Sicily—an outgrowth of the wanderings of the Normans outside their homeland, which became a center for the translation of scientific treatises and home of some of the earliest universities.

The Normans in European History (1915), his first book on this medieval research, consists of a series of eight lectures given originally at the Lowell Institute and later repeated at the University of California. The book retains the lecture style and

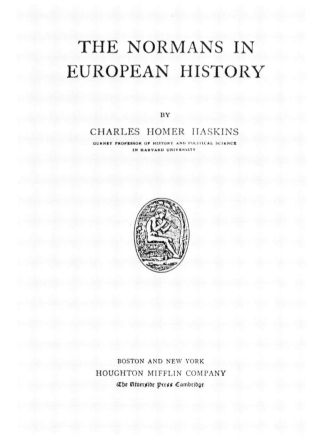

THE NORMANS IN
EUROPEAN HISTORY

BY

CHARLES HOMER HASKINS

GURNEY PROFESSOR OF HISTORY AND POLITICAL SCIENCE
IN HARVARD UNIVERSITY

BOSTON AND NEW YORK
HOUGHTON MIFFLIN COMPANY
The Riverside Press Cambridge

Title page for Haskins's first book on medieval history, a pathbreaking analysis of Norman culture and its contributions to the development of Europe

is filled with amusing and illustrative anecdotes drawn from his sources. On the firm foundation of these manuscript sources Haskins builds his story of the importance of the Normans in the development of European culture. His purpose was to place the Normans into the context of the development of Europe, emphasizing their contributions to culture.

Haskins offers many new and stimulating ideas in the pages of this, the first broad analysis of the Normans as a separate and distinct culture which made an important mark on the European scene. His conclusions have generated scholarly debate that has continued to the present day. Haskins was the first to emphasize the Viking background as important to the development of their progeny the Normans. He proposed that when William the Conqueror won England, he created not just the English kingdom (as English historians customarily held) but a Norman Empire, which included Normandy and England and lasted until King John lost Normandy in 1204. Further, he wanted to distinguish Normandy from the rest of France; whereas French historians tended to regard it as merely a French province, Haskins emphasized its unique character and the ways in which, culturally, it was separate from France. Finally, he was the first to draw the attention of English and Continental scholars to the significance of the Norman kingdoms in Italy and Sicily as extensions of the same Norman-French culture that had been transferred to England. Haskins pointed to striking parallels between the achievements of the Normans in England and in the Mediterranean and to the connections between these areas. Taking as examples kings Henry II of England and Roger the Great of Sicily, he proposed that the Normans' greatest impact on Europe was first in the magnitude of their conquests: at the height of their power—circa 1166, one hundred years after the conquest of England—they held "half of Italy, two thirds of France, and the whole of England; and they had made a beginning on Ireland and Scotland." Haskins also emphasized the abiding political institutions that they created: in 1166 the two largest, most complex, and best-organized kingdoms in Europe were Norman England and Norman Sicily. Finally, Haskins noted, the brilliant composite culture of Sicily was one of two vital conduits (the other was Spain) for the transmission of Arabic, Greek, and Byzantine culture to the West.

What Haskins had done with *The Normans in European History* was approach the whole sweep of European medieval history from a new perspective, transcending the narrow nationalistic confines to which French, English, and Italian scholars had limited themselves in studying their own histories to see the Normans in a European context. It was this all-encompassing vision of the sweep of European history that distinguished his work from that of his contemporaries, changed and broadened their views, and marked his emergence as a great historian.

An anonymous reviewer in the *American Historical Review* concluded that there were "but few books which combine, to such an extent . . . the virtues of good historical writing; wide and exact knowledge, rare skill in the presentation of facts, and a style which in addition to Norman strength and orderliness possesses the qualities of elegance and genial humor."

Haskins had already won the respect of his colleagues at home and abroad with his concise and rigorously researched scholarly articles. Some of these, together with some new research, he gathered together and published in what he conceived of as a companion volume to his first book. It appeared under the title *Norman Institutions* in 1918 and consisted of a history of Normandy under the Conqueror, his sons Duke Robert Curthose and kings William Rufus and Henry I; his grandson Stephen of Blois (later King Stephen of England); his grandson-in-law Geoffrey Plantagenet; and his great-grandson King Henry II. A final chapter dealt with the early Norman jury, and appendices followed which included previously unpublished documents.

Norman Institutions, clearly intended for the "scientific" scholars of the minutiae of institutional history, was as creative and innovative in its conceptions as *The Normans in European History* but in very different ways. Whereas the first book was broadly interpretive, the second was concerned with very specific issues and problems. Haskins set out to investigate the Norman origins of English institutions. He found in the process that in almost every case pre-Conquest Norman practices preceded post-Conquest English practices and were the foundation for many important constitutional developments that later took place in England, including the political system of feudal monarchy and the jury trial. As Haskins concluded, "Where Normandy sowed, England and all English-speaking lands were to reap." The major English institution which Haskins did not find in pre-Conquest Normandy was the Chancery—the royal "writing" office that produced official documents. Haskins went on to trace the similarities of Norman and English governments as the two developed along parallel lines, often administered in a single royal court under the Conqueror, his sons or grandsons. The widely lauded creation of the foundation of the English common law by Henry II—the "father of English law"—proved to have had its real groundwork in the practices of the second Henry's grandfather, Henry I, as well as in Norman practices.

Haskins wrote at a time when English historians had been debating for about forty years whether English institutions had their origins in Norman or Anglo-Saxon practices, and the debate had been following political lines. Whigs such as Edward A. Freeman wanted to see the origins of parliamentary government in old Anglo-Saxon institutions such as the Witan (the council of warriors who advised and elected the Anglo-Saxon kings) and the fyrd (the national army, called up in a kind of draft of all able-bodied men). Tories such as John Horace Round wanted to see Norman origins for English parliamentarianism—an affirmation of the English aristocracy that traced its roots back to the Norman Conquest. What Haskins, an American, achieved was to collect for the first time, from a diligent search of Norman archives, every scrap of evidence—fragmentary though it is—and subject this collection to the most intense, judicious, and unbiased scrutiny in the best tradition of scientific history, publishing many of the documents for the first time. The debate over Norman or Anglo-Saxon origins was to continue for two generations, losing its political configurations as time progressed. But by the 1950s further research and analysis had validated most of Haskins's conclusions; and *Norman Institutions* remains the foundation for all subsequent scholarly investigation of medieval Normandy.

When the book first appeared, James Tait seems to have been so impressed that his review filled four pages of the *English Historical Review*—an extraordinary length for a book review, and a tribute to the wealth of material in Haskins's book. Although Tait concluded by saying that Haskins did no more than confirm and add supporting evidence to what was already known (a reaction also of Sir Frank Stenton in his *History* review), his careful and lengthy analysis contradicts this judgment and may perhaps be attributed to his own ambivalence toward an American's dealing so thoroughly and competently with materials which proved almost conclusively what Tait's English colleagues had only suspected before. Haskins himself saw the book partially as the detailed documentation of concepts he had advanced in *The Normans in European History*. Sir Frank Stenton, however, concluded that it had "established the main features of one of the most interesting experiments in government achieved in all the early Middle Ages."

Haskins interrupted his work to serve President Woodrow Wilson as an adviser and aide in the negotiations for peace at Versailles at the end of World War I. Wilson had been Haskins's close friend at Johns Hopkins, and he regarded Haskins's intimate knowledge of Europe, his fluency in European languages, and his powerful intellect as superb qualifications for his appointment. As early as 1917, shortly after the United States entered the war against Germany, Wilson asked Colonel Edward M. House to initiate a study of problems involved in structuring a peace treaty. House gathered together a group of advisers—mostly university professors—who began investigating the issues and interests of each of the countries of Europe. Traveling by night from Boston to Washington, sometimes as often as once a week, Haskins became one of the leading members of this group, known as "The Inquiry." Haskins directed the work of the committee relating to the settlement along the northwestern frontiers of Germany—Belgium, Denmark, Alsace-Lorraine, the Rhine, and the Saar. As the war ended, Haskins and most of the other members of the commission—plus perhaps two hundred more advisers—were attached to the American delegation at the Paris Peace Conference, 1918-1919. Here Haskins became chief of the Western Division and helped structure the peace agreement on the areas of Europe which he had earlier been commissioned to study.

It is clear from the book *Some Problems of the Peace Conference* (1920), written by Haskins and his Harvard colleague Robert Howard Lord to explain the workings of the conference, that Haskins played a continuous and important role at Paris. What is clear from unpublished letters, but little known and certainly not explained in his and Lord's book, is that Haskins served as Wilson's interpreter in the president's meetings with the French prime minister Georges Clemenceau. Haskins's role was more than that of a functionary, for he served Wilson in a special capacity. Whereas Wilson had to be discreet and reserved, Haskins could often be bold and assert ideas which, emanating from the president himself, might be at some risk. Moreover, Haskins was fluent in French, Wilson far less so. Thus Haskins served in a special advisory capacity to Wilson and in a diplomatic role in his dealings with one of the conference's most

important and influential heads of state—and certainly the strongest personality—Clemenceau. It was Haskins who advanced the solution which was eventually accepted for the problems with the Saar: that the Saar be placed under the government of the League of Nations for fifteen years, at the end of which a plebiscite would determine its fate. This solution illustrates Haskins's generally pro-French attitude during the negotiations, which must have enabled him to work well with Clemenceau; it also demonstrates Haskins's reasonable attitude and the responsibility he felt to be fair and just. The Germans, however, came to regard the treaty as a *diktat*, and eventually the "peace without victory" became a "victory without peace."

On his return to the United States in January 1920, Haskins and Lord were persuaded to discuss the Paris Peace Conference and the treaty that resulted at the Lowell Institute. From the series of eight lectures presented, they constructed their book to reach a wider audience. Haskins wrote the introductory chapter outlining the tasks and methods used at the conference, describing in much vivid detail the course of the meetings and the characters of key personalities involved in the negotiations. Typically, he used colorful anecdotes to illuminate some of the problems caused by the delegates' personal idiosyncrasies and quirks, but always he wrote in a tone of respect, and often, as was his wont, with gentle and affectionate humor. Characteristically, too, Haskins generally remained silent on his own role at the conference, but it is clear from his eyewitness accounts and intimate knowledge of the workings of the extensive and often tedious meetings that he was present at many of the most important negotiations. This book was the first to be published on the Paris Peace Conference. Clive Day, also a delegate to Paris, reviewed it for the *American Historical Review*, commenting that "at this early date it sets a standard of workmanship which should discourage rivalry by authors less well prepared, and should save the public from much printing that its publication has made unnecessary."

Haskins and Lord, delegated representatives to the Peace commission on the problems they discuss, had sifted through vast amounts of material to offer a clear presentation of the problems faced, the solutions reached, and the probable outcome, in their opinion, of these settlements. Their own meticulous and carefully documented scholarship illustrates the manner in which the delegation must have prepared for the conference and the way in which the Paris negotiations themselves must have been conducted. Surely never before in history had the methods of "scientific" historians been applied to practical diplomatic problems—except perhaps by Wilson himself. This concern for diplomacy was, however, a weakness of the book, for Lord and Haskins discreetly refrained from indicating the attitude of the various powers that were party to the negotiations and from estimating the share that each power had in formulating the final version of the treaty. Understandably, because of their own roles in the negotiations, the importance of gaining approval of the treaty and the League of Nations in the United States (a goal which was never achieved), and the delicacy of the subject of the relative influence of each of the major powers, the authors wisely left this kind of analysis to future historians.

Although Haskins's efforts in Paris were valuable and might have led to his appointment as governor of the Saar or to a high post in the diplomatic service (he was offered an ambassadorship), he chose instead to return to his position at Harvard. During the years of his diplomatic work the flow of his publications in medieval history and on the subject of education had never ceased. Shortly after the war he also published at least two articles on the problems of the Peace Conference in *Foreign Affairs Quarterly*. But it was at Paris that the very first signs of the illness that was to darken his final years appeared. Whether he chose to return to academic life for this or other reasons, his final years were filled with honors, and, in fact, his major and most innovative work was yet to be done. He received honorary degrees from the universities of Strasbourg (1919), Padua and Manchester (1922), Paris (1926), Louvain (1927), Caen (1932), Harvard (1908 and 1924), Wisconsin (1910), and from Allegheny College (1915). He was made an officer of the French Legion of Honor and commander of the Order of the Crown of Belgium and received decorations from Denmark and Italy as well. During his career, he had also been made a fellow of the American Philosophical Society and of the American Academy of Arts and Sciences, corresponding member of the Royal Historical Society of England, and of the academies of Barcelona, Brussels, Rouen, and Caen. He was elected to the Accademia Pontifica di Archeologia and to Société des Antiquaires of Normandy and France; he was corresponding fellow of the British Academy and a foreign associate of the Institut de France and the Royal Belgian Academy. He served as president of the Medieval Academy of America (1926-1927) and of the American Historical As-

sociation (1922), as chairman of the American Council of Learned Societies (1920-1926), and as vice-president of the Massachusetts Historical Society (1922-1932). He was offered the post of president of at least four universities, including M.I.T. and Johns Hopkins. These he declined, as he had declined government posts in 1920. It was this very year, 1920, the same year in which his book on the Peace Conference appeared, that his first article referring to the twelfth century renaissance appeared in the *American Historical Review*. This topic was to occupy him for the rest of his life and to gain him further recognition as a great historian.

By 1922 Haskins had learned that the stirrings of illness which he had experienced in Paris were the first manifestations of Parkinson's disease. From this year until Haskins's death in May 1937, the disease grew progressively worse and in the last years of his life nearly incapacitated him physically but not mentally. From 1922 to 1929, however, he led an astonishingly active and productive life. It almost seems as though he were trying to cram a lifetime of work into the few short years remaining to him. It was during this period that he governed three of the major scholarly organizations in the United States almost simultaneously; he continued as dean of the Graduate School of Arts and Sciences until 1924, taught until 1931, and routinely published book reviews, edited the American Historical series, and wrote numerous articles as well as four major books, the last of which appeared in 1929. The year 1929 was the dividing line, when he seems to have passed from relatively normal activity into the life of a semi-invalid.

In 1923, the year after Haskins learned the exact nature of his illness, his book *The Rise of Universities* appeared. The book, collecting the Colver Lectures Haskins had delivered at Brown, was based on work he had probably done, at least in part, while he was a student himself and was designed to appeal particularly to student audiences. While no revolutionary or surprising new theories emerge in this book, as they had in earlier works, *The Rise of Universities* is nevertheless rich in fascinating, previously unpublished source material illuminating aspects of medieval university life. It is doubtful that this small masterpiece will ever be surpassed as an engaging, timeless portrait of the university, and it is not surprising that *The Rise of Universities* became Haskins's most popular and most widely read work. Nevertheless, when it first appeared it received virtually no reviews—only here and there a notice of its publication.

The following year, 1924, Haskins's *Studies in*

the History of Mediaeval Science was published. Haskins had been engaged in research on intellectual history since the beginning of his studies and had published many of the chapters of this book as articles, some of them inspired by his interest in the excursions of the Normans into Sicily. Although the articles collected in *Studies in the History of Mediaeval Science* were independently written, the volume achieves a connectedness similar to that of *Norman Institutions*, which was compiled in basically the same way. And like *Norman Institutions*, this book is serious, scientific scholarship meant to be read mainly by experts well-versed in Greek as well as in Latin. A good half of the book consists of lengthy source quotations from unpublished manuscripts. These manuscripts, painstakingly gathered from archives all over Europe—from Spain, Sicily, England, France, Germany, and Italy—Haskins uses to trace the transmission of scientific knowledge from its entry points in Spain and Sicily through its diffusion throughout the schools and courts of Europe. Rigorously thorough in his search for relevant manuscripts, meticulous and restrained in his analysis and interpretation of them, Haskins won again the high praises of scholars at home and abroad. *Studies in the History of Mediaeval Science* marked the zenith of Haskins's scholarly reputation as a scientific researcher. It was in his review of this book that Powicke claimed that Haskins possessed an English mind and compared him to the great British scholars Poole and Round. Haskins's studies reveal that Arab and Greek scientific knowledge began to pass to the West far earlier than had been suspected, through major translating centers in Spain, to which Norman and French knights traveled to aid in the campaign to drive the Muslims from their bastions and reestablish Christian kingdoms. At these centers scholars who had journeyed with great initiative and through great dangers translated works from Arabic to Spanish to Latin, collaborating in the search for information which they would then take to their homelands to be copied and disseminated. At the same time, scholars in Sicily had organized an even more sophisticated "school" of direct translation from Greek and Arabic to Latin, under the official sponsorship of King Roger the Great, whom Haskins had earlier shown in his *Normans in European History* to have anticipated the much better known Frederick II in remarkable political achievements. Roger, Haskins makes clear in *Studies in the History of Mediaeval Science*, also set the pattern for Frederick's scientific and cultural achievements. A surprising number of English scholars traveled to both

translation centers, including Adelard of Bath, who brought the abacus back to the court of Henry I of England (1100-1135) and thus contributed much to the development of the Exchequer (or treasury department, the first in Europe). What emerges from Haskins's book is not the fact that medieval scientists made any great discoveries on their own or engaged in scientific research as we know it, but that they laid the foundation for the work of future European scientists by the kind of work in which they did engage—the tedious and difficult collection, translation, and dissemination of bits and pieces of knowledge gleaned from the Greeks and the Arabs, who had preserved the works of the ancient Greeks and in some areas augmented them with their own investigations. Interestingly, the task and purpose of these scholars almost mirrors Haskins's own in collecting remnants of their manuscripts. Haskins doubtless felt some affinity with these medieval scholars. In the Latin prefaces to their renditions of the manuscripts they discovered, which Haskins quotes at great length, a sense of their intellectual excitement and their determination to discover every scrap of knowledge which they could find filters through. Like Haskins himself, they were engaged in one of the greatest intellectual adventures of their time, and while Haskins never explicitly states this, the concept permeates the whole of his book.

Three years after publication of *Studies in the History of Mediaeval Science*, in 1927 the third of Haskins's more general books appeared: *The Renaissance of the Twelfth Century*. This was to become his most controversial book, though it is also considered by many to be his greatest work. Like *The Normans in European History*, it was a broad overview. But whereas the first book contemplated the sweep of all European history, this work focused on only the twelfth century, which Haskins was the first to identify as a period of "renaissance" comparable to and preceding the one in Italy. Haskins wanted to refute the idea that "the Middle Ages, that epoch of ignorance, stagnation, and gloom, stand in sharpest contrast to the light and progress and freedom of the Italian Renaissance which followed." Medievalists, especially art historians and students of medieval literature, were well aware that the twelfth century was a period of great creativity, for Gothic art and the literature of courtly love had long been appreciated and indeed enjoyed a vogue in the Romantic revival of the nineteenth century. For Haskins, however, such appreciation was not enough. "How could there be a renaissance in the Middle Ages," he continues, "when men had

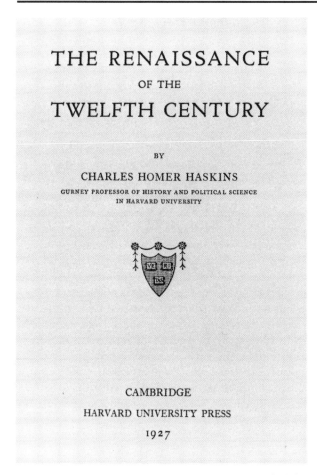

THE RENAISSANCE

OF THE

TWELFTH CENTURY

BY

CHARLES HOMER HASKINS

GURNEY PROFESSOR OF HISTORY AND POLITICAL SCIENCE
IN HARVARD UNIVERSITY

CAMBRIDGE

HARVARD UNIVERSITY PRESS

1927

Title page for Haskins's most controversial book, in which he refutes the idea that "the Middle Ages, that epoch of ignorance, stagnation, and gloom, stand in sharpest contrast to the light and progress and freedom of the Italian Renaissance which followed."

Ages clearly had produced great art, but Gothic art, and even the earlier Romanesque, had diverged so greatly from Roman practices in concept and execution that it clearly represented a distinctly nonclassical genre, much admired in its own right for its beauty and creativity. The creative adventures in vernacular literature in the Middle Ages, too—the epic and the romance—contain scarcely a trace of classical influence. But Haskins chose not to discuss these creative aspects. He deals first with the Burckhardtian topics—intellectual centers, the collection and dissemination of manuscripts of the classics in books and libraries, and the teaching of classical authors in the new schools springing up all over Europe around and during the 1100s. He had searched the manuscript sources with his accustomed thoroughness to find references to classical authors and found that knowledge of a significant number of these writers was indeed widespread. Creative writing in the Latin language ranged from poetry to history and was often based on classical sources as models. At this point Haskins went beyond Burckhardt and included in his definition of things classical jurisprudence, philosophy, and science—not merely art and literature. Haskins went beyond Burckhardt in a second way: unlike Burckhardt, he chose to admire not only those in the Middle Ages who revived, preserved, and used classical models but also the medieval creators of new modes of invention, whether these were based on classical, paraclassical, or nonclassical conceptions. Thus, for example, he devoted a chapter of the book to the beginnings of universities, thoroughly unclassical in their conception and organization, but nonetheless essential to the proliferation and spread of classical learning.

The book received a mixed reception. Powicke, in the *English Historical Review*, was apparently somewhat perplexed by *The Renaissance of the Twelfth Century*. Although he praised Haskins as a great teacher and a great scholar and expressed gratitude "for the author's mature reflections upon the bearing of his highly specialized work and upon its relation to the period as a whole," he did not discuss Haskins's concept of the Twelfth-Century Renaissance at all, limiting his remarks to somewhat minor criticisms and omissions. Powicke nevertheless concluded that "every one will wish to read [it] for himself." It may also be significant that this book was reviewed in the short notices—three-quarters of a page as opposed to the four pages the *English Historical Review* allowed James Tait to comment on *Norman Institutions*. The *Speculum* review by L. J. Paetow, was, however, ebullient in its praise, her-

no eye for the joy and beauty and knowledge of this passing world, their gaze ever fixed on the terrors of the world to come?" He quotes John Addington Symonds's view of an age when "humanity had passed, a careful pilgrim, intent on the terrors of sin, death, and judgment, along the highways of the world, and had scarcely known that they were sightworthy, or that life is a blessing."

It is this Burckhardtian notion of medieval ignorance and darkness, as opposed to Renaissance knowledge and light—which Jacob Burckhardt himself had drawn from Renaissance thinkers including Petrarch—that Haskins addresses. His choice of a title was a direct challenge to the followers of Burckhardt, and the battleground which he chose was the field of Latin secular literature, the revival of which was the basis for Burckhardt's claims to a "renaissance" or rebirth. The Middle alding the book as the beginning of a new intellectual movement, describing its conclusions as intricate, brilliant, and profound, and remarking upon Haskins's "style which will charm many readers." L. R. Loomis's review in the *American Historical Review* likewise abounded in praise: the book "shows the master hand in the breadth and sweep of its plan, and in the authenticity of its material, [but] still is written with sufficient simplicity to please a layman with only a general acquaintance with the Middle Ages." Like Powicke, Loomis seems to have regarded the book as an attempt at popularizing medieval history, and like Powicke, he had some criticisms of the chapter on philosophy. While in Loomis's view this chapter had been broadened too much to cover political theory, the dialectical method, and freedom of thought, in Powicke's estimation Haskins had erred by slighting certain philosophers. Nevertheless, Loomis found several chapters—especially those on intellectual centers and historical writing—original and imaginative, creating "a mirror of an age."

Haskins's last "popular" book had a considerable impact on the study of medieval history. It generated a significant amount of controversy and dissent, but it also stimulated energetic discussions of the concept of a Medieval Renaissance, most recently at a 1977 conference cosponsored by Harvard University and UCLA, with twenty-six papers by such eminent scholars as Sir Richard Southern, Georges Duby, Jean Leclerq, and Peter Dronke. This conference resulted in the publication of a book, *Renaissance and Renewal in the Twelfth Century* (1982), edited by R. L. Benson and Giles Constable. An earlier conference with a symposium, at the annual meeting of the Medieval Academy of America in 1950, foreshadowed this international tribute to Haskins's work. Haskins's arguments have found their way into books too numerous to mention, ranging from general considerations of historiography, such as Herbert Muller's *The Uses of the Past* (1952), to specialized books considering the problem of defining renaissances, such as *The 12th Century Renaissance* (1969), edited by C. Warren Hollister. Many medievalists were inspired to reexamine all the evidence possible to verify, modify, or broaden Haskins's conclusions. Sometimes these efforts to expand Haskins's insights reached a point where they became distorted. Medievalists began discovering "renaissances" everywhere in the Middle Ages—in the Northumbrian cultural blossoming in the Age of Bede in England, in Charlemagne's Carolingian Empire, and in the Ottonian kingdom a bit later. Some medievalists even

began to question whether the Italian Renaissance was really a renaissance at all and again began to use the older term—*Quattrocento* (1400s)—to designate the period. Renaissance scholars such as the art historian Irwin Panofsky were led eventually to reject or modify the concept of multiple renaissance, and to defend the uniqueness of the Italian Renaissance, but Haskins's book compelled them to define their terms much more rigorously than before.

Wherever the truth may lie in the continuing debate over the definition of the concept *Renaissance*, the criteria for determining whether one has taken place, and indeed the value of the term itself, it is abundantly clear that *The Renaissance of the Twelfth Century* prompted several generations of historians to re-evaluate the periods of history they studied and indeed to reconsider the whole notion of periodization. Haskins inspired an abundance of new research to illuminate the twelfth century more fully. The "Haskins Thesis" has stood the test of time extremely well. Marcia Colish, in her comments on the Twelfth-Century Renaissance at the 1984 American Historical Association Centennial Session to honor Haskins, concluded that "Haskins and his vision of the 12th Century Renaissance are alive and well today. . . . [He] lives in those medievalists who find diversity in the 12th century exhilarating, not problematic. His legacy is bright in those scholars who embrace the task of grasping interrelationships, where they exist, and who are not tempted by the illusion of a fictive homogeneity. . . . The Haskins legacy is a living legacy, which continues to offer a guide and a mandate for present and future work in medieval intellectual history."

Haskins's final book, *Studies in Mediaeval Culture*, appeared in 1929. Together with *Studies in the History of Mediaeval Science*, this work, mostly a collection of previously published articles on medieval intellectual history, presents the documentation and scientific studies underlying the theories expressed in *The Renaissance of the Twelfth Century*, and much of the documentation, in an expanded form, that appeared in *The Rise of Universities*. It concludes with tributes by Haskins to Henry Charles Lea and Charles Gross. Reviews of this last book uniformly acknowledge Haskins's scholarly achievements and confirm the reputation for excellence he had gained by this date. Powicke commented on Haskins's "vivid glimpse into the great world," his "energetic scholarship which has enabled him to produce work beyond the reach of criticism and, as so little work can claim to be, immune from the corrosive touch of time." Loren C. MacKinney, in *American Historical Review,* found that "every chapter contains rare treasure." Ephraim Emerton, in *Speculum,* called the work "characteristic of the qualities that have given to its predecessors their great and deserved reputation." In Emerton's review, at last, tribute was given to Haskins's original and stimulating work on medieval students and universities. Emerton succinctly summarized the tone and character of Haskins's attitudes toward the subjects of his study in all his works: "The general reader, whose ideas of the Middle Ages are of a time of universal stupidity and dullness, will be surprised at the evidence of humane activity reflected here. He will, perhaps, be led to ask how it could possibly be that these very lively human boys could grow into a class of intellectual dullards, how these young experimenters in the qualities of metals should develop minds impervious to the suggestions of a truly scientific method, or how this army of entertainers, traders, pilgrims, and message-bearers could wander in and out of all corners of Europe with eyes blinded to the obvious facts of the world about them. The answer he will get here is: 'They didn't.' " It is this message that Haskins had been implying from the beginning of his career, and it shines forth in the vitality of all his work.

Haskins's own vitality began to fail him in 1928 and 1929, when illness forced him to reduce the number of courses he was teaching at Harvard and at Radcliffe. In the summer of 1929 he was forced to decline an invitation to give the Ford Lectures at Oxford, too lame to travel. At home, he worked on proofs for *Studies in Mediaeval Culture,* played a few games of croquet with his sons, and remarked that he was not "picking up strength as usual" in Maine. Walking to his office back in Cambridge was exhausting, so he decided to teach at home. He retired altogether in 1932, completing thirty years of teaching at Harvard. By the end of 1932 he was almost totally confined to his house and front yard. It was also in that year that he ceased writing.

In these closing years, life for Haskins was far from congenial. By this time his children had reached adolescence, and Haskins tried for as long as he could to supervise their welfare. Even though he could not walk far, he would visit their schools by car to assure himself of their proper education. He never complained and took his disabilities in stride. Witnesses to his illness have described his ability to adapt to his unfortunate last years as "heroic." He was able to rise from bed and sit for only

six hours a day, but even when nearly bedridden by 1936, he could not be idle. He received letters and dictated replies. He read or was read to three to four hours a day. One or two friends or colleagues would stop by each day. George, his eldest son, remembers his going over Greek I-stem verbs "to keep my mind sharp." When George was away, Haskins would sometimes dictate letters to him in fluent classical Latin.

Despite the tragedy of his illness Haskins continued to function at the utmost limits of his intellectual strength until the end. He lived to see his two sons graduate—one aged nineteen, the other twenty—from Harvard College with highest honors, George having given the commencement oration to an audience of some 6,000 persons. He also saw published, and could read with pride, George's first book, written at the age of nineteen, on the beginnings of the English Parliament, and was especially pleased that other research was on its way to publication in journals for which he himself had written. The day before he died he did know that George had been invited to give the Lowell Lectures in Boston the next year, at the age of twenty-three. Later that day, as Haskins's son George reports, when his wife, Clare, returned from a college committee meeting, he said briefly and in French: "C'est la mort qui vient." He died at home on 14 May 1937, of bronchial pneumonia and acute circulatory failure. His funeral services on 17 May packed the Harvard Church to overflowing.

Two regrets Haskins expressed in his last years: he had wanted very much to learn Arabic to enhance his ability to examine documents pertinent to the transmission of Islamic culture to the West; and, connected with this desire, he had wanted to complete his study of England and Sicily in the twelfth century—a project begun as early as 1910 and virtually cancelled after he had to refuse the invitation to lecture at Oxford on this subject in 1929. On his death, he was mourned on both sides of the Atlantic. Important obituaries appeared in the *New York Times,* the *London Times,* the *Boston Evening Transcript, Speculum,* the *American Historical Review,* and the *English Historical Review.* A special tribute to his stature was a *New York Times* editorial which appeared a few days after his death.

Haskins's energy and vitality, his intellectual astuteness and his creative genius had helped to shape the character of both undergraduate and graduate education in the United States. His careful and meticulous—but above all voluminous—scholarship and the suggestive ideas emerging from his creative analyses had sparked medievalists both in the United States and abroad with new energy and curiosity, infusing a generation of English scholars with new concepts to absorb, new questions to answer, and new fields to research and inspiring a burst of medieval studies in the United States on an unprecedented level that continues to this day. Not least among his contributions to the burgeoning of scholarly interest in the Middle Ages were the many graduate students who passed through his classes and later spread throughout the country to educate students of their own on the Haskins model. One of the founders of many professional societies and governor of most of them, he helped to establish professionalism in history in the United States. And finally, his role at the Paris Peace Conference of 1918-1919 put him near the heart of the most important political events of his day, in which he functioned as an important shaper of events. Despite these numerous achievements and the expenditure of energy, time, and work necessary for their successful completion, Haskins retained the most attractive human qualities. He was beloved by his family, friends, colleagues, and students, and he was generous in returning their affections unreservedly. His personal charm and gentle humor endeared him to students, scholars, and to readers he would never meet. His classic works are models. In the "scientific" books and articles, his scholarship stands out; in the more general interpretive books his narratives and his analyses are artful. In 1981 the Charles Homer Haskins Society for Viking, Anglo-Saxon, Anglo-Norman, and Angevin History

was founded as a tribute to his life and works. In the renascence of medieval studies and in the study of history in the United States, no one contributed more than Charles Homer Haskins.

Bibliography:

Charles H. Taylor and John H. LaMonte, eds., *Anniversary Essays in Mediaeval History, by Students of Charles Homer Haskins, Presented on His Completion of Forty Years of Teaching* (Boston & New York: Houghton Mifflin, 1929), pp. 389-398.

References:

R. P. Blake, G. R. Coffman, and E. K. Rand, "Charles Homer Haskins," *Speculum*, 14 (July 1939): 413-415;

Edward M. House and Charles Seymour, eds., *What Really Happened at Paris: The Story of the Peace Conference, 1918-1919* (New York: Scribners, 1921);

William E. Lingelback, "Charles Homer Haskins," in *The American Philosophical Society Year Book, 1937* (Philadelphia: American Philosophical Society, 1938), pp. 356-357;

Samuel Eliot Morison, ed., *The Development of Harvard University Since the Inauguration of President Eliot, 1869-1929* (Cambridge: Harvard University Press, 1930);

F[rederick] M[aurice] Powicke, "Charles Homer Haskins," *English Historical Review*, 52 (October 1937): 649-656;

Josiah Cox Russell, *Twelfth Century Studies* (New York: AMS Press, 1978).

Hermann E. von Holst
(19 June 1841-20 January 1904)

Clyde N. Wilson
University of South Carolina

SELECTED BOOKS: *Verfassung und Demokratie der Vereinigten Staaten von Amerika*, 5 volumes (Düsseldorf: J. Buddeus, 1873-1891); translated as *The Constitutional and Political History of the United States*, 8 volumes (Chicago: Callaghan, 1876-1892);

John C. Calhoun (Boston & New York: Houghton Mifflin, 1882);

John Brown, edited by Frank Preston Stearns (Boston: Cupples & Herd, 1883);

Das Staatsrecht der Vereinigten Staaten (Freiburg: J. C. B. Mohr, 1885); translated by Alfred Bishop Mason as *The Constitutional Law of the United States of America* (Chicago: Callaghan, 1887);

The French Revolution Tested by Mirabeau's Career; Twelve Lectures on the History of the French Revolution, Delivered at the Lowell Institute, Boston, Mass., 2 volumes (Chicago: Callaghan, 1894).

Hermann E. von Holst (University of Chicago Archives)

Hermann Eduard von Holst's works are now largely and deservedly unread except as an object lesson in the transience of historical interpretations. However, he was the first fully trained, professional, academic historian to devote major attention to the national history of the United States, and he long influenced the views of American history, especially of the Civil War era, that were held on both sides of the Atlantic.

Holst was born at Fellin in Livonia in the dominions of the czar of Russia, in what later was to become the Estonian Soviet Socialist Republic. Despite the fact that his family had been in Baltic Russia for five centuries, Holst was German through and through. His father, Valentine von Holst, was a Lutheran minister who died when Holst was in secondary school, leaving his wife, Marie Lenz von Holst, and their family of ten children in poverty. It was only by considerable sacrifice and privation that Holst was able to complete studies at Heidelberg University, where he received his doctorate in the same year that the Civil War ended in America.

Holst's interest was in modern history and his mentor was Ludwig Haüsser, a leading academic advocate of German unification under Prussian leadership. The graduate returned to Russia with an appointment in modern French history at the University of St. Petersburg. However, during the repression that followed the attempted assassination of Czar Alexander II in 1866, Holst, in Germany, published opinions critical of the Russian government and found himself persona non grata in his homeland. In 1867 he departed for the United States as a steerage passenger in preference to a prospective Siberian holiday.

Holst lived in New York City for several years. He was at first reduced to manual labor, which, along with the privations of his student days, is said to have permanently undermined his health. After a while he prospered modestly as a tutor and newspaper correspondent, and he became a Republican campaign orator during the election of 1868. However, despite the prestige of European advanced degrees in America and the influence of a large and respectable German-American community, he was unable to secure an academic position.

The mid-nineteenth century courses of development of the United States and Germany seemed to Holst and many others to be similar. In America there had recently been a victory of national unity under progressive principles over forces of decentralization and conservatism. The same process was under way in Germany. Thinking on these lines, Holst conceived that a study of American institutions would be instructive and soon moved on to make American history his life's work.

The progress of unification in Germany not only suggested to Holst his major historical work, it gave him the opportunity to pursue it as well. When the University of Strasbourg passed from French to German control at the end of the Franco-Prussian War, Holst was made a professor there. He returned to Europe in 1872, taking with him a New England bride, Annie Isabelle Hatt, a graduate of Vassar. He set to work on his multivolume study which is known in English under the general title of *The Constitutional and Political History of the United States* (1876-1892). The appearance of the first German volume of this work in 1873 won him an even more prestigious appointment at the University of Freiburg.

At Freiburg Holst remained until 1892. He engaged in politics under the patronage of the Grand Duke of Baden and continued to publish volumes of his multivolume history. During this period he also wrote in English and published in America studies of John C. Calhoun (1882) and John Brown (1883) and made two triumphant lecture tours in America. His Continental style and dramatic oratory attracted attention, and he was as well known in America as any historian of the day, receiving frequent invitations to lecture and write on current subjects as well as history. In 1892, when the University of Chicago was organized with Rockefeller money, Holst became head of the history department. He remained at Chicago until shortly before his death, when he returned to Europe.

To say that Holst's attitude toward American history enthusiastically agreed with that of Republican, antislavery Northerners would be an understatement. For Holst American history was a struggle between the forces of light—that is, nationalism, centralism, progress, capitalism, antislavery, and the Republican party—and the forces of darkness, which he identified totally with the South, slavery, and state rights. For him slavery was not an undesirable, obsolete system that had grown up and persisted in the South, it was a demonic force which was specifically responsible for every effect and influence in American history of which he disapproved. This evaluation of the causes and issues of the Civil War in terms of the virtue of the winning side did not differ greatly from what was conventional at the time, but Holst went beyond any other respectable historian in the relentless Germanic didacticism and dogmatism with which he presented the case.

Despite its title and vast extent, *The Constitutional and Political History of the United States* is not a comprehensive history of the American Constitution and politics. It is really focused almost entirely on the sectional conflict that resulted in the Civil War, as indicated by the fact that four entire volumes were devoted to the 1850s and only the first to all of American history prior to 1828. In regard to the 1850s Holst's research was massive and unprecedented and was presented with great powers of synthesis and exposition. However, his limited focus on the sectional polemics of the late prewar period only reinforced Holst's dogmatism and partisanship. Given his ignorance of American colonial and early national history, he could not possibly understand in historical perspective either of his two main objects of study, slavery and state rights. This ignorance, reinforced by his Germanic penchant for nationalism, led him to assume, dogmatically but with little foundation, that there was no historical basis for state sovereignty and that slavery could have been easily done away with except for the machinations of an evil party.

Holst's most significant work, besides the multivolume history, was his 1882 biography, *John C. Calhoun*, commissioned by John T. Morse, Jr., for the American Statesmen series. It was the first scholarly treatment of Calhoun, and its interpretation remains influential in some quarters. The study was not a conventional biography but a telescoped version of the ideas presented in *The Constitutional and Political History*. J. Franklin Jameson, a leading American historian, remarked in 1900 that Calhoun remained as unknown after the publication of the book as he had before, and the publisher added to later editions a preface admitting that "this volume differs from all the other volumes" of the American Statesmen series. "In it the narrative element is subordinated to other purposes, and the personal element appears hardly at all." The "biography" deals only with Calhoun's public career, and it is essentially an extended criticism by the author of the subject. Holst had a begrudging respect for Calhoun and considered him a fallen angel who, throughout his career, had merely personified one hopelessly evil idea, slavery.

Because he was an early professionally trained historian, Holst has sometimes been mistakenly labeled as a member of the "scientific" school of historians of the late nineteenth century. If "scientific" is taken only to mean that he engaged in extensive and systematic research, that claim is true. But in all other respects Holst is really an example of a late generation of romantic historians rather than an early generation of scientific ones. In fact, his few virtues as a writer are related to his romanticism. His dogmatism and partisanship dominated his larger, interpretive themes, but he analyzed factual events reasonably objectively and thoroughly and did not intentionally take cheap shots at the figures he criticized. His highly personalized style often exhibited liveliness and irony. For example, he contrasted Calhoun favorably with politicians of a later time: "He did not owe his position to the grace of King Caucus and the favor of his grandees, the washed and unwashed patriots of the primary meetings. He therefore did not know and understand everything by intuition, as this privileged class of mortals do, but was obliged to study and reflect upon the subjects with which he had to deal as a legislator."

In the same year that the last volume of Holst's *Constitutional and Political History of the United States* was published, 1892, the first volume of James Ford Rhodes's *History of the United States from the Compromise of 1850* appeared. By that time it was obvious to all that the once-standard account of American history espoused by Holst was passing along with his generation, to be replaced by a more deliberately evenhanded and restrained interpretation.

References:

Eric F. Goldman, "Hermann Eduard von Holst: Plumed Knight of American Historiography," *Mississippi Valley Historical Review*, 23 (March 1937): 511-532;

Michael Kraus, *The Writing of American History* (Norman: University of Oklahoma Press, 1963), pp. 192-198;

Bert James Loewenberg, *American History in American Thought: Christopher Columbus to Henry Adams* (New York: Simon & Schuster, 1972), pp. 449-450, 482-489;

Charles R. Wilson, "Hermann Eduard von Holst," in *The Marcus W. Jernegan Essays in American Historiography*, edited by William T. Hutchinson (Chicago: University of Chicago Press, 1937), pp. 60-83;

Clyde N. Wilson, Introduction to Hermann E. von Holst's *John C. Calhoun* (New York & London: Chelsea House, 1980), pp. xv-xxx.

Papers:
Holst's papers are at the University of Chicago.

Helen Hunt Jackson

(15 October 1830-12 August 1885)

Barry W. Bienstock

See also the Jackson entry in *DLB 42, American Writers for Children Before 1900.*

SELECTED BOOKS: *Verses,* as H. H. (Boston: Fields, Osgood, 1870; enlarged, Boston: Roberts Brothers, 1874);

Bits of Travel, as H. H. (Boston: Osgood, 1872);

Bits of Talk About Home Matters, as H. H. (Boston: Roberts Brothers, 1873; London: Low, 1873);

Saxe Holm's Stories, as Saxe Holm (New York: Scribner, Armstrong, 1874);

The Story of Boon, as H. H. (Boston: Roberts Brothers, 1874);

Mercy Philbrick's Choice, anonymous (Boston: Roberts Brothers, 1876; London: Low, 1876);

Bits of Talk, in Verse and Prose, for Young Folks, as H. H. (Boston: Roberts Brothers, 1876);

Hetty's Strange History, by the author of *Mercy Philbrick's Choice* (Boston: Roberts Brothers, 1877);

Bits of Travel at Home, as H. H. (Boston: Roberts Brothers, 1878);

Saxe Holm's Stories, second series, as Saxe Holm (New York: Scribners, 1878);

Nelly's Silver Mine: A Story of Colorado Life, as H. H. (Boston: Roberts Brothers, 1878);

A Century of Dishonor: A Sketch of the United States Government's Dealings with Some of the Indian Tribes, as H. H. (New York: Harper, 1881; London: Chatto & Windus, 1881); enlarged edition (Boston: Roberts Brothers, 1885)—includes *Report on the Condition and Needs of the Mission Indians of California* (1883);

Mammy Tittleback and Her Family: A True Story of Seventeen Cats, as H. H. (Boston: Roberts Brothers, 1881);

The Training of Children, as H. H. (New York: New York & Brooklyn Publishing Company, 1882);

Report on the Condition and Needs of the Mission Indians of California, by Jackson and Abbot Kinney (Washington, D.C.: Government Printing Office, 1883);

The Hunter Cats of Connorloa (Boston: Roberts Brothers, 1884);

Helen Hunt Jackson

Ramona (Boston: Roberts Brothers, 1884; London: Macmillan, 1884);

Easter Bells, as H. H. (New York: White, Stokes & Allen, 1884);

Zeph: A Posthumous Story (Boston: Roberts Brothers, 1885; Edinburgh: Douglas, 1886);

Glimpses of Three Coasts (Boston: Roberts Brothers, 1886);

Sonnets and Lyrics (Boston: Roberts Brothers, 1886);

Between Whiles (Boston: Roberts Brothers, 1887);

A Calendar of Sonnets (Boston: Roberts Brothers, 1891);

Pansy Billings and Popsy, as H. H. (Boston: Lothrop, 1898).

OTHER: *Bathmendi: A Persian Tale. Translated for*

the Children from the French of Florian, as H. H.
(Boston: Loring, 1867);

*Letters from a Cat. Published by Her Mistress for the
Benefit of All Cats and the Amusement of Little
Children*, edited by Jackson as H. H. (Boston:
Roberts Brothers, 1879).

Praised in the nineteenth century for poetry
and prose which has now slipped into obscurity,
Helen Hunt Jackson is remembered for her chronicles of the mistreatment of the American Indian,
A Century of Dishonor (1881), and the novel *Ramona*
(1884), which remain glowing testaments of her
contribution to American history and literature.
Both books remain in print one hundred years
after publication, and it is difficult to discuss Indian
reform without invoking the name of Helen Hunt
Jackson.

One of the most prolific women writers in the
nineteenth century, with over twenty books and
hundreds of poems, book reviews, essays, and
travel sketches, Helen Hunt Jackson was born to
Nathan Welby and Deborah Waterman Vinal Fiske
on 15 October 1830. She was the eldest of two girls;
two boys died in infancy. Helen Fiske spent her
first fourteen years in Amherst, Massachusetts,
where her father taught languages and moral philosophy at Amherst College. Professor Fiske had
studied at Dartmouth College and Andover Theological Seminary but decided against a career in
the Congregational ministry. His religious orthodoxy, however, permeated the family home. Jackson rejected the strict Calvinism of her childhood,
dabbled in spiritualism in her later years, and never
joined an institutional church. She found some ca-
thartic use for her religiously oppressive childhood
memories in her two books of *Saxe Holm Stories*
(1874, 1878). In fact, autobiography formed the
basis for a great deal of her writing, and the impact
of personal misfortune would move her into an
active and successful literary career.

In 1844 her mother died of tuberculosis, and
failing health forced her father to resign his position and seek a cure in the Middle East, where he
died three years later. The Fiske girls, Helen and
her sister Anne, were entrusted to different relatives and distinct fortunes. They were never to have
a close relationship. Helen was educated at the Ips-
wich Female Seminary, north of Boston, and the
Spingler Institute in New York City. Her schooling
ended in 1850 with no indication of the literary
success that was to follow.

What followed in the decade to come was the
domestic life of wife and mother, but tragedy

would continue to plague Helen Fiske. On 28 October 1852 she married Edward Bissell Hunt, the
brother of Washington Hunt, who was then governor of New York. Her husband was a career army
officer in the corps of engineers, rising from the
rank of lieutenant to major. The nomadic career
of a soldier permitted no permanent home, and
the Hunts lived what Helen Hunt referred to as a
life of "scatterdom." The couple's first-born son,
Murray, died at the age of eleven months in 1854.
In 1863 Major Hunt died from suffocation while
experimenting with a "sea-miner" for launching
torpedoes underwater. The final blow fell two years
later when her sole surviving son, Warren, better
known as Rennie, died. Separated from her sister
upon the death of her mother, losing an infant
during the early years of her marriage, and within
a two-year period losing her husband and her
much-loved Rennie, the usually ebullient Hunt fell
into a great despair, from which friends feared she
might not recover.

Out of the depths of her unhappiness came
the beginning of her literary apprenticeship. In
1866 Helen Hunt settled in Newport, Rhode Island. A woman of extraordinary will and ability,
and cultivated by a close circle of friends, including
Thomas Wentworth Higginson in Newport and
childhood friend Emily Dickinson from Amherst,
she began to write poems and essays. Her first well-
known poem was published in the *Nation* three
months after Rennie's death. According to her
biographer Ruth Odell: "out of the death of her
child grew her first poems, cries of despair at her
loss." Her personal loss and love of children inspired a series of children's stories. *Bathmendi*, a
translation from the French and the first of her
many books for children, was published in 1867.
Helen Hunt never became reconciled to her childless existence, a theme she voiced often in her stories. Two of her creations, Mercy Philbrick and
Hetty Gunn, despair over childless lives. Other
parts of her life were fictionalized in "The Elder's
Wife," in which Draxy Miller, a loving wife and
mother of one child, loses her husband in an accident. By several accounts, the reactions of Draxy
and her son closely reflect those of the author and
her son Rennie after Major Hunt's death. Draxy,
however, becomes a preacher, whereas Helen Hunt
turned to writing as "the only digging for which I
have any capacity."

Helen Hunt's earliest publications were of
verse, travel sketches, children's stories, and book
reviews. Eschewing publicity and disliking her al-
literative name, she published under the pseud-

onyms Marah, Rip Van Winkle, Saxe Holm, and H. H., as well as anonymously in the Roberts Brothers No-Name series. Her first published prose sketch appeared in the New York *Independent*, for which she wrote more than 300 articles and book reviews. She contributed to numerous other periodicals, including *Hearth and Home*, the *Atlantic Monthly*, the *New York Evening Post*, *Scribner's Monthly*, the *Christian Union*, the *Riverside Magazine for Young People*, and *St. Nicholas*.

From 1868 to 1870 she traveled abroad, writing the pieces later published in *Bits of Travel* (1872). Her first book of poems, *Verses*, appeared in 1870. During the next fifteen years she published in most of the leading magazines. Her poems were praised by Ralph Waldo Emerson. Noting that they "have rare merit," he reprinted three of them in his 1875 anthology *Parnassus*. *Verses* was favorably reviewed in *Scribner's* and the *Atlantic Monthly*.

Helen Hunt proved to be an astute businesswoman. She published extensively and made certain that she was well paid for her efforts. In her later years she earned between three and four thousand dollars a year. "Cash is a vile article," she once noted, "but one thing is viler, and that is a purse without any cash in it."

During the winter of 1873-1874 she traveled to Colorado Springs. She had suffered bouts of diphtheria and dysentery, and friends suggested the Colorado retreat as a good place to recuperate. There she met and married William Sharpless Jackson, a Pennsylvania Quaker who resided in Colorado Springs, where he had become a successful banker and railroad promoter. The couple married on 22 October 1875, providing her the first permanent home since her childhood. The marriage also offered Helen Hunt Jackson considerable financial security which enabled her to travel extensively and devote a considerable portion of her last years to American Indian reform.

While visiting friends in Boston in 1879, she attended a lecture by a Ponca chief named Standing Bear. The Poncas, a peaceful Siouan tribe, had signed a treaty with the United States government in 1865 guaranteeing them a reservation along the Missouri, north of the Niobrara River. In 1868 the federal government mistakenly ceded the entire Ponca reservation to the Sioux, who had traditionally been the enemies of the tribe. United States policymakers responded to Ponca objections by removing the tribe to the Indian Territory, where they were settled on the Quapaw agency. The hardship of forced removal took its toll, and misery, disease, and death followed. Standing Bear took

the body of his dead son, a victim of malaria, and followed by other tribesmen, headed north in the spring of 1879. The Poncas got as far as Omaha, Nebraska, where they were invited to rest with the Omaha Indians.

Thomas Henry Tibbles, the assistant editor of the *Omaha Herald*, mounted a campaign in the East to support the Poncas. He sent Standing Bear on the lecture circuit with Bright Eyes (Suzette La Flesche, later Suzette Tibbles), an Omaha Indian girl.

Jackson was deeply moved by what she heard in November 1879. Feeling a Quakerly "concern" to fight against Indian injustice ("I cannot think of anything else from morning to night"), she engaged in a heated correspondence with Carl Schurz, the secretary of the interior. Despite evidence to the contrary, Jackson was convinced that Schurz was responsible for the recent wrongs perpetrated against the American Indian. To bolster her argument she spent months in the Astor Library researching the history of federal Indian policy failure which she published in 1881 as *A Century of Dishonor*. The book opens with a discussion of tribal sovereignty and a legal history of treaty proceedings. The second part of the work offers minihistories of United States dealings with seven tribes—the Delawares, Cheyennes, Nez Percé, Sioux, Poncas, Winnebagoes, Cherokees. The third part is entitled "Massacres of Indians By Whites." In her conclusion Jackson comments that it "makes little difference. . . . where one opens the record of the history of the Indians; every page and every year has its dark stain." Therefore, she believed it was not necessary to offer a comprehensive history of United States-Indian relations, because the "story of one tribe is the story of all." She condemned American politicians and policymakers for failing to recognize Indians' legal claims and failure to abide by treaty obligations. In the conclusion she offers a demographic breakdown of American Indian populations and censures the American government because there "is not among these three hundred bands of Indians one which has not suffered cruelly at the hands either of the Government or of white settlers."

According to Francis P. Prucha, a leading authority on late-nineteenth-century Indian reforms, *A Century of Dishonor* is "a strange book, a disorganized cluttered compilation of fragments, which sets forth the story of the government's dealings with seven tribes. It is a polemic work, not balanced history, and everywhere there is evidence of the haste with which the book was put together."

Jackson denied that the book was a history. To produce such a work, she declared, "would take years and volumes." She subtitled the book a "sketch." "I give an outline of the experience of each tribe straight through by itself. . . . All the heart and soul I possess have gone into it." For the four years that remained of her life after *A Century of Dishonor* was published, she would be known as the chief publicist of the Indian reform movement.

In 1882 President Chester A. Arthur appointed Jackson and Abbot Kinney of Los Angeles special commissioners. The two were empowered to investigate the plight of the Mission Indians of California and suggest reforms necessary to ameliorate their conditions. The fifty-six-page report was sent to the Department of the Interior, published by the U.S. government in 1883, and included in an edition of *A Century of Dishonor* that appeared in 1885. The Mission Indians were being displaced and maltreated as a result of America's acquisition of California. The report offered ten proposals to improve social conditions for the Indians, many of whom had been reduced to homeless vagabonds. The new secretary of the interior Henry M. Teller ignored the Jackson-Kinney Report, which prompted Jackson to seek an alternative means of bringing these Indians' beleaguered status to the attention of the American people. She would attempt to arouse the conscience of the American people just as Harriet Beecher Stowe had done in *Uncle Tom's Cabin*. The result of her labor was her most important novel and her best-selling book, *Ramona* (1884). "If I can do one-hundredth part for the Indians as Mrs. Stowe did for the Negro, I will be thankful," Jackson commented soon after the publication of the book.

Ramona offers a picturesque description of life on a large California estate shortly after American occupation. The culture Jackson portrays is one in the twilight of its existence. Señora Moreno presides over the estate with her son Felipe and her adopted daughter, Ramona, a beautiful young woman of mixed-blood—half-Indian, half-white. The second half of the book chronicles the mistreatment of the Mission Indians. Ramona marries Alessandro, an Indian of noble character. The marriage is opposed by Señora Moreno, and so the couple must elope and face a tragic future. The land upon which Alessandro's people live is given over by the court in San Francisco to white settlers. The Indians lose their cattle and horses to pay for the court costs. The landless Indians are harassed by greedy American frontiersmen, and Ramona's child dies because a government surgeon refuses

to help. The grief-crazed Alessandro is killed by an American man, and Ramona barely escapes death from fever. The novel ends with what historian Allan Nevins refers to as "an artistic blunder." Ramona is rescued by the ever faithful Felipe who marries her. Thus the tragic tale is blunted by a happy ending, an ending which seriously undercuts Jackson's message. Alessandro and Ramona were grievously wronged by rapacious Americans, and the wrongs they suffered were yet to be corrected by the American government. But the reader is left with an upbeat conclusion, a happy marriage and a promising future not in tune with the message that Jackson meant to get across to her readers. Jackson noted that in *A Century of Dishonor* she "had tried to attack the people's conscience directly" but in *Ramona* she "had sugared my pill, and it remains to be seen if it will go down." It may well be that Jackson added several teaspoons of sweetener too many to this ultimately saccharine tale.

Jackson commented that "I did not write *Ramona*. It was written *through* me. My lifeblood went into it—all I had thought, felt, and suffered for five years on the Indian question. I shall never write another novel." She was right. While she lived for another year and continued to turn out travel sketches and essays, started and abandoned another work of fiction, and thought of writing an Indian story for children, she never completed another novel. In 1885, after a series of debilitating illnesses and a fractured leg, Helen Hunt Jackson succumbed to cancer. She died in San Francisco on 12 August 1885.

Author of more than twenty books and hundreds of articles, Helen Hunt Jackson is remembered for the two books she considered her most significant contributions. "My *Century of Dishonor* and *Ramona* are the only things I have done for which I am glad now." For historians, *A Century of Dishonor* and *Ramona* remain important artifacts of late-nineteenth-century Indian reform, but the question remains of how influential they were in shaping government policy. Historians are not united on an answer, but it is safe to say that the books, while important in arousing the conscience of some Americans, did little to produce any specific legislation. *A Century of Dishonor* was published in 1881. Jackson sent each member of Congress a copy, but if they read it and were moved by its argument, there is no real evidence. No reform legislation came out of the Congress of 1880. Not until 1887 and the Dawes Act would legislation be passed, and its provision for immediate citizenship was not endorsed by Jackson in her book. While she offered little in the way of constructive proposals, she did note that Indians were not ready for citizenship. A process of tutelage must first take place. On that issue her views were clearly out of sync with the institutionalized reform movements which developed in the 1880s. Clearly an organization such as the Indian Rights Association was far more instrumental than Jackson's books in shaping federal Indian policy in the closing decades of the nineteenth century. As for claims that *A Century of Dishonor* was a path-breaking work, these also must be put to rest. It was not sui generis. A year earlier, George Manypenny had published *Our Indian Wards*, a diatribe against the United States Army, the arm of government which Manypenny blamed for America's grievous Indian policy.

Ramona was clearly the more popular of the two books. It has gone through more than three hundred printings, as well as many stage and screen productions. The book was received with ringing endorsements and some mixed notices. The *North American Review* called it "unquestionably the best novel yet produced by an American woman." The *Atlantic Monthly* was highly enthusiastic. The *Nation* applauded Jackson's noble effort ("all extremely well meant") but criticized the novel's lack of structure and the anticlimactic happy ending. Modern critics concur. According to Allan Nevins, *Ramona* "bears evidence of the hasty writing of a passionate woman eager to throw her message upon paper. The construction is so ill-planned that the reader is sometimes puzzled by a failure to observe even the temporal order of events. . . . Yet with all its faults *Ramona* has the indispensable virtue of vitality. . . . despite passages of confusion and unreality the book as a whole leaves an impression of fiery truth." Did this fiery truth affect policy makers in Washington, D.C.? Probably not. Here again, the Indian Rights Association with its active lobby pressured for legislation improving conditions for California's Mission Indians. Helen Hunt Jackson publicized the issues, but other, more concerted efforts were brought to bear to create the necessary legislation—legislation which Jackson did not live to see, although she died certain that it was coming.

Four days before she died she wrote to President Grover Cleveland: "From my deathbed I send you a message of heartfelt thanks for what you have already done for the Indians. I ask you to read my 'Century of Dishonor.' I am dying happier for the belief I have that it is your hand that is destined to strike the first steady blow toward lifting this burden of infamy from our country and righting the wrongs of the Indian race."

The *Nation* eulogized Helen Hunt Jackson, noting that next to Harriet Beecher Stowe she was the most admired American woman writer. A woman who did not publish a word until she was thirty-five and then turned out a large body of books, essays, and poems, and who refused to involve herself in a cause and then in the last years of her life became a zealous "woman with a hobby," Helen Hunt Jackson made contributions to literature and history that are among the most important the nineteenth century has to offer.

Biography:
Ruth Odell, *Helen Hunt Jackson* (New York & London: Appleton, 1939).

Reference:
Allan Nevins, "Helen Hunt Jackson, Sentimentalist vs. Realist," *American Scholar*, 10 (Summer 1941): 269-285.

Papers:
Most of Jackson's papers are at the Huntington Library, San Marino, California.

Henry Charles Lea

(19 September 1825-24 October 1909)

Robert B. Patterson
University of South Carolina

SELECTED BOOKS: *The First Duty of the Citizen. The Grandeur of the Struggle and Its Responsibilities. Southern Principles* (Philadelphia: Privately printed, 1863);

The Record of the Democratic Party, 1860-1865 (N.p., 1865);

Superstition and Force: Essays on the Wager of Law—The Wager of Battle—The Ordeal—Torture (Philadelphia: H. C. Lea, 1866; revised and enlarged, 1870, 1878, and 1892);

An Historical Sketch of Sacerdotal Celibacy in the Christian Church (Philadelphia: Lippincott, 1867; enlarged, Boston: Houghton Mifflin, 1884); revised as *History of Sacerdotal Celibacy in the Christian Church*, 2 volumes (New York: Macmillan, 1907; London: Williams & Norgate, 1907);

Studies in Church History: The Rise of the Temporal Power—Benefit of Clergy—Excommunication (Philadelphia: H. C. Lea/London: Low, Son & Marston, 1869); enlarged edition (Philadelphia: H. C. Lea's Son, 1883)—adds the essay "The Early Church and Slavery";

Constitutional Reform. A Letter to John Price Wetherill, Esq. (Philadelphia: Privately printed, 1872);

Translations and Other Rhymes (Philadelphia: Privately printed, 1882);

International Copyright. An Open Letter (Philadelphia, 1884);

A History of the Inquisition of the Middle Ages, 3 volumes (New York: Harper, 1888; London: Low, Marston, Searle & Rivington, 1888);

Chapters from the Religious History of Spain Connected with the Inquisition (Philadelphia: Lea Brothers, 1890);

Is There a Roman Catholic Church? An Excursus in Scholastic Theology (Philadelphia: Dornan, 1891);

A History of Auricular Confession and Indulgences in the Latin Church, 3 volumes (Philadelphia: Lea Brothers, 1896; London: Sonnenschein, 1896);

The Dead Hand: A Brief Sketch of the Relations Between Church and State with Regard to Ecclesiastical

Henry Charles Lea

Property and the Religious Orders (Philadelphia: Dornan, 1900);

The Moriscos of Spain, Their Conversion and Expulsion (Philadelphia: Lea Brothers, 1901; London: Quaritch, 1901);

A History of the Inquisition of Spain, 4 volumes (New York: Macmillan/London: Macmillan, 1906-1907);

The Inquisition in the Spanish Dependencies; Sicily—Naples—Sardinia—Milan—the Canaries—Mexico—Peru—New Granada (New York: Macmillan/London: Macmillan, 1908);

Minor Historical Writings and Other Essays, edited by Arthur C. Howland (Philadelphia: University of Pennsylvania Press/London: Oxford University Press, 1942).

OTHER: "Indulgences in Spain," in *Papers of the American Society of Church History*, 1 (1889), pp. 129-171;

"The Martyrdom of San Pedro Arbués," in *Papers of the American Historical Association*, 3 (1889), pp. 433-453;

A Formulary of the Papal Penitentiary in the Thirteenth Century, edited by Lea (Philadelphia: Lea Brothers, 1892);

"The Absolution Formula of the Templars," in *Papers of the American Society of Church History*, 5 (1893), pp. 37-58;

"The Eve of the Reformation," in *Cambridge Modern History*, 13 volumes (Cambridge: Cambridge University Press, 1902-1912), I: 653-692;

"Ethical Values in History," in *Annual Report of the American Historical Association for the Year 1903*, 2 volumes (Washington, D.C.: Government Printing Office, 1904), I: 53-69;

Materials Toward a History of Witchcraft, collected by Lea, edited by Arthur C. Howland, 3 volumes (Philadelphia: University of Pennsylvania Press, 1939).

Henry Charles Lea must be considered one of the most remarkable men in the American scholarly community of the nineteenth century. His reputation rests chiefly upon voluminous histories of the medieval Church. To the distinguished contemporary English historian Lord Acton, who reviewed Lea's *History of the Inquisition of the Middle Ages* for the *English Historical Review* in 1888, the American had produced a work which "will assuredly be accepted as the most important contribution of the new world to the religious history of the old." Various of Lea's books were translated into German, French, and Italian. He received honorary degrees, memberships, and offices in learned societies in the U.S. and Europe and was elected president of the American Historical Association in 1903. Lea also is notable in the history of American historical writing for being among the leaders in applying and promoting the new scientific methodological techniques of documentary analysis and criticism. Yet for all of Lea's involvement in the world of scholarship, he never held an academic post.

Lea's scholarly contributions and interests were by no means limited to history. His passion for research first was directed toward science. By the age of fifteen, he published the first of nine

articles and reviews which appeared between 1841 and 1851 and reputedly added new data to chemistry and conchology. From 1841 to 1882, Lea published some twenty-seven works of poetry and literary criticism in periodicals such as the *Southern Literary Messenger* and the *Knickerbocker*. In what might be called his political phase, Lea published about one hundred and sixteen articles, pamphlets, and letters to editors relating to issues such as support for the Union effort in the Civil War, for reform of the Civil Service, and for reform at various levels of government, especially in his native city, Philadelphia. Lea was the author of the Chace Copyright Act of 1891. His advice also was sought by several U.S. presidents.

An enduring commitment to professional and public service was still another dimension of Lea's almost boundless energy. Lea actively supported, in some cases helped to found, and not infrequently held leadership positions in many learned and political organizations. Illustrative of Lea's devotion to the preservation of the Union and of his

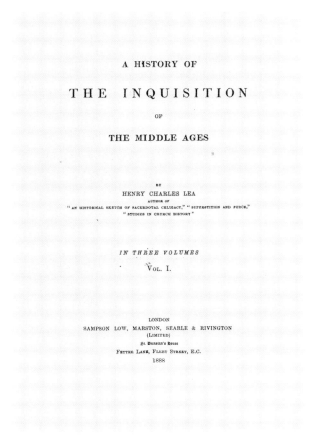

A HISTORY OF

THE INQUISITION

OF

THE MIDDLE AGES

BY

HENRY CHARLES LEA

AUTHOR OF
" AN HISTORICAL SKETCH OF SACERDOTAL CELIBACY," " SUPERSTITION AND FORCE,"
" STUDIES IN CHURCH HISTORY"

IN THREE VOLUMES
VOL. I.

LONDON
SAMPSON LOW, MARSTON, SEARLE & RIVINGTON
(LIMITED)
St. Dunstan's House
Fetter Lane, Fleet Street, E.C.
1888

Title page for a volume from the first British edition of the work Lord Acton described as "assuredly . . . the most important contribution of the new world to the religious history of the old"

passion for political reform were his efforts on be-half of the Union League, the Citizens Municipal Reform Association, and the Civil Service Reform Association. Although a staunch Republican, Lea put aside party affiliation to promote political re-form in Philadelphia and elsewhere. He sent a do-nation to the European Old Catholic movement which was generated by opposition to doctrines enunciated by the First Vatican Council (1869-1870); and he encouraged several individuals who broke with the Catholic Church. Yet earlier, in 1844, Lea personally stood guard to protect Cath-olic church property in Philadelphia from nativist attacks. Lea belonged to about twenty-three learned societies and served as either president or vice-president of the American Historical Associ-ation, the Wycliffe Society (American branch), the Historical Society of Pennsylvania, and the Amer-ican Academy of Political and Social Science.

Much of Lea's life was devoted to a business career in his family's publishing house, under whose imprint many of his own historical works appeared. Lea joined the firm founded by his ma-ternal grandfather, Mathew Carey, in 1843. In 1851 he succeeded his father as a partner. From 1865 to 1880, Lea was solely responsible for car-rying on the business, which he did in his own name as H. C. Lea & Co. On at least two occasions, Lea's health broke from the strain of his overexertions and forced him to retire from the business. The first of these, when Lea was twenty-two, led to the emergence of history as his principal scholarly in-terest.

Henry Charles Lea came from an old colonial Philadelphia family which already had distin-guished itself in the world of scholarship and pub-lishing by the early nineteenth century. His paternal ancestor, John Lea, had accompanied Wil-liam Penn on his second voyage to his new colony on board the *Canterbury* in 1699. Lea's father, Isaac, was a famous naturalist who was awarded a doc-torate of laws degree from Harvard University in 1852. Lea's mother, Frances Anne Carey, whom Isaac Lea married in 1821 in Philadelphia, was the daughter of the prominent Philadelphia publisher Mathew Carey, a onetime Irish patriot whose American publishing career had been aided by a $400 loan from LaFayette. Henry Charles Lea was the third of four children. He married his first cousin Anna Caroline Jaudon in 1850. Two of their sons also became associated with the Lea publishing house.

There are striking parallels between several behavioral patterns followed by Lea's parents and ones found in Henry Charles Lea's career. Isaac Lea joined his father-in-law's publishing firm while continuing his scientific studies. Henry's religious independence is perhaps prefigured in his father's willingness to sacrifice membership in the Society of Friends in order to serve in a musket company during the War of 1812. Both Lea's parents changed their original religious affiliations and ul-timately became Episcopalians. Frances Carey had been a Roman Catholic, and whatever Isaac Lea's beliefs were at the time of his marriage to Frances, the ceremony was a Roman Catholic one. Henry Charles Lea became a Unitarian, though he re-tained nominal Episcopalian membership. Among the scholarly models for Lea were his father and his uncle, Henry Charles Carey, an economist of note who at one time served as president of the family publishing business. Lea's mother and father gave him his first direction into the world of learning. Frances Lea taught her son the Greek alphabet when he was six years old, and Isaac Lea stimulated the boy's first interest in science.

Given his scholarly achievements, Lea's lack of formal education is certainly one of his notable qualities. Except for a brief period, he was either instructed privately, particularly by a tutor, Eugen-ius Nulty, or was self-taught. The American me-dievalist D. C. Munro, who knew Lea, claimed that he taught himself the scientific historical method he championed. Lea, who knew Latin, Greek, and many other languages, is said to have learned Ger-man at sixty and Dutch at eighty. The keys to Lea's prolific literary achievements were his insatiable ap-petite for study and a firm adherence to a regular routine for writing.

The first of Lea's physical breakdowns influ-enced his evolution into a medieval ecclesiastical historian. During his convalescence Lea read the French chronicler Jean Froissart. Froissart stimu-lated his curiosity about medieval law and the Latin Church as keys to understanding medieval civili-zation. The Church became Lea's preoccupation. Lea's publishing in the field of medieval history began rather modestly in 1858 with a review of Sir Francis Palgrave's *History of Normandy and of En-gland* in the *North American Review*. The literary tidal wave only occurred after the end of the Civil War.

True to the new scientific method of historical study, Lea prided himself on basing his descrip-tions and analyses upon the sources themselves. His essay collection *Superstition and Force* (1866) is an excellent illustration of this methodology in prac-tice. In the course of his investigations, Lea accu-

BY THE SAME AUTHOR—Just Published.

I.

SUPERSTITION AND FORCE:

ESSAYS ON THE WAGER OF LAW, THE WAGER OF
BATTLE, THE ORDEAL, AND TORTURE.

THIRD EDITION, REVISED.

In one handsome volume. royal 12mo., of 552 pages, extra cloth, $2 50.

The copious collection of facts by which Mr. Lea has illustrated his subject shows in the fullest manner the constant conflict and varying success, the advances and defeats, by which the progress of humane legislation has been and is still marked. This work fills up with the fullest exemplification and detail the wise remarks which we have quoted above. As a book of ready reference on the subject it is of the highest value.—*Westminster Review*, Oct. 1867.

This is a book of extraordinary research. Mr. Lea has entered into his subject *con amore*; and a more striking record of the cruel superstitions of our unhappy Middle Ages could not possibly have been compiled. . . . As a work of curious inquiry on certain outlying points of obsolete law, "Superstition and Force" is one of the most remarkable books we have met with.—*London Athenæum*, Nov. 3, 1866.

One of the gloomiest chapters in the history of mankind is that of the miseries which have resulted from their errors in the search for truth, and the false methods adopted to discover it. And there are few more striking episodes in this chapter than that which Mr. Lea has set before us in his excellent volume.—*North American Review*, Oct. 1866.

II.

AN HISTORICAL SKETCH

OF

SACERDOTAL CELIBACY IN THE CHRISTIAN CHURCH.

In one handsome octavo volume of 600 pages, extra cloth, $3 75.

This subject has recently been treated with very great learning and with admirable impartiality by an American author, Mr. Henry C. Lea, in his *History of Sacerdotal Celibacy*, which is certainly one of the most valuable works that America has produced. Since the great history of Dean Milman, I know no work in English which has thrown more light on the moral condition of the Middle Ages, and none which is more fitted to dispel the gross illusions concerning that period which Positive writers and writers of a certain ecclesiastical school have conspired to sustain.—*Lecky's History of European Morals*, Chap. V.

In freshness and exactness of detail, in conscientious citation of authorities, in the impartiality with which all possible sources of information have been searched, in learning and scholarly finish, it is absolutely unapproached by any similar treatise which has issued from the American press. Indeed, the number of foreign historical works which have equalled it in these particulars might be readily counted on the fingers —*Quarterly Journal of Psychological Medicine*, Oct. 1867.

Thus, his chapter on the Anglican church is perhaps the most connected and most satisfactory account of our own Reformation, as to the question of celibacy or marriage, that could be found —*Quarterly Review*, Oct. 1869.

Publisher's advertisement for new editions of two works by Lea

mulated a large library of printed sources and transcriptions of manuscripts obtained from agents in Europe. After his death this collection, together with his own letters and manuscripts and the furnishings of his library, was given to the University of Pennsylvania, where the library in its reconstructed state survives as a monument to his scholarship.

Many of Lea's works generated considerable criticism from some Roman Catholic circles. To cite a single example, *Studies in Church History* (1869) portrayed the papacy on the eve of the First Vatican Council as a human invention endowed with powers which had in part been won on the basis of forgeries. Contrary to Lea's own protestations of impartiality, he seldom failed to guide readers to his desired conclusion or to pass judgment on some of the episodes he had related. A magnificently

sweeping moralization appears in *Studies in Church History:* "Had it [the Church] been true to the law which it professed to administer; had it shunned the vulgar ambitions of power and wealth, and had it taught by precept and example the evangel of love, Christendom would not now, in the nineteenth century after the birth of the Redeemer, be groping as blindly as ever over the as yet insoluble problems of existence."

Lea believed in an evolutionary Christianity which departed from primitive simplicity and was transformed through the acquisition of various legal powers into a system of despotism. As Lea wrote to the French archaeologist Salomon Reinach, the Catholic Church became "a political system adverse to the interests of humanity." Doubtless this kind of drift in Lea's writings was what enhanced their popularity with European anticlericals. It could be, however, that Lea's editorializing was a manifestation of his passion for reform at work, applied to the church instead of secular politics. Correspondence cited by E. A. Ryan in "The Religion of Henry Charles Lea" (1951) indicates that Lea never desired to "shake the confidence of anyone in the faith in which he had been bred"; nor did Lea wish to assume "responsibility to guide any soul." Perhaps he voiced his reformer's intent when he wrote in *Studies in Church History* that the church's "real friends are those whom she regards as her worst enemies." Subsequent scholarship may have altered some of Lea's assertions and softened some of his judgments, and passages of his prose may appear to a twentieth-century reader as overly rhetorical. Nevertheless, the praise of Lord Acton, who was a Roman Catholic, remains well deserved.

Biography:

Edward Bradley, *Henry Charles Lea: A Biography* (Philadelphia: University of Pennsylvania Press, 1931).

References:

Lord Acton, "Review: *A History of the Inquisition of the Middle Ages,* by Henry Charles Lea," *English Historical Review,* 3 (October 1888): 773-788;

Paul Maria Baumgarten, *Henry Charles Lea's Historical Writings: A Critical Inquiry into their Method and Merit* (New York: Wagner, 1909);

E. P. Cheney, "Henry Charles Lea," in *Proceedings of the British Academy,* 5 (1911-1912), pp. 517-521;

C. H. Haskins, "Tribute to Henry Charles Lea," in

Proceedings of the Massachusetts Historical Society,
43 (1909), pp. 183-188;

E. A. Ryan, S. J., "The Religion of Henry Charles
Lea," in *Mélanges; Joseph de Ghellinck S. J.,* 2
volumes (Gembloux: Éditions J. Duclot,
1951), II: 1043-1051.

Papers:
Lea's manuscripts and correspondence are at the
Henry Charles Lea Library, University of Pennsylvania.

Henry Cabot Lodge
(12 May 1850-9 November 1924)

William C. Widenor
University of Illinois at Urbana-Champaign

SELECTED BOOKS: *Life and Letters of George Cabot*
(Boston: Little, Brown, 1877);

A Short History of the English Colonies in America (New
York: Harper, 1881);

Alexander Hamilton (Boston: Houghton Mifflin,
1882);

Daniel Webster (Boston & New York: Houghton Mifflin, 1883);

Studies in History (Boston & New York: Houghton
Mifflin, 1884);

George Washington, 2 volumes (Boston & New York:
Houghton Mifflin, 1889);

Boston (London & New York: Longmans, Green,
1891);

Historical and Political Essays (Boston & New York:
Houghton Mifflin, 1892);

Speeches (Boston & New York: Houghton Mifflin,
1892); enlarged as *Speeches and Addresses,
1884-1909* (Boston & New York: Houghton
Mifflin, 1909);

Hero Tales from American History, by Lodge and
Theodore Roosevelt (New York: Century,
1895);

*Certain Accepted Heroes and Other Essays in Literature
and Politics* (New York & London: Harper,
1897);

The Story of the Revolution, 2 volumes (New York:
Scribners, 1898; London: Constable, 1898);

The War with Spain (New York & London: Harper,
1899);

A Fighting Frigate, and Other Essays and Addresses
(New York: Scribners, 1902);

A Frontier Town, and Other Essays (New York: Scribners, 1906);

Henry Cabot Lodge, circa 1900

One Hundred Years of Peace (New York: Macmillan,
1913);

Early Memories (New York: Scribners, 1913; London: Constable, 1913);

*The Democracy of the Constitution, and Other Addresses
and Essays* (New York: Scribners, 1915);

Two Commencement Addresses (Cambridge: Harvard
University Press, 1915);

War Addresses, 1915-1917 (Boston & New York:
Houghton Mifflin, 1917);

The Senate of the United States, and Other Essays and Addresses, Historical and Literary (New York: Scribners, 1921);

The Senate and the League of Nations (New York & London: Scribners, 1925).

OTHER: "The Land Law of the Anglo-Saxons," in *Essays in Anglo-Saxon Law,* edited by Henry Adams (Boston: Little, Brown/London: Macmillan, 1876), pp. 59-119;

The Works of Alexander Hamilton, edited by Lodge, 9 volumes (New York & London: Putnam's, 1885-1886);

The Federalist, edited by Lodge (New York & London: Putnam's, 1888);

André's Journal; An Authentic Record of the Movements and Engagements of the British Army in America from June 1777 to November 1778 as Recorded Day to Day by Major John André, edited by Lodge, 2 volumes (Boston: Privately printed, 1903);

"Force and Peace," in *Annals of the American Academy of Political and Social Science,* 60 (1915), pp. 197-212;

"Francis Parkman," in *Proceedings of the Massachusetts Historical Society,* 56 (1923), pp. 319-335;

Selections from the Correspondence of Theodore Roosevelt and Henry Cabot Lodge, edited by Lodge, 2 volumes (New York: Scribners, 1925).

PERIODICAL PUBLICATIONS: "Critical Review of Von Holst's *Constitutional and Political History of the United States,*" by Lodge and Henry Adams, *North American Review,* 123 (October 1876): 328-361;

"Limited Sovereignty in the United States," *Atlantic Monthly,* 43 (February 1879): 184-192;

"True Americanism," *Harvard Graduates' Magazine,* 3 (September 1894): 9-23;

"Our Blundering Foreign Policy," *Forum,* 19 (March 1895): 8-17;

"Our Duty to Cuba," *Forum,* 21 (May 1896): 278-287;

"One Hundred Years of the Monroe Doctrine," *Scribner's Magazine,* 74 (October 1923): 413-423.

Henry Cabot Lodge had a long and controversial political career as representative and senator from Massachusetts from 1887 to 1924 and as majority leader of the Senate from 1918 until his death. His prominence as a leader of the Republican party, culminating in his leadership of the opposition to the Wilsonian version of the League of Nations following World War I, has left his reputation as historian in eclipse. But, in fact, he was one of America's very first professionally trained historians, and he produced a large body of historical writing, some of it remarkably innovative for its day and much of it widely read.

Lodge was born in Boston on 12 May 1850, the only son of John Ellerton Lodge, a prosperous merchant involved in the China trade. His mother was Anna Cabot, granddaughter of George Cabot, the prominent Federalist leader. Born into a society and class that was convinced of its superior virtue and culture, Lodge became for many of his contemporaries the quintessential Bostonian, a representative of both the best and the less-attractive characteristics of Brahmin society. He was educated at private schools that placed great emphasis on the classics and on the mastery of Latin and Greek. His undergraduate years were marked more by social than by academic distinction, and he graduated from Harvard in 1871 without any definite career plans. He probably had other preoccupations. On the day after his graduation he married his cousin, Anna Cabot Mills Davis, daughter of Rear Admiral Charles H. Davis, and together he and his bride embarked on a year-long trip exploring the sights and societies of Europe.

It was at this point in his life that Lodge sought the advice of his former Harvard history teacher Henry Adams, who strongly urged upon him the choice of a "historico-literary" career, emphasizing the attractions of addressing the great questions—what men are and have been driving at—and concluding with the admonition that Lodge would have to work hard and master the new German historical method of diligent and careful research. Lodge appears to have sought to model his own career closely on that of Thomas Babington Macaulay, a course which permitted both literary and political pursuits. On his return from Europe he enrolled at the Harvard Law School from which he received his law degree in 1874. But it was Henry Adams's influence which was probably decisive. When Adams himself returned from Europe in 1873 to resume the editorship of the *North American Review* and continue his teaching career at Harvard, he took young Lodge under his wing and appointed him assistant editor of the *Review.* Lodge also enrolled in Adams's advanced class on medieval institutions. At the *Review,* Adams taught Lodge to write with simplicity and precision, and at Harvard he instructed Lodge in the virtues of the new German historiography. With two other students, Ernest Young and

J. Laurence Laughlin, Lodge was part of what was probably the first real graduate seminar in history in the United States, and out of that endeavor emerged *Essays in Anglo-Saxon Law,* edited by Adams and containing Lodge's dissertation on land law. The volume appeared in 1876, the same year that Lodge received his Ph.D. from Harvard. *Essays in Anglo-Saxon Law* reflected Adams's preoccupation with German method and thinking and was devoted to the now-discredited notion that English and American law and political procedures had Teutonic origins, that there was a strong link between ancient German tribal practices and modern constitutional liberties.

There is evidence that Adams intended Lodge for a teaching career, and Lodge did teach American colonial history at Harvard from 1876 to 1879. But Lodge himself was determined on a public career, and it was the same Henry Adams who fanned the fires of Lodge's interest in politics by giving him an important role in the Independent political movement of 1876. Lodge never abandoned his interest in scholarship for a career in politics. Rather his interest in history and in politics developed in tandem, and it probably never occurred to him to try to separate one from the other.

Lodge's history, even his early work which clearly displayed the influence of Adams, always had a strong political tone. Adams warned him that unless he organized his history around some faith in general principles or some theory of the progress of civilization, he was destined to write a history defending those historical figures or movements whose prejudices coincided most closely with his own. Detachment was never Lodge's strong suit. He took his methodology from Adams but his purpose from Francis Parkman and others who looked upon history as the special preserve of Boston and its Brahmin aristocracy. Lodge's early historical writing shows painstaking research and documentation far superior to the standards of his day, but from the first his methodology was ever the servant of a deep-seated political and social purpose.

To his credit he usually admitted as much. In his first book, a justificatory biography of his great-grandfather and most illustrious ancestor entitled *Life and Letters of George Cabot* (1877), he stated his intention to present the Federalist position "in the strongest and clearest light" and went on to admit to an interest in extolling the virtues of men and manners now out of fashion in the bustling, brawling democracy of post-Civil War America. History had special attractions for Lodge's class, race, and

region, and this was the more so in an era when traditional Massachusetts society was reeling under the assaults of the new industrialism and of massive immigration and was beginning to doubt its role in a nation which seemed to accept lightly the corruption and jobbery of the Grant administration. In his *Life and Letters of George Cabot,* Lodge did more than exalt his own ancestry; he also investigated the sources of New England's special character and distinction and its seeming monopoly on culture and civic virtue. In sum, he took up history with a profoundly conservative purpose in an effort to preserve standards, values, and institutions that he thought were threatened with extinction.

Perhaps his most interesting and innovative work was his next book, *A Short History of the English Colonies in America* (1881), which was based on fresh and original economic and social source materials that Lodge had assembled for his lectures at Harvard. Both in its emphasis on the importance of economic history and in its attempt to depict manners, customs, and social conditions it was far in advance of its time. The depth of the research involved made such an impression on Moses Coit Tyler, a Cornell faculty member and pioneer literary historian, that he quickly adopted it as a text for his new course on the colonial period. But *A Short History of the English Colonies in America* also had its political and social purposes. The contrasts Lodge made between the society of New England and that of the Southern colonies could easily be read as an explanation for why the North won the Civil War.

The Civil War had coincided with Lodge's most impressionable years, and he always admitted that it gave a special flavor and intensity to his patriotism. The war also stimulated his interest in history, for to Lodge an interest in history was proof of national consciousness and recognition of the fact that a nation had come to its place in the world. Like Henry Adams, and under the abiding influence of the Romantic historians, Lodge tended to interpret all of American history as the growth and advance of the national principle. But for New Englanders, their belief in moral progress temporarily restored by the Northern victory, the triumph of the principle of national unity was easily transposed into a vindication of the values represented by the civilization of New England and the democracy of Plymouth. It was both appealing and comfortable for New Englanders to interpret their ascendancy as a function of superior character, and that led readily to a preoccupation with the historical conditions of its development. Several of

Lodge's early books, including *Studies in History* (1884), *Boston* (1891), and *Historical and Political Essays* (1892), are products of this generational state of mind. He always betrayed, in the succinct expression of Henry Adams, "the consciousness that he and his people had a past, if they dared but avow it." Temporarily at least, in the atmosphere of post-Civil War conservative resurgence, they dared.

Especially important for Lodge was the fact that the Civil War had called into question the Jeffersonian, states' rights, democratic school of thinking that had long dominated American historiography. Like many of his fellow New Englanders, he was strongly attracted to a revisionist historiography epitomized by the remark of Lodge's cousin and close friend, John T. Morse, Jr., who reportedly said, "Let the Jeffersonians and Jacksonians beware! I will poison the popular mind!" The object was a rehabilitation of American conservatives, particularly the Federalists, to the end of demonstrating the necessity for the preservation of the traditions and conservative habits of thought that had permitted the United States to survive its trials, and, more specifically, to show that events of the period 1800-1815 and of the Civil War had forced the Jeffersonians to rule "in the manner and after the methods prescribed by Hamilton." The message to be conveyed was that Hamiltonian leadership and methods would always be indispensable to the American democracy. Though Lodge had a personal stake in the rehabilitation of his most distinguished ancestor, George Cabot, his efforts were part of a shift in the thinking of a whole generation of Bostonians, and soon after the early biography he turned his attention to such leading figures as Washington and Hamilton in an effort to demonstrate that the Federalists had possessed "a greater amount of ability than was ever displayed by all other political parties in America."

Research now began to take a back seat to political and social purpose. Lodge began a long collaboration with John T. Morse, Jr., editor-in-chief of the American Statesmen series, who assigned to Lodge the writing of the biographies of Hamilton, Washington, and Webster. The series was by any standards of the day a popular and financial success. Lodge told a reporter in 1907 that his biography of Hamilton had sold over 35,000 copies and was still in demand. None of Lodge's three contributions to the series betrayed much in the way of new findings based on additional research, but all reflected a new emphasis on style and readability. Macaulay's influence was now par-

amount, as evidenced by Lodge's pronouncement that "the only history the world will ever read is the history that is literature." Lodge wanted an audience and knew how to reach it.

The historical reputation of Federalism was intimately bound up with that of Hamilton, and Lodge was an eager participant in his rehabilitation; after the biography *Alexander Hamilton* appeared in 1882, Lodge produced a nine-volume edition of Hamilton's *Works* in 1885 and 1886. Both Lodge's *Alexander Hamilton* and his later, two-volume life, *George Washington* (1889), are particularly revealing of his combined historical and political purpose. The great and long-hidden secret of America's political success was now openly alleged to be the inherent conservatism of its people and institutions. But it was not easy to find an audience for a conservative and aristocratic history in a liberal and democratic country. Offense was under the circumstances the best defense; it was, as Henry Adams once told Lodge, "always safe to abuse Jefferson." The Civil War had dealt the Jeffersonians a strong blow. Their belief in states' rights and weak government was now out of fashion, and Lodge sought to build on that foundation. He was continually at pains to demonstrate the Jeffersonians' inability to devise a workable foreign and national security policy and their general incapacity for truly national leadership. Today, many of Lodge's pronouncements on the Jeffersonians seem revealingly partisan and unduly harsh, but such strictures were common among the post-Civil War generation. In fact, many of Lodge's subsequent stands in national politics, such as his advocacy of a strong navy and his opposition to compulsory international arbitration, have obvious antecedents in his historical appraisals of the failings of the Jeffersonians. His biographies of both Hamilton and Washington demonstrate a preoccupation with foreign policy problems and are replete with references to the necessity of maintaining a strong military establishment and of avoiding what he termed a "peace at all risks" policy. The recurrent problems of the American democracy in those areas were ever the conservatives' likeliest opportunity.

For Lodge the overriding object of history was to teach political wisdom. History thus was a substitute for philosophy and often for religion as well. All his life he preached its value, and what he said in his capacity as president of the Massachusetts Historical Society in 1921 was often foremost in his mind, namely that "there never was a time when reverence for and knowledge of the past were more necessary than at this moment to deal with the great problems of the present and to encourage hopes and stimulate preparation for the future." The result was that over the years his writing took on an increasingly didactic tone. Sometimes it even took on the trappings of moral drama. His history of *The War with Spain* (1899) reflects all the prejudices of the romantic historians and is one long paean to the supposedly progressive historical forces of Protestantism, republicanism, and nationalism. History, Lodge believed, had much to teach Americans, ahistorical people that they were, but could only do so if they revered it and used it to demonstrate the limits of human possibility. Lodge had a particularly strong sense of historical continuity. From his conservative perspective the basic problems of human existence were recurrent; the great and underlying qualities which made and saved men and nations did not change.

It followed naturally that those qualities required continual cultivation. One way of encouraging that cultivation was by exhortation, by repeated jeremiads urging the American people to respect and be guided by past virtue, and Lodge seldom missed an opportunity for such rhetorical appeals. Another way was to write a kind of idealistic history that held up as a model for oncoming generations the great heroes of the American historical experience. Though in theory Lodge always emphasized the power of the movements which engaged great masses of people, he himself never wrote that kind of history. The appeal of writing the history of great men was always too great. No nation was exempt from the need for inspired leadership, and as a result he often saw his role as one fostering in the next generation a strong sense of national sentiment and of the possibility of heroic achievement. Several of his books fall into this category, *A Fighting Frigate* (1902), *Certain Accepted Heroes* (1897), and especially *Hero Tales from American History* (1895), which he wrote in collaboration with Theodore Roosevelt. Even Lodge realized that using history to inculcate the kind of heroic ideal to which the preindustrial aristocracy of the United States was naturally drawn greatly reduced its value as scholarship, but he and many of his generation never hesitated to pay that price.

Though some writers have claimed that Lodge abandoned a career in history for one in politics, he always considered the two as complementary aspects of a public career. True, his active engagement in politics took its toll on his work in history. He entered Congress in 1887, was elected to the United States Senate in 1893, and remained in the Senate until his death in 1924, serving as both Republican majority leader and as chairman of the Senate Foreign Relations Committee. His writing gradually became more strident and more partisan in tone, sometimes descending almost to the level of Republican party campaign tracts. But as he noted in his journal in 1890: "Some days ago Theodore [Roosevelt] said to me 'we must write our side; they think that history will be written by them or their successors who will take their—i.e., the mugwump view of us.'" To the end of his life Lodge displayed a determination not to let that happen, and both of his last contributions, *Selections from the Correspondence of Theodore Roosevelt and Henry Cabot Lodge* and *The Senate and the League of Nations* published in 1925, should be viewed in that light. Certainly, Lodge always viewed history as a political weapon, and his supposed lack of objectivity has brought down a torrent of criticism on his head. But despite the protestations of his many detractors, it is also true that academic historians have always had difficulty separating their history from their politics. To Henry Adams's accolade that Lodge had the singular merit of being interesting, one might well add, and of not being a hypocrite.

Biographies:

Charles S. Groves, *Henry Cabot Lodge: The Statesman* (Boston: Small, Maynard, 1925);

William Lawrence, *Henry Cabot Lodge: A Biographical Sketch* (Boston: Houghton Mifflin, 1925);

Karl Schriftgiesser, *The Gentleman from Massachusetts: Henry Cabot Lodge* (Boston: Little, Brown, 1944);

John A. Garraty, *Henry Cabot Lodge: A Biography* (New York: Knopf, 1953).

References:

John A. S. Grenville and George Berkeley Young, *Politics, Strategy, and American Diplomacy: Studies in Foreign Policy, 1873-1917* (New Haven: Yale University Press, 1966);

James E. Hewes, Jr., "Henry Cabot Lodge and the League of Nations," in *Proceedings of the American Philosophical Society*, 114 (1970), pp. 245-255;

John T. Morse, Jr., "Henry Cabot Lodge," *Harvard Graduates' Magazine*, 33 (March 1925): 439-455;

Charles G. Washburn, "Memoir of Henry Cabot Lodge," in *Proceedings of the Massachusetts Historical Society*, 58 (1925), pp. 324-376;

William C. Widenor, *Henry Cabot Lodge and the Search for an American Foreign Policy* (Berkeley: University of California Press, 1980).

Papers:
Lodge's papers are at the Massachusetts Historical Society.

Alfred Thayer Mahan
(27 September 1840-1 December 1914)

Robert Seager II
University of Kentucky

SELECTED BOOKS: *The Gulf and Inland Waters* (New York: Scribners, 1883; London: Low, 1899);

The Influence of Sea Power Upon History, 1660-1783 (Boston: Little, Brown, 1890; London: Low, Marston, Searle & Rivington, 1890);

The Influence of Sea Power Upon the French Revolution and Empire, 1793-1812, 2 volumes (Boston: Little, Brown, 1892; London: Low, Marston, Searle & Rivington, 1892);

Admiral Farragut (New York: Appleton, 1892; London: Low, Marston, Searle & Rivington, 1892);

The Life of Nelson: The Embodiment of the Sea Power of Great Britain, 2 volumes (Boston: Little, Brown, 1897; London: Low, Marston, 1897); revised and enlarged (Boston: Little, Brown, 1899; London: Low, Marston, 1899);

The Interest of America in Sea Power, Present and Future (Boston: Little, Brown, 1897; London: Low, Marston, 1897);

"Major Operations of the Royal Navy, 1762-1783," in *A History of the Royal Navy*," edited by William L. Clowes, 7 volumes (London: Low, Marston, 1897-1903), III (1898): 353-565; republished with a new introduction as *The Major Operations of the Navies in the War of American Independence* (Boston: Little, Brown, 1913; London: Low, Marston, 1913);

Lessons of the War with Spain, and Other Articles (Boston: Little, Brown, 1899; London: Low, Marston, 1899);

The Problem of Asia and Its Effects Upon International Policies (Boston: Little, Brown, 1900; London: Low, Marston, 1900);

The Story of War in South Africa, 1899-1900 (London:

Alfred Thayer Mahan (U.S. Naval War College)

Low, Marston, 1900); also published as *The War in South Africa* (New York: Collier, 1900);

Types of Naval Officers Drawn from the History of the British Navy; With Some Account of the Conditions of Naval Warfare at the Beginning of the Eigh-

teenth Century, and of Its Subsequent Development During the Sail Period (Boston: Little, Brown, 1901; London: Low, Marston, 1902);

Retrospect and Prospect: Studies in International Relations, Naval and Political (Boston: Little, Brown, 1902; London: Low, Marston, 1902);

Sea Power in Its Relations to the War of 1812, 2 volumes (Boston: Little, Brown, 1905; London: Low, Marston, 1905);

From Sail to Steam: Recollections of Naval Life (New York & London: Harper, 1907);

Naval Administration and Warfare, Some General Principles, With Other Essays (Boston: Little, Brown, 1908; London: Low, Marston, 1908);

The Harvest Within: Thoughts on the Life of a Christian (Boston: Little, Brown, 1909; London: Longmans, Green, 1909);

The Interest of America in International Conditions (Boston: Little, Brown, 1910; London: Low, Marston, 1910);

Naval Strategy, Compared and Contrasted with the Principles of Military Operations on Land: Lectures Delivered at U.S. Naval War College, Newport, R.I., Between the Years 1887 and 1911 (Boston: Little, Brown, 1911; London: Low, Marston, 1911);

Armaments and Arbitration, or the Place of Force in the International Relations of States (New York & London: Harper, 1912).

OTHER: "Some Neglected Aspects of War," in *Some Neglected Aspects of War, by Captain A. T. Mahan . . . Together with The Power that Makes for Peace, by Henry S. Pritchett . . . and The Capture of Private Property at Sea, by Julian S. Corbett . . .* (Boston: Little, Brown, 1907).

In 1890 Captain Alfred Thayer Mahan, an obscure American naval officer, published a book which revolutionized the way statesmen of the world's major powers looked at the relationship of naval power, foreign policy, and national survival in a state system that was becoming increasingly volcanic. Soon translated into German, French, Russian, and Japanese, Mahan's *The Influence of Sea Power Upon History, 1660-1783* quickly became the handbook of those political and military leaders who came to believe, during the two decades before World War I, that the power, prosperity, and historical survival of the nation state (their own in particular) depended in substantial measure on policies embracing imperialism and colonialism; and that such policies related specifically to what Mahan in his book called "command of the sea."

It is certainly not overstating the case to argue that *The Influence of Sea Power Upon History, 1660-1783* powerfully affected the thinking and behavior of those statesmen responsible for the outbreak of the Spanish-American War, the Russo-Japanese War, and World War I. In this sense, it was one of the few truly significant books written by an American in the nineteenth century.

Mahan was born at the U.S. Military Academy in West Point, New York, eldest son of Mary Helena Okill Mahan and Dennis Hart Mahan, professor of civil and military engineering, dean of faculty at the Academy, and the author of seminal works on field fortifications and infantry tactics. Mahan grew to young manhood in a home filled with books and journals and in an atmosphere of drums, bugles, and marching men. His was a world of Duty-Honor-Country ruled by a stern father who was as dedicated a practitioner of absolute discipline in his own household as he was in his classes and at parade. How this rigid upbringing affected young Mahan is not known. He scarcely mentioned his father or the West Point years in his autobiography, *From Sail to Steam* (1907).

At age twelve Mahan was placed in St. James's School, an Episcopal boarding school in Hagerstown, Maryland. Two years later his father entered him in Columbia College in New York City. In September 1856, at age sixteen, he joined the third (sophomore) class at the U.S. Naval Academy in Annapolis. The navy's unwise decision permitting him to skip the fourth (freshman) class year at Annapolis was based on the fact that he had already had two years of college-level work at Columbia. He thus joined a group of twenty-eight young men (winnowed from forty-nine) who had survived the fierce hazing of the plebe year and had already formed their cliques. As a third classman, Mahan experienced no hazing. Consequently, from the moment he arrived at the Naval Academy he was an outsider, a marked man. He remained an outsider until his graduation, second in the class of June 1859.

Mahan never made any secret of the fact that he considered the Academy's rote-memory curriculum to be wholly lacking in breadth, intellectual challenge, and interest. Instead of studying, he read history and romantic novels, chased Annapolis girls, and delighted in expressing his contempt for the institution to all who would listen. The fact that he was exceptionally bright, handsome, articulate, arrogant, and through his father well-connected in the service, did not endear him to his classmates; nor did his perverse practice of giving them demerits for minor infractions. During the final months of his senior year fully half of his classmates severed all personal relations with him, placing him in "Coventry." In sum, Mahan's Naval Academy experience was the beginning of his life-long hatred of the very navy which would later hold him and his writing in the highest esteem.

His career at the Academy also foreshadowed the fact that, while he had a first-rate mind, he was to the end of his life a contentious, often disagreeable man. Those who came to know Mahan in the navy considered him conceited, aloof, pompous, quick to anger, intolerant of lesser intellects, and unwilling to accept or profit from criticism. His dedicated Episcopalianism shaded into a religiosity that was as tiresomely egocentric as his narrow Victorian morality was pervasive. Throughout his life there were, by his own count, only two men he thought of as friends, and he saw little of either of them over the years. He had not a single close friend in the U.S. Navy. As his daughter Ellen recalled, using the words of Rudyard Kipling, he was "The Cat That Walked By Himself."

During the Civil War, Lieutenant Mahan found himself on blockade duty, an unheroic fate if ever there was one. After the war he endured service at a succession of equally dreary and irrelevant duty stations on shore and on obsolete ships at sea. It was on board one such vessel, the *Iroquois*, while she was attached to the Asiatic Station (1867-1869), that Lieutenant Commander Mahan, the executive officer, returned to reading the history that he had enjoyed at the Naval Academy. During this same period, he discovered that he could not handle liquor, that he hated and feared the sea, that he had a propensity for seasickness, and that he suffered severe headaches and skin disorders when his vessel encountered heavy weather. In addition, he learned that he was thoroughly disliked by the other officers, that his distaste for naval life was extreme, and that he was not much of a marlinspike seaman. Indeed, the three ships Mahan commanded after the *Iroquois* all suffered grounding, collision, or maritime embarrassment of some kind. Indeed, as a ship handler and shipmate he was a disaster. He spent much of the remainder of his career attempting to avoid assignment to sea duty.

He was, however, professionally trapped in the navy. By 1870, when he returned to the United States from the *Iroquois* cruise, he was thirty years old, had been in the navy for fourteen of those years, and was without any trade, skill, or training that was not naval. But since he needed the salary that the navy paid, especially after his marriage in

1872 to Ellen Lyle Evans and the births of his three children—Helen Evans (1873), Ellen Kuhn (1877), and Lyle Evans (1881)—he felt he had no choice but to remain in service.

In 1871 there began for Mahan another round of service on leaky ships and at various corruptly managed shore installations as the postwar navy sank to the lowest professional, operational, and ethical level in its history. It was during one of these tedious tours, that of navigation officer at the New York Navy Yard in Brooklyn from 1880 to 1883, that Commander Mahan wrote his first book.

For reasons unknown, he was approached by Charles Scribner's Sons to prepare a volume for their hastily conceived and executed series The Navy in the Civil War. Mahan's contribution to the series was titled *The Gulf and Inland Waters* and published in 1883. So desperately did he need the $600 Scribners offered for the job, he was willing to crank out the book in the brief five-month period that the publisher allowed him. "As I wanted the money," he remarked, "I consented with grave misgivings as to whether I could do justice to the subject, but believing I would probably do as well as another who would accept the same time [limit]."

Considering the haste with which he executed Scribners' commission, Mahan did indeed do justice to his topic in *The Gulf and Inland Waters*. It is a solid book, one that is still useful. While it is sadly deficient in literary style (like almost all of his subsequent books), it was firmly based on such official records as were then available in the War Record Office in Washington as well as on eyewitness accounts of both Union and Confederate participants. Further, it argued the sensible hypothesis that Union naval control of the Gulf of Mexico and of the Mississippi, Tennessee, and Red rivers had contributed enormously to bringing down the Confederate enemy in what Mahan was certain had been a just war. "Of course I don't pretend to believe that I have no bias," he admitted; "I only claim that I did my utmost to speak the truth."

Nowhere in *The Gulf and Inland Waters* is there any suggestion of the sea power hypothesis that Mahan would bring to the attention of the world's statesmen in 1890. The book is straightforward narrative history and was well received in both the military and civilian press. Most important, in a navy just beginning a tenuous and belated transition from sail, wood, and smooth bores to steam, steel, and rifled cannon, it marked Mahan as one of a coterie of officers capable of researching, organizing, understanding, and writing acceptable naval history.

Mahan with his firstborn daughter, Helen Evans Mahan

The leading member of that coterie was Captain Stephen B. Luce, the navy's premier reformer, scholar, and intellectual in the 1870s and 1880s. In 1884 he founded the Naval War College in Newport, R.I., and in 1885 and 1886 he served as its first president. The college was, as he conceived it, a postgraduate school "for the study of the Science of War" at which student officers would also study "the great naval battles of history, even from the earliest times, which illustrate and enforce many of the most important and immutable principles of War."

Luce had read *The Gulf and Inland Waters*, which prompted him in July 1884 to arrange for Mahan's assignment to the College faculty to teach naval history and naval tactics. Mahan would commence his duties there in September 1885. At the time Luce notified him of his selection, Mahan was commanding the *U.S.S. Wachusett*, a wooden sieve

attached to the South Pacific Squadron which operated mainly on the west coasts of South and Central America. He hated every minute he was on board the decrepit vessel, and he regarded his pending reassignment to Newport as an act of deliverance by the man whose protégé he would soon become. Unfortunately for Mahan, a series of minor crises in Ecuador, Panama, and El Salvador, all involving threats to the lives and property of American citizens, resulted in U.S. naval interventions which tied the *Wachusett* to her station. Not until August 1885 did the vessel reach San Francisco. There she was mercifully decommissioned.

In October 1885, Mahan officially joined the faculty of the Naval War College. But since the 1885 session, the College's first, had begun in September, and since Mahan had had no opportunity to prepare for his classes, he was placed on detached duty and ordered to work up the lectures in naval history and tactics he would begin to deliver in 1886. For a period of ten months, during which he was promoted to captain, he lived in New York City. There he researched and wrote the lectures that would become the foundation of his *The Influence of Sea Power Upon History, 1660-1783*. In undertaking this task he drew mainly upon secondary source materials at the New York Public Library. These dealt with the maritime histories, in war and peace, of Spain, Holland, France, and England, mainly the last, in the seventeenth and eighteenth centuries as those nations, with their magnificent fleets of sail, built their overseas empires and struggled with one another for mastery of the sea lanes that joined mother countries to their colonies.

Mahan had already discovered the theme around which to organize this data. Soon after learning that he was to go to the Naval War College he had begun preliminary reading for the intellectual task that lay ahead. One afternoon in November 1884, while reading Theodor Mommsen's *The History of Rome* (1854-1856) in the small library of the English Club in Lima, Peru, Mahan stumbled onto the historical insight that radically changed the course of his naval career, revolutionized the study of naval history, and made his name a household word during America's imperialist period. He later described that awesome moment of discovery as divinely inspired: "To me, continuously seeking, came from within the suggestion that control of the sea was an historic factor which had never been systematically appreciated and expanded. For me . . . the light dawned first on my inner consciousness; I owed it to no other man." In May 1885, when the *Wachusett* was showing the flag in Central American waters, he explained in a letter to Luce just how he intended to flesh out and apply his great discovery: "I meant to begin with a general consideration of the sea as a highway for commerce and also for hostile attacks upon countries bordering on it, dwell upon principal commercial routes— then consider sources of maritime power or weakness—material, personnel, national aptitude, harbors with their positions relative to commercial routes and enemies coasts. I proposed after to bring forward instances, from ancient and modern history, of the effect of navies and the control of the seas upon great or small campaigns. Hannibal, for instance, had to make that frightful passage of the Alps, in which he lost the quarter part of his original army, because he did not control the sea."

From this beginning Mahan went on to preach, as a writer for both professional and lay audiences, the doctrine that command of the sea, or the lack thereof, determined the relative power, prosperity, security, and glory of nations; and that no other single factor had so influenced the course of human history as had the creation, existence, and use of power at sea. In one way or another, in his classes and public lectures, in his many books and articles, Mahan confidently documented a thesis he had embraced even before beginning research—one which called stridently for the construction of a great U.S. Navy and the acquisition of the overseas naval bases necessary to its swift strategic deployment in time of national danger. Needless to say, his subsequent choice of corroborating evidence was necessarily selective, indeed, highly so.

Nor was his sea power hypothesis original. In Mahan's most mature formulation, the sea power hypothesis was an eclectic body of doctrine about the importance of maritime factors in the waxing and waning of empires, composed of ideas earlier suggested in varying ways by Themistocles, Thucydides, Xenophon, Francis Bacon, Walter Raleigh, Theodor Mommsen, William F. P. Napier, John R. Seeley, Stephen B. Luce, and even by the obscure Ensign William G. David, USN. David's prize essay in the 1882 *Proceedings of the U.S. Naval Institute* paralleled in significant ways several of Mahan's principal arguments in the early 1890s on the nature of the geographical, material, and demographical base the United States needed to develop in order to become a great maritime power. In David's view, the U.S. would have to have a numerous merchant marine and a great navy to protect it as it transported the nation's growing industrial production to receptive, ever-expanding markets throughout the world.

The Influence of Sea Power Upon History, 1660-1783 was published by Little, Brown, the Boston firm that would handle all but four of Mahan's subsequent books. It was an instant success, mainly because of the opening chapter, added at the last minute to make the book "more popular," which argued that the United States possessed all the elements, historical, industrial, and geographical, to become a great world sea power; and that the achievement of such power was absolutely crucial to the nation's future economic health and military security. Not only did the volume sell well; it also attracted favorable attention to Captain Mahan as one of the world's leading naval theorists, and it augmented the credibility of the nation's untried New Navy, which began its renaissance in 1882 and was moving steadily toward respectability by 1890.

To sharpen the point of his arguments and to reach a still larger audience, Mahan published "The United States Looking Outward" in the December 1890 issue of the *Atlantic Monthly*. This was the first of a series of popular articles in the 1890s in which he proclaimed the need to end the nation's post-Civil War isolationism and to begin its participation in international trade and politics. Such participation would require a substantial maritime establishment, naval and merchant, as well as a national commitment to the concept of commercial empire.

To capitalize on his unexpected success, increase his royalty income, broaden his magazine readership, and avoid assignment to sea duty, Mahan, now in his second term as president of the Naval War College (he had first held the office from 1886 to 1889), rushed to completion in 1892 two additional volumes:*The Influence of Sea Power Upon the French Revolution and Empire, 1793-1812* and *Admiral Farragut*. The first, based more solidly on primary source material than Mahan's 1890 book, was another triumph for the author. British reviewers were particularly kind, perhaps because Mahan attributed the ultimate defeat of the tyrant Bonaparte to the Royal Navy.

The biography of Admiral David G. Farragut, however, was a critical and financial disaster. It was shaped by Mahan's conviction that biography should teach moral lessons to the rising generation. As such, the book was little more than a superficial Victorian morality tale emphasizing the saintly Farragut's marital fidelity, his honesty and decency, his professional brilliance, and his reliance upon God. Indeed, at a critical juncture in his description of the Battle of Mobile Bay, Mahan quoted an exchange between God and the admiral having to do with a difficult tactical decision. "O God, who created man and gave him reason," Farragut is said to have prayed, "direct me what to do. Shall I go on?" And it seemed, the admiral himself recalled, "as if in answer a voice commanded, 'Go on.'"

As poor a book as *Admiral Farragut* was, it was not the reason that Captain Mahan was packed off to sea in 1893. His aggressive navalism, which by this time included a strident advocacy of the annexation of Hawaii in the public prints, made him an embarrassment to the anti-expansionist Cleveland administration; furthermore, he had been on shore since 1885 and was due regular rotation to a sea-going billet; and finally, in the words of Rear Admiral Francis M. Ramsay, who, despite Mahan's pleas, ordered him to the command of the *U.S.S. Chicago*, "It is not the business of a Naval officer to

write books"—at least not for the purpose of avoiding sea duty.

The *Chicago* command, which took Mahan to England and the Mediterranean in 1893 and 1894, was a blessing in disguise. He was lionized by the British naval establishment and nobility, introduced to Queen Victoria and to her visiting cousin the kaiser, and praised by the British press for the sagacity of his views on navies and empires, especially England's. More important, the trip afforded him the opportunity to examine much of the primary source material he would use in a later laudatory biography of Lord Nelson.

A poor fitness report from Rear Admiral Henry Erban, commanding officer of the European Station, correctly charging that Captain Mahan was far more interested in his research, writing, and socializing on shore than he was in properly running his vessel, produced some awkward professional moments for the world-renowned "Philosopher of Sea Power." But this crisis subsided, and in 1896, soon after the *Chicago* returned to New York, Mahan retired from the U.S. Navy. He had served forty thoroughly disagreeable years.

His departure from the navy on an annual retirement stipend of $3,375 made it imperative that he orient his future writing more to the realities of the literary marketplace than to the service of Poseidon and Clio. Having earlier discouraged any interest his two daughters might have had in men and confident they would obey his wishes and remain unmarried unless God chose specific mates for them, he undertook to provide them with inheritances that would enable them to live out their lives both comfortably and alone. He was also determined to provide his entire family with the niceties of upper-middle-class existence. These would include a winter residence in Manhattan and a summer place on Long Island, the convenience of three or four house servants, participation in the cultural life of New York City, and occasional tours of the Continent.

To manage all this financially, Mahan took pen in hand. Soon after his retirement he decided he would concentrate on producing articles for well-paying popular magazines. He would write and publish them as rapidly as possible, relating their subject matter to the headlines of the hour, particularly as the news of the day focused on contemporary political, diplomatic, and military events at home and abroad. For his "potboilers," as he called them, he received an average of five cents a word, or about four hundred to five hundred dollars per article. The most successful of these were collected in books from which he received additional royalties. Among the most important of these were *Lessons of the War with Spain, and Other Articles* (1899), *The Problem of Asia and Its Effects upon International Policies* (1900), *Naval Administration and Warfare, Some General Principles, With Other Essays* (1908), and *Armaments and Arbitration, or the Place of Force in the International Relations of States* (1912). From his retirement in 1896 to his death in 1914, Mahan published 107 articles, seventy-one of which were subsequently reprinted. Indeed, most of Mahan's writing for magazines was published, republished, or recycled in some way. His study was a veritable factory producing what he and various magazine editors thought the public wanted to read. His articles, often slapped together and rushed to press in time to capitalize on the headline of the hour, were especially in demand at the end of the Spanish-American war, during the Boer and Russo-Japanese wars, and throughout the military and diplomatic crises that preceded the outbreak of World War I.

Taken together, these potboilers advocated a U.S. Navy second only to Britain's, the acquisition of strategically situated naval bases and coaling stations in the Caribbean and Pacific, an interoceanic canal in Central America (built, fortified, and controlled by the United States), the participation by American businessmen and missionaries in Europe's competition for the markets and souls of China and the Chinese, and the need for Anglo-American rapprochement and cooperation in a world rendered increasingly unstable by the growing power and arrogance of Germany and Japan. Mahan wrote also of the nature and conduct of war, emphasizing its historical inevitability, the scientific principles that controlled it, and its contributions to human progress. He warned his countrymen of the dangers to the United States and to the entire Christian world that were inherent in various fuzzy-headed schemes promoting international leagues of nations, compulsory arbitration, disarmament and arms control. His service on the five-man U.S. delegation to the First Hague Peace Conference in 1899 gave him an opportunity to practice what he preached, while providing still more grist for his literary mill.

Anglophile, professional Episcopalian, self-taught historian, seasick naval officer, Victorian moralist, capitalist without capital, warrior who never heard a gun fired in anger, Mahan preached imperialism at five cents a word to those Americans who would listen. There is no evidence, however,

that he was a member of the decision-making inner circle of the American imperialist movement. He was never consulted in the planning stages of imperialist policy formulation by leaders like Theodore Roosevelt, Henry Cabot Lodge, or John Hay. No one asked him before the fact what he thought of America's declaration of war on Spain in 1898 or solicited his opinion on the subsequent decision to annex the Philippines; he was never consulted as to whether the U.S. should promote a revolution in Panama in 1903 or intervene in the Dominican Republic in 1904 or proclaim the Open Door Policy in China in 1899 and 1900 or reinterpret the Monroe Doctrine to permit preventative intervention in Caribbean America. Mahan cheered, justified, explained, and defended decisions and activities such as these in his articles—but always after the fact. He was an enthusiastic backer of American imperialism, not a planner or sword arm. Put simply, he needed the money that the debate over imperialism in America provided him, and he stimulated that debate not only in his own financial interest, but also because he was intellectually and emotionally committed to the imperialist side.

No records of his literary income have survived. Nevertheless, an educated guess based on comments in his private correspondence would place his combined annual income (retirement, book royalties, and magazine fees) at no less than $6000. In an era (1900-1910) of long hours (nearly 60 per week), low wages (20 to 25 cents an hour) and paltry annual incomes—factory worker ($497), schoolteacher ($410), federal employee ($1,030)—Mahan's income from the navy, from Little, Brown, and from such magazines as *Collier's*, *McClure's*, *Harper's* and *Scribner's* was comfortable.

His best work by far during his retirement years was his *The Life of Nelson: The Embodiment of the Sea Power of Great Britain*. First published in 1897, it is a two-volume exercise in hero worship. But it is also unusually well written, solidly grounded in primary source material, and comprehensive in scope. The reviews were almost universally enthusiastic, and Mahan's life of Nelson was another financial success.

In only one particular did the book merit criticism; and this was in Mahan's insistence that Nelson, like Farragut, was nearly perfect in every way, not only professionally, but morally and spiritually as well. Obviously he was not. His tawdry sexual liaison with Lady Hamilton, by whom he fathered an illegitimate daughter, and his hasty court-martial and hanging of turncoat Neapolitan Admiral Francesco Caracciolo in June 1799, without a semblance of due process, were gaping holes in Nelson's armor that Mahan unwisely attempted to cover up. He thus explained Nelson's adulterous relationship with Emma Hamilton as the result of mental aberration caused by a superficial scalp wound he had suffered at the Battle of the Nile in August 1798. The dispatch of Caracciolo was attributed by Mahan to a direct order from the absent Ferdinand I, self-proclaimed ruler of the Kingdom of the Two Sicilies.

British reviewers of *The Life of Nelson* laughed politely at Mahan's naiveté in the matter of Nelson's sexual involvement with Emma Hamilton; on the other hand, they utterly demolished his treatment of the Caracciolo case, mainly with the observation that Nelson had no clear order from Ferdinand or from anyone else in his comic-opera government to hang the officer. Mahan, however, was not one to accept criticism, even deserved. Not only did he enter into an unnecessary and acrimonious dispute with his British critics, principally Francis P. Badham, but he also brought out a revised and enlarged edition of his *Life of Nelson* in 1899. It included additional documentation, which, in Mahan's view, proved him absolutely correct in his interpretation of the Caracciolo matter. It did not; and to make matters worse, the revised edition sold poorly.

Not surprisingly, his experience with *The Life of Nelson*, like the earlier one with *Admiral Farragut*, convinced him that biography was simply not his forte: "I find biography . . . far harder work than philosophizing over history. . . . the handling of an immense amount of material . . . greatly taxes me, for my strength has been, as far as I can judge, rather in singling out the great outlines of events and concentrating attention upon them, than in the management of details. . . . The expenditure of labor has been much greater than on the same amount of product in other books; from which I reason that a biography is not an economical use of brain power for me." He never again attempted biography.

In the midst of the so-called Badham Contention over the Nelson volumes, Mahan was called out of retirement and ordered home from a family tour of Europe to serve on the Naval War Board during the war with Spain. In this assignment, which had to do with U.S. naval strategic war planning and operations, he served honorably and usefully from 9 May to 20 August 1898. He also wasted no time turning this opportunity to his literary and financial advantage. The Naval War Board was near the vortex of the war effort, and within a few

weeks of his arrival in Washington Mahan was being courted by S. S. McClure of *McClure's* magazine, Robert U. Johnson of *Century* magazine, and William Randolph Hearst of the *New York Journal* to write a series of articles which viewed the war from his own perspective and that of the Board. As he explained the pleasures of his merchandising dilemma to Johnson on 17 May, "You come second in order of application to me, and there is a third now." That he would have something of real value to sell was obvious. "I am forced to know now a good deal of what goes on, and am making my mental comments on the operations, as illustrative of the theory and practice of war." As it turned out, Mahan heartily disliked Hearst's brand of yellow journalism and quickly dismissed his offer of a dollar a word. McClure outbid Johnson (at "my price," Mahan boasted), and from December 1898 through April 1899 five of Mahan's hastily written articles on the naval operations of the war appeared in *McClure's* magazine. Later in 1899 Little, Brown brought out in book form his *Lessons of the War with Spain, and Other Articles*. Good paydays were had by all. The outbreak of the Boer War in October 1899 and of the Russo-Japanese War in February 1904 resulted in more profits. Mahan quickly put together a book entitled *The Story of War in South Africa, 1899-1900* (1900) and five well-paid articles for *Collier's Weekly* dealing with the second conflict. Both projects were rushed to completion with little more research than a scanning of daily newspaper accounts of land and sea operations.

In spite of such shaky publications as these, Mahan's prestige as a historian continued to grow. In 1902 he was elected president of the American Historical Association, and in December of that year, at the Association's annual meeting in Philadelphia, he delivered his presidential address, "Subordination in Historical Treatment." Mahan spoke at a time when the profession was teeming with historians searching for the "Laws" of history or for more or less discernible "cycles" and "influences" in history, especially in American history. Andrew D. White, John Fiske, Frederick Jackson Turner, and the three Adams brothers—Brooks, Henry, and Charles Francis, Jr.—were all involved in this quest, as were Halford J. Mackinder and John R. Seeley in England. Mahan was in good company. He had already discovered and proved one "influence" in history, that of sea power, and his presidential address was classroom instruction in how his colleagues might discover and apply other such influences.

At one level, his address was a plea to the

Mahan with his wife, Ellen Lyle Evans Mahan, and their daughters, 1906

profession to write the kind of popular history that would present "large, simple ideas" in such manner "that the wayfaring man, whom we now call 'the man in the street' shall not err therein." At another, it was a defense of the methodology by which he had tested and demonstrated the correctness of the "central idea" he had conceived in Lima in 1884—that sea power had decisively influenced the course and direction of human history. He thus argued that it was the duty of historians to search for, discover, and test other central ideas that might provide equally useful insights into the nature and processes of history. The methodology of testing and verifying demanded, said Mahan, the "artistic grouping of subordinate details around a central idea." Indeed, historians using his subordinationist approach would discover that "each particular incident and group of incidents becomes . . . a fully wrought and fashioned piece, prepared for its adjustment in its place in the great mosaic which the history of the race is gradually fashioning under the Divine overruling." Given his parallel belief that history was nothing less than "the plan of Providence . . . in its fulfillment," it was important, Ma-

han insisted, that historians join him in discerning and studying those central ideas in history. Because if and when they were verified by subordinationist methodology, they would comprise nothing less than the central themes, or foundation stones, in the fashioning of the "great mosaic" that was God's continuing revelation of Himself to man. Subordinationist methodology was thus the link between the central ideas of historians and the overriding central themes of history.

One such central theme, of course, was Mahan's own discovery of the influence of sea power upon history. This was a central idea he had elevated to the status of central theme by the proper application of his subordinationist research techniques. He was certain that other ideas awaited similar conceptualization and verification as themes. And he also believed that "some favored mind" would eventually achieve a "final great synthesis" of all the historical themes permeating the Universe. Properly synthesized, "they will present a majestic ideal unity corresponding to the thought of the Divine Architect, realized to his creatures." Put another way, Mahan's historian, were he to use proper subordinationist methodology, could become one with God.

At the same time, he speculated that there were other possible central ideas that might ascend to the level of themes. One such idea, Mahan suggested, might be an explanation of conflict and progress in history in dialectical terms. Specifically, he pointed to "the conflict of two opposites, as in the long struggle between freedom and slavery, union and disunion in our own land; but the unity nevertheless exists. It is not to be found in freedom, not yet in slavery, but in their conflict it is. Around it group in subordination the many events, and the warriors of the political arena, whose names are household words among us to this day." Another central idea with prospects of becoming a central theme in history is mentioned in Mahan's spiritual autobiography, *The Harvest Within: Thoughts on the Life of a Christian* (1909), written partly in propitiation for the cowardice he felt he had shown in late 1907 in the face of the excruciating pain caused by a botched prostatectomy. It was "that man today is susceptible of an enthusiasm for Jesus Christ resembling, but surpassing, that which has been shown in past times for this or that historical character in many nations." Still another central idea worthy of subordinationist evaluation, said Mahan, was the influence of territorial expansion on U.S. history. Unfortunately, Mahan died before he could apply subordinationist methodology to either Enthusiasm for Jesus or to Manifest Destiny. That both would have risen to central theme status in Mahan's eager hands seems likely. Subordinationism, properly employed, was, after all, an exact historiographical tool. As he explained in 1907: "Facts won't lie if you work them right; but if you work them wrong, a little disproportion in the emphasis, a slight exaggeration of color, a little more or less limelight on this or that part of the grouping and the result is not truth, even though each individual fact be as unimpeachable as the multiplication table."

On the inevitability of war in human history Mahan worked the facts right. He looked not to dialectical explanations for the persistence of war; nor to Social Darwinist or Capitalist Conspiracy interpretations of it. Instead, his study of the past, recent and distant, told him that mankind's historical record was heavy with evidence that periods of peace in history mainly provided convenient and necessary breathing spaces between wars, rather than the converse notion that wars were unwanted and unwelcome interruptions of peace. Moreover, his own experience confirmed this. Among his first

recollections was that of the West Point garrison returning from the Mexican War. Among his last were the early naval battle reports from World War I. Between the two, he had personally served in the Civil War and the Spanish-American War and he had written extensively on the Boer and Russo-Japanese conflagrations as they were being fought. Not surprisingly, therefore, Mahan came to believe that the study of war was the study of history, that war was inherent in human behavior.

It was this conviction, supplemented by his earlier exposure at the Naval War College to Luce's belief in "the Science of War" and its "immutable principles," that persuaded him also to search for the historical principles applicable to warfare, particularly to the strategy and tactics of war at sea. This he did in tens of thousands of words over the years, most particularly in *Naval Strategy, Compared and Contrasted with the Principles of Military Operations on Land* (1911), and, with less focus and cohesiveness, in his *Naval Administration and Warfare, Some General Principles, With Other Essays* (1908). In Mahan's eyes the basic principles of war were essentially two, both of which he adapted from Henri Jomini's brilliant *Précis de l'art de la guerre* (*The Art of War*, 1836). This was the leading text of its day governing the strategy and tactics of land armies, and from it Mahan borrowed the "lessons" that he applied to fleet naval operations. His conclusions were that (1) fleets which situate themselves at geographical positions in or near the "strategic center" of a given war, thus affording themselves the greatest amount of offensive mobility or the greatest measure of defensive flexibility, usually win the major battles that determine the outcome of the wars which influence the course of history; (2) a fleet in battle that can maneuver (concentrate) its vessels (guns) in such a way as to bring for a decisive moment a greater part of its firepower against lesser parts of the firepower of its enemy will invariably win the action. Unfortunately for Mahan's later reputation as a tactician, neither of these principles was particularly applicable to steel, steam, and all-big-gun navies on the eve of World War I, however relevant they might have been in the age of sail and to Royal Navy squadrons commanded by the incomparable Nelson.

In working out his principles of naval warfare, Mahan simply did not take into account the revolution in naval technology that occurred from 1890 to 1910. From a tactical standpoint he was a child of the age of sail who never grew up. He also believed in a strategy of bringing an enemy into one "Big Battle" at sea, a decisive Trafalgar or

Tsushima that would bring instant "command of the sea" to the victor, and with it victory in the war. He would never have understood a Jutland, which was a peculiar combination of strategic victory and tactical defeat; nor a Midway, where the surface forces were never in direct contact. In fine, he failed to grasp the strategical and tactical implications of aircraft, submarines, wireless telegraphy, and naval guns mechanically sighted and fired. He opposed the development of the all-big-gun battleship in the U.S. Navy with such bullheadedness as to cause an irreparable break with President Theodore Roosevelt, one of his early admirers. By 1910 his influence within the officer corps of the Navy had waned. He was a back number.

But not to his loyal readership. When World War I broke out Mahan rushed into print in *Leslie's Weekly* with an article cheering on the British and predicting their ultimate victory through an effective blockade of Germany followed by a glorious victory in a Big Battle of surface fleets that would gain them control of the strategic center of the war that was the North Sea. Magazine editors hurried to secure his services, two offering him the princely sum of $100 per week for a regular column on the war in Europe. But the biggest paydays his potboiling career ever promised were not to be. Mahan was abruptly silenced by Woodrow Wilson's order of 6 August 1914, forbidding all officers, active or retired, from "public comment of any kind upon the military or political situation on the other side of the water." This was in conjunction with the president's naive policy of attempting to insure American neutrality in the war by thought, word, and deed. Mahan protested the gag order vigorously but to no avail. A little more than three months later he was dead, the victim of a heart attack.

Mahan has fared much better with the U.S. Navy since his death in 1914 than he did while in service or on the retirement list. A naval vessel and several shore installations carry his name today. Officers and midshipmen are urged to read his books. His picture hangs in various navy libraries and reading rooms. He has, it seems, achieved naval sainthood of sorts, even though nothing in his enormous literary output speaks with relevance to contingency naval war planning in the nuclear age. His comments on strategy, tactics, weapons, and logistics are virtually useless to naval theorists in the final decades of the twentieth century. His thoughts about history, philosophy of history, and historical methodology can only be classified today as rather quaint.

Still, there lingers within the U.S. Navy and in the nation as a whole the uneasy feeling, traceable in some measure to Alfred Thayer Mahan, that "command of the sea," whatever that means, is important to national security; and that a nation without a respectable navy in the hair-trigger state system of the nuclear age is a minnow among sharks. That uneasiness will remain, and properly so, until someone can show that Mahan was wrong when he insisted that war, not peace, is the normal historical condition of men, tribes, and nations, rather than the other way around. Perhaps it is not surprising that nine of his books have recently been republished.

Letters:
Letters and Papers of Alfred Thayer Mahan, edited by Robert Seager II and Doris D. Maguire, 3 volumes (Annapolis: Naval Institute Press, 1975).

Bibliographies:
William E. Livezey, *Mahan on Sea Power* (Norman: University of Oklahoma Press, 1947), pp. 301-311;
Robert Seager II and Doris D. Maguire, eds., *Letters and Papers of Alfred Thayer Mahan* (Annapolis: Naval Institute Press, 1975), III: 731-732, 827-831.

Biographies:
Charles C. Taylor, *The Life of Admiral Mahan* (New York: Doran, 1920);
William D. Puleston, *The Life and Work of Captain Alfred Thayer Mahan* (New Haven: Yale University Press, 1939);
Robert Seager II, *Alfred Thayer Mahan* (Annapolis: Naval Institute Press, 1977);
Seager, "Biography of a Biographer: Alfred Thayer Mahan," in *Changing Interpretations and New Sources in Naval History*, edited by Robert W. Love, Jr. (New York: Garland, 1980), pp. 278-292.

References:
Kenneth J. Hagan, "Alfred Thayer Mahan," in *Makers of American Diplomacy*, edited by Frank J. Merli and Theodore A. Wilson, 2 volumes (New York: Scribners, 1974), I: 279-305;
William E. Livezey, *Mahan on Sea Power* (Norman: University of Oklahoma Press, 1947);
Peter Paret, Gordon A. Craig, and Felix Gilbert, eds., *Makers of Modern Strategy* (Princeton University Press, forthcoming 1986);

Julius W. Pratt, "Alfred Thayer Mahan," in *The Marcus W. Jernegan Essays in American Historiography*, edited by William T. Hutchinson (Chicago: University of Chicago Press, 1937), pp. 207-226;

Richard S. West, *Admirals of American Empire* (Indianapolis: Bobbs-Merrill, 1948).

Papers:
The largest collections of Mahan's papers are at the Naval War College, Newport, Rhode Island, and at the Library of Congress in the Mahan Collection and other collections.

John Bach McMaster

E. Stanly Godbold, Jr.
Mississippi State University

BIRTH: Brooklyn, New York, 29 June 1852, to James and Julia Anna Matilda Bach McMaster.

EDUCATION: B.A., College of the City of New York, 1872; M.A., 1873; C.E., 1875.

MARRIAGE: 14 April 1887 to Gertrude Stevenson; children: John Bach, Jr., Philip Duryee.

AWARDS AND HONORS: Litt.D., University of Pennsylvania, 1894; elected member of National Institute of Arts and Letters, 1899; LL.D., Washington and Jefferson College, 1901; President of the American Historical Association, 1905-1906; LL.D., University of Toronto, 1907; Litt.D., Princeton University, 1925.

DEATH: Darien, Connecticut, 24 May 1932.

SELECTED BOOKS: *Bridge and Tunnel Centres* (New York: Van Nostrand, 1875);

High Masonry Dams (New York: Van Nostrand, 1876);

A History of the People of the United States, from the Revolution to the Civil War, 8 volumes (New York: Appleton, 1883-1913);

The Life, Memoirs, Military Career and Death of General U. S. Grant, With War Anecdotes and Freely Drawn Extracts from His Autobiography (Philadelphia: Barclay, 1885);

Benjamin Franklin as a Man of Letters (Boston & New York: Houghton Mifflin, 1887; London: Kegan Paul, Trench, 1887);

The Origin, Meaning, and Application of the Monroe Doctrine (Philadelphia: Altemus, 1896);

John Bach McMaster, 1888 (Historical Society of Pennsylvania)

The Venezuela Dispute (New York: The New-York Times, 1896);

With the Fathers: Studies in the History of the United States (New York: Appleton, 1896;

The University of Pennsylvania Illustrated [by McMaster] *and a Sketch of Franklin Field* [by H. Lausatt Geyelin] (Philadelphia: Lippincott, 1897);

A School History of the United States (New York &

Cincinnati: American Book Company, 1897; revised and enlarged, 1920);

A Primary History of the United States (New York & Cincinnati: American Book Company, 1901; revised and enlarged, 1919);

Daniel Webster (New York: Century, 1902);

The Acquisition of Political, Social and Industrial Rights of Man in America (Cleveland: Imperial Press, 1903);

A Brief History of the United States (New York & Cincinnati: American Book Company, 1907);

The Life and Times of Stephen Girard, Mariner and Merchant, 2 volumes (Philadelphia & London: Lippincott, 1918);

The United States in the World War, 2 volumes (New York & London: Appleton, 1918, 1920);

A History of the People of the United States during Lincoln's Administration (New York: Appleton, 1927).

OTHER: "Thomas Babington Macaulay," in *Library of the World's Best Literature, Ancient and Modern*, edited by Charles D. Warner, 30 volumes (New York: Peale & Hill, 1896-1897), XVI: 9381-9386;

"The Teaching of History," in *Annual Report of the American Historical Association for the Year 1896*, 2 volumes (Washington, D.C.: Government Printing Office, 1897), I: 258-263;

"A Century of Struggle for the Rights of Man," in *Proceedings of the New York State Historical Association*, 1 (1901), pp. 65-79;

John Fiske, *Modern Development of the New World*, completed by McMaster (Philadelphia: Lea Brothers, 1902);

"The Struggle for Commercial Independence," in *The Cambridge Modern History*, 13 volumes (Cambridge: Cambridge University Press, 1902-1912), VII: 305-334;

"The Growth of the Nation," in *The Cambridge Modern History*, 13 volumes (Cambridge: Cambridge University Press, 1902-1912), VII: 349-377;

"Commerce, Expansion, and Slavery, 1828-1850," in *The Cambridge Modern History*, 13 volumes (Cambridge: Cambridge University Press, 1902-1912), VII: 378-404;

The Trail Makers: A Library of History and Exploration, edited by Edward Gaylord Bourne with consulting editor McMaster, 17 volumes (New York: Barnes, 1904-1905);

"Old Standards of Public Morals," in *Annual Report of the American Historical Association for the Year 1905*, 2 volumes (Washington, D.C.: Govern-

ment Printing Office, 1906), I: 55-70;

"The Present State of Historical Writing in America," in *Proceedings of the American Antiquarian Society*, new series, 20 (1910), pp. 420-426;

"The Princeton Period of John Bach McMaster," in *Proceedings of the New Jersey Historical Society*, 57 (1939), pp. 214-230.

PERIODICAL PUBLICATIONS: "The Struggle for the West," *Lippincott's Monthly Magazine*, 49 (June 1892): 758-771;

"The Election of the President," *Atlantic Monthly*, 78 (September 1896): 328-337;

"Senate Shorn of Early Dignity by Primaries, Says Noted Historian," *New York Herald-Tribune*, 22 June 1930, II: 1, 3;

"Young John Bach McMaster: A Boyhood in New York City," *New York History*, 20 (July 1939): 316-324;

"Reliving History: John Bach McMaster as an Army Clerk," *Journal of the American Military Institute*, 4 (Summer 1940): 127-128.

John Bach McMaster was a pioneering historian who believed that people themselves, not institutions and wars alone, were the proper subject of written history. He discovered the daily newspaper as a legitimate source of historical knowledge, and he thought that a straightforward narrative was the best way to reveal the intriguing and inspiring story of the people of the United States. An ardent nationalist, he saw a need for an extensive, comprehensive history of his country that would inform the citizenry, generate pride and loyalty, and contribute to the nation's growth and improvement. His impact upon the writing and study of history was enormous. A university professor who influenced a generation of scholars, he was the first major American historian to describe the lives of the common people. He also wrote textbooks that were widely adopted at both the primary and secondary levels. Those who read his books learned a great deal about the virtues of the people of the United States, but they probably knew little about the warmth, modesty, and integrity of the man who had become their teacher.

John Bach McMaster was born in Brooklyn, New York, on 29 June 1852, to James and Julia Anna Matilda Bach McMaster. His mother was the daughter of Robert and Margaret Cowan Bach. Robert Bach had arrived in New York City from Hereford, England, in 1796; he became an enterprising merchant who specialized in medical remedies and eventually expanded his business into a major pharmaceutical firm. Bach was married to Margaret Cowan of Newry, Ireland, and they built a luxurious home in Brooklyn on the spot where one end of the Brooklyn Bridge now stands. Their daughter Julia was married to a promising young artist, Frederic W. Philip, but he died only four months after the wedding. After five years of young widowhood, in 1845, she married James McMaster.

James McMaster had a colorful past. Of Scottish descent, he was born in New York State and was reared by an indomitable widowed mother who ran a boardinghouse near Saratoga Springs. As a young man he drove a pack of mules across central Mexico, trading with Indians; later, with a half brother, he founded a banking house in New Orleans. He withdrew from the bank to buy Oak Lawn, a large plantation on the Mississippi River about a dozen miles south of New Orleans and adjoining the property of P. G. T. Beauregard, the future Confederate general. Here he successfully grew cane and manufactured it into sugar. His wife, Julia, lived at Oak Lawn with him, but the transplanted New Yorkers frequently returned to their native state for long visits. After the death of her second child at Oak Lawn, Julia McMaster never went south again. Her third son, John, was born in the home of his grandfather Bach in Brooklyn. Shortly after John's birth, his father sold the plantation and financed the sale himself. The Civil War ended the payments completely, but he organized a petroleum company in the North that provided him with a relatively good income during the war. The family lived in a good neighborhood first at East Fourteenth Street, then at East Sixtieth Street in Manhattan. They frequently passed their summers in a dwelling on a well-planted acre at the corner of 120th Street and Second Avenue in Harlem.

Growing up in New York City before and during the Civil War exposed young John McMaster to a kaleidoscope of American life. He was fascinated by ordinary people engaged in their daily routines. He was vividly aware of the war; he knew that his father had owned African slaves whose morals his mother had attempted to reform, but he did not see the plantation in the South until long after the war had ended. His own loyalty was to the Union. The story of his grandfather Bach's mercantile career was a part of his daily life, and he pieced together the details of the McMasters' past through his own investigations and from his mother who shared her memories with him. Kin to both Southern planter and Northern merchant,

heir to personal tales of frontier adventure and international life, alert and curious in a lively city during a major historical event, the future historian was developing an appreciation for the changing complexity of life in the United States.

John McMaster attended the public schools of New York City. As a student at Grammar School No. 40, he enjoyed his history books as much as he enjoyed throwing snowballs at other boys on a wintry day. He read and collected dime novels, which he circulated to others for a penny a day. He played games in vacant lots, watched the military heroes in blue uniforms on parade, listened to the presidential campaign speeches of 1860, and later at the White House shook hands with Abraham Lincoln. On that occasion he heard a Unionist from New York State say to Lincoln. "Up from where I come from we think that God and Abraham Lincoln are going to save the country." And he heard Lincoln reply, "My friend, you are half right." In 1865, the year Lincoln was assassinated, McMaster was graduated from the grammar school and entered the New York Free Academy, or school for advanced students; in 1866 its name was changed to College of the City of New York.

McMaster was only thirteen when he entered the Free Academy, a school without dormitories that was attended by students from all economic classes. He enrolled in the "Introductory Class," which served as a transition from grammar school to college. Then he moved on to the college curriculum. He was popular with the other students. He was elected president of the Phrenocosmian Society, a literary club; president of Delta Kappa Epsilon, a fraternity concerned with student politics; president of his senior class; and to membership in Phi Beta Kappa. His worst experiences occurred during his junior year, which he had to repeat. His father's oil business failed, and it was necessary for McMaster to spend long hours operating a lithograph machine to help support the family. In college he found both history and his history teacher boring, and he concentrated on the sciences, in which he excelled. He was graduated with a bachelor of arts degree in 1872 and remained at the college with a teaching assistantship in English, which enabled him to earn a master of arts degree in 1873.

While he was a senior in college, McMaster made his decision to write a history of the people of the United States. His inspiration came largely from the experiences of his family and ancestors and especially from the events of his own life. He wanted to know why the owners of neighboring plantations in Louisiana would be on opposite sides in the war. To find out, he read *The American Conflict* (1866) by Horace Greeley. That book raised more questions, and he turned to Francis Parkman's *La Salle and the Discovery of the Great West* (1879) and to the multivolume histories of the United States published by George Bancroft (1834-1875) and Richard Hildreth (1856-1860). He concluded that no satisfactory history of the people had been written. The summer after his graduation in 1872 he stumbled across a copy of Thomas Babington Macaulay's *The History of England from the Accession of James the Second* (1849-1861); he became fascinated, thinking that the history of the United States was just as interesting and wondering why no similar history had been written. Filled with the enthusiasm of a lad of twenty, McMaster vowed that he would write it.

While teaching English, McMaster dabbled at taking notes for his history, but he was to have many interruptions. In 1873 his father died. He did not have the money to go to Europe to earn a Ph.D., nor was he able to study under one of several European-trained historians in the United States. His first history seminars were to be those which he himself conducted. McMaster's inspiration had been largely experiential, and his training was to follow a similar line. In 1873 he accepted an appointment as chief clerk and civil assistant to Major George L. Gillespie of the United States Army Corps of Engineers. His job was to lead a small survey party to the battlefields at Winchester, Cedar Creek, and Waynesboro, Virginia. His findings were to be given to General Philip H. Sheridan who was writing his memoirs with the aid of a grant from Congress. McMaster picked up relics from the battlefields, interviewed eyewitnesses, and apparently decided that historical geography would be an important part of his history. He lived in filth and squalor in a dilapidated hotel, described Winchester as a town of "pigs" and "niggers," was repulsed by a Methodist camp meeting that he attended, and completed his assignment on a sarcastic and disillusioned note. From the battlefield McMaster was sent to Chicago, where he prepared one of the topographical maps that appeared in Sheridan's *Personal Memoirs* (1888), but most of his work consisted of being a secretary for Gillespie. He thought Sheridan, whom he met in Chicago, was "a hot tempered, ugly-faced, long-armed little Irishman." He did not find any heroes in this assignment, and he was planning to write a history without heroes.

The Panic of 1873 ended the Congressional appropriation for Sheridan's memoirs and forced McMaster out of work. He returned to New York to live with his mother. He passed his mornings tutoring for pay the children of James Roosevelt and Abram S. Hewitt. In the afternoons he worked in the office of the engineer who had laid out Central Park and drew a topographical map of New York State, for which he was not paid. He decided to pursue his career in engineering, and he earned a degree in civil engineering from his alma mater in 1875. He continued to combine his interests in history, engineering, and teaching. He wrote two technical booklets, *Bridge and Tunnel Centres* (1875) and *High Masonry Dams* (1876), for the Van Nostrand Science series. After reading Henry Buckle's *History of Civilization in England* (1857-1861), he produced a manuscript entitled "The Struggle of Man with Nature," but he was unable to find a publisher and later destroyed the work. He read widely in history, science, literature, noting in the works of the realist writers of his day a shift of focus from heroes to the common people, a change which he hoped to exploit in his history.

In January 1877 McMaster accepted an appointment as instructor of civil engineering at the John C. Green School of Science at the College of New Jersey, later Princeton University. The salary of $350 per term, plus room and board in one of the dormitories, gave him a comfortable living. And some years later he could take pride in the fact that he had lived two floors above an undergraduate named Woodrow Wilson. But he did not like life in Princeton; he was lonely, the other faculty members had little to do with him, and the young women apparently did not find him very interesting. He was quiet, shy, sarcastic, ambitious, and bored. But he was delighted in the summer of 1878 when the director of the E. M. Museum at the college invited him to lead a fossil-collecting expedition. He was thrilled by the natural beauty of the Wyoming wilderness and more so by the opportunity to observe life west of the Rockies. He talked to pioneers, rode long hours in a saddle, narrowly escaped an attack by a "she-cougar," and generally experienced the kind of life in the West that other historians only wrote about. Back at Princeton, however, he quickly lapsed into sarcasm about the studying and teaching of civil engineering. "Teaching lunk-heads to survey farms, and rivers, and railroads," he wrote his future wife, "is not so much fun as it looks."

During the six years he spent at the College of New Jersey, however, McMaster was doing more than teaching "lunk-heads"; he was quietly fulfilling his dream to write a history of the American people. During the summers and his leisure hours he read the histories of Bancroft and Hildreth, biographies, state histories, and memoirs. Since none of them satisfied him, he sought more information in the repositories within his range. The American Antiquarian Society at Worcester, Massachusetts, gave him unlimited access to its extensive files of newspapers; Frederick D. Stone of the Historical Society of Pennsylvania gave him the key to the building; and both the New York and Massachusetts historical societies allowed him limited use of their collections. McMaster thought that the Library of Congress, then located in the Capitol, "resembled nothing so much as an old-fashioned second-hand book shop," but he spent many hours taking notes on the volumes that the librarian piled on his table. By 1881 the first volume of *A History of the People of the United States, from the Revolution to the Civil War* was complete.

McMaster personally carried the bulky, longhand manuscript from publisher to publisher until finally, in the summer of 1881, D. Appleton and Company agreed to read it. Their readers disapproved, and the company ignored the manuscript until Daniel Appleton himself decided to take it home. He read it aloud to guests at a party, whose attention it easily captured. Since Appleton valued the opinion of intelligent readers above that of the learned critics, he offered McMaster a contract. It was Appleton who suggested the title that would capture the imagination of the reading public.

The title promised that this volume would be a history of the "people," and the table of contents confirmed that readers would learn about the education and habits of New England farmers, the bigotry and poverty of ministers, the dress of the inhabitants of Philadelphia, the cost of books in Virginia, the sad state of jails and prisons, the invention of balloons, the Barbary piracies, and the character of Benjamin Franklin, as well as the major political and diplomatic events from 1783 through 1789. The appearance of the first volume of his history in 1883 catapulted McMaster from obscure, shy teacher of civil engineering to prominent historian. Despite a few hostile reviews, the book was warmly received; it went into a fourth edition within three months. Six weeks after publication George Bancroft himself sent McMaster a letter "welcoming" him into the fold of American historians. Nonhistorical writers, too, found much to praise in McMaster's history. McMaster, who had taught English and sprinkled his history with literary references, was particularly happy to receive the compliments of Charles Dudley Warner, an important writer and critic of his day.

The instant fame of his first volume brought about major changes in McMaster's life. He was offered a newly created position as professor of American history at the Wharton School of Finance and Economy at the University of Pennsylvania. He immediately accepted, noting in his diary on 21 June 1883, "Left Princeton, Thank God forever." Thus he became one of the first professors of American history in a college or university. As his reputation increased, McMaster had other offers, including the presidency of the University of Illinois, but he declined all of them in order to be free to teach seminars and to continue to produce the subsequent volumes of his history. He remained at the University of Pennsylvania for thirty-seven years until his retirement in 1920.

Once settled in Philadelphia, McMaster set about accumulating enough money to marry Gertrude Stevenson of Morristown, New Jersey. For several years she had been his principal correspondent. She was the person with whom he shared his private thoughts about his life and work and for whom he made fun of himself. The letters, complemented by many visits, had led to a romance. Driven to increase his income, McMaster produced the second volume of his history in 1885, gave tedious public lectures for a fee, and agreed to write a literary biography of Benjamin Franklin. Finally, on 14 April 1887, at the age of thirty-four, he was married to Gertrude Stevenson. McMaster was short, with an oversized head and reddish-blond hair. He had once caricatured himself to Gertrude as looking like "a watermelon on a stalk," and his students had nicknamed him "The Tack." But Gertrude found him lovable, and theirs was a good marriage that lasted. In time they settled in a residence at 2190 DeLancey Street and became the parents of two sons, John Bach, Jr., and Philip Duryee. McMaster seems to have taken much pleasure in his family whom he affectionately referred to as "The Big Four."

When away from home McMaster revealed very little about himself to his professional associates. His colleagues found him relatively uncommunicative and something of a man of mystery. McMaster's favorite social activity was to attend the Franklin Inn Club, where he could eat lunch and spend hours talking with other local men of letters. At the university, however, he apparently had little to say and frequently ignored committee assignments. He did serve one term as vice-president of the faculty club, and he occasionally made speeches

From a letter dated 22 July 1883 in which McMaster caricatured himself for his future wife, Gertrude Stevenson (Eric F. Goldman,
John Bach McMaster: American Historian, *1942)*

representing the university if he thought the task was unavoidable. His motivation to complete his history was so strong that he attempted to guard against as many unwelcome intrusions as possible.

As a teacher, McMaster was neither exciting nor dynamic. The general public and undergraduates who heard him lecture thought he was dull, difficult to hear, and very boring. The human-interest aspect of his written history was surprisingly lacking in his lectures. But he was very successful as a teacher of graduate seminars, where his enthusiasm for research and new forms of presentation was infectious for bright students. He could be brutally insulting to lazy and dull students, but he seemed never to tire of the company of those who shared his energy and excitement for history. Among the professional historians who studied under his instruction were Herbert E. Bolton, Edward S. Corwin, Ellis Paxson Oberholtzer, William Warren Sweet, and Claude H. Van Tyne. These, and others, eventually became accepted authorities of their generation on various areas of American history. McMaster had drilled them in the importance of writing monographs upon which the more comprehensive histories such as his own could accurately be based.

At the annual meeting of the American Historical Association in 1896, McMaster participated in a panel discussion on the teaching of history. He thought that young people in the United States should study the history of their country so that they could "distinguish between truth and falsity," understand "that there is such a thing as a temperate and hasty judgment," and revise their judgments "by the processes of time." He thought that the four elements needed for teaching were teachers, students, textbooks, and time. Regretting that all students could not be exceptional and time unlimited, he suggested that such handicaps could be overcome with proper teachers and texts. He therefore recommended that all teachers be educated and professionally trained and that textbooks be competently written.

McMaster devoted most of his comments on the panel to the content of textbooks. He argued that the colonial period should be covered very briefly but that great attention should be paid to the Declaration of Independence. Students who were informed about Whig thought of the late eighteenth century would understand the Declaration and the American Revolution. Students should also learn that the population centers of Boston, Philadelphia, Baltimore, and the South were founded by people who were "utterly distinct

from each other." As individuals from these centers moved westward there developed "two sets of people who utterly failed to understand each other, and to a large extent do not do so to the present day." The use of maps and census reports, a discussion of the War of 1812, and a description of contemporary means of transportation would enable students to understand the pace at which westward migration took place. Then, McMaster continued, the student should be "presented with certain ideas" that would "enable him to see that, while our ancestors drew up the famous Declaration of Independence they made something which they could not practice." The American Historical Association, McMaster concluded, should concentrate not only on promoting the teaching of history in college but also upon the production of satisfactory textbooks for schools at every level.

McMaster was already engaged in writing textbooks. In 1897 he completed *A School History of the United States*. Some of his critics accused him of having written to please the Grand Army of the Republic, but generally the text met with success and was widely adopted, especially in the Northern states. Although it was readable, it was too advanced for many schools. Therefore, McMaster produced *A Primary History of the United States* in 1901. In 1902 one of his texts was translated into Spanish, and in 1903 his *School History*, supplemented by material written by Kendric Charles Babcock, was adapted by the California State Board of Education as *New Grammar School History of the United States*. McMaster dominated much of the textbook market in the North and the West for more than a decade. His approach was topical, and he tended to emphasize social history as he did in his massive account of the American people.

Interspersed with his textbooks and the continuing volumes of his history, McMaster produced a variety of other writings. His *Benjamin Franklin as a Man of Letters* appeared in 1887. It was the first attempt to treat Benjamin Franklin as a writer. Unwilling to present Franklin as a hero, McMaster criticized Franklin's lack of morality, his arguments in favor of paper money, his desire for wealth, and the apparent inconsistencies between what he practiced and what he preached. Nevertheless, he recognized Franklin's skill as a writer and vigorously recommended the reading of his autobiography, which he judged to be "the very best" of its kind. He thought it admirable that Franklin had risen from a humble background to a position of eminence, and especially that Franklin was "the only man who wrote his name at the foot of the Declaration of Independence, at the foot of the Treaty of Alliance, at the foot of the Treaty of Peace, and at the foot of the Constitution under which we live."

As a prominent historian, McMaster was drawn into commenting upon several events of his day. Great Britain's controversy with Venezuela in 1895 over the boundary of British Guiana elicited from him a 4000-word piece published as *The Origin, Meaning, and Application of the Monroe Doctrine* (1896) and a pamphlet entitled *The Venezuela Dispute*, which appeared the same year, criticizing the British. When the Cuban revolution ignited the Spanish-American War in 1898, McMaster lectured on "Expansionism," offered his services as an engineer, and generally excited his students to his own level of feverish nationalism. He thought that the patriotism which the war fostered was benefit enough from it. McMaster never experienced military service, but he became a champion of military preparedness and expansion. He found the expansion of the United States at the end of the century consistent with American tradition, and his arguments from the perspective of history were welcomed within the inner circles of the Republican party. McMaster himself was becoming an American institution.

In 1913 the eighth volume of *A History of the People of the United States, from the Revolution to the Civil War* was published. That work had consumed much of McMaster's energy for the past thirty years. On Saturday night, 22 November 1913, a large number of friends and admirers gathered for dinner at the Historical Society of Pennsylvania to congratulate McMaster and to help him celebrate. Silas Weir Mitchell, a prominent historical novelist, presided. The guests included James Ford Rhodes, the governor of Pennsylvania, dignitaries from Princeton, the University of Pennsylvania, and the City College of New York, and several of McMaster's former students. Theodore Roosevelt, William Howard Taft, and Woodrow Wilson sent warm greetings. A nephew of Thomas Babington Macaulay commended the American historian in a letter from England, and the literary world, represented by William Dean Howells, Walter Hines Page, and others, joined in the praise. McMaster himself wryly wondered if perhaps so many people had read some of his volumes only because the committee in charge of the celebration had urged them to do so. Nevertheless, he was moved by the attention, and more important, his history had become a permanent part of American historiography.

When asked how he had written his work,

McMaster in 1913 (Historical Society of Pennsylvania)

McMaster was not very helpful. He had resisted imposing an interpretation or philosophy upon his history. When called upon to give public lectures, he talked about history, not about historiography. He had had no special training in his craft. In brief comments before the American Historical Association in 1904 he argued that "real history" could not be written "by following with precision any number of parallel lines." The investigator, he said, must not limit his concentration to changes taking place in only one area of human endeavor; "all social and industrial conditions" must be considered because many factors bore upon constitutional and political change.

The clues to how McMaster wrote his history must be gathered from the work itself. He used printed works, diaries, letters, memoirs, and especially newspapers. His heavy dependence upon newspapers was innovative; his colleague William A. Dunning jokingly noted that McMaster had added to the task of historians "the burdensome duty of going through all the newspapers of the day." McMaster's research, even in newspapers, was not comprehensive. He used only what was available in the repositories that he visited, which meant newspapers largely from the Middle States and New England. Although the South and Southwest were also represented, his research in their newspapers was very limited. He was careless with his footnotes, perhaps in part yielding to George Bancroft's advice not to be too generous in giving away his sources. In some sections of his writing it is nearly impossible to check his documentation, and in others he followed his sources so closely as to approach plagiarism. His style was usually that of the smoothly flowing, realistic narrative, but he was capable of abrupt conclusions and rough transitions. The sheer size of his eight volumes would perhaps make inevitable the presence of errors of fact and lapses of style, but the acclaim he won in his lifetime and the newness of his approach to history won for him a prominent and permanent place in American historiography.

Although McMaster denied having a philosophy of history, his work was the product of the early formative experiences of his life. Above all, he wrote a social history, a history without heroes in which the masses of people themselves were given the credit for building and preserving a strong nation. He examined the Middle States, New England, the South, and the West. He noted the significance of westward migration in the social and political development of the United States, but he did not celebrate it with the passion of Frederick Jackson Turner. He had little use for the disorderly mobs of Andrew Jackson's time or for Jackson's political maneuvers. Nevertheless, the advance of democracy, which McMaster never defined clearly, seemed to him to approach realization of the principles of the Declaration of Independence and to contain none of the horrors of which the British accused it in the 1820s. Although McMaster was more interested in describing than interpreting the social scene, his account of the routine lives of American citizens during the age of Jackson seems to imply that this was a time of progress.

The significance of democracy to McMaster rested with the establishment of a government of and by the people, not with a perennial agitation for individual rights. McMaster was not a reformer; he had no patience with the radical groups in American history. The government that had been established under the Constitution and had been preserved by the Civil War was good enough for him. He concluded his final volume with Abraham Lincoln's promise to the people upon the occasion of his first inauguration that he would preserve, protect, and defend the Union. What was impor-

tant about the presidents, according to McMaster, was not that they were presidents, but that they exemplified the crucial principle that a common man could win and execute the position. The legislative branch of the government, McMaster thought, was far more important. The lesson which he wanted students of his history to learn was how their ancestors had participated in building such a model nation; readers should be thankful and understand that they, too, however seemingly insignificant, were part of the process of history. His faith was in the ultimate rightness of the people, in their ability to succeed as individuals and as groups. It was such a faith in himself at age twenty that had enabled him to complete at age sixty-one his self-assigned task.

For a man of his accomplishments, McMaster was remarkably modest. His history without heroes was in a sense an extension of his shy, almost reclusive, but confident, personality. Although he wrote biographies of Ulysses S. Grant, Benjamin Franklin, Daniel Webster, and Stephen Girard, he found more to criticize than to praise in famous men. The hastily written, anecdotal *Life, Memoirs, Military Career and Death of General U. S. Grant* (1885) praised Grant only for saving the Republic, and *Benjamin Franklin as a Man of Letters* celebrates its subject's writing and contributions to the establishment of democratic institutions, but not his life. McMaster admired Daniel Webster, but his 1902 biography of Webster focused upon Webster's defense of the Constitution, not upon his whole life. The later, commissioned biography entitled *The Life and Times of Stephen Girard, Mariner and Merchant* (1918) contains more praise of Philadelphia than it does of its subject. Individual psychology played no role in McMaster's history; he is remembered for his history of the people, not for his biographies. If McMaster could accomplish what he did with his modest background, he perhaps reasoned, then anyone in the right place at the right time might have done the same things that Grant, Franklin, Webster, and Girard did. In fact, McMaster apparently did not think there was any personal magic in his own accomplishment; he taught his students that they could do the same thing he had done and do it better.

By the time his history was complete, McMaster had already received the recognition of his profession. He had served as president of the American Historical Association in 1905-1906 and as editor of the *American Historical Review* from 1895 through 1899. In 1899 he had been elected to membership in the National Institute of Arts and

Letters. He had achieved his major goals and was free now to enjoy his family and to continue teaching and writing monographs. In May 1914, taking his wife and sons, he sailed for Europe. They were in London when Archduke Franz Ferdinand was assassinated, and they were in Germany as the first effects of war became evident there. After several months of frightening experiences during which they lost their money and luggage and often found it difficult to secure lodging, the McMasters finally succeeded in booking passage for home.

McMaster settled down to write the biography of Stephen Girard, the merchant and mariner from Philadelphia in the early years of the nation. Since the biography was to be official, McMaster had complete use of thousands of surviving manuscripts and letters. The result was his best biography, containing much useful information about the business practices and social milieu of Girard's era, though the man himself tended to become lost in McMaster's indiscriminate and extensive use of long quotations from the voluminous primary sources. McMaster did not distinguish himself with the publication in 1918 and 1920 of two volumes entitled *The United States in the World War*. He had succumbed to the pressure of teachers who wanted information to use in their classrooms, and he had done little more than to put together in chronological order articles from newspapers and official documents.

Meanwhile, McMaster was becoming increasingly occupied with changes in his personal life. On 1 March 1915, John Bach McMaster, Jr., died of pneumonia a few months before he was to graduate from the University of Pennsylvania Law School. In 1920, at the age of sixty-eight, McMaster retired from teaching. To the first historian to have combined the teaching and writing of history, the end of his teaching career must have come with the gloom of finality. Then, on 30 June 1922, Gertrude McMaster died of a heart attack. McMaster was left with only Philip, then married and successfully established at the Rockefeller Institute for Medical Research.

With the need to fill his days with something that could absorb his attention, McMaster returned to his history of the people and produced in 1927 another volume, *A History of the People of the United States during Lincoln's Administration*. He busied himself with his diary and composing memoirs, most of which were never published, but the pressures of age and loneliness bore down upon him. He

moved to Darien, Connecticut, to live with Philip and his wife. He died there on 24 May 1932 and was buried a few days later in Philadelphia. At the time of his death he was a well-known citizen, and with the passage of time, students of United States history and biography would learn that John Bach McMaster's own life and achievements were as vital as anything he wrote about in his history of the American people. His contributions to knowledge and methodology have been surpassed, but his prominence in historiography remains secure because he was a pioneer.

Eric F. Goldman's *John Bach McMaster: American Historian*, first published in 1942 and reprinted in 1971, is the work of a modern historian who shared McMaster's interest in social history and who had access to numerous McMaster papers that are not generally available. The continuing importance of this biography, complete with a definitive list of McMaster's printed writings and speeches and a preliminary analysis of the famous *History*, attests to the historical and human significance of John Bach McMaster as a man of history and of letters.

Bibliography:

Eric F. Goldman, *John Bach McMaster: American Historian* (Philadelphia: University of Pennsylvania Press/London: Oxford University Press, 1942; republished, New York: Octagon Books, 1971), pp. 179-184.

Biography:

Eric F. Goldman, *John Bach McMaster: American Historian* (Philadelphia: University of Pennsylvania Press/London: Oxford University Press, 1942; republished, New York: Octagon Books, 1971).

References:

William T. Hutchinson, "John Bach McMaster, Historian of the American People," *Mississippi Valley Historical Review*, 16 (June 1929): 23-49;

Hutchinson, "John Bach McMaster," in his *The Marcus W. Jernigan Essays in American Historiography* (Chicago: University of Chicago Press, 1937), pp. 122-143;

Ellis Paxson Oberholtzer, "John Bach McMaster, 1852-1932," *Pennsylvania Magazine of History and Biography*, 57, no. 1 (1933): 1-31.

John T. Morse, Jr.

(9 January 1840-27 March 1937)

David Alan Lincove
Ohio State University

SELECTED BOOKS: *A Treatise on the Law Relating to Banks and Banking, With an Appendix Containing the National Bank Act of June 3, 1864, and Amendments Thereto* (Boston: Little, Brown, 1870; revised and enlarged, 1879);

The Law of Arbitration and Award (Boston: Little, Brown, 1872);

Famous Trials: The Tichborne Claimant, Troppmann, Prince Pierre Bonaparte, Mrs. Wharton, The Meteor, Mrs. Fair (Boston: Little, Brown, 1874);

The Life of Alexander Hamilton, 2 volumes (Boston: Little, Brown, 1876);

John Quincy Adams (Boston & New York: Houghton Mifflin, 1882);

Thomas Jefferson (Boston & New York: Houghton Mifflin, 1883);

John Adams (Boston & New York: Houghton Mifflin, 1884);

Benjamin Franklin (Boston & New York: Houghton Mifflin, 1889);

Abraham Lincoln, 2 volumes (Boston: Houghton Mifflin, 1893; London: Osgood, McIlvaine, 1893);

Life and Letters of Oliver Wendell Holmes, 2 volumes (Boston & New York: Houghton Mifflin, 1896; London: Low, 1896);

Memoir of Colonel Henry Lee: With Selections From His Writings and Speeches (Boston: Little, Brown, 1905);

Thomas Sergeant Perry: A Memoir (Boston & New York: Houghton Mifflin, 1929).

OTHER: *American Statesmen Series*, edited by Morse (32 volumes including index, Boston: Houghton Mifflin, 1882-1900; 8 volumes republished, London: Low, 1882-1887);

"Memoir of Thornton Kirkland Lothrop," in *Proceedings of the Massachusetts Historical Society*, 47 (May 1914), pp. 425-444;

"Lord Charnwood's 'Life of Abraham Lincoln,'" in *Proceedings of the Massachusetts Historical Society*, 51 (1917), pp. 90-105;

"Memoir of Henry Lee Higginson," in *Proceedings*

of the *Massachusetts Historical Society*, 53 (1920), pp. 105-127;

"Memoir of Henry Cabot Lodge," in *Proceedings of the Massachusetts Historical Society*, 58 (1924-1925), pp. 99-110;

"Memoir of James Ford Rhodes," in *Proceedings of the Massachusetts Historical Society*, 60 (March 1927), pp. 178-192;

"Moorfield Storey: A Memoir," in *Proceedings of the Massachusetts Historical Society*, 63 (June 1930), pp. 288-301;

"Incidents Connected With the American Statesmen Series," in *Proceedings of the Massachusetts*

Historical Society, 64 (November 1931), pp. 370-388;

"Recollections of Boston and Harvard Before the Civil War," in *Proceedings of the Massachusetts Historical Society*, 65 (October 1933), pp. 150-163.

PERIODICAL PUBLICATION: "William Channing Gannett," *Harvard Graduates' Magazine*, 32 (March 1924): 425-429.

There was a period of transition in biographical writing during the last quarter of the nineteenth century. The concentration on literary style and the marked tendency toward biased accounts slowly gave way to more serious historical research and objectivity displayed by a growing number of authors. John T. Morse, Jr.'s biographical writing and the American Statesmen series which he edited generally reflected the changing nature of writing at the time. As editor and popular biographer, he contributed to the broadening of the American reading public's interest in the American past.

John Torrey Morse, Jr., was born in Boston on 9 January 1840. He was the eldest of three sons born to John Torrey Morse, a merchant engaged in the East India trade, and Lucy Cabot Jackson Morse, the daughter of Charles Jackson, lawyer and justice of the Supreme Judicial Court of Massachusetts. Both parents came from distinguished families highly regarded in Boston society. Morse grew up amid wealth and was always able to live a life of leisure. Like much of Boston's aristocracy at that time, the Morses were Unitarians. Morse did not appear to be deeply affected by religion, although he placed strong emphasis on morality, fairness toward fellow men, achievement, and the power of logic in his analysis of contemporaries and of men in American history. He attended high school at Dixwell, a private day school which compared well with other elite college preparatory schools in the Boston area. By the time Morse graduated and went on to Harvard College in 1856, Dixwell was one of Boston's most respected prep schools, which, along with Boston Latin, contributed about twenty-five percent of the freshman class at Harvard.

By the middle of the nineteenth century, Harvard had become an extension of Boston's elite society, which held a near monopolistic preserve over the college's facilities, benefits, governing boards, and instructional staff. The student body consisted mostly of young men from wealthy families, many of them from the Boston area. It was in this en-

vironment that Morse lived, studied, and socialized from 1856 until he received an A.B. in classics and English in 1860. His experiences at Harvard, the friends he made, and the elite nature of his educational and social background had a lasting impact on his future in law and literature.

The year after Morse graduated from Harvard was a critical year in American history. The Civil War began in 1861, but even though Morse, at twenty-one, was at a prime age for enlisting in the Northern army, he avoided enlistment. In a letter to his cousin and close friend Henry Cabot Lodge in August 1904, he expressed some guilt about having avoided military service. "The sight of the throngs of veterans quite stirred even my sluggish emotions; and for the thousandth time I asked myself why I stayed at home in those days." He answered his own question in 1921 in a letter to the Reverend William C. Gannett. In 1859, wrote Morse, he met Fanny Pope Hovey, daughter of Boston merchant George Otis Hovey. They fell in love, thus making it clear to him that he required a profession so that he could ask for Miss Hovey's hand in marriage. "Even the Civil War," wrote Morse, "failed to tempt me into a diversion." On 10 June 1865, three years after Morse had established his law practice, the couple married. They eventually had two sons, Cabot Jackson and John Torrey III, and adopted a daughter, Charlotte Gertrude Silber Morse.

Morse chose a legal career under pressure from his family. After leaving Harvard, he studied for two years in the law office of John Lowell. In 1862 he gained acceptance to the Massachusetts bar and promptly established an independent practice, which he retained until 1866. From that time until he left the legal profession in 1880, he practiced law in partnership with Darwin Erastus Ware. By one account, Morse was a "moderately successful lawyer" during his eighteen-year career. He also published several articles in the *North American Review* and the *American Law Review* on legal issues, mostly relating to international law and popular trials. These same concerns appeared in three books that he produced from 1870 to 1874: *A Treatise on the Law Relating to Banks and Banking* (1870), *The Law of Arbitration and Award* (1872), and *Famous Trials* (1874). The first was perhaps the most notable book; it went through six editions by 1928. Morse revised and enlarged it in 1879 before subsequent updatings by Frank Parsons, James N. Carter, and Harvey C. Voorhees. Despite the appearance of an active, successful career in law, Morse felt dissatisfied. The practice of law bored him and his time spent writing articles and books was, perhaps, a reflection of his desire to find other interests. In 1931, long after retiring, he expressed his dissatisfaction: "I hated law with all my wicked little heart."

Before leaving law practice completely, Morse found other activities to divert his attention. In 1876 he won election to the Massachusetts House of Representatives on the Republican ticket as a representative for the Back Bay district of Boston. But apparently Boston politics suited his temperament no better than the law. He served only one term. In 1879 he was elected to the Board of Overseers, one of the major governing boards of Harvard College. Morse served from 1879 to 1891. Membership on the Board, which represented the alumni, was an honor conferred on graduates prominent in business, finance, or alumni activities. The Board, however, was only a part-time interest for Morse. By the time he retired from law at the age of forty, his interest in literature and American history, particularly in important statesmen, had led him to a new career.

Morse's career in literature began during the 1870s. For three years, from 1879 to 1883, Morse and Henry Cabot Lodge coedited the *International Review*, a journal that included articles on literature and art and some belles lettres. Foreign writers frequently contributed, but American authors predominated. John Fiske, Oliver Wendell Holmes, John Greenleaf Whittier, and Henry Lee Higginson were among those whose work appeared regularly in the journal. Lodge resigned his position in 1881, and in 1884, the year after Morse left the editorship, the *International Review* ceased publication.

In 1876 Morse published his two-volume *Life of Alexander Hamilton*. The work was well received and long held to be the standard work on Hamilton, although not every review was laudatory. The *Nation* described Morse's biography as a "frank panegyric" characterized by an excessively popular, undignified tone. The biography of Hamilton marked the beginning of Morse's long career as a popular biographer, a career which lasted until nearly 1930 when Morse was well into his years as an octagenarian. His contemporaries, particularly during the last quarter of the nineteenth century, considered him to be both a biographer and historian, perhaps because of the view then prevalent that biographical writing was a branch of history if not the core of history itself. Morse's increasing interest in biography and history was characteristic of the period after the Civil War. Several of his contemporaries, particularly those Harvard graduates such as Lodge and Henry Adams who began to write about American history, influenced him. Morse remarked at a meeting of the Massachusetts Historical Society in 1917 that the Civil War changed the apathetic mood of Americans about their history. After the war "it seemed that a country worthy of preservation by such an expenditure of human and financial sacrifice ought also to be worth knowing about."

Morse recognized that the war had spurred the public's desire to know about great Americans, and he had the skill to respond to this development. The American Statesmen series was introduced in 1882. Morse claimed that he got the idea for the series while reading books in the English Men of Letters series (1878-1919), edited by John Morley. A similar approach, Morse reasoned, might prove successful for dealing with American statesmen. Exactly when he decided to act on his idea is not clear, but it was probably in 1881 when he took his plan to his friend Henry Holt, believing Holt and his New York City publishing house to be more progressive than "any of the old conservative firms." But Holt doubted that such a series would be commercially successful. He saw very little precedent for the wide appeal of books on American history and biography. Holt's reservations did not deter Morse. As a result of a chance meeting with retired publisher James T. Fields, the project got new life. Actually, Fields had had the same idea as Morse; he insisted, however, that Morse was the right man for the job. With Fields's assistance, Morse got an interview with Henry O. Houghton of Houghton Mifflin and found Houghton very enthusiastic about the proposal. On the day of the interview, the contract for the series was set in a rough draft and a verbal agreement had been made.

From 1882 to 1898 the series developed to include twenty-eight biographies covering the period from Benjamin Franklin and the American Revolution to Thaddeus Stevens and Reconstruction after the Civil War. In 1898 Houghton Mifflin published a new, updated edition of the series in thirty-one uniform volumes available only through subscription for $1.25 each. For this edition the volumes were reorganized by period: "Revolutionary Period": *Benjamin Franklin* by John T. Morse, Jr., *Samuel Adams* by James K. Hosmer, *Patrick Henry* by Moses Coit Tyler, and *George Washington*, 2 volumes, by Henry Cabot Lodge; "Constructive Period": *John Adams* by John T. Morse, Jr., *Alexander Hamilton* by Henry Cabot Lodge, *Gouverneur*

Morris by Theodore Roosevelt, *John Jay* by George Pellew, and *John Marshall* by Allan B. Magruder; "Jeffersonian Period": *Thomas Jefferson* by John T. Morse, Jr., *James Madison* by Sydney Howard Gay, *Albert Gallatin* by John Austin Stevens, *James Monroe* by Daniel C. Gilman, *John Quincy Adams* by John T. Morse, Jr., and *John Randolph* by Henry Adams; "Domestic Politics: The Tariff and Slavery": *Andrew Jackson as a Public Man* by William Graham Sumner, *Martin Van Buren* by Edward Morse Shepard, *Life of Henry Clay*, 2 volumes, by Carl Schurz, *Daniel Webster* by Henry Cabot Lodge, *John C. Calhoun* by Hermann E. von Holst, *Thomas Hart Benton* by Theodore Roosevelt, and *Lewis Cass* by Andrew Cunningham McLaughlin; "Civil War and Reconstruction": *Abraham Lincoln*, 2 volumes, by John T. Morse, Jr., *William Henry Seward* by Thornton Kirkland Lothrop, *Salmon Portland Chase* by Albert Bushnell Hart, *Charles Francis Adams* by Charles Francis Adams, Jr., *Charles Sumner* by Moorfield Storey, and *Thaddeus Stevens* by Samuel Walker McCall.

From 1901 to 1917 Houghton Mifflin published a second series which included six biographies in eight volumes, grouped under the period title "Reunited Nation—Growth and Prosperity": *Ulysses S. Grant* by Louis Arthur Coolidge, *John Sherman* by Theodore Elijah Burton, *James Gillespie Blaine* by Edward Stanwood, *Thomas Brackett Reed* by Samuel Walker McCall, *John Hay*, 2 volumes, by William Roscoe Thayer, and *Life of William McKinley*, 2 volumes, by Charles Sumner Olcott. Morse did not edit the second series, but eventually the eight volumes were integrated with the first series. The publisher enhanced the 1898 edition and later volumes with portraits and other illustrations. Each volume included its own index, but in 1900 Houghton Mifflin published a one-volume index and chronology of American history by Theodore Clarke Smith for use with the first thirty-one volumes, and in 1917 it was revised by George Burnham Ives to include later volumes.

The great task of getting the series started was assumed mainly by Morse. Henry O. Houghton gave him complete authority over the project and showed keen interest in its development. Houghton sometimes made suggestions regarding subjects and authors and was available to help solve difficult problems as they occurred. Morse also received assistance from his cousin Henry Cabot Lodge. "We discussed every move together," wrote Morse in his eulogy of Lodge in 1924. "He was almost co-editor."

The first tasks in commencing the series were

1885 publisher's advertisement for the series Morse modeled on John Morley's English Men of Letters. *Although William Dorsheimer's biography "in preparation" never appeared, a volume on* Martin Van Buren *by Edward Morse Shepard was added to the series in 1888.*

deciding how it would be organized, which American statesmen would be covered, and who might best write each volume. Looking back on this time at the age of ninety-one, Morse explained that the criteria for selecting biographical subjects went beyond the caliber and standing of a man personally. "Even more important might often be the matter of the measures and policies with which he happened to have been connected. For I regarded it as a function of the series that, when complete, it should present such a picture of the development of the country that the reader who had faithfully read all the volumes would have a full and fair view of the history of the United States told through the medium of the efforts of the men who had shaped our national career. The actors were to develop the drama." Morse also wrote that the American Statesmen series represented the United States in a positive light, emphasizing the impact of great men, the nation's progress, and the growing strength of the country. Morse disqualified men such as Stephen A. Douglas and Andrew Johnson, because Douglas had been judged a political failure, and Johnson seemed too weak a figure, compared with William H. Seward, Thaddeus Stevens, and Charles Sumner, around which to base the story of Reconstruction.

In the biographical sketch of Morse in the *Dictionary of American Biography*, Oscar Handlin criticizes Morse for his failure to clarify the scope of the series and for his selection of subjects. Handlin emphasizes that Morse first conceived of history as "a succession of the lives of great men; and he indignantly rejected the notion that there might be a place for Aaron Burr in such a gallery." As the series progressed, however, he moved toward the belief that "the individual was less important than the forces working upon him." In his introduction to volume one of the 1898 edition of the series, Morse thus explained that he chose Patrick Henry as representative of the pre-Revolutionary South and included John Randolph based on the belief that his career illustrated the characteristics of Congress during the early nineteenth century.

The task of matching biographical subjects with authors proved to be difficult for Morse. Lodge aided him in the selection of authors, because Lodge had a wider acquaintance with writers. Not counting Morse, of the twenty-five authors who contributed to the American Statesmen series, twelve graduated from Harvard College and most of them resided in the Northeast, particularly Massachusetts. Notable exceptions were German-born Carl Schurz and Hermann E. von Holst and English-born George Pellew, although Pellew did attend Harvard. The authors came from several professions, including law, education, theology, journalism, and politics. Law, in particular, was part of the background of several authors, including Edward Morse Shepard and Moorfield Storey, although others, such as Samuel Walker McCall and Henry Cabot Lodge, went from law to other careers in journalism, literature, and politics. Several widely known authors contributed to Morse's series, including Sydney Howard Gay, editor of the *New York Tribune* and the *New York Evening Post*, James K. Hosmer, professor of rhetoric and English literature, and the influential historians Albert Bushnell Hart and Henry Adams. Collectively, these men were highly educated but, for the most part, conservative and parochial in outlook.

Although Morse claimed to consider carefully the appropriateness of each author for a given subject, the process of commissioning volumes was often quite casual and haphazard. For example, he assigned the volumes on George Washington and Gouverneur Morris by accident. Morse wanted to write the biography of Washington himself and had done considerable work on his manuscript before abruptly abandoning his plan during a conversation with Lodge. Lodge appeared very despondent and expressed gloomy feelings about his political future to his friend. "Suddenly," wrote Morse, "he turned and said: 'John, if you haven't allotted the Washington definitely to anyone else, I wish you would let me do it.'" Despite Morse's own desire to write the book, he responded to Lodge's request by offering the project to him. This was a difficult moment for Morse, because he considered Washington to be the prize subject in the whole series. After Lodge left in a cheerful mood, Morse picked up his manuscript and threw it into the fire. The Gouverneur Morris volume was put into the works one day when Lodge and Theodore Roosevelt appeared uninvited at Morse's residence shortly before lunch. As the three men approached the lunch table, Lodge pulled Morse aside and suggested that Roosevelt be allowed to write the life of Gouverneur Morris for the series. Morse responded with astonishment that Morris did not belong in the series. Lodge seemed to agree but explained that Roosevelt had nothing to do and needed the money. Morse gave in and assented to both Morris and Roosevelt.

During the entire period that he spent as editor of the American Statesmen series, from 1881 until 1900, Morse turned down only one manuscript. Colonel Allan Magruder, a Virginia Civil War veteran, wrote to Morse requesting permission to write the biography of John Marshall. Although Morse knew nothing about Magruder, he had heard of the Magruder family, and he decided that a writer from Virginia would help diversify his corps of authors in the series. When Morse received the manuscript, he rejected it because it had been plagiarized from *The Lives and Times of the Chief Justices of the Supreme Court of the United States* (1855-1858) by Henry Flanders. After Magruder's daughter pleaded with Morse to accept the volume due to the family's poverty, his heart softened. Morse edited the volume himself, and it was published in 1885 under Magruder's name. Morse seemed satisfied with the final product, but in 1885 Lippincott, Grambo, who held the copyright on Flanders's book, charged Houghton Mifflin with plagiarism. The charge proved to be correct, embarrassing both Morse and his publisher. Morse personally settled the matter by paying Lippincott, Grambo $500 which he said came from his own account. Ellen Ballou, however, contradicted this claim in *The Building of the House: Houghton Mifflin's Formative Years* (1970), in which she wrote that the company accepted the charge. Morse never told Magruder about the episode and refused to blame him for it. Magruder was, Morse declared, "a strictly honorable man, and he certainly never had the slightest idea that he had in the least degree impugned on the proprieties." In the same year a charge of plagiarism was directed at James K. Hosmer's *Samuel Adams* by the *St. Louis Globe*, Hosmer's home newspaper. Houghton defended both Hosmer and Morse, and apparently the charges were dropped.

Morse's editorial experience with the *International Review* apparently did not prepare him for some of the problems as editor of a large ongoing series. He expressed exasperation with the slow response of many of the authors, because he expected the biographies to be churned out in a matter of months. When manuscripts did not appear within six months to a year after they were assigned, he felt betrayed. Even more irritating to Morse was his belief that most of the contributors considered their participation in the series as a great service to him. Morse believed that he was paying the contributors, "my writers," a compliment. "They did not in the least appreciate the embarrassment which they caused me by their dilatoriness. . . . Thus there occurred awful hiatuses in the publication, and my series was disfigured by long naps, or interludes, most humiliating to the apparently incompetent editor." Despite this comment, Morse later wrote that his relationship with all contributors was "thoroughly cordial and friendly."

When the American Statesmen series began in 1882, George Mifflin told Morse that he hoped to keep the volumes in print for at least ten or twelve years. But the series was a much bigger success than expected. Many books were still available in the early 1930s, some of them nearly fifty years past their original imprint. *Cumulative Book Index, 1928-1932* listed the entire forty-volume set, consisting of the 1898 edition plus later volumes, as available for seventy-five dollars. The authors' original contracts with Houghton Mifflin offered them $500 cash per volume published or twelve and one-half cents per volume sold. Most authors took the latter option and benefited greatly. In 1907 Henry Cabot Lodge told a news reporter that his biography of Alexander Hamilton published in 1882 had sold thirty-five thousand copies and was still in demand.

The great appeal of the series was due in part to the continued growth of the reading market in American history and biography and to the respect many readers had for Boston publishers and authors. Of the twenty-eight biographies published in the 1898 edition, eighteen were written by New England authors, sixteen of whom were from Boston. The American Statesmen series was one example of New England's domination of the American literary scene, a phenomenon which reached its peak during the last quarter of the nineteenth century and added to the prestige of Morse's series. Also, many students found the American Statesmen biographies informative and delightful reading. The books long remained useful for both teaching and scholarship, although the works in the series generally have been criticized for their popular nature and their lack of documentation and objectivity. Edward H. O'Neill wrote in *A History of American Biography, 1800-1935* (1935) that because the volumes were generally well written and included most of the major national political figures in American history, the series was the most important group of political biographies published in America in the nineteenth century. Morse's direction of and contributions to the series probably influenced Harvard's decision to grant him an honorary doctorate in 1911.

Morse contributed five biographies to the American Statesmen series from 1882 to 1893: *John Quincy Adams* (1882), *Thomas Jefferson* (1883), *John Adams* (1884), *Benjamin Franklin* (1889), and the two-volume *Abraham Lincoln* (1893). These biographies established Morse as a professional, popular biographer of significant stature. The principal reasons for Morse's success, wrote Edward H. O'Neill, were his personal, sympathetic style of writing and his suppression of the traditional eulogistic or panegyric approach. Morse's work represented "conventional biographical writing at its best or near it." He exemplified the growing number of biographers during the 1880s and 1890s who, in response to the post-Civil War call for more realism in literature, showed more interest in facts and a greater appreciation for the spirit of scientific inquiry developing among historians. Morse and other biographers attempted to present their subjects in a lifelike manner. Morse's writing reflected the changing style of the period. Although he generally approached his biographical subjects sympathetically, he did not hesitate to criticize as well as to compliment them. However, he did not have training in historical research. His works were usually based on secondary sources and whatever primary sources were readily available. Research on the subject's life and the relevant events of the time was insufficient, and emphasis was placed on narrative style, an important ingredient for popular appeal.

Morse showed a conservative bias in his writing by focusing mainly on the political lives of his subjects, and he evaluated them based on his ideas about what a statesman ought to be. He placed great value on a man's moral character, the sturdiness of his principles, his leadership qualities, and his strength and skill to accomplish whatever needed to be done. Judged against these guidelines, the subjects of Morse's biographies for the American Statesmen series may be divided into three groups: Benjamin Franklin and John Quincy Adams represented great statesmen; John Adams and Thomas Jefferson were average statesmen; and Abraham Lincoln was a statesman and great leader, yet a man of mystery.

Benjamin Franklin and John Quincy Adams were considered exemplary statesmen, because they showed true patriotism, constantly gave their time and energy to public service, and had some success at shaping United States opinion on certain issues. Franklin was depicted as the first great American and a representative, in moral and intellectual terms, of the American nation. The chief motive of his life, wrote Morse, was to promote the welfare of mankind, whether through serving as a Pennsylvania public official, helping to create the new nation, or representing its interests in France and England. Although Morse was criticized for errors of fact due to his heavy reliance on James Parton's earlier *Life and Times of Benjamin Franklin* (1864), historian Paul Leicester Ford wrote in his 1889 review in the *Nation* that Morse offered the best work on Franklin's political career available.

Morse's *John Quincy Adams* emphasized Adams's great statesmanship due to the "honorable," "dignified" manner with which he conducted American foreign relations as president and earlier as secretary of state and minister to several European nations. His switch from the Federalists to the Republicans as a United States senator from Massachusetts showed only his desire to fight for his principles without bending to the party line. Morse

cleared Adams of any unethical acts resulting from his election as president in the House of Representatives in 1825. Adams's most glorious period followed his presidency, when for many years he served Massachusetts in Congress, most notably as a champion of the antislavery cause. Although Morse did not credit Adams with many lasting accomplishments, he depicted him as a statesman out of the ordinary, with a unique character respected even by his enemies. This book, the first of Morse's contributions to the American Statesmen series, received favorable reviews. Both the *Nation* and the *New York Times* applauded the work's organization and candid, readable style. The reviewer in the *Times* complimented Morse for his "faithful and valuable political sketch" of Adams's career.

Although in his 1883 and 1884 biographies Morse viewed John Adams and Thomas Jefferson as statesmen, he criticized the manner in which they participated in public service. John Adams's chief accomplishment, wrote Morse, was his defense of the Declaration of Independence during debate in Congress in June and early July 1776. Adams showed "cool judgement and statesmanlike comprehension." He promoted independence more efficiently than any other patriot. But from that time until the end of his career, Adams showed very little political skill. Despite his diplomatic assignments in Europe during the Revolution, he had none of the qualities needed by a diplomat. His restiveness and aggressive temperament generated controversy in diplomatic proceedings, and these traits hurt him during his terms as vice-president and president. Morse devoted only forty-six pages to Adams's presidency. Though Adams served the country well, he was constantly embroiled in controversy with Alexander Hamilton, and this conflict constituted the major roadblock to a more fruitful term of office. Adams was also hampered, wrote Morse, by a tendency to value his own self-interests rather than the interests of the public. The reviewer for the *New York Times* disputed Morse's general criticism of Adams and warned readers to beware of accepting false impressions about Adams's character. The *Nation*, however, emphasized the positive qualities of Morse's book, particularly its "succinct" and "simple" account which was highly appropriate to a series of popular biographies. The reviewer complimented Morse for his sympathetic, judicious tone.

Of the five biographies that Morse contributed to the series, his work on Thomas Jefferson was the most biased. In a letter to Henry Cabot Lodge in 1881, Morse wrote that some of the subjects in the series might suffer partisan evaluations. "Let the Jeffersonians and the Jacksonians beware! I will poison the popular mind!!" Morse, like most New Englanders, believed that Jefferson was an unrealistic political ideologist and radical. His only accomplishment was bringing his political faction to supremacy by winning the presidential election of 1800. Despite his professed belief in small government and his severe criticism of the financial policies of the Federalists, Jefferson, Morse pointed out, made no changes when he became president. In fact, he built on the policies he earlier opposed. He favored the extraconstitutional Louisiana Purchase in 1803 and became nothing short of a dictator of his policies to Congress. Morse discredited Jefferson as an administrator, believing that the presidency was not his forte. Furthermore, Morse wrote that Jefferson believed in strong government only when he and his political followers could run it. In describing Jefferson as a notorious political visionary, Morse criticized the Declaration of Independence as a "too broad and high-sounding generalization" and ridiculed Jeffersonian ideas about the structure of government and recurring revolution. Although Morse's biography of Jefferson generated a very positive review in the *Nation*, the reviewer for the *New York Times* faulted Morse for his lack of sympathy with Jefferson and his grudgingly offered praise. The book included "for the most part a series of amusing and captious criticisms" which failed to give an honest picture of Jefferson.

The last of Morse's contributions to the series appeared in two volumes in 1893. *Abraham Lincoln* was his most ambitious work. Morse not only sought to tell Lincoln's life story, which included an analysis of Lincoln's character and a discussion of difficult national issues before and during the Civil War, but he also attempted to describe the administration of the war and the important battles. Morse pictured Lincoln as the greatest man of the Civil War period. Although Lincoln had a solitary, stern character, his honesty, fairness, and disapproval of revenge made him extraordinarily suited to lead the country during a long crisis. Despite his lack of experience with national politics, he had courage, patience, and self-confidence which aided him in directing the nation. Morse believed that Lincoln's repugnance for slavery was tempered by political realism. Lincoln, and the North in general, viewed the Civil War as a struggle to preserve the Union, torn apart by the issue of slavery. This attitude was clear, wrote Morse, in Lincoln's theory of reconstruction for the Southern states, which probably would have been a better plan than the Reconstruction which actually occurred after his death.

According to Edward H. O'Neill, Morse's work on Lincoln was one of the few books which gave a complete record of Lincoln's life in narrative form, and for this reason, it was a valuable contribution to Lincoln biography at the time. Lincoln had become the subject of many biographies since his death in 1865. Most of the early ones, which appeared through the 1870s, either tried to destroy Lincoln or eulogize him, generally confirming public opinion that the man was larger than life. Later, due to tremendous research and writing efforts in the 1880s and early 1890s, biographies of Lincoln took on a more realistic tone. William H. Herndon, the major Lincoln researcher of the period and author of *Abraham Lincoln: True Story of a Great Life* (1892), provided the basis for many books about Lincoln. In an attempt to provide a true picture of Lincoln, Morse used Herndon's work and several other published biographies as sources, and based on the evidence, came to an independent interpretation of Lincoln and the Civil War period. A review in *Critic* considered the distillation of many sources to be the book's chief value. O'Neill found Morse's style and presentation so pleasing that he referred to the book as the "most distinguished piece of writing on Lincoln that we have in the nineteenth century."

Most of the contemporary reviewers acclaimed Morse's biography of Lincoln. The great merit of the book, wrote John J. Halsey in the *Dial*, was the analysis of Lincoln's life and character and of his ability to communicate with the general populace, even while he was president. The reviewer for the *New York Times* agreed, stating that "after Herndon [this is] the best book on Lincoln written within twenty years. In particular, the *Times* reviewer emphasized Morse's ability to find continuity in Lincoln's life, from a poor, difficult youth to the years as national leader during a period of crisis. At each stage of his career, Morse concluded, Lincoln seemed to understand and express the thoughts of his generation. This observation, noted the reviewer, was the "finest specimen of biographical insight shown by Mr. Morse. It gives us, also, a key to the spirit which pervades the whole work." Morse "is content always to take the man as he was and to find his greatness a thing wholly compatible with the facts. . . ." The reviewer for the *Critic*, however, regretted Morse's admitted difficulty with truly understanding Lincoln's personality and mo-

American Statesmen

ABRAHAM LINCOLN

BY

JOHN T. MORSE, JR.

IN TWO VOLUMES

VOL. I.

BOSTON AND NEW YORK
HOUGHTON, MIFFLIN AND COMPANY
The Riverside Press, Cambridge

Frontispiece and title page for the last of Morse's five contributions to the American Statesmen series

tives for action. Morse described his subject as at bottom an unfathomable mystery.

Morse continued as editor of the American Statesmen series until the completion of the first series in 1900. He spent most of the next thirty-seven years in retirement, but he continued to write an occasional book or magazine article. In 1896 he had produced *Life and Letters of Oliver Wendell Holmes;* his *Memoir of Colonel Henry Lee* appeared in 1905 and *Thomas Sergeant Perry: A Memoir* in 1929. The Holmes family asked Morse to write the biography of the well-known novelist, poet, and biographer not long after Holmes's death in 1894. For the next fifty years, this two-volume work, with the prestige of an authorized biography, served as the basis of other studies of Holmes's life. As a close friend of the family, particularly of Oliver Wendell Holmes, Jr., Morse had cooperation in gaining access to much of Holmes's correspondence. In his work Morse sought to describe Holmes's long, var-

ied career, his personality, his thoughts, and his place in Boston's literary society. Holmes's letters made up most of the work, which Morse rounded out with anecdotes. For the most part, the correspondence was the central focus of the work, rather than a source of supporting information. This format was characteristic of many literary biographies during the late nineteenth century, including Samuel Thomas Pickard's *Life and Letters of John Greenleaf Whittier* (1894) and Samuel Longfellow's *Life of Henry Wadsworth Longfellow* (1886). Contemporary reviewers considered the publication of the Holmes biography something of an event, since it scrutinized and applauded the life of one of New England's most beloved men.

The memoirs of Colonel Henry Lee and Thomas Sergeant Perry were both eulogistic works about two Harvard graduates and well-known Boston residents. Perry was a world traveler, thinker, and writer, while Lee was a Union officer during the Civil War and later an author. Both wrote many letters to their friends and associates, and many of these were printed in Morse's two books. Morse also included several eulogies written by Lee after the deaths of friends. Both books received favorable reviews. Henry Steele Commager, reviewing *Thomas Sergeant Perry: A Memoir* in the *New York Herald-Tribune*, described the work as a charming biography and a "labor of love and devotion."

Morse spent his many years of retirement at his home in Needham, Massachusetts. He loved nature and enjoyed walks, riding horseback, and boating, even when he reached his eighties and nineties. Morse enjoyed his relationship with friends, particularly with his cousin Henry Cabot Lodge, with United States Supreme Court Justice Oliver Wendell Holmes, Jr., and with the subject of his 1929 memoir, Thomas Sergeant Perry. He communicated with these men and others in letters and at activities of social, literary, and historical organizations. Morse held membership in the Massachusetts Historical Society, American Historical Association, National Institute of Arts and Letters, Somerset and Algonquin clubs of Boston, and the Country Club of Brookline, Massachusetts. Morse, along with many others from the social and literary establishment of Boston, attended The Club, a dinner and discussion group held the first Friday of each month from about 1870 to 1930. Among the members were such well-known men as Henry Adams, John Fiske, Charles Hale, William Dean Howells, Henry James, Francis Parkman, and James Ford Rhodes. Morse was particularly active in the Massachusetts Historical Society and frequently delivered addresses at the Society's meetings. Friends often called on him to eulogize recently deceased fellow members. On two such occasions he produced brief biographical sketches of Henry Cabot Lodge and James Ford Rhodes, published in 1924 and 1927 in the Society's *Proceedings.*

During his long retirement, Morse often wrote about his past, but his tone was usually self-deprecating. In letters to Lodge and Justice Holmes, he expressed dissatisfaction with what he had accomplished and wished he had been more productive. But he was proud of his American Statesmen series and its great success. Speaking before the Massachusetts Historical Society at the age of ninety-one, Morse credited the series with "blazing the way for such noble and impressive work as was appearing or was about to appear from [John] Fiske, [James Ford] Rhodes, and [John Bach] McMaster." Clearly, the American Statesmen series formed the centerpiece of Morse's career as both editor and biographer. The series exemplified the style of popular biographical writing at the end of the nineteenth century and contributed greatly to the growing interest in American history and biography well into the twentieth century.

On 27 March 1937 Morse died at his home in Needham, Massachusetts, at the age of ninety-seven. He was buried at Mt. Auburn Cemetery, Cambridge.

Reference:

Alexander W. Williams, "The Letters and Friends of John T. Morse, Jr.," in *Proceedings of the Massachusetts Historical Society*, 79 (1967), pp. 97-108.

Papers:

The Massachusetts Historical Society in Boston owns Morse's papers and some correspondence and scrapbooks for the period 1859 to 1935.

Gustavus Myers

(20 March 1872-7 December 1942)

Gary W. McDonogh
New College of the University of South Florida

BOOKS: *History of Public Franchises in New York City, Boroughs of Manhattan and the Bronx* (New York: Reform Club Committee on City Affairs, 1900?);

The History of Tammany Hall (New York: Privately printed, 1901; revised and enlarged, New York: Boni & Liveright, 1917);

History of the Great American Fortunes, 3 volumes (Chicago: Kerr, 1909-1910);

Beyond the Borderline of Life: A Summing Up of the Results of the Scientific Investigation of Psychic Phenomena, with an Account of Professor Botazzi's Experiments with Eusapia Paladino, and an Abstract of the Report of the Cross-references by Mrs. Piper, Mrs. Verrall and Others Which So Influenced Sir Oliver Lodge in His Decision in Favor of the Spiritistic Hypothesis (Boston: Ball, 1910);

History of the Supreme Court of the United States (Chicago: Kerr, 1912);

History of Canadian Wealth (Chicago: Kerr, 1914);

The German Myth: The Falsity of Germany's "Social Progress" Claims (New York: Boni & Liveright, 1918);

Ye Olden Blue Laws (New York: Century, 1921);

The History of American Idealism (New York: Boni & Liveright, 1925);

America Strikes Back; A Record of Contrasts (New York: Washburn, 1935);

The Ending of Hereditary American Fortunes (New York: Messner, 1939);

History of Bigotry in the United States (New York: Random House, 1943).

Gustavus Myers

Gustavus Myers was a social reformer who used meticulous historical research to criticize the failure of American society to live up to its expressed ideals of freedom, democracy, and tolerance. He attacked those who he believed corrupted these values and celebrated the struggle of the American people to improve their nation. Myers wrote for a popular audience, rather than fitting into mainstream academic historiography, although he only received widespread acceptance for his works near the end of his life. He focused on the rigorous collection of facts and the organization of narrative rather than on synthesis or argument; many of his works are voluminous compilations. His studies of Tammany Hall and of the American elite have been recognized as classics. While he was not a direct influence on modern social or radical historians, both his concern for the critical lessons of the past and his convictions had an impact on his contemporary audience, as even his critics conceded in the 1930s and 1940s.

Little is known about Myers's early life beyond the information given in his own accounts. Born in Trenton, New Jersey, where his peripatetic family had moved from Virginia, he was the youngest of the five children of Abram and Julia Hillman Myers. His father rarely lived with the family, and Myers alternated his time in an impoverished home with institutional care. His brother Jerome went on to become a well-known painter, although he does not mention Gustavus in his autobiography.

Myers went to work in a factory at the age of fourteen, cutting short his formal education. At nineteen, he secured a job with the *Philadelphia Record*, and a year later he moved to New York City to continue his journalistic work. Myers felt that these experiences "had a profound awakening influence in early life in shaping my sympathy for the underdog and clearing my vision in youthful years to the effects of oppressive environment and social injustice in general. My developing grievance was not so much personal as social, resulting in a spirit of rebelliousness against conditions which racked so many people in my immediate view."

In New York Myers became involved in reform groups and socialist politics. His first work, *History of Public Franchises in New York City*, was published under the aegis of New York's Social Reform Club; it appeared first in the March 1900 issue of the journal *Municipal Affairs* and was later separately published. In *History of Public Franchises* Myers established the pattern for much of his later work: systematic collection of facts from statutes, newspapers, and legislative investigations to document the history of wrongdoing. In this case, he concentrated on the private appropriation of public services in the city, favoring remunicipalization, with more recompense to the city and much stricter regulation.

He followed this attack on past corruption in New York City with a history of Tammany Hall and its role in urban politics. Myers chronicled the misdeeds of the Tammany Society from its inception in the late eighteenth century through his own time. Pressure from Tammany made it difficult to find a publisher for the work. Myers finally produced *The History of Tammany Hall* (1901) through public subscription, but because few copies were printed, the edition soon became unavailable. The book has become a basic source on Tammany. Recent scholarship, however, has raised the question of how much influence Myers's friends—the liberal reformers James B. Reynolds, James W. Pryor, and Milo Roy Malthie—had on the work.

Myers married Genevieve Whitney in 1904, supporting his family, which eventually included two daughters, with writings for periodicals. In

1907 he joined the Socialist party. He also devoted time and research in the decade 1900 to 1910 to the preparation of his three-volume *History of the Great American Fortunes* (1909-1910). The book continued his exposure of those who had manipulated the American system in order to gain personal and family wealth. His targets ranged from the landowners and shippers of the early days, to the Astors and Fields, to industrial and railroad barons such as the Vanderbilts, Goulds, and Morgans. The dubious early careers of each of Myers's subjects were set forth as the foundations of later gentility and power. Again, publishers were nervous, but the work was finally issued by C. H. Kerr, a socialist publisher in Chicago. *History of the Great American Fortunes* was met with scathing reviews from much of the popular press. Academics criticized its socialist tone and impassioned partisanship. Yet, republished by the Modern Library in 1936 in the midst of the New Deal, it was regarded as a pathbreaking work because of its detailed and demythologized survey of the origins of the major American fortunes. The republication did inspire a detailed reply to Myers's charges against the Morgans by Robert G. Wasson. Wasson pointed to lacunae in the use of primary sources and to Myers's extreme emphasis on the culpability of J. P. Morgan. Ironically, although Wasson claimed that the book was shoddy and unpopular, he documented its widespread influence on historical literature, on the press, and among intellectuals.

Two equally unpopular critical works followed the analysis of the American elite. *History of the Supreme Court of the United States* (1912) showed how this body had failed to promote American ideals because of its acceptance of institutions and power groups. *History of Canadian Wealth* (1914) traced the roots of the oligarchic families of Canada from trapping to land to railroads. Myers thus became classed with the muckrakers. He and his work were repeatedly criticized by major newspapers, including the *New York Times*. During this same general period Myers produced *Beyond the Borderline of Life* (1910), a venture into psychology and spiritism.

Myers's actions and writings began to show striking changes. In 1912 he quit the Socialist party. Only a few years later, writing for his former enemies at the *New York Times*, he decried the failure of European socialists to unite and prevent war. During World War I he turned his investigative acumen to attacking Germany's claim to having produced an ideal social welfare state. He presented evidence of the exploitation of farmers, workers, and their families, as well as of the failure of the German government to provide adequate social insurance. He aimed to undercut German prestige while refuting an American sense of inferiority. His articles were originally prepared for the League for National Unity and serialized by the Federal Committee on Public Information. In 1918, under the title *The German Myth*, they were published in book form.

As Myers became more pro-American in tone, his earlier work was reevaluated. A second, revised and enlarged edition of *The History of Tammany Hall* appeared in 1917, fueling controversies attending a mayoral race in which a Tammany candidate was running. The book was not only approvingly reviewed, but it was also quoted in a *New York Times* editorial.

These trends toward Americanism and wider public acceptance of Myers's work continued in 1921 with the publication of *Ye Olden Blue Laws*, a critical review of restrictions on freedom of religion, press, dress, and speech in the colonial and post-Revolutionary period. The work, too, was cordially received as an antidote to the Volstead Act. The *New York Times* appreciated this work as a depiction of an aristocracy attempting to impose laws against the popular will. But, significantly, Myers was now celebrating the popular will rather than vilifying the elite.

Myers's patriotic zeal peaked in *The History of American Idealism* (1925), which was greeted by the press as a signal of his complete conversion. In this compact text Myers looked at the values of American democracy represented by universal public education, religious liberty, the abolition of slavery, and the destruction of aristocracies at home, as well as by the defense of peace and liberty abroad. He traced the difficulties that had surrounded the emergence of these ideals, with special emphasis on the nineteenth century. The result was a portrait of the triumph of ideals over both the nation's European roots and those who would try to undermine democracy at home.

In his study of idealism Myers criticized Europeans who denigrated the U.S. They became the primary focus of his *America Strikes Back* (1935), perhaps the most enthusiastically received of his books in its day. In this work Myers refuted charges leveled by foreign critics, especially the British, that America was a haven for materialism and its corollaries such as greed, political corruption, and lack of culture. He replied with copious examples of the greed and other failings of European states and their inability to overcome these problems. Myers believed that self-correction was a hallmark of

America's superiority. He even found kind words for a former nemesis, J. Pierpont Morgan. Although *America Strikes Back* remains of some interest as a history of the Black Legend of America, the book now appears extremely defensive.

In 1939 Myers produced *The Ending of Hereditary American Fortunes*, a work whose title seems to hark back to his more fiery days of the beginning of the century. Myers did include lengthy stories of abuses perpetrated by hereditary wealth, but he concentrated on reforms made within the American system and suggested laws to eradicate all inheritance and castes. He lauded Franklin D. Roosevelt's New Deal efforts in particular.

Myers's final work, *History of Bigotry in the United States* (1943), perhaps retained more of his earlier spirit, balanced by his belief in idealism. He said that he had become interested in the topic in the 1920s after his work on blue laws, but he was unable to complete his research until he was awarded a Guggenheim fellowship in 1941. In his book he traced religious intolerance in the United States from European colonization through the Know-Nothings, the Ku Klux Klan, and the anti-Semitism of the 1930s. Myers returned to his recurrent theme of the failure of American society to live up to its dreams. Despite efforts to combat it, bigotry had not been eliminated in American life. Again, as in most of Myers's works, the compilation of facts dominates the narrative, with little synthesis.

Myers did not live to see publication of his work on bigotry. He collapsed shortly after handing in the manuscript in August 1942; in December he died of a cerebral hemorrhage. In his obituary in the *New York Times* he was remembered for his works on Tammany Hall and American wealth, books which had originally led traditional historians and established newspapers, including the *Times*, to reject him as a radical.

Myers's place in American historiography is in many ways paradoxical. He lacked academic status and even popularity for much of his career. He was attacked for his dogmatism, prolixity, and failure to synthesize, and he often claimed that academic historians pirated his researches without acknowledgment. And while he seemed to shift from radical criticism of the United States to a more conciliatory tone in the 1920s and 1930s, it is ultimately on the early works that his enduring reputation has been built.

Yet if there is paradox, there is also consistency. Even in his study of Tammany Hall, Myers saw the ability of the New York populace to raise an outcry and reject political malfeasance as a healthy sign. After documenting abuses against American ideals, he returned to the affirmation of those ideals. Underlying all his works was a profound belief in democracy, freedom, and tolerance, and a passionate dedication to meticulous historical research to demonstrate the relevance of the past to the present and future of such ideals. Gustavus Myers's works are interesting predecessors for modern social histories of power.

References:
John Chamberlain, *Farewell to Reform: The Rise, Life and Decay of the Progressive Mind in America* (New York: Liveright, 1932);

David C. Hammack, *Power and Society: Greater New York at the Turn of the Century* (New York: Russell Sage, 1982);

Robert G. Wasson, *The Hall Carbine Affair: A Study of Contemporary Folklore* (New York: Privately printed, 1941).

John G. Nicolay

(26 February 1832-26 September 1901)

John Hay

(8 October 1838-1 July 1905)

Mark E. Neely, Jr.
Louis A. Warren Lincoln Library and Museum

See also the Hay entry in *DLB 12, American Realists and Naturalists.*

BOOK BY NICOLAY AND HAY: *Abraham Lincoln: A History,* 10 volumes (New York: Century, 1890).

SELECTED BOOK BY NICOLAY: *The Outbreak of Rebellion* (New York: Scribners, 1881).

SELECTED BOOKS BY HAY: *Jim Bludso of the Prairie Belle, and Little Breeches* (Boston: Osgood, 1871);
Pike County Ballads and Other Pieces (Boston: Osgood, 1871);
Castilian Days (Boston: Osgood, 1871; revised edition, Boston & New York: Houghton Mifflin, 1890; revised again, Boston & New York: Houghton Mifflin, 1903; London: Heinemann, 1903);
The Bread-winners: A Social Study, anonymous (New York: Harper, 1884; London: Warne, 1884);
Poems (Boston & New York: Houghton Mifflin, 1890);
Addresses of John Hay (New York: Century, 1906);
The Complete Poetical Works of John Hay (Boston & New York: Houghton Mifflin, 1916);

Lincoln and the Civil War in the Diaries and Letters of John Hay, selected with an introduction by Tyler Dennett (New York: Dodd, Mead, 1939);
The Blood Seedling and Other Tales: The Uncollected Fiction of John Hay, edited by George Monteiro (Providence: Cut Flower Press, 1972).

OTHER: *Abraham Lincoln: Complete Works, Comprising His Speeches, Letters, State Papers, and Miscellaneous Writings,* edited by Nicolay and Hay, 2 volumes (New York: Century, 1894);
"The Civil War, 1861-1865," by Nicolay, in *The Cambridge Modern History,* 13 volumes (Cambridge: Cambridge University Press, 1902-1912), VII: 443-548;
"The North During the War," in *The Cambridge Modern History,* 13 volumes (Cambridge: Cambridge University Press, 1902-1912), VII: 568-602.

John George Nicolay and John Milton Hay produced one of the best and most comprehensive histories written in America in the nineteenth century. Nicolay was born in Essingen, Bavaria, but came to America in 1838 with his parents, John Jacob and Helena Nicolay, and four other Nicolay children. The family lived in Ohio, Indiana, and

Missouri before settling in Pike County, Illinois, where John Jacob Nicolay and his sons operated a flour mill. By the late 1840s both of Nicolay's parents had died. Nicolay spent one year as a clerk in a White Hall, Illinois, store before going to work as a printer's devil for the *Pittsfield* (Illinois) *Free Press*, which was Whig in politics.

In 1851 in Pittsfield Nicolay met and became a friend of his future collaborator, John Hay, who was preparing for college at a local academy. Hay, the son of Dr. Charles Hay and Helen Leonard Hay of Salem, Indiana, moved on from Pittsfield to college at Springfield, Illinois (1852-1855), and then to Brown University (B.A., 1858), while Nicolay remained at work in Illinois.

In 1854 Nicolay became the owner of the *Free Press*. Journalism very often led to involvement in politics in those days, and in 1856 Nicolay sold the newspaper to become, in 1857, a clerk in the office of Illinois Secretary of State Ozias M. Hatch. Both Nicolay and Hatch were solid Republicans. Since Abraham Lincoln was an "assiduous student of election tables" and these were kept in the secretary of state's office, Nicolay soon made Lincoln's acquaintance. In 1858 he wrote a pamphlet attacking the record of Lincoln's rival for the United States Senate in that historic election, Stephen A. Douglas.

Two years later, as a correspondent for a Missouri newspaper, Nicolay attended the Chicago convention which nominated Lincoln for the presidency. Though he was disappointed that he was not chosen to write a campaign biography of the Republican nominee, the increased volume of mail Lincoln was receiving as his party's standard-bearer necessitated hiring a private secretary, and Nicolay got the job. When Lincoln won the election in November, correspondence again increased greatly, and Nicolay needed help. Hay, who had been reading law at his uncle's office in Springfield, had campaigned actively for Lincoln. Nicolay hired Hay, and the two young men became President Lincoln's private secretaries in Washington.

Nicolay and Hay had as good a vantage point as anyone from which to observe the Lincoln administration. Although they took their meals in town, they lived in the executive mansion. They screened most of Lincoln's White House visitors, sorted his mail, prepared daily news summaries, and occasionally wrote letters for the president. The life was tough and lonely, but Nicolay and Hay lived it in good spirits, spicing their sometimes grimly depressing days with humor and irony. When the president was out of earshot, they called him the "Tycoon," and they referred to his wife,

whom neither liked, by much less flattering names.

Nicolay's and Hay's jobs were not menial, and the history of the administration they later wrote was not at all a backstairs at the White House affair. They were discreet as secretaries, and they would be discreet as historians. From time to time each was entrusted with government missions. Nicolay helped negotiate Indian treaties and "watched proceedings" at the 1864 Republican convention; Hay attempted to organize a reconstruction government in Florida, investigated fifth-column movements in Missouri, and met Confederate peace commissioners in Canada in 1864.

It is likely that Nicolay and Hay had a book in mind almost from the beginning of their work in Washington. Hay kept a diary, and Nicolay wrote occasional private memoranda on the president's conversations. Both received foreign appointments from Lincoln before his assassination, and after getting his papers in order after his death, both men were in Europe for a time. In 1865 Nicolay married Therena Bates of Pittsfield and went to Paris, where he served as consul from 1865 to 1869. Hay became Secretary of the U.S. legation in Paris in 1865, chargé d'affaires in Vienna in 1867, and secretary of the legation at Madrid in 1868. While he was in Europe Hay, who had published poetry, essays, and at least one story during the early 1860's, continued to write for American periodicals. His essays based upon his experiences in Madrid were included in his 1871 book *Castilian Days*.

Nicolay returned to the United States in 1869. He tried journalism again and applied for a consulship at Bogota in 1872, advertising himself to President Ulysses S. Grant more or less as a stalwart whose appointment would help stem the tide of Lincoln's old Illinois friends toward the Liberal Republicans. Grant turned him down, but in 1872 Nicolay did gain appointment as marshal of the United States Supreme Court, a Washington sinecure which left him plenty of time for research.

Hay returned to the U.S. in 1870 and accepted a position with the *New York Tribune*, to which he contributed daily editorials as well as his first regional poems, "Little Breeches" and "Jim Bludso (of the Prairie Belle)." In 1874 he married Clara Louise Stone, daughter of affluent Ohioan Amasa Stone.

By the early 1870s, both Nicolay and Hay were ready to begin writing a history of the Lincoln administration. The main obstacle was Robert Todd Lincoln's possession of his father's papers. By 1875 Nicolay had gained access to the papers and the men were at work. In addition to having

John G. Nicolay (left) and John Hay with President Lincoln, photographed 8 November 1863 by Alexander Gardner

at their disposal crucial sources that, as it turned out, no one else would be allowed to see until 1947, Nicolay and Hay were personally well equipped to write the history. Hay was already a published author, and Nicolay was a journalist who would see his book *The Outbreak of Rebellion* published as the first volume of Scribners Campaigns of the Civil War series in 1881. Nicolay, because of his government job, and Hay, because of wealth gained by marriage, had time for research and writing. Both men were intelligent, conscientious, and thorough.

Abraham Lincoln: A History took fifteen years to complete. During that time Hay served as assistant secretary of state under Rutherford B. Hayes (1879-1881) and produced his only novel, *The Bread-winners: A Social Study*, which was published anonymously in 1884. Nicolay's infant son died in 1878; his wife died in 1885. Only a daughter, Helen, survived. Eye trouble plagued him. He worried constantly about being scooped (by Lin-

coln's Secretary of the Navy Gideon Welles, for example) on certain episodes of the Lincoln administration, and he worried that Robert Lincoln might let someone else see the papers.

Robert Lincoln did not release any papers, but he did have to approve the manuscript. Not much evidence exists to show what bearing this requirement had on the text, but most scholars believe that Robert Lincoln's influence was not great—after all, Nicolay and Hay admired Abraham Lincoln almost as much as his son did.

The collaboration was serene, and the fact that the two men exchanged drafts and blended their styles so well makes it impossible to say who wrote which parts of the history. In 1885 Nicolay and Hay sold serial rights to their material to *Century* magazine for $50,000. This sum was widely reputed to have been the largest ever paid for a series of magazine articles, but Hay pointed out that, after deducting the expenses incurred in gathering materials for the enormous project, each man had earned only $1.50 per day for his work. Over a third of *Abraham Lincoln: A History* appeared in the magazine from November 1886 through February 1890, and it increased *Century*'s circulation considerably.

Nicolay and Hay's work appeared in ten octavo volumes in 1890. Five thousand copies were sold by subscription, and considering that it was such a lengthy and serious work, it sold at a respectable rate for many years. Contemporary reviewers generally took note of the staggering bulk of *Abraham Lincoln: A History*, and even friendly critics, like the one for the *Chautauquan*, understood that in Nicolay and Hay's "long contemplation of their subject, . . . he [Lincoln] assumed to them at times moral proportions somewhat unnaturally exalted, and . . . they represent him as standing habitually on a higher round of the ladder of perfection than is possible for humanity." In truth, Nicolay and Hay lacerated Lincoln's opponents, referring, for example, to General P. G. T. Beauregard's "lurid Creole rhetoric."

Modern historians often quote Hay's letter to Nicolay asserting that in their treatment of General George B. McClellan "it is of the utmost moment that we should seem fair to him, while we are destroying him." Why that letter should seem so telling is not clear, for Nicolay and Hay made little pretense of liking McClellan, who was Lincoln's opponent in the 1864 presidential race. In fact, they treated him with scorn and sarcasm. Noting the fact that McClellan's report on Antietam exaggerated the number of his own troops, the authors were quick to add: "It is true he could afford it, as in the same estimate he very nearly doubled the number of the enemy." Of McClellan's views on a strategic question which bitterly divided him and Lincoln, the authors wrote caustically: "Except when he was in Washington, he always regarded its possible capture as a trifling affair."

In addition to the pro-Lincoln bias, *Abraham Lincoln*, perhaps because of its sprawling comprehensiveness, had only one other overriding interpretive bias, and that one was against the Radical wing of the Republican party. This slant is controversial and more difficult to deal with because it is unclear whether Lincoln viewed the Radicals in the same way that Nicolay and Hay did. If he did not, then it could be argued that Nicolay and Hay, through their own dislike of the Radicals, fostered a historical myth of great difficulties between Lincoln and the Radicals. On the other hand, Nicolay and Hay were in the executive mansion and may

well have rendered accurately a tone of feeling picked up from the president himself. All that can be said for certain is that Hay used much stronger language to describe the Radicals than Lincoln did. He regularly referred to them in his diary and letters as "Jacobins," a phrase later picked up by antiradical historians. The president, however, did not use such terms and specifically told campaign biographer Henry J. Raymond in 1864 that the phrase "*the Jacobinism of Congress*" had been falsely attributed: "I do not remember using [it] literally or in substance, and . . . I wish [it] not to be published in any event."

Despite the obvious pro-Lincoln bias of Nicolay and Hay's work, in *The Lincoln Theme and American National Historiography* (1948) David M. Potter astutely notes that "the fullness and the candor of the record is astonishing." Nicolay and Hay "seldom distorted the record, seldom misrepresented Lincoln's position," but "they always defended that position whatever it might be." An important example of that defense is their treatment of the Emancipation Proclamation, which for some unaccountable reason they wished to call "Mr. Lincoln's Edict of Freedom." After describing Lincoln's gradual decision to issue the proclamation and the process of composing the final document, Nicolay and Hay note that "several eminent lawyers have publicly questioned the legal validity of Mr. Lincoln's Edict of Freedom." Then they launch their defense: "Mr. Lincoln's own conception and explanation of the constitutional and legal bearings of his act": "There is little difficulty in arriving at this. His language, embodied in a number of letters and documents, contains such a distinct and logical exposition of the whole process of his thought and action, from the somewhat extreme conservatism of his first inaugural to his great edict of January 1, 1863, and the subsequent policy of its practical enforcement, that we need but arrange them in their obvious sequence." The sequence which follows may be *logically* obvious but it is conspicuously *not* chronological and includes citations from various letters and papers written on 4 April 1864; 26 August 1863; 17 August 1864; and 2 September 1863 (in Nicolay and Hay's order). This is unusual in a historical work otherwise marked by careful attention to chronology and frequently given to defending Lincoln's actions by lecturing the reader on the oft-forgotten pressures of the moment.

Notably absent in each of the two chapters on the Emancipation Proclamation is any reference to Lincoln's starchy letter of 22 September 1861 to

Orville Hickman Browning, explaining why the president had overruled General John C. Frémont's unauthorized military order for emancipation in Missouri in 1861. In that letter Lincoln said flatly: "Can it be pretended that it is any longer the Government of the United States—any government of constitution and laws—wherein a general or a president may make permanent rules of property by proclamation? I do not say Congress might not, with propriety, pass a law on the point, just such as General Frémont proclaimed. I do not say I might not, as a member of Congress, vote for it. What I object to is, that I, as President, shall expressly or impliedly seize and exercise the permanent legislative functions of the Government." To be sure, Nicolay and Hay did not suppress this document which seems to undermine Lincoln's later position in the Emancipation Proclamation. They had quoted the letter in full two volumes earlier, and they had defended it, saying that "no real distinction of principle exists between his criticism of Frémont's proclamation and the issuing of his own." They had to refer to the letter to Browning because, diligent researchers that they were, they knew that its text had already been printed in 1882 in *The Proceedings of the Illinois Bar Association.*

Nicolay and Hay admit only "a marked and acknowledged change of policy between the date of the Browning letter and the date of his preliminary Emancipation Proclamation" (exactly one year). The policy shift stemmed from the fact that emancipation would help win the war in 1862 after many military defeats and would have apparently hindered the war effort in 1861, when keeping slave-holding Kentucky in the Union was essential. Nicolay and Hay offered other explanations of the legal difference between the Emancipation Proclamation and Frémont's proclamation, several of them definitely worth historical consideration: "The difference between these extra-military decrees of Frémont's proclamation and Lincoln's acts of emancipation is broad and essential. Frémont's act was one of civil administration, Lincoln's a step in an active military campaign; Frémont's was local and individual, Lincoln's national and general; Frémont's partly within military lines, Lincoln's altogether beyond military lines; Frémont's an act of punishment, Lincoln's a means of war; Frémont's acting upon property, Lincoln's acting upon persons. National law, civil and military, knew nothing of slavery, and did not protect it as an institution. It only tolerated State laws to that effect, and only dealt with fugitive slaves as 'persons held to service.' Lincoln did not, as dictator, decree the abrogation

of these State laws; but in order to call persons from the military aid of the rebellion to the military aid of the Union, he, as Commander-in-Chief, armed by military necessity, proclaimed that persons held as slaves within rebel lines should on a certain day become free unless rebellion ceased." The authors thus defend mightily—but on altogether different grounds from those on which they later defended the Emancipation Proclamation itself, where the standard is "Mr. Lincoln's own conception and explanation of the constitutional and legal bearings of his act."

The fact of the matter is that by his "own conception and explanation" Lincoln changed constitutional principle between 22 September 1861 and 22 September 1862. But Nicolay and Hay would not admit or could not see that fact, because in their *Abraham Lincoln* the president is always "by nature so singularly frank and conscientious, and by mental constitution so unavoidably logical, that he could not, if he had desired, do things or even seem to do them by indirection or subterfuge." Remarkably, just after quoting Lincoln's answer to Horace Greeley's "Prayer of Twenty Millions," in which the president appeared to say that he would not issue an emancipation proclamation precisely one month before he did, and just before quoting his reply to a Chicago religious delegation, to whom he seemed to describe an emancipation proclamation as a document like "the Pope's bull against the comet," Nicolay and Hay describe Lincoln as "by nature . . . frank and direct."

Yet, however doubtful the conclusions the authors draw from the record, as David Potter says, the record is all there in Nicolay and Hay's history, and along with it are numerous valuable insights, too often overlooked by modern scholars who ignore Nicolay and Hay's work as biased official history. Their description of Lincoln's mentality in the remarkable period before the issuing of the preliminary proclamation seems quite sensitive:

> Under this enforced necessity for further postponement of his fixed purpose [to issue the proclamation], in addition to his many other perplexities, the President grew sensitive and even irritable upon this point. He was by nature so frank and direct, he was so conscientious in all his official responsibilities, that he made the complaints and implied reproaches of even his humblest petitioner his own. The severe impartiality of his self-judgment sometimes became almost a feeling of self-accusation, from which he found relief only by a most searching analysis of his

own motives in self-justification.

In this period under review this state of feeling was several times manifested. Individuals and delegations came to him to urge one side or the other of a decision, which, though already made in his own mind, forced upon him a reëxamination of its justness and its possibilities for good or evil. Imperceptibly these mental processes became a species of self-torment, and well-meaning inquirers or advisers affected his overstrung nerves like so many persecuting inquisitors. A phlegmatic nature would have turned them away in sullen silence, or at most with an evasive commonplace. But Lincoln felt himself under compulsion, which he could not resist, to state somewhat precisely the difficulties and perplexities under which he was acting, or, rather, apparently refusing to act; and in such statements his public argument, upon hypothesis assumed for illustration, was liable to outrun his private conclusion upon facts which had controlled his judgment.

If this analysis is only a defense, it is at least an artful one, and it may well contain genuine psychological insight.

That is not to say that Nicolay and Hay were given, as Lincoln's law partner William H. Herndon was in the 1889 biography he wrote with Jesse Weik, to uninformed speculation about Lincoln's psyche. Nicolay and Hay had not been counselors, intimates, and advisers. They had been private secretaries only. In dealing with many of the most important policies of the administration, they worked the way other historians did. They read the relevant documents and drew conclusions based on those documents. They rarely buttressed their conclusions about Lincoln with recollections of personal conversations or personal glimpses of the president at work; and then only when those conversations or glimpses had been recorded in writing by Nicolay or Hay at the time of their occurrence.

Nicolay and Hay were not methodological pioneers, and yet their method was sound and meritorious under the circumstances. In the beginning they attempted what today would be called oral history. This approach was a natural one and one which no doubt appealed to these two men who lacked any formal training in history. They were not writing ancient history, but rather were chronicling, albeit with system and accuracy, the events of the previous decade. The distinctly unschooled and woolly-headed Herndon also turned to oral history almost immediately after Lincoln's death,

interviewing dozens of old settlers who had known Lincoln in his youth. He thought that his training as a courtroom lawyer would make him a shrewd enough judge of witnesses to steer him clear of error.

Nicolay and Hay had no such confidence, and they quickly lost all faith in oral history. After the magazine publication of their work, when men who could remember the events described in the articles complained about them, Hay, who combined an acid wit with considerable literary ability, snorted at the "pig-headed contradiction we have to go through on the part of conceited old men with bad memories, who have been lying for twenty years." Nicolay and Hay's devotion to documentary accuracy was so thoroughgoing that, as Benjamin P. Thomas says, "they came to distrust their own recollections, unless they were confirmed by memoranda or other written evidence."

In one respect, they carried their documentary dedication too far. Richard Watson Gilder, the *Century* editor, pleaded with the authors for more details of Lincoln's personal, everyday life, but Nicolay and Hay stuck to the high road of solemn political and administrative history. That was a loss both to the future of Lincoln biography (which was forced to rely more on the overly bucolic and folksy anecdotes in *Herndon's Lincoln*) and to Nicolay and Hay's own work. Those occasional chapters which focus closely on Lincoln are far livelier than the rest and make memorable reading.

A good example is "Lincoln Reëlected." Here, in a chapter which stresses "the dignity and self-control with which Mr. Lincoln held himself aloof from the work of the canvass" and the even-handedness with which he aided legitimate party nominees whether they were particularly friendly toward him or not, Nicolay and Hay offer some charming glimpses of the man. When Lincoln and Secretary of War Edwin M. Stanton learned that the veterans' vote from Washington's Carver Hospital had the heaviest proportion of votes for McClellan of any veterans' returns, the president turned to the secretary and said, "That's hard on us, Stanton! They know us better than the others."

Nicolay and Hay were men who appreciated a sharp wit, and they had occasionally been doubtful about the president's sometimes rustic taste in humor. In "Lincoln Reëlected" they quoted Lincoln's notation on a letter which warned him of a complicated strategy in one locality whereby Democrats would abstain from voting: "More likely to abstain from stopping once they get at it." Despite Hay's Ivy League education, the authors were willing to let Lincoln speak in his own less refined voice. They retold an anecdote that Lincoln had recounted on election night, describing a near fall on a Springfield path "worn hog-backed and . . . slippery." Yet they left out the homely detail (which can be found in Hay's diary) that at midnight, while awaiting the election returns, the little group had a supper of fried oysters which the "President went awkwardly and hospitably to work shovelling out" for the rest of the party.

This eminently readable and image-filled chapter provides a contrast with the many chapters in which Lincoln is not even mentioned, or is mentioned only in passing. These chapters, covering military campaigns exclusively, have been criticized ever since Nicolay and Hay wrote them. The editors at *Century*, who had considerable expertise in military matters as the orchestrators of the series of reminiscences which became the monumental *Battles and Leaders of the Civil War* (1888), urged Nicolay and Hay to steer clear of straight military narrative. The editors kept finding errors, thought that the two authors were more or less out of their element, and liked best the chapters with Lincoln in them. So do most modern readers. But Nicolay and Hay were adamant in thinking the story incomplete without the background narrative. Paul M. Angle, who edited a one-volume abridgment of their history in 1966, more or less agreed with them, praising *Abraham Lincoln: A History* as "one narrative that covers the whole great sweep of events—political developments, South as well as North; military campaigns, not only in the East but also in the often-neglected West and Southwest; the naval war; emancipation; military government and the problems it occasioned; foreign affairs; reconstruction; Lincoln's assassination and funeral."

By any standard, the achievement of Nicolay and Hay is worthy of note in the history of American historical writing. What they wrote endures and is still useful to modern historians, though of course in a limited way, because they were eyewitnesses to the historical events they wrote about. Their collaborative effort advanced Lincoln scholarship, as David Potter rightly says, more than any other work on Lincoln, because they had access to sources that others would not see for over fifty years, and because they surpassed other Lincoln writers of the era in education in the broadest sense of the word. Their work also revealed their own

era. It is instructive to note, for example, that in their beautifully written final chapter on "Lincoln's Fame" Nicolay and Hay had already concluded that "the wide chorus" of popular opinion held that Lincoln's achievements were "equaled by Washington alone."

Nicolay and Hay's work was among the greatest American historical works of the era, meriting comparison in thoroughness, clear writing, documentary method, advance over previous scholarship, and enduring worth with Henry Adams's *History of the United States of America During the Administrations of Thomas Jefferson and James Madison* (1884-1891).

Letters:
Letters of John Hay and Extracts from Diary, edited by Clara Stone Hay and Henry Adams, 3 volumes (Washington, D.C.: Privately printed, 1908);
Lincoln and the Civil War in the Diaries and Letters of John Hay, edited by Tyler Dennett (New York: Dodd, Mead, 1939).

Biographies:
William Roscoe Thayer, *The Life and Letters of John Hay* (Boston & New York: Houghton Mifflin, 1915);
Tyler Dennett, *John Hay: From Poetry to Politics* (New York: Dodd, Mead, 1933);
Helen Nicolay, *Lincoln's Secretary: A Biography of John G. Nicolay* (New York: Longmans, Green, 1949);
Kenton J. Clymer, *John Hay: The Gentleman as Diplomat* (Ann Arbor: University of Michigan Press, 1975).

References:
David M. Potter, *The Lincoln Theme and American National Historiography* (Oxford: Clarendon Press, 1948);
Benjamin P. Thomas, *Portrait for Posterity: Lincoln and His Biographers* (New Brunswick, N.J.: Rutgers University Press, 1947).

Papers:
The Nicolay-Hay Collection at the Illinois State Historical Library, Springfield, contains the surviving correspondence and notes pertaining to *Abraham Lincoln: A History*.

Ellis Paxson Oberholtzer

(5 October 1868-8 December 1936)

L. Moody Simms, Jr.
Illinois State University

SELECTED BOOKS: *The Referendum in America* (Philadelphia: Printed by Burk & McFetridge, 1893; enlarged and updated, New York: Scribners, 1900; enlarged and updated again, 1911);

Die Beziehungen zwischen dem Staat und der Zeitungspresse im Deutschen Reich (Berlin: Mayer & Miller, 1895);

The New Man: A Chronicle of the Modern Time (Philadelphia: Levytype, 1897);

Robert Morris: Patriot and Financier (New York & London: Macmillan, 1903);

Abraham Lincoln (Philadelphia: Jacobs, 1904);

The Literary History of Philadelphia (Philadelphia: Jacobs, 1906);

Jay Cooke: Financier of the Civil War, 2 volumes (Philadelphia: Jacobs, 1907);

Philadelphia: A History of the City and Its People, A Record of 225 Years, 4 volumes (Philadelphia & Chicago: Clarke, 1912);

A History of the United States Since the Civil War, 5 volumes (New York: Macmillan, 1917-1937);

The Morals of the Movie (Philadelphia: Penn, 1922).

OTHER: Joshua L. Chamberlain, ed., *University of Pennsylvania: Its History, Influence, Equipment and Characteristics*, biographical editing by Oberholtzer, 2 volumes (Boston: Herndon, 1901, 1902);

American Crisis Biographies, edited by Oberholtzer, 15 volumes (Philadelphia: Jacobs, 1904-1915);

The Book of the Pageant, October 9th, 1908, arranged by Oberholtzer (Philadelphia: Printed for the Committee by Jacobs, 1908);

Henry Clay, by His Grandson Thomas Hart Clay, completed by Oberholtzer (Philadelphia: Jacobs, 1910);

Official Pictorial and Descriptive Souvenir Book of the Historical Pageant, October Seventh to Twelfth, 1912, compiled with notes and adaptation to the field by Oberholtzer (Philadelphia: Historical Pageant Committee of Philadelphia, 1912).

Ellis Paxson Oberholtzer (Historical Society of Pennsylvania)

PERIODICAL PUBLICATIONS: "The First American Novelist," *Journal of American History*, 1, no. 2 (1907): 236-240;

"John Bach McMaster, 1852-1932," *Pennsylvania Magazine of History and Biography*, 57 (January 1933): 1-31.

Ellis Paxson Oberholtzer was among the many students who passed through John Bach Mc-

Master's classes at the University of Pennsylvania during the late 1880s. Under his mentor's influence, he turned in time—as editor, biographer, and historian—to historical writing. He edited the American Crisis Biographies series, wrote a volume on the literary history of Philadelphia, and completed biographies of Robert Morris and Jay Cooke. Oberholtzer had already brought out the early volumes of *A History of the United States Since the Civil War* when McMaster published the final volume of his own *History of the People of the United States* in 1927. Giving a copy of the book to Oberholtzer, McMaster said: "There, I have come up to you. It is for you to go on." Oberholtzer did go on, bringing his narrative history to the assassination of William McKinley.

Born at Cambria Station, Chester County, Pennsylvania, on 5 October 1868, Ellis Paxson Oberholtzer was the elder of two children of John Oberholtzer, a merchant, and Sara Louisa Vickers Oberholtzer, a poet, novelist, and leader in the movement for school savings. He was well educated and had entrée to the upper-class circles of Philadelphia. Upon graduation from the University of Pennsylvania in 1889, he joined the staff of the *Philadelphia Evening Telegraph*. While working for the *Evening Telegraph*, Oberholtzer also attended graduate school at Pennsylvania, receiving a Ph.D. in history in 1893 with a dissertation on *The Referendum in America*. Published the same year, the work describes what had been done to graft this form of democracy onto the American political system. Later updated editions (1900, 1911) included material on the initiative and the recall. Though the work was invoked at times to help extend these reforms across the United States, its author seemed to prefer the role of scientific investigator to that of advocate.

Oberholtzer went to Europe in September of 1893. Though his itinerary included several countries, he spent most of his time in Germany. During his European sojourn he wrote travel articles for the *Evening Telegraph* and completed a book on journalism in Germany entitled *Die Beziehungen zwischen dem Staat und der Zeitungspresse im Deutschen Reich*, published in 1895. Returning to the United States after some eighteen months of study and travel, he worked for a while as editor of the *Manufacturer* in Philadelphia before becoming literary editor, first at the *Philadelphia Times*, then at the *Public Ledger*.

As an editor, Oberholtzer continued to work with historical topics. He served as biographical editor for a work entitled *University of Pennsylvania:*

Its History, Influence, Equipment and Characteristics, which was edited and supervised by Joshua L. Chamberlain and published in 1901 and 1902. His *Robert Morris: Patriot and Financier* was published in 1903, twelve years after the appearance of an earlier study of Morris, William Graham Sumner's *The Financier and the Finances of the American Revolution*. Though his volumes were comparatively thorough for their day, Sumner's method of organizing his study limited its usefulness. Oberholtzer took advantage of Morris's letter-books and the diary of the Office of Finance—primary sources unavailable to Sumner—but his analysis of Morris was much less profound. Because of his persuasive presentation, however, Oberholtzer rather than Sumner became the recognized biographer of Morris.

The Philadelphia publisher G. W. Jacobs and Company chose Oberholtzer as editor of the American Crisis Biographies series which was to deal primarily with figures of the Civil War era. He wrote two biographies in the series, one of Abraham Lincoln and another of Jay Cooke. Though workmanlike, Oberholtzer's *Abraham Lincoln* (1904) added little to existing knowledge. It was quickly buried in the ever-growing body of Lincoln literature.

While working on the American Crisis project, Oberholtzer produced *The Literary History of Philadelphia* (1906). In this local history, he expressed strong regional and ethnic preferences. Himself a Philadelphian, descendant of the early Pennsylvania melting pot—"dissidents like the Quakers," "German sectarians," "belligerent Scotch-Irish and other Gaels," and "more formal Church of England men"—Oberholtzer was extremely conscious of belonging to the Philadelphia aristocratic tradition. The work reflects the provincialism of an upper-class Philadelphian as well as a general narrowness of social and economic outlook, traits which appear even in his later multivolume *History of the United States Since the Civil War*.

Appearing in the American Crisis Biographies series, Oberholtzer's two-volume *Jay Cooke: Financier of the Civil War* (1907) was one of the first scholarly biographies in American business history. One contemporary reviewer maintained that Oberholtzer's volumes "offer themselves as a standard work of reference," though another faulted the author for being an "undiscriminating admirer of Jay Cooke." Oberholtzer's work was largely superseded by Henrietta Larson's study (*Jay Cooke: Private Banker*, 1936) based on extensive records and sound economic analysis. Yet Larson recommended the earlier work, largely because its author had quoted generously from Cooke's letters which were later lost.

Oberholtzer also wrote in 1907 "The First American Novelist," an article dealing with the early Pennsylvania writer Charles Brockden Brown. In connection with the American Crisis Biographies project, he completed the volume on *Henry Clay* (1910), which had been undertaken initially by Clay's grandson Thomas Hart Clay. Like the earlier Lincoln volume in the same series, this biography contributed nothing new to existing knowledge about Clay. Oberholtzer's *Philadelphia: A History of the City and Its People, A Record of 225 Years* appeared in four volumes in 1912; it represented a natural outgrowth of his previous literary history of the city.

Among Oberholtzer's interests were historical pageants. He managed two in Philadelphia (1908, 1912) and one at Valley Forge (1928). Examples of his work in this area can be found in such volumes as *The Book of the Pageant, October 9, 1908* (1908) and the *Official Pictorial and Descriptive Souvenir Book of the Historical Pageant, October Seventh to Twelfth, 1912* (1912), both dealing with the Philadelphia pageants. The former volume was arranged by Oberholtzer; the latter contained a text by Francis Howard Williams and Oberholtzer's notes and adaptation to the field.

As secretary of the Pennsylvania Board of Motion Picture Censors (1915-1921), Oberholtzer worked to restrict the treatment of sex in the cinema. Eventually, however, Oberholtzer's zeal led to his dismissal by Governor William C. Sproul, under pressure from powerful interest groups. The experience prompted the publication in 1922 of Oberholtzer's *The Morals of the Movie*, in which he argued that a large school of motion-picture makers worked feverishly to produce something unusual and different for a sensation-jaded public. He maintained that a movie's usual short run, plus the inadequacy of local methods of police inspection, made censorship before exhibition the only practical way of dealing with the problem.

Oberholtzer's principal achievement was his five-volume *History of the United States Since the Civil War* (1917-1937), much of it written at the Historical Society of Pennsylvania where his mentor John Bach McMaster had an office. Oberholtzer began his work with the year 1865, where McMaster's *History of the People of the United States* came to an end. Though he devoted more attention to politics than McMaster permitted, he used much of the master's formula—describing rather than analyzing the history of the American people as a social entity. Uti-

lizing newspapers, pamphlets, congressional documents, and manuscript collections, Oberholtzer piled details mass upon mass, without attempting much in the way of broad interpretation and conclusions.

The impartiality and the inspiration that generally characterized McMaster was absent in his disciple. Oberholtzer once expressed preference for James Schouler's methods, which were not "impartial between right and wrong, honorable and dishonorable conduct." Giving very little acknowledgment to the parallel researches of Schouler, James Ford Rhodes, William A. Dunning, and others, his own work did not much alter the picture of Reconstruction (one finds the familiar revisionist pattern of vindictive Radicals using blacks as an instrument of power against white Southerners) and its aftermath. Though there were and still are admirers of Oberholtzer, and though his works have been republished, reviewers in scholarly journals such as the *Mississippi Valley Historical Review* and the *American Historical Review* were for the most part severely critical of each volume.

Volume one of Oberholtzer's *History of the United States Since the Civil War* was published by Macmillan in 1917. Dealing with the years 1865 to 1868, it reports the efforts of President Andrew Johnson to implement Abraham Lincoln's conciliatory Reconstruction policies, the revulsion of the North against the South's "Black Codes," and the rise of the Radical Republican congressional opposition, with its "conquered provinces" theory. Among the most interesting chapters in the first volume are those on social conditions in various parts of the country. A tragic picture of degradation and misery, with few signs of economic reconstruction, is painted in "The South after the War." Striking in its contrast with the chapter on Southern poverty, "The Triumphant North" describes prices, immigration, and the material wealth of the region. A reviewer for the *Bookman* called volume one "a storehouse of detail," but, faulting Oberholtzer, the *Nation* instructed its readers that "the historian must be more than a reporter." In the *American Historial Review*, William A. Dunning began by praising the chapters on the South, West, and North, and Oberholtzer's style and spirit, but he went on to observe that volume one was mostly political history written by an author who assassinated reputations, saw only one side of a controversy, and attacked the motives of those on the other side.

The second volume of the *History* appeared in 1922. Covering the years 1868 to 1872, it describes Johnson's further disputes with Congress, his impeachment and trial, Ulysses S. Grant's first term and the era's "moral blindness," the rule of the Carpetbaggers and the rise of "protective associations" such as the Ku Klux Klan in the South, and the sovereignty in the North of such political bosses and robber barons as Jay Gould, James Fisk, Jr., and Cornelius Vanderbilt. When writing about the Johnson impeachment proceedings, Oberholtzer was hostile to the congressional Radicals. His accounts of the men he believed to be political and economic despoilers—Gould, "Boss" William M. Tweed, Fisk—revealed his strong moral indignation. Edward Stanwood, writing in the *American Historical Review*, commented negatively on the author's exaggerated attention to the scandalous tendencies of the times.

Oberholtzer married Winona McBride on 19 November 1926 (they had no children). The same year saw the publication of volume three of his *History*, which covered the years 1872 to 1878. Among other matters, it is devoted to Grant's second term, the Panic of 1873, the Rutherford B. Hayes administration, which removed Federal troops from the South and ended Reconstruction, and the Indian uprisings in the Far West. In this volume the author attacks Grant's second administration as a "coarse and venal regime." In *The Writing of American History* (1953), Michael Kraus has noted that Oberholtzer had a high regard in his youth for E. L. Godkin, editor of the *Nation;* he maintains that Godkin's reform crusades of the later nineteenth century and his "moral force" continued to influence the writing of Oberholtzer, as is evident in his assessment of Grant. The *American Historical Review* assigned volume three to Walter L. Fleming, a disciple of Dunning, for review. While conceding that numerous sources had been consulted, Fleming held that the volume was superficial in many areas and that there was no evaluation of important social and economic factors.

Volume four of Oberholtzer's *History*, dealing with the period 1878 to 1888, appeared in 1931. It discusses the "infirm character" of the James A. Garfield administration; the surprisingly "discreet, conservative and just" Chester A. Arthur administration; and the independence, honesty, and "responsible understanding of public duty" demonstrated by the first Grover Cleveland administration. Oberholtzer's preferences are obvious throughout; for example, free silver advocates are given short shrift. Though a critic in the *Review of Reviews* found that the fourth volume, "like its predecessors, shows profound research and ample

documentation," T. C. Smith, writing in the *American Historical Review*, criticized Oberholtzer's superficiality and Victorian moralizing.

The fifth and final volume of the *History* was published posthumously in 1937. Covering the years 1888 to 1901, it characterizes Benjamin Harrison's administration as efficient, honest, paternalistic, and protectionist; Cleveland's second administration is viewed as sound on the tariff, money, and civil service reform but ignorant and tactless in foreign affairs. Oberholtzer considered William Jennings Bryan "a race bigot" rather than a "mountebank" and William McKinley a mere recorder of the flow of popular thought. The *American Historical Review* gave the final volume of Oberholtzer's history to Allan Nevins, who was working on a multivolume history of the coming of the Civil War in all of its political, economic, social, diplomatic, and cultural complexity. Finding little to praise, Nevins attacked the volume's superficiality, undigested facts, upper-class bias, deep prejudices, and failure to understand the laborer and the farmer. Writing in the *Mississippi Valley Historical Review*, E. D. Ross and John D. Hicks were no more enthusiastic than Nevins.

Throughout his *History*, Oberholtzer revealed a talent for selecting fascinating details about the social setting. In treating Reconstruction, for instance, he depicted uneasy social contacts between Southern whites and Northern visitors, the plight of poor whites, vindictive Southern belles, and the boycott of the Yankee schoolmarms. The volumes contain good accounts of the oil booms, industrial growth, and mushrooming cities such as Chicago. Unfortunately, Oberholtzer's readers frequently found themselves overwhelmed by this massing of detail.

Oberholtzer revealed marked prejudice in dealing with a wide variety of topics. The entire black race was seen as savage and shiftless. Though Oberholtzer was candid in his treatment of lynchings and other brutalities against blacks, he explained them in terms not only of bitter economic rivalry between whites and blacks but also of black criminality. He maintained that the peoples of the new immigration, being of a lower order of mankind, were repellent to those who were further advanced on the social scale and who had higher standards of living. Although the severity of the recurrent economic depression from 1873 to 1896 was briefly mentioned, labor and unions were usually discussed only in terms of violence and threats to property. For Oberholtzer, it was axiomatic that the common man was incapable of solving complex economic and social problems. Therefore, it was a mistake to give the vote to blacks and recent immigrants.

In 1932 Oberholtzer lashed out at the criticism which his work and McMaster's had undergone from the exponents of "interpretive" history. Complaining that the critics were too much concerned with the question of social justice, he championed the cause of "factual" history which, in his opinion, he and McMaster had written. Yet, for Oberholtzer, factual history need not be impartial history (Oberholtzer believed that McMaster leaned heavily toward impartiality); thus, not surprisingly, value judgments abound in Oberholtzer's work.

Despite his strong regional and ethnic prejudices, in choosing the subject of his major work—and in keeping with the general trend among historians from the Middle Atlantic states—Oberholtzer evinced a traditionally nationalist viewpoint. Following in the footsteps of such nationalist historians as Rhodes, Hermann E. von Holst, and McMaster, he produced one of the last big narrative histories of the United States written between the Civil War and the present day. By the time the last volume was published in 1937, however, fellow historians tended to agree that the *History* was out of step with twentieth-century historiography. More modern historians preferred a synthesis of materials rather than a mere accumulation of facts.

In addition to his historical research and writing, Oberholtzer had other interests. He was a member of the Valley Forge Historical Commission from 1925 to 1935. He was also active in the English-Speaking Union, an organization whose goal was the development of closer relations with Great Britain. At various times, he served as secretary of the Transatlantic Society of America and of the Scottish Memorial Association and as corresponding secretary of the Historical Society of Pennsylvania. Oberholtzer also participated in Philadelphia's social and cultural life as secretary of the Franklin Inn Club for men with literary or artistic interests.

On 8 December 1936, nearly twenty years after the publication of the first volume of his *History of the United States Since the Civil War*, Oberholtzer went to the Historical Society of Pennsylvania to check the manuscript of his fifth volume. Before he could get to the task, he died of a heart attack, just inside the door of the building where he had worked almost daily for so many years. He was buried in Philadelphia's West Laurel Hill Cemetery.

Over twenty years in the writing, Oberholtzer's major work, *A History of the United States Since the Civil War*, was rather old-fashioned in its manner and outlook by the time of its completion. Nevertheless, it is the only large-scale treatment of American history from 1865 to 1901. And though it has received more criticism than praise, it remains an informative and, in its own way, honest performance.

References:

Michael Kraus, *The Writing of American History* (Norman: University of Oklahoma Press, 1953), pp. 226-227;

Edward N. Saveth, *American Historians and European Immigrants, 1875-1925* (New York: Columbia University Press, 1948), pp. 188-191;

Harvey Wish, *The American Historian: A Social-Intellectual History of the Writing of the American Past* (New York: Oxford University Press, 1960), pp. 145-147.

Papers:

A collection of Oberholtzer's manuscripts and newspaper clippings pertaining to his work is at the Historical Society of Pennsylvania in Philadelphia.

Herbert L. Osgood

(9 April 1855-11 September 1918)

Alexander Moore
University of South Carolina

BOOKS: *Socialism and Anarchism* (Boston & London: Ginn, 1889);

The American Colonies in the Seventeenth Century, 3 volumes (New York & London: Macmillan, 1904-1907);

The American Colonies in the Eighteenth Century, 4 volumes (New York: Columbia University Press, 1924-1925; London: Oxford University Press, 1924-1925).

OTHER: "The Classification of Colonial Governments," in *Annual Report of the American Historical Association for the Year 1895* (Washington, D.C.: Government Printing Office, 1896), pp. 615-627;

"The Study of American Colonial History," in *Annual Report of the American Historical Association for the Year 1898* (Washington, D.C.: Government Printing Office, 1899), pp. 61-76;

"Report on the Public Archives of New York," in *Annual Report of the American Historical Association for the Year 1900*, 2 volumes (Washington, D.C.: Government Printing Office, 1901), II: 67-250;

"The Society of Dissenters founded at New York in 1769," edited by Osgood, in *American Historical Review*, 6 (April 1901), pp. 498-507;

Minutes of the Common Council of the City of New York, 1675-1776, edited by Osgood, 8 volumes (New York: Dodd, Mead, 1905);

Preface to *The Records of the Virginia Company of London—The Court Book, from the Manuscripts in the Library of Congress*, edited by Susan M. Kingsbury, 4 volumes (Washington, D.C.: Library of Congress, 1906-1935);

"United States—History, 1578-1783," in *Encyclopaedia Britannica*, eleventh edition, 29 volumes (Cambridge & New York: Cambridge University Press, 1910-1911), XXVII: 663-684.

PERIODICAL PUBLICATIONS: "England and the Colonies," *Political Science Quarterly*, 2 (September 1887): 440-469;

"The Political Ideas of the Puritans," *Political Sci-*

ence *Quarterly*, 6 (March 1891): 1-28; 6 (June 1891): 201-231;

"The Prussian Archives," *Political Science Quarterly*, 8 (September 1893): 495-525;

"The Corporation as a Form of Colonial Government," *Political Science Quarterly*, 11 (June 1896): 259-277; 11 (September 1896): 502-

533; 11 (December 1896): 694-715;

"The Proprietary Province as a Form of Colonial Government," *American Historical Review,* 2 (July 1897): 644-664; 3 (October 1897): 31-55; 3 (January 1898): 244-265;

"The American Revolution," *Political Science Quarterly,* 13 (March 1898): 41-59;

"Connecticut as a Corporate Colony," *Political Science Quarterly,* 14 (June 1899): 251-280;

"England and the American Colonies in the Seventeenth Century," *Political Science Quarterly,* 17 (June 1902): 206-222;

"New England Colonial Finance in the Seventeenth Century," *Political Science Quarterly,* 19 (March 1904): 80-106.

As a professor at Columbia University and a writer of American history, Herbert Levi Osgood helped to accomplish and then to exemplify a quiet but profound revolution in the American historical profession. Osgood realized as a youth that he was destined for historical scholarship. He proceeded through secondary, undergraduate, and graduate education almost uninterruptedly and then found a professorship and a scholarly home at a major university. This pattern has become familiar to subsequent generations of historians but was markedly different from the eclectic educations and varied livelihoods of many of Osgood's nineteenth-century predecessors. Early in his career Osgood struck upon his primary field of research. With few diversions he devoted a thirty-year career to an exhaustive study of British political and imperial institutions in colonial North America from the first British settlements in 1578 to the treaties of Paris and Hubertusberg in 1763. Osgood's three-volume *The American Colonies in the Seventeenth Century,* published in 1904 and 1907, and his four-volume *The American Colonies in the Eighteenth Century,* published posthumously in 1924 and 1925, epitomized the scholar's life and his historical vision.

Osgood pioneered a dispassionate, comparative approach to the study of Anglo-American political and economic institutions that focused less on major historical events than on processes and congeries of events that wrought historical changes. He took the drama out of American history and replaced it with a realistic account of the British experience in colonial America. There are fewer heroes and villains in Osgood's writings than in the writings of any American historians before or since him. His student at Columbia George L. Beer and a younger historian at Yale University, Charles M. Andrews, took up Osgood's historical vision and

applied it to their own work. These two, plus Osgood, make up what is sometimes called the imperial school of American historians because they lifted colonial American history from its patriotic, xenophobic isolation and placed it within an Anglo-American and global context.

Herbert Levi Osgood was born on 9 April 1855, at Canton, Maine, the son of Stephen and Joan Staples Osgood. He was in the eighth American generation descended from John Osgood who emigrated from England to Massachusetts in 1638. Osgood received his secondary education at Wilton Academy, Andover, Maine, and took his bachelor's and master's degrees, in 1877 and 1880 respectively, at Amherst College. There he studied with John W. Burgess, the German-educated historian of nineteenth-century America. In 1880 Osgood began his doctoral work in history at Yale University, where he studied with another German-educated scholar, William Graham Sumner. He spent a year at Yale and then, following the examples of Burgess and Sumner, studied at the University of Berlin in 1882 and 1883. Although he did not study with Leopold von Ranke, the famous philosopher of history and historian of the Renaissance, he met the man and attended the lectures of Ranke's intellectual heirs, Gustav Schmoller, Adolph Wagner, and Rudolph Gneist. Osgood adopted for himself a Rankean historical methodology of strict objectivism derived from research in primary historical sources. In a review of one of Ranke's books Osgood paid homage to the man and his method. "He had . . . the loftiest conception of the duty of the historian to discover the truth and to state it with absolute impartiality. Again and again in his letters and elsewhere does he rebuke partisanship and insist upon thoroughness in research and objectivity in statement. This is the priceless lesson which his life and work have taught the scientific world."

Returning from Germany, Osgood transferred his doctoral studies to Columbia University whither Burgess had moved to found the political science department. Osgood completed and saw the publication of a dissertation on *Socialism and Anarchism* in 1889 and immediately set off for a year's research in London and the British Public Record Office. When he returned in 1890, he joined the history faculty at Columbia. Osgood taught European history for five years and developed a course on the English colonies prior to the American Revolution. When he was promoted to full professor in 1896 he shifted all of his attention to American colonial history, using his course on the colonies as the centerpiece for his research and teaching. Investigation of the American colonies was nearly his sole occupation from 1896 until his death on 11 September 1918.

Osgood married Caroline Augusta Symonds of Pownall, Vermont, on 22 July 1885, and the couple had two sons, Edward and Harold Symonds, and a daughter Marian Stickney. In 1915 Marian Osgood married Dixon Ryan Fox, one of her father's students and a historian of New York politics. Fox later wrote a brief, eulogistic biography of his father-in-law and performed a more important act of filial piety when he edited and secured the publication of Osgood's *The American Colonies in the Eighteenth Century.*

Apart from his historical labors, Osgood's biography is largely a conventional recitation of names, dates, and a few places. As do many modern scholars, Osgood apparently lived for and through his profession. Most of his life was defined by the rhythms of a university amid the modest trials and rewards of professional scholarship.

Osgood's reputation justly rests upon his seven volumes of writings on American colonial history. However, he also wrote numerous essays and book reviews, particularly early in his career, on British and Continental European topics. He was a member of the editorial board of the *Political Science Quarterly* from 1891 until his death, and that periodical was his most important scholarly forum prior to publication of *The American Colonies in the Seventeenth Century.* Before publishing his dissertation in book form in 1889, Osgood published the complete text of it in two *Political Science Quarterly* articles, "Scientific Socialism—Rodbertus" (December 1886) and "Scientific Anarchism" (March 1889). These articles displayed fully the effects of Osgood's studies in Germany and his grasp of sophisticated European political philosophy. They also recorded his rejection of "scientific" political thought in favor of an Anglo-American philosophy based upon tradition and experience.

Karl Rodbertus was a pre-Marxian socialist who analyzed society in terms of a class struggle impelled by a dialectic of "spirit, will, and matter." He believed that modern capitalism was anarchistic, irrational, socially and morally destructive. A disciple of Georg W. F. Hegel and a theist, he also believed that the "German-Christian State" was the apogee of social evolution. Rodbertus expected the German-Christian State to institute a socialism that would end the class struggle without the Armageddon anticipated by Karl Marx. Osgood explicated Rodbertus's ideas and compared them to Marxist thought without subjecting them to too

much criticism. He rather blandly observed that neither Rodbertus nor Marx properly appreciated "the incalculable service rendered to society by freedom of competition."

"Scientific Anarchism" was a study of the anarchist theories of Pierre J. Proudhon, Mikhail Bakunin, and a group of Americans that included Josiah Warren, Stephen P. Andrews, and Benjamin R. Tucker. Osgood divided the anarchist thinkers into two groups, individualists and communists. The first group included the Proudhonists and the Americans. They believed in natural rights, social contract, and extreme forms of personal liberty. Many established utopian communities as alternatives to modern repressive society. The communists took their revolutionary program from Marx and Engels's *Communist Manifesto* and the romantic, nihilistic theories of Bakunin and Nikolai Chernyshevski. Most were Russian intellectuals enamored of terrorism and personal "acts of will" against a monolithic czarist State.

Osgood rejected the theoretical premise of anarchism that there had been or ever could be a form of human society that predated organized governments. For him the existence of governments was and always would be coterminous with human society. Despite this rejection, Osgood admired the intellectual purity, if not the pragmatism, of the Americans and Proudhonists. He saw a logical place for their thought in the modern world, especially in the United States. "The minds and the writings of our revolutionary heroes were full of the theory of natural rights and social contract. The founder of one of our political parties was a living embodiment of that theory. The anarchists ask for no better statement of their premises than the opening sentences of the Declaration of Independence."

Osgood reviewed for the *Political Science Quarterly* numerous works of European historians and economists. These included a study of Marxist economics by Georg Alder, Karl Lamprecht's *Deutsches Wirtschaftsleben im Mittelalter,* Albert Schaeffle's economic essays, and Leopold von Ranke's *Zur Eigenen Lebensgeschichte.* Some French works were Henri Doniol's *Histoire de la participation de la France à l'établissement des Etats-Unis d'Amérique,* and Albert Sorel's *L'Europe et la Révolution Française.* He also reviewed works by American and British writers on English constitutional history, military history, geography, political science, and the philosophy of history. Among these were Stephen R. Gardiner's *History of the Great Civil War,* Philip Alexander Bruce's *Economic History of Virginia in the Sev-*

enteenth Century, Charles H. Firth's edition of *The Clarke Papers*, and George Bernard Shaw's *Fabian Essays in Socialism*.

As he concentrated his study upon Anglo-American institutions, Osgood gradually abandoned his writing and reviewing of European historiography. This narrowing of focus revealed itself in his essays. Through them he developed the historical concepts that undergirded his life's work. This is not to suggest that he abandoned his interest in European thought or his intellectual freedom from American historical cant fostered by his European experiences. In fact his seven volumes are strongly grounded in comparative political science and empirical criticism.

"England and the Colonies," published in the *Political Science Quarterly* in 1887, expressed Osgood's attitude toward the methodological failings of his American historian-predecessors and outlined the rationale of the imperial school. He invoked Ranke to criticize his predecessors and then proposed through an impartial study of primary historical evidence to elucidate "the constitutional relations existing between England and her colonies, and to show that the supremacy of King and Parliament over them was complete, that control was exercised in every department of governmental activity, judicial, legislative, ecclesiastical, military; that the right of the mother country to this control was uniformly asserted until the fortunes of war compelled her to acknowledge America as an independent nation." Two tenets of the imperial school of historians were immediately apparent: emphasis on comparative studies of the institutions that linked America and England and a repudiation of American chauvinism. With this latter tenet came a reluctance to assign blame to the English for "causing" the American Revolution.

Osgood divided colonial American history into two periods, the first settlements in 1578 to 1688 and 1688 to the Declaration of Independence. He chose 1688, the year of the Glorious Revolution, as his dividing point because that year saw a constitutional and diplomatic revolution in Europe that radically altered Anglo-American relations. The Glorious Revolution completed a process of consolidation of colonial governments under royal control. The demonstrated supremacy of Parliament over the Crown brought the colonies increasingly under Parliamentary control. The Revolution also brought England and her colonies into full participation in William III's wars against Louis XIV and the French. North America and the West Indies soon became important war zones. In "En-

gland and the Colonies" Osgood identified what he called the "neglected period" of American history, the years from 1690 to 1763. His posthumously published *The American Colonies in the Eighteenth Century* went far to remedy that neglect.

Two long essays, "The Corporation as a Form of Colonial Government," published in the *Political Science Quarterly* in 1896, and "The Proprietary Province as a Form of Colonial Government," published in the *American Historical Review* in 1897 and 1898, provided the framework for Osgood's *The American Colonies in the Seventeenth Century*. Osgood divided colonies into two groups, corporate and proprietary colonies, not on the basis of their origins (both stemmed from royal charters) but according to their internal political institutions. Massachusetts, Connecticut, and Rhode Island were corporate colonies because their corporations, or charter-holders, were virtually identical with their local governments. Virginia, the two Carolinas, Maryland, and Pennsylvania were proprietary because the charter-holders for the most part remained in England and delegated the governance of their colonies to resident officials.

The corporate colonies were virtually self-governing and, by choice, as isolated as possible from London authorities. They had been established as homes for religious nonconformists seeking refuge from oppression in England. Unified in purpose and in possession of their charter documents, the New England colonies became "laboratories for liberty." The proprietary colonies were more disparate in origin and political development. Virginia, New Jersey, and the two Carolinas were founded as economic ventures. Political power rested with the proprietors but was geographically removed from the colonies and was often subordinated to the profit motive. Legislative, judicial, and executive institutions developed in the proprietary colonies, but they were often in conflict with the proprietors and sometimes one with another. Maryland and Pennsylvania were founded as religious havens but the disparity between their idealistic origins and their pragmatic and even cynical local authorities, as well as an absentee center of power, hampered local development. Virginia's charter was revoked in 1624, and from then until the Declaration of Independence the colony was governed directly by the king as a royal province. New York was also a royal province. Conquered from the Dutch in 1664, it was granted as a proprietary colony to James Stuart, Duke of York. When James ascended the English throne in 1685 New York became a royal province.

Osgood also identified the dynamic of historical change during the seventeenth century. The American colonies, whether corporate or proprietary, suffered continuous attacks by royal authorities upon their independence. The Navigation Acts, Board of Trade, High Court of Admiralty, royal garrisons, and writs of quo warranto and scire facias all aimed to bring the colonies under the aegis of a London-centered economic and political empire. The colonies struggled against imperial encroachment, but by the end of the century most had surrendered at least some part of their sovereignty.

In 1904 Osgood produced the first two volumes of *The American Colonies in the Seventeenth Century*. They were a history of the British American colonies from the first voyages of Humphrey Gilbert and Sir Walter Raleigh in 1578 to about the year 1690. Subtitled "The Chartered Colonies, Beginnings of Self-Government," the volumes fleshed out the arguments Osgood had made in his two important articles. In the preface to volume one Osgood clearly stated his vision of American history in the seventeenth century: "Institutionally considered, the history of the American colonies falls into two phases or periods. The two phases appear in the system of chartered colonies and the system of royal provinces, with the transition from one to the other. This comprises all there is in the constitutional history of that period. The meaning of the period, its unity and diversity, the character of the colonies as special jurisdictions, as well as their relations with the sovereign imperial power will become sufficiently clear if these subjects are properly treated."

The corporate colonies of Virginia and New England were the subjects of volume one. Volume two contained histories of the proprietary provinces of Maryland, the Carolinas, East and West Jersey, and Pennsylvania. The books are dryly written, devoid of anecdote, replete with long, uninterrupted paragraphs, and have neither maps, illustrations, nor bibliographies. In physical appearance and in presentation of their subjects, the books represent stolid, Germanic scholarship at its best and worst. Volume two contains a cumulative index and both of the volumes have long, detailed tables of contents to facilitate comparative reading. The first two thirds of each volume were given over to a chronological narrative history of each colony while the last third contained a series of comparative studies of specific local institutions. In these latter chapters Osgood investigated the judicial, fiscal, executive, military, and ecclesiastical establish-

ments in the several colonies. The final chapter in each volume was a study of Indian-white diplomacy in the seventeenth century.

Volume three was published in 1907 and subtitled "Imperial Control, Beginnings of the System of Royal Provinces." In it Osgood examined the machinery of imperial control and how it was brought to bear upon the individual colonies. This machinery included the Board of Trade, the Navigation Acts, and the official visitations of the government agent Edward Randolph, as well as the mercantilist theories that undergirded British empire-building. Volume three also carried the story of the royal provinces of Virginia and New York to the 1690s. Osgood investigated Bacon's Rebellion in Virginia, Coode's Rebellion in Maryland, and Leisler's Rebellion in New York not only as local events but also in terms of the impact they had in England. Conversely, he explicated at great length the influence of the Glorious Revolution upon the colonies.

The American Colonies in the Seventeenth Century is comprehensive. Its combination of chronological narrative and topical studies makes it useful for reference. Readers can find in it accurate political histories of all of the British colonies in the seventeenth century as well as insightful commentaries on colonial institutions. A chapter in the first volume on "The Land System in the Corporate Colonies of New England" is paired with "The Land System of the Later Proprietary Provinces" in volume two to present a thorough study of colonial land policies. Together these chapters demonstrate the manner in which Osgood used his studies of "institutions" to elucidate broader aspects of colonial history. In New England the corporations owned the land and distributed it in a rational, organized fashion. They sometimes granted it outright or sold it to individuals but more often they made free town-size grants to groups of immigrants seeking to build communities. This form of land system encouraged cooperation among neighbors, orderly settlement patterns, and fostered social homogeneity. In contrast, in the proprietary colonies, land was owned and distributed by absentee proprietors who sought foremost to profit from their ownership. They granted large tracts of land to individuals with a provision for payment of quit rents. This system pitted new immigrants against one another and all new arrivals against older established settlers, in competition for the best lands. It also encouraged widely dispersed plantation settlement instead of orderly town growth. Problems of payment and collection of quitrents were continual sources of friction between settlers and proprietors that occasionally precipitated local rebellions.

After finding his life's work in the 1890s, Osgood permitted himself few diversions from the study of colonial history. However, he made two noteworthy forays into the domains of the archivist and the documentary editor. In 1900, as a member of the Public Archives Commission of the American Historical Association, he supervised a survey and then wrote a book-length "Report on the Public Archives of New York" which was published in the *Annual Report of the American Historical Association* (1901). This report was one of a series of surveys of state and local archives sponsored by the Association, but Osgood's was by far the most comprehensive. It was intended to be not only a committee report but also a research tool. Osgood and a research staff of Columbia University graduate students surveyed the Dutch and English colonial records at Albany, the municipal records of New York City, and the records of the counties that surround the city. Arranged according to approved archival techniques respecting the provenance or origins of these records, the report constituted an administrative history of New York government. Another notable aspect of the report was Osgood's collation of the manuscript records with published historical sources, primarily Edmund B. O'Callaghan's *The Documentary History of the State of New-York* (1849-1851) and his *Documents Relative to the Colonial History of the State of New-York* (1853-1887).

While engaged in work for the report Osgood discovered the minutes of the Common Council of New York City, a series of municipal records that continued unbroken from 1675 to 1776. When he found them in 1900 Osgood described them as "the most important single body of unprinted records relating to the history of New York as an English city" and called for their prompt publication. Osgood heeded his own call and five years later produced an eight-volume edition of *Minutes of the Common Council of the City of New York, 1675-1776* (1905). The *Minutes* recorded the day-to-day proceedings of the governing body of New York City. They contain a wealth of primary information on all aspects of colonial urban society from the issuing of business licenses and enforcement of health regulations to municipal defense in wartime and the city's role in the first days of American independence. A massive index of more than three hundred pages made thousands of personal names and occupations available to historians and genealogists.

From 1907 until his death in 1918 Osgood

bent his attention to one purpose, completion of a work on the eighteenth century to complement *The American Colonies in the Seventeenth Century*. When he died he had nearly finished a four-volume study of the colonies from 1690 to 1763. All that he lacked was two chapters, one on the institution of slavery and the other a comparative study of imperial administration in Ireland, the West Indies, and North America and a formal conclusion. Osgood's son-in-law and biographer, Dixon Ryan Fox, undertook to edit the nearly complete manuscript and to find a publisher. Osgood had believed that he had a firm publishing contract with Macmillan and Company, but he had been in error. Fox had to wait six years and secure funds from Dwight W. Morrow, one of Osgood's former students, to finance publication of the work by Columbia University Press. *The American Colonies in the Eighteenth*

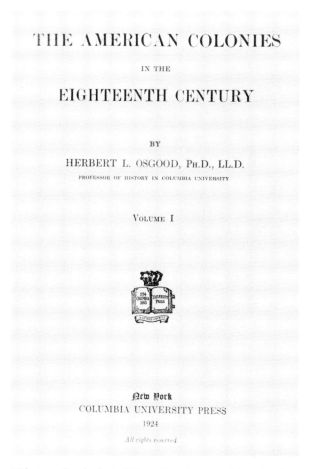

THE AMERICAN COLONIES

IN THE

EIGHTEENTH CENTURY

BY

HERBERT L. OSGOOD, Ph.D., LL.D.

PROFESSOR OF HISTORY IN COLUMBIA UNIVERSITY

VOLUME I

New York

COLUMBIA UNIVERSITY PRESS

1924

All rights reserved

Title page for the first of Osgood's volumes studying the eighteenth century in the context of "Four Intercolonial Wars," a term he coined to describe the series of conflicts between France and Great Britain from the 1680s to 1763

Century was published in 1924 and 1925 and took its place as the completion of Osgood's comprehensive study of Anglo-American institutions from 1578 to 1763.

In 1887 Osgood had characterized the era from the Glorious Revolution to the treaties of Paris and Hubertusberg in 1763 as the neglected period of American history. This neglect stemmed partly from the fact that the era seemingly possessed no unifying theme and partly from the fact that no American historian had performed sufficient research with the primary sources in Great Britain to write authoritatively upon it. Osgood's imperial vision of the American colonies gave him a methodological key to comprehending the era. Also, his youthful research trip to England and two later visits as a senior scholar gave him a command of the British sources sufficient to write with authority.

The imperial perspective in his second work was even more pronounced than in his first one. The first volume of *The American Colonies in the Eighteenth Century* set the stage. It contained chapters on the development of imperial institutions after the Glorious Revolution. These included the advent of ministerial governments that derived their strength from Parliament, not from the king. The ministerial system supplanted earlier, less formal institutions that had their basis in the king's household. A long study of the Board of Trade demonstrated that that institution achieved its most effective (and intrusive) form in 1696. The Board consolidated in its hands the formerly dispersed reins of imperial administration.

As he had in *American Colonies in the Seventeenth Century,* Osgood divided the eighteenth century into periods that accorded not with local colonial events but with events that took place on a global scale. He divided the work into four sections that corresponded with the "Four Intercolonial Wars," a term he coined to describe the series of wars between France and Great Britain that lasted from the 1680s until 1763. He abandoned as misleading the customary names of these wars: King William's War (1689-1697), Queen Anne's War (1702-1713), the War of Jenkins' Ear (1739-1748), and the French and Indian War (1755-1763). The four intercolonial wars were simply episodes in "a prolonged duel between France and England for supremacy and incidentally for the possession of North America."

Osgood's organization of American history upon a European chronology rested upon his observation that the one great theme which underlay the neglected period of American history was the competition between France and England for hegemony in Europe and North America. In truth, if Osgood had carried his study through the era of the American Revolution, he might have argued that the Revolution itself was partly a phase in an even more prolonged Anglo-French struggle that did not end until 1815.

Volume one of *The American Colonies in the Eighteenth Century* recorded events from 1690 to the Treaty of Utrecht in 1713, the eras of the first and second intercolonial wars. In America those eras comprehended the witchcraft mania in Massachusetts, political factionalism in New York, Maryland, and South Carolina, as well as the military history of the two wars. Osgood continued his practice of appending topical studies to the end of each of his volumes and, in volume one, he addressed the subjects of Indian-white diplomacy on the Allegheny frontier, piracy in the New World, and the production of naval stores in America.

Volume two carried Osgood's chronological study to 1740 and contained topical studies on the Church of England in America and colonial immigration. The narrative portion recorded the 1719 revolution of South Carolina against the rule of the lords proprietors and the transition of the two Carolinas to royal provinces.

Volume three reached 1748, the end of the Third Intercolonial War. It marked a departure for Osgood from his almost exclusively secular interests. Four chapters were devoted to religious topics, specifically, relations between Anglicans and Nonconformists in the colonies, church-state politics, and a long study of the theology and social impact of the Great Awakening. Volume three also recorded the founding and early history of the Georgia province. Contrary to the trends of British empire-building throughout the seventeenth and eighteenth centuries, Georgia was founded as the proprietary province of General James Oglethorpe and the Georgia Trustees. Osgood called the event "a step backwards" and "an odd mingling of the crude and primitive and of the later and developed features of colonial policy." The Georgia colony was a unique experiment that combined the benevolence of the Georgia Trustees toward the English poor and a militaristic plan to erect a marcher province between Spanish Florida and the southern English colonies.

Volume four completed Osgood's study of the neglected period. It carried the historical narrative to the fall of Quebec in 1762 and ended abruptly with the surrender, on 8 September 1763, of the French in Canada to the British. The only topical study in the volume was a survey of westward expansion into the Old Northwest and of the Albany Congress at New York in 1754.

Osgood's seven volumes were highly praised at the time of their publication. Both titles were awarded Columbia University's Loubat Prize for the best work on North American history or geography in the years of their publication and received a full measure of critical acclaim. Charles M. Andrews, Osgood's immediate successor as America's foremost imperial historian, observed that both *The American Colonies in the Seventeenth Century* and *The American Colonies in the Eighteenth Century* were comprehensive in scope and detailed sometimes to a fault. Andrews recognized that the works were pathbreaking in intention as well as in accomplishment, but they were so austere, complicated, and, for modern tastes, old-fashioned, they would not be read by many students or scholars. Andrews's prediction came true, aided by the fact that his own four-volume *The Colonial Period of American History*, published from 1934 to 1938, which covered much the same ground as did Osgood's seven volumes, is lucidly, even elegantly, written.

Osgood's works are currently out of print, and it is unlikely that they will come back into historiographical vogue. Multivolume institutional histories, despite the recent works of Jack M. Sosin and Stephen S. Webb, are out of fashion. With their long, involved tables of contents, utter lack of pictures, maps, tables, or appendices, and sheer weight, Osgood's histories are especially antique. Osgood took much from the writings of John G. Palfrey, the historian of New England, and from the historian of South Carolina, Edward McCrady. These two were his intellectual peers and Osgood acknowledged his debt to them. However, in terms of historical conclusions based fully on research in primary sources, and in terms of freedom from American nationalistic prejudices, Osgood was indeed a pioneer.

Biography:
Dixon Ryan Fox, *Herbert Levi Osgood—An American Scholar* (New York: Columbia University Press, 1924).

References:
E. C. O. Beatty, "Herbert Levi Osgood," in *The Marcus W. Jernegan Essays in American Historiography*, edited by William T. Hutchinson (Chicago: University of Chicago Press, 1937), pp. 271-293;

Homer J. Coppock, "Herbert Levi Osgood," *Mississippi Valley Historical Review*, 19 (December 1932): 394-403.

Papers:
A collection of Herbert Levi Osgood's papers, mostly research notes and transcriptions of documents, is at the Columbia University Library, New York City.

James Ford Rhodes

(1 May 1848-22 January 1927)

Richard M. McMurry

North Carolina State University

SELECTED BOOKS: *History of the United States from the Compromise of 1850* [1850-1854] (New York: Harper, 1892; London: Macmillan, 1892);

History of the United States from the Compromise of 1850 [1854-1860] (New York: Harper, 1892; London: Macmillan, 1892);

History of the United States from the Compromise of 1850 [1860-1862] (New York: Harper, 1895; London: Macmillan, 1895);

History of the United States from the Compromise of 1850 [1862-1864] (New York: Harper, 1899; London: Macmillan, 1899);

History of the United States from the Compromise of 1850 [1864-1866] (New York: Macmillan, 1904; London: Macmillan, 1905);

History of the United States from the Compromise of 1850 to the Final Restoration of Home Rule at the South in 1877 [1866-1872] (New York: Macmillan, 1906; London: Macmillan, 1907);

History of the United States from the Compromise of 1850 to the Final Restoration of Home Rule at the South in 1877 [1872-1877] (New York: Macmillan, 1906; London: Macmillan, 1907);

Historical Essays (New York: Macmillan, 1909; London: Macmillan, 1910);

Lectures on the American Civil War, Delivered Before the University of Oxford in Easter and Trinity Terms, 1912 (New York: Macmillan, 1913; London: Macmillan, 1913);

History of the Civil War, 1861-1865 (New York: Macmillan, 1917);

History of the United States from Hayes to McKinley, 1877-1896 (New York: Macmillan, 1919; London: Macmillan, 1919);

The McKinley and Roosevelt Administrations, 1897-1909 (New York: Macmillan, 1922; London: Macmillan, 1923).

From the mid-1890s until World War I, James Ford Rhodes dominated Americans' understanding of their recent past to a degree unmatched by any historian before or since. Unlike most historians, whose work deals with other times or other

James Ford Rhodes, late 1870s

places, Rhodes wrote a massive history of his own country during his own lifetime—the last half of the nineteenth century and the first years of the twentieth. Hundreds of thousands of Rhodes's readers had participated in the events he narrated and came to look upon him as *the* scholar who gave meaning to the experiences of their lives.

Because Rhodes mirrored so well his own class and time, he will always be an important figure in American social and intellectual history. Because he stands as a transitional writer between the great literary historians and gentlemen scholars of the nineteenth century and the professional historians of the twentieth, and because his interpretation of the Civil War-Reconstruction period was for so long so dominant, Rhodes and his work will remain important in American historiography. Because his ideas had such influence on the popular mind that he helped shape American political, economic, social, and racial policies, he is an important part of the background of United States history in the first half of the twentieth century.

Born near Cleveland, Ohio, on 1 May 1848, Rhodes was the son of New England parents. His father, Daniel Pomeroy Rhodes, migrated from Vermont to Ohio where he prospered in the iron and coal businesses and in the development of railroads, utilities, financial institutions, and real estate. Daniel Rhodes was a New England Yankee, who believed in thrift, hard work, and individualism; a deist, who left the religious training of his children to his wife; an active Democrat; and a supporter and cousin of Illinois Senator Stephen A. Douglas, the leading Democratic politician of the 1850s. Daniel Rhodes's wife, Sophia Lord Russell Rhodes, from a Connecticut family, was a loving mother, a devout Episcopalian, and a cheerful embodiment of mid-nineteenth-century womanly virtues. To indoctrinate her four children she depended on the Bible and the Episcopal prayer book.

From his parents Rhodes inherited a Puritan-like respect for the proprieties, a firm belief in the existence of an absolute moral order (which closely resembled the milieu of his upper-middle-class family), and an appreciation for the virtues of the Democratic Party. Because of his family's wealth and standing, he enjoyed an unusual degree of economic, social, and emotional stability. Too young to serve in the Civil War and to a large extent sheltered by family circumstances from the turmoil of mid-nineteenth-century America, Rhodes imbibed and, with one notable exception, remained faithful to his inherited values throughout his life. His interpretation of American history was, to a significant extent, affected by those values.

Educated first by private tutors and then in the Cleveland public schools, Rhodes went in 1865 to the University of the City of New York (later New York University). In New York the serious young man spent much time studying history and, inspired by professors Benjamin N. Martin and John William Draper as well as by reading the works of the great historians, resolved to become an historian.

In 1866 Rhodes, in compliance with his father's wishes, transferred to the University of Chicago (an earlier school, not the present institution of the same name). At Chicago he studied metaphysics, developed a taste for English literature, and began the practice of reading the *Nation,* a journal, he once wrote, "of civilization and good

political morals." The *Nation* was an upper-middle-class magazine that generally championed "progress," honesty in public life, and property rights and was hostile to agrarianism, socialism, and organized labor. Rhodes read the magazine for most of his adult life; it reflected and reinforced the basic values he had acquired from his parents, and it sought to apply those values to the issues of the day.

After a year of study at Chicago, Rhodes accompanied his father on a European tour. At the urging of the elder Rhodes, the young man agreed to abandon his plans for a literary life and to go to work in the family business. He traveled in Europe, studying metallurgy in Berlin and visiting mines and iron and steel works in Germany and Great Britain. In 1869, after returning to the United States, Rhodes was sent to study the prospects for developing iron and coal deposits in Georgia, Tennessee, and North Carolina.

In 1872 Rhodes married Ann Card, the daughter of one of his father's early business partners. Although his wife was a semi-invalid for much of her life, Rhodes's marriage seems to have been a happy one which provided him the same family stability he had known as a child. From all indications Ann Rhodes was an amiable woman, devoted to her husband and their son.

Two events in 1875 were of great importance in Rhodes's life. His father's death freed him from his commitment to business, and he decided to abandon the Democratic Party. In 1872 Rhodes had cooperated with the Liberal Republicans, the reform faction of the party, in support of the Democratic presidential candidate Horace Greeley. Three years later, when the Ohio Democrats espoused inflationary "soft money," Rhodes quietly terminated his affiliation with the party of his father and became a Republican, the party then most often identified with the supremacy of the national government and big business. For the rest of his life he oscillated from one party to the other. In 1884 he was a Grover Cleveland Democrat. Later he became a friend and supporter of Theodore Roosevelt. In 1912 he voted for Woodrow Wilson, but in 1916 he returned to the Republican fold. "I started life," Rhodes said in 1919, "a strong Democrat, then I became a strong Republican, then a lukewarm Democrat, and now I suppose I am a lukewarm Republican."

In 1874 Rhodes entered into a partnership with his brother Robert and his brother-in-law Mark Hanna. The partnership sold the iron and coal produced by its own mines and furnaces and also acted as a commission merchant for other producers. Despite the economic depression of the mid-1870s, the firm flourished. In the years after his father's death Rhodes saw in his prosperity the opportunity to revive his earlier dream. He had never abandoned his reading and had been active in the cultural and literary life of Cleveland. Now he determined to accumulate enough money to provide for himself and his family and then withdraw from business to pursue the intellectual life that he had given up years before. Inspired by a reading of Richard Hildreth's *History of the United States of America* (1856-1860), he resolved to write a history of the country. Even while still involved with the partnership, Rhodes began to read and to collect material.

In 1885, having accumulated what he regarded as a sufficient sum (estimated at up to $500,000), Rhodes threw off "the shackles of business," invested his funds, and prepared "to devote myself to dearer and higher work." He now planned to write a history of the United States from 1850 to 1885. The work would cover the years from the Compromise of 1850 to the first inauguration of Grover Cleveland and the return to power of the Democrats. The central theme would be the issue of slavery which, he wrote, had engrossed the national attention for eleven years before the Civil War. Rhodes's purpose was "to recount the causes of the triumph of the Republican party in the presidential election of 1860, and to make clear how the revolution in public opinion was brought about that led to this result." Cleveland's inauguration, Rhodes thought, would be a "fitting close to this historical inquiry, for by that time the great questions which had their origin in the war had been settled as far as they could be by legislative or executive direction."

For six years Rhodes labored on his history. Then, in 1891, after the first two volumes were completed, he moved from Cleveland to Cambridge, Massachusetts. The relocation was motivated by a desire to be at what he regarded as the center of American culture and perhaps by resentment because his work did not have an appreciative audience in Cleveland. In Cambridge Rhodes would be near great universities, good libraries, and appreciative intellectual companions, and the family could be together while his son attended Harvard. Until his death on 22 January 1927, Rhodes lived in the Boston area, although he was frequently absent, traveling for pleasure, business, or health. He was happy in Boston, where his wealth and civility won him acceptance by such upper-crust groups as the Massachusetts Historical Society, the cheering section at Harvard football games, and some of the city's private dinner clubs. He had, in a very real way, come home.

Although he wrote several dozen articles and essays and a few other books, Rhodes's reputation as an historian rests upon his massive work originally entitled *History of the United States from the Compromise of 1850*. The first two volumes, covering the years 1850-1854 and 1854-1860, were published in 1892. Volume three (1860-1862) was published in 1895; volume four (1862-1864) in 1899; and volume five (1864-1866) in 1904. Volumes six (1866-1872) and seven (1872-1877) were both published in 1906 with the title *History of the United States from the Compromise of 1850 to the Final Restoration of Home Rule at the South in 1877*.

Rhodes worked diligently at his chosen task, poring over travel accounts, published autobiographies, and works by other historians. He made extensive use of newspaper material (although in many cases he quoted it from secondary sources) to give himself what he called "the spirit of the times." With the help of friends and hired research assistants, Rhodes plowed through his sources. Much of the research, however, was in his own extensive library. He made but limited use of manuscripts and exerted very little effort to obtain information that might be available from groups outside his own socioeconomic class. He began the actual writing in 1888 and then employed Titus Munson Coan, a professional writer and literary adviser, to help polish the style of his work.

The first volumes of Rhodes's *History* appeared at a time when his audience was ready for a fresh understanding of the Civil War. For thirty years the writing about that conflict had been done by participants in the war. Most of these writers had sought to place guilt for the coming of the war on their opponents. Northerners wrote about "the Rebellion," which, they maintained, had been the result of a conspiracy by wicked slaveowners who wanted to extend their rule over the entire country. Southerners described a "War Between the States" in which their gallant section struggled against hopeless odds to defend its rights against the aggressions of fanatical Northern abolitionists who did not understand the South and who would destroy her institutions, disrupt her society, and abolish her constitutional rights. These works (sometimes called the "we was right" school of Civil War historiography) frequently echoed the bitterness of the war years and were often little more than apologias for their authors' conduct.

By the 1890s much of the passion generated by the war was beginning to cool. Many of the political and military leaders—often the most vituperative and unforgiving belligerents of the war years—were dead. The surviving veterans, boys and young men during the war, found it easier to remember the camaraderie of soldier life rather than the hatreds and fears of the prewar years. Their children were busy with their own lives and, when they thought about the Civil War at all, were interested in its larger background and meaning rather than in the often petty questions that had exercised their elders. They all were affected by the nationalism and the hoopla that accompanied the centennials of the War for Independence and the Constitution. Much of the book-reading public was economically well-to-do and imbued with the idea of progress—the belief that things were getting better—and with a sense of pride and strength that grew from the nation's emergence as a great industrial power. New issues—the Populist movement, imperialism, the closing of the frontier, urbanization, industrialization, labor unrest—all seemed to indicate that the disputes of the 1860s had been left behind and could now be explained in a calm manner that would satisfy both North and South. The economic troubles of the early and mid-1890s led many worried Americans to seek in the past some assurance that their nation was based on eternal moral values and that it would survive. Conversely, confident and happy Americans, enjoying the prosperity at the end of the century, wanted assurances that their economic/social order rested on a firm foundation. Sectional reconciliation was in the air during the last decade of the nineteenth century as groups in the North united with those of like mind in the South to deal with new problems.

Years later historians looking back at their predecessors would see a new interpretation of the Civil War emerging from this environment and would call it the "nationalist school" of Civil War historiography. Rhodes, by chance, was the right historian in the right place at the right time with the right connections to appeal to readers of the 1890s, and he came to embody the "nationalist" interpretation. He was a Republican and a Democrat, a successful businessman turned man of letters, and a Northerner whose inclination and brief personal experiences and travels in the South in the 1860s and 1870s had made him sympathetic to that region. Equally important was the fact that Rhodes was an upper-middle-class man who shared the basic values of educated Anglo-Saxon Americans in both sections.

"All the right," Rhodes once observed, "is never on one side and all the wrong on the other." The basic attitude reflected by this statement was the foundation of Rhodes's obvious desire to be fair to both North and South. That attitude set Rhodes's *History* apart from most earlier works. Believing himself to be a completely disinterested scholar, Rhodes thought that he could weigh issues fairly and pass judgments that would provide his readers with the truth. The truth as Rhodes saw it was to be found in the standards by which he and other upper-middle-class Americans lived—the standards and values that Rhodes had inherited from his parents. The historian, he believed, should serve as "a fair-minded and intelligent guide" who would direct the layman to these truths. Outside the framework of his values there was no truth and very little that was even worthy of note. Rhodes, good, uncritical Victorian that he was, could hold such beliefs in complete innocence.

Rhodes accepted the dominant American ideas about nationalism, progress, race, and, to a large extent, economics. In common with most of his white countrymen he regarded the Anglo-Saxon United States as superior in virtually every way to all other nations. This idea had long been a staple of American sermons, speeches, and editorials, and it permeated such standard works as George Bancroft's *History of the United States from the Discovery of the American Continent to the Present Time* (1834-1875). "If one were to name the period of history during which men generally were most happy and prosperous," Rhodes asserted in the mid-1880s, "he could hardly fail to designate our country as the place, and the time as that from the adoption of our Constitution to the present, making the exception of the twenty years from 1850-1870."

In common with most educated Americans of the day, Rhodes accepted the "scientific truth" that blacks were inherently inferior to whites. "The ignorant foreign vote," Rhodes asserted, was responsible for whatever corruption was to be found in American politics. The gold standard was the proper policy for the United States—it was both economically and morally sound. The Constitution of the United States, except for its provisions recognizing slavery, had been a "perfect work." Rhodes's America was a happy, fortunate land. It was, in reality, closely circumscribed; to a large degree it resembled the society of upper-middle-class Cleveland and Boston.

When Rhodes applied his basic assumptions to the history of mid-nineteenth-century America, he produced an interpretation that found wide acceptance among his readers. Like most Americans of similar background, he believed his age to be "a century of progress and light." Human slavery had been antithetical to the moral, ethical, and religious standards of the age and was "utterly condemned at the tribunal of modern civilization."

"Of the American Civil War," Rhodes declared in a famous sentence, "it may safely be asserted that there was a single cause, slavery." The struggle, he believed, had been one of the antislavery North versus the proslavery South. In committing itself to the defense of human bondage, the antebellum South was simply wrong. (Rhodes discarded the idea that the Confederates had been fighting for the abstract principle of state rights.) Unlike most earlier Northern writers, however, Rhodes did not seek to place the guilt for slavery or the war on individual Southerners or even exclusively on the South. Both England and the Northern states, he pointed out, had played a major and profitable role in establishing and maintaining slavery. Slavery was, in fact, a tragedy of the South, not its crime.

Once he had absolved the South and individual Southerners from exclusive moral guilt for slavery, Rhodes found much about Southern society to admire. He praised the region's famed hospitality, and he lauded Robert E. Lee, "Stonewall" Jackson, and other Southerners. Southern planters, he once wrote, "were high-spirited gentlemen, with a keen sense of honor, showing itself in hatred of political corruption . . . and a reverence for and readiness to protect female virtue. Most of them were well educated and had a taste for reading. . . ." Rhodes depicted Civil War battles as heroic struggles between brave men in blue and gray. He even abandoned the pro-Northern label of "the Rebellion" and referred to the struggle as "the Civil War."

As a schoolboy in Cleveland, Rhodes had once argued against the Emancipation Proclamation. In 1865 he had accompanied the widow of Stephen A. Douglas when she called on President Andrew Johnson, and he had listened sympathetically as the chief executive recounted his troubles with the Radical Republicans who were attempting to foist "negro rule" on the South. Rhodes long had opposed Negro suffrage, and in 1905 he declared that blacks were about a million years behind whites.

Once slavery was abolished and no longer a threat to the moral fiber of the nation, Rhodes thought, the Southern people should have been permitted to work out their own system of race relations. In effect Rhodes drew a distinction between slavery and what his generation dubbed "the race question." Slavery was immoral and beyond the pale of nineteenth-century civilization. It was injurious to the nation. Exclusion of blacks from most aspects of American life, on the other hand, was desirable—even necessary—because such banishment merely prevented an inferior race from corrupting white society.

With these attitudes, which were shared by such leading contemporary historians of Reconstruction as William A. Dunning, Rhodes viewed the years after the Civil War largely from the perspective of a Southern white who had resumed his loyalty to the Union. "No large policy in our country," he wrote, "has ever been so conspicuous a failure as that of forcing universal negro suffrage upon the South." The overthrow of Radical Reconstruction in 1877 was, Rhodes believed, the "triumph of Southern intelligence and character."

In effect, Rhodes praised the North's stand against slavery and for the preservation of the Union, all the while empathizing with the white South's position on Reconstruction. Each side was portrayed as having taken the correct and successful stand on the issues that were most important to it and for the ultimate welfare of the nation—emancipation and preservation of the Union for the North, and the maintenance of white supremacy for the South. No wonder that Rhodes received praise from both sections. No wonder that he became a symbol of "balanced judgment and fairness" in the writing of history.

Rhodes's massive work touched on many facets of mid-nineteenth-century America not directly related to the major story that he was telling. These asides were sometimes intended to add interest or to enliven the narrative; often, however, they also reflected Rhodes's personal beliefs and reinforced similar ideas and prejudices in the minds of his readers. This was especially true of the adjectives that Rhodes attached to his nouns. For example, he included in volume three of his history a long chapter filled with praise of American businessmen and business values and offering such homilies as "an honest striving for wealth is better than idleness; and habits of industry, acquired in the pursuit of riches . . . may be directed to the most noble aims." Only "hard money," he wrote, was "honest money," and therefore the issuing of greenbacks in the 1860s had been a "scheme . . . at war with economic truths." Such sentences reflected Rhodes's own business ethos, and his readers could hardly miss the point that their patriotic duty was to support political candidates who favored the true policies of "hard money" and support for business (usually the Republicans, but also such Democrats as Grover Cleveland).

Rhodes chose to emphasize the fact that some of the historical figures he believed to have been scoundrels were Jews. He stressed Jewishness in his treatment of the Southern politician Judah P. Benjamin, the Northern financier Jay Gould, and Governor F. J. Moses of South Carolina, though he made no mention of the religious persuasion when dealing with non-Jewish scoundrels. The blacks of the Reconstruction era were, in Rhodes's view, propertyless and ignorant barbarians who "simply acted out of their nature" and were manipulated by "knavish white natives and . . . vulturous adventurers who flocked from the North." In the Reconstruction South "intelligence and property stood bound and helpless under negro-carpet-bag rule."

Rhodes's attitude toward minorities was insensitive rather than vicious, and in making such remarks he articulated and sanctified with his scholarship beliefs that were already widely held. Because his books were especially influential among teachers, journalists, ministers, and others who played major roles in molding public opinion, Rhodes's views helped shape public policy.

Rhodes's *History* was interesting, well-written, and popular. Reviewers of the early volumes who were critical usually took issue with one facet of his work and praised the remainder. Frederick Jackson Turner, for example, took Rhodes to task for ignoring the role of the West in the sectional struggle. Charles Francis Adams, Jr., pointed out that Rhodes lacked any real understanding of diplomatic and military matters. Several writers criticized his description of slavery for being too similar to the abolitionists' writings. Others faulted Rhodes for concentrating too much on slavery or on political, military, and constitutional history; for his treatment of Stephen A. Douglas; for giving too much emphasis to such spectacular events as slave rescues and draft riots; or for his probusiness bias. On the whole, however, the *History* was well received, and Rhodes was even likened to Thucydides and Tacitus. In 1898 he was elected president of the American Historical Association. He was also awarded prizes for his books and chosen for membership in such scholarly groups as the American Association for the Advancement of Science, the American Philosophical Society, and the British Academy. Universities from England to California showered him with honorary degrees.

Originally Rhodes had planned to carry his *History* through 1885, but as volumes six and seven neared completion, he grew tired and became convinced that he lacked the "basic knowledge" necessary to deal with the new issues that arose in the 1880s. Despite these beliefs, Rhodes, soon after he completed volume seven, began to consider a continuation of his *History*. In 1907 he began work on the eighth volume, entitled *History of the United States from Hayes to McKinley*. While he worked on this book Rhodes also produced *Historical Essays* (1909), *Lectures on the American Civil War* (1913), and *History of the Civil War, 1861-1865* (1917). He received a Gold Medal from the American Academy of Arts and Letters in 1910 and a Pulitzer Prize in 1918. Ostensibly the award was for *History of the Civil War;* in reality, it was for all of his work to that date.

Work on these three books—which, in truth, were often little more than excerpts from the *History*—other writing projects, lectures, travel, poor health, and a more relaxed work schedule combined to delay completion of *History of the United States from Hayes to McKinley, 1877-1896*. It was not published until 1919. Rhodes's last major work was

Rhodes in 1920, crayon portrait by John Singer Sargent

The McKinley and Roosevelt Administrations, 1897-1909, the ninth volume of the *History*. It was published in 1922.

In terms of both time and quality, these last two volumes were separated by a wide gap from Rhodes's earlier books. For one thing, Rhodes's health had begun to fail rapidly, and after 1908 his work was frequently interrupted by illness. He was also distressed by the deaths of his brother, his sister, and other relatives and friends. Economic troubles and the failure during the 1912-1914 recession of some of his business interests added to his woes. World War I shattered his faith in Western civilization in general and in "progress" in particular. Rhodes, who abhorred even scholarly controversy as ungentlemanly, found himself an inviting target for those who differed with his interpretation of American history. In 1917 the *Journal of Negro History* published two articles by John R. Lynch, a black former Republican political figure of the Reconstruction era, on the "Historical Errors of James Ford Rhodes." Nor was an elderly man of Rhodes's background and temperament pleased with the rambunctious activities of early-twentieth-century black militants, labor organizers, suffragettes, immigrants, and other vulgarians who were scrambling to improve their status in American society.

Rhodes's last volumes, which generally received very harsh reviews, were the work of a tired man, displeased and probably frightened by the changes in his society, who, one senses, forced himself to complete a dreary task for which he had but little enthusiasm. The result was far more a shallow political chronicle of the 1877-1909 period than an interpretative history. Rhodes simply had little interest in history that dealt with such matters as industrialization, urbanization, and the rise of finance capitalism. He therefore contented himself with a rather superficial narrative of politics and made little effort to delve below the surface to portray the underlying causes of political activities.

The last two volumes also were marred by Rhodes's tirades against those who did not subscribe to his standards of gentlemanly behavior and those who held different ideas—especially different economic ideas. He therefore described the leaders of an 1877 railroad strike as "tramps, communists, criminals and outcasts—the dregs of society." In describing an 1886 bomb-throwing incident, Rhodes commented: "All thoughtful citizens must have been interested to note that six of the eight who stood trial [for the bombing] were Germans, as was also the thrower of the bomb. . . .

When the Germans came to America they translated liberty into license." On the other hand, Rhodes had high praise for the men who upheld proper standards of conduct and policy. Grover Cleveland, William McKinley, and Rhodes's friend Theodore Roosevelt were all fine men, and the last named was an outstanding president. Mark Hanna, Rhodes's brother-in-law and friend, was praised both for his personal characteristics and also for his successful effort to save the country from the evils of unsound monetary policy in the 1896 presidential election.

The obvious flaws, prejudices, and other weaknesses of Rhodes's historical works do not render them valueless. His account of Reconstruction—although it fell out of favor among historians after 1930—was the "first comprehensive treatment of that period based on what appeared to be critical use of available sources and carried out according to the existing standard of historical scholarship." The wide praise which his *History of the United States from the Compromise of 1850* received before World War I is testimony to the fact that it satisfied a need that many Americans felt for a usable past. Rhodes was one of the first writers to call attention to race as an important issue in nineteenth-century American history. Later historians—most of whom differed with Rhodes's views on race—developed the theme and made it a major factor in historical interpretaton. Parts of Rhodes's last two volumes draw on personal acquaintance with some of the prominent men of the period and are therefore of considerable value as raw material for other writers. His works themselves are useful as sources for social and intellectual historians who study the ideas and attitudes of upper-middle-class Americans of the late nineteenth and early twentieth centuries.

Rhodes's misfortune was not that he deluded himself into believing that he was an objective, disinterested scholar, for all historians fall prey to that belief, or that his interpretations were superseded by later works, for this, too, is the fate of all historians. Rather, the tragic thing about Rhodes was that he apparently lived in almost complete isolation from the great intellectual revolution of the 1890-1914 period that changed so many ideas in history and in such fields as physics, economics, anthropology, biology, and psychology. Rhodes, after all, was born in the year in which the Mexican War ended, and he lived into the year in which Charles Lindbergh flew solo across the Atlantic. He lived too long and in an environment too isolated from the sweeping changes of his time.

Bibliography:
"A Complete Bibliography of the Writings of James Ford Rhodes," in *James Ford Rhodes: The Man, the Historian, and His Work*, by Robert Cruden (Cleveland: Press of Western Reserve University, 1961), pp. 278-283.

Biographies:
Mark A. DeWolfe Howe, *James Ford Rhodes: American Historian* (New York: Appleton, 1929);
Robert Cruden, *James Ford Rhodes: The Man, the Historian, and his Work* (Cleveland: Press of Western Reserve University, 1961).

Reference:
John David Smith, "James Ford Rhodes, Woodrow Wilson, and the Passing of the Amateur Historian of Slavery," *Mid-America*, 64 (October 1982): 17-24.

Papers:
Collections of Rhodes's papers are at the Massachusetts Historical Society and at Duke University.

James Harvey Robinson

John Braeman
University of Nebraska at Lincoln

BIRTH: Bloomington, Illinois, 29 June 1863, to James Harvey and Latricia Maria Drake Robinson.

EDUCATION: A.B., Harvard University, 1887; A.M., Harvard University, 1888; Ph.D., University of Freiburg, 1890.

MARRIAGE: 1 September 1887 to Grace Woodville Read.

AWARDS AND HONORS: LL.D., University of Utah, 1922; L.H.D., Tufts College, 1924; president, American Historical Association, 1929.

DEATH: New York, New York, 16 February 1936.

SELECTED BOOKS: *The Original and Derived Features of the Constitution of the United States of America* (N.p.: Privately printed, 1890); republished as "The Original and Derived Features of the Constitution," in *Annals of the American Academy of Political and Social Science*, 1 (1890), pp. 203-243;
The German Bundesrath. A Study in Comparative Constitutional Law (Philadelphia, 1891);
Petrarch: The First Modern Scholar, by Robinson with the collaboration of Henry Winchester Rolfe (New York & London: Putnam's, 1898);
An Introduction to the History of Western Europe (part one, Boston & London: Ginn, 1902; republished with part two, Boston & London: Ginn, 1903; revised and enlarged, 2 volumes, 1924, 1926);
The Development of Modern Europe: An Introduction to the Study of Current History, by Robinson and Charles A. Beard, 2 volumes (Boston: Ginn, 1907, 1908; revised and enlarged, 1929, 1930);
"The Fall of Rome": Some Current Misapprehensions in Regard to the Process of Dissolution of the Roman Empire. An Address Read Before the New England History Teachers' Association at Hartford, April 27, 1906 (Boston: New England History Teachers' Association, 1907);
History: A Lecture Delivered at Columbia University in the Series on Science, Philosophy and Art, January 15, 1908 (New York: Columbia University Press, 1908);
An Outline of the History of the Intellectual Class in Western Europe (New York: Privately printed, 1911; revised, New York: Marion Press, 1914, 1915); revised again as *An Outline of the History of the Western European Mind* (New York: Marion Press, 1919);
The New History: Essays Illustrating the Modern Historical Outlook (New York: Macmillan, 1912);
Outlines of European History, 2 volumes, by Robinson, Beard, and James Henry Breasted (Boston: Ginn, 1914); volume one revised as *History of Europe, Ancient and Medieval*, by Rob-

James Harvey Robinson

inson and Breasted (Boston: Ginn, 1920; revised again, 1929); volume two revised and republished as *History of Europe, Our Own Times, the Eighteenth and Nineteenth Centuries, the Opening of the Twentieth Century and the World War*, by Robinson and Beard (Boston: Ginn, 1921; revised again, 1927);

Medieval and Modern Times: An Introduction to the History of Western Europe from the Dissolution of the Roman Empire to the Opening of the Great War of 1914 (Boston: Ginn, 1916; revised and enlarged, 1918, 1926, and 1934);

The Last Decade of European History and the Great War, Designed As a Supplement to "The Development of Modern Europe," by Robinson and Beard, and "An Introduction to the History of Western Europe," by James Harvey Robinson (Boston: Ginn, 1918);

The Mind in the Making: The Relation of Intelligence to Social Reform (New York & London: Harper, 1921; revised, London: Cape, 1923);

A General History of Europe. From the Origins of Civilization to the Present Time, by Robinson, Breasted, and Emma Peters Smith (Boston: Ginn, 1921); republished as *Our World Today and Yesterday* (Boston: Ginn, 1924);

The Humanizing of Knowledge (New York: Doran, 1923; revised, 1926);

The Ordeal of Civilization: A Sketch of the Development and World-Wide Diffusion of Our Present-Day Institutions and Ideas (New York & London: Harper, 1926);

The Human Comedy As Devised and Directed by Mankind Itself (New York & London: Harper, 1937).

OTHER: "Sidgwick's Elements of Politics," in *Annals of the American Academy of Political and Social Science*, 3 (1892), pp. 211-222;

Constitution of the Kingdom of Prussia, translated with an introduction and notes by Robinson, in *Annals of the American Academy of Political and Social Science*, 5, supplement (September 1894);

"Ought the Sources to be Used in Teaching History?," in *Proceedings of the Second Annual Convention of the Association of Colleges and Preparatory Schools in the Middle States and Maryland* (N.p., 1894), pp. 38-44;

The French Revolution, 1789-1791, edited by Robinson (Philadelphia: University of Pennsylvania Department of History, 1894);

"The Tennis Court Oath," in *Annual Report of the American Historical Association for the Year 1894* (Washington, D.C.: Government Printing Office, 1895), pp. 541-547;

The Napoleonic Period, edited by Robinson (Philadelphia: University of Pennsylvania Department of History, 1895);

The Period of the Early Reformation in Germany, edited by Robinson and Merrick Whitcomb (Philadelphia: University of Pennsylvania Department of History, 1895);

The Restoration and the European Policy of Metternich (1814-1820), edited by Robinson (Philadelphia: University of Pennsylvania Department of History, 1896);

"The Teaching of European History in the College," in *Annual Report of the American Historical Association for the Year 1896*, 2 volumes (Washington, D.C.: Government Printing Office, 1897), I: 265-276;

The Pre-Reformation Period, edited by Robinson (Philadelphia: University of Pennsylvania, Department of History, 1897);

"Mediaeval and Modern History in the High School," in *Fifth Yearbook of the National Herbart Society for the Scientific Study of Teaching* (Chicago: University of Chicago Press, 1899), pp. 42-68;

Protest of the Cour des Aides of Paris—April 10, 1775,

edited by Robinson (Philadelphia: University of Pennsylvania Department of History, 1899);

"Sacred and Profane History," in *Annual Report of the American Historical Association for the Year 1899*, 2 volumes (Washington, 1900), I: 527-535;

Readings in European History: A Collection of Extracts from the Sources Chosen with the Purpose of Illustrating the Progress of Culture in Western Europe Since the German Invasions, edited by Robinson, 2 volumes (Boston: Ginn, 1904, 1906);

"The Conception and Methods of History," in *Congress of Arts and Science, Universal Exposition, St. Louis, 1904*, edited by Howard J. Rogers, 8 volumes (Boston: Houghton Mifflin, 1905-1907), II: 40-51;

Readings in Modern European History: A Collection of Extracts from the Sources Chosen with the Purpose of Illustrating Some of the Chief Phases of the Development of Europe During the Last Two Hundred Years, edited by Robinson and Beard, 2 volumes (Boston: Ginn, 1908, 1909);

"The Reformation," in *Encyclopaedia Britannica*, eleventh edition, 29 volumes (Cambridge: Cambridge University Press, 1910-1911), XXIII: 4-22;

"Religion," in *Whither Mankind: A Panorama of Modern Civilization*, edited by Beard (New York: Longmans, Green, 1928), pp. 264-286;

"The Age of Surprises," in *The Drift of Civilization: By the Contributors to the Fiftieth Anniversary Number of the St. Louis Post-Dispatch* (New York: Simon & Schuster, 1929), pp. 15-31;

"Civilization," in *Encyclopaedia Britannica*, fourteenth edition, 24 volumes (London: Encyclopaedia Britannica Company, 1929), V: 735-741;

"John Dewey and Liberal Thought," in *John Dewey, The Man and His Philosophy: Addresses in Celebration of His Seventieth Birthday Delivered in New York* (Cambridge: Harvard University Press, 1930), pp. 153-171.

PERIODICAL PUBLICATIONS: "France of To-Day," *Political Science Quarterly*, 13 (December 1898): 687-693;

"The French Declaration of the Rights of Man, of 1789," *Political Science Quarterly*, 14 (December 1899): 653-662;

"Popular Histories, Their Defects and Possibilities," *International Monthly*, 2 (July 1900): 47-73;

"The Neglect of the Church by Historians," *Political Science Quarterly*, 15 (December 1900): 667-674;

"The Elective System Historically Considered," *International Quarterly*, 6 (September-December 1902): 191-201;

"The Study of the Lutheran Revolt," *American Historical Review*, 8 (January 1903): 205-216;

"The Cambridge Modern History," *Political Science Quarterly*, 18 (December 1903): 681-687;

"Recent Tendencies in the Study of the French Revolution," *American Historical Review*, 11 (April 1906): 529-547;

"The Ancestry of the Liberal Arts," *Columbia University Quarterly*, 12 (March 1910): 200-204;

"The Significance of History in Industrial Education," *Educational Bi-Monthly*, 4 (June 1910): 376-389;

"Aulard's Political History of the French Revolution," *Political Science Quarterly*, 26 (March 1911): 133-141;

"The Relation of History to the Newer Sciences of Man," *Journal of Philosophy, Psychology and Scientific Methods*, 8 (16 March 1911): 141-157;

"Is Mankind Advancing?," *Survey*, 26 (6 May 1911): 247-252;

"The Spirit of Conservatism in the Light of History," *Journal of Philosophy, Psychology and Scientific Methods*, 8 (11 May 1911): 253-269;

"War and Thinking," *New Republic*, 1 (19 December 1914): 17-18;

"What is National Spirit?," *Century*, 93 (November 1916): 57-64;

"The Still Small Voice of the Herd," *Political Science Quarterly*, 32 (June 1917): 312-319;

"The Threatened Eclipse of Free Speech," *Atlantic Monthly*, 120 (December 1917): 811-818;

"The Philosopher's Stone," *Atlantic Monthly*, 123 (April 1919): 474-481;

"The New School," *School and Society*, 11 (31 January 1920): 129-132;

"Mr. Wells's Gospel of History," *Yale Review*, new series, 10 (January 1921): 412-418;

"Is Darwinism Dead?," *Harper's*, 145 (June 1922): 68-74;

"The Humanizing of Knowledge," *Science*, 56 (28 July 1922): 89-100;

"The Seven Greatest Americans," *American Magazine* 95 (June 1923): 13-15, 136, 138, 142;

"Freedom Reconsidered," *Harper's*, 147 (October 1923): 577-585; 147 (November 1923): 769-777;

"After Twenty Years," *Survey*, 53 (1 October 1924): 18-21;

"How Did We Get That Way?," *Harper's*, 153 (August 1926): 265-272;

"The Drift of Human Affairs," *Harper's*, 153 (September 1926): 426-433;

"The Newer Ways of Historians," *American Historical Review*, 35 (January 1930): 245-255;

"John Dewey and His World," *Harvard Teachers Record*, 2 (February 1932): 9-16.

James Harvey Robinson retains an honored place in the annals of American historiography as the champion of, and leading spokesman for, the "New History." His challenge to the "scientific history" that was the dominant orthodoxy among the first generation of American professional historians in the late nineteenth century revolved around a complex of interrelated propositions. In the first place, he called for broadening the scope of historical study beyond politics, wars, and formal institutions to include the full range of mankind's activities and experiences. Second, he proclaimed that history must deal with the dynamic rather than the static. The crux of what he would call the "genetic" approach was that history should be viewed not as a series of discrete events and occurrences, but rather as a process of continuing, and continuous, development. Accordingly, the historian should go beyond simply describing what had been to explaining how things had come about. As a corollary, Robinson looked to the social sciences for explanatory tools. Even more radical was his ambition to make history itself an instrument for social progress. That quest became his deepest passion— a passion that would transform him from practicing historian to, in the words of one commentator, a "preacher of history."

Robinson was born on 29 June 1863, in Bloomington, Illinois, the fifth of six children to survive infancy, four boys and two girls, of James Harvey and Latricia Maria Drake Robinson. His father, a well-to-do banker who traced his ancestry back to the Pilgrims, died when Robinson was eleven, leaving him financially independent. His mother was the strong-minded and religiously orthodox daughter of a Presbyterian minister. After attending the local public schools, Robinson enrolled in the nearby Illinois State Normal School. There was first kindled his fascination with the wonders revealed by science. That enthusiasm in turn marked the first step on the path that would lead him to abandon the Christian faith of his upbringing. Moved by a youthful wanderlust, he took off in 1882 for a year's tour in Europe. After his return to Bloomington, he worked first as a store

clerk, then in the family bank. When his younger brother Benjamin went off to Harvard in the fall of 1884, Robinson decided to join him there. After finishing his bachelor's degree in three years, he married, on 1 September 1887, Grace Woodville Read, the daughter of a successful Bloomington hardware merchant. She died in 1927; the couple had no children.

Robinson stayed on at Harvard for a fourth year to work on a master's degree in history. After receiving his A.M. in 1888, he went to Germany, again to join his brother, who was studying botany at Strasbourg. After one semester there, he transferred to the University of Freiburg to work under Hermann E. von Holst. Although he had started out in French history, Holst was best known for his multivolume *The Constitutional and Political History of the United States*, which had begun to appear in German in 1873. Expanding his Harvard master's paper, Robinson wrote his dissertation on *The Original and Derived Features of the Constitution of the United States of America*. He was awarded the Ph.D. and saw his dissertation published in 1890. The next year he spent in Germany studying and traveling with his wife. While there he met the University of Pennsylvania economist Simon N. Patten, who was so impressed that he arranged for Robinson's appointment as lecturer in history at Pennsylvania starting in the fall of 1891. The following year he was promoted to associate professor. Along with his teaching responsibilities, Robinson served as associate editor of the *Annals of the American Academy of Political and Social Science*. In 1895 he was appointed professor of European history at Columbia University. Technically, the appointment was at Barnard College under an arrangement whereby he would divide his time between the women's school and Columbia. And he was acting dean of Barnard in 1900-1901.

At Pennsylvania and during his first years at Columbia, Robinson's teaching centered around four major areas: the Middle Ages, the Renaissance, the Protestant Reformation, and the era of the French Revolution and Napoleon. He was a highly effective and stimulating teacher with a knack for conveying his own enthusiasm for learning. "Upon set notions, sacrosanct prejudices, solemn convictions, derived from conventional ways of viewing things bygone," recalled one student who worked with him in the early Columbia years, "Robinson cast an incredulous, critical eye." His reputation was as an exponent of German-style *Quellenkritik:* the reconstruction of the past through the minute and painstaking examination of what

Robinson termed "the best original sources." He was assiduous in pushing for library purchase of "contemporaneous" pamphlets and available printed documentary collections. He was unsparing in his reviews of writers who had failed to use primary materials. "[N]o correction of details," he observed about one work found guilty of that fault, "could make a book satisfactory which neglects the chief sources of our knowledge of the period with which it deals." Even when moving away from late-nineteenth-century scientific history, he continued to affirm that critical analysis of the documents "is the most scientific phase of historical investigation, both in its spirit and results."

Robinson applied the same technique even at the undergraduate level. In 1894 he produced a translation, with an introduction and extensive explanatory notes, of the Prussian constitution. That same year he joined with his colleagues Edward P. Cheyney and Dana C. Munro to begin a series of Translations and Reprints from the Original Sources of European History, published by the University of Pennsylvania Department of History. His contributions dealing with the Protestant Reformation, the period of the French Revolution and Napoleon, and the post-1815 reaction were twenty- to forty-page-long pamphlets made up of brief excerpts from mostly well-known sources. More substantial was his 1899 edition—with an accompanying English translation by his wife—of the 1775 *Remontrances*, or "Protest," of the Paris Cour des aides to illustrate the abuses leading to the French Revolution. Exposure to "the experiences of eyewitnesses," he believed, would stimulate student interest because of their "vividness." It would, moreover, provide more insight into the spirit of a given time than any secondary account could possibly do and promote understanding of how the historian proceeded. In Robinson's view, simply teaching history as an "inflexible dogmatic statement of facts" for rote memorization reinforced students' tendency to accept what they read as gospel. "Can we afford," he asked, "to encourage the spirit of blind acceptance when discrimination

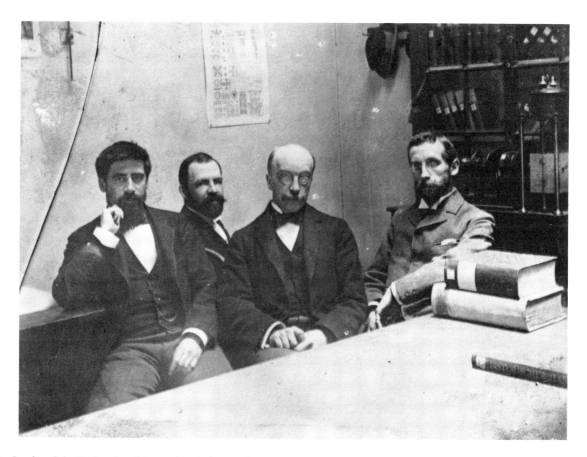

The faculty of the University of Pennsylvania history department, early 1890s: Edward P. Cheyney, Dana C. Munro, John Bach McMaster, and James Harvey Robinson (University of Pennsylvania Archives)

is so essential amidst the ever increasing mass of literature which is submitted to us yearly and monthly?"

The goal of training students in critical thinking animated Robinson as a member of the subcommittee on history, civil government, and political economy of the Committee of Ten appointed in 1892 by the National Educational Association to examine the high school curriculum. His major contribution was the suggestion that the fourth year include the intensive study of a special period involving work with primary sources to force the student "to use his own wits," to strengthen his "critical powers," and to promote a "healthful skepticism." His larger justification for the study of history similarly remained with the liberal-education rationale of the time. He rebutted the notion that the study of the past could provide a guide to forecasting the future. "If such prophetic insight were once possible it is no longer so. Our century is too different from all that has preceded it to permit anything except the vaguest inferences." The value of historical study lay instead in broadening one's cultural horizons. "When the past, with all its bewildering spectacle of human enterprise and efforts is opened before us, . . ." he told a meeting of educators, "ought we not to see in it a divine protest against all national bigotry, and an easy acquiescence in the propriety of the merely familiar? . . . of all the good lessons which history should teach us, this lesson of cosmopolitan sympathy is far the most important and far-reaching." Or as he put the matter more broadly, the "real" purpose of education was "the cultivation of those faculties which promise to be the greatest source of satisfaction to ourselves and our friends as the years go on."

Looking back at the end of his life, Robinson confessed his inability to explain the influences that led him to adopt a radically different conception of history. But the starting point appears to have been his work with Holst. A product of the Prussian historical school and its ideological partner, the historical school of jurisprudence, Holst taught that a nation's political and legal institutions were the unique product of its particular historical experience. Applying that approach in his dissertation, Robinson denied that the United States Constitution was the result of "abstract principles," or simply copied from European models. On the contrary, the new governmental structure represented a "natural development" from the American people's "home experience." To underline the distinctive features of the American form of govern-

ment, he examined in his follow-up study, *The German Bundesrath* (1891), how Germany's different historical experience had resulted in a different kind of federal system. Inasmuch as "the political institutions of a nation must be relative to its social and economic status," he concluded, "the attempt to lay down general principles of government applicable to every country, and even to a single country in every stage of its development, must always prove futile." Since every country was in "a constant state of flux," the outcome was a continuing process of "readjustment between the political institutions and the constantly changing social and economic life of the nation."

Robinson found the same lesson taught by evolutionary biology: life was an endless process of ongoing, cumulative change. Just as the biologist traced the evolution of the plant and animal worlds, the historian's task was "the awakening of the consciousness that man changes." And he saw the three major watersheds—or "transitional periods"—in the transformation of medieval into modern Europe: the Renaissance, the Protestant Reformation, and the French Revolution. His major contribution in the first area was his 1898 translation of selections from the writings of the fourteenth-century humanist Petrarch "to show," as he explained to a publisher, "the contrast between the characteristic culture of the Middle Ages and that of Modern times." While hailing the Italian polymath as "one of those incomparable leaders of humanity who . . . have directed men's thoughts into new channels for ages to follow," Robinson's accompanying commentary simultaneously underlined how Petrarch, like his time, remained a mixture of the old and the new: "He was mediaeval as well as modern. He belonged both to the present and the future." Robinson applied this "law of historical continuity" to the Reformation—first in a survey of recent scholarship in the *American Historical Review*, then for the lay public in the eleventh edition of the *Encyclopaedia Britannica*—by showing how its roots lay in "the conditions in Germany during the fifty years preceding Luther's secession from the Roman Church."

Robinson made the most thoroughgoing application of this approach to the subject that became the concentration of his own researches—the French Revolution. He laid down as the "chief task" for the student of that upheaval "the painstaking investigation of the often obscure causal relations of events, the tracing of gradual and inevitable development where only seemingly spasmodic and erratic outbursts have previously been noticed."

Take, for example, the Declaration of the Rights of Man. Placing that manifesto "in its historical setting" revealed that the declaration was no exercise in mere abstract speculation; each of its provisions was a "concrete and positive" response to a long-condemned "crying evil." And as Robinson dug more deeply into the sources, he expanded the scope of his analysis. To "appreciate properly the place of the Revolution among the great transformations of history," he concluded, "it will be necessary to bring the history of France from 1789 to 1800 into organic relation not only with the Ancien Régime but with the developments throughout Western Europe of the half-century immediately preceding. . . ." Nor could explanation of the "gestation" of "the most decisive and general readjustment to meet new and altered conditions of which we have any record" deal exclusively with the political sphere. Required was examination of "manners, customs, conditions, and property-holding."

A complex of influences contributed to this broadening of Robinson's perspective. Voltaire, who was Robinson's intellectual hero if any one person could be given that accolade, had pioneered in formulating a cultural interpretation of history that focused upon changes in men's customs. Robinson was familiar with and admired German historian Karl Lamprecht's *Kulturgeshichte;* he thought the attempt by his University of Pennsylvania colleague John Bach McMaster to place American history in a broad social context "a really great historical work." Probably still more crucial was the role of Simon N. Patten, whose 1899 *The Development of English Thought* was a path-breaking exploration of the relationship between the material conditions of life and men's ideas and beliefs. As regards the French Revolution, he was much impressed by the neo-Marxist analysis by French socialist leader Jean Jaurès in his *Histoire socialiste* of how the coming to power of the bourgeoisie represented a necessary readjustment of political and social institutions to the new industrial mode of production. But his own treatment owed most to Alexis de Tocqueville's *L'Ancien Régime et la Révolution* (1856); the Revolution was the culmination of a long process of decay in the feudal/aristocratic/corporate institutions of the old regime with the accompanying radicalization of public opinion; its result was the transformation of France into a modern democratic state based upon a uniform and centralized administrative system, equal rights, and individual liberty.

At the same time, Robinson's involvement in curricular reform sharpened his awareness of the faults in the standard European history manuals. Most were factually unsound, written without knowledge of the latest secondary accounts, much less of the primary sources. Rather than explaining why men had acted or believed as they had, the existing texts condemned or praised by the standard of present-day values—a tendency most striking in the Protestant-inspired denunciations of the medieval Church. The shortcomings of an institution, Robinson admonished, may explain why that institution was modified or discarded, but not why it was accepted. Worse than such moralizing was the narrow focus upon political, dynastic, and military matters, with the resulting piling up of meaningless names and dates. Man was more than simply a soldier, subject, or ruler. Thus, history should aim to become "the limitless science of past human affairs"; its realm should include "everything true about everything which man ever did, or thought, or hoped, or felt." The corollary was that the historian must avoid the simply picturesque or spectacular. Just as the natural scientist looked to find regularities, the historian must direct his attention to "normal conduct"—must pick out from the mass of human experiences those facts that will reveal "the prevailing interests, preoccupations and permanent achievements of the past."

In response to the problem of inadequate school texts, Robinson decided—apparently in the late 1890s—to write his own college-level survey of European history starting with the fall of Rome. After sounding out publishers, he contracted with the Boston publishing firm of Ginn & Company to edit a new history textbook series. His contribution, *An Introduction to the History of Western Europe*, was published in two parts, in 1902 and 1903. The work would dominate the European history text market for a generation, selling approximately 250,000 copies. The text reflected not simply Robinson's extensive reading in the latest scholarship but his own mastery of the primary sources. At the same time, he had a lucid and even vivid writing style. The result was a rare combination of factual authoritativeness and readability. More important, his book had what most texts, then and now, lack—an overarching conceptual framework that kept the work from degenerating into a mere chronicle. In his opening pages, he explained his guiding principles: to concentrate upon the key institutions, patterns of behavior, and beliefs; to deal "sympathetically" with "the convictions and habits of men and nations in the past"; and to treat not simply politics but also "economic, intellectual, and artistic achievements." The unifying thread was the transformation of medieval into modern Europe. The reviewer for the *American Historical Review* summed up the near-universal professional approval, calling Robinson's work "the best manual of general European history which has yet appeared in English."

The first part, published separately in 1902, was devoted to the Middle Ages; the rest to developments since. Robinson showed how feudalism evolved to fill the vacuum left by the collapse of the *pax Romana*. After tracing the rise of the Church during the later Roman Empire, he gave a sympathetic treatment of the Church's role as the source of solace amid the hardships of daily life, as the bulwark of peace amid the lawless anarchy of the times, and as the preserver of civilization against a threatening barbarism. Rather than detailing the petty squabbles of kings and nobles, he emphasized the positive achievements of the Middle Ages: the rise of the universities, the magnificent cathedrals, the beginnings of vernacular literature, the emergence of the nation state, the revival of commerce, and the rise of towns. He went on to extoll the Renaissance as marking "a very great and fundamental change" in men's attitudes and values: a shift in the focus of men's interests to this world in contrast with the otherworldliness of the medieval period. He was more ambivalent about the Reformation. He played down the newness of Luther's ideas and underlined how many of his supporters were animated more by worldly than religious motives; but he remained sufficiently within the Protestant tradition to affirm that the result was to "inaugurate a fundamental revolution in many of the habits and customs of the people." His own sympathies were most strongly with "the marvelous transformations produced by the French Revolution"—"a great and permanent reform" that replaced "vicious institutions—relics of bygone times and outlived conditions"—with "a modern and more rational order."

Innovative as *An Introduction to the History of Western Europe* was, there were still major gaps. Art, literature, and men's intellectual constructs after the Renaissance were largely ignored. Treatment of the eighteenth-century philosophes was limited to their role in laying the groundwork for the French Revolution by exposing the abuses of the ancien régime. There was nothing about the commercial revolution of the sixteenth century, nothing about the rise of the bourgeoisie. The work was similarly traditional in its slighting of the post-Napoleonic period. Seventeen pages were devoted to a sketchy account of political developments between the Congress of Vienna and the 1848 revolutions; a follow-up chapter dealt with the unification of Germany and Italy. The final chapter on "Europe of To-day" allocated four pages to the rise of modern science from Roger Bacon in the thirteenth century, another eight to the industrial revolution and its accompanying social problems. Most striking, and perhaps the major reason for the work's ready acceptance, was the extent to which Robinson remained within late-nineteenth-century orthodox assumptions regarding the historical process—what John Higham has aptly termed "conservative evolutionism." If the explicit theme was change, his underlying premise was "the *unity* or *continuity of history*." He thus downplayed the extent to which even the French Revolution involved a sharp break with the past: its contribution lay in doing away "with abuses of which the whole nation was heartily tired." His moral was "that no abrupt change has ever taken place in all the customs of a people, and that it cannot, in the nature of things, take place."

The catalyst that brought Robinson to aspire to make history into a conscious and explicit instrument for reform was his growing feeling, shared by many of his background and milieu, that things were out of joint in the United States. That feeling affected the University of Pennsylvania even in the 1890s. Robinson's former teacher at Illinois Normal Edmund J. James was aspiring to make Pennsylvania's Wharton School into an agency for the scientific investigation of current political, social, and economic problems; Simon N. Patten was formulating his analysis of how the promise of abundance made possible by technological advance was being frustrated by outmoded beliefs and values that were holdovers from a bygone age. Moved by the same reform impulse, Robinson expressed his sympathy with the economists of the new school who were challenging the "hopelessly closed circle of the English classical school," indicted the defenders of laissez-faire for ignoring "the causes tending towards a more complete social organization," and lamented that the rigidity of the U.S. Constitution impeded the required adjustment to the "profound changes" that had taken place in the United States. As the insurgent spirit picked up momentum after the turn of the century, he appears instinctively to have asked what contribution the historian could make to human betterment. "Each generation has new questions to put to the past," he declared in 1903—and then pointedly added: "To-day we grow impatient over fifty pages devoted to the ceremonies accompanying the

AN INTRODUCTION TO THE

HISTORY OF WESTERN EUROPE

BY

JAMES HARVEY ROBINSON
PROFESSOR OF HISTORY IN COLUMBIA UNIVERSITY

*History is no easy science;
its subject, human society,
is infinitely complex.*

FUSTEL DE COULANGES

WITH SUPPLEMENT

GINN AND COMPANY
BOSTON · NEW YORK · CHICAGO · LONDON
ATLANTA · DALLAS · COLUMBUS · SAN FRANCISCO

PAGE FROM AN ILLUMINATED MANUSCRIPT

*Frontispiece and title page for the 1918 edition of Robinson's college-level textbook chronicling European history from the fall of
Rome. The supplement, covering World War I, updated the work, originally published in two parts, 1902 and 1903.*

abdication of Charles V, and ask how Brussels managed its schools or disposed of its sewage."

The upshot was that Robinson became a leading exponent of revamping the curriculum to devote more time to the recent period in order, as Robinson put it, "to explain the great problems of the present." When he was named to the Committee of Five appointed by the American Historical Association in 1907 to reexamine the teaching of history in the high schools, his lobbying for fuller attention to "dealing with our own times" was instrumental in the committee's adoption of a recommendation for the introduction of a new one-year course in modern European history. And at the behest of Ginn and Company, he undertook to write a text covering from the time of Louis XIV on for the growing number of similar college-level courses. Aware of his own lack of expertise in the post-1815 years, he took as collaborator his younger colleague at Columbia Charles A. Beard. The resulting two-volume *The Development of Modern Europe: An Introduction to the Study of Current History* appeared in 1907 and 1908. As Robinson had done for *An Introduction to the History of Western Europe*, the authors provided a companion collection of documentary sources entitled *Readings in Modern European History* (1908, 1909). The Robinson-Beard history was enthusiastically received. "There is no better text-book for the nineteenth century than this," one reviewer declared. "It is as solid and informing," another reported, "as it is interesting and clever." Although its departures from the conventional might "shock some conservative temperaments," many others would hail the work "as a new evangel."

Sales totaled 78,600 copies for the first volume of the text, 88,000 for the second. Although it did not match the sales of *An Introduction to the*

History of Western Europe, The Development of Modern Europe had an even more revolutionary impact upon the teaching of history. The authors set forth in bold fashion "the claims of this new manual to be regarded as an adventurer in the educational world." One difference from the existing texts was that Robinson and Beard downplayed "purely political and military events" to put heavier emphasis on "the more fundamental economic matters." A "second trait of novelty" was "the happy reunion of the eighteenth and nineteenth centuries, which should never have been put asunder by the date 1789. . . . It was the eighteenth century which set the problems of progress and suggested their solutions, leaving to its successor the comparatively simple task of working them out in detail and making fuller application of them." The work pictured the major forces responsible for the "modernization" of Western Europe as the rise of science, the ideas of the Enlightenment, the French Revolution, and the "still more fundamental" transformation wrought by the Industrial Revolution. But its most striking feature was the aim of illuminating "the existing forms of government and social life" by showing how "they came to be." The authors, the preface declared, "have consistently subordinated the past to the present. It has been their ever-conscious aim to enable the reader to catch up with his own times; to read intelligently the foreign news in the morning paper; to know what was the attitude of Leo XIII toward the social democrats even if he has forgotten that of Innocent III toward the Albigenses."

How much of the work was Robinson's, how much Beard's, is difficult to ascertain. Beard, who even at the height of his reputation continued to look up to Robinson as "a very wise old owl," accorded the elder man primacy. Robinson's principle of historical continuity underlay the emphasis given to the eighteenth-century sources of nineteenth-century developments. His hand was likewise reflected in the sympathetic treatment of the Catholic Church's historic contribution to European civilization, in the praise given the eighteenth-century philosophes for undermining the old regime and preparing the new, and in the account of the French Revolution. On the other side, the importance accorded commercial rivalries in eighteenth-century power struggles had no parallel in *An Introduction to the History of Western Europe;* Robinson himself would acknowledge that the increased stress put upon the role played by the quest for markets and investment opportunities in nineteenth-century European overseas expansion was

Beard's doing, the result of his reading of English economist John A. Hobson's seminal *Imperialism* (1902). Beard similarly appears responsible for the exaltation of the contributions of modern science: its liberation of mankind from "the shackles of error and superstition," its promise "for infinitely improving our human lot." And the protean influence assigned the Industrial Revolution as the single most important force in transforming Western European habits, ideas, and ways of living was even more strikingly Beard's contribution.

This vision of science and technology as the twin engines of "modernization" still gives *The Development of Modern Europe* a contemporary ring more than three-quarters of a century later. What dates the work as a product of its own time is the optimism suffusing its pages. The battle for popular government had been largely won; so too the struggle to achieve the basic human rights of freedom of speech, press, and assembly, liberty of occupation and abode, equality before the law, and religious toleration. Even Russia "appears to be on the verge of modifying its ancient system of despotism"; contact with the West was speeding reforms in the long stagnant civilizations of Asia. Scientific knowledge was increasing at an accelerating pace, and the new technology developing in its wake promised an ever-rising level of material well-being. Although "imperial ambition and patriotic pride have led to a steady increase in the armies and navies of Europe," stronger counterforces were making men "less and less inclined to warlike pursuits." The major problems remaining were the persistence of poverty and the accompanying growth of the socialist movement. But governments had already done much in the way of social legislation, while the growing awareness of "the evils of our present organization" gave "hope that many shocking inequalities may gradually be done away with."

In the years that followed, the two men—though remaining personal friends—took different intellectual paths. Beard went on to apply the "economic interpretation," or "the theory of economic determinism" (he used the terms interchangeably), to explain the past. Under Beard's influence, Robinson appeared to lean in that direction. In his 1908 Columbia University lecture *History*, he hailed Karl Marx for having made the "first and greatest contribution to the scientific study of history." While not explaining everything, economics "serves to explain far more of the phenomena of the past than any other single explanation ever offered." But his attraction to the economic interpretation of history was a transitory phase. Man was no more exclusively an economic than a political animal. Robinson's ambition to understand man in his full complexity underlay his interest in what he termed "the history of culture": "a history of the inner man, his range of knowledge, his tastes, his ideas of the world, and of himself." The content of his course offerings underwent a like shift from political history to an emphasis upon cultural and intellectual developments. The new focus reinforced his dissatisfaction with the traditional periodization of European history along chronological lines into so many self-contained time blocks. And as early as 1904 Robinson broke with that framework to introduce his famous course surveying the "Intellectual History of Western Europe."

Robinson did not take a great-books approach concentrating upon the high-level ideas of the major thinkers. His aim was rather to delineate the beliefs, values, and assumptions held by the commonality of more or less educated laymen. Significantly, he came to title the course the "History of the Intellectual Class in Western Europe." When first introduced, the course covered from the breakup of the Roman Empire to the French Revolution. But his wish to link the past with the present impelled him to extend the time span to include late-nineteenth-century and early-twentieth-century developments. More important, he was led by the genetic principle to push the starting date back first to the Greeks, then to the civilizations of the ancient Near East, finally to prehistoric man. "The Middle Ages, . . ." he would explain, "appear from a cultural standpoint, to be a sort of attenuated later Roman Empire. And the later Roman Empire witnessed the lapsing of borrowed Greek culture; and the Greeks, we now know, were pretty dependent on all the wonders that were achieved by Egyptians and Western Asiatics, who built on the fundamental discoveries of neolithic mankind, whom we must recognize incredible progressives compared with their predecessors. It took the race, with its humble origins, so long to make a hatchet to be held in the hand, then so long to set it in a handle, then so long and so recently to set the handle in the hatchet!"

Robinson's interest in the problem of cultural transmission drew him to the newer social sciences for explanatory tools. The findings of "prehistoric archeology" shed light upon "the whole perspective of *modern* change" by revealing how man during the thousands of years before written records existed had laid "the foundations of our present civ-

ilization." The study by anthropologists of the customs, beliefs, and institutions of primitive societies put into sharper relief the distinctive features of our own society. The work in comparative religion was demonstrating how every religion—including Christianity—was a "complex syncretism" of old and new. The "animal" psychologists, such as E. L. Thorndike of Columbia Teachers' College, were making possible differentiating those aspects of human behavior that were culturally derived from "the more primitive instincts which we inherit from our animal ancestors." His highest enthusiasm was for social psychology. Thus, he extolled George Herbert Mead for showing how the individual's "ego" was a "social product" resulting from this association with others and Gabriel Tarde for demonstrating how all that went to make up civilization was transmitted by "imitation." "Indeed," Robinson underlined, "the great and fundamental question of how mankind learns and disseminates his discoveries and misapprehensions—in short, the whole rationale of human civilization as distinguished from the life of the anthropoids—will never be understood without social psychology. . . ."

Robinson had a restless, inquiring mind that was constantly spinning off new ideas. But he lacked the drive for their systematic implementation. While the source of the difficulty remains not known, the evidence indicates that he was prone to recurring bouts of paralyzing depression—what he called "a fatigue neurosis." For a time he worked upon a comparative study of constitutional development in France, Germany, and the United States. Then he turned to expanding *An Introduction to the History of Western Europe* into an in-depth, multivolume account, but he abandoned that project. To "tell over the old tale a little better and a little more correctly than it has been told," he confessed to his publisher, "does not seem to me worth while." His new plan was "far more original and illuminating . . . really essentially novel": to reexamine European history "in the light of the past twenty-five years of achievement in anthropology, sociology and archeology and use as a cannon [sic] of selection those phases of the past that have some assignable relation to our interests and endeavors today." He, however, had a larger ambition than simply explaining past change. His hope was that history, refashioned along proper lines, could promote future change. "History has always adapted itself more or less servilely and unconsciously [sic] to the demands of the times. It has not yet adapted itself to our present needs and I am anxious to make a beginning toward an exploitation of the past in the interest of progress."

But the same mental block that would throughout his life keep Robinson from finishing any major research project prevented completion of the full-scale synthesis he had envisaged. *The New History*, when it appeared in 1912, was no more than a collection of loosely linked essays—mostly previously published articles revised to "illustrate a rather definite and novel point of view." Much of the text, therefore, consisted of reiteration of themes he had earlier developed. He reaffirmed that "history, in order to become scientific, had first to become historical"—that is, apply the "genetic" approach rather than traditional "episodal treatment of the past." And he called upon historians to substitute for the Rankean ideal of *"wie es eigentlich gewesen"* the goal of showing *"wie es eigentlich geworden":* to explain "how it really came about" rather than to describe "how it really was." He repeated his pleas for expanding the scope of historical study to include all of mankind's multifarious activities and experiences; he reemphasized the contribution that the social sciences could make to historical understanding. But the central theme—and what gave the work its éclat—was his appeal for the historian self-consciously to join in the contemporary struggle for human betterment. "The present," he proclaimed, "has hitherto been the willing victim of the past; the time has now come when it should turn on the past and exploit it in the interests of advance."

Robinson was too sophisticated simply to apply analogies from the past to the present. He similarly realized the impossibility of deriving historical laws like those in biology or physics, given the fragmentary data left from the past, the historian's inability to test experimentally his findings, and man's "devious ways and wandering desires." But history still had lessons to teach. His major target was the hallowed conservative dogma of the immutability of human nature. History showed how "the most extraordinary variety has existed and still exists in the habits, institutions, and feelings of various groups of mankind." That which the radical wished to alter and the conservative to preserve were not "constant and unalterable elements in our native outfit," but were the "artificially acquired" products of *"human nurture."* Most important, history revealed the extent of the progress that had been made. Although that progress was most strikingly exemplified in man's growing knowledge of, and thus control over, the natural world, there had been a steady advance toward a

more just social order. "Hitherto," Robinson concluded triumphantly, "the radical has appealed to the future, but now he can confidently rest his case on past achievement and current success. He can point to what has been done, he can cite what is being done, he can perceive as never before what remains to be done, and, lastly, he begins to see, as never before, how it will get done."

Drawing upon sociologist Lester Frank Ward's distinction between genetic and telic evolution, Robinson emphasized that until recently human progress had been largely *"unconscious."* For the bulk of man's existence on the planet, gains in the arts and skills of civilization were the accidental results of man's animal propensities of curiosity, tinkering, and imitation. What distinguished man from the lower animals was his unique ability to transmit his discoveries from generation to generation. While the Greeks were the first people to "use their minds freely," Greek thought became bogged down in the dead end of metaphysical speculation. In contrast with his formerly sympathetic account of the positive achievements of the Middle Ages, Robinson now dismissed those centuries as a time of intolerance, blind reliance upon accepted authority, and neglect of this world in favor of the next. Even the Renaissance "transcended relatively few of the ancient superstitions"; the Protestant reformers were still more the prisoners of the medieval outlook. The breakthrough came in the seventeenth century with the rise of experimental science and the accompanying belief that man's increasing knowledge could be purposefully applied to the improvement of his estate. These twin developments—science and the "idea of the possibility of indefinite progress through man's own conscious efforts"—inaugurated the modern age of ever-accelerating human advance.

At a philosophical level, Robinson owed much to William James, still more to his Columbia colleague and friend John Dewey. While an undergraduate at Harvard, he had been deeply impressed by James's conception that the mind was not a passive receptacle but an active force capable of intervening in, and thereby changing, the temporal process. For James, thinking was activated when the individual faced an unexpected or unfamiliar situation. Dewey's contribution was his call for society to apply the same creative intelligence for adapting to new conditions. Like Dewey, Robinson was convinced that the "inertia" of inherited beliefs and habits constituted the major obstacle to social progress; like Dewey, he rested his hopes for the future upon application of what he loosely—

or, to be more accurate, metaphorically—called the scientific method. But what gave *The New History* its impact was its message of reassurance to a generation torn between anxiety and hope. In the final pages Robinson cast off the historian's role to assume the mantle of prophet. History, he exulted, revealed "a mysterious unconscious impulse"—the *élan vital* of French philosopher Henri Bergson—at work that "has always been unsettling the existing conditions and pushing forward, groping after something more elaborate and intricate than what already existed." Most important, Robinson concluded, we now "realize that we can cooperate with and direct this innate force of change which has so long been silently operating"; we now know "that the conscious reformer who appeals to the future is the final product of a progressive order of things."

Published at the height of the progressive era, this paean to rationally guided social change struck a responsive chord. Although *The New History* only sold approximately 5,000 copies, this figure does not indicate the extent of its influence. Its message was most widely disseminated via the Committee on Social Studies of the Commission on the Reorganization of Secondary Education set up in 1913 by the National Education Association. Robinson was not simply a member of the committee, but was quoted extensively in its 1916 report. The committee took as its guiding principle that the role of social studies in the high school was to "contribute to the social welfare of the community." And its recommendations would set the pattern for the high school curriculum for at least the next generation. While the committee's most radical innovation was its recommendation of a new one-year course at the twelfth-grade level in "Problems of American Democracy" that would incorporate political science, economics, and sociology, history continued to occupy the center stage. But the history envisaged was Robinson's brand. Whereas one year was alloted to European history up through the middle of the seventeenth century, one year each was given to European history since and to American history. "History, too," the committee chairman explained, "must answer the test of good citizenship." Therefore, "recent history is more important than that of ancient times; the history of our own country than that of foreign lands; the record of our own institutions and activities than that of strangers; the labors and plans of the multitudes than the pleasures and dreams of the few."

At first Robinson's optimism survived the shock of World War I. As was true for most Amer-

ican academics, his sympathies lay with the Allies. Placing major responsibility for the conflict upon Germany, he blamed its educational system for inculcating, even among its intellectual elite, "archaic" notions of Teutonic supremacy, the virtues of war, and blind loyalty to the state. And he supported American entry, seeing "no way to win the Germans from their disastrous scheme of life, except through defeat." While the conflagration made "clear that a complete reconstruction of our institutions is absolutely essential," Robinson continued to hope that good might yet result. "The crisis or unexpected 'fix' in which a creature finds itself," he rationalized, "furnishes the test of its capacity of readjustment. In the case of man, crisis centers attention on unobserved or ill-understood factors in a situation and may happily lead to more complete control and thus to escape from pressing difficulties. The present war is a crisis of unprecedented magnitude, and is inevitably promoting thinking of unprecedented variety and depth in regard to man's woes, their origin, nature and remedy." That faith inspired his 1917 *Atlantic Monthly* article "The Threatened Eclipse of Free Speech," warning against making the war an excuse for repressing the free inquiry and discussion required for successfully adapting to new conditions. Resistance by "distracted revolutionaries," he emphasized, "cannot check the process; they can serve only to render the adjustments slower, more bungling and circuitous. . . ."

Hope soon turned into disillusionment. Despite his own prowar sympathies, Robinson himself became the target of attacks by superpatriots because of his too-balanced treatment of the background of the conflict in his 1916 high school textbook *Medieval and Modern Times.* He was appalled by Columbia's firing of three antiwar faculty; he was further alienated by his friend Charles A. Beard's resignation in protest. With the Columbia experience underlining, as he put it, "the obstacles which stand in the way of good work in our great universities as they are now organized," Robinson took the lead in promoting a "free and independent school of social science, designed to bridge the gap between the intellectual and capitalistic classes and the so-called working classes." He brought into the planning Beard, *New Republic* editor Herbert Croly, economists Wesley C. Mitchell and Alvin Johnson, and former Barnard College dean Emily James Putnam. To guarantee academic freedom, the new institution's board of trustees would include members from the faculty and be limited to dealing with financial matters. There would be no professional administrators; policy would be left to the democratic vote of the faculty. To avoid the intellectual fragmentation of the existing spectrum of university courses, the curriculum would deal exclusively with the problems of human behavior and social organization. What most appealed to Robinson was that the students would be adults who came not for the pecuniary advantages of a degree but from a wish to learn.

The New School for Social Research opened its door in February 1919. That spring Robinson, who was chairman of the executive board, resigned his Columbia professorship to devote his full time to the project. The faculty included, along with Robinson, Beard, and Mitchell, Thorstein Veblen in economics, Franz Boas's disciple A. A. Goldenweiser in anthropology, Horace M. Kallen in philosophy, and Harry Elmer Barnes in history. Despite what seemed a promising beginning, the New School was beset with worsening difficulties. From the start the founders had differing aims. Croly envisaged a Fabian-like think tank turning out practical solutions to current problems; Beard and Mitchell wanted major emphasis upon research; Robinson saw its function as teaching young adults to think critically. Personality conflicts among the instructional staff made faculty self-government unworkable. The absence of degree-granting authority limited its ability to attract serious students. Exacerbating these difficulties was the New School's shaky financial position. With the institution on the brink of collapse, Alvin Johnson took over its management, instituted a more traditional administrative structure, and introduced new courses, mostly of the popular psychology and self-improvement type, to attract fee-paying students. Disappointed at this new direction—and convinced by the similarly disillusioned Beard that he could exert more influence via his writing than from the podium—Robinson withdrew from active involvement.

Robinson's most ambitious—and most successful—attempt to reach a wide audience came in 1921 with the publication of *The Mind in the Making*. This work reflected his dismay—or, to be more accurate, his apprehension—over what he bitterly termed "current stupidities and partisanship." The hope of reformers that the war would speed realization of their dreams of social reconstruction were dashed when the Wilson administration inaugurated the return to normalcy that would be continued by its Republican successor. The economy was in disarray: the postarmistice runaway inflation had provoked bitter labor-management strife and was followed by a sharp recession beginning in mid-1920. The war-inflamed passion for conformity spurred a continuing assault upon all those not measuring up to one hundred percent Americanism. Written in this atmosphere, *The Mind in the Making* was suffused with a sense of crisis. "The world seems to demand," Robinson lamented, "a moral and economic regeneration which it is dangerous to postpone, but as yet impossible to imagine, let alone direct." Whereas *The New History* had exuded confidence in the inevitability of progress, the dominant theme of the new book was the obstacles in the way of achieving it. History was no longer the triumphant record of man's past advance; the historian was, rather, struck with "the ease with which ancient misapprehensions are transmitted," with "the difficulty of launching a newer and clearer and truer idea of anything."

In form *The Mind in the Making* purported to trace historically the development of civilization in its broad sense: men's language, arts, skills, and techniques, their institutions, beliefs, and ideas—all, in short, that differentiated contemporary man from his animal forebears. As in *The New History*—though in more long-winded fashion—Robinson described how for most of mankind's existence such progress that was achieved was due largely to accident rather than to conscious direction. The application of what he alternatively but synonymously termed "Intelligence," the "scientific attitude," or "critical thought" was a recent phenomenon, dating from the seventeenth-century scientific revolution. The crucial question, therefore, for the historian aspiring to explain *"wie es eigentlich geworden"* is why the emergence of the new complex of attitudes associated with experimental science and the idea of progress. But Robinson failed even to deal with that problem. And in contrast with his former reputation for careful scholarship, he was guilty of sloppiness on factual details. The history side had become so much trimming; his purpose was to write a tract for the times—or what Robinson acknowledged in a moment of self-reflection, "a sort of apologia pro vita." The crux of the message was that while the new technology resulting from rapidly increasing scientific knowledge had revolutionized the environment, men's institutions and values had not kept pace; "unless thought be raised to a far higher plane than hitherto," he warned, "some great setback to civilization is inevitable."

Robinson drew upon his wide reading in the social sciences for explanation of this cultural lag.

The so-called animal psychologists had demon-strated the continued influence upon human be-havior of man's simian heritage. The Boas school of anthropologists confirmed the findings of the social psychologists about how the larger part of an individual's opinions and standards was the prod-uct "of unthinking absorption from the social en-vironment." Freudian psychoanalytical theory—which Robinson hailed as offering important new insights into human behavior—revealed the extent to which conduct and thinking were influenced by "hidden impulses and desires and secret longings." Even much of so-called reasoning was simply "ra-tionalizing": *finding arguments for going on believing as we already do.* With a bow to John Dewey, Thor-stein Veblen, and Italian sociologist Vilfredo Pare-to, Robinson dismissed as rationalizations "almost all that had passed for social science, political econ-omy, politics, and ethics in the past." His largest debt was to the English anthropologist E. B. Tylor, whose landmark work, *Primitive Culture* (1871), had showed how much in modern civilization was an anachronistic holdover from a more backward age. "*In general,*" Robinson underscored, "*those ideas which are still almost universally accepted in regard to man's nature, his proper conduct, and his relations to God and his fellows are far more ancient and far less critical than those which have to do with the movement of the stars, the stratification of the rocks and the life of plants and animals.*"

Everywhere Robinson looked he found the stultifying effects of outmoded and obsolete ways of thinking. He echoed Havelock Ellis in denounc-ing the "impurity complex" about sex inherited from the Christian fathers and the Middle Ages. He lamented how at the time improvements in transportation and communication were knitting the peoples of the globe into ever closer interde-pendence, nationalism had produced the bloodiest war in history. A participant in the discussion group that became the nucleus of the Foreign Pol-icy Association, he poured scorn upon the senators who had opposed American membership in the League of Nations for blindly clinging to "old no-tions of noble isolation and national sovereignty" that may have been suitable a century before but which had become "magnificently criminal." His sharpest attack was against the wastefulness and injustices of the existing industrial order. He was much taken with Veblen's indictment of how the predatory values of businessmen blocked full uti-lization of modern technology to produce abun-dance for all; his reading of the English socialist R. H. Tawney sharpened his condemnation of

"The Sickness of an Acquisitive Society." Nor was there any issue on which critical thinking was more sure to suffer attack. "Business indeed has almost become our religion. . . ." But there was no way, he declared, "the present system can be made to work satisfactorily on the basis of ideas of a hundred or a hundred thousand years ago."

In what appeared an anticlimax, however, Robinson had no proposals to make beyond the cultivation of "*a critical open-minded attitude.*" "I have no reforms to recommend," he admitted, "except the liberation of Intelligence, which is the first and most essential one." Although many readers were disappointed at this failure to spell out remedies for the ills he so graphically portrayed, Robinson's justification was that the study of man and his ways still remained in its infancy. "One cannot but feel a little queasy when he uses the expression 'social science,' " he confessed, "because it seems as if we had not as yet got anywhere near a real science of man." Any proposed solutions for social problems, therefore, could be no more than temporary and provisional. The more important reason for Robin-son's failure to offer solutions was that he was no radical in the conventional political sense. Reveal-ing is the fact that when he drew up his list of the greatest Americans, he ranked Theodore Roose-velt second to Lincoln among the political leaders. And he was as hostile to the dogmatisms of the left as to the standpattism of the right. "I am no social reformer," he confided to a former student. "I be-lieve that intelligence underlies the kind of good-ness we most need nowadays in making fresh adjustments. I have a tendency to share and impart what I learn but no great anxiety to 'better' my fellow-beings. That desire has come to seem a very arrogant and crude enterprise based usually upon some suspicious psychic mechanism. Reformers of the more fanatical type approach paranoiacs."

Although not wishing "to be confused with the naive uplifter," Robinson was too warmly sym-pathetic a person to fall into the easy cynicism of the detached observer of human follies. His am-bition remained "the humanizing of science, or rather, of our best knowledge, which is what science is, not merely so-called natural science." What was new was the elitist twist given this ambition. The moral he drew from history in *The Mind in the Mak-ing* was that man by nature was timid, unadven-turous, enamored of the tried and true and suspicious of the new. Progress was due to the handful of exceptional individuals who stood apart from, and against, the average of their kind. Much of the book's popularity lay in its appeal to the self-appointed enlightened who took pride in their superiority over the common lot of their fellows. And Robinson's own disillusionment with the vox populi was heightened by the rising tide of the Fundamentalist attack upon evolutionary theory, a campaign which he saw as a threat to science, the scientific outlook, and thus the possibilities of any further advance. He reacted by placing the major blame for the repression of dissent upon the tyranny of mass opinion; he even equated democracy with "herd" rule. "Now," he complained, "in all plans for general betterment we have for the first time in the history of the world to take in everybody. We have to listen to everyone's objections and take account of everyone's prejudices and make head against everybody's ignorance. We have to meet the tastes of the most tasteless and overcome the fears of the most cowardly."

In one sense, however, Robinson thought the intellectual inertness of the multitude an advantage. Since only a small number—"a few hundred thousand at best in our broad land," he estimated—were even interested in "problems of general significance," all that was required was to convert that minority of opinion shapers and "the majority would spontaneously accede and follow." He put forth his plan in an address to the June 1922 meeting of the American Association for the Advancement of Science and then expanded it into the book *The Humanizing of Knowledge*, published the following year. In this work he pictured as the major obstacle to social reconstruction the failure of even most educated laymen to grasp the significance of the new discoveries about man and his world. Scientific work had become increasingly compartmentalized and fragmented; most scholars wrote for a narrow audience of fellow specialists. The solution, therefore, was "a new class of writers"—"re-assorters, selectors, combiners and illuminators"—to explain to the layman "what is already known or in the way to get known." Robinson arranged with the Workers Education Bureau of America to sponsor a series of 200- to 300-page popularizations of the more important recent work in the natural and social sciences. His list of proposed authors included Dewey, Veblen, Ellis, behavioral psychologist J. B. Watson, and astronomer Harlow Shapely and physiologist Walter B. Cannon from Harvard; the titles of the proposed volumes included *Evolution, Starlight, Glands, The Green Leaf, The Atom, Social Life of Insects, Old Age,* and *Economics*.

At the same time Robinson reaffirmed that history, properly written, had its own vital contribution to make. The enemy was reverence for the past: "The old drags us down like a chronic disease. . . ." The historian could, and should, free mankind from bondage to its continued sway by showing how much of what people had once believed eternal truths had fallen by the wayside. Most important, the historian could, and should, expose the obsolescence of current beliefs by showing "their often quite stupid origin." "We cannot," he summed up, "attack our political, religious, economic, educational and social standards directly. . . . They may all, however, issue into a clearer light when we think how everything that now goes on has come about. So history might be the great illuminator. As yet it is highly imperfect; but someday it might well become the most potent instrument for human regeneration." As an example of what he had in mind, Robinson pointed to Veblen's analysis in his *Absentee Ownership* (1923) of the state as an instrument of exploitation by, and for, the ruling class. He was even more enthusiastic about the indictment of religious intolerance, nationalist prejudices, and selfish privilege by H. G. Wells in his "wondrous" *The Outline of History* (1919-1920). And Wells, finding a kindred spirit, reciprocated by contributing an introduction to the 1923 British edition of *The Mind in the Making*, hailing Robinson's "leadership"—"at once bold and sceptical"—in challenging men's obsolete "assumptions."

As the 1920s went on, Robinson retreated from the public sphere into his own private world. When he did write for publication, his targets were the repressiveness of the middle-class family that was the staple of the popularized Freudianism dominant in the decade, the narrowness of small-town life as revealed by novelists such as Theodore Dreiser, Sherwood Anderson, and Sinclair Lewis, and the continued strength of Christian "superstitions." By mid-decade the public issues that had formerly loomed so large may not have been solved, but at least they had become not immediately menacing. The Locarno agreements raised new hopes for an era of peace ahead. The prosperity of the Coolidge years appeared to promise relief from the worst abuses of industrial society. Even Fundamentalism as a political force appeared on the wane. But the deeper reason for Robinson's withdrawal into near-silence during his last years was that he felt the strains of the same culture shock in the face of accelerating change that he described. During the early years of the century, he recalled in nostalgic, even elegiac, tones, the historian lived in a stable world that looked forward to the triumph of liberalism, democracy, and nationalism and saw in the advance of science and technology the guarantee of unlimited future progress. Those verities were gone: "our old moorings are lost and we are tossed about on the waves of illimitable doubt. Former assurances turn into questions; and solutions into problems."

No question proved more troublesome for Robinson than the problem of the validity of historical knowledge. Notwithstanding his calls for a "New History," Robinson had remained wedded to the methodological assumptions of late-nineteenth-century scientific history. When revising the Rankean ideal, he retained the *"eigentlich"*: the goal was to explain how things "really" came about. As time passed, he began to edge toward relativism. "What onlookers call 'impartial' history and professionals call 'objective,' " he chided, "is merely history without an object." More radically, he denied the possibility of "a search for facts regardless of any preferences or aims, except the discovery of raw truth"; he went so far as to acknowledge that historians' selection of facts was influenced by "many unrecognized assumptions." But he still affirmed that their duty was to provide as "authentic" an account as possible "based upon the best and most critical information we can get." History, in short, "may be both true and useful." By his 1929 American Historical Association presidential address, however, he had abandoned even that hope. Man, he reminded his startled audience, has always been prone to rationalizing, to putting the most favorable gloss upon his behavior; "a certain duplicity or dissimulation has been an inevitable concomitant of human development from a wild beast." How then can we take at face value the records left from the past? "In dealing with a great part of human history," he answered, "we must be contented with the face and appearance of things, and can not hope to gain much knowledge of what was carrying on underneath."

Robinson died on 16 February 1936, of a heart attack at his home on Riverside Drive in New York City. He left an unfinished manuscript that his former student Harry Elmer Barnes saw through the press the following year under the title *The Human Comedy As Devised and Directed by Mankind Itself*. The bulk of the text appears to have been written years before. Large chunks were taken almost verbatim from earlier published books and articles. Those segments gave the work its aura of optimism about the future if men could emancipate themselves from outmoded ways of thinking. But he now admitted that the possibility of that happening was a matter of faith rather than a histor-

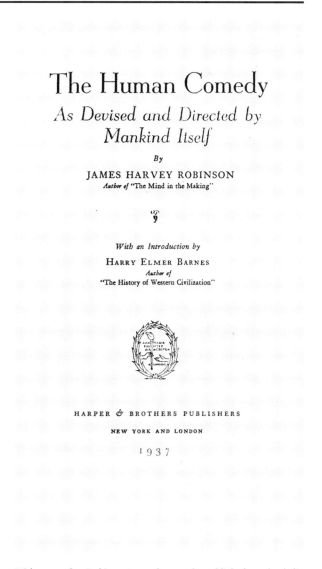

Title page for Robinson's posthumously published work, dedicated "To Edward Potts Cheyney, Fellow Student of the Comedy"

ically validated certainty. And when Robinson dealt with contemporary developments his disenchantment and pessimism were painfully apparent. He assailed the New Deal for shying away from the planning required for achieving an economy of abundance; the Roosevelt administration's program remained based upon "the bankrupt and discredited 'pain economy' of scarcity." He was dismayed at the triumph of totalitarianism in Europe, Stalin's as much as Hitler's and Mussolini's. Given the apathy and ignorance of the masses— "the majority of men range from mediocrity to imbecility"—he questioned the continued viability of democracy even in the United States. Perhaps if management of the crucial economic sphere were turned over to Veblen's technocrats, "a chastened democracy might suffice as a means of political control for other aspects of life." And his hopes for averting a repeat of the disaster of World War I were strained by the "ominous evidence to the contrary right now."

What overall evaluation can be made of Robinson? As a champion of the "New History," he made an important contribution to freeing American historical scholarship from its late-nineteenth-century rigid factualism, narrow legal/constitutional/institutional focus, and stylistic aridity. Through his involvement in curricular reform at the high school level, even more through his textbooks, he did much to improve the quality of historical instruction. His most direct impact was in the classroom. His success as a teacher was a triumph of personality over style. Although he had a sharp, if dry, wit, he exploited no dramatic tricks. He stood with his arms closed looking up at the ceiling, speaking in a slow drawl; his lectures were discursive, even rambling. But a quarter of a century of undergraduates—at least the brighter ones—came out of his courses with a deepened appreciation of man's long struggle to gain mastery over himself and his world. And students in his graduate seminars found his mixture of solid training in research techniques with iconoclasm toward conventional pieties a stimulating experience. The list of those whom he influenced reads like a who's who in the development of intellectual and social history in the United States: on the American side, Charles A. Beard, Arthur M. Schlesinger, Sr., Dixon Ryan Fox, and Harold U. Faulkner; on the European side, Carl L. Becker, Lynn Thorndike, James T. Shotwell, Carlton J. H. Hayes, Preserved Smith, Harry Elmer Barnes, and J. Salwyn Shapiro.

His published legacy is, however, thin. Although highly regarded by contemporaries for the depth and breadth of his learning, he produced no major work of research that could serve as a model for the "new history." His much-talked-of magnum opus tracing the intellectual history of Western Europe never materialized and appears never to have been pursued in any systematic way. His high school texts were simply abridged versions of his college-level surveys. And while the exigencies of the marketplace forced him to update those works, there were no significant revisions in approach or substance. As a result, his texts had lost by the 1920s their innovative quality as they were overtaken by rivals which followed in a more thoroughgoing way

the path that he had pioneered. Similarly dated are what should be termed his philosophical speculations on the meaning of human existence. Robinson was no profound thinker; his forte was in picking up the latest fashions in thinking that would appeal to the intellectual class of his own time. His optimism, his belief in the possibility of unlimited progress through science and the application of the scientific method, fitted the mood of the Progressive Era. In the 1920s he appealed to the self-consciously enlightened who felt beleaguered by the forces of obscurantism. The Depression-spurred fascination with social engineering stimulated a flurry of renewed interest in his work during the 1930s. Since then, however, his books have languished, largely unread, upon the library shelves.

Robinson's most lasting influence has been upon the rationale for why one should study history. Only the New Left goes so far as to take the position that the historian should consciously enlist in the barricades to fight for the good, the true, and the beautiful. And most present-day historians concede that history offers no more than an imperfect guide because no two situations are exactly alike. Still, the dominant theme in current discussions of the value of history remains the conviction that knowledge of the past can shed light upon present conditions by revealing their sources and can thereby improve our ability to shape the future. Historians continue to assume that man is a rational being capable of learning from his experiences, and that all problems are solvable through the application of intelligence. As declining enrollments in history courses demonstrate, however, many present-day students do not accept these comfortable, and comforting, assumptions. Nowhere is the gap between the current generation and Robinson's more strikingly revealed than in the contemporary disillusionment with science. What can be more ironical than when extolling the possibilities of future scientific advance, Robinson took as his prime example the blessings that would result when physicists unlocked the secrets of the atom. By unleashing that force, science raised anew—and in more perplexing fashion than Robinson could imagine—the question of what is the good of history.

Bibliography:

A Bibliography of the Faculty of Columbia University 1880-1930 (New York: Columbia University Press, 1931), pp. 91-97.

Biography:
Luther V. Hendricks, *James Harvey Robinson: Teacher of History* (New York: King's Crown Press, 1946).

References:
Harry Elmer Barnes, "James Harvey Robinson," in *American Masters of Social Sciences: An Approach to the Study of the Social Sciences Through a Neglected Field of Biography,* edited by Howard W. Odum (New York: Holt, 1927), pp. 321-408;

Crane Brinton, "The New History: Twenty-Five Years After," *Journal of Social Philosophy,* 1 (January 1936): 134-153;

Luther V. Hendricks, "James Harvey Robinson and the New School for Social Research," *Journal of Higher Education,* 20 (January 1949): 1-11, 58;

John Higham and others, *History* (Englewood Cliffs, N.J.: Prentice-Hall, 1965);

J. R. Pole, "The New History and the Sense of Social Purpose in American Historical Writing," *Transactions of the Royal Historical Society,* fifth series, 23 (1973): 221-242;

Rae W. Rohfeld, "James Harvey Robinson and the New History," Ph.D. dissertation, Western Reserve University, 1965;

Dorothy Ross, "The 'New History' and the 'New Psychology': An Early Attempt at Psychohistory," in *The Hofstadter Aegis: A Memorial,* edited by Stanley Elkins and Eric McKitrick (New York: Knopf, 1974), pp. 207-234;

Morton G. White, *Social Thought in America; The Revolt Against Formalism* (New York: Viking, 1949);

Esmond Wright, "History: The 'New' and the Newer," *Sewanee Review,* 49 (October-December 1941): 479-491.

Papers:
Most of Robinson's papers disappeared after his death. Notebooks of his European travels in the early 1890s are at the Columbia University Library. Some correspondence may be found in the Central Files of Columbia University and among the papers of many contemporary historians.

Theodore Roosevelt

(27 October 1858-6 January 1919)

J. W. Cooke
Tennessee State University

*SELECTED BOOKS: *The Summer Birds of the Adirondacks in Franklin County, N.Y.,* by Roosevelt and H. D. Minot (Salem, Mass.: Privately printed, 1877);

Notes on Some of the Birds of Oyster Bay, Long Island (New York: Privately printed, 1879);

The Naval War of 1812; or, The History of the United States Navy during the Last War with Great Britain (New York: Putnam's, 1882); republished as *The Naval Operations of the War Between Great Britain and the United States* (London: Low, 1910);

Hunting Trips of a Ranchman (New York & London: Putnam's, 1885; London: Kegan Paul, Trench, 1886);

Thomas Hart Benton (Boston: Houghton Mifflin, 1886);

Essays on Practical Politics (New York & London: Putnam's, 1888);

Gouverneur Morris (Boston & New York: Houghton Mifflin, 1888);

Ranch Life and the Hunting-trail (New York: Century, 1888; London: Unwin, 1888);

The Winning of the West; An Account of the Exploration and Settlement of Our Country from the Alleghanies to the Pacific, 4 volumes (New York: Putnam's, 1889-1896);

New York (London & New York: Longmans, Green, 1891);

The Wilderness Hunter: An Account of the Big Game of the United States and Its Chase With Horse (New York: Putnam's, 1893);

Hero Tales from American History, by Roosevelt and Henry Cabot Lodge (New York: Century, 1895);

American Ideals, and Other Essays, Social and Political (New York & London: Putnam's, 1897);

The Rough Riders (New York: Scribners, 1899; London: Kegan Paul, Trench, Trübner, 1899);

Oliver Cromwell (New York: Scribners, 1900; London: Constable, 1900);

---

* This list excludes separately published speeches and other brief pamphlets.

Theodore Roosevelt. This portrait by Underwood & Underwood was purportedly Roosevelt's favorite photograph of himself (The Bettmann Archive)

The Strenuous Life: Essays and Addresses (New York: Century, 1900; London: Richards, 1902);

California Addresses (San Francisco: California Promotion Committee, 1903);

Outdoor Pastimes of an American Hunter (limited edition, New York: Scribners, 1903; New York: Scribners, 1905; London: Longmans, Green, 1905; enlarged, New York: Scribners, 1908);

Addresses and Presidential Messages of Theodore Roo-

sevelt, 1902-1904 (New York & London: Putnam's, 1904);

Good Hunting (New York & London: Harper, 1907);

Addresses and Papers, edited by Willis Fletcher Johnson (New York: Sun Dial, 1908);

The Roosevelt Policy; Speeches, Letters and State Papers, Relating to Corporate Wealth and Closely Allied Topics, of Theodore Roosevelt, 2 volumes (New York: Current Literature, 1908); enlarged edition, edited by William Griffith, 3 volumes (New York: Current Literature, 1919);

Outlook Editorials (New York: Outlook, 1909);

African Game Trails, An Account of the African Wanderings of an American Hunter-Naturalist (New York: Scribners, 1910; London: Murray, 1910);

African and European Addresses (New York & London: Putnam's, 1910);

American Problems (New York: Outlook, 1910);

The New Nationalism (New York: Outlook, 1910);

Realizable Ideals (The Earl Lectures) (San Francisco: Whittaker & Ray-Wiggin, 1912);

Theodore Roosevelt: An Autobiography (New York: Macmillan, 1913);

Progressive Principles: Selections from Addresses Made During the Presidential Campaign of 1912, edited by Elmer H. Youngman (New York: Progressive National Service, 1913);

History as Literature, and Other Essays (New York: Scribners, 1913; London: Murray, 1914);

Life-histories of African Game Animals, 2 volumes, by Roosevelt and Edmund Heller (New York: Scribners, 1914; London: Murray, 1915);

Through the Brazilian Wilderness (New York: Scribners, 1914; London: Murray, 1914);

America and the World War (New York: Scribners, 1915; London: Murray, 1915);

A Book-lover's Holidays in the Open (New York: Scribners, 1916; London: Murray, 1916);

Fear God and Take Your Own Part (New York: Doran, 1916; London: Hodder & Stoughton, 1916);

Americanism and Preparedness. Speeches, July to November, 1916 (New York: Mail and Express Job Print, 1916);

The Foes of Our Own Household (New York: Doran, 1917);

National Strength and International Duty (Princeton: Princeton University Press, 1917);

The Great Adventure: Present-Day Studies in American Nationalism (New York: Scribners, 1918; London: Murray, 1919);

Average Americans (New York & London: Putnam's, 1919);

Newer Roosevelt Messages: Speeches, Letters and Magazine Articles Dealing with the War, Before and After, and Other Vital Topics, edited by William Griffith (New York: Current Literature, 1919);

Roosevelt in the Kansas City Star: War-time Editorials by Theodore Roosevelt (Boston & New York: Houghton Mifflin, 1921);

Campaigns and Controversies (New York: Scribners, 1926);

East of the Sun and West of the Moon, by Roosevelt and Kermit Roosevelt (New York & London: Scribners, 1926);

Literary Essays (New York: Scribners, 1926);

Social Justice and Popular Rule: Essays, Addresses, and Public Statements Relating to the Progressive Movement (New York: Scribners, 1926);

Theodore Roosevelt's Diaries of Boyhood and Youth (New York & London: Scribners, 1928);

Colonial Policies of the United States (Garden City: Doubleday, Doran, 1937);

The Hunting and Exploring Adventures of Theodore Roosevelt, edited by Donald Day (New York: Dial, 1955).

Collection: *The Works of Theodore Roosevelt*, National Edition, 20 volumes (New York: Scribners, 1926).

Theodore Roosevelt was probably America's closest approximation to a man of letters who was also a man of affairs. Roosevelt possessed an extraordinarily strong intellect coupled with the energies and aggressiveness of a Renaissance prince. Such a combination in American public life is rare and a little alarming. It was perhaps well for the republic that the twenty-sixth president was a moral man and a confirmed republican.

A prolific author, he wrote on such diverse topics as the bird life of the Adirondacks, ranching in Dakota Territory, hunting big game on two continents, exploring in South America, the Spanish-American War, the Progressive movement, military preparedness, his own life, and, incidentally, American and English history. He also reviewed fiction and nonfiction for such magazines as the *Atlantic Monthly, Scribner's,* and the *Outlook* and carried on a voluminous correspondence with dozens of friends, admirers, scholars, politicians, and with his own children.

No one is able to say when Roosevelt's interest in the American past began, but it is plausible to assume that he was early stimulated by stories of ancestral exploits. The Roosevelts and the Bullochs were both families of long residence in the United

States, and many of them had played an honorable role in its wars and politics. They were people of substance and not unconscious of their good repute. The youthful Roosevelt was also an enthusiastic reader. The novels of Mayne Reid and J. G. Wood and the *Niebelungenlied*, for instance, remained vivid for him throughout his life. Francis Parkman's *France and England in North America* was also a childhood delight, and the Boston historian (whom Roosevelt later called "the greatest—of our two or three first class historians who devoted himself to American history") was probably the most important literary influence in directing Roosevelt's curiosity toward his country's history.

The War for Southern Independence, that most tragic and intense of American conflicts, raised questions in the young Roosevelt's mind that continued to preoccupy him throughout his life. His father was a firm supporter of the Union; his mother favored the Confederate cause. Grandmother Bulloch and his Aunt Anna, both residents of the Roosevelt household, also declared for the Confederates, and two of his mother's brothers served with distinction in the Confederate Navy. Childhood visits to Europe and the Near East enlarged his intellectual horizon and suggested in still other ways the uniqueness of his native land.

A well-nourished childhood curiosity about the past flowered during his Harvard years (1876-1880), although there were no upper-division courses in American history. The young patrician had only a semester's exposure to the discipline during his sophomore year when he was required to attend two weekly lectures given by a Mr. Macvane and to read Edward A. Freeman's *General History of the World* (to page 272), Henry Flanders's *An Exposition of the Constitution of the United States*, and Alexander Charles Ewald's *The Crown and its Advisors*. Roosevelt, however, continued what Edmund Morris has called his "avidly eclectic reading" and earned a reputation among his classmates for his knowledge of the American past. TR, however, wanted to become a naturalist after the fashion of John James Audubon or C. Hart Merriam, but instruction leading to such a career was not to be had at Harvard. Altogether, Roosevelt later complained, there was little in his studies that "helped me in after-life." It is significant that he devoted a good deal more space in his *Autobiography* (1913) to the boxers he had known, and to Will Dow and Bill Sewall, two Maine guides of his acquaintance, than to President Charles W. Eliot and the Harvard faculty.

His last two years at Harvard were made un-

usually difficult by two tumultuous events. First, his father ("the best man I ever knew") died. This had the effect of cutting the young Roosevelt off from the most vivid, trusted, and influential interpreter of the past he had ever known. And second, he married the Boston beauty Alice Hathaway Lee.

Before marriage he had already written one or two chapters of his first full-length book, *The Naval War of 1812; or, The History of the United States Navy during the Last War with Great Britain* (1882). He continued research while honeymooning in Europe and received much help from uncle Irvine Bulloch, ex-Confederate midshipman and Liverpool merchant. After the Roosevelts returned to the United States, claimed Owen Wister, TR completed the book "mostly standing on one leg at the bookcases in his New York City house, the other leg crossed behind, toe touching the floor, heedless of dinner engagements and the flight of time." The publishers (G. P. Putnam's Sons) received the manuscript on 3 December 1881, one month after Roosevelt had been elected to the New York Assembly. He was twenty-three.

Reviews were favorable, and the book went through three editions within a year of publication. Royalties were minimal, but the young American was signally honored when the British publisher of William L. Clowes's *A History of the Royal Navy* asked him to write the chapter devoted to the War of 1812 for the next edition.

The Naval War of 1812 announces several recurring themes of Roosevelt's historical writing. Perhaps influenced by Henry Adams, he condemned Jefferson and Madison for their "criminal neglect" of the armed forces, although he later admitted to William P. Trent that he had perhaps been too hard on Jefferson. He offered a patriotic, though reasoned, account of U.S. naval successes in the conflict and expressed unstinting admiration for the fighting tars who achieved them. Valor always claimed his respect. His praise for the Kentucky and Ohio frontiersmen who fought and died under General William Henry Harrison as "hardy and restless pioneers of our race" and his mistaken assumption that Major General Sir Edward Pakenham's defeat below New Orleans could be attributed to Tennessee sharpshooters foretell his continuing admiration for westerners. Roosevelt showed himself to be an Anglo-Saxonist, given to viewing the "lesser breeds" with a certain condescension, and a Federalist-Whig who nevertheless professed a belief in the common man's reliability. His pronounced penchant for moralizing also makes its appearance in *The Naval War of 1812*.

Roosevelt's life underwent a second tumultuous turn in 1883 with the birth of his first child, Alice, and the almost simultaneous deaths of his wife and mother on the same day, 14 February 1884. He first sought release from his pain by immersing himself in politics and then, in the summer of 1884, turned to the demanding, intensely physical life of a rancher in the Dakota Territory. He spent his winters in New York. Thanks to the influence of Henry Cabot Lodge, Roosevelt was asked to write a biography of Thomas Hart Benton for the American Statesmen series. The manuscript was written, says historian John Gable, "between hunting trips and work on the range, far from libraries and manuscript collections," and completed in three or four months. "I feel," wrote TR with some embarrassment, "a little appalled over the Benton. . . ."

Nevertheless, the book was published in 1886 and received generally favorable reviews. Regrettably, it is almost entirely political history; there is precious little of "Old Bullion" outside the Senate.

Roosevelt on a roundup, Minnesota, 1885 (photograph by Ingersoll)

In the recounting of Benton's early years in Tennessee and Missouri, there is obvious respect for the fierce courage of the Trans-Appalachian pioneers, a limited concern for the red men, a strong sense of the inevitability of a white victory in any contest with the Indians, and a continuing fascination with the ethnic and racial diversity of American life. Altogether, *Thomas Hart Benton* is a superficial book, best read as a preparatory exercise for the multivolume *Winning of the West*.

Roosevelt returned to the East for good shortly after publication of *Thomas Hart Benton*. Its success persuaded John T. Morse, Jr., editor of the American Statesmen series, to solicit a second volume from Roosevelt. *Gouverneur Morris* was written in 1887 (mostly at Oyster Bay, Long Island, after his marriage to Edith Kermit Carow, with whom he had a large and energetic family of children). The biography was published the following year. Although denied access to the Morris papers by the family, Roosevelt made good use of the Timothy Pickering, John Jay, and Jared Sparks collections, and the Morris diary. The book remained the "standard work for many decades" according to John Gable, although it is uneven and sometimes superficial. Yet *Gouverneur Morris* displays two of Roosevelt's most significant strengths as a historian: a passionate interest in individuals rather than in such amorphous abstractions as movements or forces and a real talent for social history. His chapters on French society before the Revolution are vivid and well written. And, of course, Roosevelt moralized. Books were proving a "bully pulpit."

In March 1888, Roosevelt signed a contract with Putnam's for what would one day be *The Winning of the West*—a project he intended to span the years between Daniel Boone's migration across the Appalachians (1767) and the Battle of San Jacinto (1836). The origins of Roosevelt's interest in this particular time and in these particular people is conjectural. Edmund Morris plausibly suggests that his reading of Parkman and of James Bryce's *The American Commonwealth* (1888), the "racial variety of the West" which he encountered as a rancher, and his reading of Western history helped determine the emphasis.

Volume one (written at his Oyster Bay estate Sagamore Hill and published in 1889) was finished before Christmas 1888, just after the election of President Benjamin Harrison for whom TR had campaigned. Roosevelt at once began volume two and completed the manuscript on 1 April 1889, immediately prior to assuming his duties as U.S. civil service commissioner in Washington. He was acutely aware of the importance of what he was doing. "I know," he wrote George H. Putnam in January 1890, "that my chance of making a permanent literary reputation depends on how I do this big work. . . ." Volume three was completed in 1894; the fourth and final volume was published two years later. Although TR made some preparation for two more volumes, they never appeared. His narrative ends with Pike's Expedition of 1807.

Appropriately, the first volume is dedicated to Roosevelt's acknowledged master, Francis Parkman. "If there be a text," TR wrote in the introduction, "it is that the coming in of the whites [to the Trans-Appalachian region] was not to be stayed by any force in America." The spread of the English-speaking peoples across the world, he wrote, was the most significant event of the last three centuries. Roosevelt was fond of comparing the epic migrations of the Germanic peoples with those of American westerners. The ferocity and mobility of the latter astounded and delighted him. "The fathers," he wrote in a typical passage, "followed Boone or fought at King's Mountain; the sons marched south with Jackson to overcome the Creeks and beat back the British; the grandsons died at the Alamo or charged to victory at San Jacinto."

Roosevelt found the white-Indian struggle fascinating. He was no uncritical admirer of the native American. They were, he believed, more ferocious than either the Zulu or the Maori. Although their cruelties were sickening, their courage was magnificent. Their conquerors, the frontiersmen, were no less esteemed. Significantly, Roosevelt referred to himself as a "frontiersman." He was not disposed to apologize for the victors. "The most ultimately righteous of all wars," he proclaimed, "is a war with savages, though it is apt to be also the most terrible and inhuman." The Indians, he believed, had subsequently been treated with an unparalleled generosity by the victors.

In his political analysis (an inconsequential part of these volumes) Roosevelt remained the good Federalist-Whig. He deplored the impotence of the Confederation government, for instance, and praised the centralizing features of the Constitution. And he expressed an honest but conventional admiration for Washington and Lincoln, the greatest of all Americans in his opinion.

Roosevelt preferred to write of the Trans-Appalachian West. The finest and most brilliant writing he ever did is found in those chapters that deal with the "men of the Western Waters" at war, their day-by-day existence, and their unique mindset.

These chapters were truly, as he wrote, a "labor of love."

The Winning of the West was reviewed respectfully. Writing in the *American Historical Review*, Frederick Jackson Turner (later to become a friend of TR's) noted Roosevelt's inadequacies: an insufficient use of foreign sources and the famous Draper Collection of Western material at the Wisconsin State Historical Society, a relative indifference to institutions (the Vandalia and Yazoo companies, for example) in the development of the frontier, hasty proofreading, faulty use of citations and sources, and what Turner called "occasional whipping together of material." The author was accused of being a romantic (whatever the term may have meant) and a moralizer who used history "as a text for a sermon to a stiff-necked generation." He was, moreover, unfair to Thomas Jefferson. Yet Turner liked much of what he read. He praised Roosevelt for exercising the skills of a "practised historian." *The Winning of the West* was a "real service" because its author had "rescued a whole movement of American development from the hands of unskilled annalists. . . ."

While researching and writing *The Winning of the West*, Roosevelt also undertook the history *New York*, published in 1891 as part of the Historic Towns series edited by Edward A. Freeman. A preoccupation with ethnicity and a new concern for the "social dynamics" of immigration characterize the book. Roosevelt's flair for social history was also evident. Yet the book is decidedly aware of the present. The author warns of the "grinding poverty" endured by elements of the city's population and expresses concern for a "seeming increase in . . . inequality." The intelligent and virtuous were lectured on their civic duties.

Public life, however, continued to exercise a superior fascination for Roosevelt. He accepted a position as president of the Board of Police Commissioners of New York City in 1895, but left in relief two years later to become assistant secretary of the navy. He resigned this office in May 1898 at the commencement of the Spanish-American War, helped organize and train the Rough Riders, served with conspicuous bravery in Cuba, and returned home in September. Two months later he was elected governor of New York. TR soon proved himself to be a strong, independent executive with decided opinions of his own. These qualities did not endear him to Republican "boss" Thomas Collier Platt, who engineered Roosevelt's nomination to the vice-presidency in 1900 to get him out of New York.

Roosevelt as assistant secretary of the navy, a post he accepted in 1897 and resigned in 1898 at the outbreak of the Spanish-American War (photograph by Clinedinst, Washington, D.C.)

TR continued to maintain at least a nodding acquaintance with Clio (surely not a very jealous mistress) by writing a biography of Oliver Cromwell (1900). "The more I have studied Cromwell," Roosevelt wrote Charles Scribner, "the more I have grown to admire him. . . ." Roosevelt expressed great esteem for Puritan political thought and interpreted the English Civil War as a device for purifying the English soul. *Oliver Cromwell* was not a major work. Roosevelt was at his best when he wrote of war and of the Puritan mind. Cromwell remains shadowy and remote. This was the last and one of the least of his historical monographs.

Roosevelt's accidental accession to the presidency after William McKinley's assassination in 1901 came after he had ended serious study of the American past. He continued, however, to correspond with historians and to deliver confident judgments on the craft. The historian of the future, he had pontificated in a letter of February 1900, must be a "great literary man" who made his narrative "readable." A more revealing letter was written to the English historian George Otto Trevelyan in 1904. Roosevelt deplored the tendency among his-

torians to avoid the vivid and alive in favor of the drab. This comment led him into a series of strictures on that "preposterous little organization," the American Historical Association. Its membership, he asserted, was largely comprised of "conscientious, industrious, painstaking, little pedants" who believed that research was all in all. There was not a thinker or synthesizer like Parkman among them. "Mere dry-as-dust fact-collecting methods" were not sufficient; the historian must be able to write. Objectivity and dullness were not synonymous. Thomas Babington Macaulay was praised more than once, as was Trevelyan's *American Revolution* (1899-1907), "the best account of the Revolution written by anyone."

When TR left the presidency in 1909 he traveled to Africa for an extended hunting safari, carrying fifty or sixty books for extracurricular reading. He returned to the United States via western Europe the next year. While visiting England the twenty-sixth president delivered the Romanes Lecture at Oxford, "Biological Analogies in History." The greatest need of the moment, he declared on that occasion, was a "literature of science which shall be readable." Yet the historian of the future must also possess the "scientific spirit"; that is, he must be knowledgeable about biology and, especially, evolution. Certain parallels, he warned, existed between the "birth, growth, and death of societies in the world of man" and similar cycles in the nonhuman world. Historians did not yet understand why societies declined, but there were several widely recognized danger signs to be seen currently in the West: particularism, "soft luxury" or the desire of men to escape the competition of life through retirement, an increasing reliance on public welfare, and, most ominous of all, a declining birthrate. Only through a defense of the family and property rights, only through self-discipline, could the English-speaking peoples avoid falling victim to their own "passions and follies."

Two years later, in 1912 (about one month after he lost his bid for the presidency on the Progressive party ticket to Woodrow Wilson) Roosevelt delivered his presidential address to the assembled members of the American Historical Association. The "painstaking little pedants" had elected him to head their organization, and the ex-president obliged them with a by-now-familiar description of how history ought to be written, and who ought to write it. Historians, he argued, must be capable stylists and synthesizers as well as researchers. They should understand the method of science and possess broad human sympathies as well. They must, perforce, be great moralists because history serves a dual purpose: inspiring Americans with examples of heroism and unselfishness and helping them make responsible decisions concerning their country's future.

The last seven years of Roosevelt's life were spent in exploring the jungles of Brazil, and in a bitter, protracted warfare with Woodrow Wilson, a man he came eventually to despise. He continued to read omnivorously and to write on contemporary affairs. Like his earlier books, these last efforts are infused with a passion for understanding and explicating the American past. He loved his country beyond all reason, and he sought to inform and inspire his countrymen with the passion and the glory that was their heritage. He died in his sleep early on the morning of 6 January 1919, of an embolism in the coronary artery.

Roosevelt was, as Elwyn B. Robinson put it, a "gentleman amateur" who conceptualized and wrote American history as a form of romantic art. He was also an unsentimental conservative who cherished much of his country's history (slavery was a notable exception), and he shared this love with those of his fellow Americans who read his books and reviews or who heard his words. Yet he recognized that certain admirable types—the Boones, Seviers, and Clarks, for instance—could no longer recur. The violent individualism that had characterized the "men of the Western Waters" and their descendants was no longer possible in an urban, industrialized, ethnically diverse nation. Nor, by analogy, was that of the John D. Rockefellers and J. P. Morgans. These bold entrepreneurs must be disciplined and restrained. Otherwise, what was best in the American character, its morality and initiative, would be destroyed. It was the function of government (in the proper hands, of course) to discipline the crass materialism that threatened the moral basis of the American republic. Like Edmund Burke, Roosevelt sought to reform in order to conserve. His study of American history, therefore, served his country (and himself) in two ways: it helped Americans understand who and what they were, and it offered a model of heroism and moral probity to inspire their actions. For Roosevelt, the past imposed an obligation, but it also held out a form of assurance: if Americans did not fall below the standards of the Fathers, all would be well.

Letters:

Theodore Roosevelt's Letters to His Children, edited by Joseph Bucklin Bishop (New York: Scribners, 1919);

Letters from Theodore Roosevelt to Anna Roosevelt Cowles, 1870-1918 (New York & London: Scribners, 1924);

Selections from the Correspondence of Theodore Roosevelt and Henry Cabot Lodge, 2 volumes (New York: Scribners, 1925);

Letters to Kermit from Theodore Roosevelt, 1902-1908, edited by Will Irwin (New York & London: Scribners, 1946);

Letters of Theodore Roosevelt, edited by Elting E. Morison, 8 volumes (Cambridge: Harvard University Press, 1951-1954).

Biographies:

Henry Pringle, *Theodore Roosevelt: A Biography* (New York: Harcourt, Brace, 1931);

Carleton Putnam, *Theodore Roosevelt Volume One: The Formative Years, 1858-1886* (New York: Scribners, 1958);

William Henry Harbaugh, *The Life and Times of Theodore Roosevelt,* revised edition (New York: Collier, 1963).

References:

Howard K. Beale, *Theodore Roosevelt and the Rise of America to World Power* (Baltimore: Johns Hopkins Press, 1956);

John Morton Blum, *The Republican Roosevelt* (Cambridge: Harvard University Press, 1961);

Thomas G. Dyer, *Theodore Roosevelt and the Idea of Race* (Baton Rouge & London: Louisiana State University Press, 1980);

John Gable, Introduction to Roosevelt's *Gouverneur Morris,* American Bicentennial Edition (Oyster Bay, N.Y.: Theodore Roosevelt Association, 1975);

Joseph L. Gardener, *Departing Glory: Theodore Roosevelt as Ex-President* (New York: Scribners, 1973);

Dewey Grantham, ed., *Theodore Roosevelt* (Englewood Cliffs, N.J.: Prentice-Hall, 1971);

Herman Hagedorn, *The Roosevelt Family of Sagamore Hill* (New York: Macmillan, 1964);

Edmund Morris, *The Rise of Theodore Roosevelt* (New York: Coward-McCann & Geoghegan, 1979);

George E. Mowry, *The Era of Theodore Roosevelt, 1900-1912* (New York: Harper, 1958);

Elwyn B. Robinson, "Theodore Roosevelt: Amateur Historian," *North Dakota History,* 25 (January 1958): 5-13;

Robert W. Sellen, "Theodore Roosevelt: Historian With a Moral," *Mid-America: An Historical Review,* 41 (October 1959): 223-240;

Harrison Johnson Thornton, "Theodore Roosevelt," in *The Marcus W. Jernigan Essays in American Historiography*, edited by William T. Hutchinson (Chicago: University of Chicago Press, 1937), pp. 227-251.

Papers:
The Theodore Roosevelt Collection is at the Library of Congress.

J. Thomas Scharf
(1 May 1843-28 February 1898)

Joseph G. Dawson III
Texas A&M University

BOOKS: *The Chronicles of Baltimore; Being a Complete History of "Baltimore Town" and Baltimore City from the Earliest Period to the Present Time* (Baltimore: Turnbull Brothers, 1874);

History of Maryland, Prepared for the Use of the Public Schools of the State, by Scharf and William H. Browne (Baltimore: Turnbull Brothers, 1877);

History of Maryland from the Earliest Period to the Present Day, 3 volumes (Baltimore: Piet, 1879);

Oration Delivered on the 11th of October 1880, the Opening Day of the Grand Celebration of the 150th Anniversary of the Founding of the City of Baltimore (Baltimore: Press of the Sun Printing Office, 1880);

History of Baltimore City and County from the Earliest Period to the Present Day: Including Biographical Sketches of Their Representative Men (Philadelphia: Everts, 1881);

History of Western Maryland, Being a History of Frederick, Montgomery, Carroll, Washington, Allegany, and Garrett Counties from the Earliest Period to the Present Day; Including Biographical Sketches of Their Representative Men, 2 volumes (Philadelphia: Everts, 1882);

History of Saint Louis City and County, from the Earliest Periods to the Present Day: Including Biographical Sketches of Representative Men, 2 volumes (Philadelphia: Everts, 1883);

History of Philadelphia, 1609-1884, by Scharf and Thompson Westcott, 3 volumes (Philadelphia: Everts, 1884);

History of Westchester County, New York, Including Morrisania, Kings, Bridge, and West Farms, Which Have Been Annexed to New York City, 2 volumes (Philadelphia: Preston, 1886);

Deer Park and Oakland: Twins of the Alleghanies (Baltimore: Lorborn, 1887);

History of the Confederate States Navy from Its Organization to the Surrender of its Last Vessel (New York: Rogers & Sherwood, 1887; San Francisco: A. L. Bancroft, 1887; Atlanta: W. H. Shepard, 1887);

History of Delaware, 1609-1888, 2 volumes (Philadelphia: Richards, 1888);

J. Thomas Scharf.

Report of J. Thomas Scharf, Commissioner, from December 1st, 1885, to January 1st, 1888, to Governor Elihu E. Jackson, with a Series of Carefully Prepared Articles on Maryland's Resources, with a Description of Every County in the State and the City of Baltimore (Annapolis: Printed by J. Young, 1888);

Orkney Springs, Shenandoah County, Virginia. Its Attractions as a Summer Resort. Its Baths, Hotels, Cuisine, Amusements, Scenery . . . and the Medical Virtue of Its Waters (Philadelphia: Everts, 1890);

An Historical Address Delivered at the Unveiling of the Monument Erected by the State of Maryland to the Memory of Leonard Calvert, the First Governor of Maryland (Baltimore: Medairy, 1891);

The Natural and Industrial Resources and Advantages of Maryland, Being a Complete Description of All the Counties of the State and the City of Baltimore (Annapolis: Printed by C. H. Baughman, 1892).

American writer and critic H. L. Mencken (1880-1956) called his native Maryland "the most average of states," but J. Thomas Scharf would have profoundly disagreed. From the first to the last of his career Scharf wrote about Maryland—the subject he knew and liked the best. In addition, he wrote histories of other localities and states and an account of the Confederate States Navy. Scharf developed a formulaic and detailed approach to preparing his comprehensive histories, making use of newspaper files as well as a variety of documents and records.

Born in Baltimore on 1 May 1843, the son of bookkeeper and lumber company owner Thomas G. Scharf and his wife Anna Maria McNulty Scharf, John Thomas Scharf attended parochial schools in St. Peter's parish and Calvert Hall, a private academy. In 1859 Scharf began working for his father, but the Civil War cut short his business career. Scharf enlisted in the 1st Maryland Artillery on 29 July 1861 and fought for the Confederacy. Serving as an enlisted man with his battery in the major battles of the eastern theater, Scharf suffered wounds at the second battle of Bull Run (August 1862) and at Chancellorsville (May 1863). Hospitalized after Chancellorsville, he considered other ways to serve the South and applied for a commission in the struggling Confederate navy. On 20 June 1863 Scharf was appointed midshipman, and, recovered from his wounds, he eventually served on gunboats at Charleston and Savannah. According to Anna Habersham, a young girl Scharf ro-

manced in Savannah, he cut "a beautiful figure" in his nautical outfit; she described him as "very short but well formed." Faced with boring shore duty, Scharf resigned his commission in late 1864 and returned to Richmond, becoming involved in some scheme to carry Confederate dispatches to Canada. He never made it north; Union soldiers captured him at Port Tobacco, Maryland, in February 1865, and he was imprisoned in Washington, D.C., and might have been tried as a spy. However, on 25 March 1865 Scharf gained parole, and President Andrew Johnson granted him a pardon six months later.

After the war Scharf worked in Baltimore, married, and eventually found his real vocation—writing history. Employed for a time by his father, Scharf also read law to prepare for the state bar examination. In 1869 he became an aide to Maryland governor Oden Bowie; this position brought Scharf the honorary rank of "colonel," a title he delighted in using. On 2 December 1869 he married Mary McDougall, daughter of a Baltimore businessman, by whom he eventually had three children. While practicing law Scharf began writing articles for newspapers and magazines on various aspects of Baltimore and Maryland history. In 1874 he accepted the job of city editor of the *Baltimore Evening News*, later working as managing editor of the *Baltimore Sunday Telegram* and, subsequently, the *Baltimore Morning Herald*. Quitting his law practice, Scharf turned to journalism and historical writing.

Scharf's first book was *The Chronicles of Baltimore* (1874). Similar in format to a respected older work, Thomas Griffith's *Annals of Baltimore* (1824), Scharf's *Chronicles* was an encyclopedic compilation of information on all aspects of Baltimore—including commercial developments—more a reference work than a literary history. The book used a chronological format with years studding the page margins like signposts and employed lengthy quotations from newspapers, magazines, pamphlets, and state and city documents. Thus, Scharf's first book exhibited one of his strong points as a historian—the ability to assemble sources on which to base his work. On the other hand, Scharf seemed to have difficulty in evaluating his historical materials and often quoted entire documents rather than trying to analyze them, a stylistic and organizational shortcoming of several nineteenth-century historians.

The Chronicles of Baltimore (which sold for five dollars per copy from the publisher or through the author) was well received locally, and it elicited favorable comments from Benson J. Lossing, author of *The Pictorial Field-Book of the Revolution* (1850-1852) and editor of the journal *Historical Record,* who wrote that such "local histories will make up the best materials for general history." Prompted by the positive response, Scharf set to work on a comprehensive history of the entire state of Maryland.

Scharf busily collected more documents and solicited information from numerous individuals with knowledge of the state's history. Furthermore, the enterprising author sought and won the support of the Maryland legislature in 1876 to underwrite the project by committing the state to purchase 300 copies of the completed work at ten dollars per set. On another tack, Scharf, in association with William H. Browne, rushed to produce *History of Maryland, Prepared for the Use of the Public Schools of the State* (1877), published the same year that the colonel was elected to the state legislature. Meanwhile, proceeds from the school history evidently provided some funds for him to complete the multivolume *History of Maryland from the Earliest Period to the Present Day* (1879).

In the *History of Maryland* Scharf surveyed the state's geography, Indian tribes, first settlers, and religious background, filling entire pages with lengthy quotations from his prized personal archives. In Scharf's history, Marylanders founded towns and cities, established churches, fought in wars, battled raging epidemics, bought and sold slaves. Scharf's style was often verbose and flowery, but, in contrast to his *Chronicles of Baltimore,* he included more of his own prose. For example, in the *Chronicles* he had used a long magazine account on the British bombardment of Fort McHenry in the War of 1812. In *History of Maryland,* Scharf himself described the famous episode, writing that the "proud waving of that flag can never be forgotten by those who saw it. It told everything at a glance; and the feeling which it excited was most happily expressed by Francis Scott Key in a burst of genuine poetry which is destined to live as long as the history of our nation shall be read or told." Writing about the central event of his generation, Scharf titled a long chapter "The War for the Union," but it and the chapter on Reconstruction were written from the author's strong pro-South perspective. Although Maryland had not seceded, Scharf claimed that it was treated as a "conquered province" lorded over by Federal Provost Marshal William J. Fish, whom Scharf labeled "a brutal ruffian and debauchee." The author continued: "Nor can we enter into the details of the insults, wrongs, and outrages that were daily and hourly committed upon the people of the State, for the remembrance still rouses indignation too hot for the calmness of impartial history." In Scharf's opinion, one of the main results of the Civil War "was the emancipation of the negroes; a measure pregnant with important consequences, not all of which are yet clear," but he doubted "whether the negroes, as a body, have been helped" by emancipation. Scharf could not decide how to end his book. The last chapter was a grab bag, jumbling together politics, colleges and schools, and the great railroad strike of 1877.

In many respects *History of Maryland* is Scharf's most important work on his native state. It was a nineteenth-century tour de force and was republished in 1967. Hailed for years as the best reference on Maryland's history, the three-volume work has been complimented by modern historians as a treasure trove of source materials. For instance, W. Stull Holt, author of the sketch on Scharf in the *Dictionary of American Biography,* remarked that *History of Maryland,* despite the writer's "many prejudices," was recognized as a "comprehensive treatment of the subject and one which historians still consult." In 1929 Matthew P. Andrews, in his *History of Maryland: Province and State,* called Scharf an "indefatigable, if unscientific, gatherer of information" and relied on Scharf's work. Aubrey C. Land (in *Maryland: A History,* 1974, edited by Richard Walsh and W. D. Fox), evaluated Scharf's three-volume set as "old fashioned and leisurely but full and detailed" and appreciatively noted that it printed "many scarce letters and documents in full." Carl Bode, in a brief treatment of the state's history *(Maryland,* 1978), labeled Scharf's volumes as "old-style local history abundantly detailed."

Playing upon his growing popularity as Maryland's historian, Scharf immediately launched into a new project to improve upon his first book about Baltimore. Using a procedure that he was honing to a fine point, Scharf personally contacted or sent letters to dozens of persons who might provide information on aspects of the city's past, such as early settlers, historic firsts, old buildings, church and religious activities, clubs and organizations, businesses and industries, and also prominent men of recent years, for Scharf had decided to include portraits and pen sketches of civic leaders. In order to help manage his growing historical and literary enterprises, Scharf employed a staff of low-paid associates. For his 1881 *History of Baltimore City and County from the Earliest Period to the Present Day* and subsequent local histories, he solicited the writing of individuals who contributed (usually at no fee) short articles on specific topics. These individuals usually made their contributions because they wanted to be a part of the project and because it was a way to have their material published in a book, giving them some measure of prestige. Having decided to mention dozens of civic leaders, Scharf believed that he had to rely on friends or relatives of the men for information on their lives and accomplishments. But, as Edward G. Howard has noted in the introduction to a 1971 edition of Scharf's history of Baltimore, it was always Scharf who had the final responsibility for arranging, editing, omitting, or completely rewriting any material submitted to him for his local histories. The more people he mentioned, the more books Scharf was likely to sell by subscription.

The *History of Baltimore City and County* allowed Scharf to dwell on one of his favorite topics, his hometown: "Surrounded by rugged hills, hemmed in by boisterous water-courses, and flanked by malarious marshes, there seemed little prospect that the rough hamlet planted on this apparently unpropitious site would rise to the dignity of metropolitan honors." Of course, Scharf packed the new city history with facts—the basis for street names, when buildings were built, and lists of citizens who served on various committees and commissions—and presented chapters on the founding of the city, the American Revolution, the War of 1812, "Privateers and Armed Vessels," city government, education, banks, businesses, newspapers, music, literary figures (including Francis Scott Key and John Pendleton Kennedy), attorneys, and doctors, while devoting considerable space to the Civil War. One of the highlights of the volume was Scharf's description of the role of the U.S. Army in the 1877 railroad strike: "Companies I and F were followed and accompanied by a dense and infuriated crowd that repeatedly attacked them, the soldiers replying by an irregular fire, so that the rattle of musketry, the crash of broken windows, and the yells of the crowd mingled in frightful dissonance. Here and there lay wounded and bleeding men along the line of march. . . ."

History of Baltimore City and County evidently marked another financial and popular success for Scharf, though how much of a success it was in either respect is difficult to say without the records of the publishing company. The book was published a year after the city celebrated its sesquicentennial. Scharf had been one of the organizers of the celebration, and if his books had not been money-makers, publishers would not have continued to market them; letters at the Maryland His-

torical Society in the Scharf collection indicate that many persons praised the author and encouraged his continued production. Several later authorities have been forthright in saying that the *History of Baltimore City and County* was their starting point for research. A note in the fall 1972 issue of the *Maryland Historical Magazine* marked the 1971 republication of the book: "Long the standard history of the area, it is a comprehensive work, treating the political, cultural, and social aspects of the times." Sherry H. Olsen, in her *Baltimore: The Building of an American City* (1980), indicated that she "freely used Baltimore's great chroniclers and interpreters" (meaning Thomas Griffith and Scharf), and Gary L. Browne cited Scharf's works on Maryland in his *Baltimore in the Nation* (1981). In his introduction to the 1971 republication, Edward G. Howard called Scharf's tribute to Baltimore "his masterpiece of purely local history" that remained valuable to social historians and genealogists because of the many short biographies of the city's prominent men.

Having successfully concentrated on the history of his own state, Scharf logically wanted to continue tapping this natural market, and so he began a book about western Maryland, using his usual procedure for gathering information. Scharf also set to work on the first of two major projects, neither of which were ever completed. The first of these fruitless ventures was a proposed "Complete History of the Railroads of the United States." In assembling materials on railroads, Scharf wrote to several men, among them Benson J. Lossing, journalist and author Murat Halstead, and A. R. Spofford, librarian of Congress. Complications involved in such an extensive project seem to have prevented Scharf from finishing it. The other unfulfilled project, which developed later, was a biography of Jefferson Davis.

Pressing ahead over the more familiar ground, Scharf succeeded with *History of Western Maryland* (1882). Scharf's book covered six counties and stressed more than ever "representative men," devoting many pages to descriptions, accounts of accomplishments, and illustrations of merchants, politicans, physicians, and ministers. Of all the events Scharf wrote about, the Civil War again received the most attention. In 1968 *The History of Western Maryland* was republished, chiefly for its genealogical value.

By the 1880s Scharf's reputation for the success of his formula-histories had spread beyond Maryland's boundaries. Working with his Philadelphia publishing house, Scharf contracted to write a book on St. Louis, Missouri. The Maryland colonel corresponded with individuals who might help answer questions about St. Louis and the history of the upper Mississippi River Valley, including historian Francis Parkman and Lyman C. Draper of the Wisconsin State Historical Society. *History of Saint Louis City and County, from the Earliest Periods to the Present Day* (1883), two imposing leather-bound, gold-stamped volumes, contained discourses on the growth of the vicinity of St. Louis from its prehistoric days to the late nineteenth century—the founding of the city, Indians, Spanish and French influence, territorial government, railroads, businesses, education, amusements, and, of course, the Civil War. In his preface, Scharf credited several contributors who had written various chapters, including "Art and Artists," "Literature and Literary Men," and the "Medical Profession." The book devoted attention to many distinguished men whose biographies were based on information supplied by their families. To his credit, Scharf placed St. Louis in the framework of national, regional, and state history; his was not just a narrow focus on the metropolis itself.

History of Saint Louis City and County spread Scharf's name among contemporaries in a different region of the country, and many modern historians have cited the work, including Edwin C. McReynolds *(Missouri: A History of the Crossroads State,* 1962), William E. Parrish *(Missouri Under Radical Rule,* 1965), William E. Foley *(A History of Missouri: Volume I, 1673-1820,* 1971), Perry McCandless *(A History of Missouri: Volume II, 1820-1860,* 1972), and S. K. Troen and G. E. Holt, editors *(St. Louis,* 1977). The author of the most comprehensive history of the state, David D. March *(The History of Missouri,* 4 volumes, 1967), frequently quoted from Scharf's work on St. Louis.

Next, Scharf capitalized on the efforts of another historian, Thompson Westcott, in the production of their *History of Philadelphia, 1609-1884* (1884). For thirty years Westcott had been collecting documents on Philadelphia and for twelve years (1865-1877) he had written a weekly column on the city's history in the *Philadelphia Sunday Dispatch.* Working together, the two historians assembled, edited, and wrote a mammoth three-volume memorial to the city. Westcott contributed nine complete chapters and pages on "many other minor subjects." In the preface, Scharf thanked the many local authorities who had provided chapters or pages on such subjects as "Religious Denominations," "Municipal Government," "Education," "Bench and Bar," "The Medical Profession," "Dis-

tinguished Women," and "Literature and Literary Men." The result was a grand overview of Philadelphia from its earliest settlement into the 1880s. The *History of Philadelphia* added to Scharf's stature as an historian in the 1880s and provided a reference source for several twentieth-century books, including Horace M. Lippincott's *Philadelphia* (1926), Carl Bridenbaugh's *Rebels and Gentlemen: Philadelphia in the Age of Franklin* (1942), James W. Livingood's *The Philadelphia-Baltimore Trade Rivalry, 1780-1860* (1947), and Sam B. Warner, Jr.'s *The Private City: Philadelphia in Three Periods of its Growth* (1968).

Meanwhile, Scharf had plunged into several projects simultaneously. He took steps that resulted in the publication of two more histories using his formulaic approach, the two-volume *History of Westchester County, New York* (1886) and a twenty-four-page booklet on two Maryland towns, *Deer Park and Oakland: Twins of the Alleghanies* (1887). Entering public service again, he became Maryland's commissioner of the State Land Office, holding that political plum from 1884 to 1892. In that capacity he had access to thousands of state documents and records, some of which ended up in the colonel's private collection. In 1899, for example, he sold the manuscript proceedings of the Maryland Convention of 1774 for one hundred dollars to supplement his own income. Furthermore, Scharf withheld hundreds of other state documents from the land office files.

During the mid-1880s Scharf had been laboring to consummate what was his most original book, *History of the Confederate States Navy* (1887). As usual, he employed his formula of contacting all persons who could provide documents or information about his subject; the correspondence began in January 1884. It came as no surprise to his readers that Scharf took the Southern side, and, like the colonel's other books, *History of the Confederate States Navy* contained many documents printed in toto, extensive quotations from newspaper accounts, and dozens of illustrations. In such a big book (more than 800 pages) Scharf had opportunities to demonstrate his literary skills, and he was at his best in describing the famous duel between the *U.S.S. Monitor* and the *C.S.S. Virginia (Merrimack):* "Discharging workmen as the *Virginia* moved into the channel, Flag-officer [Franklin] Buchanan turned her prow into waters swarming with enemies, and covered with the line-of-battle ships that had never lowered their flag to an enemy." Indicating some malaise with the new military technology, Scharf contended that "the poetry

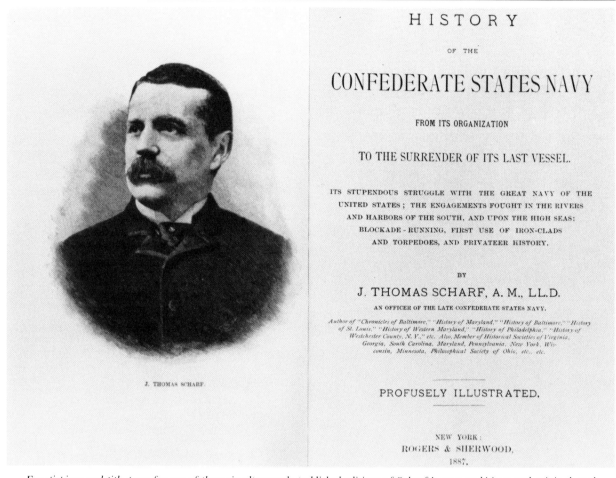

Frontispiece and title page for one of three simultaneously published editions of Scharfs's most ambitious and original work

of a naval battle was not there; it was simply a game of enormous iron bolts hurled upon thick iron plates from iron guns of heretofore unknown dimensions." He concluded that "the contest was not between ships but between metal monsters." Scharf opened a strong account of "The Confederate States Cruisers" as follows: "In many respects the most interesting chapter of the history of the Confederate navy is that of the building and operation of the ships-of-war which drove the merchant flag of the United States from the oceans and almost extirpated their carrying trade." But the author missed an excellent opportunity to write a dramatic narrative about the fall of Fort Fisher at Wilmington, North Carolina, instead joining together a string of quotations about the battle. Three different firms published Scharf's navy book simultaneously in 1887, and a second edition appeared in 1894.

Royce G. Shingleton, in his book *John Taylor Wood: Sea Ghost of the Confederacy* (1979), called

Scharf "a Civil War veteran who, unlike Thucydides, could not remain objective when writing about the war in which he participated." In fact, Scharf took pleasure in writing to former Confederate president Jefferson Davis that in chapter four ("Privateers") he had "rubbed it in quite hard on the United States naval authorities." Nevertheless, despite Scharf's lack of objectivity and his mistakes in relating some naval engagements, Shingleton judged that Scharf's book "remains the best general account of the southern naval effort."

A host of historians dealing with the Civil War navies have noted their debt to Scharf. William M. Robinson, Jr., in *The Confederate Privateers* (1928), pointed out some errors Scharf made in identifying ships, but held that the book was a "monumental history." Frank L. Owsley in *King Cotton Diplomacy* (1931; revised edition, 1959) cited Scharf, as did Joseph T. Durkin in *Stephen R. Mallory, Confederate Navy Chief* (1954); Durkin reckoned that Scharf's was "still the best all-around history of the Confederate Navy, although it leaves much to be desired." Virgil C. Jones obviously relied on Scharf to reconstruct several episodes in *The Civil War at Sea* (3 volumes, 1960-1962). Sounding a critical note, Frank J. Merli remarked in his *Great Britain and the Confederate Navy* (1970) that Scharf's was "an extended but haphazard treatment." James M. Merrill referred to *History of the Confederate States Navy* in his books *The Rebel Shore* (1957) and *Battle Flags South* (1970), as did William N. Still in *Iron Afloat: The Story of the Confederate Armorclads* (1971), Rowena Reed in *Combined Operations in the Civil War* (1978), and Warren F. Spencer in *The Confederate Navy in Europe* (1983). Tom H. Wells, in *The Confederate Navy: A Study in Organization* (1971), criticized Scharf's history for being "rambling and sometimes inaccurate," and Wells found that the former midshipman tended to accept "uncritically the statements of participants and is sometimes inconsistent." Even so, Wells pointed out that Scharf's was "the only full-length treatment of the subject," and William C. Davis, in *Duel Between the First Ironclads* (1975), indicated that Scharf's book was one of the most useful books available. Demonstrating its continuing value and popularity, *History of the Confederate States Navy* was republished in 1969 and 1977.

Hard on the heels of the navy book, Scharf completed his last major study, *History of Delaware, 1609-1888* (1888), and devoted increasing attention to his other fruitless endeavor, the biography of Jefferson Davis. *History of Delaware* took a broad approach to the state's development, from prehistoric geology and geography to the politics and cultural and social activities of the 1880s. Once more Scharf relied on responses to questionnaires and the assistance of staff and contributors to fill the work's two volumes. The result has held up remarkably well. In the twentieth century, historians still look to Scharf's work, with Carol E. Hoffecker *(Delaware,* 1977) contending that "among the multivolume state histories the best is still J. Thomas Scharf, *History of Delaware.*" John A. Munroe *(Colonial Delaware,* 1978), however, was more critical, judging that "the most comprehensive history of Delaware covering the entire colonial period has long been *History of Delaware, 1609-1888,* by J. Thomas Scharf, *et al.* . . . This is a strange work, astonishing at once for its contents, which sometimes include otherwise lost original materials, and for its omissions." Munroe added in his own *History of Delaware* (1979) that while Scharf's book included "sections on every village and every hundred . . . unfortunately its facts are not always accurate and

it seldom offers any analysis or interpretation of the myriad of facts that it presents."

Throughout Scharf's literary career it really had never been his purpose to be particularly analytical or critical, and undoubtedly his proposed biography of Jefferson Davis would not have been critical of its subject. But as biography it was an extraordinary undertaking for Scharf, and it is unfortunate that the work was never completed. The colonel entered into negotiations about a book with the crusty old president and visited him in Mississippi during the summer of 1886. Telling Davis that he wanted "to controvert all the lies that have been told about you," Scharf intended to present his subject in the best possible light. By June of 1887 Davis said that he was ready for Scharf to conduct another interview, and the author planned to send a stenographer to Davis's home to take down the president's answers to a lengthy list of questions. However, Davis flew into a rage when he learned that Scharf had prematurely published a partial account of the 1886 summer interview in the *Baltimore Morning Herald*. According to Davis, Scharf had distorted or embellished parts of the conversation, which the president thought were reserved only for the "preparation of [the] proposed biography." Scharf apologized profusely for the blunder, related how he had purchased newspaper files and documents in support of the biography, and wanted to proceed on the book as planned. Evidently the two men maintained a correspondence during the next two years, at least to within a few months of Davis's death on 6 December 1889. A few days later, on 13 December, Scharf signed a contract with publisher J. A. Hill of New York for the Davis biography, to have been completed by 1 August 1890. Hill expected Scharf to get Mrs. Varina Davis to cooperate and bless the project.

Unfortunately, Scharf never finished the book on Davis. Distractions—literary (he considered undertaking a state history of Rhode Island), business, and political—got in the way. Whatever the case, in June 1891 Scharf donated most of the documents in his private archives, including some Maryland state records, to the Johns Hopkins University. The *Johns Hopkins University Circular* of June 1891 proudly announced "Colonel Scharf's Gift of an Important Historical Collection," and in the same periodical L. P. Powell wrote that the donation had been made "with the hope that it may become the nucleus of one of the greatest libraries of Southern Americana in this country." (During the 1930s and 1940s many of these documents were placed at the Maryland Historical Society but some remained at the university's archives. By then the Southern Historical Collection at the University of North Carolina was becoming the most important depository for Southern historical papers.)

In 1892 Scharf produced his last book, *The Natural and Industrial Resources and Advantages of Maryland*, but he lost his job at the State Land Office. *The Natural and Industrial Resources* was a promotional book touting the economic potential of the state and Baltimore. Subject or topic headings such as "Central Maryland," "Western Maryland," "The Eastern Shore," "Baltimore: A Solid City," and "Baltimore's Trade of Today" were used in the text. Contrasted with the possibilities of the biography of Jefferson Davis, this was a disappointing last book.

In 1893 Scharf acted as manager of Maryland's exhibit at the World's Columbian Exposition in Chicago. Moving to New York later that year, he became special federal inspector of Chinese immigration. He held that job until 1897, when the administration of Democrat Grover Cleveland gave way to that of Republican William McKinley. After losing the federal sinecure, Scharf practiced law in New York City, where he died 28 February 1898.

In a 1983 article, Richard J. Cox described Scharf as "one of the ablest practitioners of the subscription or memorial history business of the last years of the nineteenth century." Several of his works have been republished in the twentieth century. Scharf's books inspired the readers' interest in history and presented a wealth of facts and information written in the flowery style of the day. Several of Scharf's books devoted considerable space to personalities—former or contemporary leaders of a city or state—introducing readers to the influential men of the area. Scharf was one of the first American historians who consistently used newspapers as a primary source. He succeeded in assembling mountains of documents, many of which were quoted at length, leading many twentieth-century researchers to refer to Scharf's works. Scharf's *History of the Confederate States Navy* remains a particularly valuable contribution to the literature of the Civil War.

References:

Richard J. Cox, "A Century of Frustration: The Movement for a State Archives in Maryland, 1811-1935," *Maryland Historical Magazine*, 78 (Summer 1983): 106-117;

Francis B. Culver, "The War Romance of John Thomas Scharf," *Maryland Historical Magazine*, 21 (September 1926): 295-302;

Edward G. Howard, Introduction to *History of Baltimore City and County*, by J. Thomas Scharf (Baltimore: Regional Publishing, 1971);

Morris L. Radoff, "An Elusive Manuscript—The Proceedings of the Maryland Convention of 1774," *American Archivist*, 30 (January 1967): 59-65;

Radoff, Foreword to *The History of Maryland*, by J. Thomas Scharf (Hatboro, Pa.: Tradition Press, 1967);

Frank F. White, Jr., ed., "Correspondence of Jefferson Davis and J. Thomas Scharf," *Journal of Mississippi History*, 10 (April 1948): 118-131.

Papers:

Scharf's personal papers are at the Museum and Library of Maryland History of the Maryland Historical Society, Baltimore.

James Schouler

(20 March 1839-16 April 1920)

Clyde N. Wilson
University of South Carolina

SELECTED BOOKS: *A Treatise on the Law of Domestic Relations; Embracing Husband and Wife, Parent and Child, Guardian and Ward, Infancy, and Master and Servant* (Boston: Little, Brown, 1870);

A Treatise on the Law of Personal Property, 2 volumes (Boston: Little, Brown, 1873, 1876);

A Treatise on the Law of Bailments, Including Carriers, Innkeepers and Pledge (Boston: Little, Brown, 1880);

History of the United States of America Under the Constitution, 7 volumes (volumes 1-4, Washington: Morrison, 1880-1889; revised, New York: Dodd, Mead, 1904; volumes 5-7, New York: Dodd, Mead, 1891-1913);

A Treatise on the Law of Executors and Administrators (Boston: Soule & Bugbee, 1883);

A Treatise on the Law of Wills (Boston: Soule, 1887);

Thomas Jefferson (New York: Dodd, Mead, 1893);

Historical Briefs (New York: Dodd, Mead, 1896);

Constitutional Studies. State and Federal (New York: Dodd, Mead, 1897);

Alexander Hamilton (Boston: Small, Maynard, 1901);

Americans of 1776 (New York: Dodd, Mead, 1906);

Ideals of the Republic (Boston: Little, Brown, 1908).

James Schouler

As a historian James Schouler's industry, ambition, and opportunity exceeded his ability. Though well known and applauded in his own day, his reputation has faded into obscurity except within the esoteric confines of historiographical study. He was among the last of those nineteenth-century gentlemen scholars who aspired to write a comprehensive history of the United States. Thanks to independent means and forty years of work he succeeded, although his ambition, as well as the methods with which he carried it out and the viewpoints he adopted, were obsolete long before he had finished.

Schouler was born in West Cambridge (later Arlington), Massachusetts. His father, William Schouler, a minor Whig politician and newspaper editor, had come from Scotland as a child. His mother, Frances Eliza Warren, was of an established New England family. During James Schouler's youth the family moved to Ohio. Its economic position was such that Schouler could attend Harvard only with some difficulty, but he managed to graduate in 1859. After teaching school for a while, he began to prepare for the law.

The political revolution of 1860 brought success and prosperity to the family. William Schouler allied himself with the rising Republican party, returned to Massachusetts, and during the Civil War held the position of adjutant general of the state. Given wartime expansion, the position was one of great potential influence and profit. (The future president Chester A. Arthur was adjutant general of New York at the same time.) Meanwhile, James Schouler finished his legal preparation and was admitted to practice, taking time out for a short-term enlistment in the Union army, which was spent in relative inactivity with a Massachusetts regiment on the coast of North Carolina.

The war made the Schoulers' fortune as it did that of many others. They opened an immensely profitable law practice in the management of claims for veterans' benefits. While the father corralled claimants in Boston, the son opened a Washington office from which he could prosecute claims and other cases. At the same time James Schouler, who never lacked industry, began to write extensively on legal subjects. From 1871 to 1873 he edited the quarterly *United States Jurist,* and in 1870 he began publishing a series of legal treatises and textbooks which were successful and profitable.

By 1873 prosperity was so established that the father could retire and the son could devote his time primarily to the research and writing of history, though he continued to produce legal works and to lecture in law schools. James Schouler's real ambition had always been literary, and as early as 1866 he published a historical article entitled "Our Diplomacy during the Rebellion" in the *North American Review.* William Schouler had written extensively in periodicals and newspapers and had published a two-volume *History of Massachusetts in the Civil War* (1868, 1871). James Schouler's own interest in the political history of the republic had been stimulated by his experiences in Reconstruction-era Washington. As an increasing deafness made law practice inconvenient, he was encouraged to turn more and more to the satisfaction of historical and literary interests.

In the first volume of his *History of the United States of America Under the Constitution,* Schouler declared that his goal was to meet a national need. George Bancroft's monumental history had ended with the adoption of the Constitution. It was Schouler's self-declared mission to carry on, to systematically record and expound the events which the republic had undergone from the founding of the national government through the recent end of Reconstruction. Unfortunately, Schouler's abilities as a writer and a thinker were far inferior to Bancroft's. What for Bancroft was a noble commission was for Schouler a personal hobby. Further, in desiring to provide a comprehensive narrative of American national history, Schouler had competition from several other writers who aspired to fill the void that he had noted.

Those who have sought to find things to praise in Schouler's work have pointed out that he gave "intimations" of an awareness of social and economic history in occasional chapters in his *History* and in articles that were collected in 1906 as *Americans of 1776.* However, his social and economic material was poorly integrated into what was generally a political narrative, and John Bach McMaster had already far outstripped him in that area. Schouler was slightly less dogmatic than Hermann E. von Holst but also more superficial. He lacked ability to adapt to changing public attitudes and perspectives in as subtle a manner as James Ford Rhodes. In some ways Schouler resembles Edward Channing, another Massachusetts scholar who published a multivolume history of the U.S. slightly after Schouler (1905-1925). However, Channing had a firm academic base and absorbed to some extent the multiplying monographic research and the new perspectives of the day. Though his writing was as personal and prejudiced as Schouler's, it was more sophisticated.

It is perhaps not too harsh to say that Schouler was pedestrian as a writer and an organizer of his material. One would be hard put to find a passage in his works suitable for quotation today except as a negative example. He was also a fairly unimaginative researcher, though an assiduous one. His *History* is basically a straightforward political narrative, written in a vein of personal opinion rather than as a work of literary art or scholarly detachment. In interpretation Schouler did not differ radically from the conventional ideas of the day. He recounted American history from the viewpoint of a New Englander and a Republican, though he did have the merit of representing a variant viewpoint within this narrow segment of opinion. The seventh volume of the *History,* which dealt with Reconstruction and drew upon personal experiences, has often been adjudged the best. In it Schouler was less sympathetic to the Radical Republicans than others had been and more sympathetic to the Johnson-Seward faction and their Reconstruction policies. He was almost alone among Northern writers of the time in defending Andrew Johnson. By the same token, he was slighty less adulatory of Alexander Hamilton and slightly less hostile to what could be called a Jeffersonian position than were other writers of the time. It was perhaps this tendency that led Schouler into one of his few research innovations. He was among the first historians to make use of the manuscripts of non-Republicans, such as James Monroe, Martin Van Buren, James K. Polk, and Andrew Johnson, that had been collected at the Library of Congress.

The first volume of the *History* was published in 1880 when Schouler was forty-one. The fifth appeared in 1891 when he was fifty-two, and the last in 1913 when he was seventy-four. The first four volumes were published by a minor Washington firm. The last three were published by Dodd, Mead, which also issued revised versions of the earlier volumes. Most of this work was accomplished without any academic affiliation, although from 1891, on invitation of Herbert Baxter Adams, Schouler lectured regularly at Johns Hopkins.

Long before Schouler's major work was complete, serious historical writing in America came to be dominated by trained academic specialists who aspired to greater objectivity and more disciplined methods. Schouler was treated respectfully but unenthusiastically by the professionals, and in 1897 he served as president of the American Historical Association. Interestingly, his presidential address was not devoted to history but was used as the occasion to propose a new, limited Constitutional convention which would draft amendments to the United States Constitution. The amendments Schouler favored involved increased popular participation in elections, restrictions on imperialistic ventures and on the power of aliens, and conservative monetary safeguards.

The professionals' attitude toward Schouler is perhaps indicated by a review written by a leader among them, William A. Dunning of Columbia University. Considering Schouler's sixth volume, which dealt with the Civil War, Dunning praised the book as a "singularly well-proportioned narrative," but also observed that as an account of the Civil War the book was "a generation too late." Dunning then presented several pages of specific analysis to show that on point after point Schouler's generalizations were merely repetitions of partisan attitudes of an earlier day which neither took account of newly accumulated knowledge nor contributed anything original to the understanding of the war.

Schouler took note of changing ideas about history without paying much heed to them. In his *Historical Briefs* (1896), a collection of previously published articles, he gave some philosophical attention to the meaning and use of history and the ways in which it should be pursued. His observations were thoughtful and honest but not very inspired. He defended his approach without being either intellectually penetrated or emotionally antagonized by criticisms of it.

Schouler married Emily Fuller Cochran of Boston in 1870 but left no children. With part of his fortune he endowed a chair in history and political science at Johns Hopkins.

References:
Biography of James Schouler, in his *Historical Briefs* (New York: Dodd, Mead, 1896), pp. 169-310;
Lewis E. Ellis, "James Schouler," in *The Marcus W. Jernegan Essays in American Historiography*, edited by William T. Hutchinson (Chicago: University of Chicago Press, 1937), pp. 84-101;
Michael Kraus, *The Writing of American History* (Norman: University of Oklahoma Press, 1963), pp. 198-202;
Bert James Loewenberg, *American History in American Thought: Christopher Columbus to Henry Adams* (New York: Simon & Schuster, 1972), pp. 501-504;
Harvey Wish, *The American Historian: A Social-Intellectual History of the Writing of the American Past* (New York: Oxford University Press, 1960), pp. 213-218.

Papers:

Schouler's papers are at the Massachusetts Historical Society.

Edwin R. A. Seligman

(25 April 1861-18 July 1939)

John Braeman
University of Nebraska at Lincoln

SELECTED BOOKS: *Two Chapters on the Mediaeval Guilds of England: An Essay in Economic History* (New York: Pearson, 1884);

On the Shifting and Incidence of Taxation (Baltimore: American Economic Association, 1892); revised and enlarged as *The Shifting and Incidence of Taxation* (New York: Published for the Columbia University Press by Macmillan, 1899; revised and enlarged again, New York: Columbia University Press, 1910, 1921);

Progressive Taxation in Theory and Practice (Baltimore: American Economic Association, 1894; revised and enlarged, Princeton: American Economic Association, 1908);

Essays in Taxation (New York & London: Macmillan, 1895; revised and enlarged, 1913; revised and enlarged again, 1921);

The Economic Interpretation of History (New York: Columbia University Press/London: Macmillan, 1902);

Principles of Economics, With Special Reference to American Conditions (New York: Longmans, Green, 1905; revised and enlarged, 1907);

The Income Tax: A Study of the History, Theory, and Practice of Income Taxation at Home and Abroad (New York: Macmillan, 1911; revised and enlarged, 1914);

The Next Step in Tax Reform; Presidential Address of Edwin R. A. Seligman, LL.D., Delivered at the Ninth Annual Conference of the National Tax Association, San Francisco, August 11, 1915 (Ithaca, N.Y.: National Tax Association, 1915?);

How to Finance the War, by Seligman and Robert Murray Haig, Columbia War Papers, first series, no. 7 (New York: Division of Intelligence and Publicity of Columbia University, 1917);

The House Revenue Bill: A Constructive Criticism, Columbia War Papers, first series, no. 16 (New York: Division of Intelligence and Publicity of Columbia University, 1917);

Our Fiscal Difficulties and the Way Out (Albany, 1919);

Curiosities of Early Economic Literature: An Address to His Fellow Members of the Hobby Club of New

Edwin R. A. Seligman

York, by Edwin R. A. Seligman (San Francisco: Privately printed, 1920);

Currency Inflation and Public Debts: An Historical Sketch (New York: Equitable Trust Company, 1921);

Debate on Capitalism vs. Socialism, by Seligman and Scott Nearing (Girard, Kans.: Haldeman-Julius, 1921);

The Allied Debts: A Constructive Criticism of Secretary Hoover's Views (New York, 1922);

The League of Nations (New York, 1924);

Essays in Economics (New York: Macmillan, 1925);

Studies in Public Finances (New York: Macmillan, 1925);

The Economics of Instalment Selling: A Study in Consumers' Credit, with Special Reference to the Automobile, 2 volumes (New York & London: Harper, 1927);

Double Taxation and International Fiscal Cooperation; Being a Series of Lectures Delivered at the Académie de Droit International de la Haye (New York: Macmillan, 1928);

The Economics of Farm Relief: A Survey of the Agricultural Problem (New York: Columbia University Press, 1929);

Price Cutting and Price Maintenance: A Study in Economics, by Seligman and Robert A. Love (New York & London: Harper, 1932);

A Report on the Revenue System of Cuba, by Seligman and Carl S. Shoup (Habana: Talleres Tipográticos de Casara, 1932);

Public Education and a Reformed Tax System (DeKalb, Ill.: Industrial Arts Print Shop, 1933).

OTHER: "Continuity of Economic Thought," in *Science Economic Discussion* (New York: Science Company, 1886), pp. 1-23;

"Economists," in *Cambridge History of American Literature*, 4 volumes, edited by William P. Trent and others (New York: Putnam's, 1917-1921), IV: 425-443;

"Edwin R. Seligman" [autobiography], in *Die Volkswirtschaftslehre der Gegenwart in Selbstdarstellungen*, edited by Felix Meiner, 2 volumes (Leipzig: Felix Meiner, 1924, 1929), II: 117-160;

"Die sozial Ökonomie in den Vereinigten Staaten," in *Die Wirtschaftswissenschaft nach dem Kriege: neunundzwanzig Beiträge über den Stand der deutschen und auslandischen sozialökonomischen Forschung nach dem Kriege (Festgabe für Lujo Brentano zum 80)*, edited by Moritz J. Bonn Melchior Palyi, 2 volumes in one (Munich: Duncker & Humblot, 1925), II: 59-78;

"The Early Teaching of Economics in the United States," in *Economic Essays Contributed in Honor of John Bates Clark*, edited by Jacob H. Hollander (New York: Macmillan, 1927), pp. 283-320;

"History and Economics," in *The Social Sciences and Their Interrelations*, edited by William F. Ogburn and Alexander Goldenweiser (Boston: Houghton Mifflin, 1927), pp. 177-188;

"What Are the Social Sciences?," in *Encyclopaedia of the Social Sciences*, edited by Seligman and others, 15 volumes (New York: Macmillan, 1930-1935), I: 3-7.

PERIODICAL PUBLICATIONS: "Railway Tariffs and the Interstate Commerce Law," *Political Science Quarterly*, 2 (June 1887): 223-264; (September 1887): 369-413;

"The Living Wage," *Gunton Institute Bulletin*, 1 (26 March 1898): 257-268;

"On Some Neglected British Economists," *Economic Journal*, 13 (September 1903): 335-363; (December 1903): 511-535;

"Economics and Social Progress," *Publications of the American Economic Association*, third series, 4 (February 1903): 52-70;

"Social Aspects of Economic Law," *Publications of the American Economic Association*, third series, 5 (February 1904): 49-73;

"The Federal Income Tax," *Political Science Quarterly*, 29 (March 1914): 1-27;

"The Committee on Academic Freedom of the American Association of University Professors," *Educational Review*, 50 (September 1915): 184-188;

"The War Revenue Act," *Political Science Quarterly*, 33 (March 1918): 1-37;

"Our Association—Its Aims and Its Accomplishments," *Bulletin of the American Association of University Professors*, 8 (February 1922): 90-110;

"The Social Theory of Fiscal Science," *Political Science Quarterly*, 41 (June 1926): 193-218; 41 tember 1926): 354-383.

Edwin Robert Anderson Seligman is today primarily remembered as an economist. Even as an economist, however, he is regarded as a secondary figure. By temperament a middle-of-the-roader, he advanced no radical new theories, founded no school. He is typically identified as a pioneer in the study of public finance and taxation. But this categorization fails to do justice to the breadth of his interests, the scope of his involvements, and the extent of his contributions. The major intellectual influence shaping his thinking was the German historical school of economics, with its emphasis upon the relativity to time and place of economic institutions and doctrines. He was a leading—perhaps the leading—authority of his day on the history of economic thought. At the same time, he played a key role in directing the attention of American scholars to the importance of economic factors in history. But he remained aware that the economic realm constituted no more than a part of human existence. And he recognized, as he put it in 1905, how history showed "that religious, political and ethical considerations have profoundly modified economic action itself."

Seligman was born on 25 April 1861 in New York City, the eighth of nine children born to Joseph and Babette Steinhardt Seligman. His father, a German Jew who had come to the United States in 1837, was founder and head of the influential private international banking house of J. & W. Seligman & Company. Seligman was educated at home until age eleven, then attended Columbia Grammar School, and at fourteen entered Columbia College. In his senior year, he came under the influence of John W. Burgess. Encouraged by Burgess, he went to Germany for advanced study after receiving his A.B. in 1879. After one semester at the University of Berlin, he transferred to the University of Heidelberg. There he worked under Karl Knies, one of the founders of the German historical school of economics. Knies attacked the classical economists of the English school for their deductive approach, their assumption of an abstract economic man moved exclusively by self-interest, and their rigidly laissez-faire views. More broadly, Knies denied the existence of immutable and universally applicable natural laws of economics. As Seligman summed up Knies's position: "the economic theories of any generation must be regarded primarily as the outgrowth of the peculiar conditions of time, place, and nationality, under which the doctrines were evolved."

After three semesters at Heidelberg, Seligman spent a year in France studying at the Sorbonne and the École Libre des Sciences Politiques. Returning to the United States in 1882, he enrolled in Burgess's recently founded School of Political Science at Columbia while simultaneously pursuing a degree in the Law School. He received his M.A. and LL.B. in 1884; he was awarded the Ph.D. cum laude the following year. His doctoral dissertation, *Two Chapters on the Mediaeval Guilds of England*, published in 1884, went beyond the narrow institutional-legal focus of the day to deal with the larger political, economic, and social context of guild development. In the fall of 1885, he began his long teaching career at Columbia as a prize lecturer. He was appointed adjunct professor of political economy in 1888 and was promoted to full professor of political economy and finance in 1891. That year he inaugurated the Columbia University Studies in History, Economics, and Public Law as a vehicle for the publication of dissertations written by students in the Faculty of Political Science; he served as the series editor for twenty-nine years. In 1901 he became chairman of the Department of Economics

and Social Science. Three years later he was named the first incumbent of the newly established McVickar Professorship of Political Economy—a position that he held until his retirement in 1931.

Seligman's erudition was legendary. Along with having a solid grounding in the classics, he read German, French, Italian, Spanish, Russian, and Dutch. His most famous course offering at Columbia—and what became the major focus of his own scholarly interest—was the history of economic thought. He amassed one of the world's foremost collections of materials on the subject, specializing in works from the sixteenth through the eighteenth centuries. His 1903 articles in the *Economic Journal* "On Some Neglected British Economists" were landmarks in showing the existence of a rich body of early-nineteenth-century British writings on economics that not simply challenged the precepts of the classical school but foreshadowed modern developments in the field. Later Seligman wrote pioneering accounts of the study and teaching of economics in the United States. But he was continually drawn from pure scholarship by his commitment to utilizing knowledge as an instrument for social betterment. "Our efforts," he explained to Columbia's president in 1895, "have hitherto been directed almost exclusively to material ends. We have been largely dominated by the need of subduing the natural forces of this vast continent, and of developing its economic resources. Wealth rather than welfare has been our aim. We are only now waking up to the need of more spiritual, intellectual and moral aims. Science, therefore, has a far greater role to play with us in the future than it has played in the past. . . ."

In 1885 Seligman joined with a group of largely German-trained economists and socially minded clergy to found the American Economic Association and became the organization's treasurer. In a dig at the "speculation" of the classical school, the Association called for resting economics upon "the historical and statistical study of actual conditions." And its "statement of principles" challenged the prevailing laissez-faire orthodoxy by explicitly announcing: "We regard the state as an agency whose positive assistance is one of the indispensable conditions of human progress." Although smoothed over at the launching, there were underlying differences between Seligman and many of his cofounders. In the first place, he retained a deep respect for the contributions of the giants of the classical tradition. Second, he did not feel the attraction for socialism that exerted a strong pull—at least at that time—upon such men as Richard T. Ely, Henry Carter Adams, and even John Bates Clark. Most important, Seligman wished to make the Association into an inclusive body encompassing all economists, regardless of views, that would have as its primary goal the promotion of research. Accordingly, he played a leading role in the dropping of the "statement of principles" to smooth the way for older school economists to join. His presidency (1902 and 1903) marked the culmination of the transformation of the Association into a broadly based, purely professional organization.

Although a defender of capitalism, Seligman was no devotee of the unrestrained free market. He hoped that the productive achievements of capitalism could be maintained while eliminating its abuses through the growth of a sense of social responsibility. A longtime member of the Society for Ethical Culture, Seligman had a strongly religious strain that took the shape of a broadly humanitarian moral idealism. After his return from European study, he financed an experiment in voluntary producers' cooperatives among New York tailors. In 1885 he joined with several philanthropists to organize a company for building low-rent model tenements. At a time when unions were widely regarded with suspicion and hostility, he defended the right of workers to organize and bargain collectively. He was the first prominent American economist to endorse the doctrine of the living wage. And during the Progressive era, he worked through the National Civic Federation to promote labor-management cooperation. In 1902 he became one of the founders of Greenwich House, a social settlement modeled on London's famed Toynbee Hall. Although he was thoroughly assimilated, he supported the work of the Educational Alliance in improving the condition of New York's Eastern European Jewish immigrants. From 1911 to 1914, he was the chairman of the National League on Urban Conditions Among Negroes (renamed the National Urban League).

Although active in such private volunteer organizations, Seligman acknowledged that government had a major role to play. As early as 1887, he announced that the day of free competition was over, that large-scale combinations were here to stay, and that, therefore, government regulation was required to prevent abuses. He went on to endorse prohibition of child labor, maximum hour and even minimum wage laws, and adoption of a comprehensive program of social insurance—including insurance against illness. In a more philosophical vein, he pictured, and thus rationalized,

the expansion of governmental responsibilities as the long-term direction of history. In "primitive society," he elaborated, defense was "the only consideration." As society became ever more complex, "public needs" expanded accordingly. First came the demand for "better roads, for more canals, for improved methods of communication." At a later stage, "the less material ends of government are recognized. Education must be provided, hospitals and asylums must be erected, and the sanitary conditions must be looked after. Finally comes the immense growth of the modern state, with its new functions due partly to the industrial revolution, partly to the growth of democracy. . . ." He even took as his test for judging government assumption of any function "the extent that the activity in question is recognized by the prevalent public opinion as of really fundamental importance to the entire community."

Probably Seligman's most significant contribution to reform lay in the area of tax policy. A major target was the doctrine of the diffusion of taxation, which held that all taxes were shifted ultimately to the consumer in the form of higher prices. Seligman admitted that the argument was correct for taxes on commodities—such as tariffs and sales taxes—although even in those instances how much could be shifted depended upon the elasticity of supply and demand. But he concluded that there was no way of shifting the burden of inheritance taxes, a tax on business profits, or a general income tax. Even more important was his development of the principle of "faculty"—that is, ability to pay—as the basis for taxation. At first, he narrowly limited its scope. While acknowledging that "the theory of progressive taxation . . . corresponds to the demands of ideal justice," he denied the practicability of its application to property, income, or even corporation taxes. His one exception was on inheritance, "which, just because of its accidental or unearned nature, is a most fitting subject of taxation." By 1911, however, he had come to support a federal income tax incorporating "the principle of graduation." And he hailed the graduated income and excess of profits taxes of the 1917 War Revenue Act as reflecting "democratic principles hitherto unrealized in fiscal history."

In the larger realm of economic theory, Seligman never accepted the sharp distinction between the deductive and inductive methods that for a time was so hotly debated between new and old school economists. He was temperamentally attracted to a middle ground between "those extreme votaries of the historical school who see no good but in

Photograph used as the frontispiece for Edwin Robert
Anderson Seligman, 1861-1939, *a collection of memorial
addresses and tributes to Seligman published in 1942*

details" and "the uncompromising adherents to the
undiluted doctrines of the classicists." As a result,
he became an early convert to the theories of marginal utility and productivity formulated by his Columbia colleague John Bates Clark. And his 1905
textbook, *Principles of Economics, With Special Reference to American Conditions*, became an important
transmitter of the marginalist approach. But he
took pains to underline that such concepts as "normal rate of interest," "normal wages," or "normal
price" applied to the "largely hypothetical" situation of "static conditions." In the real world, however, "conditions are continually changing or
dynamic. The law is one of movement, not of rest."
When studying economics, therefore, "we must endeavor first to ascertain how the particular relations
have come to be what they are; secondly, to explain
what are the conditions of the problem as it actually
exists; and, finally, to forecast the probable changes
in the institutions as a result of an alteration in the
conditions of the problem."

Even more important, Seligman made the

centerpiece of his own approach the German historical school's gospel of the interrelatedness of all
human activities. Take, for example, his analysis of
the problem of economic value. Value was a measure of "utility"—that is, "capacity to satisfy a want."
Although utility at the individual level was exclusively a psychological matter, market value was the
measure of utility set by "society as a whole." "At
bottom," he explained, "it is demand which sets in
motion those forces which result in giving a thing
value. The social demand for a thing is due to the
uses to which it can be put. But the uses to which
it can be put depend not only upon the thing to be
used but on the individuals who use it." A savage
would have no use for a watch except possibly as
a trinket. "People now want more things of different kinds than in the earlier stages of society." And
the things that people want "depend in the last
resort upon their aesthetic, intellectual and moral
conditions. The physical appetite of civilized man
differs from that of the savage only in its being
more refined—that is, more aesthetic. It differs not
in quantity, but in quality. His other appetites also
change with the development of civilization. The
economic life is therefore ultimately bound up with
the whole moral and social life."

While placing the study of economics in a
broad social context, Seligman was simultaneously
calling upon historians to pay more attention to the
role of economic factors. His plea appeared first in
a four-part series of articles in the *Political Science
Quarterly* in 1901 and 1902; their revision appeared
in book form in 1902 under the title *The Economic
Interpretation of History*. His target was the narrowly
legal-institutional focus dominant among late-nineteenth-century "scientific" historians—an approach given its classic expression in English
historian Edward A. Freeman's dictum that "history is past politics." Although expressing his gratification at evidences of a growing awareness that
"political history is only one phase of that wider
activity which includes all the phenomena of social
life," Seligman pointed out that there still remained
the question of "the fundamental causes of this
social development—the reason of these great
changes in human thought and human life which
form the conditions of progress." His answer was:
"The existence of man depends upon his ability to
sustain himself; the economic life is therefore the
fundamental condition of all life. . . . What the conditions of maintenance are to the individual, the
similar relations of production and consumption
are to the community. To economic causes, therefore, must be traced in last instance those trans-

formations in the structure of society which themselves condition the relations of social classes and the various manifestations of social life."

Seligman traced the antecedents of his "thesis" to the pioneering analyses of the conditioning influence exerted by the physical environment upon human life by Giovanni Battista Vico, Montesquieu, and the nineteenth-century British historian Thomas H. Buckle. He likewise acknowledged the contribution made by American anthropologist Lewis Henry Morgan in showing how changes in the form and condition of property transformed family relationships. But he hailed Karl Marx as "in the truest sense the originator of the economic interpretation of history." Seligman had a more extensive knowledge of the then-available corpus of Marx's work than probably any other American scholar of the time. He tracked the development of Marx's thinking through his early writings. He relied even more heavily upon Friedrich Engels's later explanatory glosses on the master. As a matter of fact, his summary exposition of his position was a close paraphrase of Engels. He largely dismissed Marx's economic theorizing as erroneous. He even more painstakingly denied any "necessary connection" between the economic interpretation of history and socialism. "One can be," he assured his readers, "an 'economic materialist' and yet remain an extreme individualist." He focused instead upon, and paid homage to, Marx's formulation of the principle "that all relations of society depend upon changes in the economic life and more particularly in the modes of production."

Seligman rightly explained that Marx meant by the mode of production not simply the existing state of technology but "the conditions of production in general." He relied upon Engels's more open-ended exegesis to deny that Marx was guilty of a philosophical monism that made economic factors the exclusive agent of social and intellectual change. He similarly acquitted Marx of postulating an iron-clad determinism that excluded the possibility of men shaping the course of events. Whether this reinterpretation reflected Marx's own position is debatable. But the strategy allowed Seligman to rebut critics with the reply that they misunderstood the true import of the economic interpretation. "The economic interpretation of history, correctly understood," he declared, "does not claim that every phenomenon of human life in general, or of social life in particular, is to be explained on economic grounds." On the contrary, "the actual form of the social organization is often determined by

political, legal, philosophical and religious theories and conceptions." And while "political, legal, religious, literary and artistic development rests on the economic," all simultaneously "react upon one another and on the economic foundation." He even left room for the "great man"—although he added the qualification that "the great man influences society only when society is ready for him. If society is not ready for him, he is called, not a great man, but a visionary or a failure."

Seligman devoted the largest part of his defense of the economic interpretation to answering the indictment that the theory denied the role of "ethical and spiritual forces in history." He extolled the "ethical teacher" as "the scout and the vanguard of society." But the preacher—like the great man—could have an impact only if the times were ready. "It is always on the border line of the transition from the old social necessity to the new social convenience that the ethical reformer makes his influence felt. With the perpetual change in human conditions there is always some kind of border line, and thus always the need of the moral teacher, to point out the higher ideal and the path of progress. Unless the social conditions, however, are ripe for the change, the demand of the ethical reformer will be fruitless." The most important prerequisite for moral progress was the improvement of men's material well-being. "Human life," he explained, "has thus far not been exempt from the inexorable law of nature, with its struggle for existence . . . due to the pressure of life upon the means of subsistence. . . . Civilization indeed consists in the attempt to minimize the evils, while conserving the benefits of this hitherto inevitable conflict between material resources and human desires. As long, however, as this conflict endures, the primary explanation of human life must continue to be the economic explanation—the explanation of the adjustment of material resources to human desires. This adjustment may be modified by aesthetic, religious and moral, in short, by intellectual and spiritual forces; but in the last resort it still remains an adjustment of life to the wherewithal of life."

There is no question that Seligman's *Economic Interpretation of History* contributed in a major way to making the economic interpretation of history respectable in the United States, partly by disassociating the theory from socialism, partly by repudiating its more deterministic implications. His direct influence on American historical scholarship, however, is difficult to assess. In his *An Economic Interpretation of the Constitution of the United States* (1913), Charles A. Beard quoted Seligman in justification of his application of an economic interpretation to the founding fathers. But there was a radical difference in Beard's and Seligman's treatments of the crucial question of motivation. Beard embraced a reductionism that made men's views the reflection of their economic self-interest. Wittingly or not, he re-enthroned the "economic man" of classical economics. By contrast, Seligman denied that human beings were moved exclusively by the drive to maximize their material welfare. On the contrary, he found innumerable examples in history when individuals, even masses of men, have acted from other than economic motives. "A full analysis of all the motives that influence men, even in their economic life," he underlined, "would test the powers of the social psychologist." And for the most part, the writers of American "Progressive history" would follow the Beardian model rather than Seligman's subtler approach.

Seligman's influence lay more in the realm of the larger intellectual climate of opinion. He had imbibed from the German historical school awareness of the relativity of economic institutions. What most attracted him to Marx was how Marx had expanded this approach to make all aspects of human existence—even human consciousness itself—historical products. Therein lay the major contribution of Seligman's own work: its affirmation that "man, like everything else, is what he is because of his environment, past and present." In his 1902 American Economic Association presidential address, he applied this principle to attack the long-dominant conviction of American historical uniqueness. The mid-nineteenth-century expression of that belief—given its classic statement by George Bancroft—pictured American history as the unfolding of God's providential plan. The late-nineteenth-century scientific historians did no more than substitute for God's hand the Teutonic idea of liberty. Seligman dismissed such eulogizing of America's "distinctive mission" as filiopietistic conceit. "We think with complacency," he scoffed, "that there is something inherent in our democracy; we look back upon the achievements of our colonial struggles as the obvious consequence of the Puritan character; we congratulate ourselves upon our love of liberty. . . . What we do not see is the essential relativity of all these phenomena, the dependence of them all on the shifting conditions of time and place."

American democracy, he went on to elaborate, "was the result, not of the Puritan ancestry, but of the economic conditions. The Puritans had nothing to do with the beginnings of democracy in the mediaeval communes, or with its development amid the Alps of Switzerland or the dunes of Holland. . . ." He likewise deflated the "so-called Anglo-Saxon love of liberty." Where the "economic environment" made slavery profitable—as in the American South—there "took but a few generations for the sturdy and liberty-loving patriots of England and Scotland to become sincere and devoted believers in the necessity and the beneficence of slavery." The same applied to "the boasted Anglo-Saxon individualism." In the beginning years of the nation, Americans faced with wresting a living from poor soil in an inhospitable climate did not hesitate to turn to government for help. "But when the mountains had been crossed and the fertile valleys of the Middle West had been reached, there came a wondrous change. Conscious of their new opportunities, the citizens now desired only to be left alone in their quest for prosperity." Where different conditions prevailed—as in Australia—socialism or its near equivalent was the result. Even in this country, under the transforming force of industrialization, "the theory of extreme individualism is passing away."

Paradoxically, Seligman's embrace of "historicism" (that is, the assumption that all human phenomena can be explained historically) came at the time when many European thinkers were recoiling from what seemed its disturbing relativist implications. Neither Seligman nor his readers, however, felt such qualms because he assimilated relativism to the long-standing American faith in progress. Seligman was confident that the future would not simply be different from the past, but would be better. He admitted that there were those taking a more pessimistic view who saw ahead the decline, decay, and final dissolution that past civilizations had experienced. But he himself found forces at work that "differentiate modern industrial society from all its predecessors." The advance of science and technology carried the promise of achieving abundance for all. The growing economic interdependence of the countries of the world would eliminate national power rivalries and war. Most important, "the existence of the democratic ideal" bore the seeds of a new conception of society based upon justice and harmony. "The social unrest of to-day," he concluded in a burst of optimism, "with all its disquieting and deplorable incidents, is on the whole a salutary symptom. It is but the labor-pains in the birth of the new industrial order which has been in the making for the past few generations. . . ."

However shallow such optimism may appear

to a later generation, this faith in evolutionary progress was a source of strength for Seligman. A leading defender of academic freedom, he chaired the committee of the American Economic Association that investigated, and in 1901 condemned, the dismissal of sociologist Edward A. Ross by Stanford University because of his advocacy of reform. He was one of the founders of the American Association of University Professors (AAUP) in 1915; he chaired the committee that drew up its landmark report on academic freedom and academic tenure (1915). In a world "where well nigh everything is in a state of flux . . . ," he explained in his 1921 AAUP presidential address, "how fatal to human progress would it be if the slightest brake were put on the effort of the human mind to convert the unknown into the known!" He himself showed a continual willingness to re-examine and adapt his own thinking to meet new conditions. In the 1920s he was a leading exponent of American assistance—including cancellation of the Allied war debts—to promote European recovery. And in the crisis of the Great Depression, he challenged the budget balancers by calling for large-scale public-works spending to revive the economy. "In policy as in analysis," Joseph Dorfman, the leading student of the history of American economic thought, has concluded, "Seligman moved just ahead of prevailing doctrines. . . ."

The catholicity of his interests was perhaps most strikingly revealed in what became the major focus of his energies toward the end of his career—the publication of the monumental fifteen-volume *Encyclopaedia of the Social Sciences* (1930-1935). He was chief promoter, leading fund-raiser, and editor in chief. He recruited a group of contributors who represented the widest possible range of viewpoints and constituted a who's who of the world's leading scholars. Reflecting his concern over the fragmentation of the study of human behavior along narrow disciplinary lines, in introductory remarks to the *Encyclopaedia* Seligman defined "What Are the Social Sciences?" in broad terms as "those mental or cultural sciences which deal with the activities of the individual as a member of a group." Included with what he termed "the purely social sciences" (political science, economics, law, anthropology, penology, sociology, and social work) were such ancillary fields as psychology, linguistics, philosophy and ethics, education, geography, art, and even biology. And he assigned to history a place of honor as the foundation stone of the field. With the expansion of its scope in recent years to encompass the manifold aspects of human life, "history has

become an indispensable source of material for the interpretation of all manner of social processes."

Seligman married Caroline Beer, the sister of historian George Louis Beer, in 1888; the couple had four children—Eustace, Mabel, Violet, and Hazel. On the surface Seligman looked like the epitome of the dignified European-style professor, down to his neatly trimmed beard. Beneath this exterior, however, was an extremely warmhearted person known for his generosity to graduate students and younger colleagues. He was not simply a good person, but a good citizen as well. He was a founder of the City Club and an active participant in its work for civic improvement. From 1900 to 1902 he was secretary of the Committee of Fifteen, whose exposure of the corrupt links between prostitution and the New York police paved the way for Seth Low's successful 1901 mayoral campaign against Tammany Hall. He was chairman (1907-1910) of the board of trustees of the New York Bureau of Municipal Research, the nation's pioneering research institute in public administration. Widely regarded as the country's foremost authority on public finance and taxation, he acted as expert consultant to a host of official bodies from the municipal to the international level. His reputation for balance and fair-mindedness assured his views a respectful hearing by the press and public officials. He died on 18 July 1939, of coronary thrombosis, at his summer home in Lake Placid, New York. As a former student eulogized, probably "no academic economist, by voice and pen, has ever reached and influenced so many of his contemporaries."

Letters:
"The Seligman Correspondence," edited by Joseph Dorfman, *Political Science Quarterly*, 56 (March 1941): 107-124; 56 (June 1941): 270-286; 56 (September 1941): 392-419; 56 (December 1941): 573-599.

Bibliography:
A Bibliography of the Faculty of Political Science of Columbia University 1880-1930 (New York: Columbia University Press, 1931), pp. 25-43.

References:
Joseph Dorfman, *The Economic Mind in American Civilization*, 5 volumes (New York: Viking, 1946-1959);
Edward Robert Anderson Seligman, 1861-1939 (Stamford, Conn.: Printed at the Overlook Press, 1942);

R. Gordon Hoxie and others, *A History of the Faculty of Political Science, Columbia University* (New York: Columbia University Press, 1955).

Papers:
Seligman's extensive papers are in Special Collections, Columbia University Library, New York, New York.

J. Allen Smith

(5 May 1860-30 January 1924)

John Braeman
University of Nebraska at Lincoln

BOOKS: *The Spirit of American Government, A Study of the Constitution: Its Origin, Influence and Relation to Democracy* (New York & London: Macmillan, 1907);

The Growth and Decadence of Constitutional Government (New York: Holt, 1930; London: Williams & Norgate, 1930).

OTHER: "The Multiple Money Standard," in *Annals of the American Academy of Political and Social Science*, 7 (1896), pp. 1-60;

"Recent Institutional Legislation," in *Proceedings of the American Political Science Association for the Year 1907* (1908), pp. 141-151;

"Effect of State Regulation of Public Utilities upon Municipal Home Rule," in *Annals of the American Academy of Political and Social Science*, 53 (1914), pp. 85-93.

PERIODICAL PUBLICATIONS: "The Relation of Oriental Immigration to the General Immigration Problem," *Bulletin of the American Economic Association*, fourth series (April 1911): 237-242;

"Municipal vs. State Control of Public Utilities," *National Municipal Review*, 3 (January 1914): 34-43.

Published in 1907 as the Progressive movement was moving into high gear, J. Allen Smith's *The Spirit of American Government* attracted a flurry of attention with its thesis that the country's current ills came from a designedly undemocratic Constitution. But he faded back into obscurity until his longtime friend and University of Washington colleague Vernon L. Parrington dedicated the first

two volumes of his influential *Main Currents in American Thought* (1927) to "J. Allen Smith Scholar Teacher Democrat Gentleman." In his third volume (1930), Parrington identified Smith as a pioneer in shattering the myths surrounding the nation's fundamental law that underpinned the status quo. Following this lead, the custodians of the American liberal pantheon elevated Smith to its ranks. Walton H. Hamilton eulogized *The Spirit of American Government* as "a breath of fresh air" that swept away the conventional wisdom's "comfortable assurance of fundamental principles and eternal verities"; Eric F. Goldman hailed the work as "a revolutionary . . . landmark in our political thought." While acknowledging how later scholarship had revealed shortcomings, Cushing Strout in 1965 found the book "still has precious value as one of the most characteristic and influential expressions of the Progressive temper in its intellectual and moral effort to bring itself into vital connection with the national inheritance."

James Allen Smith was born on 5 May 1860 at Pleasant Hill, Cass County, Missouri. His mother was Naomi Holloway, the daughter of a Virginia slaveholder who had moved to western Missouri near present-day Kansas City. His father, Isaac James Smith, was a former sea captain turned farmer. Although owning only one or two slaves, the family was pro-Confederate in its sympathies. In 1863 the Smiths were forced to leave their farm by a military order expelling the settlers from the area to deny local assistance to pro-Confederate guerrillas. They moved in with relatives in Kansas City. Shortly after the war, Isaac Smith built a home at the edge of Kansas City on that part of the Holloway property willed to his wife. But he could do no more than eke out a bare living on the new farm. These experiences intensified Naomi Smith's bitterness over the Union victory, reinforced her tendency to romanticize the gentility of the antebellum Southern way of life. This home atmosphere left its mark. Reflecting his own yearning for distinction, Smith legally changed his name to the less commonplace J. Allen. He retained Southern attitudes about the Negro's place; he favored restrictions on the entry of Orientals and the new immigrants from southern and eastern Europe; he felt uncomfortable in personal contacts with workingmen. And the legacy of allegiance to the Lost Cause contributed to his sense of alienation from the main currents of post-Civil War America.

Smith's frail health—he suffered from chronic shortness of breath—probably contributed to his viewing education as a way out of the drudgery of farm life. After going through the primary grades in a country school near his parents' farm, he attended Kansas City High School. Graduating "in the highest class," he taught school in order to save the money to go to college. In the fall of 1883 he enrolled at the University of Missouri in Columbia. He majored in the "Arts" course—a "slightly modified" version of the traditional classical curriculum. His teachers were intellectually orthodox. The text for his political economy class was Francis Wayland's *The Elements of Political Economy* (1837): laissez-faire clothed in the garb of Christian moralism. His political science course took a legalistic approach to the Constitution based upon Sir William Blackstone and Chancellor James Kent. Despite his absence from campus for much of his second year because of the death of his father, he graduated in June 1886 in the "First Rank." That fall he entered the university's Law Department; he received his LL.B. in June 1887 and proceeded to open a law office in downtown Kansas City. But he was not successful—or happy—at the bar. Not simply did he find the petty details of a minor practice at odds with his idealized vision of the lawyer's role, but, in addition, the growing political ferment of the time drew him to the study of contemporary social and economic problems.

At Missouri, Smith first showed his maverick streak by becoming a leader of a student revolt against the university's authoritarian president. When his political economy professor warned the class against Henry George's *Progress and Poverty* (1879), he promptly read the book. Although Smith never became a single-taxer, George's indictment of existing conditions made a deep impress upon his mind. Along the way, Smith also abandoned the

Southern Baptist faith of his youth. Vocal in his hostility toward organized religion as a pillar of the established order, he would never become a member of any church. The major turning point in life was his marriage on 26 November 1890 to Doris J. Lehmann of Maywood, Missouri. Her outgoing personality complemented his own shyness and reserve; more important, she encouraged him to give up the law to pursue his intellectual ambitions. He had taken advantage of Kansas City's rapid population growth to borrow money to build rental housing on the family farm. The resulting income allowed him in the fall of 1892 to begin graduate work at the University of Michigan under economist Henry Carter Adams. Influenced by the German school of historical economics, Adams defended labor unions, supported protective legislation for women and children, and favored a positive role for government "to maintain the beneficent results of competitive action while guarding society from the evil consequences of unrestrained competition."

Smith was awarded the Ph.D. in June 1894. Taking as his major field "Finance," he wrote his dissertation on the money question. The money question was the hottest political issue of the day. And Smith had a direct personal interest because the Panic of 1893 wiped out his savings and forced him to sell his rental properties to pay off the mortgage. Smith's approach in his dissertation, "The Multiple Money Standard," was influenced by American scientist-turned-economist Simon Newcomb and English economists W. Stanley Jevons and Alfred Marshall. Still, the work represented an imaginative, and in Joseph Dorfman's view, an "extremely suggestive" break with prevailing opinion. The late-nineteenth-century American debate on the money question revolved around three alternatives—the gold standard, international bimetallism, and the free coinage of silver at a 16:1 ratio to gold. By contrast, Smith denied the adequacy of any metallic-based currency. The difficulty with such currency was that its value constantly fluctuated with supply and demand, producing disruptive price fluctuations. "If gold rises in value," he explained, "or what is the same thing, the total demand for money becomes greater than the supply, the total demand for commodities is correspondingly diminished, and a fall in general prices ensues. If gold falls in value, the result is an increased demand for commodities and a rise in general prices." Thus, "fluctuations in the value of money are the cause of the paroxyms of modern industry."

The gist of his proposed remedy was a government-managed legal tender paper currency whose supply would be expanded or contracted to coincide with ups and downs in general commodity prices. When prices rose, the currency supply would be contracted; when prices fell, the currency supply would be expanded. The result would be a medium of exchange of almost constant value, a stable price level, and uninterrupted long-term economic growth. Smith was no advocate of free silver; on the contrary, he emphasized its inadequacies. But his denunciation of "gold monometallism" sufficed to brand him with the taint of intellectual heresy. The dissertation would not be without its future influence. The distinguished Yale economist Irving Fisher would draw upon Smith when formulating his "compensated dollar" plan whereby the gold value of the dollar would be periodically readjusted to maintain price stability. And proposals along similar lines would gain popularity during the Great Depression. At the time, however, the work attracted scant attention even though Henry Carter Adams arranged for its publication in March 1896 in the *Annals of the American Academy of Political and Social Science*. In part, Smith's scheme involved a larger degree of governmental control than even most liberal-minded contemporary economists could accept; in part, interest in the money question faded with the post-1896 return of prosperity. Most important, nearly everyone who counted in American economics regarded a self-regulating metallic standard as the only practicable monetary system.

Unable to find a suitable academic position for the fall of 1894, Smith stayed on at Michigan as Adams's teaching assistant, and Doris Smith returned to work as a secretary. That spring he accepted an offer of a professorship at Marietta College in southern Ohio. The school's president, John Simpson, a clergyman active in the Social Gospel movement, wanted someone of "liberal views" to teach economics and sociology and promised Smith a free hand. But Simpson was forced out as president. Although Smith was reappointed for a second year, the trustees voted in March 1897 not to renew his contract. The official reason given was the institution's financial difficulties. Smith's salary had been provided by private contributions outside of regular college funds; now this support was withdrawn. The college's hiring of a part-time replacement at a higher salary than Smith was receiving indicates, however, that more was involved. Smith himself had no doubt that the trustees were moved by hostility toward his politics. "They are," he complained bitterly, "partisan Republicans, are interested in gas and other monopolies, and would like to see the teaching in this college subordinated to their own private interests. It is probable that I should have found no difficulty in remaining here had I been willing to defend protection, unregulated private ownership of monopolies, and the gold standard. As it was a case of intellectual prostitution or giving up my position, I preferred the latter."

Fortunately, he was offered the chair of history and political science at the Populist-dominated University of Washington. Although history was split from the department of political and social sciences in 1898, Smith still had the responsibility for single-handedly covering economics, political sociology, and American "political institutions." By that time, the major focus of his own interests had shifted from economics to political science. The gradual addition of new faculty to the department eventually allowed him to devote the bulk of his time to instruction in that area, with particular emphasis on municipal government and reform. Although Smith generally shied from direct personal involvement in politics, he nevertheless became a focal point of controversy. He first became a target of attack because of his support for municipal ownership of Seattle's street railways and utilities. Complaints about his radicalism were given new force with the publication by the Macmillan Company in 1907 of *The Spirit of American Government*. In the preface, Smith boldly laid out his thesis: that "the real spirit and purpose" of the Constitution was "its inherent opposition to democracy." His own purpose in writing the book, he explained, was "to strengthen and advance the cause of popular government by bringing us to a realization of the fact that the so-called evils of democracy are very largely the natural results of those constitutional checks on popular rule which we have inherited from the political system of the eighteenth century."

Smith pictured the impetus behind adoption of the Constitution as a "conservative reaction" against the democratic impulse unleashed by the American Revolution. He did not feel any compulsion to present a philosophical justification for democracy; its value was assumed as a self-evident truth. And his definition of its meaning was simply "the principle of majority rule." Majority rule presupposed not only "political equality" (that is, universal suffrage) but "supremacy of the legislature." Applying that standard, he found the early state constitutions, and even the Articles of Confederation, more democratic than the new Constitution. He pointed to abundant examples of how the Constitution imposed limits upon the popular will: the difficulties in the way of amendment; indirect election of the president and United States senators; and an appointive federal judiciary irremovable except by impeachment. He even assailed equal representation in the Senate as further evidence of the framers' antidemocratic bias. But the major target of his animus was the "system of checks and balances"—which he stigmatized as the antithesis of "popular government." "We must," he admonished, "either recognize the many as supreme, with no checks upon their authority except such as are implied in their own intelligence, sense of justice and spirit of fair play, or we must accept the view that the ultimate authority is in the hands of the few."

In one sense, *The Spirit of American Government* was hardly novel. The discussion of the limits imposed by the Constitution on governmental authority for the protection of person and property was a staple of late-nineteenth-century legal commentary. While at Michigan, Smith himself had taken as his minor field "Comparative Constitutional Law" and studied under probably the most influential expositor of the constitutional limitations theme, Thomas M. Cooley. There was, similarly, wide acceptance that the architects of the Constitution harbored a deep suspicion of unrestrained popular majorities. The founding fathers' "distrust of government in which the people would have free sway," University of Chicago professor Andrew C. McLaughlin observed dismissively, was nothing more than a commonplace "to the student of American constitutional history." Where Smith diverged from the mainstream was in the conclusion that he drew—or, to be more accurate, in the value judgments that he made. Defenders of property rights extolled the barriers against majority rule raised by the Constitution as its cardinal virtue. Even those who did not go so far paid homage to the Constitution as a work of farsighted statesmanship; agreed that the new republic faced a crisis threatening its continued existence; and found the framers' attitudes justified by the experiences under the Articles of Confederation or, at a minimum, understandable given the dominant values of the age.

By contrast, Smith dismissed the critical-era rationale as so much propaganda. He pilloried the men of the convention as reactionaries even for the time, finding their handiwork more immunized against popular influence than even the eigh-

teenth-century British government had been. He explained away whatever concessions were made to vox populi as no more than bows to political expediency. Most important, he portrayed the supporters of the Constitution as a band of conspirators guilty of misrepresentation and unscrupulous political tactics. Nowhere was Smith more on the offensive than in his treatment of the Supreme Court. Like many reformers of the day, he directed his sharpest attack against the Court's power of judicial review: "A more powerful check upon democratic innovation it would be hard to devise." But he denied that the Court had usurped that power. To thwart the popular will was its intended role from the start. The ambiguity of the constitutional text was a disguise. The framers realized that "to give to the judiciary the power to veto legislation . . . by an express provision of the Constitution . . . . would have disclosed altogether too clearly the undemocratic reactionary character of the proposed government and thus have prevented its adoption. . . . It was by controlling the Executive and the Senate, and through these the appointment of Supreme judges, that they expected to incorporate this power in the Constitution and make it a permanent feature of our political system."

Smith proceeded to ascribe to the poisoned root of the Constitution all the ills facing the United States. The Senate was a millionaire's club that stood as an immovable barrier against reform legislation at the national level. The federal judiciary narrowly circumscribed the regulatory powers of the states. Simultaneously, municipal self-government was denied by the legal fiction that made cities creatures of the state and thus at the mercy of special interest-dominated state legislatures. This lack of home rule was, Smith held, "the main cause of corruption and inefficiency in municipal government." He acknowledged that there had taken place developments not foreseen—much less wanted—by the framers. A new democratic upsurge during the Jacksonian era had forced removal of property qualifications for voting. But the defenders of minority rule had neutralized this gain by propagandizing the public into accepting the Constitution as the embodiment of democratic principles. Thus sanctified in popular veneration, the system of checks and balances was extended to the state and local levels. The result was to nullify the ability of the parties—another departure from the governmental system envisaged by the framers—to implement their programs. Because the parties were thus denied meaningful power, the outcome was the public apathy that has "allowed a small selfish minority to seize the party machinery."

Even by the standards of the day, *The Spirit of American Government* lacked scholarly weight. Smith's evidence for the antidemocratic purposes of the framers consisted of quotations selected from the published convention debates—many from delegates who ended up refusing to endorse the Constitution. He made Alexander Hamilton into the moving spirit behind the new frame of government and treated the New Yorker's views as representative of the delegates as a body, notwithstanding the convention's rejection of Hamilton's plan. He consulted no archival sources; even his knowledge of the published secondary materials was spotty. He showed no awareness of Richard Hildreth's *The History of the United States of America* (1856-1860) or Orin G. Libby's *The Geographical Distribution of the Vote of the Thirteen States on the Federal Constitution* (1894)—to note two works whose analyses of the socioeconomic divisions over the Constitution would have provided support for his own interpretation. Part of Smith's difficulty stemmed from the inadequacy of the University of Washington Library. But the deeper problem was that Smith lacked the capacity for genuine historical thinking: he studied the past not in its own terms but as grist for a jeremiad directed at the present. This same polemical thrust marred his treatment of the current American political scene. Although capable of shrewd observations, he was not so much a realist explaining how things actually worked as an ideologue preaching what should be.

Not without reason, therefore, the work failed to make much of a stir among scholars. Those who were enthusiastic, like sociologist Edward A. Ross or economist Richard T. Ely, lacked expertise in the subject. Most of those who had the necessary background—even the reform-minded—were unimpressed. Smith is remembered today primarily as a forerunner of, and major influence on, Charles A. Beard's *An Economic Interpretation of the Constitution of the United States* (1913). But that reputation appears not warranted. The two were poles apart on the crucial issue of motivation—a difference that Parrington grasped more astutely than many later commentators. Smith portrayed the framers as animated by an abstract antidemocratic ideology; Beard linked their distrust of popular majorities to their economic class interests. Smith did allude to how supporters of the Constitution represented "the wealth and culture of the colonies"; he did suggest that the document's purpose was "to perpetuate the ascendancy of the property-holding class"; he even affirmed that "constitutional forms are always largely the product and expression of economic conditions." But he failed to develop these scattered references in any systematic way. While he quoted James Madison's analysis of the sources of faction in *The Federalist*, number 10, he did so simply as evidence of the framers' hostility to "majority rule." There is no inkling in Smith of Beard's distinction between reality and personality. Nor did he deal with the influences that Beard emphasized when explaining the movement for the Constitution: the fathers' public securities holdings, the agitation for paper money and stay laws, or even Shay's Rebellion.

The Spirit of American Government was, however, a popular success, selling thirteen thousand plus copies—more, for example, than Herbert Croly's *The Promise of American Life* (1909) or Beard's work on the Constitution. The Chautauqua Institute included Smith's book in its 1911-1912 home-study course, which resulted in the distribution of another eight thousand copies. Most of the reviews in newspapers and general magazines were favorable, and enthusiastic raves came from leading reform activists and publicists. Smith tapped the same mood exploited by the muckraking journalists: the suspicion of sordid realities hiding behind a respectable facade. Probably at least equally responsible for the book's appeal was how Smith gave the appearance of radicalism without its substance. In the economic sphere, he called for governmental action "to the end that the product of industry may be equitably distributed." But what he meant was simply the familiar goal of "equality of opportunity." Nor did his substantive recommendations go beyond the Jeffersonian-Jacksonian demand for the elimination of "special privileges." A like gap existed between his indictment of the structural defects in the existing political system and the reforms proposed. While advocating the standard nostrums of the direct primary, the initiative and referendum, and the recall, he placed his major emphasis upon popular election of United States senators. Once the Senate was "democratized," he assured, there would be no difficulty in bringing even the judiciary "into line with the popular movement."

During Smith's years there, the University of Washington was not a major center for graduate training. But he was a highly popular undergraduate lecturer who inspired many of his students to go on to careers in scholarship and public service. Although he was the target of recurring attack, the support he enjoyed among students and faculty and from reform and labor groups in the state protected him against the loss of his position. Smith served as acting dean of the College of Liberal Arts in 1911 and as dean of the Graduate School from 1909 until 1920. Nevertheless, his last years at Washington were far from happy. He ran afoul of the university's authoritarian new president, Henry Suzzallo, over Suzzallo's ambition to institute a new program in business administration. Given his exalted view of the function of education—"laying a suitable foundation for right thinking on the part of the people"—Smith opposed the university's offering courses in what he described as "individual wealth getting." In retaliation, Suzzallo in 1917 divided the Political and Social Science Department into separate departments of political science, sociology, and economics. The reshuffle left Smith to handle political science by himself, assisted at most by one or two ill-trained instructors. Personal tragedies aggravated the situation. His daughter Elfreda—born 1 January 1898—was left paralyzed by an attack of poliomyelitis. A son Allen died in infancy from influenza. In 1918 Smith himself was found to have developed serious heart trouble. And as his health rapidly deteriorated, he was torn with anxiety about the financial welfare of his family.

At the same time he watched with growing dismay the direction of public affairs. Although not publicly expressing his feelings, he strongly opposed American intervention in World War I. He viewed the conflict as no more than a struggle between rival imperialisms—a struggle born of the quest by "big business interests" for profitable markets. He was convinced that American involvement would spell the doom of further reform at home. That involvement was proof of how the president could abuse his powers to plunge the country into war regardless of the majority's wish for peace. The results of U.S. entry into the conflict confirmed his worst forebodings. He was appalled by the repression of antiwar dissenters followed by the antiradical crusade of the post-Armistice red scare. He found the Versailles Treaty a betrayal of the idealistic goals used in official rhetoric to justify American participation, saw the League of Nations as a device to safeguard the spoils grabbed by the victors. The war led to the increased aggrandizement of executive power, gave further impetus to business concentration and consolidation, and accelerated the country's militarization. Warren G. Harding's election to the presidency signaled the death of the reform impulse of the preceding years. In response to such developments, Smith labored on a new book that would explain what had gone

wrong. As a latter-day Jeffersonian, he found the answer readily at hand. "The recent world war and the political changes that accompanied and followed it," he explained to a former student, "convinced me that extreme centralization of political power is one of the greatest dangers confronting this country today."

At his death on 30 January 1924 Smith had finished all except a planned concluding chapter of *The Growth and Decadence of Constitutional Government*. His daughter Elfreda—who had served as his secretary—could not find a publisher willing to take a chance on the manuscript until Henry Holt and Company did so in 1930. The contrast of this later work with *The Spirit of American Government* was striking. As he had in the first book, Smith pictured the central theme of American history as "a constant struggle between conservatism and liberalism." But its substance was transformed from a conflict between the supporters of majority rule

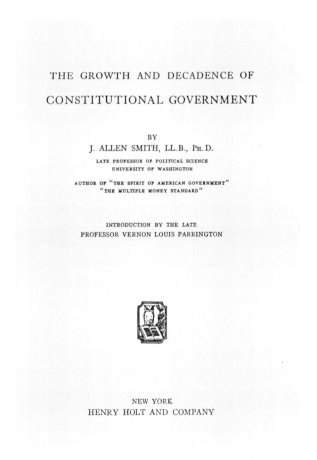

THE GROWTH AND DECADENCE OF

CONSTITUTIONAL GOVERNMENT

BY

J. ALLEN SMITH, LL.B., PH.D.

LATE PROFESSOR OF POLITICAL SCIENCE
UNIVERSITY OF WASHINGTON

AUTHOR OF "THE SPIRIT OF AMERICAN GOVERNMENT"
"THE MULTIPLE MONEY STANDARD"

INTRODUCTION BY THE LATE
PROFESSOR VERNON LOUIS PARRINGTON

NEW YORK
HENRY HOLT AND COMPANY

Title page for Smith's posthumously published book, in which the central theme of American history is described in terms of "a struggle between those who would limit and diffuse political power and those who would centralize and extend governmental authority" and the defenders of elite control into "a struggle between those who would limit and diffuse political power and those who would centralize and extend governmental authority." He no longer contrasted the antidemocratic views of the framers of the Constitution with the democratic spirit of the American revolutionists. Rather, he emphasized the almost universal fear of "unlimited authority of any sort." Eighteenth-century "liberal political philosophy" assumed the existence of "a law of nature . . . guaranteeing certain rights to the individual"; this "theory of natural law, natural rights, and individual liberty not only served to justify the Revolution, but also constituted the philosophic foundation of the American political system." While acknowledging "the people as the only source of legitimate authority," the Declaration of Independence and early state constitutions recognized that the limits imposed by natural law applied even to "the democratic state."

Smith's treatment of the Constitution in *The Growth and Decadence of Constitutional Government* was diametrically opposite to his account in *The Spirit of American Government.* No longer was Hamilton portrayed as spokesman for the convention; his enthusiasm for a centralized government was now found not to be shared by most of the delegates. The "check and balance plan" was transformed from the major source of the country's ills into a wise and necessary safeguard against "governmental absolutism." Judicial review was not the crowning arch of the system of checks and balances but its antithesis, given the absence of any limits upon the judiciary's exercise of the crucially important "constitution-interpreting power." And that power was usurped by the Supreme Court. While "some influential members" hoped for that result, Smith argued that "there is no ground for believing that this viewpoint was accepted by the convention as a whole, or even by an influential class of that time." In *The Spirit of American Government* he had presented the real—though disguised—aim of the framers as establishment of the "complete supremacy of the general government." Now he denied the existence of any such ambition. Although the framers wanted a stronger central government than that provided by the Articles of Confederation, "there was no intention to make it supreme." As shown by the application of the name "Federal" to the new governmental structure, their purpose was "to make the division of power between the states and the general government such that neither would be able to encroach on the other."

The source of current ills, therefore, was not the Constitution but the departures made from its principles. Following John C. Calhoun—who more even than Jefferson emerges as his intellectual hero—Smith placed much of the blame upon the failure of the framers to provide a workable mechanism by which the states could resist encroachments by the federal government upon their position. In *The Spirit of American Government,* he had stigmatized that omission as "not a mere oversight"; now the failure was a mistake made in "good faith." The Supreme Court remained a favored target. But Smith's heaviest fire was directed not so much against the Court's hostility to democratic reform as at the "way in which the judiciary has aided in the growth of federal power at the expense of the state." And more explicitly than in *The Spirit of American Government,* he made his principal villain "the capitalist class." "Organized wealth" spearheaded the push to strengthen the national government vis-à-vis the states because the farther removed a government was from the average citizen the easier domination by a minority would be. This motive explained why "the well-to-do classes" resisted municipal home rule. The same "big business interests" were behind the League of Nations. Popular control was sufficiently difficult to attain within a single nation; "it would be infinitely more difficult for the people of the world as a whole, hampered as they are by differences in race, culture, language, and religion, to exercise any effective control over the policies of such a league."

Despite his attacks on "the capitalistic system," Smith had no sympathy for socialism. His animus was against the concentration of power in any form. "Industrial consolidation" not only meant exploitive "monopoly profits" but also threatened "political democracy." Thus, he called for more vigorous antitrust action to restore "a régime of free competition." In the political sphere, he called for the maximum possible devolution of authority to the local level. This Jeffersonian bias was not new. The difference lay in Smith's rationale for governmental decentralization: the protection of "individual liberty." Whereas in *The Spirit of American Government* he had accepted as axiomatic the rightness of the majority will, now he was no longer so sure. The pages of *The Growth and Decadence of Constitutional Government* were sprinkled with laments about the public's lack of "sufficient civic intelligence." Although he placed much of the blame upon business domination of the media, his disillusionment ran more deeply. The popular hysteria against dissent during and after the war had shattered his formerly optimistic faith in "the masses" by exposing what he called their "blind instinctive fear" of any challenge to their cherished beliefs. Human nature was such that no one could be safely trusted with unlimited power. "Popular majorities, no less than public officials," he warned, "are prone to take into their own hands as much power as circumstances permit." And "the majority may be fully as intolerant of dissenting opinion as kings and aristocracies have always been."

Sales of *The Growth and Decadence of Constitutional Government* were disappointing, in the range of two to three thousand copies. Former admirers of Smith found the new work puzzling, even an embarrassment. In his introduction to *The Growth and Decadence of Constitutional Government*, even fellow Jeffersonian Vernon L. Parrington largely ignored the work at hand in favor of extolling the contribution made by *The Spirit of American Government* to the Progressive movement. Most reviewers took the same tack, or worse, dismissed the book as irrelevant to the current situation of the country. The reason for this chilly reception was the message, not the medium. *The Growth and Decadence of Constitutional Government* had major flaws: thin research, a conspiratorial view of history, and vagueness about how to achieve its goals. But *The Spirit of American Government* suffered from the same faults. And compared with Smith's first book, his second and final one had a sounder grasp of the purposes of the founding fathers and showed a more perceptive awareness of the limits presented by the human condition to the fulfillment of millenarian dreams. The trouble was that *The Growth and Decadence of Constitutional Government* appeared at a time when the Great Depression was converting

much of the public to belief in an expanded federal government as the pathway to salvation. No group became more enamored of that faith than the intellectuals, and none has remained more loyal to the gospel of activist government. Not surprisingly, therefore, *The Spirit of American Government* retains a reputation beyond its importance while *The Growth and Decadence of Constitutional Government* languishes in historiographical oblivion.

References:
Eric F. Goldman, "J. Allen Smith: the Reformer and His Dilemma," *Pacific Northwest Quarterly*, 35 (July 1944): 195-214;
Thomas C. McClintock, "J. Allen Smith and the Progressive Movement: A Study in Intellectual History," Ph.D. dissertation, University of Washington, 1959;
McClintock, "J. Allen Smith, A Pacific Northwest Progressive," *Pacific Northwest Quarterly*, 53 (April 1962): 49-59;
Cushing Strout, Introduction to Smith's *The Spirit of American Government* (Cambridge: Belknap Press of Harvard University Press, 1965), pp. xiii-lxvi.

Papers:
There is a small collection of Smith's papers at the University of Washington Library, Seattle. Smith appears rarely to have made copies of his outgoing letters or saved his incoming correspondence, and much of what he had kept was lost after his death. What remains consists mostly of copies of unpublished speeches and papers and scrapbooks of newspaper clippings.

Alexander H. Stephens

(11 February 1812-4 March 1883)

John C. Roberson
University of South Carolina

SELECTED BOOKS: *Speech of Mr. A. H. Stephens, of Georgia, against the Tariff Bill. Reported by the Committee of Ways and Means. Delivered in the House of Representatives, May 7, 1844* (Washington, D.C.: Printed by John Towers, 1844);

Speech of Mr. Stephens, of Georgia, on the Joint Resolution for the Annexation of Texas, Delivered in the House of Representatives, January 25, 1845 (Washington, D.C.: Printed by Gales & Seaton, 1845);

Speech of Mr. Stephens, of Georgia, on the Subject of the Mexican War, Delivered in the House of Representatives, U.S., June 16, 1846 (Washington, D.C.: Printed by J. & G. S. Gideon, 1846);

Speech of Mr. A. H. Stephens, of Georgia, on the Land Bill. Delivered in the House of Representatives of the U.S., July 7, 1846 (Washington, D.C.: Printed by J.& G. S. Gideon, 1846);

Speech [on the Mexican War] *In the House of Representatives, Feb. 12, 1847* (Washington, D.C.: Printed by J. & G. S. Gideon, 1847);

Speech of Mr. Stephens, of Georgia, on the War and Taxation. Delivered in the House of Representatives of the U.S., February 2, 1848 (Washington, D.C.: Printed by J. & G. S. Gideon, 1848);

Speech of Mr. A. H. Stephens, of Georgia, on the Territorial Bill, Delivered in the House of Representatives of the United States, Aug. 7, 1848 (Washington, D.C.: J. & G. S. Gideon, 1848);

Texas and New Mexico. Speech of Hon. A. H. Stephens, of Georgia, in the House of Representatives, Friday, August 9, 1850, on the President's Message of August 6, 1850, Concerning Texas and New Mexico (Washington, D.C.: Printed at the Congressional Globe Office, 1850);

Homestead Bill—The State of Parties—and the Presidency. Speech of Hon. A. H. Stephens, of Georgia, on the State of the Country. Delivered in the House of Representatives, April 27, 1852 (Washington, D.C.: Printed by John T. Towers, 1852);

Address of Hon. Alexander H. Stephens Before the Few and Phi Gamma Societies of Emory College, Oxford, Ga., on Commencement Day, July 21, 1852

(Washington, D.C.: Printed by John T. Towers, 1852);

Speech of the Hon. A. H. Stephens, of Georgia, in the House of Representatives, February 17, 1854, on Nebraska and Kansas (Washington, D.C.: Printed at the Sentinel Office, 1854);

Kansas-Nebraska—The Recent Elections: Speech of Hon. A. H. Stephens, of Georgia, Delivered in the House of Representatives, December 14, 1854, in Reply to the Remarks of Mr. Mace, of Indiana, on Giving Notice of His Intention to Introduce a Bill to Restore the Missouri Compromise (Washington, D.C.: Printed at the Congressional Globe Office, n.d.);

Georgia and Ohio Again. Speech of Mr. Stephens, of

Georgia, in Reply to Mr. Campbell, of Ohio. Delivered in the House of Representatives, January 15, 1855 (Washington, D.C.: Printed at the Congressional Globe Office, 1855);

Extracts from the Speech of the Hon. Alex. H. Stephens, Delivered at Appling (Ga.) on the 11th July 1855 (New Orleans: Printed at the Office of the Louisiana Courier, 1855);

Letters of Hon. A. H. Stephens and Rev. H. H. Tucker, on Religious Liberty (Atlanta: C. R. Hnleiter, 1855);

Speech of Hon. Alex. H. Stephens, of Georgia, on the Kansas Election. Delivered in the House of Representatives, February 19, 1856 (Washington, D.C.: Printed at the Congressional Globe Office, 1856);

Kansas Contested Election. Speech of Hon. A. H. Stephens, of Georgia, Delivered in the House of Representatives, March 11, 1856, on the Resolution from the Committee of Elections Asking for Power to Send for Persons and Papers in the Kansas Election Case (Washington, D.C.: Printed at the Congressional Globe Office, 1856);

Speech of Hon. Alexander H. Stephens, of Georgia, on the Bill to Admit Kansas as a State under the Topeka Constitution. Delivered in the House of Representatives, June 28, 1856 (Washington, D.C.: Printed at the Congressional Globe Office, 1856);

Speech of Hon. Alexander H. Stephens, of Georgia, on the Report of the Kansas Investigating Committee, in the Case of Reeder against Whitfield. Delivered in the House of Representatives, July 31, 1856 (Washington, D.C.: Printed at the Congressional Globe Office, 1856);

Speech of Hon. Alexander H. Stephens, of Georgia, on the Presidential Election of 1856; the Compromise of 1850; and the Kansas-Nebraska Act of 1854. Delivered in the House of Representatives, January 6, 1857 (Washington, D.C.: Printed at the Congressional Globe Office, 1857);

The Neutrality Laws. Speech of Hon. A. H. Stephens, of Georgia, in the House of Representatives, January 13, 1858, on the Neutrality Laws and the Arrest of General Walker, by Commodore Paulding (Washington, D.C.: Printed at the Congressional Globe Office, 1858);

The Lecompton Constitution, report by Stephens for the House of Representatives Select Committee of Fifteen, 10 March 1858 (Washington, D.C., 1858);

Speech of Hon. Alexander H. Stephens, of Georgia, on the Admission of Minnesota and Alien Suffrage. Delivered in the House of Representatives, May 11, 1858 (Washington, D.C.: Printed at the Congressional Globe Office, 1858);

Admission of Oregon. Speech of Hon. Alexander H. Stephens, of Georgia, in the House of Representatives, February 12, 1859 (Washington, D.C.: Printed at the Congressional Globe Office, 1859);

Speech Delivered in the City Hall Park, Augusta, Georgia, on Saturday Evening, September 1, 1860 (Augusta?: Printed by L. Towers, 1860?);

Speech for the Union, by Alexander H. Stephens, now Vice-President of the Confederacy, Delivered at Milledgeville, Georgia, in November 1860, Before the Members of the Georgia Legislature (Baltimore: Woods, 1860?);

The Great Speech of Hon. A. H. Stephens, Delivered Before the Georgia Legislature, on Wednesday Night, March 16th, 1864, to Which Is Added Extracts from Governor Brown's Message to the Georgia Legislature (Milledgeville, Ga., 1864);

An Address, Delivered at Crawfordville, on the Fourth of July 1864 (Augusta: Printed at the Chronicle & Sentinel Office, 1864);

Address of Hon. Alexander H. Stephens, Before the General Assembly of the State of Georgia, 22nd February, 1866 (Milledgeville, Ga.: Printed by Nisbet, Barnes & Moore, 1866);

A Constitutional View of the Late War Between the States: Its Causes, Character, Conduct and Results Presented in a Series of Colloquies at Liberty Hall, 2 volumes (Philadelphia & Cincinnati: National Publishing Company/Chicago & St. Louis: Zeigler, McCurdy, 1868-1870);

The Reviewer Reviewed. Reply of Hon. Alexander H. Stephens, to the Baltimore Leader's Notice of the "Review" of the "War Between the States, etc." by Albert Taylor Bledsoe (Philadelphia, 1868);

Conservative Views. The Government of the United States: What Is It? Comprising a Correspondence with Alexander H. Stephens, Eliciting Views Touching the Nature and Character of the Government of the United States, the Impolicy of Secession, the Evils of Disunion, and the Means of Restoration, by Stephens and J. A. Stewart (Atlanta: Franklin Printing House, 1869);

Alexander H. Stephens on the Study of Law. Letter to a Class of "Liberty Hall" Law Students (Atlanta: Daily Sun Steam-Power Presses, 1871);

The Reviewers Reviewed; A Supplement to the "War Between the States," Etc., With An Appendix in Review of "Reconstruction," So Called (New York: Appleton, 1872);

A Compendium of the History of the United States from the Earliest Settlements to 1872. Designed to Answer the Purpose of a Text Book in Schools and

Colleges as Well as to Meet the Wants of General Readers (New York: E. J. Hale/Columbia, S.C.: W. J. Duffie, 1872; revised, 1874; revised again and enlarged, 1883);

Address of Hon. Alexander H. Stephens [on the Letters of Junius], *Before the Literary Societies of the University of Georgia, August 4th, 1873* (N.p., 1873?);

Speech of Hon. Alex. H. Stephens, of Georgia, on the Repeal of Increased Congressional Pay, Delivered in the House of Representatives of the United States, December 11, 1873 (Washington, D.C.: Printed by John H. Cunningham, 1873);

Speech of Hon. Alex. H. Stephens, of Georgia, on the Civil Rights' Bill, Delivered in the House of Representatives of the United States, in Congress Assembled, 8th of January, 1874 (Washington, D.C.: Printed by John H. Cunningham, 1874);

Carpenter's Picture, Lincoln and Emancipation. Speech of the Hon. Alexander H. Stephens, of Georgia, in the House of Representatives, 12th of February, 1878 (Washington, D.C.: Printed by Darby & Duvall, 1878);

The Trade Dollar. Speech of Alex. H. Stephens, of Georgia, Delivered in the House of Representatives, Thursday, 19th June, 1879, as Revised and Abridged by Himself, on the Exchange of Trade-Dollars for Legal-Tender Silver Dollars (Washington, D.C.: Printed by R. O. Polkinhorn, 1879);

Speech of Alexander H. Stephens, of Georgia, in the House of Representatives, February 19, 1880, against Riders on Appropriation Bills (Washington, D.C., 1880);

A Comprehensive and Popular History of the United States, Embracing a full account of the Discovery and Settlement of the Country; the History of each of the Colonies until their Union as States; The French and Indian Wars; the War of the Revolution; the War of 1812; the Long Period of Peace; the Mexican War, the Great War Between the North and South, and its Results; the Centennial of Our Independence; the Assassination of President Garfield; and Events down to the Present Time (Philadelphia & Chicago: National Publishing Company, 1882);

Recollections of Alexander H. Stephens: his diary kept when a prisoner at Fort Warren, Boston harbour, 1865; giving incidents and reflections of his prison life and some letters and reminiscences, edited with a biographical study by Myrta Lockett Avary (New York: Doubleday, Page, 1910).

OTHER: "Speech of Hon. A. H. Stephens, Delivered in the Hall of the House of Representatives of Georgia, Nov. 14, 1860;" "African Slavery, The Corner-stone of the Southern Confederacy;" "Speech of Hon. A. H. Stephens, at Atlanta, Ga., April 30, 1861;" and "Speech of Hon. A. H. Stephens, at Richmond, Va., April 22, 1861" in *Echoes from the South: Comprising the Most Important Speeches, Proclamations, and Public Acts Emanating from the South during the Late War*, edited by Edward A. Pollard (New York: E. B. Treat, 1866), pp. 7-44, 77-102, 157-165, and 191-195;

Henry Cleveland, *Alexander H. Stephens, in Public and Private* (Philadelphia: National Publishing Company, 1866)—includes speeches and letters by Stephens;

Richard Malcolm Johnston and William Hand Browne, *Life of Alexander H. Stephens* (Philadelphia: Lippincott, 1878)—includes speeches by Stephens;

"Government," in *Johnson's Universal Cyclopaedia*, 8 volumes, edited by Charles Kendall Adams (New York: Appleton, 1893-1897), III: 861-863.

PERIODICAL PUBLICATIONS: "The Hampton Roads Conference," *New Eclectic*, 6 (August 1870): 175-196;

"Tribute to General Lee," *Southern Magazine*, 8 (January 1871): 45-46;

"The Letters of Junius," *International Review*, 4 (September 1877): 601-613;

"The Count of the Electoral Vote for President and Vice-President," *International Review*, 5 (January 1878): 102-113;

"Negro Suffrage," *North American Review*, 128 (March 1879): 250-257;

"My Impression of General Robert Edward Lee," *Southern Bivouac*, 1 (February 1886): 536-542.

Alexander Hamilton Stephens is a relatively well-known figure in history, primarily because of his position as vice-president of the Confederacy. However, his antebellum and postbellum careers probably deserve as much if not more attention than his service during the Civil War. Stephens served a long tenure as a United States Congressman in the late antebellum period, which was especially noteworthy, and a shorter term in Congress following the war, which merits some attention. He was also important as an orator, legal theorist, practicing attorney, and historian. Although his main achievement as a historian was his two-volume treatise on constitutional theory and history, *A Constitutional View of the Late War Between the States*, he also produced a high school textbook on American history and a general survey of American history. The importance of Stephens as a political figure has obscured his literary career.

Throughout his life, Stephens was profoundly affected by his frail physique, superior intelligence, and unusual psychology. He was abnormally small as a child and did not reach his full height of five feet ten inches until he was in his late twenties. As an adult, his weight was usually in the nineties, and associates often referred to him as "Little Aleck" or "Little Ellick." Until he reached the age of thirty-five strangers sometimes mistook Stephens for a young man in his teens. His frail constitution contributed to his susceptibility to numerous diseases. Stephens had to struggle constantly to maintain life itself and at times spent months in bed recovering from illness or injury. His complexion was sallow in youth and took on a mummified appearance as he grew older. Like the the the fictitious character Cyrano de Bergerac, Stephens regarded himself as having a superior mind and worthy soul encased in a hideous frame. He suffered at times from depression and obsession with death, but he was able to overcome melancholy with self-esteem derived from his intellectual activities. His voice was shrill and musical, often described as sounding like a flute, though it could be easily heard in a crowd of five thousand. Although Stephens never married or had any lengthy love affairs, he was chivalrous toward women and believed that their educational opportunities should be improved. Stephens's physical incapacities contributed to this intellectual development by giving him more time to read and meditate on works of political philosophy. His bodily infirmities and frequent severe pain did not sour his temperament or dampen his concern for his fellow man. In his latter years, Stephens was liberal in his works of philanthropy and generous in hospitality.

Stephens was named for his grandfather Alexander, a Scottish supporter of the Stuarts who came to Pennsylvania in 1746 and served there during the Revolutionary War before migrating to the rapidly developing yeoman-dominated area of middle Georgia in 1784. His son Andrew Stephens became a Methodist schoolmaster and farmer in that area. Alexander Stephens was born on his father's farm near Crawfordville on 11 February 1812, the third child in the family. Within a month of his birth, his mother, Margaret Grier Stephens, died.

The following year Andrew Stephens married Matilda Lindsey. Among the several children added to the family by this union was Linton, the youngest, who was born in 1823. He eventually became Alexander's ward, his most intimate associate, and a prominent Georgia lawyer. Andrew Stephens, whom Alexander admired and respected, died when his son was fourteen, and his death was immediately followed by that of his wife. In the parceling out of the children among relatives, Alexander Stephens was sent to the home of an uncle in Washington, Georgia. In 1827 Stephens began study at the Washington Academy. The most influential teacher at the school was Alexander Hamilton Webster, a Presbyterian minister, from whom Stephens took the middle name of Hamilton. Following the completion of his studies and his affiliation with the Presbyterian Church, Stephens was sponsored by the Presbyterian Education Society of Washington as a student at Franklin College, which is now the University of Georgia. In college Stephens studied the traditional liberal arts curriculum and prepared to become a Presbyterian minister, but before his graduation as valedictorian in 1832, he renounced his intention of becoming a minister. However, he repaid the education society in Washington for its financial support.

After short stints as a schoolmaster in Madison and a tutor on a plantation near Sunbury, Stephens settled in Crawfordville. He purchased the library of the town's retiring lawyer and began to study law in solitude. Stephens claimed that he was attracted to the legal profession because "discussion and argument are my delight." His performance on the bar examination was described as the most outstanding that his examiners, William H. Crawford and Joseph H. Lumpkin, had ever witnessed. As a lawyer, Stephens displayed an eloquence and persuasiveness which could influence the emotions of those in the courtroom. He practiced in the circuit courts of northeastern Georgia and declined to accept litigants who he felt were not entitled to a favorable judgment.

Stephens's political career began in 1836 with election to the Georgia House of Representatives. Although opposed to nullification and the formation of local vigilance committees, Stephens campaigned as an opponent of the Jackson administration and denounced Jackson's 1833 force bill which was aimed at coercing South Carolina into accepting a federal tariff that clearly favored the industrial North. In the legislature, Stephens aligned himself with the political faction of George M. Troup, which had become an element of the national Whig Party by 1840. He supported the building of the Western & Atlantic Railroad, connecting Georgia to Chattanooga and the grain-growing and livestock-producing areas of Tennessee, Kentucky, and the old Northwest. Stephens voted for an increase in appropriations for the state university, the creation of a state-supported system of public schools, and the establishment of Macon Female College, which was the first college in the world to graduate women with degrees in science. In the legislature Stephens mastered the skills of political oratory, parliamentary procedure, and partisan organization. He won election as a state senator in 1842, but his term as senator was cut short by his elevation to the U.S. House of Representatives.

At the time Stephens was chosen for Congress, Georgia still elected its congressmen on a statewide basis, contrary to the procedure mandated by Congress in the preceding session. Although he easily defeated his opponent in a statewide Whig victory, a controversy arose when the congressmen from Georgia arrived in Washington to be seated. As an early expression of the uncompromising purity of his constitutional principles, Stephens actually argued against the legality of his own election. The matter was finally settled by the seating of the congressmen from Georgia and the implementation of a district system of representation for future elections in Georgia.

In Congress Stephens began his career as a follower of Henry Clay and his "American System," which proposed internal improvements, protective tariffs, and a national bank. Although Stephens supported Clay for president in 1844, he soon parted company with Clay on the issue of annexation of Texas. Stephens voted to annex Texas in 1845, but he strongly opposed the recognition of the Rio Grande as the southern boundary of Texas and President James K. Polk's handling of the situation. Stephens placed responsibility for the outbreak of the Mexican War on what he termed Polk's "imprudence, indiscretion, and mismanagement." He opposed the annexation of Mexican territory to the United States for fear that the issue of slavery would be rekindled in Congress, which in turn would lead to greater sectional divisiveness and then to "desolation, carnage and blood."

Stephens's fear was soon realized when in 1846 David Wilmot introduced into Congress the famous Wilmot Proviso, stipulating that territory won in the Mexican War be closed to slavery. For four years controversy raged in Congress and re-

percussions were felt throughout the U.S. During this period Stephens engaged in the emotional rhetoric of a fire-eater. In early 1848 Stephens delivered a one-hour speech in the House which was a vituperative condemnation of Polk, "the greatest enemy of the people," who was waging "a war against the Constitution of the country!" Stephens won the acclaim of a young congressman from Illinois, Abraham Lincoln, who called this the best short speech he had ever heard and one which had brought tears to his eyes. When congressmen from Northern states continued to oppose the introduction of slavery into the territory won from Mexico, Stephens replied that when the government was "brought into hostile array" against the South, then he was "for disunion openly, boldly and fearlessly [and] . . . for revolution." It was also during this period of controversy that Stephens barely avoided duels with three men and was severely injured in a knife attack by Judge Francis Cone of Georgia.

Efforts toward a compromise on the sectional controversy in 1848 were defeated as Stephens led Southern Whigs in opposition to the Clayton Compromise which would have allowed the federal courts to decide the issue of slavery in the Mexican Cession. Stephens claimed that the passage of the compromise would have been tantamount to abandonment of the cause by Southerners and hoped that its defeat would help Zachary Taylor increase his electoral votes in the South during the presidential campaign. As an early supporter of the Taylor candidacy, Stephens had high hopes when Taylor entered the White House. However, Stephens and most Southern Whigs were dismayed when Taylor endorsed the Wilmot Proviso. Following the death of Taylor and the passage of the Compromise of 1850, Stephens returned to Georgia to encourage Georgians to accept the new compromise. With his friends Robert Toombs, a Whig, and Howell Cobb, a Democrat, Stephens was instrumental in the formation of a new political organization in Georgia, the Constitutional Union party. Under its banner, they promoted the Georgia Platform, which Stephens was instrumental in framing. It incorporated a reluctant acceptance of the Compromise of 1850 and stated that the Union was secondary in importance to the principles which it was designed to perpetuate. Moreover, the Georgia Platform provided for secession if slavery was abolished in the District of Columbia, if any new state was refused admission because it recognized slavery, if slavery was prohibited in the Utah or New Mexico territories, or if the fugitive slave laws were repealed or weakened. With the passage of the Compromise of 1850, the Georgia Platform and other similar measures, the sectional controversy tended to subside somewhat for a few years.

In 1845 Stephens acquired full possession of the house in which he had lived since 1834 as the result of the settlement of an estate. He called it Bachelor's Hall until 1859, when he changed the name to Liberty Hall. It is located in Crawfordville, a small town which is the county seat of Taliaferro (pronounced Tolliver) County. In 1841 Stephens bought the nearby farm on which he had been born. These possessions, along with about twenty slaves, made him a man of substantial means, but he was still far from being a great planter. Liberty Hall was also the home of Stephens's widowed sister and some of his younger relatives. Stephens exercised great hospitality and proved to be a benevolent master, and neighbors often referred to his slaves as "Stephens' Free Negroes."

The presidential election of 1852 caused the demise of the Constitutional Union party of Georgia. Stephens led a movement among Southern Whigs to declare their lack of support for the Whig presidential candidate, Winfield Scott, because of his failure to endorse the Compromise of 1850. As a gesture of his nonsupport, Stephens voted for the deceased Daniel Webster for president in 1852, and majorities in four counties of his congressional district followed his lead. This marked the end of Stephens's association with the Whigs, whose organization would soon disintegrate.

During the 1850s Stephens, like many Southerners, became more defensive of the institution of slavery. In 1845 Stephens claimed that he was "no defender of slavery in the abstract," but by the early 1850s he was defending slavery on sociological and biblical grounds. He claimed that the abolitionists were "at war with the works of the Creator."

Following the sectional controversy over the Wilmot Proviso and the Compromise of 1850, Stephens gradually came to embrace the idea of "popular sovereignty" in the territories, a concept espoused by Democrats, including Stephen Douglas. When Douglas's Kansas-Nebraska bill came before the House of Representatives, Stephens gave a speech strongly endorsing it. When the bill became bogged down in committee with proposed amendments, Stephens, by a master stroke of parliamentary tactics, moved to strike the enabling cause. This motion took precedence over the proposed amendments and caused the bill to be reported unfavorably on the floor of the House. Despite the unfavorable report, the House pro-

ceeded to vote in favor of the bill by a vote of 113 to 100. Although Stephens called the passage of the Kansas-Nebraska Act "the greatest glory of my life," it brought an uproar in the Northern states which resulted in a severe loss for the Democrats in the fall elections of 1854, and in the long term it gave Southerners nothing of real value.

Following the demise of the Whig Party, the Know-Nothings filled their place as the opposition to the Democrats in the South and enlisted most of the Whigs' former supporters. Stephens bitterly opposed the Know-Nothings in his district because of the secrecy of the party and their hostility to foreigners and Catholics. He considered the Know-Nothing Party a scheme by Northern capitalists to produce a "votingless population to do their work and perform all labor" and to make "white slaves" of immigrants. Stephens faced strong opposition in his bid for reelection in 1855 and had to do some strenuous campaigning. It was during a speech in Augusta in this campaign that Stephens made the often-quoted remark, "I am afraid of nothing on earth . . . except to do wrong. I would rather be *defeated* in a good cause than to *triumph* in a bad one." Stephens carried his district with fifty-five percent of the vote, the lowest percentage he had ever received in his political career.

The long struggle over the admission of Kansas as a state and the violent scenes in Congress which accompanied it caused Stephens to become discouraged with that body. In 1857 Stephens refused an opportunity to become Speaker of the House and in 1859 he decided to retire from Congress. Although some of the biographers of Stephens have quoted him as saying "there was bound to be a smash-up on the rail-road, and I resolved to jump off at the first station," others have stated that Stephens thought that the safety of the South was secure and the future would be calm when he retired. In a letter to his constituents following his retirement, Stephens decried anticipation of an "irrepressible conflict" and declared that the greatest danger was a tendency toward strife and anarchy which was caused by "unparalleled prosperity." Following his retirement from Congress, Stephens expanded his farming operations and returned to practicing law. By 1860 he was making $22,000 per year in the legal profession and his farming operations included 920 acres of land and thirty-four slaves.

Stephens was a strong supporter of Stephen A. Douglas for president in 1860. He considered Douglas a friend of Southern interests who had endangered his political career by supporting the

Kansas-Nebraska Act. Stephens was dismayed by the division of the Democratic Party at the Charleston Convention and compared the condemnation of Douglas to the crucifixion of Christ. Although Stephens actively campaigned with Douglas, he despaired over the future of the nation. Stephens thought that civil war and destruction were close at hand: "The demagogues have raised a whirlwind they cannot control." He claimed that secessionists were attempting to destroy "the best government in the world." When Lincoln was elected, Stephens was one of the few men in the South who knew him as a friend. Stephens had faith in Lincoln's integrity and told Southerners that Lincoln would administer the government with honesty and good faith.

Following Lincoln's election, the Georgia legislators invited the leading political figures of the state to address them. Stephens's address of 14 November 1860 followed secessionist exhortations. In this "Speech for the Union," his best-known address, Stephens counseled patience, recognition of the impropriety of the legislature's acting upon secession, and the calling of a conference of Southern states so that they would be united in policy. He said that he stood by the Constitution and the Georgia Platform and that the time to act would be when the Constitution was violated. However, the position of Stephens in the speech was not that of an unconditional Unionist: he stated that he would remain with Georgia in the event of secession. Although he made a gallant effort, Stephens failed to halt the march toward secession. The legislature ordered a special election for 2 January 1861 to choose delegates to a state convention.

Stephens and those in Georgia who opposed secession lost the initiative during the following weeks. Lincoln wrote to Stephens commending him on his address to the legislature, and the two men exchanged a few letters during those critical weeks. Stephens wrote Lincoln that the government had no right to coerce a state against its will. Stephens was reluctantly elected to the convention of the state, and there he gave an oration of fifteen minutes, saying that the "point of resistance should be the point of aggression." Stephens voted against the ordinance of secession but signed it once it had been passed, so that unity could be preserved and civil warfare avoided within Georgia. In the North, fraudulent versions of Stephens's speech to the convention were circulated widely.

In February Stephens went to Montgomery as a delegate to the convention to form the Confederate government. There he was instrumental in framing the Confederate Constitution. Stephens approved of most of the few variations from the U.S. Constitution in the Confederate document, such as the single six-year presidential term, the single-item veto, and the seating of cabinet members on the floor of Congress. However, he opposed the prohibition against states which did not recognize slaveholding. There are several reasons why Stephens was chosen as the Confederate vice-president: the importance of Georgia within the Confederacy; the consolation to Georgia after two of her favorite sons, Toombs and Cobb, were passed over for the top position; the fact that Stephens was a recognized leader of the former conditional Unionists and Whigs in the lower South; and the hope that a conservative man in the second position would encourage the states of the upper South to join the Confederacy.

In the early months of the Confederacy, Stephens was enthusiastic and gave several speeches which espoused Southern nationalism and contained a rather strong strain of racism. The best-known of these was his "Corner-stone Speech," delivered in Savannah on 21 March 1861. He called the formation of the Confederacy a bloodless revolution which had as its immediate cause the controversy over the status of blacks in American society. Stephens stated that the idea of the equality of races was an error and that the cornerstone of the Confederacy rested upon racial inequality. Stephens advocated equality among whites and equal opportunity for business enterprises based upon a fair return for honest labor. He accused the Republicans of the duplicity of opposing the addition of slave states to the Union while being equally determined to regain slave states which had been lost. Stephens claimed that Northerners wanted the spoils of slavery through heavy taxation. His "Corner-stone Speech" was given wide circulation in the North, Great Britain, and France where the address could have done harm to the Confederate image.

Following the firing upon Fort Sumter, Stephens predicted one of the bloodiest civil wars in history which would lead America to ruin. Nevertheless, he spoke at Washington, Georgia, in June of 1861 and called upon Southerners to display "the valor of free men battling for country, for home, for everything dear as well as sacred." This speech, as well as many others which he delivered during the Civil War, shows the rhetoric of nationalism which was so influential in Europe in the nineteenth century.

As the war progressed, the Confederacy enacted certain commonly invoked wartime measures such as conscription, suspension of the writ of habeas corpus, and martial law. Stephens held Jefferson Davis responsible for these measures and believed that Davis sought a despotic reign or dictatorship which would destroy all of the liberties for which Southerners were fighting. He also felt that the influence of West Point was dominant in the Confederate administration, an influence which tended to dampen enthusiasm and spirit in the fighting men and transform them into machines. He showed great concern for the wounded and often visited the hospitals in Richmond. During the latter part of the war Stephens spent much of his time in Georgia, where he, his brother Linton, and Robert Toombs gave support to the administration of Governor Joseph E. Brown in opposition to the Confederate government. Some historians, including Frank L. Owsley, E. Merton Coulter, and Burton Hendrick, place much, if not all, of the responsibility for the defeat of the Confederacy on Stephens, Brown, Governor Zebulon Vance of North Carolina, and other leaders of opposition to the Davis administration. William P. Trent thought that Stephens as vice-president was too much of a theorist and not enough of a practical statesman.

The last service of Stephens to the Confederacy was as leader of the delegation to the Hampton Roads Peace Conference in February 1865. At the conference Stephens hoped for a restoration of the status quo antebellum but honored the instructions of Jefferson Davis which required recognition of Southern independence. Soon after the failure of the conference, Stephens departed for his home in Georgia. He was arrested by Union soldiers on 11 May 1865 and was sent to Fort Warren in Boston Harbor. There he was held for over four months without an indictment or trial.

While imprisoned, Stephens wrote a journal which was published posthumously in 1910 as the *Recollections of Alexander H. Stephens*. In the journal Stephens elaborated his critical opinions of the Confederate president and Congress. About all that Stephens gave Davis credit for were good intentions. As for himself, Stephens claimed to be the unsurpassed constitutionalist: "No one ever lived with stronger feelings of devotion to the Constitution of the United States and the Union under it than myself." He professed to care very little for the Union without the rights and guarantees of the Constitution, and stated that he had been opposed to antebellum laws in the Southern states which prohibited the education of slaves. Stephens con-

fessed to being unenthusiastic about organized religion but at Fort Warren continued his daily practice of reading from the Bible. Although Stephens was not often humorous, he told the story of some companions at Fort Warren "whose nature it is to stick to you closer than a brother and to keep you awake all night." He added, "Of course, I mean bedbugs."

Stephens returned to Crawfordville following his release from Fort Warren in October 1865. In February 1866 he addressed the Georgia legislature and advocated a policy of patience and forbearance until "the passion of the day should subside." He advised Georgians to accept the abolition of slavery as an irrevocable fact. Stephens thanked the blacks of Georgia for faithful service during the war and asked that legislation be passed to protect them. He maintained that the social aspects of racial relations were more important than the economic loss involved in emancipation. Stephens praised Andrew Johnson as a man of constitutional principles and hoped for the restoration of good government as the key to prosperity and "great human achievements." The full text of this speech was later an appendix to Stephens's *A Comprehensive and Popular History of the United States.* (1882).

The Georgia legislature chose Stephens in early 1866 to represent the state in the United States Senate, but he was refused his seat as were other representatives from the former Confederate states. In April 1866 Stephens testified before the Joint Reconstruction Committee of Congress and objected to the requirement that the Southern states ratify the Fourteenth Amendment before their representatives be admitted to Congress. Stephens said that he would not be opposed to limited suffrage for the freedmen but that Georgians would regard general black suffrage as the worst "political evil as could befall them." Southerners had expected an immediate restoration of constitutional government once the Confederate cause was abandoned, he claimed, so that postwar problems could be discussed in common council. By opposing the reunion of the Southern states to the United States under the Constitution, Stephens said that the "former unionists" had become "practical disunionists." He favored a settlement based upon "the principles of mutual convenience and reciprocal advantage on the part of the states," which were the principles upon which the Union under the Constitution was established. By recognition of "the separate sovereignty of the several states," Stephens thought that other problems would solve themselves in a "self-adjusting, self-regulating" manner. This testimony before Congress was also published as an appendix to *A Comprehensive and Popular History of the United States.*

As the Reconstruction measures became more stringent in 1867, Stephens's attitude toward the government became hostile and he counseled Southerners to resist. He compared Congressional Reconstruction to the French Revolution and said that constitutional liberty was in the "very throes and agonies of death." However, he disapproved of the Ku Klux Klan and warned that mob law would only worsen social tensions. In 1868 Stephens wrote a series of articles for the *Augusta Chronicle and Sentinel* encouraging Georgians to accept the fact of Republican rule and to work for change through political channels. Stephens favored a redemption based upon "the old line Democratic Jeffersonian ideas and principles." The presidential election of 1872, in which many Southerners, unlike Stephens, supported the Liberal Republican Horace Greeley, alienated Stephens from most of those who became Georgia's post-Reconstruction leaders.

Following the rejection of Stephens by Congress in 1866, he began his literary career in earnest. At the encouragement of a Philadelphia publisher, Stephens began to write the first volume of *A Constitutional View of the Late War Between the States* in December 1866. Stephens spent the greater part of 1867 working on what was to become his magnum opus and went to Philadelphia at the end of the year to meticulously correct proof pages. The first volume, published in 1868, was a great success on the book market. Over 67,000 copies were sold by 1871. Many readers purchased the volume, whose cover title read only *The War Between the States*, expecting an exciting account of battles or at least a record of the internal administration and intrigues of the Confederate government. Many readers were disappointed to find a thorough treatise on constitutional history and political philosophy. Encouraged by burgeoning sales, Stephens began working on the second volume in 1868. However, in early 1869 he was seriously injured by a heavy iron gate which fell upon him as he tried to open it. Stephens was never able to walk again without the aid of crutches, and the progress on the second volume was curtailed. Nevertheless, he completed the second volume in 1870, which was published with the first volume by the National Publishing Company of Philadelphia and others. The sales of the combined volumes—only slightly more than 20,000 copies in the first year—showed

that readers were becoming weary of constitutional and legal "battles." All told, however, Stephens made a healthy sum of $35,000 on the work.

In his introduction to *A Constitutional View of the Late War Between the States*, Stephens established as his purpose the presentation of historical principles involved in the establishment of American government. He emphasized that principles, which "like truths are eternal, unchangeable and immutable," would constitute his subject matter. The entire work totaled over fourteen hundred pages, and the text made use of what Stephens called the "Colloquial style." Using Cicero's *Tusculan Disputations* as a model throughout the book, Stephens created dialogues between three fictitious Northern guests at Liberty Hall and himself. By presenting his message in this unusual manner, Stephens claimed that he could demonstrate both sides of legal arguments "more clearly and forcibly" than in a standard narrative form. Perhaps Stephens's experience in the court room influenced his decision to adopt this format, with him and his three guests as argumentative lawyers and the reader as the judge. The three fictitious guests at Liberty Hall were Judge Bynum, a radical Republican from Massachusetts; Professor Norton, a conservative Republican from Connecticut; and Major Heister, a "war Democrat" from Pennsylvania. Stephens claimed that he engaged in similar conversations with actual Northern visitors to Liberty Hall during the early Reconstruction years. At the end of each dialogue, or colloquy, Stephens persuades his guests to acknowledge his constitutional history and theory as the ultimate truth.

Despite its unusual format and unwieldy size, *A Constitutional View of the Late War Between the States* is a depository of Stephens's political thought and of American constitutional history from the perspective of state sovereignty. Stephens was extremely thorough with his documentation, and he incorporated lengthy quotations from the state conventions that ratified the Constitution, Congressional speeches, and the published writings of Washington, Jefferson, Hamilton, Madison, and Webster. The citations in *A Constitutional View* reveal that Stephens conducted an immense amount of research and was widely read in classical, enlightenment, and contemporary writings. Notably absent were the Supreme Court decisions of John Marshall. Other historians from whom Stephens drew information included Benson J. Lossing, John W. Draper, Henry S. Randall, and George Bancroft. Stephens included twenty-six appendices which contained not only the major constitutional documents which established American government but also obscure political speeches, the Georgia Platform, Roger B. Taney's decision in the 1861 case *Ex Parte Merryman*, a description of the burning of Columbia, and "A Prayer for Peace" by an imprisoned Marylander. As an aid to finding the way through the tome, Stephens included an index, which was uncommon for works of history in the nineteenth century.

The foundations of Stephens's political thought can be traced to a lengthy appendix in St. George Tucker's *Blackstone's Commentaries* (1803) entitled "View of the Constitution of the United States." Stephens called it the clearest short exposition of the concept of state sovereignty. Tucker held that the United States was an association of states, or a confederacy "in fact as well as theory," and that each member state "is still a perfect state, still sovereign, still independent," and still capable of resuming full political power within its bounds. Stephens always maintained that he was a disciple of Thomas Jefferson and a supporter of the principle of local self-government within a republic. In a letter to a political associate in Georgia, Stephens expressed a belief in Tucker's theory of confederation and in Jeffersonian terms wrote that the "strength of all governments, and particularly republics, is in the affections of the people." Stephens thought that with the support of the people, the unity of a confederation was secure but that when the central government assumed "supreme power in the land," treated member states as "mere provinces," dispensed "favors with a partial hand," taxed some states for the aggrandizement of others, or attempted to "transcend its powers," then the confederation was in danger. These ideas were greatly expanded, supported, strengthened, and documented in Stephens's *A Constitutional View of the Late War Between the States*.

The basic thesis which Stephens maintained in his work was that sovereignty, or ultimate and original political power, resided with the people of each individual state. He held that the formation of the United States under the Articles of Confederation and under the Constitution was a compact among the states, which was terminable by a member state if the terms of the compact, in that state's judgment, were violated. In other words, Stephens sought to justify the theory of secession on historical and legal grounds.

Stephens defined sovereignty as paramount authority which is an "inherent, absolute power of self-determination." He claimed that sovereignty originated from the social forces and self-interests of a political body. Furthermore, Stephens maintained that sovereignty "cannot be rightfully interfered with by any other similar body, without its consent." Sovereignty was not divisible, according to Stephens, but sovereign powers were divisible, and their division by delegation of certain powers to the central government served as proof that the source of sovereign powers still existed unimpaired. By the social forces of a political body, Stephens essentially meant the people, a body of citizens. He believed that citizens were equal and were the ultimate source of political power. Those who were chosen to represent the people in government were considered servants of the people.

Stephens agreed with Jean Jacques Rousseau that laws were a means of checking the rule of force. Therefore, constitutions not only established the mechanics of government, but they also provided for individual liberties. Stephens believed that individual liberty ultimately strengthened the state because it contributed to making each individual more productive and contented. Contrarily, a state made up of restless and dissatisfied individuals was a state ripe for overthrow by revolution.

The right to vote frequently and intelligently was held by Stephens to be a characteristic essential to a healthy state. He was not a strong believer in political parties but realized that a two-party system usually developed within a republican state. Ideally, Stephens believed in the existence of several small parties, or no parties at all, and thought that such a development could be encouraged by requiring more than a bare majority to pass new legislation. He pointed out that it was usually the majority party which advocated a liberal interpretation of constitutional law as a means of increasing its power within the government and maintaining the political ascendancy. Stephens was a strong believer in the strict interpretation of the Constitution and upon this basis he rejected the idea of implied powers.

Stephens was one of the foremost authorities on the U.S. Constitution. He reportedly knew virtually every word in the document. In *A Constitutional View of the Late War Between the States* he presented one of the best studies of the origins and ratification of the Constitution which had been written up that time. In maintaining that the Constitution was a compact among the states, Stephens argued that the states were separate political units under the Articles of Confederation and were recognized as such by Great Britain in the Treaty of Paris in 1783. Stephens presented in copious quantities the various debates and documents within each state on the ratification of the Constitution. He argued, and his evidence indicated, that at several ratifying conventions of the states, delegates did not believe that they were giving up their sovereignty nor entering into a consolidated republic. Stephens showed that some of the states, in their ratification resolutions, explicitly reserved the right to resume the full powers of government while some powers were being delegated to the central government under the Constitution. Stephens argued that the Constitution, being a compact among the states, was revocable, like a contract in equity law, by any signatory following a single breach. According to Stephens, a convention of the people of a state could judge whether a breach had occurred and could then rescind the state's obligations by withdrawing from the compact. He defended secession in the abstract and maintained that it was a peaceful means of revolution. Interestingly enough, Stephens did not agree with John C. Calhoun on the right of a state convention to nullify a federal law which it believed to be unconstitutional.

Stephens did not believe that republics should engage in wars: "Fields of carnage may make men brave and heroic, but seldom tend to make nations virtuous or great." He held that wars were "never right or justifiable on both sides." Instead of conquests by military force, Stephens explained that a republic could "properly enlarge only by voluntary accessions." He admonished with equal ferocity both Abraham Lincoln and Jefferson Davis in regard to successive steps toward the establishment of military "despotism": conscription of soldiers, impressment of provisions at arbitrary prices, suspension of the writ of habeas corpus, and, finally, declaration of martial law. Furthermore, he charged Lincoln with "duplicity and fraud" in his communications with Confederate commissioners immediately prior to the attack on Fort Sumter. Stephens compared the Lincoln administration to the French "Reign of Terror" and accused Lincoln of worshiping the Union with "religious mysticism" while totally misunderstanding "its structure and formation in logic." While maintaining that slavery was only the immediate precipitant of the war, Stephens believed that the fundamental causes had to do with the principles of government. The tenacity of Stephens as a legal metaphysician was proven by his conviction that Union soldiers were fighting for centralized government over *all* of the states and that Confederate soldiers were fighting for the state sovereignty of *all* of the states.

Stephens was certainly not a believer in eco-

nomics as the determinant of political institutions. However, he did touch upon a few economic issues in *A Constitutional View of the Late War Between the States.* He strongly advocated the protection of property rights. On the tariff issue, he favored low duties which he claimed had enhanced nationwide economic growth in the antebellum period. Stephens implied that the protective tariff had been used to help manufacturing industries while it harmed the agricultural economy. He also believed that the tariff could be legitimately used against foreign nations which had placed high duties on American goods.

Antebellum slavery was defended by Stephens in *A Constitutional View of the the Late War Between the States.* He often referred to Southern slavery as "slavery so-called" because it differed from slavery in ancient times. The slaves of antiquity had no rights in court and were of the same race as the masters, according to Stephens. Slavery in the South was called by him a system of "legal subordination of the African to the Caucasian race . . . regulated by law as to promote . . . the best interests of both races" and to produce "reciprocal service and mutual bonds." He compared the condition of the Southern slaves favorably to that of free blacks in the North. Stephens's ideas on the social system of the Old South were similar to what some modern historians, such as George M. Fredrickson, J. Mills Thornton, and John McCardell, have referred to as a herrenvolk democracy with only blacks as slaves and equality among whites. Stephens cared nothing for an aristocracy.

The response of the critics to the publication of *A Constitutional View of the Late War Between the States* was mixed. The weekly journal the *Nation* complimented Stephens on his sincerity and dignified tone but attacked him on the grounds that he was impractical. The reviewer claimed that only an extremely patient reader who was willing to listen to endless philosophical arguments that "two and two make five" would find Stephens interesting. In London the *Saturday Review* gave Stephens a laudatory review. It commended Stephens on his combining the qualifications "of the lawyer, the historian, and the statesman" and cited his work as a "masterpiece of constitutional reasoning and political disquisition." Horace Greeley in his *New York Tribune* attacked Stephens by holding that secession and revolution were completely different processes and that "secession was the work of a violent, subversive, bullying, terrorizing minority" which stifled the majority in the South.

The most vehement criticism of *A Constitu-*

Springfield, Ills. Nov. 30. 1860

Hon. A. H. Stephens

    My dear Sir.

        I have read, in the newspapers, your speech recently delivered (I think) before the Georgia Legislature, or its assembled members. If you have revised it, as is probable, I shall be much obliged if you will send me a copy—

        Yours very truly

        A. Lincoln.

Letter from President-elect Lincoln requesting a copy of Stephens's "Speech for the Union," delivered 14 November 1860 at Milledgeville, Georgia (Henry Cleveland, Alexander H. Stephens, in Public and Private, *1866) tional View* came from Albert Taylor Bledsoe, editor of the *Southern Review* in Baltimore and perhaps a more unreconstructed Southerner than Stephens. In the pages of his October 1868 review, Bledsoe accused Stephens of "bookmaking," or padding a one-dollar book with so much extraneous material as to make it a four-dollar book. Bledsoe called the work a "joint production of Stephens and scissors," and retitled one chapter "The Bowels of *Elliot's Debates* with small scraps of Mr. Stephens' brains." He claimed that Stephens wrote without passion about a contest in which the stakes had been of an "appalling magnitude." Stephens was presumptuous in believing that the book was a profound work of philosophy, according to Bledsoe, and he criticized Stephens for limited use of *The Federalist,* which Bledsoe claimed to be the most important record relating to the nature of the Constitution.

Stephens was not the type of man to let criticism of his cherished work go unanswered or to allow the adversary last word. He produced another complete book in 1872 with the curious title of *The Reviewers Reviewed.* This volume included not only Stephens's replies to his critics, but also long excerpts from their reviews, the rejoinders of the critics, the surrejoinders of Stephens, the text of two speeches by Linton Stephens on Reconstruction, and other miscellaneous documents. Stephens replied to Greeley that the use of "Federal bayonets" to support *very bad government*" proved erroneous Greeley's assertion that a Southern majority favored the Republican administration. In a riposte to Bledsoe, Stephens accused him of "hot-bloodedness" and maintained that the South might have been better off had Bledsoe, as assistant secretary of war in the Confederacy, displayed more "calm good sense" and less "fiery passion and personal prejudices." Stephens questioned Bledsoe's ever having read James Madison's Report on the Virginia Resolutions (1800) and stated that the debates on the Constitution, at both the federal and state levels, were more important than *The Federalist.* Stephens resented being accused of reconstructing history by logic and asked if a straitjacket were not appropriate for Bledsoe.

In yet another volley of acrimonious penmanship, Bledsoe reviewed *The Reviewers Reviewed* in his journal for July 1872. Bledsoe accused Stephens of denying the right of secession in his speech to the Georgia legislature on 14 November 1860. He thought that Stephens was confusing the right of secession with the right of revolution. Bledsoe claimed that it was "part of his very humble mission in the world to attack wind-bags, and bladders, and all that sort of inflated thing." Bledsoe advised Stephens to read James Madison in order to understand the importance of the balance of power between the sections in the antebellum period. He closed by stating that he had to leave unnoticed many of Stephens's blunders, including "his feeble defence of the splendid part performed by Scissors in the production of his great work."

A Constitutional View of the Late War Between the States has received varied evaluations from scholars. William P. Trent, a turn-of-the-century historian, described the work as an able exposition, calm in tone, but too theoretical. In his *Southern Statesmen of the Old Régime* (1897), Trent maintained that Stephens endeavored to fit the actual administration of government to a theory and neglected the evolutionary development of the American people. Nemias Beck, a scholar in the field of oratory, thought that it was dry, uninspired, and essentially legalistic, yet remained a clear and well-documented presentation of the Southern point of view. Gamaliel Bradford, in *Confederate Portraits* (1914), called Stephens's work "a learned book, an awe-inspiring book, as dead as a volume of eighteenth-century sermons." Richard M. Weaver, a disciple of the Vanderbilt Agrarians, claimed that Stephens was trying to identify with the struggle for constitutional liberty throughout the world. Weaver called *A Constitutional View of the Late War Between the States* "a remarkable *tour de force*; verbose . . . repetitious . . . voluminous . . . unyielding and fundamental." One of Stephens's biographers, Rudolph Von Abele, admired the calm and dignified tone of the book but criticized it as intolerably dull except for "those interested in legal abstractions." Stephens's most ardent defender was Vernon Louis Parrington, an early-twentieth-century intellectual historian who wrote *Main Currents in American Thought* (1927-1930). He called Stephens's work an outstanding study of the origins of the Constitution; a showcase of clear, confident, and simple truths; and the most convincing scholarly monument to states' rights.

Following the publication of the second volume of *A Constitutional View of the Late War Between the States* Stephens began work on an American history school textbook so that Southern children would be protected "from further imposition as well as dependence upon Northern primary books." Stephens spent a year and a half preparing the work which appeared in 1872 as *A Compendium of the History of the United States from the Earliest Settlements to 1872* It was a relatively short and elementary work which included questions at the end

Liberty Hall, Stephens's home in Crawfordville, Georgia

of each chapter but no documentation. The textbook was a modest success financially and was printed by several different publishers in numerous editions, some of them revised and/or enlarged, during the late 1870s and early 1880s. When not involved in politics during this period, Stephens was busy at Liberty Hall adapting his school textbook into a more scholarly general survey. He employed the assistance of six secretaries on the project.

The general survey appeared in 1882 with the title of *A Comprehensive and Popular History of the United States*. It has also been referred to as the *Pictorial History of the United States*, the title which appeared on the leather binding. Although neglected by literary critics at the time and by most historians for over a hundred years, the book is an essential supplement to the political and historical thought of Stephens and does have some intrinsic merit. Stephens conducted a substantial amount of research for the volume, considering what was available to him. The literary style of the volume was often verbose and legalistic. The book was

slightly over a thousand pages in length and liberally illustrated.

Stephens began by explaining that his underlying purpose was to instruct people in "the nature, principles and limitations of government" so that they could enjoy and maintain constitutional liberty. Beginning with the Indians, the work contained a detailed account of American history from Stephens's viewpoint. Occasionally Stephens gave the reader some observations from his perspective as vice-president of the Confederacy. He maintained that the war had become a stalemate in early June 1863 and that he had advocated a negotiated peace. Stephens was uninformed on the invasion of Pennsylvania until he returned to Richmond from Georgia. Thereupon he strongly opposed the invasion because it "would greatly excite the war spirit" in the North. On the prisons, Stephens revealed that Confederates were anxious for exchanges and Federals were not. He also revealed that 22,576 out of 270,000 Federal prisoners died in Confederate hands while 26,436 out of 220,000 Confederate prisoners died in Federal hands. He cited an 1866 report of Secretary of War Edwin M. Stanton as the source of this information. For the Reconstruction period, Stephens had kind words for Andrew Johnson and placed the cause of the Panic of 1873 upon the demonetization of silver.

In his concluding remarks Stephens candidly confessed that it was not within the range of his work to treat economic, social, moral, or intellectual history. As a final plea to Americans, Stephens tried to show that centralized government destroyed the ancient Roman Empire and asked Americans to choose between "true greatness in human development" under local self-government or the "overthrow and destruction" of liberty under centralized government.

In addition to the theme of decentralized government, Stephens placed undue emphasis upon death. The narrative was interrupted to include death notices of many prominent public figures. Stephens went into considerable detail on the deaths of presidents but for some reason, strangely, left out the death of Martin Van Buren. He dealt with a few nonpolitical events such as the invention of the telegraph and an unusual blackout over the country on 19 May 1780, a phenomenon which he attributed to a yellow vapor. In terms of sales *A Comprehensive and Popular History of the United States* was a dismal failure.

In addition to his published volumes Stephens made occasional contributions to various journals of public opinion. In an 1879 article on "Negro Suffrage" in the *North American Review*, Stephens took issue with James G. Blaine's assertion that blacks were being denied the right to vote in the South. Stephens defended the one-dollar poll tax in Georgia as a wise measure to aid education and one which applied equally to all voters. He cited cases of vote purchasing and accused Blaine of being disappointed because blacks were not voting the way the Republicans expected them to.

The 1876 presidential contest between Rutherford B. Hayes and Samuel J. Tilden was one in which several electoral votes were disputed. It was settled in favor of Hayes by an election committee chosen by Congress. The controversy over the disputed election prompted Stephens to write an article in 1878 for the *International Review* on electoral reform. Stephens held that the Constitution did not intend for Congress to accept each electoral vote as legitimate if there was evidence to the contrary. Citing a letter written by Vice-President Thomas Jefferson, Stephens stated that Jefferson upheld the legality of congressional action to resolve disputed elections. On this ground Stephens advo-

cated the passage of a law providing for the settlement of disputed elections in the future by a joint vote of both houses of Congress. Reviewing the 1876 election, Stephens maintained that a majority of Americans thought that the decision of the election committee was inconsistent with the facts and testimony but that the decision was accepted in obedience to the majesty of the law and to avoid civil disorders.

For *Johnson's Universal Cyclopaedia* (1895) Stephens wrote an article entitled "Government" which is probably the best short exposition of his political theories. After going through some semantic gymnastics on definitions, Stephens postulated that government was the inherent power of self-determination and self-control for self-preservation in an organized society. He wrote that sovereignty was an attribute of will and power which corresponded to the mind in a human being. He defined a constitution as the organic structure of government which may be written or unwritten. Stephens rejected Jeremy Bentham's idea of the "greatest good for the greatest number" and advocated the "greatest good for all." He warned against the dangers of a tyrannical majority. Stephens delineated the difference between civil liberties and political rights; he provided the examples of women and minors who enjoyed the former but not the latter. Equality required the fair administration of justice, which was the great regulator in the government of human affairs, according to Stephens. He maintained that justice produced peace, quiet, order, and happiness in communities. Stephens endorsed the division of government into legislative, judicial, and executive branches: "independent, co-equal and co-ordinate departments."

The classification of governments was divided into the single types and confederated types by Stephens. He named monarchies, aristocracies, democracies, and republics as single governments. He distinguished between pure confederacies, in which the central government has no power over the citizens of the various states, and the confederated republic, in which the central government has limited power over citizens. Stephens favored the latter and called the United States a confederated republic, a nation of nations.

Stephens was bitterly denounced by Richard Taylor, former Confederate general and son of Zachary Taylor, in his personal memoirs, *Destruction and Reconstruction*. Taylor said that Stephens had "an acute intellect attached to a frail and meagre body" and a "mind in a state of indecent exposure." Taylor belittled Stephens's "Corner-stone Speech" and criticized him for dwelling on the vices of the embattled Confederacy "with the impartiality of an equity judge." In his customary fashion Stephens made a biting retort to Taylor in the pages of the *International Review*. Stephens defended his "Corner-stone Speech," said that he stayed out of military affairs early in the war, and called Taylor's judgment distorted by "fancy and imagination." This type of literary jousting between former Confederates was frequent during the Reconstruction period.

A biographical sketch of Meredith Poindexter Gentry, taken directly from an appendix to *A Comprehensive and Popular History of the United States*, was published posthumously in the *Confederate Veteran* for June 1906. Gentry, from Tennessee, was a Whig colleague of Stephens in Congress during the antebellum period who, like Stephens, bolted the party in 1852. In Stephens's sketch Gentry was described as a greater orator than Patrick Henry.

Although most men would have retired from politics following such an experience during the Civil War and early years of Reconstruction, Stephens could never sit on the sidelines. In 1871 he invested much of the money that he had made on the publication of *A Constitutional View of the Late War Between the States* in the *Atlanta Sun* newspaper. From its pages Stephens denounced the Reconstruction program, Georgia Republicans, and the New Departure Democrats. The newspaper failed in 1873 and damaged Stephens's finances severely, but it did help him get back into the political limelight. When Congress restored full political rights to former Confederates in 1872, Stephens began campaigning for a U. S. Senate seat against former Confederate general John B. Gordon. Although Gordon defeated Stephens, the latter regained his old seat in the House of Representatives in early 1873. A year later Stephens opposed the Civil Rights Act on the grounds that Georgia blacks did not want social equality or mixed race relations. As a postbellum congressman Stephens worked for monetary reform, a more equitable tax system, and better prices for agricultural products. Most of his congressional speeches in this period dealt with the constitutionality of measures under consideration.

The death of his brother, Linton, in 1872 caused Stephens tremendous grief. His health declined steadily and he was eventually confined to a wheelchair. During a long and severe illness in 1876, an erroneous report of Stephens's death was widely circulated. However, he continued to live, on what has been said to be only medicine and will

power. That same year Stephens began an extensive remodeling and enlargement of Liberty Hall which included the addition of a carbide gas lighting system. However, the routine of life there had changed very little from antebellum times. Almost all of the former slave families remained. For the centennial Fourth of July Stephens was treated to a serenade by about three thousand black Sunday School students from Taliaferro and neighboring counties. In a short speech from his front porch he commended them on the progress which they had made since emancipation and encouraged the youthful singers to advance their education.

Stephens found enough strength to continue his duties as congressman in the late 1870s. His speech in 1878 at the unveiling of a painting by Francis B. Carpenter commemorating the Emancipation Proclamation was praiseworthy. It was during Stephens's last days on Capitol Hill that a newspaper reporter made the following amusing

Stephens as governor of Georgia. He was elected in autumn 1882 and died shortly after his inauguration, in March 1883

and oft-quoted observation: "A little way up the aisle sits a queer-looking bundle. An immense cloak, a high hat, and peering somewhere out of the middle is a thin, pale, sad little face. This brain and eyes enrolled in countless thicknesses of flannel and broadcloth wrappings belong to Hon. Alexander H. Stephens, of Georgia. How anything so small and sick and sorrowful could get here all the way from Georgia is a wonder. If he were to draw his last breath any instant you would not be surprised. If he were laid out in his coffin, he needn't look any different, only the fires would have gone out in those burning eyes. Set, as they are, in the wax-white face, they seem to burn and blaze. Still, on the countenance is stamped that pathos of long-continued suffering which goes to the heart. That he is here at all to offer the counsels of moderation and patriotism proves how invincible is the soul that dwells in this shrunken and aching frame." Stephens retired from Congress for the second time in 1882. However, because of a split in the ranks of the Democratic party in Georgia, some of his old friends begged him to run for governor. Without extensive campaigning Stephens won the governorship handily. He was strongly supported by small- and middle-class farmers on what was clearly a Jeffersonian platform.

Governor Stephens was the featured speaker at the sesquicentennial celebration in Savannah on 12 February 1883. True to his principles, this wisp of a man on his last thread of life spoke in favor of a glorious future when Americans would realize that their country was a confederation of "wheels within wheels," a union of local units "separate as the billows but one as the sea." On the Savannah trip Stephens was chilled by a draft from a broken window on a carriage or railroad car. After three weeks of serious illness he died in Atlanta on 4 March 1883 at the age of seventy-one.

Stephens's intellect was his greatest source of strength throughout life. Often described as "a brain without a body," he had a fine memory for minute details and an ability to analyze figures and statistics; he could remember names as easily as faces. His reading, which was intensive as well as extensive, was primarily in history, political theory, and law. He was committed to principles of law, order, and justice which he regarded as timeless. His systematic reasoning was strictly of the deductive type: from accepted general principles he constructed positive specifics. Foremost among his principles was the idea of constitutional liberty. To him this principle resided not in some vague or misty conception of legal philosophy but in con-

crete laws or clauses of the Constitution which produced real and visible effects upon individuals, institutions, and society. Some observers have assigned to Stephens the role of a closet scholar or pure theorist rather than that of a practical leader. Certainly Stephens was not a compromiser, opportunist, or traitor and he would have rejected modern pragmatism. Stephens sought to establish for posterity certain immortal truths, but because his subject was justice, a value-related idea, his efforts often belied him. His view of the legal world was from within, and he often disregarded the influences from other sources. Because he expended great efforts to arrive at his own conclusions, Stephens was always reluctant to admit that he was mistaken. He believed that good character was the key to salvation.

As a speaker, Stephens was earnest and convincing. Although observers often described him as beginning a speech with a "squeak," he would soon shift to a mellifluent clarity and thought-provoking wit. Until confined to a wheelchair he used all the tricks of oratory, including arm-waving and body movement. Stephens knew the dangerous powers of oratory and never descended to demagoguery. He believed that eloquence was the art of selecting and fitting the rhetoric to the proper time, place, and circumstance. Stephens thought that the purpose of oratory was to induce conviction.

As a writer Stephens did not reach the great heights which he did in other pursuits. "Writing is not my forte," he once told Linton. He defended definite ideas with a vast array of evidence, arguments, and logic, but he was not a creative political thinker like Hamilton, Jefferson, or Calhoun. He was an able analyst but not a true political philosopher. Although well read in American history, Stephens was relatively uninformed on the history and current developments of Europe. He believed that the record of civil administration was just as important as that of military conflicts, which at the time attracted more attention from historians. Stephens wrote that the purpose of the historian was thorough research, proper selection of material, and scholarly writing "so as to erect . . . an enduring monument, . . . [an] artistic presentation . . . both agreeable and instructive."

In their judgments of Stephens and his impact upon history, historians have never reached a consensus. Some of his fiercest attackers have been Southerners such as William E. Dodd, Frank L. Owsley, and E. Merton Coulter. Owsley believed that Stephens and the antiadministration cohorts contributed substantially to the defeat of the Confederacy. Owsley claimed that Stephens only used state sovereignty and constitutionalism as a cover for partisan agitation and personal animosity: he "harbored as much personal venom in his diminutive frame as one could well imagine in a Georgia rattlesnake." Gamaliel Bradford and Nemias Beck agreed that Stephens's excess of conviction and his inflexibility in principles prevented him from becoming an even greater statesman and contributed to his frequent quarrels. Edmund Wilson, a scholar of American literary history, described Stephens as an eighteenth-century man who was intellectually related to the political theorists of the French Revolution. Rudolph Von Abele, one of Stephens's biographers, charged him with lack of vision in believing that the Constitution could stop the flood of economic and social change in the nineteenth century. Most historians have agreed with Jasper Reid, a scholar of political theory, that Stephens was not a good executive or administrator and that he failed as a modern war leader. Burton J. Hendrick, in his *Statesmen of the Lost Cause; Jefferson Davis and His Cabinet* (1939), labeled Stephens a "fanatic" and "supreme egoist." One of the most complimentary defenders of Stephens was his early-twentieth-century biographer, Louis Pendleton, who called Stephens a genius who "rose to power and fame from humble circumstances."

Stephens was a true believer in Jeffersonian democracy as a legal principle without emphasis on its social and economic foundations. He was a strong advocate of individualism and local self-government. His background on a small farm in rural Georgia and his acquisition of a modest farm on the outskirts of Crawfordville probably contributed to his ideal of individuals solving problems for themselves and building up their estates by their own skills, talents, and labor. This represented a strong streak of the yeoman ideal in the legal thought of Stephens. He observed the political system from the perspective of a lawyer, and to a great extent, thought of it as being a world unto itself.

To Stephens, state sovereignty was not a matter of expediency but a matter of conviction. The legal theory and constitutional history contained in *A Constitutional View of the Late War Between the States* are fairly convincing. Those who have rejected Stephens's arguments in their entirety have sometimes come perilously close to the position that "might makes right." On the other hand, the Civil War experience demonstrated that legal trends tend to follow, and indeed be shaped and influenced by, economic, political, and military power. Stephens could not fathom this reality. *A Constitutional View of the Late War Between the States* had many shortcomings and it probably would have had more impact if it had been published before the Civil War. Nevertheless it will always stand as a monument to the ideal of decentralized government.

Letters:

"The Correspondence of Robert Toombs, Alexander H. Stephens and Howell Cobb," edited by Ulrich B. Phillips, in *Annual Report of the American Historical Association for the Year 1911*, volume 2 (Washington, D.C.: Government Printing Office, 1913).

Biographies:

Henry Cleveland, *Alexander H. Stephens, in Public and Private. With Letters and Speeches, before, during and since the War* (Philadelphia: National Publishing Company, 1866);

Richard Malcolm Johnston and William Hand Browne, *Life of Alexander H. Stephens* (Philadelphia: Lippincott, 1878; revised, 1883);

Louis Beauregard Pendleton, *Alexander H. Stephens* (Philadelphia: Jacobs, 1908);

Eudora Ramsay Richardson, *Little Aleck: A Life of Alexander H. Stephens, the Fighting Vice-President of the Confederacy* (Indianapolis: Bobbs-Merrill, 1932);

Rudolph Radama Von Abele, *Alexander H. Stephens: A Biography* (New York: Knopf, 1946);

James Z. Rabun, "Alexander H. Stephens, 1812-1861," Ph.D. dissertation, University of Chicago, 1948;

Thomas Edwin Schott, "Alexander H. Stephens: Antebellum Statesman," Ph.D dissertation, Louisiana State University, 1978.

References:

Nemias Bramlette Beck, "Alexander H. Stephens: Orator," Ph.D dissertation, University of Wisconsin, 1937;

Gamaliel Bradford, *Confederate Portraits* (Boston: Houghton Mifflin, 1914), pp. 151-181;

Nash K. Burger and John K. Bettersworth, *South of Appomattox* (New York: Harcourt, Brace, 1959), pp. 144-172;

Jesse T. Carpenter, *The South As a Conscious Minority, 1789-1861: A Study in Political Thought* (New York: New York University, 1930);

Howard Carroll, *Twelve Americans: Their Lives and Times* (New York: Harper, 1883), pp. 429-473;

E. Merton Coulter, *The Confederate States of America, 1861-1865* (Baton Rouge: Louisiana State

University Press & the Littlefield Fund for Southern History of the University of Texas, 1950);

Ray F. Harvey, "The Political Theory of Alexander Hamilton Stephens," M.A. thesis, University of Oklahoma, 1930;

Burton J. Hendrick, *Statesmen of the Lost Cause; Jefferson Davis and His Cabinet* (New York: The Literary Guild of America, 1939), pp. 57-70, 80-84, 417-432;

Warren Lee Jones, "Alexander Hamilton Stephens: Governor of Georgia, 1882-1883," M.A. thesis, University of Georgia, 1942;

Hans Kohn, *American Nationalism: An Interpretive Essay* (New York: Macmillan, 1957), pp. 108-113;

Lewis H. Machen, "The Personality of Alexander H. Stephens," *Southern Magazine*, 1 (December 1899): 469-478;

Horace Montgomery, *Cracker Parties* (Baton Rouge: Louisiana State University Press, 1950);

Frank Lawrence Owsley, *States Rights in the Confederacy* (Chicago: University of Chicago Press, 1925);

Vernon Louis Parrington, *Main Currents in American Thought: An Interpretation of American Literature from the Beginnings to 1920*, volume two: *The Romantic Revolution, 1800-1860* (New York: Harcourt, Brace, 1930), pp. 82-93;

Michael Perman, *Reunion Without Compromise: The South and Reconstruction, 1865-1868* (London: Cambridge University Press, 1973);

Perman, *The Road to Redemption: Southern Politics, 1869-1879* (Chapel Hill: University of North Carolina Press, 1984);

Jasper Braley Reid, Jr., "The Mephistopheles of Southern Politics: A Critical Analysis of Some of the Political Thought of Alexander Hamilton Stephens, Vice-President of the Confederacy," Ph.D. dissertation, University of Michigan, 1966;

Richard Taylor, *Destruction and Reconstruction: Personal Experiences of the Late War*, edited by Charles P. Roland (Waltham, Mass.: Blaisdell, 1968), pp. 21-22;

William P. Trent, *Southern Statesmen of the Old Régime: Washington, Jefferson, Randolph, Calhoun, Stephens, Toombs and Jefferson Davis* (New York: Crowell, 1897), pp. 197-253;

Richard M. Weaver, *The Southern Tradition at Bay: A History of Postbellum Thought* (New Rochelle, N.Y.: Arlington House, 1968), pp. 124-129;

Edmund Wilson, *Patriotic Gore: Studies in the Literature of the American Civil War* (New York: Oxford University Press, 1962), pp. 380-437.

Papers:

There are collections of Stephens's papers at the Georgia State Department of Archives and History in Atlanta, the University of Georgia, Emory University, Duke University, the Southern Historical Collection of the University of North Carolina at Chapel Hill, the Library of Congress, the Historical Society of Pennsylvania, and the Manhattanville College of the Sacred Heart in Purchase, New York.

Ida M. Tarbell

(5 November 1857-6 January 1944)

Mary E. Tomkins
Michigan State University

BOOKS: *A Short Life of Napoleon Bonaparte* (New York: McClure, 1895); republished as *McClure's Complete Life of Napoleon* (London: McClure, 1895); enlarged as *A Life of Napoleon Bonaparte* (New York & London: McClure, Phillips, 1901)—adds a biographical sketch of Josephine Bonaparte;

Madame Roland: A Biographical Study (New York: Scribners, 1896; London: Lawrence & Bullen, 1896);

The Early Life of Abraham Lincoln, by Tarbell, assisted by J. McCan Davis (New York: McClure, 1896);

The Life of Abraham Lincoln, Drawn from Original Sources and Containing Many Speeches, Letters and Telegrams Hitherto Unpublished, 2 volumes (New York: McClure, Phillips, 1900);

The History of the Standard Oil Company, 2 volumes (New York: McClure, Phillips, 1904; London: Heinemann, 1905);

He Knew Lincoln (New York: McClure, Phillips, 1907);

Father Abraham (New York: Moffat, Yard, 1909);

The Tariff in Our Times (New York: Macmillan, 1911);

The Business of Being a Woman (New York: Macmillan, 1912);

The Ways of Woman (New York: Macmillan, 1915);

New Ideals in Business: An Account of Their Practice and Their Effects Upon Men and Profits (New York: Macmillan, 1916);

The Rising of the Tide: The Story of Sabinsport (New York: Macmillan, 1919; London: Macmillan, 1919);

In Lincoln's Chair (New York: Macmillan, 1920);

Boy Scouts' Life of Lincoln (New York: Macmillan, 1921);

He Knew Lincoln, and Other Billy Brown Stories (New York: Macmillan, 1922);

Peacemakers—Blessed and Otherwise: Observations, Reflections and Irritations at an International Conference (New York: Macmillan, 1922);

In the Footsteps of the Lincolns (New York & London: Harper, 1924);

Library of Congress

The Life of Elbert H. Gary: The Story of Steel (New York & London: Appleton, 1925);

A Reporter for Lincoln: Story of Henry E. Wing, Soldier and Newspaperman (New York: Macmillan, 1927);

Owen D. Young: A New Type of Industrial Leader (New York: Macmillan, 1932);

The Nationalizing of Business, 1878-1898 (New York: Macmillan, 1936);

All in the Day's Work: An Autobiography (New York: Macmillan, 1939).

OTHER: *Napoleon's Addresses: Selections from the*

Proclamations, Speeches and Correspondence of Napoleon Bonaparte, edited by Tarbell (Boston: Knight, 1897);

"The Parents of Lincoln," in *Abraham Lincoln. A Souvenir of Lincoln's Birthday, February 12, 1907* (New York: Lincoln Farm Association, 1907), pp. 17-24;

Selections from the Letters, Speeches and State Papers of Abraham Lincoln, edited by Tarbell (Boston: Ginn, 1911).

Ida Minerva Tarbell is recalled as the writer who blew the whistle on the first and most powerful trust in America. *The History of the Standard Oil Company*, her most important work, was published in 1904 and immediately convinced the public that the Standard Oil Company and its imitators in other industries threatened the underpinning of democracy—equal opportunity. The Supreme Court of the United States eventually concurred; in a 1911 decision the Court decreed the breakup of Standard Oil. Tarbell became known as the Joan of Arc of the oil regions, a historian who not only recorded history but also helped powerfully to shape it.

The pioneering drive that characterized Tarbell's career came from English and Scottish ancestors who arrived in the midst of the wilderness of seventeenth-century New England. Many of them continued to press westward in a restless search for a perfect life in a perfect place. In 1857 Ida Tarbell was born at one of these western posts, the Erie County, Pennsylvania, farm of her maternal grandparents, known only to history as the McCulloughs. Her mother, Esther Ann Tarbell, had remained with her parents while Franklin Tarbell, Ida's father, searched for new farmland in Iowa. The Panic of 1857 prevented the Tarbells' migration, and Franklin returned to the McCullough farm. News of the discovery of oil in 1859 by Edwin L. Drake near Titusville, Pennsylvania, about forty miles south of the McCullough place, sent Franklin Tarbell on a new quest and launched the Tarbell family into the oil age. The alert Tarbell went to the site of the oil strike, sized up the immense potential richness of the discovery, and decided to stay. He invented the wooden tanks first used to store the oil, prospered, and became an oil prospector and driller.

In 1860 Franklin Tarbell built a shanty near the oil fields for his family, now including Ida's brother Willie, in a settlement soon to be called Rouseville. By the time Ida was thirteen it was clear to her parents that a rowdy settlement was no place to raise children. They moved in 1870 to Titusville, a settled town with public schools suitable for their children, who, with the birth of Sarah, numbered three. A fourth child, Franklin, had died in Rouseville of scarlet fever. But the imprint of the oil frontier town on Ida Tarbell's mind went deep. She had seen her mother and father and like-minded parents build a neighborhood Methodist church in Rouseville and create a stable community around it to insulate their children from the riotous atmosphere of the boom town. She had absorbed their reliance on the family as the basic unity of that community. She had seen determined mothers impose order on a chaotic community, and she had watched fathers as they applied their frontiersmen's ingenuity to a new industry and through cooperation bring it under productive control. These experiences she never forgot, and the sex roles she had observed remained constants in her social thought, as did the beneficial effects of willing cooperation in business.

At first Ida Tarbell's frontier ways conflicted with the strict expectations of her eighth-grade teacher in Titusville. Schooling in Rouseville had been easygoing. In the new environment the child reacted to the unaccustomed yoke of regular attendance by frequently playing hooky and rarely doing homework. Finally the teacher reprimanded her balky pupil. Tarbell responded by settling down and becoming a model student, and she remained one throughout high school, where she developed her early interest in botany.

During her high school days, John D. Rockefeller and his associates in the Standard Oil Company swiftly completed a takeover of the Pennsylvania oil regions. Franklin Tarbell remained bitterly opposed to Rockefeller's business standards and monopolistic goals, a stand that eventually led to the end of his own business career. Although many able independent drillers joined Standard, Tarbell refused to consider such a move, outraged by crooked schemes such as the South Improvement Company. Through this scheme, Standard meant to ruin competitors by high freight rates arrived at in collusion with the railroad companies, while at the same time receiving from the railroads secret rebates from their own and their rivals' shipments. This particular scheme was discovered in time to prevent its implementation, but Tarbell and his daughter remained convinced that Standard gained control of the oil industry through such unfair and illegal means. Burned into her consciousness was, in her words, "a hatred of privilege" that became a hallmark of her later work.

Tarbell's parents were open to the idea of her entering college following graduation from high school, for they were aware of the new currents of the time. They attended lectures and summer sessions at the Methodist-sponsored camp at Lake Chautauqua, New York, that had grown into an important cultural institution. Her mother had long been an advocate of woman's rights, and income from her father's investments provided the wherewithal. The decision was made easier by the proximity of Allegheny College, a small Methodist-affiliated liberal arts school only thirty miles from Titusville in Meadville, Pennsylvania.

By this time young Ida Tarbell had rejected Methodism in favor of Spencerian evolutionary theories, but prudently kept these new ideas to herself. Allegheny College had recently become coeducational, and she was the only woman in her freshman class. Her college years were rewarding; she profited from her academic program, majored in biology, and managed to avoid what she considered the pitfall of marriage. She graduated in 1880, aware that her desire to continue her studies in biology at the graduate level would remain a dream.

What was the reality? For women there were two alternatives: marriage, already ruled out, and teaching. She took a teaching job at Poland Union Seminary, not far away across the Ohio border. She stuck it out for two years of overwork and pay so low she had to borrow from her father in order to survive. Defeated and disillusioned, she quit and went home to face again two alternatives, marriage or spinsterhood as her parents' dependent. An opportunity soon came along that rescued her from both fates and launched her, in 1883, on her career.

The family's Chautauqua connections came to her aid in the person of the Reverend T. L. Flood, a Methodist minister well known in Titusville and the editor of the Chautauqua Assembly's magazine, the *Chautauquan*. At the Tarbells' Sunday dinner table he recruited Ida to annotate difficult passages in texts used in correspondence courses that were carried in the magazine. Soon she became so involved that she moved back to Meadville, the magazine's headquarters. During the next few years she learned the nuts and bolts of putting together a magazine, from editing to typesetting to writing articles. Though Flood never granted her the title, in reality she became the managing editor.

By 1890, at age thirty-three, Tarbell had outgrown her native region and her work. During her stint on the magazine she had written a few articles on women prominent in the French revolutionary period, developing a resolve to study the period and women's role in it more closely. That ambition meant going to Paris. Two of her female coworkers agreed to accompany her, and before long she was busy studying historiography at the Sorbonne and doing research at the Bibliothèque Nationale, focused on Madame Marie Jeanne Roland, an activist in the Revolution whose papers had recently been deposited there. Meanwhile Tarbell supported herself by selling free-lance features about Parisian life to American newspapers. Her work caught the eye of Samuel S. McClure, proprietor of McClure's Syndicate, which marketed some of her writing. One day he swept into her tiny Latin Quarter apartment and hired her as a writer for his new venture, *McClure's* magazine, designed as a livelier, less expensive version of the *Century* magazine.

Like the pioneer she was, Tarbell accepted McClure's offer and in 1893 returned home to Titusville to complete her book on Roland while awaiting assignment. She did not have long to wait. In August 1894 McClure ordered her to write a biography of Napoleon Bonaparte in time for serial publication in *McClure's* starting in November. Undaunted, Tarbell moved to Washington, D.C., to work with Gardner Green Hubbard, owner of the Napoleon portraits to be featured in the series. Her research base was the Library of Congress. While Tarbell herself considered her scholarship sketchy, the public loved the series. *McClure's* circulation doubled. The articles were soon published in book form as *A Short Life of Napoleon Bonaparte* (1895) and remained popular for many years. The second edition, published in 1901, included a generally favorable biographical sketch of Josephine Bonaparte. In this study, as in that of Napoleon, Tarbell denigrated the aristocratic bias of the Bonapartes that took special privilege as a right, but both biographies are fast-paced, accurate, and informative. The Hubbard portraits covered Napoleon's career from 1796 to 1815, and Tarbell concentrated on that period. Her treatment conveys the tragic nature of Napoleon's rise and fall and emphasizes his constructive role in modernizing French governance and laws. Her open prejudices in favor of democracy and of a subservient role for women seem unduly heavy-handed, though doubtless they seemed right and proper to her readers.

Encouraged by the success of Tarbell's Napoleon biography, Scribners published *Madame Roland: A Biographical Study* in 1896. The book did not sell well, but it is a benchmark in Tarbell's development as a historian/biographer. Madame Ro-

Tarbell (seated at left) with fellow members of the Chautauquan *staff, 1888*

land, Girondist celebrity of the French Revolution, was executed at the height of the Reign of Terror in 1793 by the radical Jacobins who wrested control from the moderates of the Gironde. Tarbell's study of the Revolution confirmed the antirevolutionary stance that was a logical part of her evolutionary philosophy. While her antifeminist bias, denying an active political role to women, skews her assessment of Roland's short career in politics, the book is solidly researched, containing much material never before available. Tarbell's narrative skill propels the book to its conclusion, Roland's execution and her husband's consequent suicide. To these events she was not willing to grant tragic stature. Perhaps unrealistically, she berated the Girondists for not engineering a compromise that could have resulted in a constitutional monarchy.

Tarbell's next assignment, a biography of Abraham Lincoln, brought her more fame and the magazine more fortune. In it she generated the myth of Lincoln as the representative American: a frontiersman. Tarbell's own frontier childhood made it natural for her to glorify Lincoln's, until then soft-pedaled by biographers of his own generation. The biography reflected the spirit of the 1890s that was in harmony with the thesis of Frederick Jackson Turner's famous 1893 address, "The Significance of the Frontier in American History." Her research for the Lincoln biography was extensive. Aided by J. McCan Davis, she unearthed fresh documents, photographs, and anecdotes, enough of the last to furnish material for a lifetime of feature articles and a dependable source of income. *The Early Life of Abraham Lincoln*, crediting both Tarbell and Davis, appeared in *McClure's* in 1895 and was published in book form the following year. The series was so popular that it led to *The Life of Abraham Lincoln*, also serialized, and published in 1900. Her biography, well researched despite the fact that Robert Todd Lincoln had denied access to the Lincoln papers, appealed to the majority of readers unwilling to wade through the ponderous authorized ten-volume biography by John G. Nicolay and John Hay. Tarbell's *Life of Abraham Lincoln* remained a standard work until 1947, when the Lincoln papers finally were released to scholars.

Around 1900 McClure and his staff, which included Ray Stannard Baker and Lincoln Steffens, became restless; their circulation had resulted so far mainly from their popular imitation of the more sedate *Century*. They were seeking originality, a new direction in journalism that would attract readers. McClure assigned Tarbell to cover the history of Standard Oil, Baker to probe the practices of labor unions, and Steffens to sniff out municipal corruption. Together these three produced a critique of big business, big labor, and municipal politics that was pivotal in energizing the Progressive reform movement. From 1902 to 1904 their articles revealed to readers eager for more the injustices and corruption that permeated business and its handmaidens, labor and politics, and lambasted the sleazy morality that tolerated them.

Tarbell focused relentlessly on the Standard Oil Company and its founder John D. Rockefeller. She avoided the mistakes of Henry Demarest Lloyd, whose *Wealth Against Commonwealth* had mounted the first attack on Standard Oil in 1894. Lloyd's fiery jeremiad was too bitter, too slanted, too conspiratorial in tone to win the credence granted Tarbell's coolness and relative objectivity. Lloyd's did not identify his villains; Tarbell named names. Lloyd's accuracy was suspect; Tarbell's facts were impeccably documented. Unrelieved evil was the focus of Lloyd's account; Tarbell's treatment of corporate behavior was more balanced. Her Rockefeller came off as an American Napoleon, a maverick genius. Lloyd had shot from the hip and missed; Tarbell took careful aim and hit the bull's-eye. Her target was identical to Lloyd's: the threat of big business to democracy. Critics have faulted Tarbell's moralistic bias, but none has disproven her facts. *The History of the Standard Oil Company*, published in 1904, marks the high point of Tarbell's achievement and probably that of muckraking journalism. While some muckrakers, including Steffens, despaired of capitalism and turned to socialism, Tarbell remained convinced that capitalism and democracy were not incompatible, given adequate government regulation of business. The connection between her book and the 1911 dissolution by the Supreme Court of Standard's holding company was pointed out by American historian Charles D. Hazen: "Miss Tarbell is the only histo-

rian I have ever heard of whose findings were corroborated by the Supreme Court of the United States." The Pennsylvania oil regions had been avenged by one of their own.

Tarbell's career began a gradual decline in 1906. After a policy dispute with the tempestuous and erratic McClure, most of his staff, including editor John S. Phillips, Tarbell, Baker, and Steffens, quit. They bought the *American* magazine from Frederick L. Colver and started production of a magazine that imitated the one they had helped bring to great popularity and influence.

Tarbell's first series in the *American* capitalized on her fame as a historian of business. Entitled *The Tariff in Our Times*, it ran intermittently from 1906 to 1911, the year of its publication in book form. As if aware that the muckraking movement was fading, Tarbell interrupted the tariff series for long intervals to concentrate on the "Woman Question," a red-hot issue of the day, and by the time the tariff book appeared, the era of reform journalism was over. Yet *The Tariff in Our Times* is an excellent companion to *The History of the Standard Oil Company*. The tariff series outlined the history of the protective tariff from the Civil War to 1909, the year of the Payne-Aldrich Act imposing the highest tariffs ever. Tarbell emphasized the connections among protective tariffs, big business, and the Republican party. She revealed the costs to consumers and labor, costs previously concealed by slick propaganda. As she had in *The History of the Standard Oil Company*, Tarbell lashed out at special privilege as a despoiler of democracy. She concluded that "one cannot in the end separate morals and economics, for all that people do is moral in the sense that the welfare of a society as a whole depends on it." This secularized morality generated the power of her best work and formed the basis for all of her writing. Tarbell's strong point was not economics, and she felt *The Tariff in Our Times* was deadened by the immense research that it entailed. Nevertheless, the book is characteristic of her analytical skill and ability to present dense material clearly and effectively.

It has always been difficult to reconcile Tarbell's belief in equal opportunity with her view on women's equality. In her day woman suffrage had come to symbolize equality, and Tarbell's antisuffrage views flew in the face of women's demands for equality under the law. Since the welfare of society as a whole was her prime concern, it could be argued that woman suffrage seemed to Tarbell, as a gradualist, a revolutionary threat to the family and therefore to a stable society. She resorted to a deistic naturalism to explain her view: "The central fact in a woman's life, Nature's reason for her, is the child, his bearing and rearing. There is no escape from the divine order that her life must be built around this constraint, duty, or privilege, as she may please to consider it." Sigmund Freud put it more succinctly: "Anatomy is destiny."

From 1909 through 1913 Tarbell wrote three series of articles on women. Two, "The American Woman" and *The Business of Being a Woman*, appeared in the *American*. The second was published in book form in 1912. The third, *The Ways of Woman*, was serialized in the *Ladies' Home Journal* and published as a book in 1915. The first was a history of the rise in women's status as a result of the Revolutionary War and the Civil War, both of which created public roles for women as nurses and community workers; the second ingeniously applied factory efficiency methods and new technology to housework; the third argued that women should be content to limit their sphere of activity to family and community. A recent feminist theory holds that Tarbell accepted the fact of male dominance as a necessary norm, believing that women were not up to full equality. In that case, she must have regarded herself as an anomaly. But it would seem, rather, that she believed in an evolutionary approach which took into account the welfare of society as a whole. She predicted, accurately, that woman suffrage would make little social impact.

Just as she differed with feminists about woman suffrage, she disagreed with labor leaders about unions, convinced that confrontation between labor and management could not produce lasting cooperative production. She spelled out her views in her last series for the *American* magazine in 1914 and 1915. It was entitled "The Golden Rule in Business" and was published in 1916 as *New Ideals in Business: An Account of Their Practice and Their Effects Upon Men and Profits*. In this work Tarbell explained and defended the scientific management methods of pioneer efficiency expert Frederick W. Taylor and argued persuasively that Taylor's methods, properly used and applied in good faith, could improve working conditions, wages, and profits without adversarial unionism. The series was her acknowledgment that muckraking had accomplished its purpose of reform. Thereafter she shifted her emphasis from the evil of business to the good.

Previous to American entry into World War I Tarbell had advocated peace but, true to form, refused to become a militant peace advocate. In 1917 she accepted Woodrow Wilson's appointment to the Women's Committee of the Council of National Defense. Her only novel was about the shift in public sentiment in the American Midwest from pro-peace to prowar. The novel, *The Rising of the Tide: The Story of Sabinsport*, published in 1919, was a fictionalized documentary and a flop, both artistically and commercially. Tarbell's material would have been put to better use in a series of articles about the growth of war sentiment. She was no novelist, nor was she of the right generation to write about the war that had swept away her world. However, she had been in Paris as an observer at the Peace Conference, had become disillusioned about the European victors' intentions, and had emerged a lifelong advocate for Woodrow Wilson's League of Nations.

Lacking now a secure base of operations like *McClure's* or the *American*, Tarbell became a freelance writer and lecturer. Her great store of Lincoln stories furnished material for books and articles throughout the 1920s. Her change in attitude toward business became particularly evident in two biographies. Her laudatory biography *The Life of Elbert H. Gary: The Story of Steel* appeared in 1925 and was considered by many critics a betrayal of

Tarbell at seventy, photographed by Alfred Cheney Johnston

her views in *The History of the Standard Oil Company*. But she maintained she had not changed; business had. Likewise, her biography of General Electric Company's chairman of the board, *Owen D. Young: A New Type of Industrial Leader*, published in 1932, was taken to be a campaign biography of the man considered a likely candidate to contest Franklin D. Roosevelt for the presidential nomination. It was not, but it well could have been. Tarbell sincerely believed that the old American Anglo-Saxon business order had been rehabilitated by men like Gary and Young. She became increasingly critical of Roosevelt's experimentalism and regretted the rise of the CIO as a threat by big labor to stable industry.

Tarbell's last major history of business was published in 1936, when she was seventy-nine years old. It was *The Nationalizing of Business, 1878-1898*, volume 9 of the distinguished A History of American Life series edited by Arthur M. Schlesinger, Sr., and Dixon Ryan Fox. The fact that Tarbell was invited to contribute to this series is ample evidence of respect for her among academic historians, who by 1936 were largely predominant in the field of history. Such respect was well earned, for Tarbell was a pioneer historian of business. Schlesinger had approached Tarbell about the project in 1923 and she only reluctantly agreed to undertake it. She was not comfortable with the academic format and theoretical perspective of professional historians, and the kudos to be earned were perhaps not as compelling as were the wider sales to be gained from a popular format. However, the book when it appeared matched the high quality of the series as a whole. It contains a dense and informative overview of the change during the period 1878 to 1898 from small local or regional businesses to national corporations. Although the work is heavily burdened with tightly organized facts, there are flashes of Tarbell's earlier fire at times. In her conclusion she tartly points out that "[Andrew] Carnegie's strong man still occupied the saddle" of the national economy. She had not modified her opinion of the bad old days.

All in the Day's Work, her autobiography, was published in 1939 near the end of her long and productive life. In it she vividly recalls the youth that prepared her for her career. Self-revelation was not easy for Tarbell, and her care to observe the proprieties results in lack of color. But apparent to a careful reader is a sophisticated and tolerant awareness of the ways of the world. The latter part of the autobiography is a chronicle of her many activities as a writer and public figure, and a reader sees that the author did indeed live by work and loved it as her zest for what she did comes through. From her restrained account of her life emerges the portrait of a woman her old friend Ray Stannard Baker once accurately described as "beautiful with virtue."

Ida Tarbell died of pneumonia at the age of eighty-six in a Bridgeport, Connecticut, hospital near her home. She was returned to Titusville to rest in Woodlawn Cemetery among kinfolk and neighbors whose rights she had so valiantly defended.

References:

Kathleen Brady, *Ida Tarbell: Portrait of a Muckraker* (New York: Seaview/Putnam's, 1984);

Mary E. Tomkins, *Ida M. Tarbell* (New York: Twayne, 1974).

Papers:

Tarbell's papers are at Allegheny College, Meadville, Pennsylvania, at the Drake Memorial Museum, Titusville, Pennsylvania, and at Smith College, Northampton, Massachusetts.

Reuben Gold Thwaites

(15 May 1853-22 October 1913)

Steven P. Gietschier

South Carolina Department of Archives and History

SELECTED BOOKS: *Historical Sketch of the Public Schools of Madison, Wisconsin, 1838-1885* (Madison: Printed by M. J. Cantwell, 1886);

Historic Waterways: Six Hundred Miles of Canoeing down the Rock, Fox, and Wisconsin Rivers (Chicago: McClurg, 1888); revised as *Down Historic Waterways: Six Hundred Miles of Canoeing upon Illinois and Wisconsin Rivers* (Chicago: McClurg, 1902);

The Story of Wisconsin (Boston: Lothrop, 1890; revised and enlarged, 1899);

The Colonies, 1492-1750 (New York & London: Longmans, Green, 1891; revised, 1892);

Our Cycling Tour in England, from Canterbury to Dartmoor Forest, and Back by Way of Bath, Oxford, and the Thames Valley (Chicago: McClurg, 1892);

Afloat on the Ohio: An Historical Pilgrimage of a Thousand Miles in a Skiff, from Redstone to Cairo (Chicago: Way & Williams, 1897); revised as *On the Storied Ohio: An Historical Pilgrimage of a Thousand Miles in a Skiff, from Redstone to Cairo* (Chicago: McClurg, 1903);

Stories of the Badger State (New York & Cincinnati: American Book Company, 1900);

Daniel Boone (New York: Appleton, 1902);

Father Marquette (New York: Appleton, 1902);

How George Rogers Clark Won the Northwest, and Other Essays in Western History (Chicago: McClurg, 1903);

A Brief History of Rocky Mountain Exploration, with Especial Reference to the Expedition of Lewis and Clark (New York: Appleton, 1904);

France in America, 1497-1763 (New York & London: Harper, 1905);

Wisconsin: The Americanization of a French Settlement (Boston & New York: Houghton Mifflin, 1908);

A History of the United States for Grammar Schools, by Thwaites and Calvin Noyes Kendall (Boston & New York: Houghton Mifflin, 1912).

OTHER: *Proceedings of the State Historical Society of*

Reuben Gold Thwaites

Wisconsin, volumes 35-60, edited by Thwaites (1888-1912);

Wisconsin Historical Collections, volumes 11-20, edited by Thwaites (1888-1912);

Triennial Catalogue of the Portrait Gallery of the State Historical Society of Wisconsin, compiled by Thwaites and Daniel Steele Durrie, 2 volumes (Madison: Democrat Printing Company, 1889, 1892);

"Early Lead-mining in Illinois and Wisconsin," in *Annual Report of the American Historical Association for the Year 1893* (Washington, D.C.: Government Printing Office, 1894), pp. 189-196;

State Historical Society of Wisconsin Bulletins of Information, numbers 1-70, edited by Thwaites (1894-1913);

Arguments for a Joint Building for the State Historical Society and the State University, compiled by Thwaites (Madison: Democrat Printing Company, 1895);

Alexander Scott Withers, *Chronicles of Border Warfare; or, A History of the Settlement by the Whites, of North-western Virginia, and of the Indian Wars and Massacres in that Section of the State, with Reflections, Anecdotes, &c.*, edited by Thwaites (Cincinnati: Clark, 1895);

The Jesuit Relations and Allied Documents: Travels and Explorations of the Jesuit Missionaries in New France, 1610-1791; The Original French, Latin and Italian Texts, with English Translations and Notes, edited by Thwaites, 73 volumes (Cleveland: Burrows, 1896-1901);

"State-Supported Historical Societies and Their Functions," in *Annual Report of the American Historical Association for the Year 1897* (Washington, D.C.: Government Printing Office, 1898), pp. 63-71;

"Historical Outline of the Admission of Wisconsin to the Union," in *Constitution of the State of Wisconsin*, edited by Henry Casson (Madison: Democrat Printing Company, 1898), pp. 3-8;

The University of Wisconsin, its History and its Alumni, with Historical and Descriptive Sketches of Madison, edited with contributions by Thwaites (Madison: Purcell, 1900);

The State Historical Society of Wisconsin: Exercises at the Dedication of its New Building, October 19, 1900; Together with a Description of the New Building, Accounts of the Several Libraries Contained Therein, and a Brief History of the Society, edited by Thwaites (Madison: Democrat Printing Company, 1901);

Mrs. John H. Kinzie (Juliette Augusta Magill), *Wau-Bun, the "Early Day" of the Northwest*, edited by Thwaites (Chicago: Caxton Club, 1901);

Father Louis Hennepin, *A New Discovery of a Vast Country in America*, edited by Thwaites, 2 volumes (Chicago: McClurg, 1903);

"The Story of Lewis and Clark's Journals," in *Annual Report of the American Historical Association for the Year 1903*, 2 volumes (Washington, D.C.: Government Printing Office, 1904), I: 105-129;

Original Journals of the Lewis and Clark Expedition, 1804-1806; Printed from the Original Manuscripts in the Library of the American Philosophical Society and by the Direction of its Committee on Historical Documents, together with Manuscript Material of Lewis and Clark from other Sources, Including Notebooks, Letters, Maps, etc., and the Journals of Charles Floyd and Joseph Whitehouse, Now for the First Time Published in Full and Exactly as Written, edited by Thwaites, 8 volumes (New York: Dodd, Mead, 1904-1905);

Early Western Travels, 1748-1846: A Series of Annotated Reprints of Some of the Best and Rarest Contemporary Volumes of Travel, Descriptive of the Aborigines and Social and Economic Conditions in the Middle and Far West, During the Period of Early American Settlement, edited by Thwaites, 32 volumes (Cleveland: Clark, 1904-1907);

Documentary History of Dunmore's War, 1774, edited by Thwaites and Louise Phelps Kellogg (Madison: State Historical Society of Wisconsin, 1905);

Louis Armand de Lom d'Arce, Baron de Lahontan, *New Voyages to North-America*, edited by Thwaites, 2 volumes (Chicago: McClurg, 1905);

"Report of the Committee on Methods of Organization on the Part of State and Local Historical Societies," in *Annual Report of the American Historical Association for the Year 1905*, 2 volumes (Washington, D.C.: Government Printing Office, 1906), I: 249-325;

Descriptive List of Manuscript Collections of the State Historical Society of Wisconsin; together with Reports on other Collections of Manuscript Material for American History in Adjacent States, edited by Thwaites (Madison: State Historical Society of Wisconsin, 1906);

State Historical Society of Wisconsin Handbooks, numbers 1-7, edited by Thwaites (Madison: State Historical Society of Wisconsin, 1906-1913);

"The Romance of Mississippi Valley History," in *Proceedings of the Fiftieth Anniversary of the Constitution of Iowa*, edited by B. F. Shambaugh (Iowa City: State Historical Society of Iowa, 1907), pp. 113-142;

The Revolution on the Upper Ohio, 1775-1777, edited by Thwaites and Kellogg (Madison: State Historical Society of Wisconsin, 1908);

Wisconsin Historical Commission, *Original Papers*, edited by Thwaites, 7 volumes (Madison: Published for the State Historical Society, 1908-1912);

Wisconsin Historical Commission, *Reprints*, edited by Thwaites, 2 volumes (Madison: Published for the State Historical Society, 1908-1912);

"The Ohio Valley Press before the War of 1812-

15," in *Proceedings of the American Antiquarian Society*, 19 (1909), pp. 309-368;

Frontier Defense on the Upper Ohio, 1777-1778, edited by Thwaites and Kellogg (Madison: State Historical Society of Wisconsin, 1912);

"At the Meeting of the Trails: The Romance of a Parish Register," in *Proceedings of the Mississippi Valley Historical Association*, 6 (1912-1913), pp. 198-217;

Check-list of Publications of the Society, 1850-1913, compiled by Thwaites and Annie Amelia Nunns (Madison: State Historical Society of Wisconsin, 1913).

PERIODICAL PUBLICATIONS: "Osh-kosh, the Last of the Menominee Sachems," *Oshkosh Times*, 22 April 1876;

"The Black Hawk War," *Magazine of Western History*, 5 (1886-1887): 32-45, 181-196;

"Lyman C. Draper—the Western Plutarch," *Magazine of Western History*, 5 (1886-1887): 335-350;

"General David Atwood," *Magazine of Western History*, 5 (February 1887): 549-565;

"The State Historical Society of Wisconsin," *Magazine of Western History*, 7 (1887-1888): 549-560;

"The Study of Local History in the Wisconsin Schools," *Wisconsin Journal of Education*, 18 (1888): 465-476;

"The State Historical Society," *Evening Wisconsin*, 6 February 1889;

"The Historical Society: Its Relation to the People of the State, *Madison Times*, 14 February 1893;

"The Library of the State Historical Society of Wisconsin," *Library Journal*, 21 (April 1896): 175-176;

"The Story of Mackinac," *Library Journal*, 21 (December 1896): 71-78;

"Apprenticeship as a Means of Library Training," *Library Journal*, 23 (February 1898): 83-84;

"Ten Years of American Library Progress," *Library Journal*, 25 (June 1900): 1-7;

"Lewis and Clark: Discoverers of Empire," *Christendom*, 1 (1902-1903): 520-527;

"Letter of Admiral Farragut, 1853," *American Historical Review*, 9 (April 1904): 537-541;

"Newly Discovered Personal Records of Lewis and Clark," *Scribner's Magazine*, 35 (June 1904): 685-700;

"A Letter of Marshall to Jefferson, 1783," *American Historical Review*, 10 (July 1905): 815-817;

"Overland a Century Ago: The Lewis and Clark Expedition as a Feature in Westward Expan-sion and the Significance of the Present Centennial Exposition at Portland, Oregon," *Sunset Magazine*, 15 (1905): 213-224;

"Local History in the Library Story Hour," *Library Journal*, 32 (April 1907): 158-159;

"Notable Gathering of Scholars," *Independent*, 68 (6 January 1910): 7-14;

"An Outline of Mackinac History," *Wisconsin Library Bulletin*, 6 (June 1910): 55-56.

Reuben Gold Thwaites, librarian, historian, editor, and administrator, served as secretary of the State Historical Society of Wisconsin from 1887 until his death in 1913. An industrious writer, he produced an array of books and superb documentary editions that added substantially to the understanding of the American westward movement. Following the career of his illustrious predecessor, Lyman C. Draper, he used his abundant enthusiasm and dedication to advance the Wisconsin society to new levels of achievement, rivaling, if not surpassing, the accomplishments of older historical societies in the East. Most significantly he created the modern idea of the historical society, especially the publicly supported society, transforming it into an instrument for public education, freeing it from antiquarian clubbiness, and encouraging the use of its varied resources by all people.

Thwaites was born in Dorchester, Massachusetts, on 15 May 1853, to William George Thwaites and Sarah Bibbs Thwaites, recent emigrants from Yorkshire, England. Educated in the Dorchester public schools, Thwaites moved with his family in 1866 to Oshkosh, Wisconsin. For six years he worked on the family farm, taught in the Winnebago County school system, and put himself through a course of studies at the undergraduate level. Before he was twenty, he was on the staff of the *Oshkosh Times* and was sent to Baltimore in 1872 to report on the Democratic party convention that nominated Horace Greeley for the presidency.

Thwaites left the newspaper in 1874 and returned east to Yale as a special student. He took graduate courses in English literature, economic history, and international law, all the while supporting himself as a newspaper correspondent. Among his professors was William Graham Sumner, renowned economic historian and sociologist, who preached the gospel of Social Darwinism. Returning to Wisconsin a year later, Thwaites worked first for the *Oshkosh Northwestern* and then, from 1876, for the *Wisconsin State Journal*, published in Madison by David Atwood, a former Republican congressman and long an active member of the

State Historical Society of Wisconsin. Serving as city editor and then managing editor of the *State Journal*, Thwaites came to know the society's secretary, Lyman C. Draper, who selected him as his assistant and heir apparent in 1885.

For Draper, who had over more than three decades raised the society from hesitant beginnings to a position of prominence, Thwaites was the obvious choice to succeed him. Draper undoubtedly saw in his young assistant qualities he valued: efficiency and organization, easy acquaintance with public officials, familiarity with government, editorial experience, and, above all, an unbounding energy and enthusiasm for his work. When Draper announced his retirement late in 1886, he concluded his letter of resignation with the words, "It is no small gratification to me to feel assured that the laboring oar of the Society's success will fall into hands so competent by his culture, his tastes, his industry, and his habits as the gentleman you have approved, and whom you will, I doubt not, choose as my successor." The resignation was accepted with regret, and a special committee headed by Atwood nominated Thwaites, who was elected unanimously.

Understandably, Thwaites did not at first depart from the course set by Draper, who had earned for the society a firm place in the affections of the state. The new man shared with his mentor the generally accepted view of what a historical society should be: fundamentally a gentlemen's club built around a library and dedicated to gathering books, historical manuscripts, and some artifacts, often called curiosities. Some societies encouraged the preparation of scholarly papers and published collections of documents. In almost all societies, especially in the East, meetings were infrequent, dues, if there were any, went uncollected, and invitations to join were extended only to the privileged few. That Draper had enhanced this vision by his own industry and promotion and by his insistence on a state appropriation, however small, did not obscure the fact that membership was limited primarily to the Madison area and that the society, therefore, had a more moderate appeal elsewhere. Thwaites originally accepted this arrangement, but even in fulfilling Draper's plans, he began to move the society into a new era and to make it one of the state's recognized resources.

As funds allowed, he built a staff, hiring a binding clerk in 1888 and a new assistant librarian and a reading room clerk in 1889. When his own work increased, he acquired a full-time secretary and put her to work at one of the first typewriters

purchased by the society. Thwaites selected each employee himself and later spoke about his hiring practices to the Summer School of Library Science in Madison. He demanded at least a bachelor's degree, cultural compatibility with the institution's goals, and loyalty. "Remember," he once said, "you are a public servant." He often hired women and tried to make a family of his staff, regularly inviting them to congenial Saturday night suppers with his family. He had married Jessie Inwood Turville in 1882; they had one son.

Before long, Thwaites's leadership and the society's continued growth brought to the forefront the question of additional space. Draper had persistently argued in vain for a permanent, fireproof building of the society's own, but had been forced to accept nothing more than barely adequate quarters in the State Capitol. Thwaites first sought private donations, as had Draper, and then tried, almost successfully, to obtain legislative approval for a building to stand as a memorial to Wisconsin's Civil War veterans. When neither of these approaches worked, he joined with the University of Wisconsin to seek a building to be shared by the society and the university library. This strategy eventually worked, although negotiations and legislative maneuvering took several years before an architectural competition to select the best design commenced. An 1895 law apportioned a one-tenth-mill tax for the building. This raised $60,000 a year until 1899 when a final cash appropriation of $200,000 was approved.

The new building, dedicated in October 1900, gave the occupants a most modern facility and symbolized the growing professionalism of the society. The design incorporated many features suggested by Thwaites and the society's librarian, Isaac Bradley, who together had toured major libraries and submitted a report to the building commissioners. Their recommendations resulted in a stack system borrowed from Harvard, central ventilation from Yale, reading room security from Cornell, and several other adaptations. Space was allocated not only to the two principal tenants but also to the state's Free Library Commission, the Wisconsin Academy of Arts, Sciences, and Letters, and the new university School of History, established to dissuade Frederick Jackson Turner from accepting an attractive offer to move to the University of Chicago. The society agreed to maintain the building to which it held title. The university assumed half the cost of utilities, and a division of collecting spheres was worked out. The university, its holdings only one-eighth those of the society's, left Thwaites responsibility for history, genealogy, travel, economics, sociology, newspapers, English drama, and American biography. This special tie between institutions has remained strong; to this day, the society still serves as the American history library for the university's Madison campus.

Thwaites used to his best advantage the interesting fact that no university professor or student could now seek a library book without passing through the society's portals. He had in truth cultivated this connection since taking over from Draper, who was intellectually stuck in antiquarianism and had no use for modern, professional historians like Turner. Thwaites had quickly given graduate students, ninety percent of his clientele, access to the stacks in the Capitol, and he had invited professors to meet their seminars there. He purchased additional desks and chairs, tore down walls to make materials accessible, and lengthened hours of operation. Once in the new building, Thwaites had to iron out minor annoyances—noise from athletic fields, lights left on by students, prorating bills—but use of the collection grew rapidly, and the library stayed open on student demand to 10:00 P.M. six nights a week. Thwaites reckoned correctly that graduates would take their good impression of the society back to their hometowns, further boosting its popularity.

Turner and Thwaites, in fact, became very close friends, as each found in the other a kindred spirit devoted to advancing his profession. While Thwaites worked for the *Wisconsin State Journal*, he had tried to interest the young Turner, then undecided on a career, in a scheme to establish a newspaper in New Mexico or Colorado. Once Turner opted to teach history, he spent many days in the society's library. Thwaites read Turner's master's thesis to the society's 1889 annual meeting so that it could be published. In 1893 they journeyed together to Chicago for the special World's Fair Historical Congress at which Thwaites read a paper on lead mining and Turner read his masterpiece on the significance of the frontier. Later, when Harvard's Albert Bushnell Hart was planning the American Nation series, a multivolume collaborative history of the United States, he engaged the society to advise him on the proper treatment of the West, and Turner sat with Thwaites and others to do so.

Historical societies in the East had traditionally published their way to fame, and Draper had adopted this technique with gusto. His ten volumes of the *Reports and Collections of the State Historical Society of Wisconsin* were a loose amalgam of annual reports, proceedings, papers, reprints, and original documentary publications. Draper used the *Reports and Collections* to advertise his progress and, with the state paying the printing bill, made sure he had sufficient copies of each volume to trade with other libraries. In 1888 Thwaites took over, separating the *Collections* from the *Reports*, which he retitled *Proceedings*, and reserving the biennial volumes of the former for primary materials and the latter, which appeared annually, for reports and monographs. He ordered the ten volumes prepared by Draper reprinted when schoolteachers showed an increased interest in the early history of the state. Two other series edited by Thwaites were also aimed at this growing appetite for local history. The *Bulletins of Information* (1894-1913), which ran to seventy volumes during Thwaites's tenure, were circulars on a multitude of topics. The *Handbooks*, a shorter series of seven titles, began in 1906 with the publication of *A Brief Description of the State Historical Building at Madison, Wisconsin*, and ended in 1913.

Thwaites's own early writings sprang mostly from his summer travels, perhaps because he believed, like Turner, that good historical writing must be preceded by a firm knowledge of geography. Immediately after being selected secretary, he began to reread the works of Francis Parkman, and during the summer of 1887 he canoed down the Rock, the Fox, and the Wisconsin rivers. This trip led to Thwaites's book *Historic Waterways* (1888), which Turner described as "a light but charming narrative [of] the history of these rivers with his own observations of scenes and men along them." In 1892 Thwaites produced *Our Cycling Tour in England*, based upon a trip to study archives and libraries there. Another canoe voyage three years later resulted in *Afloat on the Ohio* (1897), an attempt by the author to "see with his own eyes what the borderers saw; in imagination to redress the pioneer stage and to repeople it."

Thwaites was a gifted lecturer and storyteller, both in person as he held a group spellbound with his wit and in his writing, which has been faulted for lack of critical insight. He believed in recounting the history of individual achievement more than that of institutions or governments. As a result his books are full of picturesque incidents, sharp characterization, and detailed narratives. Titles such as "At the Meeting of the Trails: the Romance of a Parish Register" and "Lewis and Clark: Discoverers of Empire" reveal his desire to convey the pageantry behind the document, the triumph of will hidden in the dusty record.

Thwaites first tried his hand at documentary editing with the publication of a new edition of Alexander Scott Withers's *Chronicles of Border Warfare* (1895). The original book, published in 1831 and intended primarily for a local audience in what is now West Virginia, had earned high praise from contemporaneous scholars. It also had ignited in the young Lyman Draper the spark to begin his own life's work, collecting and rescuing from obscurity the history of the heroes of the westward movement. In his last years Draper had been asked to prepare an updated, annotated edition of Withers's work, but this task remained unfinished at his death. The publisher soon approached Thwaites to assume the job, and he did so with some reluctance, aware that Draper's knowledge of the period had far surpassed his own. Nevertheless, he saw the work through, determined to preserve and publish Draper's notes which so often contradicted Withers's reliance on local tradition as the sole source of information.

Thwaites was a strict taskmaster who demanded much of his staff. Having picked them himself, he trained them, led them, and pushed them to match his own prodigious energy and iron will. Those who came up short of his expectations, as well as outsiders who tried to take advantage, quickly experienced his reprimand. For the most part, he combined his enormous energy to get things done with a ready smile and personal charm. Five feet seven inches tall and slightly rotund, he maintained a cheery disposition and sense of humor. His eyes sparkling behind rimless glasses, his hair rumpled, his speech easy, he made friends readily and inspired others to do their best work.

Such enthusiasm became a necessity as Thwaites tackled his second editorial project. Moving away from border warfare to a period and subject more to his taste, he compiled *The Jesuit Relations and Allied Documents* (1896-1901), which secured for him a national reputation. Thwaites obtained the cooperation of Catholic authorities, traveled to both Canada and Italy, and produced a seventy-three-volume series that included rare printed works, manuscript sources, and the invaluable annual reports, the *Relations*, filed by Jesuit missionaries with their superiors in France. In publishing what he called "one of the most thrilling chapters in human history," Thwaites added greatly to the existing sources on the work of these men and reasserted the truth that European colonization of North America had been a multinational enterprise. Coming as it did while Francis Parkman's histories were still in vogue, publication

of the *Jesuit Relations* revealed the missionaries' courage and devotion that Parkman's Protestant bias occasionally neglected. Also of significance was Thwaites's demonstration that a library team could be brought to the service of the professional historian. Translators, transcribers, proofreaders, and bibliographers—some paid by the society and some by the publisher—were assembled to produce this grand effort, still a reliable source, which Thwaites supervised while tending to other society business as well.

Thwaites's penchant for the dramatic led him rather naturally to writing biographies, two of which he produced for both scholarly and popular readers. *Daniel Boone* (1902), part of the Appleton Life Histories series, was a thorough reworking of an unfinished manuscript left by Draper, whose plans to publish a multitude of volumes never came to fruition. Thwaites edited and rewrote Draper's chapters, completed the story based on raw material collected by Draper and left to the society, and pared the result down to a readable whole. Though he feared that the book "would doubtless not have won the approbation of Dr. Draper, whose unaccomplished biographical plans were all drawn upon a large scale," Thwaites delivered a well-written volume which attracted a large audience. *Father Marquette* (1902), another in the series, though not based on Draper's work, was much the same sort of book, an exciting, popular account of an interesting subject informed by primary research and concisely written. In this case Thwaites was able to draw heavily and easily on his own work with the *Relations.*

That editorial projects, writing, and administration could go on all at once was a tribute to Thwaites's skills as an organizer, his journalistic training, and his insistence that the society be run along business lines. Each employee became a specialist and assumed responsibility for an area or department. Thwaites solicited their suggestions and intuitively grasped the best of them. He frequently attended professional conventions and took key staff members with him to exchange ideas and compare methods.

Early on, the Thwaites style transformed the society's library from "an aristocratic sanctum sanctorum," as he called it, to "an institution for the people," dedicated to the motto "We aim to be useful." All but the rarest items were made accessible, and by 1900 the library's holdings had nearly doubled to some 200,000 volumes. Draper's rate of accessions, itself an astounding 2,000 per year, was dwarfed by Thwaites's annual average of nearly

The State Historical Society of Wisconsin staff, in costume to celebrate the organization's sixtieth anniversary. Thwaites is seated in the front row; third from right at back is the Society's editorial assistant, Louise Phelps Kellogg (Iconographical Collections, State Historical Society of Wisconsin).

6,900. Ordering books and pamphlets was done systematically by class, duplicates were traded feverishly, and donations were actively encouraged. Thwaites sought materials from county clerks, from the Wisconsin Press Association, and from all members of the American Historical Association and the American Economic Association. He accepted on deposit University of Wisconsin professor Richard T. Ely's papers, the start of the society's outstanding collection of labor materials. Thwaites stopped production of the triennial printed library catalog and switched to a card catalog system. He established a binding fund to prolong the life of books, pamphlets, and newspapers. The society also published lists of its holdings by class, beginning with Civil War and slavery titles, and in 1893 Thwaites and Isaac Bradley prepared a *Bibliography of Wisconsin Authors*. The *Descriptive List of Manuscript Collections* (1906), edited by Thwaites, bridged the gap between an old card index system and the

still-to-come calendars of major collections.

When Draper died in 1891, he left his own collections of books, manuscripts, transcriptions, and notes to the society. Thwaites had the manuscripts bound into 478 volumes and then set out methodically to acquire Wisconsin sources, which Draper had ignored. By correspondence and personal visits, he collected the papers of business organizations and prominent individuals, specializing in the descendants of French pioneers. He extended this search to other American archives and then to Europe, arranging in 1897 to obtain copies of Wisconsin documents in London and Paris. Two projects were especially novel. The first, undertaken in 1887 with the university history department, inquired into the history of Wisconsin's many ethnic groups, especially those immigrants whose embarkation had been sponsored by government or business. The second, begun in 1892, sought, with the approval of the Grand Army of the Republic, to have the state's Civil War veterans contribute family histories to the society.

Even before Wisconsin began its intense experiments with progressivism, Thwaites led the historical society to play a larger role to in popular education for the general improvement of society, thereby irrevocably expanding the society's stated mission. At first, he was particularly interested in developing the society's museum, asking in 1891 for a state appropriation to hire professional staff and build new exhibits. "We can spend no less on the library," he said, "but there should be a fund for the development of the museum as well. . . . We are missing a golden opportunity in the education of the masses." Rebuffed by the legislature, he collected as best he could, relying mainly on donations and private subscription, and museum attendance rose from 35,000 in 1888 to 60,000 in 1895.

The state's semicentennial celebration in 1898 provided another chance for Thwaites to enlarge the society's educational work. A firm believer in the importance of local history, he attempted to persuade people to examine and use primary sources close at hand. For those not interested in monographs and other scholarship, he envisioned work with historic sites, markers, pageants and ceremonies, and collecting reminiscences. The legislature authorized the superintendent of public instruction to serve as historical commissioner for the semicentennial with Thwaites as an adviser and allowed local historical societies to incorporate as auxiliaries of the state society. The first *Bulletin of Information* was issued to begin preparations for the planned statewide celebration on 28 May 1898, and a second gave details for establishing auxiliaries. The outbreak of the Spanish-American War, which turned attentions elsewhere, canceled most of these observances, but Thwaites was not deterred. He personally organized several local societies, headed a conference for scholarly papers, and took the society's annual meeting on the road for the first time to Green Bay. "More and more," he said, "are the people of Wisconsin divining what a thesaurus of educational wealth rests upon these shelves and is anxious to reach their hands."

In the midst of all this activity, Thwaites was still able to withdraw to his private office to write and edit, sure that the daily operations of the society would proceed smoothly and that assistants would take care of typing, footnotes, and checking proof. He prepared new editions of two accounts of French exploration, Father Louis Hennepin's *A New Discovery of a Vast Country in America* (1903) and

the Baron de Lahontan's *New Voyages to North-America* (1905). In *France in America, 1497-1763* (1905), a volume Thwaites wrote for the American Nation series, he attempted to present a one-volume treatment that would update Parkman and "give the story of New France as it appears to modern investigators." Quite readable, the book was noted for its fine chapter on the discovery of the Mississippi River and for an interesting survey of the people of New France, their political and economic struggles. Thwaites edited *The University of Wisconsin, its History and its Alumni* (1900), a large portion of which he wrote himself, and coauthored *A History of the United States for Grammar Schools* (1912) with Calvin Noyes Kendall, the superintendent of public instruction. He also produced his second history of the state, *Wisconsin: The Americanization of a French Settlement* (1908), to complement an earlier effort, *The Story of Wisconsin*, published in 1890. Both remain respected standards. Judged solely on quantity, Thwaites had few peers.

In 1904 Thwaites took a trip to Yellowstone Park and came home to write *A Brief History of Rocky Mountain Exploration* (1904). Then, after once again familiarizing himself with geography first, he set up his editorial team to produce two more unparalleled sets of documents. The *Original Journals of the Lewis and Clark Expedition, 1804-1806* (1904-1905), in eight volumes, the last an atlas, marked the first time that these materials had been published, an effort that involved ferreting out missing documents, deciphering difficult handwriting, and correlating the several journals kept during the journey. Even more complex was the work involved in the thirty-two volumes of *Early Western Travels, 1748-1846* (1904-1907), a compilation of travel accounts and pioneer documents brought together with an exceedingly complete index so that, according to Turner, "they present a picture of the irresistible tide of American settlement flowing into the wilderness, of societies forming in the forests, of cities evolving almost under our gaze as we see them through the eyes of these travelers in successive years." In this work Thwaites was aided especially by editorial assistant Louise Phelps Kellogg, a new Wisconsin Ph.D. who would later become the only woman president of the Mississippi Valley Historical Association. She also worked on several volumes of the *Collections*, and when Thwaites convinced the Wisconsin Society of the Sons of the American Revolution to finance publication of three volumes of the Draper manuscripts, she did the basic editorial work and shared credit with Thwaites on *Documentary History of Dun-*

LORD DUNMORE
Reduced from old engraving in Wisconsin Historical Society's Library

DOCUMENTARY HISTORY

OF

DUNMORE'S WAR

1774

Compiled from the Draper Manuscripts in the
Library of the Wisconsin Historical Society
and published at the charge of the Wisconsin
Society of the Sons of the American Revolution

EDITED BY

REUBEN GOLD THWAITES, LL.D.
Secretary of the Society

AND

LOUISE PHELPS KELLOGG, PH.D.
Editorial Assistant on the Society's Staff

MADISON
WISCONSIN HISTORICAL SOCIETY
1905

Frontispiece and title page for the volume which Thwaites describes in his "Acknowledgment" as "significant in that it is the first considerable publication directly from the Draper Manuscript Collection"

more's War, 1774 (1905), *The Revolution on the Upper Ohio, 1775-1777* (1908), and *Frontier Defense on the Upper Ohio, 1777-1778* (1912). Kellogg then commenced to calendar and index the entire Draper collection, series by series, but the first calendar was not published until after Thwaites's death.

Thwaites renewed his work with Civil War veterans in time for the fiftieth anniversary of that conflict, for which the state at his urging established a five-member Wisconsin Historical Commission. It prepared a list of available sources and sought to stimulate a wide variety of activities around the state. Achievements did not measure up to goals despite the publication of several authentic eyewitness accounts, a volume on women during the war, and another on the social and economic history of the war years. The proposed general history of the state during the war never appeared.

With typical progressive zeal, Thwaites pushed hard in other directions, inspired by his belief in the perfectibility of man through broad-

based public education. He helped found the Wisconsin Library Association, local library associations, and the Free Library Commission charged with encouraging the growth of public libraries in the state. He urged local libraries to gather historical materials and to coordinate efforts with local historical societies. He actively promoted the erection of historical markers at some of Wisconsin's earliest historic places and began work to restore the territorial capitol building. The society's museum finally came into its own in 1907 when funds were secured to hire a professional curator who took over control of the collection from the janitorial staff, catalogued the objects, and installed new exhibits. Similar work was done in the new photographic collection, begun in 1905 upon the receipt of 465 photographs of Confederate officers. Thwaites and other staff members regularly spoke in schools and addressed students visiting the society on field trips. Thwaites promoted local museums as well as local libraries. Slowly membership in the society increased as the involvement with these many groups began to pay dividends. Honorary memberships, the original ploy used by Draper to solicit materials, fell by the wayside. In 1907 the legislature raised the society's operating budget from $5,000 a year to $20,000 and Thwaites's salary to $3,500 a year. Four years later, a northwest wing for the building, originally planned at the time of first construction, was authorized. Endowments and donations continued to grow, and Thwaites was able, in 1912, to overhaul completely the society's structure as he celebrated his twenty-fifth anniversary as secretary. The staff, numbering twenty-one professionals, three students, and fourteen caretakers, was henceforth organized by divisions.

All the while Thwaites was also playing a major role in national library and archival affairs, especially in the widespread effort to make available to American scholars documentary material on America held in private hands or in European archives. The American Historical Association created the Historical Manuscripts Commission to address this problem, and Thwaites served as a member from 1900 to 1906. The commission eventually published the papers of several noted Americans and gave birth to two other groups, the Public Archives Commission and the Carnegie Institution's Bureau of Historical Research. Funded by the Library of Congress, the bureau undertook work in European archives and published transcripts. The commission had an even greater impact in its domain, the records of American national, state, and local government. It published reports on the condition of public records in most of the states, and the Wisconsin report led to the first Wisconsin archives act in 1907. This simple law, heartily endorsed by Thwaites, was prompted in part by a 1904 fire in the State Capitol that would have destroyed the society had it remained in that building. It authorized any department head to transfer five-year-old records to the society, in effect making the society, a private organization dependent upon public funding, the archives of the state. After publishing its state reports, the commission turned to a consideration of archival techniques, creating in 1909 the Conference of American Archivists, which became in 1936 the Society of American Archivists.

Emphasis on popular education, the growth of museums, and new stress on the teaching of history in schools led to the need for further cooperation among historical societies, something that Thwaites had long advocated. As a member of the 1904 American Historical Association program committee, he organized an experimental conference of midwestern and southern societies to discuss common problems, particularly whether state historical societies should be private or public and whether state archives should be separate institutions. The sessions progressed so well that the group decided to organize into the Conference of Historical Societies, which evolved into the American Association for State and Local History. Thwaites chaired a committee of the conference to investigate cooperative ventures among members and recommended joint publication of documentary materials. In 1907 the American Historical Association met in Madison to help celebrate the University of Wisconsin's sixtieth anniversary. Thwaites chaired the local arrangements committee for what was really a joint convention of historians, the American Economic Association, the American Political Science Association, the American Sociology Society, and the American Association for Labor Legislation. From the American Historical Association meeting came still another committee proposing joint sponsorship of the transcription of additional European records. Thwaites, a member of the committee, pushed his own pet project, the history of the Mississippi Valley up to 1763, and Waldo Gifford Leland, already in France, was engaged to do the work. Some scholars and society administrators urged that still more be done, and they created the Mississippi Valley Historical Association. Thwaites declined to attend its inaugural meeting and refused the presidency, arguing that the American Historical Association could do all that was needed. Later he relented and served as president in 1912.

Sitting in his office on 20 October 1913, Thwaites prepared for the approaching annual meeting of the society and finished writing his annual report. The library, he could recall, now held over 350,000 volumes, three times what it had in 1887. The state appropriation, all told, stood at $70,000 a year. Ten volumes of the *Collections* had been published during his tenure and a comprehensive index readied for the press. The Draper papers were being calendared and a guide to all manuscripts had appeared in 1906. Just as important, the society had been modernized. A new building with an impending addition, a large, competent staff and administration, a professional museum, and a historic sites program were all in place. In fact, the Thwaites program in its diversity had reached out to touch a large segment of Wisconsin. That night Thwaites entered the hospital for what was first called a kidney ailment. Two days later, the society was shocked to learn that the best-known man in Wisconsin outside politics had died of a heart attack at age sixty.

When Frederick Jackson Turner returned to Madison in December to eulogize his late friend at a memorial service, he mourned his colleague's passing and credited him with being "the builder of a new type of state historical society." Historians' analyses usually require perspective, but in this case Turner was especially prescient. Thwaites's books are still somewhat respected, and his editorial series remain a cherished resource; but there can be no doubt that his greatest contribution was his vision of what a historical society should strive to be, not "an aristocratic retreat for the learned alone," as he once wrote, but "a practical assistant to intellectual activity among all classes." This democratic legacy has endured as the goals to which Thwaites aspired have become accepted standards in his profession.

Bibliography:
Frederick Jackson Turner, *Reuben Gold Thwaites: A Memorial Address* (Madison: State Historical Society of Wisconsin, 1914), pp. 63-94.

References:
Clarence W. Alvord, "A Critical Analysis of the Work of Reuben Gold Thwaites," in *Proceedings of the Mississippi Valley Historical Association*, 7 (1913-1914), pp. 321-323;

Clifford L. Lord, *Reuben Gold Thwaites and the Progressive Historical Society* (Lansing: Michigan Historical Society, 1963);

Lord, "Reuben Gold Thwaites," *Wisconsin Magazine of History*, 47 (Autumn 1963): 3-11;

Lord, "Reuben Gold Thwaites," in his *Keepers of the Past* (Chapel Hill: University of North Carolina Press, 1965);

Lord and Carl Ubbelohde, *Clio's Servant: The State Historical Society of Wisconsin, 1846-1954* (Madison: State Historical Society of Wisconsin, 1967);

Frederick Jackson Turner, *Reuben Gold Thwaites: A Memorial Address* (Madison: State Historical Society of Wisconsin, 1914).

Papers:
Thwaites's papers are at the State Historical Society of Wisconsin.

William P. Trent

(10 November 1862-6 December 1939)

L. Moody Simms, Jr.
Illinois State University

SELECTED BOOKS: *English Culture in Virginia: A Study of the Gilmer Letters and an Account of the English Professors Obtained by Jefferson for the University of Virginia* (Baltimore: N. Murray, Publication Agent, Johns Hopkins University, 1889);

William Gilmore Simms (Boston & New York: Houghton Mifflin, 1892; London, 1892);

The Study of Southern History (Nashville, 1895);

Southern Statesmen of the Old Régime: Washington, Jefferson, Randolph, Calhoun, Stephens, Toombs, and Jefferson Davis (New York: Crowell, 1897);

The Authority of Criticism, and Other Essays (New York: Scribners, 1899; London, 1899);

John Milton: A Short Study of His Life and Works (New York & London: Macmillan, 1899);

Robert E. Lee (Boston: Small, Maynard, 1899; London: Kegan Paul, Trench, Trübner, 1899);

Verses (Philadelphia: Slocum, 1899);

Progress of the United States of America in the Century (London & Philadelphia: Linscott, 1901; London: Chambers, 1903);

War and Civilization (New York: Crowell, 1901);

A History of the United States, by Trent and Charles Kendall Adams (Boston: Allyn & Bacon, 1903; revised, 1922);

A History of American Literature, 1607-1865 (New York: Appleton, 1903; London: Heinemann, 1903);

Greatness in Literature and Other Papers (New York:

Crowell, 1905; London: Harrap, 1905);

The Relations of History and Literature: An Address Delivered Before the Annual Meeting of the Virginia Historical Society (Richmond, 1906);

Longfellow and Other Essays (New York: Crowell, 1910);

An Introduction to the English Classics, by Trent, Charles L. Hanson, and William T. Brewster (Boston: Ginn, 1911; revised, 1916);

Great American Writers, by Trent and John Erskine (New York: Holt, 1912; London: Williams & Norgate, 1912);

Daniel Defoe, How to Know Him (Indianapolis: Bobbs-Merrill, 1916).

OTHER: "Notes on the Outlook for Historical Studies in the South," in *Papers of the American Historical Association*, 5 volumes (New York & London: Putnam's, 1886-1891), IV: 381-391;

"The Period of Constitution-Making in the American Churches," in *Essays in the Constitutional History of the United States in the Formative Period, 1775-1789*, edited by J. Franklin Jameson (Boston & New York: Houghton Mifflin, 1889), pp. 186-262;

"Notes on Recent Work in Southern History," in *Collections of the Virginia Historical Society*, new series, 11 (1892), pp. 47-59;

Colonial Prose and Poetry, edited by Trent and Benjamin W. Wells (New York: Crowell, 1901);

Southern Writers: Selections in Prose and Verse, edited by Trent (New York & London: Macmillan, 1905);

The Best American Tales, edited by Trent and John B. Henneman (New York: Crowell, 1907);

The Cambridge History of American Literature, edited by Trent, Stuart P. Sherman, John Erskine, and Carl Van Doren, 4 volumes (New York: Putnam's, 1917-1921).

PERIODICAL PUBLICATIONS: "Dominant Forces in Southern Life," *Atlantic Monthly*, 79 (January 1897): 42-53;

"Tendencies of Higher Life in the South," *Atlantic Monthly*, 79 (June 1897): 766-778;

"A New South View of Reconstruction," *Sewanee Review*, 9 (January 1901): 13-29.

Following his mid-career appointment to the Columbia University faculty in 1900, William Peterfield Trent won widespread recognition as a professor of English literature and as a literary historian. This fame has tended to obscure the fact that he was also a pioneering student of Southern history during the closing years of the nineteenth century.

The second of two children, William Peterfield Trent was born in Richmond, Virginia, on 10 November 1862. His older brother died in infancy. Both his parents—Peterfield Trent, a Richmond physician, and Lucy Carter Burwell Trent—were from distinguished Virginia families. As tobacco planters, merchants, landowners, and doctors, William Trent's paternal ancestors had long been influential citizens of Virginia. His grandfather Joseph Trent graduated with a medical degree from the University of Pennsylvania, and his father received his M.D. from the University of Georgia. Though Peterfield Trent prospered as a physician during the 1850s, he lost his fortune and his health during the Civil War while serving the Confederate army as a surgeon.

William Trent received his secondary education at Norwood's University School in Richmond, where his excellent academic record during the first term exempted him from paying tuition thereafter. Entering the University of Virginia in the fall of 1880, he studied history and moral philosophy, ancient and modern languages, natural history and geology, mathematics and chemistry. Among his professors were William M. Fontaine, George F. Holmes, and Charles S. Venable; fellow students included Richard H. Dabney, Oscar W. Underwood, and Woodrow Wilson. At Virginia Trent frequently wrote verse and criticism, acquiring for himself a considerable reputation as a literary critic. He served first as assistant editor and then as editor-in-chief of the *Virginia University Magazine*. After graduating from Virginia in 1883 with a bachelor of letters degree, Trent spent another year at the university, where further study of mathematics, history, and science earned him a master of arts degree.

Trent had planned a career in the law. From 1884 to 1887 he read law and taught in private schools in Richmond. In the fall of 1887, having decided against the law and in favor of a career as a university professor, he entered Johns Hopkins University for advanced graduate study in history and political science. Trent was attracted to Johns Hopkins, as were many budding scholars from the South, by the reputation of Herbert Baxter Adams, both as an outstanding teacher of history and politics and as an inspiring director of graduate studies. In addition to his work in Russian history and ancient politics with Adams, Trent studied American history with J. Franklin Jameson, finance with Richard T. Ely, and historical jurisprudence with

George H. Emmott. He was also a member of the seminary of history and political science, which was directed by Adams and included other members of the departmental faculty.

Trent's seminary paper on "The Influence of the University of Virginia on Southern Life and Thought" received praise from Adams, who included it as a chapter in his 1888 publication *Thomas Jefferson and the University of Virginia* (to which Trent also contributed a bibliography of publications by the University of Virginia faculty from 1825 to 1887). Another seminary paper by Trent dealt with "Thomas Jefferson and the Gilmer Correspondence." Adams had come into possession of some papers of Francis Walker Gilmer (1790-1826), the brilliant young Virginian who had been a friend of Jefferson's in later years and the University of Virginia's agent in Europe, charged with recruiting faculty and acquiring books and equipment. Adams encouraged Trent to edit the letters and provide background commentary; the result was

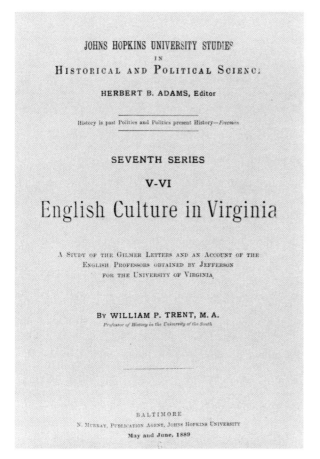

Title page for Trent's study based on letters by Francis Walker Gilmer, who served in Europe as the University of Virginia's agent in charge of faculty recruitment

English Culture in Virginia (1889). Few students made two seminary reports in one school year; however, the industrious Trent read a third paper in the spring of 1888 on "The Attitude of the Roman Catholic Church toward Education, Exhibited in the Acts & Decrees of the Third Plenary Council of Baltimore."

During his year at Johns Hopkins, Trent's admiration for Adams grew steadily. He would remain an enthusiastic supporter of the Baltimore school long after he left for Sewanee, Tennessee, where he accepted a teaching position at the University of the South in the fall of 1888. Circumstances would prevent further education, even though for a time Trent hoped to return to Johns Hopkins to complete requirements for the Ph.D.

At the University of the South Trent became acting professor of political economy and history and professor of English, even though he had taken no work in the latter field either at the University of Virginia or Johns Hopkins. Independent reading and his knowledge of languages compensated in part for his lack of formal training in English. Trent gave courses in rhetoric, English language and literature, American literature, politics, political economy, and general history. Though he came to view literature as his primary interest, he pursued history as his major objective during his early years at Sewanee. Indeed, on the title pages of his *English Culture in Virginia* and *William Gilmore Simms* (1892), he was identified as "Professor of History in the University of the South." In 1889 he contributed a study of "The Period of Constitution-Making in the American Churches" to *Essays in the Constitutional History of the United States, 1775-1789*, edited by J. Franklin Jameson.

When Trent began work at Sewanee, Southern academic historical scholarship was in its infancy. Herbert Baxter Adams had published two books on higher education in Virginia. Burr J. Ramage, Colyer Meriwether, Stephen B. Weeks, and Lewis W. Wilhelm—all Johns Hopkins men—would begin to publish contemporaneously with Trent. William A. Dunning was already at work at Columbia, but more than ten years would pass before his doctoral students began producing dissertations on the Civil War and Reconstruction period. Philip Alexander Bruce's *The Plantation Negro as a Freeman* was published in 1889; yet his first volume of five on seventeenth-century Virginia did not appear until 1895.

Realizing that historical research was at a low level and unorganized in the South, Trent in 1889 and 1891 sent inquiries to people throughout the region—including the secretaries of several hundred historical societies—to gather data on the state of historical studies. He found that no historical societies existed in Texas, Arkansas, Mississippi, and Florida. Those that did exist in the other Southern states were hampered by limited personnel, small memberships, and inadequate support. Few monographs and books were in preparation on Southern history. Concluding that there was little demand for historical studies in the South, he remained hopeful that an awakening of interest and activity was on the horizon.

Trent's optimism regarding an awakened interest in the pursuit of Southern history is revealed in his paper "Notes on Recent Work in Southern History," which he read before the Virginia Historical Society on 21 December 1891. He found encouraging historical activity in Tennessee, the Carolinas, Virginia, and Maryland. A committee of the state historical society in South Carolina had persuaded the legislature to provide funds for copying colonial records in London. The establishment of a chair in history and political science at the University of Georgia was another encouraging sign. In his paper Trent also detailed his own efforts, which led to the founding of the Sewanee Historical Society.

By 1895 the Sewanee Historical Society was defunct. The progress in developing Southern interest in Southern history was more apparent than real. Nevertheless, Trent remained optimistic and continued his efforts as a promoter of organized historical activities throughout the 1890s. Addressing the newly formed Vanderbilt Southern Historical Society in 1895, he encouraged the Nashville group to believe that it would endure and succeed.

In 1890 Trent combined historical and literary interests to write a biography of William Gilmore Simms for the American Men of Letters series edited by Charles D. Warner. Devoting much of the next two years to the task, he engaged in exhaustive research. He visited Charleston, Washington, Baltimore, and Richmond; he sought letters and reminiscences; he examined over a thousand letters to Simms and 175 of Simms's letters to such men as Beverley Tucker and Paul Hamilton Hayne. Trent compiled an extensive bibliography of Simms's work, ranging from romances and poetry to newspaper and periodical pieces. His research completed, he turned out a first draft of 850 manuscript pages in less than two months. A revision, accomplished in two weeks, cut 150 pages. Despite a heavy teaching load during much of this period, Trent met his publisher's deadline.

Seeing Simms as in most ways a typical Southerner, Trent believed that he needed to include a great deal of history in his biography in order to portray his subject adequately. Believing in the doctrine of progress, Trent maintained that slavery was the natural enemy of advancement, that it shackled the master more than the slave and thus repressed intellectual activity and retarded the development of talent.

Simms's career was a perfect example of this limitation on the antebellum Southern mind. Trent appraised Simms's prose and poetry against this background of a primitive and unprogressive South, lacking originality and imagination and uninterested even in the work of its own writers. He believed that Simms could most accurately be depicted "as the most conspicuous representative of letters the old South can boast of" rather than "as an unjustly treated poet, which he was not, or as a partially successful romancer, which he was." Trent argued that Simms, like nearly all Southern poets down to Sidney Lanier, failed to rein in his imagination. Self-control was important to an artist, but antebellum Southern life did not encourage such discipline.

Agreeing with the poet Paul Hamilton Hayne's assessment of Simms as a talented but not great prose writer, Trent took issue with Hayne's view that Simms's work would not endure. He concluded, rather, that Simms's colonial and Revolutionary romances would retain value because they were ennobling, even if they were marred by a repetition of incidents and a slipshod style.

Tempers flared when Charlestonians in particular and Southerners in general read Trent's description of Simms and the cultural condition of the antebellum South. Trent had criticized the old régime, calling attention to its backwardness and inconsistencies and charging South Carolinians with disregarding efforts to create a native literature. Writing in the *Charleston News and Courier*, F. Peyre Porcher defended South Carolinians against the charge that they had not appreciated Simms. W. Porcher Miles, formerly a congressman and president of the University of South Carolina, asserted that Trent's "New England ideas and prejudices" made him unfit to write about a South Carolinian. J. J. Pringle Smith, a historian, was incensed at Trent's attitude toward slavery and his jeering characterizations of life and thought in the Old South.

Northern critics, however, greeted Trent's

William Gilmore Simms with praise. Writing in the *Atlantic Monthly*, Theodore Roosevelt applauded the work for its literary and historical virtues. He commended Trent for being unbiased, for exhibiting a keen understanding of life in the Old South, and for demonstrating appreciation of Simms. Reviewing the biography for *Cosmopolitan*, Brander Matthews of Columbia University found Trent's work solid in research, dignified in manner, and brave in tone. Agreeing that slavery contributed greatly to the literary backwardness of the Old South, he proclaimed Trent's study as evidence that a New South had been born. Such praise from Northern reviewers gained Trent admission to celebrated literary circles.

Trent, a pioneer who helped usher the New South into existence, saw it as sharply different from the Old South. The New South was progressive, whereas the Old South had been reactionary. More recent critics believe that Trent's hatred for everything Simms's Old South stood for deeply marred his biography of the author. Reevaluating Simms, they have argued that Simms's fiction is worthy of attention. Though restrained by the convictions which popular taste imposed in his day, Simms created the only wide-ranging fictional portrait of antebellum Southern society by an acute and talented observer. As such, it stands as a unique cultural document.

In 1896 Trent married Alice Lyman of East Orange, New Jersey, with whom he eventually had two children, Lucia and William Peterfield. The same year, at the invitation of Frederick Jackson Turner and Richard T. Ely, Trent delivered a series of lectures on prominent antebellum Southerners at the University of Wisconsin. As subjects he chose George Washington, "the greatest of all Americans"; Thomas Jefferson, "the most influential of all our statesmen"; John Randolph of Roanoke, the eccentric "Heine of Virginia politics"; Jefferson Davis and John C. Calhoun, representatives of the dominant states in the secession movement; and Robert Toombs and Alexander H. Stephens, Georgians who typified Southern secessionists and unionists. Trent's study of these seven Southerners, which was published in 1897 as *Southern Statesmen of the Old Régime*, revealed him as a liberal revisionist of the South's past. He simply could not accept the traditional Southern view of slavery and the other factors which led to civil war.

Published in 1899, Trent's *Robert E. Lee* did little for his reputation as a critical historian. A small volume, it was based heavily on previous biographies of Lee and his contemporaries. The work

was in effect a tribute to Lee, pointing out many parallels in the careers of Washington and the Confederate general.

In 1892 the *Sewanee Review* was founded as a Southern critical quarterly. Trent, Benjamin W. Wells, B. Lawton Wiggins, and Thomas Gailor launched the journal, with Trent serving as editor from the second volume (1893) through the seventh (1899). Over a period of seventeen years, Trent contributed twenty-seven articles and reviews, most of them on literary subjects. An important exception was the 1901 essay "A New South View of Reconstruction," which contrasted the Southern region of 1867 with the South of 1900.

Prominence as a Southern liberal brought Trent recognition in the East. Walter Hines Page commissioned Trent to write two pieces for the *Atlantic Monthly* in 1897. "Dominant Forces in Southern Life" and "Tendencies of Higher Life in the South" explore Trent's concern for the contemporary South's politics, religion, education, manners, and morals.

Trent's major field of interest changed during the 1890s. At the beginning of the decade, he wished to gain recognition as a historian. By 1900 his enthusiasm for history had waned, while his reputation in the field of literature had grown markedly. After 1900 he rarely dealt with the history of his native section.

In 1900, on the recommendation of Theodore Roosevelt, Brander Matthews, and Nicholas Murray Butler, President Seth Low of Columbia University offered Trent a professorship of English literature. Believing that younger Southerners would carry on the historical work he had helped begin and that he would still have contact with Southern students, he accepted, beginning a long career at Columbia.

At Columbia Trent collaborated on his most important later project, *The Cambridge History of American Literature* (1917-1921). With Stuart P. Sherman and fellow Columbians John Erskine and Carl Van Doren, Trent edited this four-volume work, to which he also contributed several chapters. For a time he served as editor-in-chief of the eighteen-volume Columbia edition of *The Works of John Milton* (1931-1938). Trent had first suggested the project in 1908; in 1925 poor health forced him to resign his post. Among other works Trent produced while he was at Columbia are *A History of American Literature, 1607-1865* (1903); *Greatness in Literature and Other Papers* (1905); an anthology of *Southern Writers* (1905); *Longfellow and Other Essays*

(1910); and *Great American Writers* (1912), on which he collaborated with Erskine.

In the summer of 1927 Trent suffered a paralytic stroke which put an end to his teaching duties. He spent his remaining years as an invalid and died of a heart attack at Hopewell Junction, New York, on 6 December 1939. Among those who were studying Southern history during the latter years of the nineteenth century, Trent wrote works that his contemporaries read. He never attained greater eminence as a historian perhaps because he abandoned history for literary scholarship when his reputation was barely established. Nevertheless, his enthusiasm for the subject during the 1890s influenced Southerners of liberal principles and played a major role in the beginning of academic historical scholarship in the South.

Bibliography:

Bibliography of Trent's writings to 1901, in *Herbert B. Adams: Tributes of Friends, With a Bibliography of the Department of History, Politics and Economics of the Johns Hopkins University, 1876-1901* (Baltimore: Johns Hopkins University, 1902), pp. 135-139.

Biography:

Franklin T. Walker, "William Peterfield Trent—A Critical Biography," Ph.D. dissertation, George Peabody College for Teachers, 1943.

References:

Mary C. Simms Oliphant, Alfred Taylor Odell, and T. C. Duncan, eds., *The Letters of William Gilmore Simms*, 6 volumes (Columbia: University of South Carolina Press, 1952-1982), I: xxxiii-xxxvi;

Wendell H. Stephenson, "A Half Century of Southern Historical Scholarship," *Journal of Southern History*, 11 (February 1945): 12-15;

Stephenson, "William P. Trent as Historian of the South." *Journal of Southern History*, 15 (May 1949): 151-177.

Papers:

There are small collections of Trent's papers at Columbia and Princeton.

Moses Coit Tyler

(2 August 1835-28 December 1900)

Alexander Moore
University of South Carolina

SELECTED BOOKS: *The Brawnville Papers: Being Memorials of the Brawnville Athletic Club* (Boston: Fields, Osgood, 1869);

A History of American Literature, 2 volumes (New York: Putnam's, 1878; London: Low, Marston, Searle & Rivington, 1879); revised as *A History of American Literature During the Colonial Time*, 2 volumes (New York: Putnam's, 1897);

Patrick Henry (Boston & New York: Houghton Mifflin, 1887; revised, 1899);

Three Men of Letters (New York & London: Putnam's, 1895);

The Literary History of the American Revolution, 1763-1783, 2 volumes (New York & London: Putnam's, 1897);

Glimpses of England, Social, Political, Literary (New York & London: Putnam's, 1898).

OTHER: "The New Gymnastics as an Instrument in Education," in *The New Gymnastics for Men, Women, and Children*, by Dio Lewis (Boston: Ticknor & Fields, 1868);

Henry Morley, *A Manual of English Literature*, revised by Tyler (New York: Sheldon, 1879);

"Neglect and Destruction of Historical Materials in this Country," in *Papers of the American Historical Association*, 2 (1887): 20-22;

"The Educational Value of the Study of History," in *Library of Universal History*, 8 volumes (New York: Peale & Hill, 1897), I: iii-x.

Moses Coit Tyler

PERIODICAL PUBLICATIONS: "Mr. Emerson as a Teacher of Eloquence," *Independent*, 22 (5 May 1870);

"The Literary Labors of Charles Sumner," *Independent*, 22 (12 May 1870);

"Gentlemen and Scholars in Politics," *Independent*, 22 (22 December 1870);

"Mr. Bancroft's Last Volume," *Independent*, 26 (3 December 1874);

"Doyle's Puritan Colonies," *Literary World*, 19 (3 March 1888): 69-70;

"A Half Century of Conflict, by Francis Parkman," *Political Science Quarterly*, 7 (December 1892): 726-729;

"The Party of the Loyalists in the American Revolution," *American Historical Review*, 1 (October 1895): 24-45;

"The Life of Thomas Hutchinson," *Nation*, 62 (26 March 1896): 258-259;

"The Declaration of Independence in the Light of Modern Criticism," *North American Review*, 163 (July 1896): 1-16.

Unlike the works of many of his contemporaries, Moses Coit Tyler's *A History of American Literature* (1878) and *The Literary History of the American Revolution, 1763-1783* (1897) are not outdated. They remain today the standard works on American literature and the starting points of all modern writing on the subject. The *History* and *Literary History* are uniformly the first entries in bibliographies and the first mentioned in critical studies of American colonial literature.

Tyler surveyed and classified the full spectrum of colonial literature. His works imposed a rational order and method to American literary studies that have not been superseded. As a historian, Tyler was the first to use systematically American literature to interpret American history. His *Literary History of the American Revolution* is social and intellectual history, solidly based on the literature of the Revolution. In this work he innovated a methodology of historical research and a sophisticated historical interpretation of the American Revolution. Tyler's works demonstrate a historical imagination of the highest order tempered by thorough research and exposition.

Moses Coit Tyler was born on 2 August 1835, at Griswold, Connecticut, the son of Elisha and Mary Greene Tyler. Soon after his birth his family moved to Michigan. The Tylers settled at Detroit where his father became a moderately successful merchant. Tyler received his primary education in the state public school system and entered the University of Michigan at Ann Arbor in 1852. After a year he returned to Connecticut, where he entered the freshman class at Yale College. Upon graduating in 1857, he studied at the Yale Theological Seminary and at the Andover Seminary, New Hampshire, to prepare for the Congregational ministry.

In 1859 he was called to a congregation at Owego, New York, and on 29 October of that year he married Jeannette Hull Gilbert of New Haven. The couple had two children, Jessica, born in 1860, and Edward Scott, born in 1863. After a year at Owego, Tyler moved to a more prosperous congregation at Poughkeepsie, New York, but his ministry lasted less than two years. In 1862 Tyler suffered a physical breakdown and resigned from his congregation. At that time in his life he apparently resembled one of the scholar-types he later caricatured in *The Brawnville Papers* (1869), who despised good health and sought to become "Martyrs to Science, bemoaned and canonized by the principal Parish Sewing Societies of the civilized world."

Tyler's collapse was also an intellectual one. Like many of his Northern, clerical counterparts, Tyler had become involved in various reform movements of the day. As a youth he lectured on temperance. At Yale he was an active member of local abolition societies and an advocate of women's rights. His liberal values ultimately collided with his Calvinist profession and he abandoned the ministry. However, Tyler did not abandon religion. He converted to Episcopalianism and in 1883 was ordained an Episcopal priest.

Although Tyler supported many reform movements, his greatest enthusiasm was for physical education. Convalescing in Boston from his breakdown, he met Dr. Dio Lewis, a physical-education reformer and inventor of "musical gymnastics." Tyler credited his recovery to Lewis's system and became the reformer's most avid propagandizer. Lewis's "musical gymnastics" consisted of calisthenics and exercises with dumbbells and Indian clubs, performed to musical accompaniment, as well as dietary and hygienic reforms. Musical gymnastics was designed for men, women, and children, and was heavily tinged with Catharine Beecher's "domestic science" reforms, Sylvester Graham's dietary reforms, and feminism.

Tyler not only regained his health thanks to musical gymnastics, but he also found a new profession. He taught Lewis's system in the Boston area, gave public demonstrations, and lectured. In April 1863 Tyler traveled to England to spread the gospel according to Lewis. He remained there until the end of 1866, organizing classes, lecturing, and writing about his experiences. As a youthful clergyman Tyler had published a few lectures and sermons but his sojourn in England gave him the incentive as well as subject matter to begin writing in earnest. He contributed articles on health and hygiene to the New York magazine the *Herald of Health* and published substantial pieces on British public opinion, liberal politics, and sketches of prominent Englishmen in the *Independent* and E. L. Godkin's *Nation*.

Tyler returned to America determined to become a professional journalist and lecturer but, once back, changed his mind. Instead, in 1867, he accepted a professorship of English literature at the University of Michigan. He took immediately to teaching and scholarship and was a successful instructor. Much of his success stemmed from changes he made in the curriculum and teaching methods. He required his students to read original literature instead of secondary texts or anthologies. They then discussed interpretations rather than listen passively to lectures.

During 1867 and 1868 Tyler had written a series of articles for the *Herald of Health* entitled "Minutes of the Brawnville Athletic Club." In 1869 the collected articles were published as *The Brawnville Papers: Being Memorials of the Brawnville Athletic Club*. This was Tyler's only venture into fiction-writing, and it amply satisfied a private suspicion that he had little talent in that line. *The Brawnville Papers* was part epistolary novel and part the "records" of the "Brawnville Athletic Club," chronicling the successful attempt of the Brawnvillians to construct a public gymnasium in their village. Like a morality play, the work was peopled with stock village types, the best of whom supported the project and the others who opposed it. Thomas Richard Henry ("Tom, Dick, and Harry"), the village schoolmaster, recorded the scene. Judge Fairplay and Reverend Samuel Bland supported the gym and the virtues it represented while Deacon Snipp and Dr. Drugger opposed the project. A rustic Yankee wit, Abdiel Standish, frequently appeared to defeat Snipp and Drugger with cracker-barrel humor when Fairplay and Bland failed to do so with reasoned argument.

Although *The Brawnville Papers* had slight humor and no depth, it managed to present in a genial manner current arguments for and against physical education. Never republished, the book lacks literary merit. Tyler found it so embarrassing in later years that he destroyed the printing plates. *The Brawnville Papers* is of interest today only as a cultural artifact.

Despite his success as a teacher Tyler tried his hand once more at journalism. He resigned from the University of Michigan in 1873 and returned to New York City to become literary editor of the *Christian Union*, a liberal religious newspaper. This final journalistic fling lasted three years and had a permanent impact upon Tyler. As part of his duties he read and reviewed much American historical writing. He concluded that therein lay his talents. In 1871 he recorded in his diary: "Unless I have entirely mistaken the symptoms of a thorough and permanent determination of my whole nature, I have at last found my work. Since I reached this resolution to make the study of American history my chief literary occupation I have experienced the truth of Carlyle's words, 'Blessed is he who has found his work.'" Tyler perceived the need for "a new school of critical historical works . . . characterized preeminently by simplicity both in material and form; and that means it seeks for the whole absolute truth of history, sincerely, sceptically, untiringly, and then tries to tell it plainly."

This need was particularly acute in the field of American literary history. There were a few anthologies that concentrated on American writers in a single genre and some collections of the works of individual writers—for example Samuel Kettel's *Specimens of American Poetry* (1829) and the publications of Evart Duyckinck and Rufus Wilmot Griswold—but there were no comprehensive, critical surveys of the whole field of American literature. Tyler decided to fill this gap.

To accomplish this goal Tyler abandoned journalism in 1874 and returned to the University of Michigan. Four years later, in 1878, he produced his two-volume *History of American Literature*. In it Tyler proposed "to write the history of American literature from the earliest English settlements in this country, down to the present time" in "three or four volumes." Twenty years later he had only reached 1783.

A History of American Literature surveyed American writings from 1607 to 1765. Volume one began with Michael Drayton's 1607 farewell ode to the Virginia colonists and concluded with the poetry of Anne Bradstreet. Although Bradstreet had died in 1672, Tyler ended the volume in 1676. He did so for historical, not literary, reasons. That year marked the end of King Philip's War in New England and Nathaniel Bacon's war of extermination against the Virginia Indians. According to Tyler, these two events guaranteed the physical survival of the English colonies and insured that American literature would endure in its own right, instead of as a transatlantic species of English literature.

Volume two encompassed the years 1676 to 1765. It began with the Puritan poets and ended with an essay on intellectual life in colonial America. Again Tyler chose his closing date for historical reasons. The most important event of that year was the Stamp Act Crisis, by most estimations the beginning of the American Revolution. To Tyler it marked the end of America's literary isolation. As the colonies united to resist Great Britain politically, they abandoned their regional literary differences to form a national literature.

Tyler broke new ground with every chapter. He was the first scholar to organize the whole field of American colonial literature into genres and to write critically about representatives of each genre. In addition to poetry, drama, and essays, he studied the literature of travel and exploration, Puritan sermons, captivity narratives, almanacs, and the early colonial histories.

The volumes were arranged chronologically and divided according to geography into chapters, treating the literature of each colony from its founding to 1765. Tyler combined biographical and bibliographical information with critical comments to place each writer within his overall scheme and included generous examples of the author's works. Readers obtained a good introduction to the works of most American colonial writers, some as famous as Cotton Mather or William Byrd and others as obscure as Roger Wolcott or Samuel Keimer.

According to Tyler, Virginia was the first seat of American literature and Captain John Smith the first American writer. He admired Smith's robust Elizabethan character and saw much in his *A True Relation of . . . Virginia* (1608) that was distinctively American: Smith's sense of wonder at the New World, the aptness and wit of his language, and his "unsubmissiveness" to authority. Tyler observed this last trait in Nathaniel Bacon, John Wise, and Roger Williams and presented them as precursors to the heroic figures of the Revolutionary era.

While praising Smith and other early Virginians, Tyler addressed the question of why the center of American literature quickly shifted to New England, never to return south. He found the answer in the social, political, and economic differences between Virginia and New England. As he put it: "The germ of the whole difference between them lay in their different notions concerning the value of vicinity among the units of society." Virginians immigrated as individuals and dispersed throughout the region, hoping to establish large plantations, to become wealthy, and to imitate the English gentry. This dispersal hindered the growth of those institutions (towns, churches, and schools) which fostered literature. By contrast, New Englanders immigrated in groups and clung together in villages and congregations. This concentration facilitated the establishment of schools, printing presses, and other requisite institutions.

The shift of America's cultural center was readily apparent in his *History of American Literature*. Together his two volumes amounted to 610 pages, of which 404 were devoted to New England writers. Virginians accounted for 114 pages and writers from the Middle and Southern colonies received only the briefest treatments. Tyler may have created the best framework for the study of colonial literature but he also epitomized the notion that American literature was New England literature.

Tyler's format best suited the "practical"

genres of American literature: travel books, histories, and sermons. These accounted for the majority of colonial literature and, from their preponderance, Tyler correctly asserted that practicality, not aesthetic creativity, was the hallmark of the era. When it came to the study of imaginative literature, his critical method was less successful. Although he commented intelligently on Anne Bradstreet, Michael Wigglesworth, Urian Oakes, and Thomas Prince, his aesthetic prejudices influenced his judgment. Tyler abhorred the English metaphysical or "euphuistic" poets. Consequently he failed to appreciate Anne Bradstreet's poetics. However, he noticed her satirical vein and especially appreciated her defiance of prevailing notions of male superiority. He liked the satirical good humor of Nathaniel Ward's *The Simple Cobbler of Aggawam in America* (1647) but disapproved of its convoluted, artificial prose style. Cotton Mather was the chief colonial exemplar of "Gongorism," and Tyler was pitiless in his criticism. "The expulsion of the beautiful from thought, from sentiment, from language; a lawless and merciless fury for the odd, the disorderly, the grotesque, the violent; strained analogies, unexploded images, pedantries, indelicacies, freaks of allusion, monstrosities of phrase—these are the traits of Cotton Mather's writing, even as they are the traits of that perverse and detestable literary mood that held sway in the different countries of Christendom during the sixteenth and seventeenth centuries."

Tyler's *History of American Literature* partook heavily of the nineteenth-century Whig interpretation of history, the notion that history, especially that of England and America, recorded the progress of humanity from a benighted past to an enlightened present. Contemporary reviewers pointed out that Tyler had omitted works of law, jurisprudence, and, except for sermons, theology. Besides Tyler's New England bias, modern readers might point out that his title is misleading because he excluded all American literature not written in English.

Tyler's *A History of American Literature* was an immediate success. Upon its strength he was elected an honorary member of the Massachusetts Historical Society and American Antiquarian Society as well as of other prestigious New England learned institutions. He was invited to present a series of lectures on American literature at the Lowell Institute, Boston, and in March and April 1881 gave six lectures. While in Boston he met the city's literary elite, Ralph Waldo Emerson, John Greenleaf Whittier, and others, and was welcomed as one of their peers.

An immediate result of his visit to Boston was an agreement to publish his next book. While there, in March 1881, he contracted with John T. Morse, Jr., editor of the American Statesmen series, to write a biography of Patrick Henry. However, other obligations intervened, and at the year's end he informed Morse that he must put aside the project indefinitely. He did not return to it until 1886. By then Houghton Mifflin, publishers of the series, had voided the contract; but Morse assured Tyler that the book would be published when completed. Tyler went to work immediately and by March 1887 the manuscript was finished. *Patrick Henry* was published in September of that year.

When Tyler began his work Patrick Henry was a shadowy Revolutionary hero whose reputation had been clouded by misrepresentation. He left few original papers and apparently gave little heed to posterity. Moreover, his fame rested upon oratory at a time before accurate records of speeches could be made. As a result, his reputation depended, more than most, on hearsay and sketchy recollections. The only other biography of Henry had been written by William Wirt in 1817. Wirt had relied heavily upon the memories of Henry's friends and enemies, the most famous of the latter being Thomas Jefferson.

Toward the end of an inconsistent political career, Henry was a Federalist and opponent of the Virginia Resolutions of 1799, although he had been a prominent anti-Federalist ten years earlier. Henry's Federalism earned him Jefferson's powerful enmity and, unfortunately, Jefferson was Wirt's chief source of information. Although Wirt's *Sketches of the Life and Character of Patrick Henry* was draped in filiopietism, it crystallized a mythology of Henry that was at best damning with faint praise. According to Wirt (and Jefferson), Henry had been uneducated, a failure at business, farming, and law, and temperamentally incapable of sustained labor of any kind. Henry's one undeniable talent was for oratory and that was God-given, not earned. He was a "child of nature" who had been a hero in the early days of the Revolution but who ended his days a reactionary Federalist.

Tyler systematically demolished the Wirt-Jefferson stereotype. He had access to primary and secondary sources unavailable to Wirt and used them well to overthrow most of the Henry mythology. While Henry's formal education had not been the best available, it compared favorably with those of his contemporaries. According to Tyler, the final proof of any man's education was the use he made of it. In this regard Henry's speeches and public papers passed any tests of literacy and intelligence. An examination of Henry's legal fee-books confuted Wirt's assertion, based upon Jefferson's recollections, that Henry was a poor lawyer. Indeed these records indicated that Henry's practice had been larger and more profitable than Jefferson's own.

The familiar stories of Henry's drafting the Virginia Stamp Act Resolutions in 1765 and his "Give me liberty, or give me death" speech in 1775 gained new interest as a result of Tyler's critical methods. He analyzed Henry's text of the Resolutions and accurately described verbal changes to them in their progress through the Virginia House of Burgesses. Regarding Henry's most famous oration, Tyler collected and compared several extant versions in order to present the most authoritative text possible.

Tyler also refuted one of the worst errors surrounding Henry's political career, one that had badly tarnished his reputation. Again, this error could be traced to Thomas Jefferson. In his *Notes on the State of Virginia* (1785), Jefferson had asserted that during Henry's governorship of Virginia the House of Delegates had proposed "to create a dictator" to rule the state during the worst days of the Revolution. Jefferson had not accused Henry of conspiring to take power, but later histories, written under his aegis, had named Henry as the instigator of the proposal and the chief candidate for the dubious mantle. The story appeared in Wirt's biography, written, as Tyler sarcastically observed, under "the inestimable advantages as regards instruction and oversight furnished by Jefferson."

Patrick Henry was an early work of historical revisionism, and there are several hints in it that, given the opportunity, Tyler would have expanded his revisionist methodology to include other Revolutionary figures. He spoke of Revolutionary events and personages as having been "ingulfed in that rich mass of unwhipped hyperboles and of unexploded fables still patriotically swallowed by the American public as American history." Although Tyler admired Jefferson, the portrait of him that emerged was decidedly unflattering. At one point in his biography, Tyler quoted several pages from John Adams's diary which described a group of the Founding Fathers drinking in taverns and engaged in other mundane human activities. He did this "to bring them and their work somewhat nearer to the plane of natural human life and motive. . . ."

One of the events that forced Tyler to postpone work on *Patrick Henry* was his final career change. In March 1881, at the height of his Boston triumph, Tyler was offered a professorship of American history at Cornell University, Ithaca, New York. He accepted the offer and left the University of Michigan for the last time. The Cornell position was unique in two ways. It paid $7,000 a year, an exceedingly high salary for that era. It was also the first chair of American history ever established at an American university. Except for excursions to Europe in 1882 and 1899 Tyler remained at Cornell teaching and writing until his death in 1900.

In 1897, ten years after completing *Patrick Henry*, Tyler published his best work, *The Literary History of the American Revolution*. This new work was at once a continuation of Tyler's *A History of American Literature* and profoundly different from it. The two-volume *Literary History* began in 1763, two years prior to the Stamp Act Crisis, and concluded in 1783, the formal end of the Revolution. Tyler applied his familiar biographical cum critical method to seventy-two American writers and to a large body of anonymous literature. He published generous excerpts of the works he discussed. Again, he construed the term literature broadly to include political and religious tracts, state papers, histories, songs and ballads, prison narratives, and almanacs, as well as poetry and drama. He again argued persuasively that practicality, not aesthetics, was the driving force behind most American literature.

Despite such similarities, the *Literary History* differed from its predecessor in purpose, theme, and point of view. It was not a chronological survey of American literature but an intellectual history of the American Revolution, an event which lasted, in Tyler's view, for twenty years. He stated his purpose succinctly: "the chief aim of the first volume is to trace the development of political discontent in the Anglo-American colonies from about the year 1763 until the year when that discontent culminated in the resolve for American Independence; while the chief aim of the second volume is to trace the development of the Revolutionary struggle under the altered conditions produced by this change in its object and in its character. . . ." To accomplish this Tyler did not propose to write a political history but rather to trace "the inward history of our Revolution—the history of its ideas, its spiritual moods, its motives, its passions, even of its sportive caprices and its whims as these altered themselves at the time, whether consciously or not, in the various writings of the two parties of Americans, who promoted or resisted that great movement." In effect, he constructed an intellectual framework to study the origins and progress of the idea of the American Revolution.

American literature was begotten of "strife" rather than "tranquillity." It was "argumentative, persuasive, appealing, rasping, retaliatory. . . . a literature accented by earnest gestures meant to convince people, or by fierce blows to smite them down." In that climate political pamphlets and satirical works of poetry and drama best represented Americans' states of mind. These kinds of works predominated in *The Literary History of the American Revolution*.

Tyler outlined the arguments of Whigs Tom Paine, Benjamin Franklin, John Dickinson, and Loyalists Samuel Seabury and Daniel Leonard, and a host of others of both parties, for and against resistance to British policies prior to 1776 and, after that date, on the question of armed struggle. In Tyler's opinion, Tom Paine's *Common Sense*, published in January 1776, had the greatest influence of all writings in transforming Americans from protesters into revolutionaries. Despite its illogical, unhistorical, and legally flawed arguments, *Common Sense* was the single most important work of the Revolutionary era, excepting the Declaration of Independence. Loyalist pamphleteers offered strong arguments against resistance prior to July 1776, but after that date most of them prudently fell silent.

Because most of the poetry and drama of the era was satirical or propagandistic, Tyler's studies of the poets and dramatists were generally more successful than those in his *History of American Literature*. Sketches of Philip Freneau, Francis Hopkinson, Jonathan Odell, and Joseph Stansbury provided information on the men and their works. Tyler included excerpts from their works as well as much anonymous material. The quality of this satirical literature ranged from the well-wrought poems of Hopkinson, Freneau, and Odell, based on the most approved classical and English models to the lowest doggerel. All of it was topical; some of it was scatological; most of it had at least one good, sharp barb.

Although Tyler's *Literary History of the American Revolution* equaled his *History of American Literature* as a source book and an encyclopedic survey, it was preeminently a work of historical reinterpretation. In *The Literary History of the American Revolution* Tyler proved himself a pioneering historian as well as the foremost literary historian of his day. The American Revolution proved that there was something seriously wrong with the Whig interpretation of history. It was logically impossible for America and Great Britain to be simultaneously the apogees of modern history, especially while engaged in a destructive war against each other. Tyler wisely abandoned that theory which had permeated his *History of American Literature* and replaced it with a sophisticated analysis of the motives and actions of the literary participants in the American Revolution, Whig and Tory alike.

An immediate result of this new method was Tyler's extensive rehabilitation of the American Loyalists. As he had done in *Patrick Henry*, Tyler consciously destroyed the myths comfortably held by Americans that all Loyalists had been corrupt aristocrats, placemen, and traitors. His resurrection and sympathetic treatment of their numerous writings revealed much about the great debates that went on during the Revolutionary era and demonstrated that Loyalists had held up their end of the debates with skill, intelligence, and wit. The Loyalists had simply lost the military phase of the Revolution and had been degraded by their victors. Tyler's evenhandedness to a defeated foe, even one a hundred years dead, was new to American historical writing.

Tyler's perception of the Revolution was also new and it partook of his own natural Anglophilism. He saw the Revolution largely as a tragic misunderstanding. America and Great Britain had differed in their interpretations of a chain of events from the Massachusetts writs of assistance case in 1763 to the battles of Lexington and Concord in April 1776, but this difference had been an exception to their natural friendship. This notion placed Tyler among a group of American historians active at the beginning of the twentieth century. Commonly called the imperial school of historians, George L. Beer, Herbert L. Osgood, and Charles M. Andrews emphasized the continuity of Anglo-American history rather than the historical differences between America and England. These men looked upon the Revolution not so much as a peculiarly American event but as an incident in the collective history of England and America. They demonstrated that political errors and misinterpretations on both sides of the Atlantic, not British malice, had led to the Revolution. Their underlying theme, one that suited the temper of the United States and Great Britain at the turn of the twentieth century, was that the Revolution had been a temporary aberration, the excesses of which were best forgotten in the interests of Anglo-American fraternity.

Tyler exemplified these ideas in *The Literary History of the American Revolution,* and he carried them further. Concentrating upon the literature of the era, he realized that Americans' anxieties, fears, and presumptions of English malice had more to do with the coming of the Revolution than did any particular events. To Tyler, the Americans rebelled "not because they were as yet actual sufferers, but because they were good logicians, and were able to prove that, without resistance, they or their children would some day become actual sufferers." In this regard, Tyler's *Literary History* prefigured some of the most sophisticated modern scholarship on the Revolution. Edmund S. Morgan's *Stamp Act Crisis* (1953), H. Trevor Colbourn's *The Lamp of Experience* (1965), and Bernard Bailyn's *Ideological Origins of the American Revolution* (1967) emphasize the role of ideas, mistaken or not, disembodied from actual events, in bringing about the Revolution. Bailyn in particular develops his important thesis of American anxiety and the "logic of revolution" solely from a study of the literature of the era. Tyler had plowed that field seventy years earlier.

The Literary History of the American Revolution was well received by reviewers upon publication. Herbert L. Osgood recognized its groundbreaking approach to "a more just and scientific view of the Revolution," one that jibed with his own ideas on the subject. However, the *Literary History* drew some criticism, mostly from reviewers who saw their favorite writers discussed briefly or omitted from the work. One accurate criticism was Tyler's neglect of the Revolutionary newspaper press. Tyler's emphasis on pamphlet publications failed to account for the most common means of dissemination of ideas. Most pamphlets and a good deal of the imaginative literature of the Revolutionary era had been first published in newspapers, and readers were most likely to have seen them in that medium.

Three Men of Letters grew from Tyler's work on his literary histories. Although George Berkeley, the British philosopher, and Timothy Dwight and Joel Barlow, the "Connecticut Wits," did not fit into either of his major works, Tyler deemed them worthy of note. He wrote essays on the men which were published in 1895 as *Three Men of Letters.* The essays on Dwight and Barlow combined biography and literary criticism in Tyler's familiar style, but his essay on Berkeley was different. It had been first published in 1885 in William S. Perry's *History of the American Episcopal Church* and was republished in *Three Men of Letters* with slight alterations and a new title. Tyler examined Berke-

ley's sojourn in Rhode Island from 1729 to 1731 as part of his plan to found an American college. Berkeley sought to escape from decadent Europe to an American Arcadia. While it lacked the cohesion of his critical sketches, the Berkeley essay was a rare attempt by Tyler to psychologize its subject. The essay was also an early elucidation of the literary theme of America as a second, failed Eden.

Tyler's last book was a throwback to the beginning of his literary career. Published in 1898, *Glimpses of England, Social, Political, Literary* included twenty-eight essays Tyler had written in Great Britain in 1865 and 1866 and previously published in the *Nation* and the *Independent.* The essays included biographical sketches of John Stuart Mill, William Gladstone, Lord John Russell, and Benjamin D'Israeli, some of whom shared Tyler's liberal political beliefs. He praised like-minded British Whigs and devoted fifty-four pages to the career of John Bright.

Tyler's best essay, "On Certain English Hallucinations Touching America," was written in 1866 but had remained unpublished until 1898. Bearing in mind the date of its composition, it is Tyler's first expression of his insights concerning the American Revolution. In the essay he contended that the American Revolution had arisen from a series of misunderstandings and errors grounded in mutual ignorance, not positive evil.

Moses Coit Tyler died on 28 December 1900, at Ithaca, New York, survived by his wife and two children. The significance of Tyler's works was recognized by all of his contemporaries, as it has been by the generations of students which followed.

Letters:
Moses Coit Tyler: Selections from his Letters and Diaries, edited by Jessica Tyler Austen (Garden City: Doubleday, Page, 1911).

Biography:
Howard M. Jones, *The Life of Moses Coit Tyler. Based upon an Unpublished Dissertation from Original Sources by Thomas Edgar Casady* (Ann Arbor: University of Michigan Press, 1933).

References:
Rose Marie Cutting, "America Rediscovers Its Literary Past: Early American Literature in Nineteenth Century Anthologies," *Early American Literature,* 9 (Winter 1975): 226-251;

Richard M. Dorson, "Moses Coit Tyler, Historian of the American Genesis," *Southwest Review,* 26 (Summer 1941): 416-427;

Michael Kammen, "Moses Coit Tyler: The First Professor of American History in the United States," *History Teacher*, 17 (November 1983): 61-87.

Papers:
Moses Coit Tyler's papers, including drafts of articles, materials gathered for his publications, and research notes, as well as his commonplace books and private correspondence, are located at Olin Library, Cornell University, Ithaca, New York. A small collection of his letters is at the Bentley Historical Library, University of Michigan, Ann Arbor.

Mariana Griswold Van Rensselaer
(Mrs. Schulyer Van Rensselaer)
(21 February 1851-20 January 1934)

Robert McColley
University of Illinois at Urbana-Champaign

SELECTED BOOKS: *Henry Hobson Richardson and His Works* (Boston & New York: Houghton Mifflin, 1888);

Six Portraits: Della Robbia, Correggio, Blake, Corot, George Fuller, Winslow Homer (Boston & New York: Houghton Mifflin, 1889);

English Cathedrals: Canterbury, Peterborough, Durham, Salisbury, Lichfield, Lincoln, Ely, Wells, Winchester, Gloucester, York, London (New York: Century, 1892); republished as *Handbook of English Cathedrals* (New York: Century, 1893; London: Unwin, 1893);

Art Out-of-Doors: Hints on Good Taste in Gardening (New York: Scribners, 1893; London: Unwin, 1893; enlarged, New York: Scribners, 1925);

Should We Ask for the Suffrage? (New York: De Vinne, 1895);

One Man Who Was Content; "Mary"; The Lustigs; Corinna's Fiametta (New York: Century, 1897);

History of the City of New York in the Seventeenth Century, 2 volumes (New York: Macmillan, 1909);

Poems (New York: Macmillan, 1910);

Many Children (Boston: Atlantic Monthly Press, 1921).

OTHER: *Book of American Figure Painters*, edited by Van Rensselaer (Philadelphia: Lippincott, 1866; London: Nimmo, 1866);

Parent the Elder, *Essay on Bibliography and on the Attainments of a Librarian*, translated by Van Rensselaer (Woodstock, Vt.: Elm Tree Press, 1914);

Wilhelm Reinhold Valentiner, *The Art of the Low Countries*, translated by Van Rensselaer (Garden City: Doubleday, Page, 1914);

Introduction to *Memorial Exhibition of the Work of John Singer Sargent, New York, January 4 through February 14, 1926* (New York: Metropolitan Museum of Art, 1926).

PERIODICAL PUBLICATIONS: "Some Aspects of Contemporary Art," *Lippincott's Magazine of Popular Literature and Science*, 22 (December 1878): 706-718;

"American Fiction," *Lippincott's Magazine of Popular Literature and Science*, 23 (June 1879): 753-761;

"In the Heart of the Alleghanies," *Lippincott's Magazine of Popular Literature and Science*, 30 (July and August 1882): 84-92, 163-172;

"Parsifal," *Harper's*, 66 (March 1883): 540-556;

"Recent Architecture in America," *Century*, 28 (May, July, and August 1884): 48-67, 323-334, 511-523; 29 (January 1885): 323-338; 31 (February and March 1886): 548-558, 677-687; 32 (May, June, and July 1886): 3-20, 206-220, 421-434;

"The Art of Gardening: A Historic Sketch," 21 parts, *Garden and Forest*, 2 (1889) and 3 (1890);

"At the Fair," *Century*, 46 (May 1893): 3-13;

Mariana Griswold Van Rensselaer. Painting by William A. Cossin (Museum of the City of New York).

"Frederick Law Olmsted," *Century,* 46 (October 1893): 860-867;

"Churches and Cathedrals of France," *Century,* 49 (November 1894): 117-135; 51 (April 1896): 918-931; 54 (July 1897): 421-439; 58 (August and September 1899): 568-575, 722-735;

"Robert Louis Stevenson, and His Writing," *Century,* 51 (November 1895): 123-129;

"Places in New York," *Century,* 53 (February 1897): 500-516;

"A Suburban Country Place," *Century,* 54 (May 1897): 3-17;

"Our Public Schools," *North American Review,* 169 (July 1899): 77-89;

"New York and Its Historians," *North American Review,* 171 (November and December 1900): 724-733, 872-883;

"Midsummer in New York City," *Century,* 62 (August 1901): 483-501;

"Mr. Fiske and the History of New York," *North American Review,* 173 (August 1901): 171-189;

"With Malice Toward None," *North American Review,* 201 (May 1915): 690-693;

"Richard Watson Gilder; Personal Memories," *Outlook,* 130 (8 March 1922): 376-379;

"American Art and the Public," *Scribner's,* 74 (November 1923): 637-640.

"We need wide and accurate knowledge, calm and well-directed earnestness. The first enables us to see the world as it is; the second gives the power to 'write the vision and make it plain upon tables, that he may run that readeth it.' Such a vision, so written, is no unimportant thing. . . . It is a lay sermon, with the impulse of genius to back it. The world as it is, things as they really exist, are more interesting, more various, more dramatic, more poetical, than visionary things." With this and many another bold declaration, twenty-seven-year-old Mariana Griswold Van Rensselaer diagnosed the inability of the United States to produce truly great fiction and set forth the terms on which such fiction must be written. She would, considerably later in her career, write a series of short stories about life in New York City, which fairly well met her youthful standards. But through over forty-five years of writing she generally preferred forms and methods which allowed her to meet reality directly. Her love of the real, the concrete, the tangible led her to study painting, sculpture, architecture, gardening, and the history which expressed itself in and around such things. Van Rensselaer is remembered as a penetrating historian of the arts, as the masterful biographer of the architect Henry Hobson Richardson (1838-1886), and especially for her *History of the City of New York in the Seventeenth Century* (1909), which brings the earliest settlers of New Netherland and New York as vividly to life as the best studies of the otherwise far more amply and sympathetically described early New Englanders and Virginians.

Although her early publications were usually signed M. G. Van Rensselaer, the title pages of her books as well as her later magazine articles carried the imposing Mrs. Schuyler Van Rensselaer, a usage she maintained after many of America's literary women had abandoned it. She was born in 1851, the second of the seven children of George and Lydia Alley Griswold, whose families had migrated from Connecticut and elsewhere to find their fortunes in New York City. Mariana Griswold's life was uncommon for its many kinds of good fortune, for opportunities fully taken, and for useful tasks well performed; but it was also noteworthy for unexpected and terrible losses.

Her parents were cultivated as well as wealthy. They provided their children with excellent private instruction, which included extensive foreign travel and extended periods of living in Europe. The Griswolds were living in Dresden in 1873 when Mariana met and married Schuyler Van Rensselaer, late of Newport, Rhode Island, and Harvard College (class of 1867). He had come to Saxony to study mining and metallurgy at the Freiburg Institute. The couple made their home in New Brunswick, New Jersey, where their son George was born in 1875.

They traveled extensively in the United States, Europe, and the Mediterranean, and frequently visited Philadelphia, New York, and Boston. Mariana Van Rensselaer began to write: first, on a variety of topics, but she soon settled into specializations. The relatively new magazine *American Architect and Building News* became her most frequent outlet in the 1880s; she reviewed books in almost any language that dealt with the history of art and architecture, and she also reviewed art exhibits, both in the United States and abroad during her foreign travels. Her work as a reviewer led to a series of longer essays focusing on major artists or movements, which she placed in several of the monthly magazines which were a conspicuous feature of American life in the later nineteenth century. Some of these essays were gathered into books. Van Rensselaer also wrote an article about Richard Wagner's last opera, *Parsifal*, and a narrative of a journey through the mountains of Pennsylvania. A long and comprehensive series of articles on contemporary American architecture began appearing in *Century* in 1884. In that same year Schuyler Van Rensselaer died. Mariana moved from New Brunswick to her mother's home at 9 West Tenth Street in New York City and lived there, except for foreign travels and summer vacations, until her death fifty years later. George, her only child, died in 1894, in Colorado Springs. He was on vacation from Harvard College.

Van Rensselaer's response to disaster was, as soon as possible, to get up and do something purposeful. After completing her series on American architecture she undertook her first tightly organized work on a large scale, the biography of her friend Richardson. His death in 1886 was another personal loss, but it was hardly unexpected: Richardson had been in very poor health for years. In any case Van Rensselaer proved her merit. She took full advantage of her friendship with Richardson's widow, Julia, and of the experiences of the excellent architects who were, or had formerly

been, his assistants for the purpose of gathering all the material required for a comprehensive study. *Henry Hobson Richardson and His Works* was published in 1888.

Richard Watson Gilder's *Century* now commissioned a long and ambitious series on twelve English cathedrals, with text by Van Rensselaer and drawings by Joseph Pennell. After publication in the magazine the Century Company gathered the pieces together as a book; *English Cathedrals* (1892) was by far Van Rensselaer's most popular work, no doubt because it served as an interesting guide to prosperous Americans planning their summer travels in England. Before the work on cathedrals was completed, Van Rensselaer had also written her twenty-one-part series "The Art of Gardening: A Historic Sketch" (1889-1890) for *Garden and Forest*, a weekly paper conducted by her friend Professor Charles Sprague Sargent, Harvard botanist and curator of the Arnold Arboretum in Boston. Sargent had put his expertise to good use in his Brookline, Massachusetts, acreage, which partly inspired Van Rensselaer's book of 1893, *Art Out-of-Doors*.

In the 1890s a *Century* series on French churches maintained the quality of the earlier series on English cathedrals, but there were fewer installments, they appeared at wider intervals, and no book followed. Van Rensselaer was now traveling less; following the death of her son she developed a lively interest in her own city, especially its pressing social problems. She had known the Gilders—Richard, Jeannette, and Joseph—for years, but now she saw more of them and shared their concern with the welfare of tenement dwellers. She helped Joseph organize a settlement, where she taught working-class girls about Egyptian antiquities and modern literature. She served on commissions, and was an inspector of public schools. And she wrote lovingly but not sentimentally about New York and its people, both in descriptive essays and in short fiction. Twenty-five years after the event, she reminisced about setting out in a cab with Richard Gilder late of a hot summer's night to prowl around the tenements and observe the inhabitants sleeping on roofs and fire escapes. Van Rensselaer realized that night the characteristic aroma of the East Side was that of stale beer.

She was, then, very much a reformer so far as health, education, and welfare were concerned, but she opposed the suffragettes. She was not alone in this; like many of her contemporaries—upper-class women with independent careers—she felt that women needed to develop still further along the lines that American women had created in the nineteenth century, improving their education, their practical skills, and their own spheres of influence. In her *Should We Ask for the Suffrage?* (1895) she argued, conventionally enough, for the duty of women to nurture men and children and not to run the world's business and politics. She took this cause quite seriously, remaining active in the anti-suffrage movement until its cause was lost with the Nineteenth Amendment.

Van Rensselaer had not by any means lost interest in man-made or natural beauty; she would have a lot more to say about art before her career was over. But in the first years of the new century, her work in magazines, somewhat reduced during her period of maximum social work, now became downright scarce. She was writing what would eventually be printed on over a thousand pages, her history of New Amsterdam and New York in the seventeenth century. She had intended this to be part of a larger work, covering the entire colonial history of the city. She completed substantial fragments of her projected volumes on the eighteenth century, but none was ever published.

The history was followed by other new departures: a book entitled *Poems* in 1910, and two translations (from different languages) in 1914. Her main response to the Great War was to organize and lead a society for the relief of the French wounded. After the war she continued writing poetry, including *Many Children*, a volume for and about youngsters published in 1921. She resumed writing about art, produced three new chapters for an enlarged edition of *Art Out-of-Doors*, and contributed an introduction to a 1926 brochure for a memorial exhibition of paintings by John Singer Sargent. That proved to be her last new publication. Though in declining health, she remained at her home on West Tenth Street, regularly receiving callers until the last days of her almost eighty-three years. She had accumulated plenty of honors over the years: honorary memberships in both the American Institute of Architects and the American Society of Landscape Architects, a Doctor of Letters degree from Columbia University in 1910, and the Gold Medal of the American Academy of Letters in 1923. Her remains were placed in Brooklyn's Greenwood Cemetery, next to those of her husband and son.

It is interesting to speculate as to why so many American writers who, however talented, accomplished far less than Van Rensselaer, are better remembered today. An odd but helpful approach to the problem is to notice that many of her best friends were artists, not writers; she could celebrate their talents both then and for posterity; they could reciprocate her friendship and admiration, but, except for a lovely bas-relief by Augustus Saint-Gaudens, they did nothing to commemorate her. She did have writers for friends too, but she outlived most of them, and no one of her circle is much read today. Finally, something should be said about Van Rensselaer's peculiar modesty. She could write movingly about her friends, living or dead, but

Bas-relief of Van Rensselaer by Augustus Saint-Gaudens, 1888 (Fogg Museum, Harvard University)

even then she was completely silent about anything that might be considered private. She wrote nothing about her parents, brothers, sisters, husband, or son, and left no collection of letters. And yet the evidence is conclusive that she cultivated not fewer, but more friendships than most people can manage; she was not in any obvious sense a private or retiring person. Though her works cover a wide range of subjects, all of them except the poetry (and the story, "One Man Who Was Content," if read in a certain way) draw attention away from the writer toward the objects or events being written about. And the only unifying principle in her works seems to be that, if she saw something that clearly needed to be done and believed that she had both the opportunity and ability to do it, she would set to work. One of the rare personal statements made in her writings is the introduction to her *History of the City of New York in the Seventeenth Century*, and it is really about her ancestors, not herself: "I beg that I may not be suspected, because of the name I acquired by marriage, of any inborn partiality for the Dutch-Americans who appear in my pages. My own people were of English and Scotch origin and, until my four grandparents became citizens of New York, lived in Connecticut, New Jersey, and Maryland and on Long Island. I like to remember that the forebears of at least two of my grandparents came to America as soon as they could—with the earliest settlers of New England. But, so far as I know, the only drops of Dutch blood I can pride myself upon I get from an inconspicuous New Jersey family and from the first wife of Captain John Underhill. Underhill himself is the only ancestor with whom I have had to deal; and I trust that his spirit has not moved me to speak of him with unjust indulgence."

Whatever her subject, Van Rensselaer was likely to display a keen interest in history. A good example is the travel sketch of 1882, "In the Heart of the Alleghanies," which contains a great deal of the social and economic history of the region and an affecting retelling of the life of Demetrius, Prince Gallitzin. This Russo-German nobleman came as a young man to the United States during the presidency of George Washington, secured ordination as a Catholic priest from Bishop Charles Carroll, and became a missionary in the backwoods wilderness of the Pennsylvania mountains, eventually settling the community of Loretto. Similarly, Van Rensselaer's essays on great painters are sensitive to the times and events which influenced—or in the case of Correggio rather curiously did not influence—their work. The 1883 essay on the pro-

duction of *Parsifal* at Bayreuth gives an idea of the town before Wagner transformed it into a cultural mecca. Van Rensselaer praised the design of Wagner's theater *Festspielhaus*, an early instance of her affirming the importance of attending to functionality in architecture. *Parsifal* she found to be a noble work in every respect; she was not moved, in the fashion of Mark Twain, to jest at solemn things, but she did write, "Everything connected with Wagner's life in Bayreuth has been made to suggest his work in a degree which seems odd to people less naive than these artistic Germans, more keenly alive to the ridiculous, and less blindly wrapped in their enthusiasms. His dogs are called Wotan, Freia, and Fricka. His children, even, are named for his creations, the youngest being Siegfried. If ever a man is crushed beneath the weight of a doubly suggestive patronymic, it may well be young Siegfried Wagner."

Van Rensselaer's *Henry Hobson Richardson and His Works* remains valuable for its lucid presentation of Richardson's entire career, its generous complement of photographs and drawings, and its complete catalogue of the architect's works. The critical judgments are equally thorough and valuable; one can scarcely imagine a more judicious assessment of the significance of Richardson's career and its potential for influencing later American architecture being formed in 1888. One is also struck by the author's sensitivity to the influence of widely contrasting cultural influences on Richardson, who was from the family of a rich Louisiana planter, descended from Joseph Priestley on his mother's side, educated at Harvard and in Paris, and eventually married to a young woman from Boston.

English Cathedrals begins with chapters explaining the development of the ecclesiastical system of England, and, along with the discussion of the structure, decoration, and grounds of each cathedral, supplies a generous sampling of its history. The series of articles on gardening is still more remarkable. Evidently Van Rensselaer found the world well supplied with books on gardening from the Renaissance onward, so she wrote her entire series on gardening in the ancient and medieval worlds, ranging as far afield as India. The shorter series on French churches, undoubtedly inspired by Richardson's fascination with Romanesque architecture, is also generous with accurate glimpses into the history of locales.

In writing her *History of the City of New York in the Seventeenth Century*, Van Rensselaer was supplying a need which she had demonstrated in three articles in the *North American Review* from November 1900 to August 1901. She deplored the relative neglect of early New York history and especially the history of the city in general treatments of early American history. Though generally a writer of coolly dispassionate prose, Van Rensselaer could wax polemical when strongly moved, and Washington Irving's pseudonymous *History of New York* by Diedrich Knickerbocker was one of the things that so moved her. She suggested that "a black border should encircle the page in our annals that is dated 1809, for it records the appearance of *Knickerbocker's History of New York*. On both sides of the ocean this book was hailed as a triumph of literary art and a new glory for the new Republic. It has proved to be an enemy of the state, and its vogue a civic disaster." More constructively, she noted the appearance, beginning in 1845, of Edmund B. O'Callaghan's exhaustively detailed and accurate *The History of New Netherland* and John R. Brodhead's superb collection of documents relating to colonial New York. These, with other published and manuscript sources, made possible both a full and accurate picture of New York in the colonial period, but so far nothing had appeared which was both readable and accurate. The popular historian John Fiske made Van Rensselaer almost as cross as Washington Irving. His expansive work, *The Dutch and Quaker Colonies in America* (1899), could easily have been informed by the available documents, but, typical of Fiske's work, it perpetuated the errors and lacunae of previous secondary accounts.

Each volume of Van Rensselaer's *History of the City of New York in the Seventeenth Century* displays signs of careful planning and execution, and each has as much unity as a single volume of history can ever have. The first encompasses the entire history of New Netherland from the earliest Dutch schemes of exploration, trade, and settlement to the English invasion and conquest of 1664. The second volume bears the subtitle *New York Under the Stuarts* and ends with the death of Jacob Leisler in 1691. No summary can do justice to the breadth and depth of historical staging with which Van Rensselaer framed her story of a tiny city in a thinly populated colony, surrounded by rivals and enemies on all sides, by turns tyrannized and neglected by the inept company that owned New Netherland, repeatedly subject to murder and kidnapping by disgruntled Indians and by intrusion from fellow Europeans, especially the self-righteous saints of New England.

Van Rensselaer proved, to the degree that any study of history can prove such a thing, that the negligible little colony in a remote corner of the world somehow managed, under an obtuse Dutch company and then under the absolutist James Stuart, to develop honest and representative institutions of local government, more on the Dutch than English model, and to create a climate of cultural and religious toleration rare in the world of the seventeenth century. The second volume builds to a remarkable climax, with an extremely detailed account of the episode known as Leisler's Rebellion. The portrait of Jacob Leisler drawn here, precisely because it makes no effort to flatter him but sets his deeds and misdeeds clearly in contrast to those of his enemies, succeeds in making a tragic hero of the man.

Mariana Van Rensselaer was so extraordinary in the range of her sympathies and achievements that one is almost embarrassed at the need for a final summary and categorization. Though hardly in the mainstream of American historical writing, she does resemble the great literary historians of the nineteenth century in her cosmopolitanism, her wide general culture, and her desire to work on a large canvas, never stinting on details which bring her historical pictures vividly to life. She anticipated many of the concerns of recent historians in the attention that she gave to economic, mental, and artistic life in the history of civilization and in her ability to enter sympathetically into the lives of ordinary people.

Papers:

The New York Public Library has the records, 1915-1919, of the American Fund for French Wounded, donated by Van Rensselaer, and some incomplete manuscripts donated by her estate.

Andrew Dickson White

(7 November 1832-4 November 1918)

Damon D. Hickey
Guilford College

SELECTED BOOKS: *A Letter to William Howard Russell, LL.D. on Passages in His "Diary North and South"* (Ann Arbor: Printed by C. G. Clark, Jr., 1863; London: Stevens, 1863);

The Most Bitter Foe of Nations and the Way to Its Permanent Overthrow: An Address Delivered Before the Phi Beta Kappa Society at Yale College, July 25, 1866 (New Haven: T. H. Pease, 1866);

The Constitutional Convention: Delegates at Large. Responsibility to Small Districts. Impartial Manhood Suffrage. Remarks of Hon. Andrew D. White, of Onondaga, in the Senate (Albany: Weed, Parson, 1867);

Address on Agricultural Education Delivered Before the N.Y. State Agricultural Society, at Albany, February 10, 1869 (Albany: Published by the Society, 1869); revised as "Scientific and Industrial Education in the United States," *Popular Science Monthly*, 5 (June 1874): 170-191;

Report Submitted to the Trustees of Cornell University, in Behalf of a Majority of the Committee on Mr. Sage's Proposal to Endow a College for Women (Ithaca: Cornell University Press, 1872);

Scientific and Industrial Education in the United States. An Address Delivered before the New-York State Agricultural Society (New York: Appleton, 1874);

Paper-Money Inflation in France: How It Came, What It Brought, and How It Ended. A Paper Read Before Several Senators and Members of the House of Representatives, of Both Political Parties, at Washington, April 12, and Before the Union League Club, at New York, April 13, 1876 (New York: Appleton, 1876); revised and enlarged as *Fiat Money Inflation in France, How It Came, What It Brought and How It Ended* (New York: Appleton, 1896);

The Warfare of Science (New York: Appleton, 1876; London: King, 1876); enlarged as *A History of the Warfare of Science With Theology in Christendom*, 2 volumes (New York: Appleton, 1896; London: Macmillan, 1896);

Education in Political Science. An Address by Hon. An-

Andrew Dickson White in 1865, when he became president of Cornell University (Department of Manuscripts and University Archives, Cornell University)

drew D. White Delivered in the Academy of Music, Baltimore, on the Third Anniversary of the Johns Hopkins University (Baltimore: Printed by J. Murray for Johns Hopkins University, 1879);

James A. Garfield. Memorial Address by Andrew D. White. Delivered at a Meeting of the Citizens of Ithaca, New York, on Monday, September 26, 1881 (Ithaca: Cornell University Press, 1881);

Two Addresses at Cleveland, Ohio, 25 and 26 October, 1882 (Cleveland: Printed at the Western Reserve University Press, 1882);

The Message of the Nineteenth Century to the Twentieth

(New Haven: Printed by Taylor & More-
house, 1883);

*Some Practical Influences of German Thought Upon the
United States. An Address Delivered at the Cen-
tennial Celebration of the German Society of New
York* (Ithaca: Andrus & Church, 1884);

*An Address Delivered at the Unveiling of the Statue of
Benjamin Silliman at Yale College, June 24, 1884*
(Ithaca: Andrus & Church, 1885);

*The Presidency of Cornell University. Remarks of Andrew
Dickson White Presented in Accordance with the
Unanimous Request of the Trustees that He Would
Address Them Regarding the Election of His Suc-
cessor* (Ithaca, 1885);

*On Studies in General History and the History of Civi-
lization* (New York & London: Putnam's,
1885);

European Schools of History and Politics (Baltimore:
N. Murray, Publication Agent, Johns Hopkins
University, 1887);

*A History of the Doctrine of Comets. A Paper Read Before
the American Historical Association at its Second
Annual Meeting, Saratoga, September 10, 1885*
(New York & London: Putnam's, 1887);

*Evolution and Revolution: An Address Delivered at the
Annual Commencement of the University of Michigan, June 26, 1890* (Ann Arbor: Published by
the University, 1890);

*My Reminiscences of Ezra Cornell; An Address Delivered
Before Cornell University on Founder's Day, January 11th, 1890* (Ithaca: Cornell University,
1890);

*Instruction in Social Science. Address of President White,
1890. Remarks of President White, 1891* (N.p.,
1891);

Evolution vs. Revolution, in Politics (Madison: State
Historical Society of Wisconsin, 1897);

*The Diplomatic Service of the United States with Some
Hints toward Its Reform* (Washington, D.C.:
Smithsonian Institution, 1905);

Autobiography of Andrew Dickson White, 2 volumes
(New York: Century, 1905; London: Macmillan, 1905);

*Seven Great Statesmen in the Warfare of Humanity With
Unreason* (New York: Century, 1910; London:
Unwin, 1910).

OTHER: "Historical Instruction in the Course of
History and Political Science," in *Methods of
Teaching History*, edited by G. Stanley Hall
(Boston: Ginn, Heath, 1885), pp. 73-76;

*The French Revolution and First Empire; an Historical
Sketch*, by William O'Connor Morris, with a

bibliography and a course of study by White
(New York: Scribners, 1901).

PERIODICAL PUBLICATIONS: "Glimpses of
Universal History," *New Englander*, 15 (August 1857): 398-427;

"Jefferson and Slavery," *Atlantic Monthly*, 9 (January 1862): 29-40;

"The Statesmanship of Richelieu," *Atlantic Monthly*,
9 (May 1862): 611-624;

"The Development and Overthrow of the Russian
Serf System," *Atlantic Monthly*, 10 (November
1862): 538-552.

When the Library of Congress catalogued a
life of Andrew Dickson White under biographies
of U.S. diplomats, historians, and college teachers,
the designations college presidents and statesmen
could well have been added, for White was all of
these. The son of successful businessman and
banker Horace White and Clara Dickson White,
White was born in Homer, New York, on 7 November 1832. When he was seven the family moved
to Syracuse where White attended public and private schools. He studied at Geneva (now Hobart)
College, then Yale University, from which he was
graduated in 1853, having been elected editor of
the *Yale Literary Magazine*, member of Phi Beta
Kappa, and recipient of the Clark, Yale Literary,
and De Forest prizes. His campaign for the editorship of the "Lit" was based largely on an abolitionist platform that reflected what was for White
an enduring and passionate issue. A lifelong interest in international law was also awakened through
his studies under President Theodore Dwight
Woolsey. Following his graduation, he and class-
mate Daniel Coit Gilman accompanied Connecticut
Governor Thomas Seymour, newly appointed U.S.
minister to Russia, as unpaid attachés for a year.
A semester of study at the Sorbonne and another
at the University of Berlin, followed by travel in
Switzerland and Italy, convinced him of the value
of historical studies. Determined on a career as a
professional historian, he returned to Yale, where
he received an A.M. in 1856.

White had hoped to be named a member of
his alma mater's faculty and was distressed when
he was passed over by the largely Congregationalist
Yale Corporation because his religious orthodoxy
was suspect. He quickly found a nonsectarian alternative, the University of Michigan presided over
by Henry P. Tappan, which offered him the professorship of history and rhetoric. At Michigan,
Tappan, who also had studied in Germany, was

creating a university that offered several courses of study, welcomed students of all religious persuasions, was devoted to scholarship, and employed scholars who lectured instead of hearing recitations—all in sharp contrast to Yale. During his tenure at Michigan beginning in 1857, White furthered his reputation as a staunch, even radical, abolitionist and advocate of the Union cause in the Civil War.

In 1864 White, on leave abroad, was elected in absentia to the New York State Senate and made the chairman of its Committee on Education. In this post he persuaded fellow senator and philanthropist Ezra Cornell to donate campus, farm, and $500,000 to help establish a land-grant university under the Morrill Act of 1862. The institution, named for Cornell, was chartered at Ithaca in 1865. White, at Cornell's insistence, became its first president. Its innovations included the integration of natural sciences and technical studies with the humanities; the election of overall courses of study (but not of particular subjects) by the students; the introduction of modern languages, modern literature, history, and political science on a footing equal with the classical curriculum; and the informal sharing of social and intellectual contacts between faculty and students. Throughout the next twenty years, despite financial setbacks, Cornell prospered, and White (with several extended leaves of absence for the sake of his health or to perform other duties) emerged as a leading figure in the reform of American higher education. The university's strictly nonsectarian stance, putting "no religion" on the same basis as any religion or sect (a more liberal position than even Michigan had taken), became White's ultimate statement in response to his earlier rejection by Congregationalist Yale. It also embroiled him in a continuing controversy with religious leaders.

During several of White's leaves of absence from the university he launched his diplomatic career. A staunch Republican, he nevertheless served administrations of both parties, although his own party was in power most of the time. He became commissioner to Santo Domingo in 1871 under President Ulysses S. Grant, minister to Germany in 1878 under Rutherford B. Hayes, minister to Russia in 1892 under Benjamin Harrison and then Grover Cleveland, member of the Venezuela-British Guiana boundary commission in 1896 under Cleveland, and ambassador to Germany in 1897 under William McKinley. McKinley also appointed him in 1899 to head the American delegation to the First Hague Conference.

White's career as a politician and statesman was intertwined with his diplomatic career. In addition to serving a term in the New York State Senate, he sought unsuccessfully the Republican gubernatorial nomination in 1891 and the vice-presidential nomination in 1900. That he was considered seriously for these positions indicates both the high regard in which he was held by the public and the faithfulness of his service to his party. That he was not chosen for either major nomination reflects his own self-image and others' view of him more as a statesman than as a party politician.

White's combination of careers and his attitude toward education were expressions of his overall belief in humanity's steady progress through its development of the institutions of law. The aim of education, particularly higher education, was to develop leaders who were dedicated to public service and to the elevation and advancement of humanity. Careers in politics and international diplomacy served these ends nationally and globally. It is not surprising to discover that White's view of history and the historical profession embraced just such a view of progress and of vocation.

White's early historical writing, in his abolitionist period, attacked slavery and those who supported it. In articles written in 1862, he praised Jefferson's free-soil views and the abolition of the Russian serf system. He also lauded Cardinal Richelieu's strengthening of the French monarchy, because in weakening the nobility such a policy indirectly contributed to eventual freedom for the serfs. In each of these studies White's focus was on an individual, a great man, whose contribution to human history he evaluated in relation to its destructive impact on slavery. White also argued in an address delivered and published in pamphlet form in 1866, during Reconstruction, that aristocracy was "The Most Bitter Foe of Nations" and praised those statesmen who had attempted elsewhere to overthrow it.

White's later concerns, along with the refocusing of the nation's energies once slavery had been abolished and Reconstruction abandoned, included inflation. Again White chose history as his weapon, arguing in *Paper-Money Inflation in France*, a short book published for the 1876 presidential campaign, that paper money inflation had ruined the economy of revolutionary France. Yet a few years before, when he had seen history as a record of failed aristocracies and slavocracies, White had denied any parallel between the American and revolutionary French economies, since the latter had

Members of the American delegation to the First Hague Conference, 1899. Left to right: Stanford Newell; George F. W. Holls; head of the delegation, Andrew Dickson White; Alfred Thayer Mahan; Seth Low; and William Crozier.

too recently emerged from the oppressor's grip. In this instance White had seen history vindicating Lincoln's suppression of the South's aristocracy, even though such action had led to inflation. In his later historical writing White turned increasingly to history for an understanding of the process of social change. Particularly in his *Seven Great Statesmen in the Warfare of Humanity With Unreason* (1910), White found justification for his belief that evolutionary change was to be preferred to revolution, and that its effects were more enduring. White's biographer, Glenn C. Altschuler, suggests that White tended to view history as deterministic, approaching the view that "what is, is right," but tempered his opinion at least with an emphasis on human will, especially that of leaders, and felt that peaceful advocacy was more effective in achieving desired reform than was violence.

Like *Seven Great Statesmen*, White's best-known historical work had to do with human progress, in

this case the progress of free human inquiry, particularly in the sciences. Its enemy was theology, particularly theology based on revelation and authority, rather than on morality. *A History of the Warfare of Science With Theology in Christendom* (1896) was the result of many years of study, lectures, and articles. Begun during his Cornell presidency in reply to the attacks of the clergy on the new university's freedom of inquiry and teaching, the first, brief version of White's work was published in *Popular Science Monthly*. In 1876 it appeared in book form under the title *The Warfare of Science*. By 1896 it had grown to two volumes, and it was surprisingly popular, leading some to the conclusion that it signaled the end of a war already virtually won, at least in the academic world. The vehemence of the author's response to every criticism of the book may indicate the intensity of the feeling generated originally by Yale's religiously biased rejection of White for a professorship. Two main lines of criticism quickly formed. One pointed out that human narrowness, not theology, was responsible for having erected the barriers to scientific inquiry and that science itself was capable of just such narrowness. The other line of criticism fastened curiously on White's attempt to "save" religion by reducing it to rationalistic morality with an icing of religious language and wondered whether such a religion could or would be effective in motivating its adherents toward a more noble or ethical life than either the old religion or none at all. Indeed, to his probable chagrin, the greatest praise for White's book came precisely from those who saw all religion as useless and outmoded, if not dangerous and false. There were others, contemporaries of White, who also espoused evolutionary progress toward national and international accord, based on the teachings of Jesus. Yet the social gospel movement, with its sometimes radical utopianism, was foreign to White's temperament.

White often lent his efforts to the formation of professional organizations in history and the social sciences. *Professional* may be an inaccurate term, for White stood at a transition point between the amateur historian and the academic professional, and his organizational efforts reflected this transition. The American Social Science Association (ASSA), in which White was active, was, according to Thomas Haskell in *The Emergence of Professional Social Science* (1977), "the only central meeting place for those who were establishing authority in all the diverse areas made problematical by the growth of an urban-industrial society." It included "all three of the men who contributed most to the construction of the modern American university—[Daniel Coit] Gilman of Hopkins, [Charles W.] Eliot of Harvard, and Andrew Dickson White of Cornell." It also embraced such diverse personalities as Simon E. Balwin, organizer of the American Bar Association, and philosopher-educator John Dewey. The ASSA was responsible for organizing the National Conference of Charities and Correction, the American Public Health Association, and civil-service reform based on the merit system. Yet, Haskell notes, it was the younger generation of scholars, who came to the universities that White and the others had built, who found the ASSA too broad for their professional needs. The organization of the independent American Historical Association (AHA) in 1884 and American Economic Association in 1885 may have marked the beginning of the end for the ASSA, but it was not obvious at the time. Andrew White, ASSA president from 1888-1891, continued to support the older organization, which he had helped bring into being. He also served as first president of the new AHA, and expressed at his inauguration the view that historians should be moral teachers who point to the salient features of historical evolution as examples to their students, the future leaders of society. White's own activity on behalf of civil-service reform provided a living example of his thesis. Thomas Haskell notes that, although the AHA was from its beginning "on a more professional and more academic course" than the ASSA, "its novel character was not immediately conspicuous." Ironically, it was White the educator and college president whose influence helped to set in motion the forces that led to the eclipse of the social sciences association as the source of social reform. As with his *History of the Warfare of Science With Theology in Christendom*, the movement he espoused and helped to lead proved to be beyond his control, despite his considerable influence.

Coming from an old and prosperous American family, White seems to have felt a strong sense of noblesse oblige throughout his life. He was reared an Episcopalian. He was fond of protocol, honors, and titles, and eventually received nine honorary degrees from American and European universities: University of Michigan, 1867; Cornell, 1886; Yale, 1887; University of Jena (Germany), 1889; St. Andrew's (Scotland), Oxford, and Johns Hopkins, 1902; Dartmouth, 1906; and Hobart, 1911. White was also obsessed with public service, including military service, and argued initially that all Cornell students should wear uniforms and participate in military drills on campus. Never a man of robust health, he led a constant struggle with illness and constant fear of death. His personal combativeness may explain in part his description of the relationship between science and theology as one of warfare, in which he was an active participant. White was a domineering husband and father whose family life seems to have been as precarious and painful as his health. In 1857 he married fellow New Yorker Mary A. Outwater, who died thirty years later in 1887, two years after White stepped down from the presidency of Cornell. Of their four children, Clara, Frederick, Ruth, and Andrew, three experienced personal tragedy (including marital scandal, drug addiction, and suicide) resulting in part from their relationship with their father, and the fourth died in childhood. White's second wife, Helen Magill, whom he married in 1890, was a Quaker from Swarthmore, Pennsylvania, who detested formality and warfare, and whom White compared unfavorably to his first wife throughout their twenty-eight-year marriage, which produced one daughter, Karin. It is remarkable that a man who experienced such distress should have remained so optimistic about the direction of history, even during the World War. Yet perhaps that optimism was necessary to his continued efforts to control the chaos that seemed ever about to engulf his personal life.

For White the future looked surprisingly like the past. Despite his occasional revolutionary rhetoric, he saw little need for dramatic change in American society. The reforms he trumpeted—abolition of slavery, application of the German system to American universities, the ascendancy of science over dogmatic theology, a civil-service merit system, the formation of professional organizations—were all movements whose time had come. In fact, in almost every instance the movement moved beyond White, to his displeasure. Reconstruction, when it spoke of redistributing land from former masters to former slaves, earned his enmity. Allowing university students to elect an overall course of study did not mean for White, as it did for Eliot at Harvard, trusting them to choose individual subjects within those courses. The ethics of the Sermon on the Mount should be applied to economic affairs, but not if that meant "socialism" in any form (including William Jennings Bryan's populism). Science should be freed of religious dogma's restraints, but that should not mean the abandonment of religion by scientists. White devoted himself to the extension of civil-service reform but stopped short of joining independent Republicans or the Democrats in 1884, despite the fact that James G. Blaine, the regular Republicans' candidate, was no friend of reform. The historical profession might need its own organization, but that should not lead it to become so academically specialized that it ceased to function as part of a larger community of practical social reforms. In short, White was a reform-minded conservative whose faith in the capacity of an educated elite to lead the nation, and the world, along the path of gradual evolution toward a better life for all did not embrace radical change (except perhaps in the case of abolishing slavery, which, from another

point of view, could be seen as a movement to bring the South into conformity with a global and national status quo).

White sought to found his career on historical studies, but it was as an educator and statesman that he achieved public stature. His few historical works were essentially tracts for the times, and only *A History of the Warfare of Science With Theology in Christendom* has proved to be of enduring interest. His lively and engaging style suited well the audience for whom his books were intended. He was a major transitional figure, bridging the gap between the amateur gentleman-historian and the specialized, professional, academic historian. The system of higher education he helped to create, the professional associations he helped to found and nurture, and above all the students he taught became mainstays of the American historical profession in the twentieth century. Very few later historians have combined higher education, popular historical writing, professional competence, and public service to the extent White did, and none has ever achieved his public stature.

Bibliography:

Glenn C. Altschuler, *Andrew D. White: Educator, Historian, Diplomat* (Ithaca: Cornell University Press, 1979), pp. 287-289.

Biography:

Glenn C. Altschuler, *Andrew D. White: Educator, Historian, Diplomat* (Ithaca: Cornell University Press, 1979).

Reference:

Thomas L. Haskell, *The Emergence of Professional Social Science: The American Social Science Association and the Nineteenth-Century Crisis of Authority* (Urbana: University of Illinois Press, 1977).

Papers:

Cornell University Libraries, Department of Manuscripts and University Archives, houses White's papers, diary, and many letters.

George Washington Williams

(16 October 1849-2 August 1891)

Linda O. McMurry
North Carolina State University

SELECTED BOOKS: *The American Negro from 1776 to 1876. Oration Delivered July 4, 1876 at Avondale, Ohio* (Cincinnati: Printed by R. Clarke, 1876);

History of the Negro Race in America from 1619 to 1880; Negroes as Slaves, as Soldiers, and as Citizens, Together with a Preliminary Consideration of the Unity of the Human Family; An Historical Sketch of Africa, and An Account of the Negro Governments of Sierra Leone and Liberia, 2 volumes (New York: Putnam's, 1883);

1862—Emancipation Day—1884. The Negro as Political Problem. Oration, by Hon. George W. Williams . . . at the Asbury Church, Washington, D.C., April 16, 1884 (Boston: Printed by A. Mudge, 1884);

Memorial Day. The Ethics of War. Oration by Col. George W. Williams, at Newton, Mass., May 30, 1884. Delivered Before Charles Ward Post 62, G.A.R. (Newton, Mass.: Printed at the Office of the Graphic, 1884);

A History of the Negro Troops in the War of the Rebellion, 1861-1865, Preceded by a Review of the Military Services of Negroes in Ancient and Modern Times (London: Low, 1887; New York: Harper, 1888);

The Constitutional Results of the War of the Rebellion. An Oration. Memorial Day, May 30th, 1889, at Millbury, Mass. (Worcester, Mass.: Sanford & Davis, 1889);

An Open Letter to His Serene Majesty Leopold II, King of the Belgians and Sovereign of the Independent State of Congo (N.p., 1890);

A Report Upon the Congo-State and Country to the President of the Republic of the United States (N.p., 1890);

A Report on the Proposed Congo Railway (N.p., 1890).

Referred to by some reviewers as the "Negro Bancroft," George Washington Williams was the first serious black historian in the United States. Like George Bancroft and several other nineteenth-century historians, Williams wrote works that both reflected the gentleman-scholar roman-ticism of his era and foreshadowed the rise of the "scientific school" of history. Unlike Bancroft, however, he was not a mainstream figure, and his life and writing display many of the dilemmas of turn-of-the-century black intellectuals, who often experienced what W. E. B. Du Bois labeled the "duality" of being both a Negro and an American. Given the rampant racism of the day, few black historians could psychologically afford to pursue truth merely from a pure love of knowledge. Most felt compelled to refute erroneous assumptions that supported discrimination while attempting to win credibility from a skeptical, and sometimes hostile, scholarly community.

Few nineteenth-century historians were professionally trained, and Williams was not an exception. Many, however, came from privileged backgrounds, and although Williams's background was not as bleak as that of most blacks of his day, he did not share many of the advantages of his white colleagues. Born 16 October 1849, in Bedford Springs, Pennsylvania, he was the second child of mulatto parents, Thomas and Ellen Rouse Williams. His father was a common laborer whose search for work caused his family to move around Pennsylvania, giving young George Williams little chance for formal learning. Eventually the boy was placed in a house of refuge and learned the barbering trade. In 1863, at the age of fourteen, he gave a false name and lied about his age in an attempt to join the Union army. Initially unsuccessful, he continued his efforts until he was accepted. He served in several battles and was wounded in 1864 near Harrison, Virginia.

As is apparent in his historical writings, Williams relished army life. By some accounts, soon after being mustered out of the United States forces, he enlisted in the Mexican army. Following the capture of Maximilian in 1867, he returned to the U.S. Army, serving in the cavalry in the Comanche campaigns later that year. He was discharged in 1868 at Fort Arbuckle, Indian Territory, after he had been shot in the left lung. His army experiences later enabled Williams to depict battles vividly and to understand better the structure of military organization.

The next phase of his life and career also influenced his writing of history. Moving to St. Louis in 1868, Williams was baptized at the First Baptist Church and began to consider entering the ministry. He briefly attended both Howard University and Wayland Seminary prior to entering Newton Theological Institution in Massachusetts in September 1870. After two years of preparatory studies, Williams was admitted as a junior in theology. When he was graduated in 1874, he delivered one of the commencement addresses, a talk on "Early Christianity in Africa," that revealed his growing interest in history as well as the florid oratorical style which frequently crept into his writing.

After his ordination Williams accepted the pastorate at Boston's Twelfth Street Baptist Church, an important black congregation. His inclination to examine the past led him to write an eighty-page history of that church. His emphasis on the charitable works of the congregation was probably intended to raise funds for continued work. Fourteen months after coming to Twelfth Street Baptist, he resigned and moved to Washington, D.C., where he started a journal, the *Commoner*, for which he served as editor. The need for a black journal in the nation's capital had the support of several prominent blacks, including Frederick Douglass. By December 1875, however, Williams was forced to take a position in the city's post office to support himself.

The editorial venture could not have lasted long, for in March 1876 he became pastor of the Union Baptist Church in Cincinnati. Four months later he delivered an address at the forty-fifth anniversary of that church in which he described the origins and development of the congregation. His interest in church history continued even after he left the ministry; three chapters of his *History of the Negro Race in America from 1619 to 1880* are devoted to the African Methodist Episcopal Church, the Methodist Episcopal Church, and the Colored Baptists of America.

All of Williams's writings are tinted by his theological training. Biblical and classical references abound, and his emotional and oratorical style is distracting to many twentieth-century readers. His concept of the past is clear in his statement that "In the interpretation of history the plans of God must be discovered." It was this view as well as his prose style that helped earn him the label of the "Negro Bancroft," for George Bancroft once noted "That God rules in the affairs of men is as certain as any truth of physical science."

While in Cincinnati Williams became engaged in several secular activities which would also color his writing of history. Becoming active in Republican politics, he began the study of law at the Cincinnati Law School and in the offices of Judge Alphonso Taft. After an unsuccessful 1877 bid for a seat in the Ohio legislature, Williams resigned his pastorate and held several jobs while studying law. He became an Internal Revenue clerk and secretary in the auditor's office of the Cincinnati Southern Railway, while regularly contributing articles to the *Cincinnati Commercial* under the pen name Aristides. Elected to the state House of Representatives in 1879, Williams served as chairman of the Committee on the Library and of the Special Committee on railroad terminal facilities and was a member of the Committee on Universities and Colleges. His legal training and governmental experience were later reflected in the emphases of his writings.

During the Ohio years, 1876-1881, Williams was in the process of becoming a full-time historian. He dated his conversion to historical studies to a centennial Fourth of July oration entitled *The American Negro from 1776 to 1876* and delivered at Avondale, Ohio. "It being the one-hundredth birthday of the American Republic," he later wrote, "I determined to prepare an oration on the American Negro. I at once began an investigation of the records of the nation to secure materials for the oration. I was surprised and delighted to find that the historical memorials of the Negro were so abundant and so creditable to him." He noted that the warm response to his speech, which was published in pamphlet form, "encouraged me to devote what leisure time I might have to a further study of the subject." Frequenting the state library, the library of the Historical and Philosophical Society of Ohio, and the private library of Robert Clark, Williams became convinced that enough material was available to produce a definitive history of the Negro.

In 1881 Williams decided not to seek reelection, partly because his chances did not seem very bright and partly because of his desire to devote himself to his historical studies. He began traveling extensively, carrying out research in the East at the Library of Congress, the Lenox Library in New York, and the Boston Public Library, among other institutions. He also consulted numerous official records of such bodies as the A.M.E. Church, the U.S. War Department, and several state governments. When the adjutant-general of the army refused to give information concerning the Negro regiments in the regular army, Williams visited the Indian Territory, Kansas, Texas, and New Mexico.

Aside from that refusal, Williams apparently received an unusual degree of cooperation for a man of his color. Perhaps these responses resulted from the impression his demeanor made upon whites. George Washington Cable once described him as "a mulatto, a christian, a scholar, a man of affairs, polished, graceful, laborious in his life," and noted, "I see at last a man whose *only* Africanism is his tawny skin."

After seven years of labor Williams finished his *History of the Negro Race in America from 1619 to 1880: Negroes as Slaves, as Soldiers, and as Citizens*, which was published by G. P. Putnam's Sons in 1883. In his preface he noted that he had consulted over twelve thousand volumes, and over one thousand are mentioned in his book. He apparently also consulted newspapers, the *Congressional Record*, the *Congressional Globe*, and the *Journal of the Confederate Congress*, as well as interviewing numerous people.

Although his documentation is frequently scanty, this high level of research clearly marks him as one of the transitional figures between the romantic and scientific schools of history.

He also listed his motivations for such an effort in his preface: 1) "ample historically accurate material [is] at hand"; 2) blacks had been "the most vexatious problem in North America"; 3) "Colored people had always displayed a matchless patriotism and an incomparable heroism in the cause of America"; 4) such a study "would give the world more correct ideas of the Colored people, and incite the latter to greater effort in the struggle of citizenship and manhood"; and 5) the lack of such a history was "sufficient reason for writing one." As with most black scholars of his generation, his goals reflected his dual status. He sincerely loved history, but he also sought to improve conditions for blacks by refuting erroneous stereotypes and inspiring confidence in blacks.

His goals required him to walk a dangerous tightrope. On one side objectivity was required for credibility; on the other some emotional fervor enhanced his message. His preface reflects this dilemma. In one paragraph he noted, "Not as the blind panegyrist of my race, nor as the partisan apologist, but from a love for '*the truth of history*,' I have striven to record the truth, the whole truth, and nothing but the truth." In the next paragraph, however, he explained, "I commit this work to the public, . . . in the hope that the obsolete antagonisms which grew out of the relation of master and slave may speedily sink as storms beneath the horizon; and that the day will hasten when there shall be no North, no South, no Black, no White,—but all be American citizens, with equal duties and rights."

Williams was neither the first nor the last historian to write for a purpose, but he generally avoided the extreme pitfalls of using history to prove a point. In many cases he let the documents speak for themselves by printing them verbatim with the "desire to escape the charge of superficiality." He recognized that he might be "charged with seeking to escape the labor incident to thorough digestion," but retorted that "while men with the reputation of Bancroft and [Richard] Hildreth could pass unchallenged when disregarding largely the use of documents and the citation of authorities, I would find myself challenged by a large number of critics."

The two-volume work, totaling over one thousand pages, is divided into nine parts which contain sixty chapters. The first volume has eleven chapters on the African background, fourteen chapters on slavery in the colonies, and six on the Revolution and slavery as a political and legal problem to 1800. The second volume has three chapters on the "Conservative Era," five on antislavery agitation, five on the 1850s, seven on the Negro in the War for the Union, six on the first decade of freedom, and three on the aftermath of Reconstruction to 1880.

The scope and depth of the book marked a milestone in Afro-American history, never to be superseded. Its quality is, however, uneven. Many of the best chapters reflect Williams's background and training. His legal expertise is evident in his analysis of the Negro's legal status throughout the book and in his "retrial" of the case regarding a 1741 "Negro plot" in New York. Williams's chapters on the military involvement of blacks display both an intimate knowledge of army life and the consultation of numerous original sources. As John Hope Franklin noted in a 1946 article on Williams, "It is in his chapters on military activity that Williams rises to his full powers; and they display the inborn love for things military that lured him away from home when but a mere lad." It is difficult to know, however, if Williams's emphasis on constitutional and military history is more a product of his background or of the prevailing mode of historical writing.

The weakest parts of the book derive from his theological grounding and his inability to retain the objectivity he so diligently sought. Partly to refute arguments that blacks lacked full humanity, Williams began with Genesis. As the *Nation* reviewer noted, "a Biblical argument to prove the negro a man, seems, in these Darwinian times, more than antediluvian." Viewing history as a battle between God and the forces of evil, especially human greed, Williams's attempts to give "the facts with temperate and honest criticism" often failed. He saw Confederate General Nathan Bedford Forrest as "a cold-blooded murderer; a fiend in human form," and slavery as " 'the sum of all villanies'— the blackest curse that ever scourged the earth." There was little subtlety in his conception of those issues he considered moral ones.

Aside from his propensity to florid rhetoric, Williams's major failings in the book were errors of omission. He barely mentioned the Atlantic slave trade and gave only a sketchy review of Reconstruction. The first omission is puzzling; the second can be explained by his intention to write a separate—but never completed—study of Reconstruction. Williams was also highly critical of other writers and seemed to relish pointing out inaccuracies in their work—sometimes to the point of pettiness. One reviewer noted that Williams severely criticized authors who had already corrected their mistakes in later editions.

The reviews of *History of the Negro Race in America from 1619 to 1880* are significant. Most generally praised the book, and even the negative comments indicated a willingness to consider the work as a serious piece of historical scholarship and to judge it more on the basis of its merit than on the color of its author. As the *Atlantic Monthly* reviewer explained, "If we frankly point out its defects as well as its merits, it is because its author has honestly aimed to place it on the high plane where it can be judged by the standard of its absolute worth, without any sort of reference to 'race, color, or previous condition of servitude.' To criticize it thus impartially is a recognition of its values."

Most reviewers extolled Williams's industry but criticized his overblown writing style. Among the most favorable notices was that in the Kansas City *Review of Science*, which described Williams as "a vigorous writer and a hard student" and noted that he "succeeded in producing a work which will be the authority on the subject treated until a better one is produced, which is likely to be a long time." The London *Westminster Review* also found little to criticize, stating, "The materials have been collected with great care . . . and though a member of an oppressed race cannot be expected to write calmly about the wrongs of his people, there is no needless or offensive vituperation."

Other reviewers were less tolerant of Williams's writing style but agreed on the value of the work. The London *Academy* noted, "If the writer could make a stern resolve to be less declamatory and more grammatical, it would tell favorably on any future literary effort. The imperfections of the work, however, do not detract from the interest it possesses." The *Literary World*, published in Boston, accused Williams of reveling in adjectives to the detriment of the book, then remarked, "Yet the work shows research and mental calibre."

One commentator, however, found the book practically worthless. The critic for the *Nation* regretfully remarked that he could not "avoid assigning this history a rank below its pretensions." The reviewer claimed he "would be glad to say it was readable, but he has not found it so; or a valuable book of reference, but it is not that; or intellectually remarkable, but, by the only standard of comparison which Mr. Williams would exact, it must be judged the crude performance of a mind in no way exceptionally endowed." Indeed, he asserted, "Its total effect is that of cramming, without the power to digest or arrange."

The reviewer for the *Magazine of American History* probably best expressed the book's true significance with the statement, "No one who fails to become acquainted with the contents of this book can claim to have a full understanding of American history, to which it forms a large and indispensable contribution." Yet decades would pass before most American historians grasped the vital role of the Afro-American experience in the nation's past.

In spite of its mixed reviews, Williams's *History of the Negro Race in America from 1619 to 1880* catapulted him to prominence. He became an often sought speaker and was appointed by President Chester Arthur in 1885 as U. S. Minister to Haiti— a position he was denied by the incoming Democratic administration. Officially practicing law in Boston, Williams spent much of his remaining years in travel, beginning in 1884 with his attendance at the World Conference on Foreign Missions in London. On one of his trips to Europe he met King Leopold of Belgium, who stimulated his interest in Africa, especially the Congo. By 1885 he had written articles on African geography and testified before a U. S. Senate committee, urging the recognition of the Congo Free State. His time, however, was increasingly spent in work on his second major book.

Even before his *History of the Negro Race in America from 1619 to 1880* was published, Williams began collecting materials for a study of the role of blacks in the Civil War. His *A History of the Negro Troops in the War of the Rebellion, 1861-1865* was published by Harper & Brothers in 1888 and had a definite thesis—that blacks had displayed remarkable valor and had played a crucial role in preserving the Union. His research was again extensive, drawing on both domestic and foreign manuscript sources, oral interviews, earlier secondary works, and the *Official Records of the War of the Rebellion.*

The book contains sixteen chapters. The first two examine the role of Negro soldiers in all parts of the world from ancient times to the Civil War. The next discusses the events leading to the war and is followed by five chapters on the debate over the use of black troops, the "idiosyncracies" of the Negro, and the problems faced by black soldiers. Six chapters, undoubtedly the best in the book, detail the participation of black troops in various locations. Chapter fifteen describes the treatment of black prisoners of war, and the final chapter

presents testimonies of officers and civilian leaders praising the performance of black soldiers.

Williams was well aware of the problems of writing about the recent past, noting in his preface, "in writing of events within living memory it requires both fortitude and skill to resist the invidious influence of interested friends and actors, . . . and to avoid partisan feeling and maintain a spirit of judicial candor." Although he had participated in several of the battles he described, he "relied very little on personal knowledge, preferring always to follow the official record." Perhaps in response to his critics' complaints regarding the intemperate language in his first book, Williams exclaimed, "I have spoken plainly it is true, but I have not extenuated nor set down aught in malice. My language is not plainer than the truth, my philippic is not more cruel than the crimes exposed, and my rhetoric is not more fiery than the trials through which these black troops passed, nor my conclusions without warrant of truth or justification of evidence."

His rhetoric was indeed more restrained; the villains are clearly identified, but with more subtlety. There are still overblown phrases; however, some are quite effective, such as his description of the late 1850s: "Slavery was like a dangerous coast with hidden reefs, where wild gales and stormy breakers blow and dash. It overshadowed every other question of national importance, and against its hidden reefs and treacherous currents the fierce gales of public events seemed driving the Ship of State." Williams's penchant for vivid language was most effectively employed in his descriptions of battles and camp life. He included many interesting anecdotes, some of which were not identified by source. Indeed, footnotes are infrequent in the book, but Williams described the work as "popular history" and sometimes noted the sources in the text.

A History of the Negro Troops in the War of the Rebellion received generally more favorable reviews than Williams's earlier volumes. In *Literary World* the reviewer noted that Williams deserved "congratulations for the intelligence, discretion, and excellent workmanship with which he prepared the book." The reviewer first stated, "Considering our common impressions of the racial source of it, it is remarkably well written. The tendency to 'fine writing' which might have been expected is slight, scarcely noticeable in fact; the style is manly, modest, strong; the book presents the facts, and presents them in an orderly, dignified and impressive form."

Once again the reviewer for the *Nation* was the least complimentary. In a joint review of Williams's book and Joseph T. Wilson's *Black Phalanx*, published at about the same time, he found both books lacking in orderly arrangement but preferred Williams's account in this respect. He asserted, "Both of these books show honest intentions and a certain amount of praiseworthy diligence . . . but both show a want of method and an inability to command their own materials, so that they leave the reader with a renewed interest in the subject, but with a very imperfect sense of clear comprehension."

Perhaps Dudley Taylor Cornish best summed up the book's strengths and weaknesses in *The Sable Arm: Negro Troops in the Union Army*, published in 1956. After noting Williams's extensive research, he declared, "But with all his excellent material and preparation and in spite of his obvious ability and intelligence, his story of the evolution of Union Negro soldier policy is far from clear. . . . [The book] is rich in battlefield anecdote and color, enlivened by reports from sometimes unidentified participants, but . . . it is overwritten to the point of tediousness. Williams weakened his work by continually overstating the case for the Negro soldier; he tried too urgently to show that every Negro was a gallant hero."

In 1889 Williams was commissioned by S. S. McClure to write a series of articles on the Congo. His trips there, against the wishes of King Leopold, convinced Williams of the injustices of Belgian rule, which he detailed in two 1890 publications, *An Open letter to His Serene Majesty Leopold II, King of the Belgians and Sovereign of the Independent State of Congo* and *A Report Upon the Congo-State and Country to the President of the Republic of the United States*. He also wrote *A Report on the Proposed Congo Railway* (1890) as a result of a request by Collis P. Huntington for him to examine the issue.

After extensive travels to British and Portuguese possessions in Africa and to Egypt, Williams returned to England in the spring of 1891 to write a longer work on the Congo. That summer, however, he became ill and died of tuberculosis and pleurisy on 2 August 1891, at the Palatine Hotel in Blackpool, England. He was survived by his wife, Sarah Sterett Williams, whom he had married in June 1874, and one son.

His brief forty-two years had been productive. Williams's work, still highly regarded, became an inspiration to other black historians. In 1921 Benjamin Brawley wrote that Williams "more than once wrote subjectively but his work was, on the whole,

written with unusually good taste. After thirty years some of his pages have, of course, been superseded; but his work is ever yet the great storehouse for students of Negro history." Twenty five years later John Hope Franklin noted, "For the most part, Williams wrote with deliberate restraint; employing satire subtlely, and elaborate description where necessary to give that glow to his work which had the effect of making it vivid." Writing at about the same time as Franklin, Vernon Loggins described that prose style as a mixed blessing: "emotional effect was Williams's highest stylistic achievement and at the same time his chief pitfall. He was too articulate."

Like George Bancroft, Williams wrote popular histories intended for a mass audience. His books, therefore, were not tightly documented, and they shared with Bancroft's the florid prose and subjectivity of the romantic school, as well as a view of history as progress through divine will. These features, though they were decried by later historians, helped make history immensely readable and entertaining. Williams followed Bancroft, too, in engaging in extensive research and thus providing a bridge to the "scientific school" of history.

Williams, however, labored under a handicap not experienced by Bancroft. As a black man he found some sources closed to him and suffered the psychological duality described by Du Bois. He seemed to accept some of the racist stereotypes held by most white scholars. While extolling the achievements of ancient Africans, Williams conceded, "To the candid student of enthnography, it must be conclusive that the Negro is but the most degraded and disfigured type of the primeval African." As a Christian minister, Williams explained this descent as a turning away from God, but declared, "The false religions of Africa are but the lonely and feeble reaching out of the human soul after the true God." Unable to reject completely the view of blacks held by white society, Williams nevertheless marshaled evidence to refute it.

Like other black scholars of his era, he was unable to avoid all the pitfalls entailed in reconciling the dual role of blacks as Negroes and Americans. He wrote for both blacks and whites in a conscious effort to improve the status of Afro-Americans. John Hope Franklin emphasized Williams's "intense devotion to objectivity," but, as Earle E. Thorpe noted in 1971, that objectivity was incomplete because Williams "was interested primarily in chronicling only the *achievements* of the race." If the racial climate of the age hampered black scholarly activity, however, doctrines of "white supremacy" also tainted the work of most white historians—with much less justification.

Biography:

John Hope Franklin, *George Washington Williams* (Chicago: University of Chicago Press, 1985).

References:

Philip Butcher, "George W. Cable and George Washington Williams: An Abortive Collabo-

ration," *Journal of Negro History*, 53 (October 1968): 334-344;

John Hope Franklin, "George Washington Williams, Historian," *Journal of Negro History*, 31 (January 1946): 60-90;

William J. Simmons, *Men of Mark* (Cleveland: G. M. Revell, 1887);

Earl E. Thorpe, *Black Historians: A Critique* (New York: Morrow, 1971), pp. 549-566.

Woodrow Wilson
(28 December 1856-3 February 1924)

Marcia G. Synnott
University of South Carolina

*SELECTED BOOKS: *Congressional Government: A Study in American Politics* (Boston: Houghton Mifflin, 1885); republished as *Congressional Government: A Study of the American Constitution* (London: Constable, 1914);

The State: Elements of Historical and Practical Politics. A Sketch of Institutional History and Administration (Boston: Heath, 1889; revised, 1898; London: Isbister, 1899);

Division and Reunion, 1829-1889 (New York & London: Longmans, Green, 1893);

An Old Master, and Other Political Essays (Boston & New York: Houghton Mifflin, 1893);

Mere Literature, and Other Essays (Boston & New York: Houghton Mifflin, 1896; London: Constable, 1914);

George Washington (New York & London: Harper, 1897);

When a Man Comes to Himself (New York & London: Harper, 1901);

A History of the American People, 5 volumes (New York & London: Harper, 1902); enlarged, documentary edition, 10 volumes (New York & London: Harper, 1918);

Constitutional Government in the United States (New York: Columbia University Press, 1908);

The New Freedom: A Call for the Emancipation of the

Generous Energies of a People, edited by W. B. Hale (New York & Garden City: Doubleday, Page, 1913; London: Chapman & Hall, 1913);

Why We Are at War; Messages to the Congress, January to April, 1917 (New York: Harper, 1917);

America and Freedom: Being the Statements of President Wilson on the War (London: Allen & Unwin, 1917);

President Wilson's State Papers and Addresses, edited by Albert Shaw (New York: Review of Reviews, 1917; enlarged, 1918); enlarged again as *The Messages and Papers of Woodrow Wilson*, 2 volumes (New York: Review of Reviews, 1924);

President Wilson's Great Speeches and Other History-Making Documents (Chicago: Stanton & Van Vliet, 1917; enlarged, 1919);

In Our First Year of the War: Messages and Addresses to Congress and the People, March 5, 1917 to April 6, 1918 (New York & London: Harper, 1918; enlarged, 1918);

The Bases of Durable Peace as Voiced by President Wilson (Chicago: Union League Club, 1918);

President Wilson's Addresses, edited by George McLean Harper (New York: Holt, 1918);

Guarantees of Peace: Messages and Addresses to the Congress and the People, January 31, 1918 to December 2, 1918, together with the Peace Notes to Germany and Austria (New York: Harper, 1919);

---

* This list excludes separately published speeches and other brief pamphlets.

Woodrow Wilson during his years as professor of jurisprudence and political economy at Princeton, 1890-1902 (Princeton University Archives)

International Ideals: Speeches and Addresses Made During the President's European Visit, December 14, 1918 to February 14, 1919 (New York & London: Harper, 1919);

Hope of the World: Messages and Addresses Delivered by the President between July 10, 1919 and December 9, 1919, including Selections from His Country-wide Speeches in Behalf of the Treaty and Covenant (New York: Harper, 1920);

Woodrow Wilson's Case for the League of Nations, compiled by Hamilton Foley (Princeton: Princeton University Press, 1923).

Collections: *The Public Papers of Woodrow Wilson*, edited by Ray Stannard Baker and William E. Dodd, 6 volumes (New York & London: Harper, 1925-1927);

The Papers of Woodrow Wilson, edited by Arthur S. Link and others, 49 volumes to date (Princeton: Princeton University Press, 1966-).

OTHER: Introduction to *The Autobiography of Benjamin Franklin*, edited by John Bigelow (New York: Century, 1901), pp. v-xix;

"The Significance of American History," preface to *Harper's Encyclopedia of United States History from 458 A.D. to 1902*, 10 volumes (New York: Harper, 1902), I: xxvii-xxxii;

"State Rights (1850-1860)," in *The Cambridge Modern History*, 13 volumes (Cambridge: Cambridge University Press, 1902-1912), VII: 405-442;

"The Variety and Unity of History," in *Congress of Arts and Sciences, Universal Exposition, St. Louis, 1904*, edited by Howard Jason Rogers, 8 volumes (Boston & New York: Houghton Mifflin, 1905-1907), II: 3-20.

PERIODICAL PUBLICATIONS: "Cabinet Government in the United States," *International Review*, 7 (August 1879): 146-163;

"Committee or Cabinet Government?," *Overland Monthly*, second series, 3 (January 1884): 17-33;

"The Study of Administration," *Political Science Quarterly*, 2 (July 1887): 197-222;

Review of James Bryce's *The American Commonwealth*, *Political Science Quarterly*, 4 (March 1889): 153-169;

"Preparatory Work in Roman History," *Wesleyan University Bulletin*, no. 5 (15 October 1889): 13-15;

"Mr. Goldwin Smith's 'Views' on Our Political History," *The Forum*, 16 (December 1893): 489-499;

"The Making of the Nation," *Atlantic Monthly*, 80 (July 1897): 1-14;

"The Reconstruction of the Southern States," *Atlantic Monthly*, 87 (January 1901): 1-15;

"Politics (1857-1907)," *Atlantic Monthly*, 100 (November 1907): 635-646;

"The Road Away from Revolution," *Atlantic Monthly*, 132 (August 1923): 145-146.

Woodrow Wilson, the historian and political scientist, will always be eclipsed by Wilson, the president of Princeton University, the governor of New Jersey, and the twenty-eighth president of the United States. Had he not attained, from 1902 to 1920, positions of educational and political statesmanship, his essays and books, all of which were written between 1877 and 1907, would probably be little read today. His historical and political writings remain essential, however, for interpreting his intellectual evolution and provide significant clues to some of his subsequent successes—and failures—as a skillful practitioner of both the art and the science of political leadership. "Wilson's political thought," commented the editors of *The Papers of Woodrow Wilson* (1966-   ), "was a continuing stream that expanded as it was fed by new tributaries." The study of government and administration was one major tributary; the study of American history was another.

Had greater opportunities not called Wilson from the professorial life, he might have completed his projected great work on "The Philosophy of Politics" and even achieved the goal that he set for historians in his essay "The Truth of the Matter" of interpreting in a sweeping synthesis the life of the American people. Although Wilson does not rank with the major historians of his era, he contributed, nevertheless, in six important ways to the development of historiography and history teaching. He was one of the first historians to view sectionalism as a movement involving all regions— New England, the Middle States, the South, and the West—rather than as solely a conflict between North and South; he was the first southerner to write an objective history of the sectional crisis, in which he introduced the concept that the United States became a nation as a result of the Civil War; and he was the first southerner since the Civil War to write a general history of the United States. By bringing southern history back into the national mainstream, Wilson epitomized, in the words of his biographer Arthur S. Link, "the American as Southerner." Fourthly, Wilson deserves recognition as one of the first "public" historians in that he applied what he had learned about political institutions and their evolution to the problems of government and administration. In addition to publishing scholarly works, Wilson sought to inform a broad reading public by writing popular, stylistically embellished biographies, essays, and histories, which were noted for their epigrammatic phrases and sweeping generalizations. Reacting against the "scientific" historical writing of his own times—monographs written for other scholars— Wilson argued that history served no great purpose unless it was widely read. Until he could become a "literary politician" like Walter Bagehot—an expert on the English constitution, editor of the London *Economist*, and a conservative spokesman— Wilson would be a "literary historian." Finally, at a time when the profession of history was in its fledgling stage, Wilson played significant roles in defining the purpose and scope of historical curriculum from secondary to graduate schools. De-

spite the fact that he neither produced a historical magnum opus nor inaugurated a major school of American historiography, Wilson's eight books, dozens of essays, and hundreds of addresses attest to an energy, commitment, and influence that few "pure" academicians ever demonstrate. Judged by his own times, he was a successful historian and political scientist; judged by later generations, his greatness as a maker of history and perhaps also as a prophet has dwarfed his earlier reputation as a scholar. In his memorial on Wilson, presented to the American Historical Association on 29 December 1924, Charles M. Andrews recognized that in spite of the limitations of his published writings Wilson's insight and expression raised "his work high above the commonplace and merely superficial into the atmosphere almost of the inspired." He "was more than a purveyor of popular history or an exponent of mere literature; he was in his historical contributions as in his statesmanship an interpreter of the lives and thoughts of the American people."

Thomas Woodrow Wilson was born in Staunton, Virginia, the first son and third of four children of the Reverend Dr. Joseph Ruggles and Janet (Jessie) Woodrow Wilson. His mother had been born in Carlisle, England, of Scots parents, while his father had been born of Scots-Irish parents in Steubenville, Ohio. From his southern birthright (the South was "the only place in the world, where nothing has to be explained to me"), Wilson gained a sense of place; from his Scots-Irish ancestry, a fierce pride and combative spirit; and from his middle-western connections, an appreciation that American nationality developed from the intermingling of diverse peoples and ideas. His experience of growing up in the South during the Civil War and Reconstruction deeply impressed on him the costliness of war and the realization that history was indeed something that happened to people. In 1857 Reverend Wilson became pastor of the First Presbyterian Church of Augusta, Georgia, at which, in December 1861, the General Assembly of the Presbyterian Church in the Confederate States was convened. His father also served as a Confederate army chaplain and coordinated army relief and medical work in Georgia. After the battle of Chickamauga in September 1863, the church was turned into a hospital and its yard became a detention camp for Union prisoners. In 1870 the family moved to Columbia, South Carolina, when Reverend Wilson was appointed professor in the Presbyterian Theological Seminary and made acting minister in that city's First Presbyterian Church.

Columbia still bore the scars of its burning five years before, and thereafter, young Wilson could remember with distaste Radical Republican rule by people whom he considered either unscrupulous carpetbaggers or ignorant blacks.

Nurtured emotionally, intellectually, and spiritually by a close association with his forceful father, Wilson developed both a sense of his own powers and of God's purpose in the world. At sixteen he experienced religious conversion and became a member of the First Presbyterian Church. From that time, his thoughts and actions were directed by a belief in God's universal design. Given Woodrow Wilson's deep religious orientation, he might have been destined for the ministry had not his father experienced double reverses in his own career: first, the loss of salary as acting minister and then the undermining of his position at the Theological Seminary. In 1874 the Reverend Wilson left Columbia to accept the call of the First Presbyterian Church of Wilmington, North Carolina. Thereafter, he freed the young Wilson to make his own career choices and sought consolation in his son's later educational and literary successes.

Having been prepared in small private schools in Augusta and Columbia, Woodrow Wilson attained average grades during 1873-1874 at Davidson College in North Carolina but was forced by poor health to return home. In September 1875 he entered the freshman class at the College of New Jersey (which became Princeton University in 1896). Graduating with a B.A. in 1879, thirty-eighth out of a class of one hundred and seven, Wilson had learned as much, if not more, from his own reading, debating, and friendships as he had from formal classroom instruction. Occasionally using the name of Atticus, he wrote his first essays on great statesmen: "Prince Bismarck" (November 1877) and "William Earl Chatham," the prize biographical essay (October 1878), both published in the campus *Nassau Literary Magazine*. As a law student at the University of Virginia (September 1879-December 1880), he published two biographical essays: "John Bright," in which he defended the Englishman's support for the Union during the Civil War by his own nationalist sentiments ("because I love the South, I rejoice in the failure of the Confederacy"); and "Mr. Gladstone, A Character Sketch," in which he expressed admiration for the English statesman's qualities of leadership. An essay on "Cabinet Government in the United States," published in the *International Review* (August 1879), indicated his future promise as a student of politics.

On the basis of another article, "Committee or Cabinet Government?," in *Overland Monthly* (January 1884), Wilson was awarded a fellowship in the Department of History, Politics, and Economics at the Johns Hopkins University, which he had entered the previous autumn. Neither his three-year study of law, which ill health forced him to conclude at home in Wilmington, nor his year's law practice (1882-1883) in Atlanta in partnership with Edward I. Renick, a University of Virginia Law School graduate, had held his interest. Nevertheless, he had learned English constitutional history, and he would later acknowledge in his 1901 *Atlantic Monthly* essay on "The Reconstruction of the Southern States" that "the American historian must be both constitutional lawyer and statesman in the judgments he utters."

At Johns Hopkins, then the premier American graduate school for the scientific study of history, government, and political economy, Wilson participated in the seminary of history and political science directed by Herbert Baxter Adams, who was assisted by Richard T. Ely and J. Franklin Jameson. Wilson soon persuaded Adams to free him from the assignments given other graduate students on institutional studies of government in the thirteen colonies, so that he could devote himself to analyzing how contemporary American government worked. Wilson justified Adams's opinion that he was his most able student by the publication of *Congressional Government: A Study in American Politics* (1885), which was accepted as his doctoral dissertation the following year. Dedicated to his father, Wilson's first and most enduring book contained, together with his earlier articles on cabinet government, the core of his thinking on politics. Influenced by Walter Bagehot's *The English Constitution* (1867) and by the fact that the United States had had a succession of weak presidents for almost twenty years, Wilson argued that the separation of executive and legislative authority in the American government contributed to presidential weakness and congressional irresponsibility. Though not advocating the adoption of cabinet government, he believed that responsibility could be effectively assigned by giving cabinet members seats in Congress, a feature of the constitution of the former Confederate States of America. The strength of *Congressional Government*, like that of virtually all his other works, was interpretation, not research; Wilson included only fifty-two citations. His analysis was astute and well written, but he had not personally visited Congress. The twenty-eight-year-old author received an impressive review in the *Nation*, praise in James Bryce's *The American Commonwealth* (1888), and in 1893 one of the first John Marshall prizes awarded in recognition of the work done by members of the Johns Hopkins historical seminary. In its first year, the book sold 2,000 copies (three editions); in 1900 Wilson wrote a new preface for the fifteenth edition; by that year the book had been translated into French. He never revised the text; by 1924, twenty-nine impressions had been made. Issued by Johns Hopkins as a paperback in 1956, with an introduction by Walter Lippmann, *Congressional Government* went through four editions within eight years; another paperback edition appeared in 1981. Lippmann commended the book for its "clinical description of a recurrent disease," while Bert James Loewenberg called it, in 1972, "one of the truly significant books in the literature of American democracy."

The executive-legislative deadlocks which Wilson criticized have appeared in subsequent administrations when different parties have controlled the presidency and Congress. Moreover, despite the increased powers of the Speaker of the House and the Rules Committee, the proliferation of congressional committees and subcommittees—there were 230 in 1956—has tended to fragment responsibility as it has promoted special interests. Wilson did recognize in his last major book, *Constitutional Government in the United States* (1908), a collection of lectures he delivered at Columbia University in March and April 1907 under the auspices of the George Blumenthal Foundation, that as a result of Grover Cleveland's presidency and the Spanish-American War, the presidency had become "the vital place of action." The growth of national power permitted the chief executive "to be as big a man as he can."

Among Wilson's half dozen other important writings on political subjects was "The Modern Democratic State," composed after October 1885 but not published except in a revised version entitled "Character of Democracy in the United States" in *The Papers of Woodrow Wilson*. In the essay Wilson outlined his ideological framework. "Only history," he wrote, "can explain modern democracy either to itself or to those who would imitate it." According to the editors of *The Papers of Woodrow Wilson*, this piece "marked a turning point in the direction of his *major* scholarly and political concerns—away from preoccupation with particular constitutional forms toward much broader subjects." The catalyst of this shift was his rereading of Sir Henry Maine, Herbert Spencer, and Bagehot's *Physics and Politics* (1873) in preparation for

his history lectures at Bryn Mawr College, Pennsylvania, where he accepted a position teaching history in the fall of 1885. As he began to study systematically "the origins, development, and problems of democracy in the modern world," he saw himself as an instrument of interpretation. Why could not, he asked, "the present age write, through me, its political *autobiography?*"

At the same time that Wilson was forging his ideas about the evolution of democratic government, the "fullest form of state life," he felt intense frustration that he was not personally involved in politics. On 24 February 1885, he had complained to his fiancée, Ellen Louise Axson, the daughter of a Rome, Georgia, Presbyterian minister, that he had "a passion for interpreting great thoughts to the world" and for inspiring "a great movement of opinion." The masses of people had to be incited to "great political achievements."

Wilson married Ellen Axson on 24 June 1885, shortly before he began at Bryn Mawr. Her love gave him self-confidence until her death in 1914. Edith Bolling (Mrs. Norman) Galt, the widow whom he married on 18 December 1915, fulfilled the same supportive role in Wilson's life. After three discontented years at Bryn Mawr, where he disliked teaching women—whose intellectual powers he considered inferior to men's—and clashed with the strong-willed dean, Martha Carey Thomas, Wilson broke his contract in order to teach men at Wesleyan University in Middletown, Connecticut (1888-1890). His growing family soon included three daughters: Margaret (1886), Jessie Woodrow (1887), and Eleanor Randolph (1889). He earned an additional $500 annually by returning every February from 1888 to 1898 to deliver at Johns Hopkins a series of twenty-five lectures on public administration.

In his essays and lectures on public administration, Wilson applied what he had learned from the study of politics to the solution of practical problems. American democracy operated inefficiently, he argued in "The Study of Administration," in *Political Science Quarterly* (July 1887), and therefore it needed to borrow and modify to its own pluralistic society the authoritarian bureaucratic methods of Prussia and France. He also proposed a type of commission plan of government for cities and the municipal ownership of gas works and street railways. His recognition that Baltimore and other cities needed such municipal reforms began to broaden his generally conservative political and social outlook.

The State: Elements of Historical and Practical

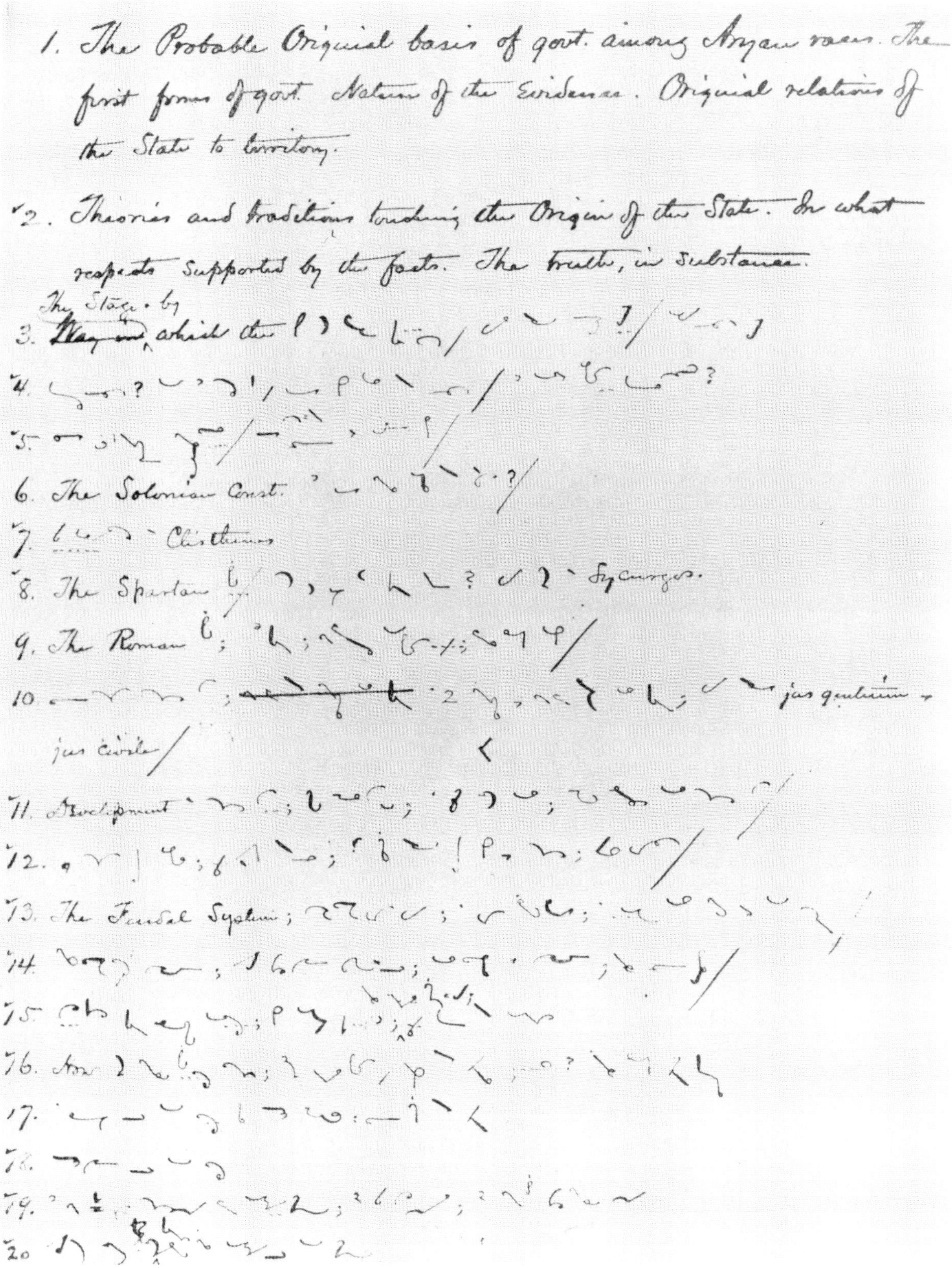
1. The Probable Original basis of govt. among Aryan races. The first forms of govt. Nature of the Evidence. Original relations of the State to territory.

2. Theories and traditions touching the Origin of the State. In what respects supported by the facts. The truth, in substance.

3. The Stage, by which the

4.

5.

6. The Solonian Const.

7. Clisthenes

8. The Spartan Lycurgus.

9. The Roman

10. jus gentium + jus civile

11. Development

12.

13. The Feudal System;

14.

15.

16. Now

17.

18.

19.

20

Wilson's notes for an outline of a chapter in The State *(1889), the college textbook that, in the words of Arthur S. Link, was probably the author's "greatest scholarly achievement" (Woodrow Wilson Papers, Library of Congress)*

Politics (1889), which D. C. Heath had commissioned him to write, was, according to Arthur S. Link, "probably Wilson's greatest scholarly achievement." Although applying Darwinian evolutionary principles to human history, Wilson repudiated laissez-faire economics and contended that the state must intervene to effect equality of opportunity. He performed a useful scholarly service, moreover, by making available to English readers what he had learned from French and German sources about political institutions in northwestern Europe. Adopted in courses at such leading universities as Harvard, Johns Hopkins, and Wisconsin, and overseas in Cambridge, England, and Bombay, India, *The State* sold over 1,000 copies a year and was republished almost annually for years. Wilson rewrote and updated it in 1898; twelve years later, Charles H. McIlwain revised the chapter on Norway and Sweden; and Edward Elliott made a final revision in 1918. It was translated into French (1902), Spanish (1904), and German (1913) and published in Paris, Madrid, and Berlin. *The State* was Wilson's major college text, but one such "dull fact book" was enough for him. After writing four chapters of a projected grammar and high school text, "The American State, Elements of Historical and Practical Politics in the United States," Wilson lost interest, preferring to devote himself to a "*novum organum* of political study."

His great work on "The Philosophy of Politics" would surpass, he believed, James Bryce's two-volume *American Commonwealth*, which he had favorably reviewed in *Political Science Quarterly* (March 1889). He commended the author for using the comparative approach in studying political institutions and for recognizing the evils that resulted from separating executive and legislative authorities. But there was still "to be accomplished the work of explaining democracy *by* America, in supplement of Mr. Bryce's admirable explanation of democracy *in* America." Wilson promised to concentrate his attention on the meaning of democracy and the development of American nationalism. His own views were in the process of change during the 1890s, a decade of economic and social tensions. In his 1889 *Atlantic Monthly* essay on the "Character of Democracy in the United States" (collected in *An Old Master, and Other Political Essays*, 1893) he saw it as "an adaptation of English constitutional government." By 1901, though acknowledging that American democracy was "an offshoot of European history," Wilson saw it as a great deal more; it was "a plain first chapter in the history of a new age."

He was not to write his work on "The Philosophy of Politics." Instead of completing this larger project, he wrote essays for magazines. The *Atlantic Monthly*, for example, paid a handsome fee for "Politics (1857-1907)." Somewhat prophetically, he described 1857 and 1907 as years "between-times, when the country had not yet consciously drawn away from its past, had not yet consciously entered its revolutionary future." On the eve of the Civil War and at the beginning of the era of Progressive reform, the United States was awaiting a realignment of political parties.

While preparing himself for the task of writing his great work on politics, Wilson spent happy and productive years at Princeton University, to which he had returned in 1890 as professor of jurisprudence and political economy. He was paid $3,000 (just $400 below the top professorial salary) and was blessed with a relatively light teaching load—after the first two years, he was required to present only four lectures a week, on public law and politics, as electives to juniors and seniors. Considerable time was devoted to the preparation of lectures, which he read for fifteen minutes each class period, but students remembered him as much for his epigrams, wit, and extensive remarks on contemporary affairs. Seven times Princeton seniors voted him "favorite professor." Offers of presidencies from other universities (Illinois, Texas, Virginia, and Washington and Lee) prompted Princeton trustees to give him a five-year contract guaranteeing him $2,500 annually above his salary. In return, Wilson, who in May 1896 had suffered a small stroke that made him unable to write with his right hand for a year, gave up his outside lecture series. (His intermittent cerebral-vascular disease caused other strokes in 1904 and 1906 and later the massive stroke of 3 October 1919, from which he never entirely recovered.) To earn money for his household, which included his wife's relatives and his father, Wilson had overextended himself with writing (earning over $4,000 in 1895) and lecturing. His lecture honorarium ranged from $50 to $400, and his essay fee ran usually from $100 to $150, sometimes to $300. For example, from October 1895 to January 1896 he received $250 for each series of six lectures that he delivered for the American Society for the Extension of University Teaching (Philadelphia) at the Brooklyn Institute of Arts and Sciences, New York, at Tarrytown, New York, and at Lancaster, Pennsylvania, on "Great Leaders of Political Thought": Aristotle, Machiavelli, Montesquieu, Edmund Burke (his new political mentor of the 1890s), Alexis de Tocqueville, and Walter Bagehot. From 1890 to 1902, he delivered more than one hundred addresses on the public lecture circuit on such topics as "Democracy" (most frequently used), "Leaders of Men," "Patriotism," "Religion and Patriotism," and "Liberty," all of which carried his message of the "gospel of order." He also found time for chapel talks at Princeton, addresses to the alumni, and for delivering the university's sesquicentennial address, "Princeton in the Nation's Service," 21 October 1896. From 1893 through 1902, Wilson wrote prolifically: nine volumes and thirty-five articles were published. They were of uneven quality, however, some marred by haste and superficiality. Yet for Wilson, it was indeed, as he put it, that "time in a man's life at which he comes to himself" by accepting both his responsibilities and limitations and by following the Christian doctrine of love and service.

Wilson's alma mater, however, would need a new and vigorous president before it could take its place among America's leading universities. In 1896 Wilson had hoped to bring Frederick Jackson Turner, a former Johns Hopkins student, from the University of Wisconsin to fill an anticipated American history chair at Princeton. But considering Turner's Unitarianism an impediment, President Francis Landey Patton and the Presbyterian trustees blocked his nomination. Wilson was so keenly disappointed by this example of religious intolerance that he thought of leaving Princeton.

The Wilson-Turner friendship and correspondence reveal that Wilson both encouraged and participated in Turner's breaking of new ground in historical interpretation. From the days in which they had stayed at the same rooming house in Baltimore, Wilson and Turner discussed and exchanged ideas. Wilson praised the paper which Turner presented to the historical seminary, 15 February 1889, on the fur trade in the Northwest, particularly in Wisconsin, for providing "the kind of atmosphere in which we can breathe." While Turner probably already had in mind the seed of what became his famous "frontier thesis," Wilson emphasized to him, in a letter of 13 August 1889, that historians had neglected the development of the national idea and the role played by the West. After hearing a draft in December 1892 of the essay on "The Significance of the Frontier in American History," which Turner read in July 1893 at the Chicago meeting of the American Historical Association, Wilson contributed the word *hither* to describe the place where the frontier began—on "the hither side of free land." Turner described his in-

tellectual relationship with Wilson in a lengthy letter written in 1919 to historian William E. Dodd: Wilson "was the older man and the riper scholar, and the greater mind. But I was bringing to him words from lands he didn't know, as he was giving me a new conception of the South, as well as a new outlook on politics in general." The Wisconsin historian came to see "the larger meaning of sectionalism as a movement between New England, Middle, Western and Southern sections, rather than between North and South." Reciprocally, Turner's ideas on the West as the least European and most American and democratic section of the country influenced Wilson's thinking about the evolutionary development of American democracy and nationalism.

In several writings Wilson indicated his affinity for Turner's kind of thinking, rather than for the scientific, institutional studies of origins taught at the Johns Hopkins historical seminary. Reviewing Goldwin Smith's *The United States, An Outline of Political History, 1492-1871* for the *Forum* (December 1893), Wilson asserted that "the history of the United States is very far from being a history of origins"; "it is a history of developments." Origins were European, while developments, "the great processes of modification . . . have really constituted the only part of our history that is distinctively our own." The American continent received European immigrants, stripped them of their inherited customs, and gave them a "radically different" life. Of all the sections, Wilson pointed to the Middle Colonies as "more distinctively American in constitution and character" than either New England or the South, and when their inhabitants moved westward, they adapted more quickly than did other settlers to the new conditions. Like Turner, Wilson concluded that the "most truly national" history was that of the West.

In his address on "The Course of American History" for the semicentennial of the New Jersey Historical Society on 16 May 1895, collected in *Mere Literature, and Other Essays* (1896), Wilson expanded on his theme that the "West" was "the great word of our history" and "the 'Westerner' . . . the type and master of our American life." On the one hand, the West intensified intersectional rivalries by making land, tariff, and slavery divisive issues. On the other, the West provided the agent of reconciliation in Abraham Lincoln, who "owed nothing to his birth, everything to his growth." Because Lincoln held all Americans in his heart, he "would have won them [southerners] back." Although he saw national history as "the history of its villages written large," Wilson preferred to discuss broad themes or great leaders rather than to engage in detailed research and analysis of local history.

In his preface on "The Significance of American History," written for *Harper's Encyclopedia of United States History from 458 A.D. to 1902* (1902), Wilson observed that the study of American history had completely changed during his own generation, from a story of the settlement, expansion, and development of a unique American nation—"a school exercise in puritan theory and cavalier pride"—to "a chapter written for grown men in the natural history of politics and society." United States history did indeed work out forces originating in England and Europe, but it was "no histrionic vindication of the Rights of Man" and the excesses of the French Revolution. In the American wilderness, European institutions were reduced to the simple forms of early village life. In time, the seeds of English polity brought with the settlers took root and led to the development of county governments. American nationality developed slowly through several different stages. Political connections with England were severed by the Revolution, but not until the War of 1812 were the United States' intellectual and psychological ties broken. The mixture of races—Europeans, Asians, and Africans—made the United States separate and distinct from other nations. Nevertheless, Wilson asserted, "nations grow by spirit, not by blood."

At a time when none of his contemporaries had been trained as a professional historian, Wilson moved easily between history and political science and contributed to both disciplines. His professional memberships and offices indicate the range of his interests: American Historical Association (member, 1884; first vice-president, 1922; and president, 1923); State Historical Society of Wisconsin (corresponding member, 1890); Phi Beta Kappa (founding member of New Jersey Beta Chapter at Princeton, 1895); American Philosophical Society (1897); American Social Science Association and National Institute of Arts and Letters (1898); American Academy of Political and Social Science (vice-president, 1898 and 1906); Alabama Historical Society (corresponding member, 1899); Circolo di Studi Sociali of the University of Genoa (foreign corresponding member, 1899); and the Hall of Fame at New York University (member of the first college of electors, 1900). Wilson published articles and reviews in *Political Science Quarterly*, which began publication in 1886; he declined to write for the *American Historical Review*, the journal of the American Historical Association first published in 1895. Nevertheless, he attended the association's annual meetings. For example, at the twelfth annual meeting of 29-31 December 1896, held at Columbia University, Wilson commented, on the same program with Andrew Cunningham McLaughlin, on Turner's paper "The West as a Field for Historical Study." Not only did Wilson approve of Turner's "dethronement of the Eastern historian" but he also vigorously defended the South from attacks by northern historians, who quoted travelers' accounts rather than visiting the region themselves. "There is nothing to apologize for in the past of the South," he asserted, "absolutely nothing to apologize for."

Proud of his southern birthright and ever ready to defend the right of southerners to fight for their principles, Wilson had earned a solid reputation as the first southerner to write an objective history of the sectional crisis. *Division and Reunion, 1829-1889*, published in the spring of 1893 as the third volume in Albert Bushnell Hart's Epochs of American History series, concentrated on the period up to the end of the Civil War, allotting only 47 of the 326 pages to the years 1865 to 1889. Slavery, which had become "indispensable" to the South, had put that region "out of sympathy" with the industrializing North. Although slavery was an anachronistic system, Wilson believed that its evils had been softened by paternalistic planters who used their leisure time to become statesmen. History was, nevertheless, on the side of the Union. Introducing new theories of secession and nationalism, Wilson argued that the North developed a new constitutional theory of national supremacy to support its industrializing economy, while the "stationary" South adhered to the state rights doctrines of the original Constitution. Historians, among them Turner, attacked this theory for failing to take into account the political reinterpretations by John C. Calhoun and other southerners as a result of the revival and expansion of cotton cultivation. In contrast, Wilson's second theory—that "the terrible exercise of prolonged" Civil War made the United States a nation—has been accepted as true. In regard to Reconstruction, he considered the effort to make the former slaves equal citizens totally misguided and accepted both the subordination and segregation of blacks as necessary conditions to insure racial harmony. *Division and Reunion, 1829-1889* received glowing reviews in the *New York Sun, Atlantic Monthly, Nation,* and *Political Science Quarterly.* It was republished frequently from 1893 to 1924; Edward S. Corwin enlarged and revised the book in 1909 and added new chapters in 1924.

Wilson declined Hart's offer to write a volume for the American Nation Series, because he wanted to work on "The Philosophy of Politics." However, he accepted Lord Acton's request that he write the chapter on "State Rights (1850-1860)" for volume seven of *The Cambridge Modern History*. Completed in December 1899 but not published until 1903, this essay was, together with *Division and Reunion*, Wilson's best historical writing. Though not based on new archival research, it eloquently expressed the contradictory principles and paradoxes inherent in winning—or losing—a Civil War: "Should the South win, she must also lose—must lose her place in the great Union which she had loved and fostered, and must in gaining independence destroy a nation. Should the North win, she would confirm a great hope and expectation, establish the Union, unify it in institutions, free it from interior contradictions of life and principle, set it in the way of consistent growth and unembarrassed greatness. The South fought for a principle, as the North did: it was this that was to give the war dignity, and supply the tragedy with a double motive. But the principle for which the South fought meant standstill in the midst of change; it was conservative, not creative; it was against drift and destiny; it protected an impossible institution and a belated order of society; it withstood a creative and imperial idea, the idea of a united people and a single law of freedom."

Whether or not one accepts Henry W. Bragdon's assessment that Wilson had ceased to be "half unrepentant Southerner and half transplanted Britisher," it is true that the study and writing of history had broadened his perspective. No doubt Wilson instinctively recognized that he could not fulfill a political mission in the United States unless he served the entire nation. As a southerner who became an American nationalist, he could help his native region rejoin the political mainstream. His wife Ellen believed he would be the South's "*greatest* son in this generation," because he would be a "more helpful son to her than any of those who cling so desperately to the past and the old prejudices."

Wilson studied history for two principal reasons: to learn what he described as its "object-lessons for the present" and to discover what the United States' mission should be. His view of what history meant was deeply influenced by his religious beliefs. "There is nothing," he said in an address on "Patriotism" in February 1903, "that gives a man more profound belief in Providence than the history of this country." Covenants and constitutions spelled out the specific roles and responsibilities that God, the nation, and the individual each assumed. In all areas of his thought—religious, political, and social—he rejected ideas and actions that separated man from God, divided states or sections from the nation, and fragmented society into classes. While the individual had to obey an absolute standard of morality, society based its ethics on the compromise of individual wills and expediency. "*Political sin*," said Wilson, was "the transgression of the law of political progress." Democracies, especially the United States, had moral missions and their greatest leaders should be Christian soldiers. Wilson could easily justify the duty of the United States to use its moral power to change the course of history.

The historian reached the height of his calling, said Wilson, in an essay published in *Century* magazine (1895) as "On the Writing of History" and later collected as "The Truth of the Matter" in *Mere Literature*, when he not only reproduced "the plan" in every nation's history but also reconstructed the life of the people. He did not revere the past for its own sake as did the antiquarians, and original research held little attraction for him. Histories, he insisted, were written for broad reading audiences, so that "the bulk of men may read and realize; and it is as bad to bungle the telling of the story as to lie, as fatal to lack a vocabulary as to lack knowledge." Since readers were "a poor jury," the historian had to digest the material first, then convey "a true impression of his theme as a whole," and interpret for them the "moral facts" of history. He should write, moreover, as if he were actually living in the time period of his subject, a method Wilson followed in his "Short History of the United States" (a project he abandoned, the content of which he incorporated into his 1902 *History of the American People*) and his 1897 biography of *George Washington*. Indeed, the 1896 *Century* essay, "On an Author's Choice of Company" (collected in *Mere Literature*), advised an author to "frequent the company in which you may learn the speech and the manner which are fit to last," but in writing "be genuinely and simply yourself." Although he never achieved "a literary life," in the sense of becoming a successful literary critic, a desire which he expressed to his wife in October 1887, Wilson did become a "literary historian."

Wilson was critical of the methods and style of other historians, both English (Thomas Babington Macaulay, Edward Gibbon, Thomas Carlyle, and John Richard Green) and American (Henry Adams, George Bancroft, John Fiske, Richard Hildreth, John Bach McMaster, Francis Parkman, James Ford Rhodes, and Justin Winsor). He had the most praise for Green's *A History of the English People* (1887), a comprehensive social history of a civilization which he chose as his model for *A History of the American People*. Wilson never fulfilled, however, the goals of scope, insight, and living narrative which he set for the ideal historian in his 1904 address on "The Variety and Unity of History" to the historical science section of the Congress of Arts and Sciences at the St. Louis Exposition.

In this, his most sophisticated statement on the discipline, Wilson divided all methods of writing history into two types: narrative history which used events to tell the large story of nations, peoples, and epochs; and historical analysis and interpretation which sought to explain the underlying causes and "silent forces" behind events by drawing upon many disciplines—politics, government, law, economics, religion, literature, art, and language. Proclaiming that "the day for synthesis has come," Wilson urged the marriage of literary art and "the conceiving imagination" (though not "the inventing imagination") with thorough scholarship. He advised the specialists to "construct their parts with regard to the whole and for the sake of the whole," so that they could cooperate with the general historians in developing a new synthesis. He found Acton's *Cambridge Modern History*, in which chapters were written by different historians, to be an important example of cooperative synthesis. Too many universities, however, trained graduate students to produce narrow dissertations before they fully grasped general history, with the result that most monographs proved "about as vital as the specimens in a museum." History should be revealed rather than simply recorded and interpretive rather than merely factual; then it would be capable of guiding statesmen, stimulating patriots, and checking tyrants.

Just as Wilson had allowed other interests and commitments to deflect him from writing "The Philosophy of Politics," so also he diverted his energies from producing a grand synthesis of American history to the writing of popular works: essays on great men, a biography of George Washington, and the lavishly illustrated five-volume *A History of the American People*. For example, Wilson composed "A Calendar of Great Americans" for *Forum* (February 1894), in which he chose Lincoln as "the supreme American of our history," who combined "rude Western strength" with "Eastern conservatism" and an understanding of the South. The other great Americans on his list were John Marshall, Daniel

Webster, Benjamin Franklin ("a sort of multiple American"), George Washington, Henry Clay, Sam Houston, Andrew Jackson ("a cyclone from off the Western prairies"), Ulysses S. Grant, Robert E. Lee (who fought "for a principle . . . scarcely less American than the principle of Union"), Patrick Henry, James Russell Lowell, and George Ticknor Curtis. He excluded from the list Alexander Hamilton and James Madison, because they remained English in their thinking; John Adams and John C. Calhoun, who were provincials; Asa Gray and Ralph Waldo Emerson, who were too universalist to be distinctly American; and Thomas Jefferson and Thomas Hart Benton, who were intellectually a "mixed breed." Whatever quarrel one might have with his selections and definition of Americanism, Wilson astutely predicted that the American of the future would be "the composite type of greatness," born of the national homogeneity that would result from the end of the frontier. From a "complete and consentaneous" nationality would "come our great literature and our greatest men."

For *George Washington*, his most sustained attempt at biography, Wilson was paid handsomely: $300 for each of the six installments serialized in *Harper's New Monthly Magazine* in 1896 and later substantial book royalties. The public loved it, but Henry Bragdon spoke for most historians when he called it "astonishingly bad" because it lacked balance (with 180 of 333 pages devoted to the 1732-1775 period), gave more attention to events of lesser importance (9 pages on General Edward Braddock's defeat, but only 2 pages on Yorktown), and painted "a saccharine picture of Colonial Virginia" in a quaint and ornate style. The biography evidently captivated Wilson's classmates, who honored him with a dinner and a copy of sculptor Jean-Antoine Houdon's bust of George Washington. Subsequently, Wilson attempted a biographical sketch in his introduction to the 1901 Century Classics edition of *The Autobiography of Benjamin Franklin*, in which he described his subject as "half peasant, only half man of letters," whose writing was "literature with its apron on." Wilson declined the offer of Richard Watson Gilder of the Century Company to write a biography of Robert E. Lee. In 1906 he submitted a proposal to Harper and Brothers, which they accepted, to write a life of Thomas Jefferson, but his energies were then completely absorbed by his battle to democratize Princeton by introducing a system of residential quadrangles.

During the heated controversy over the location of the graduate college, however, Wilson

Wilson with his first wife, Ellen Louise Axson Wilson, and their daughters (left to right), Margaret, Jessie, and Eleanor

wrote two important biographical sketches, one of Lee and the other of Lincoln. In his boyhood Wilson once saw Lee, whom he now portrayed as personifying the ideals of duty and service. Yet his presence radiated such "fire," that it was "best not incautiously to touch that man," for there was "something that makes it dangerous to cross him, that if you grapple with his mind you will find that you have grappled with flame and fire." In "Robert E. Lee," originally delivered as an address at the University of North Carolina on 19 January 1909, Wilson was, of course, describing his own personality and his reaction to alumni and faculty opposition at Princeton. Wilson's speech was published in the UNC *Record* in 1909, published separately in 1924, and collected in *Public Papers* (1925-1927). His 12 February 1909 centennial address in Chicago on "Abraham Lincoln: A Man of the People," also collected in *Public Papers*, portrayed his subject as the epitome of the morally informed leader who served both the forces of democracy and the larger interests of the whole nation. Wilson's biographical

sketches were thus partly autobiographical.

The popularity of *George Washington* made publishers eager to sign Wilson for other books. Harper and Brothers offered him a ten percent royalty on the retail price for a text on the "History of the United States for Schools," aimed particularly at southern schools. Interested in this project since 1893, Wilson completed several chapters by drawing in part on the manuscript on which he was then also working, a "Short History of the United States." When Harper and Brothers ran into financial difficulties, however, they sold their contracts for texts to the American Book Company. Wilson was unable to get his school text contract back, but under no pressure to finish, he let the project lapse. Harper and Brothers signed another contract with him for a general history of the United States, which would first be serialized in *Harper's* magazine, at $1,000 for each of twelve installments, with expected sales for the book itself to exceed 100,000. Convinced that it would be "a monumental, permanent work," as the publishers wrote to Wilson, they decided to "spare no pains or expense in making the setting worthy of the matter."

In January 1901 the first installment was published in *Harper's* magazine under the title of "Colonies and Nation: A Short History of the People of the United States," which became in revised form the first two volumes of his *A History of the American People*. But only about half the manuscript was published serially. The 280,000 words of the completed work were stretched to fill five volumes by means of generous margins, large type, almost 800 illustrations—by Howard Pyle, Howard Chandler Christy, Frederic Remington—and appendices with documents but no footnotes. Five American editions were published: in 1902 subscription, standard trade, and a special 350-copy alumni (bound in orange and black, Princeton's colors) editions; in 1910 a "popular" edition; and in 1918 a ten-volume edition, with additional sources and documents. A one-volume Swedish edition was published in 1916, followed by a two-volume French edition in 1918 and 1919. In spite of the fact that Wilson had earned over $40,000 from *A History of the American People* by 1910, he felt that Harper and Brothers had not sufficiently pushed the work and tried unsuccessfully to buy back the copyright.

For the most part, in writing his *History* Wilson drew upon printed sources for his information and used some of the material from his unpublished school and short histories. He did not do independent archival research, nor was he particularly concerned with factual accuracy. In a 26 January 1901 letter to Richard Watson Gilder, Wilson rationalized errors in the text: "I am not an historian: I am only a writer of history, and these little faults must be overlooked in a fellow who merely tries to tell the story, and is not infallible on dates." As he explained in his 1909 address on Lee, he had written the work "not to instruct anybody else, but to instruct" himself. He wanted "to find which way we were going" as a people.

Although better balanced than either *Division and Reunion* or *George Washington* because it attempted to relate American to European affairs, *A History of the American People* devoted 781 of its 1,748 pages to the era from first exploration and settlement to the adoption of the Constitution. While Wilson spent 106 pages on the Revolution, only 51 pages were given to the Civil War and a mere three and a half to the Mexican War. More space—10 pages—was allotted to the Ku Klux Klan than to the agrarian and labor movements of the

late nineteenth century. Political battles, such as Andrew Jackson's war on the Second Bank of the United States, received more attention than literature or social movements. Volume four, covering the years 1829 to 1865, repeated Wilson's interpretation in *Division and Reunion*, although he added a chapter on wartime social history, which drew heavily on Professor John Christopher Schwab's *The Confederate States of America, 1861-1865: A Financial and Industrial History of the South during the Civil War* (1901). He thus made Schwab's research available to the general public. Wilson treated the American Revolution and the Civil War objectively, but his conservative social bias showed in his uncomplimentary comments about the "multitudes of men of the lowest class from the south of Italy and men of the meaner sort out of Hungary and Poland, men out of the ranks where there was neither skill nor energy nor any initiative of quick intelligence." Although he praised the Chinese as more desirable "as workmen if not as citizens, than most of the coarse crew" of European immigrants, he described "the thrifty, skilful Orientals" as people whose "yellow skin and strange, debasing habits of life" made them seem "hardly fellow men at all, but evil spirits, rather." These comments later caused Wilson political embarrassment when he ran for the governorship of New Jersey. Actually, Wilson was willing to keep the door open to immigrants longer than many Americans. His conservative views, including admiration for Grover Cleveland and approval of the Spanish-American War, were warmly applauded. His colorful and perceptive characterizations of leaders and his literary style, somewhat less anachronistic than that of *George Washington*, also appealed to many readers.

Professional historians criticized both Wilson's lack of research and his writing, which did not convey concepts but rather impressions and atmosphere. In his May 1903 review in the *Annals of the American Academy of Political and Social Science*, Claude Halstead Van Tyne pointed out that Wilson wrote the "history of the politics of the people" rather than a history of the people, broadly conceived, an observation that George Louis Beer had also made in his *New York Critic* review of February 1903. Although the work was an "able summary," said Van Tyne, it could have been condensed into two volumes. Moreover, Wilson did not provide "more than a small measure of the results of analytical scholarship in American history." By the time "first-hand information has filtered through several secondary histories" before reaching the author, its meaning has been too frequently reversed. In the *American Historical Review* (July 1903), Frederick Jackson Turner praised Wilson's "often brilliant" style but criticized his brevity, if not superficiality, in treating "the deeper undercurrents of economic and social change." Writing in an "artistic literary form," Wilson compressed and disguised his facts to achieve a work of "interpretation." In spite of his factual errors, Turner acknowledged that Wilson was "the first Southern scholar of adequate training and power who has dealt with American history as a whole in a continental spirit."

By his own tenets of historical writing, Wilson had failed to reconstruct the life of the American people. Nevertheless, he wrote history that people paid to read: the story of great leaders, historical turning points, and the processes of political change. In addition, he also performed another service in defining the purpose and scope of the history curriculum. He was a member of the Conference on History, Civil Government, and Political Economy, which met in Madison, Wisconsin, 28-30 December 1892, to discuss and then report recommendations on the teaching of these subjects to the Committee of Ten of the National Council of Education of the National Educational Association. Since secondary schools were preparing most students "for life" rather than for college, Wilson strongly urged that they provide "a literary teaching of history," which would "put children into the spirit of the times which they are studying." Secondary school pupils should first be intrigued by the "*story*" of a country, which in the case of Rome also includes great literature; as college students they would be taught the scientific critical history of Rome. Wilson proposed an eight-year general program for the study of biography, mythology, and history (American, Greek and Roman, French, English, and civil government), with no less than three forty-minute periods per week devoted to these areas. The conference adopted the substance of Wilson's proposals, and its report, together with those of the other conferences, shaped secondary-school curricula until World War I. Wilson also served, in 1906 and 1907, as president of the Association of Colleges and Preparatory Schools of the Middle States and Maryland. His reputation as both scholar and educator was attested in 1901 when President Daniel Coit Gilman invited him to succeed Herbert Baxter Adams as professor of American and institutional history at the Johns Hopkins University. From 1887 to 1910, moreover, Wilson received eleven honorary degrees; ten were

LL.D.'s from Wake Forest College (1887), Tulane University (1898), Johns Hopkins University and Rutgers College (1902), University of Pennsylvania and Brown University (1903), Harvard University (1907), Williams College (1908), Dartmouth College (1909), and Princeton University (1910); Yale University conferred on him a Litt.D. in 1901.

After Wilson was elected president of Princeton University on 9 June 1902 he had to put aside scholarly interests. His presidential duties forced him to decline an invitation to address the meeting of the History Association of the Middle States: "I have ceased to be an historian," he explained, "and have become a man of business." But Wilson continued to apply the lessons he learned from history to university administration and then later to the governorship of New Jersey and the presidency of the United States. Just as he had criticized sectionalism as counter to the interests of the nation as a whole, so also he attacked the interests of moneyed alumni as counter to the welfare of Princeton University. As he swung decidedly toward Progressivism after 1908, he carried to the national arena his attack on selfish men of wealth and advocated that government curb the excesses of big business. In 1910 the "literary politician" was elected Democratic governor of New Jersey. While campaigning for United States president in Baltimore in April 1912, Wilson pointed to "the lesson of history . . . that every set of institutions and every nation is renewed out of the mass of unknown men." No one could predict who would become the leaders of a future generation—or its "saviors." His campaign speeches, collected in *The New Freedom* (1913), and his public addresses and state papers as president of the United States are more properly considered as historical documents rather than as his historical writings, which he set aside after 1907. He wrote one last historical essay, "The Road Away from Revolution," published in *Atlantic Monthly* as well as separately in 1923, in which he expressed several interesting observations and predictions. He correctly interpreted the Russian Revolution as "the product of a whole social system" that had denied most Russians their "rights and privileges." Only by democracy enlightened by "a Christian conception of justice," he said, could the world be made "safe against irrational revolution." He left this warning: "Our civilization cannot survive materially unless it be redeemed spiritually."

Wilson's significance as a historian is still debated, as is his role as a maker of history. In his 1967 biography, Henry Wilkinson Bragdon contended that Wilson's "reputation as a historian would be higher if he had written only *Division and Reunion*," since "none of his three books on American history is read today." Nevertheless, in the last fifteen years, his writings have been republished, both individually and as part of *The Papers of Woodrow Wilson*, the comprehensive editorial project directed by Professor Arthur S. Link of Princeton. In 1985 the following were in print: *Congressional Government; A Crossroads of Freedom: Nineteen Twelve Campaign Speeches of Woodrow Wilson; Division and Reunion, 1829-1889; Mere Literature & Other Essays; The Theory of the State*, a two-volume republication of *The State; An Old Master: And Other Political Essays;* and *On the Writing of History*—a list which demonstrates Wilson's continued appeal to readers.

Letters:
Woodrow Wilson: Life and Letters, edited by Ray Stannard Baker, 8 volumes (Garden City: Doubleday, Page, 1927-1939).

Bibliography:
Laura Shearer Turnbull, *Woodrow Wilson: A Selected Bibliography of His Published Writings, Addresses, and Public Papers* (Princeton: Princeton University Press, 1948; republished, Port Washington, N.Y. & London: Kennikat, 1971).

Biographies:
Arthur S. Link, *Wilson: The Road to the White House* (Princeton: Princeton University Press, 1947);

Henry Wilkinson Bragdon, *Woodrow Wilson: The Academic Years* (Cambridge: Belknap Press of Harvard University Press, 1967);

George C. Osborn, *Woodrow Wilson: The Early Years* (Baton Rouge: Louisiana State University Press, 1968);

John M. Mulder, *Woodrow Wilson: The Years of Preparation*, supplementary volume to *The Papers of Woodrow Wilson* (Princeton: Princeton University Press, 1978);

Edwin A. Weinstein, *Woodrow Wilson: A Medical and Psychological Biography*, supplementary volume to *The Papers of Woodrow Wilson* (Prince-

ton: Princeton University Press, 1981).

References:
Marjorie L. Daniel, "Woodrow Wilson—Historian," *Mississippi Valley Historical Review*, 21 (December 1934): 361-374;

Michael Kraus, *The Writing of American History* (Norman: University of Oklahoma Press, 1953), pp. 213-217;

Arthur S. Link, "Woodrow Wilson: The American as Southerner," *Journal of Southern History*, 36 (February 1970): 3-17;

Bert James Loewenberg, *American History in American Thought, Christopher Columbus to Henry Adams* (New York: Simon & Schuster, 1972), pp. 409-421;

George C. Osborn, "The Influence of Joseph Ruggles Wilson on His Son Woodrow Wilson," *North Carolina Historical Review*, 32 (October 1955): 519-543;

Louis Martin Sears, "Woodrow Wilson," in *The Marcus W. Jernegan Essays in American Historiography*, edited by William T. Hutchinson (Chicago: University of Chicago Press, 1937), pp. 102-121;

Wendell H. Stephenson, ed., "The Influence of Woodrow Wilson on Frederick Jackson Turner," *Agricultural History*, 19 (October 1945): 249-253;

Laurence R. Veysey, "The Academic Mind of Woodrow Wilson," *Mississippi Valley Historical Review*, 49 (March 1963): 613-634;

Francis P. Weisenburger, "The Middle Western Antecedents of Woodrow Wilson," *Mississippi Valley Historical Review*, 23 (December 1936): 375-390.

Papers:
The major collection of Wilson's papers is at the Library of Congress. There are small collections of correspondence at the Princeton University Library and some records of Wilson's Princeton presidency at the Princeton University Archives.

Justin Winsor

(2 January 1831-22 October 1897)

L. Moody Simms, Jr.
Illinois State University

SELECTED BOOKS: *History of the Town of Duxbury, Massachusetts, With Genealogical Registers* (Boston: Crosby & Nicholls, 1849);

A Bibliography of the Original Quartos and Folios of Shakespeare With Particular Reference to Copies in America (Boston: Osgood, 1876);

Shakespeare's Poems. A Bibliography of the Earlier Editions (Cambridge, Mass.: Wilson, 1879);

Historical Sketch of the Colony and County of Plymouth (Boston: Walker, 1879);

The Reader's Handbook of the American Revolution, 1761-1783 (Boston: Houghton, Osgood, 1880);

Massachusetts (Boston: Little, Brown, 1882);

A Bibliography of Ptolemy's Geography (Cambridge, Mass.: Wilson, 1884);

The Kohl Collection of Maps Relating to America (Cambridge: Library of Harvard University, 1886);

The Manuscript Sources of American History; An Address Before the American Historical Association, May 21, 1887 (New York, 1887);

The Cartographical History of the North-eastern Boundary Controversy between the United States and Great Britain (Cambridge, Mass.: Wilson, 1887);

Christopher Columbus and How He Received and Imparted the Spirit of Discovery (Boston: & New York: Houghton Mifflin, 1891; London: Low, 1891; revised, Boston & New York: Houghton Mifflin, 1892);

The Pageant of Saint Lusson, Sault Ste. Marie, 1671. An Address Delivered at the Annual Commencement of the University of Michigan, Thursday, June 30, 1892 (Ann Arbor: University of Michigan Board of Regents, 1892);

The Results in Europe of Cartier's Explorations, 1542-1603 (Cambridge, Mass.: Wilson, 1892);

Cartier to Frontenac. Geographical Discovery in the Interior of North America in Its Historical Relations, 1534-1700 (Boston & New York: Houghton Mifflin, 1894); republished as *Geographical Discovery in the Interior of North America in Its Historical Relations, 1534-1700* (London: Low, Marston, 1894);

The Mississippi Basin. The Struggle in America between England and France, 1697-1763 (Boston & New York: Houghton Mifflin, 1895); republished as *The Struggle Between England and America, 1697-1763* (London: Low, Marston, 1895);

The New-England Indians: A Bibliographical Survey, 1630-1700 (Cambridge, Mass.: Wilson, 1895);

The Westward Movement. The Colonies and the Republic West of the Alleghanies, 1763-1798 (Boston & New York: Houghton Mifflin, 1897).

OTHER: *Journal of an Expedition against Quebec, in 1775, under Colonel Benedict Arnold. By Joseph Ware, of Needham, Mass.,* edited by Winsor (Boston: Printed by Thomas Price, 1852);

The Memorial History of Boston, Including Suffolk County, Massachusetts, 1630-1880, edited by Winsor, 4 volumes (Boston: Osgood, 1880-1881);

Narrative and Critical History of America, edited with contributions by Winsor (8 volumes: volumes 3 and 4, Boston: Osgood, 1885; volumes 1, 2, and 5-8, Boston & New York: Houghton Mifflin, 1886-1889; 8 volumes, London: Low, Marston, Searle & Rivington, 1886-1889);

Was Shakespeare Shapleigh? A Correspondence in Two Entanglements, edited by Winsor (Boston & New York: Houghton Mifflin, 1887).

PERIODICAL PUBLICATION: "The Perils of Historical Narrative," *Atlantic Monthly,* 66 (September 1890): 289-302.

Justin Winsor, librarian, editor, historian, is little known among contemporary historians. His commitment to scientific and collaborative history became unfashionable long ago. But Winsor's eclipse as a historian has been paralleled by his heightened relevance to modern librarianship. His insistence on professional autonomy, his remarkable administrative skills, and his unfailing dedication remain benchmarks for professional librarians. Winsor deserves wider recognition among today's professional historians as a pioneer in their own field of study. When his masterwork, the eight-volume *Narrative and Critical History of America,* was completed, it served as a monument to those critical historians who flourished from 1848, the year the last volume of Jared Sparks's *Library of American Biography* was published, to 1889, when Winsor's final volume appeared. For some forty years, the *Narrative and Critical History of America* was an important force in the realm of historical scholarship.

Born in Boston, Massachusetts, on 2 January 1831, Justin Winsor was the son of Nathaniel Winsor, Jr., a successful merchant, and Ann Thomas Howland Winsor. He was a descendant of Samuel Winsor of Duxbury, Massachusetts, and of *Mayflower* voyager John Howland. Reminders of his colonial past surrounded him during frequent vis-

its to his father's ancestral home. Even as a boy he was proud of his Pilgrim ancestry and demonstrated an interest in the town of Duxbury.

Young Winsor briefly attended a boarding school in Sandwich, Massachusetts, and then enrolled at the Latin Grammar School in Boston. While there, he attended meetings of the New-England Historic Genealogical Society and began research for what became his first book. Growing out of Winsor's love of ancestral traditions and local lore, *History of the Town of Duxbury, Massachusetts, With Genealogical Registers* was published in 1849, the year he entered Harvard College. Based on public records, interviews, and local traditions, it reveals that Winsor had already developed some sophistication in the study of local and family history. A good balance exists between the book's narrative material and the genealogical registers. Winsor would return later in life to historical studies, but only after pursuing successive careers as a poet and literary critic and as a librarian.

Attracted by the literary profession, Winsor read widely in modern literature and biography and attended local dramatic productions while at Harvard. However, he remained uninterested in his routine assignments and early demonstrated a disdain for the prevailing classical curriculum, which he found lifeless. Growing increasingly bored and restless, he hastily composed theatrical farces and offered them—unsuccessfully—to a Boston drama company. His class standing fell and subsequent disciplinary action led to his suspension for a semester. Against his parents' wishes, he left Harvard during his senior year and did not receive his degree until fifteen years later.

In October of 1852, Winsor sailed for Europe. Spending two years in Paris and Heidelberg, he studied French and German and continued to read voraciously. He tested his new skills by translating poetry, some of which would be published after his return home. Letters to his parents dating from this period reveal that Winsor was determined to earn his living by writing. By correspondence, he also proposed marriage to Caroline Tufts Barker, a young woman he had courted while he was at Harvard.

Arriving in Boston in September 1854, Winsor launched a vigorous—and ultimately rather undistinguished—literary career. For over a decade, despite his energy and tenacity, artistic fame would elude him. Following his marriage to Caroline Barker on 18 December 1855, the couple was given quarters in his family's spacious new home on Boston's fashionable Blackstone Square. From its li-

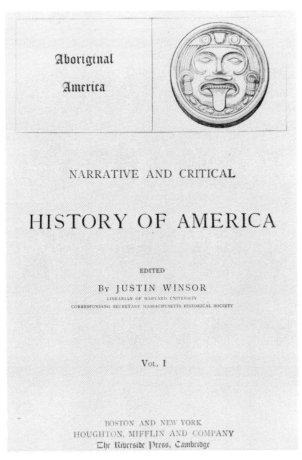

Title page for the first of Winsor's eight volumes planned to summarize and comment upon the work of scholars in all areas of American history

brary, which Winsor had copied from European models, he made his forays into the literary world.

From 1855 to 1858, the new *Crayon* magazine (New York) published thirty-five of Winsor's poems, many of them translations of German romantic poets, and twenty-six of his essays. In addition to serving as literary editor of the *Crayon* for two years, Winsor became the Boston literary correspondent for the *New York World*, supplying regular reports of publishing news. Because poor eyesight prevented him from serving in the Massachusetts militia, he remained at work in Boston during the Civil War. Winsor's letters and literary notes on a wide variety of topics—especially Shakespearean criticism and the definition of art—were published in the *Round Table* (New York) from 1863 to 1868. During the war, he drafted a lengthy manuscript (never published) on the life of David Garrick, whose career in the theater had interested him since 1850.

Though Winsor's work as a poet, essayist, and literary critic won him considerable local recognition, his prose and verse compositions were often ponderous, contrived, and laboriously rendered. His work would not survive in even the most comprehensive literary anthologies. His appreciation for great literature simply was not matched by his skills as literary artist or critic.

Winsor's management of the Boston Public and Harvard University libraries marked more significant career developments. Friendship with Lillian Woodman Aldrich led to his appointment in late 1866 to the Board of Trustees of the Boston Public Library, where he initially served on the finance committee. In 1867 his prodigious energy and family name earned him the chairmanship of the library's examining committee. With characteristic zeal, he produced an examiner's report (1867) which would be hailed in years to come as a masterwork of statistical analysis. The most thorough report ever prepared by the trustees, it reveals Winsor's remarkable grasp of the broad range of the library's activities.

When the library's superintendent, Charles Coffin Jewett, died in 1868 the trustees named Winsor temporary, then permanent, director. Though he lacked library experience, he was well suited for the post in other ways. He was ambitious and energetic; he was a proper Bostonian; he had a local reputation as a literary man; and he came from a family with financial and social connections in Boston. For Winsor, the position as director gave him a focus for his drive to be of service.

The nine years of Winsor's administration of the Boston Public Library showed a marked development in both the growth and usefulness of the library. He was interested in getting the library's books into the hands of users. His annual reports, rich in statistics and general suggestions; his innovative promotion of reading guides, popular fiction, branch libraries, Sunday opening, a shelf list with entries on cards; and his bibliographical and historical notes in the library's catalogues and bulletins focused the attention of the library world on Boston. Winsor's hallmark became his thoughtful and "scientific" approach to library management.

Playing an instrumental role in the formation of the American Library Association in 1876, Winsor was selected as its first president, a position he would hold until 1885. He also aided in the founding of the *American Library Journal* (later the *Library Journal*). Now considered America's foremost librarian, Winsor was sought for advice on almost all areas of librarianship. Having numerous foreign contacts, he earned the respect of leading European librarians. In 1877 he led the American delegation to the first International Conference of Librarians in London.

Though under Winsor's administration the Boston Public Library prospered, from time to time he became embroiled in conflicts with local authorities. In September of 1877 he resigned his post to succeed John L. Sibley as librarian of Harvard College. At Harvard, where Winsor remained until his death, he continued to concentrate on fostering use of library resources rather than on merely accumulating them. Winsor increased the influence of the library; his broad scholarship and his recognition of the new methods of instruction then coming into vogue in the college made the library, in his words, "the centre of the university system," "indispensable and attractive to all." Among his accomplishments were reclassifying books, unifying various small campus libraries under the main library, allowing stack privileges to students, enlarging the reserve collection, and improving the library facility. By way of encouraging interlibrary loans, he had published a union list of serial publications in Boston-Cambridge area libraries.

In his various library posts, Winsor worked toward liberalizing the relations between libraries and their users. In spite of his intense interest in his own institution, he found time for promoting the library movement throughout the country. "For Winsor," according to Wayne Cutler and Michael H. Harris in their introduction to a collection of Winsor's writings published in 1980, "the library was not a literary retreat from reality, but a workshop for exploring, ordering, and promoting the creative forces of human progress." "His library," they maintain, "was not so much a place or an institution, but a process, a habit of producing that was ignited by an explosive passion for knowledge and sustained by a missionary zeal for self-education."

By the time he became librarian of Harvard College, Winsor had long wanted a situation in which to pursue further historical research. He found such circumstances at Harvard, and it is likely that his contacts in the college stimulated his own historical interests. Undoubtedly, Winsor's own work proved of great value in supplementing the efforts of Albert Bushnell Hart and Edward Channing to establish the respectability of American history at Harvard.

Winsor produced a *Historical Sketch of the Colony and County of Plymouth* in 1879. Thirty years

earlier, he had published his work on Duxbury, where his paternal forebears had lived. The new volume was devoted to a study of an area connected with his maternal ancestor John Howland. Inspired by the centennial anniversary of the American Revolution, Winsor published *The Reader's Handbook of the American Revolution* in 1880. For at least the next fifty years it remained an indispensable reference source.

In New England an enterprising Boston publisher named Clarence Frederick Jewett was promoting the writing of town and county histories. He had already published under his own imprint several local histories, one of which was a cooperative work, before he approached Winsor to edit a history of Boston. Though still engaged with his *Reader's Handbook* and other work, Winsor accepted Jewett's proposition. He quickly demonstrated an exceptional executive ability as well as his extraordinary learning. After carefully planning the work, he solicited contributions on all phases of Boston's history from seventy contributing authors. He brought the project to completion in three years and ably saw through the press the four volumes which comprise *The Memorial History of Boston, Including Suffolk County, Massachusetts, 1630-1880* (1880-1881). The volumes were published by James R. Osgood and Company, to which Jewett had sold his rights. In 1897 historian Edward Channing proclaimed it to be the best work of its kind produced in any country up until that time.

During the period between the publication of Winsor's first historical work in 1849 and his renewed efforts at historical research and publication in the late 1870s and early 1880s, important changes had taken place in the writing of history in the United States. By the 1870s, the influence of Leopold von Ranke had become paramount. The great German historian had, it was thought, worked out a scientific method to arrive at objective truth; the historian had been freed from preconceived ideas. A growing number of students of America's past developed a reverence for data, for the publication of unexpurgated documents and letters, and for the straightforward presentation of events. As American historical writers ceased to consider their work as a branch of literature, they practiced critical analysis and claimed for history the exalted position given to those subjects considered scientific.

Though occasionally proposed, the cooperative writing of American history had not been used in a large project prior to Hubert Howe Bancroft's massive multivolume history of western North

America, which began to appear in 1874. During the 1880s and 1890s, the cooperative concept was utilized for three monumental series—the American Commonwealths, the American Statesmen biographies, and Winsor's *Narrative and Critical History of America.*

At the time that the first volume of *The Memorial History of Boston* appeared, Jewett suggested a new project to the busy Winsor. He proposed to sponsor a history of the United States compiled in the same manner as the Boston history. Agreeing to undertake this assignment in 1880, Winsor had some definite ideas about what the purpose and nature of such a work should be. He had no desire to make the projected volumes a "model for the general writing of history based on cooperative and critical methods." "There is no substitute," he maintained, "for the individuality of an historian." Proposing that the project be a summary of the work that had been done in every area of American history, Winsor conceived of each chapter as a monograph by the scholar "most entitled to be heard" on the specific phase of history to be covered. Given his love for facts and detail, Winsor had planned originally to edit only a critical history. Yet he feared such a work would not gain a wide audience. Modifying the overall plan of the work, he decided to include a narrative as well as a critical chapter on each topic. The narrative accounts would make the work more readable and more marketable. Subsequent scholars would profit from critical commentary on the sources. Such an arrangement enabled Winsor to bridge the growing gap between history as literature and history as science and gained him acceptance and respect from both camps.

Winsor drew up a prospectus for the *Narrative and Critical History of America* and sent it to historical societies throughout the country. His monument to critical scholarship would grow out of the materials haphazardly gathered by these organizations. The Massachusetts Historical Society, of which Winsor was a member, viewed the project with special favor. Winsor selected thirty-nine men to contribute chapters for the *Narrative and Critical History.* Only eight were from New England; the rest were scattered throughout the United States. Since the great majority were from the Atlantic states, it is not surprising that the work's emphasis falls on colonial America. Though Winsor enlisted several Harvard historians, he relied more heavily on amateur writers.

From 1885 to 1889, the *Narrative and Critical History of America* was published in eight volumes

under Winsor's editorship. His thorough acquaintance with the sources of American history and his exhaustive bibliographical knowledge are evident throughout the work. Winsor wrote about half of the *Narrative and Critical History.* In addition to providing most of the critical bibliographical essays in the work, he also wrote many narrative sections credited to others. Volumes one through five contain a history of North and South America to the eighteenth century; six and seven deal with the United States from 1763 to 1850; the last volume continues with the later history of Portuguese, Spanish, and British America. It is notable that Winsor did not think of America solely as the region comprising the United States.

The first volume in the series, subtitled *Aboriginal America,* reflects contemporary fascination with primitive America. Winsor, who had special interests in geography, cartography, and the earliest discoveries, wrote on Lahontan, Hennepin, Marquette, and Joliet. In volume six Mellen Chamberlain contributed a chapter on the American Revolution which broke new ground in emphasizing the Navigation Acts among the causes of the conflict. The work as a whole reveals the disinclination of nineteenth-century historians to deal with recent history; the Civil War, for example, is simply alluded to at the end of a chapter on the history of the Constitution by George T. Curtis. Winsor brought together some of the notes in his vast collection on the manuscript sources of American history in an appendix to the work; he also added a list of printed authorities.

Completed in 1889, the *Narrative and Critical History* is a monument to meticulous scholarship which will always be useful. The notes alone still deserve the attention of students of American history. They opened the way for many areas of historical investigation. Edward Channing maintained that Winsor "made the scientific study of American history possible by making available the rich mines of material." Even so, the series is not without flaws. Winsor's own writing lacks grace and bears the marks of hasty composition. The work as a whole reflects the interests of the period's older scholars— most of them amateurs—and is not representative of the views of contemporary younger historians. The latter pointed out in reviews the preponderance of material on the age of exploration and discovery and also noted that the narrative did not extend beyond 1850. A group of younger scholars—almost all of them academicians—was brought together under the editorship of Albert Bushnell Hart at the turn of the century to produce the American Nation series, a twenty-seven-volume collaborative work which brought American history to the end of the nineteenth century and incorporated the latest research.

The year 1884 marked the copyrighting of the first completed volumes in Winsor's *Narrative and Critical History* and the birth of the American Historical Association. Skilled amateurs were at work on Winsor's monumental project at the very moment that the pace of the professionalization of the study of history in the United States quickened. Winsor chaired the organizational meeting of the American Historical Association in 1884, and two years later, that organization named him its president.

Upon completion of his editorial labors on the cooperative histories of Boston and the Americas, Winsor reflected on "The Perils of Historical Narrative" in an 1890 article published in *Atlantic Monthly*. No scholar had a greater love of facts than Winsor; facts were indeed most important. Yet a scholar must go further, Winsor observed in his essay: "the difference between an annalist and a historian is, that the mere facts of the first as used by the latter become correlated events, which illumine each other, and get their angles of reflection from many causes external to the naked facts. These causes are the conditions of the time, which gave rise to the facts; the views of the period in which they are studied; the idiosyncracies of the person studying them. Hence no historical statement can be final." Thus Winsor was in one essential way unlike either scientific or literary historians: neither theories of evolutionary development nor of world spirit convinced him to accept historical interpretations as final truths.

Winsor followed his cooperative undertakings with works of his own focusing on the discovery and exploration of America. The first, *Christopher Columbus and How He Received and Imparted the Spirit of Discovery*, was published in 1891. It elicited some hostile criticism because of its somewhat severe estimate of the explorer's career and character. In 1894 *Cartier to Frontenac* appeared; it deals with geographical discovery in North America from 1534 to 1700. The struggle between England and France in North America from 1697 to 1763 is the subject of *The Mississippi Basin*, which was published in 1895. In Winsor's final book, *The Westward Movement*, which appeared in 1897, he traces the development of the later colonial and early national phases of American history (1763-1798).

These volumes display the ripest results of Winsor's studies. Essentially books for the scholar, they are written in a straightforward style with little literary adornment. A contemporary critic found them to contain the "very pith of history." Winsor's interest in cartography played an important part in these works. Though his initial interest in maps was incidental to his historical studies, he became absorbed in their study and eventually emerged as the foremost American cartographer of his day. Cartography enabled him to solve several historical problems which had previously seemed to defy resolution. In 1896 Winsor received a practical tribute to his reputation as an authority on geographical matters when he was asked to testify before the U.S. Arbitration Commission as an expert on the question of the boundary between British Guiana and Venezuela.

Elected president of the American Library Association for the second time in 1897, Winsor led the American delegation to the Second International Conference of Librarians in London. Assuming his role with his customary zeal, he represented the United States with strength and dignity. Following a brief illness upon his return home, Winsor died on 22 October 1897 and was buried in Boston's Mount Auburn Cemetery. The daughter of his marriage to Caroline Barker, and Winsor's only child, had died in 1895.

For the last twenty years of his life, Winsor successfully combined his historical research and publication interests with his duties as Harvard librarian. By the time of his death, the age of the amateur historian in America had drawn to a close. Yet Winsor's *Narrative and Critical History* served as a legacy from these skilled amateurs to the first generation of trained American historians, who were about to produce their own monument to scholarship, the American Nation series.

Bibliography:

W. F. Yust, *A Bibliography of Justin Winsor* (Cambridge: Library of Harvard University, 1902).

Biography:

Joseph A. Boromé, "The Life and Letters of Justin Winsor," Ph.D. dissertation, Columbia University, 1950.

References:

Edward Channing, "Justin Winsor," *American Historical Review*, 3 (January 1898): 197-202;

Introduction to *Justin Winsor: Scholar-Librarian*, edited by Wayne Cutler and Michael H. Harris

(Littleton, Colo.: Libraries Unlimited, 1980),
pp. 13-56;

Horace E. Scudder, "Memoir of Justin Winsor," in
Proceedings of the Massachusetts Historical Society,
second series, 12 (1899), pp. 457-482.

Papers:
Collections of Winsor's papers are at the Massachusetts Historical Society, the Harvard University Library, and the Boston Public Library.

Appendix

Recording the Civil War

Editor's Note

The American Civil War occurred on a vast scale, and no other period of American history is so full of dramatic events, memorable personalities, and crucial issues. The body of literature produced after 1866 by participants in the war is immense. There are hundreds of memoirs in book form by generals, admirals, lesser officers, privates, politicians, and civilians. Accounts of the activities of individual units and other specialized works number many hundreds more. Thousands of participants and observers left published records of their experiences in pamphlets, newspapers, veterans' magazines, and other periodicals—the stuff of memories and controversies for that time and the raw material for historians of later years. And this is to account only for nonfiction, not for the works of fiction writers and poets who drew upon their Civil War experiences. Two of the most significant large-scale publications of Civil War materials during the period 1866-1912 are described in this appendix. Some useful sources of further information about the Civil War literature written by participants are: Allan Nevins, Bell Irvin Wiley, and James I. Robertson, Jr., *Civil War Books: A Critical Bibliography*, 2 volumes (Baton Rouge: Louisiana State University Press, 1967, 1969); Douglas Southall Freeman, *The South to Posterity: An Introduction to the Writing of Confederate History* (New York: Scribners, 1939); Thomas J. Pressly, *Americans Interpret Their Civil War* (Princeton: Princeton University Press, 1954); Otto Eisenschiml, Ralph Newman, and E. B. Long, editors, *The Civil War*, 2 volumes (New York: Grosset & Dunlap, 1956); and Edmund Wilson, *Patriotic Gore: Studies in the Literature of the American Civil War* (New York: Oxford University Press, 1962).

The *Official Records* of the Rebellion

Richard M. McMurry
North Carolina State University

War of the Rebellion: A Compilation of the Official Records of the Union and Confederate Armies, compiled by the United States War Department, 4 series, 70 volumes (Washington, D.C.: Government Printing Office, 1881-1901);

Atlas to Accompany the Official Records of the Union and Confederate Armies, compiled by Calvin D. Cowles (Washington, D.C.: Government Printing Office, 1895);

Official Records of the Union and Confederate Navies in the War of the Rebellion, compiled by the United States Navy Department, 2 series, 31 volumes (Washington, D.C.: Government Printing Office, 1894-1927).

What was to become the greatest of the Federal government's nineteenth-century ventures into the publication of historical documents had its beginning in the frustration brought on by a relatively minor administrative problem. One of the duties required of Major General Henry W. Halleck, general-in-chief of the Federal armies from 1862 to 1864, was to submit to the secretary of war an annual report summarizing the past year's military operations. When Halleck compiled his report covering the period from late 1862 to late 1863, he was forced to omit information about "some of the engagements which our troops have had with the enemy during the past year, as no official accounts or reports of some of them could be found." This difficulty led Halleck to recommend to Secretary Edwin M. Stanton "that all these official documents and reports received since the beginning of the war be collected and published in chronological order, under the direction of the Adjutant General's Department."

Prior to the Civil War the Federal government had published many records of historical value in documents issued by the Congress. The government had also subsidized Peter Force's *American Archives* (1837-1853) and in 1861 began to issue the *Foreign Relations of the United States* series. Six months before Halleck made his recommendation, the United States Army's Surgeon General William A. Hammond began the collection of material for a medical history of the war. The antebellum publications, however, had not been directed toward the compilation of complete official histories; rather they were intended for the government's own use. *The Medical and Surgical History of the War of the Rebellion* (six volumes, 1870-1888) dealt with a very specialized subject and was never completed.

The project that grew from Halleck's suggestion resulted in the publication of vast documentary histories of the Civil War armies and navies that are indispensable sources for the military and naval history of the conflict. The collections are also important sources for studies of most other facets of the war and useful sources for many aspects of mid-nineteenth-century American history.

In January 1864 Henry Wilson of Massachusetts, chairman of the Senate Committee on Military Affairs, introduced a resolution "to provide for the printing of the official reports of the armies of the United States." At the suggestion of John D. Defrees, superintendent of public printing, the proposal was amended to provide for the publication of all significant Federal records pertaining to the Civil War. The documents were to be arranged by their dates, and ten thousand copies were to be printed. The amended resolution was approved by both houses of Congress and, on 19 May 1864, signed by President Abraham Lincoln.

The task of preparing the records for publication was given to Colonel Edward D. Townsend, assistant adjutant general of the army. (The adjutant general's office was the archive of the army and therefore custodian of the documents.) Townsend seems to have taken little interest in the project and to have worked on it just enough to avoid criticism. In the summer of 1865 his office sent eight volumes of collected reports to the public printer. Defrees, observing that the volumes did not meet the broad standards specified by the 1864 resolution, held up publication and conferred with Wilson.

Meanwhile, in the spring of 1865, Union armies had captured masses of Confederate government records, including important files from the Rebels' War, Treasury, and Post Office departments. Halleck ordered that these captured documents be collected and stored.

In May 1866 Wilson, after consultation with Defrees, introduced a resolution rescinding his earlier proposal and calling for a broader publication project that would include Confederate as well as Federal material. The resolution also provided for an editor at an annual salary of $2,500 and required him to develop a new plan for publishing the records.

President Andrew Johnson signed the resolution on 27 July 1866, and former Assistant Secretary of War Peter H. Watson was named editor. Watson, however, never performed any editorial duties, and his appointment expired in 1868. For several years the project was allowed to languish. Some thirty volumes of documents arranged by date had either been completed or were in preparation when the project came to this standstill.

Over the next few years pressure from veterans' organizations led the War Department to make occasional requests for funds to resume work on the project. In 1874 Congress voted an initial $15,000 to meet publication costs of what was by then called "The Official Records of the War of the Rebellion." (Subsequent annual appropriations, beginning in 1879, averaged about $80,000.) By the provisions of the 1874 law the publication was to include "all official documents that can be obtained by the compiler, and that appear to be of any historical value." By the end of 1877 the adjutant general's office had put together forty-seven volumes of documents. The arrangement was still by date of the documents.

The crucial development in the publication's history came in December 1877 when Secretary of War George W. McCrary, unhappy with the slow pace of the project, removed it from the adjutant general's jurisdiction and entrusted it to the Publications Office, War Records, which he put directly under his own control. Captain Robert Nicholson Scott of the 3d Artillery was made chief of the Publications Office. Scott had served as an aide to Halleck, as a professor of military science and art, as a member of an army regulations board, and as military secretary to a congressional committee engaged in reorganizing the army. He was also the author of an analytical digest of United States military law, a study that had attracted favorable attention and was probably responsible for his appointment to direct the work of the Publications Office. All in all, Scott was well suited to the task, and the final publication would be more his work than anyone else's.

Scott quickly decided to drop the cumbersome chronological arrangement of documents and to organize the publication as four series of volumes. The first series would cover the military operations of the war. The volumes in the series would be arranged according to the order in which the events took place, although some overlapping was inevitable. Each volume would bring together the reports and correspondence relating to a particular campaign or military event or to the operations in a particular area or areas during a specified time. Volume 38, for example, contained material on the 1864 Atlanta campaign. Parts 1, 2, and 3 of the volume contained the after-action reports of officers arranged by commands. For example, all reports relating to the Atlanta campaign submitted by officers of the 1st Brigade, 2d Division, Twentieth Corps, Army of the Cumberland, were brought together, regardless of the date of the reports themselves. Parts 4 and 5 of volume 38 contained correspondence. A section comprising the Federal letters and telegrams written during and pertaining to the campaign, arranged chronologically and then by commands, was followed by a section of Confederate correspondence arranged in the same way. The volume also contained "summaries of principal events" during the period of the campaign, tabular reports of strength and casualties, organizational tables, circulars, and extracts from orders. Some contemporary field sketches of fortifications and terrain were also included. Ultimately there would be fifty-three volumes in the first series (volumes 51-53 were used for documents received too late for publication in the volumes in which they belonged). Since many of the volumes contained more than one part, the total number of books in the series was 111.

The first series was to constitute by far the largest part of the publication. The second (eight volumes) was for the correspondence, reports, returns, and other documents relating to the military forces' involvement with prisoners (both military and political). The third (five volumes) was for Federal documents not included in the first two series. This material covered such topics as the mobilization, supply, and transport of Federal troops. The fourth series (three volumes) contained similar documents from the Confederates. Each volume was indexed, and the project concluded with a general index which was, in effect, an index of the indexes.

Once this plan was formally approved by secretary of war Alexander Ramsey in August 1880, work on the project went well. Scott and his successors supervised a mostly civilian clerical force, numbering 123 at its peak in 1893, that collected, copied, sorted, and prepared the documents for publication.

Early in his tenure Scott laid down the basic policies that contributed much to the ultimate success of the project. The sheer bulk of records necessitated the exclusion of many documents. One historian has observed that the American Civil War was the first conflict "to use paper on a massive modern scale." With millions of Federal telegrams on file and a three-story building bulging with captured Confederate records, there was simply too much material to include everything. Documents relating to an individual's service, Scott ruled, could not be accommodated. Such records as muster rolls, arms procurement contracts, by-name casualty lists, and quartermaster requisitions would also be omitted. By such exclusions Scott kept the size of the project within manageable bounds.

Scott also made the crucial decision that only wartime records would be published. Many former officers—especially some who harbored political ambitions—were eager to enhance their reputations by altering documents or by submitting postwar explanations of their actions. Scott, however, would not permit even the postwar correction of factual errors. The reader would therefore have the exact information on which wartime decisions had been based.

The most serious problem that Scott and his colleagues encountered had to do with Confederate material. Rebel military administration during the war had often been slipshod. Many reports had never been made, some had been made on such poor quality paper or written in such poor quality ink that they were all but illegible, and other documents had been lost, scattered, or destroyed in the closing months of the war. To overcome the shortage of Southern material the editors employed several former Confederate officers, such as ex-Brigadier General Marcus J. Wright, to convince their wartime colleagues of the project's fairness toward the South and to urge them to make available to Federal authorities documents in private possession. Other former Rebels were hired to do part of the work of compiling and editing the documents. Much Confederate material was acquired through donation or purchase. Many former Rebels, persuaded by Wright and others, were willing to allow documents in their possession to be copied. Although some of these documents were "unofficial," they were sometimes the only Southern records available, and the editors often decided to include them in order to have as complete a record as possible.

In preparing the documents for publication the editors standardized the abbreviations, the openings and closings of correspondence, and the forms of address. Sometimes they corrected the spelling and grammar. As with any project of such magnitude, there were inevitable mistakes in copying documents and in compiling statistical and organizational tables. Such errors are unfortunate but seldom of great significance. The editors did compile "additions and corrections" for each volume and published them both in the index volume and as a series of leaflets.

The first volume, with the title *War of the Rebellion: A Compilation of the Official Records of the Union and Confederate Armies*, was ready in late 1880 and made its appearance in 1881. Others were published periodically over the next two decades. The last volume (1901) was the general index to the complete set.

Some people urged the publication of a volume or volumes of photographs to accompany the documents. Publication of photographs was found to be prohibitively expensive. It proved feasible, however, to publish maps, and the preparation of an atlas was begun in 1889. As the maps were prepared, they were published in a series of forty paperbound folios from 1891 to 1895. The bound *Atlas to Accompany the Official Records of the Union and Confederate Armies* was published in 1895. Preparation of the maps was carried out under the supervision of Captain Calvin Duvall Cowles of the 23d Infantry.

During the war the armies had often operated without maps or with maps that were, at best, inaccurate. Most of the maps published in the *Atlas* were made after the battles to accompany the official reports of Federal officers. Cowles and his staff often combined maps and made many corrections in an effort to provide more complete and accurate information. While the maps in the *Atlas* are useful, they often are not the crude drawings used by commanders during the war. Many of the maps in the *Atlas* contain serious errors despite the time and effort that went into their production. The *Atlas* also contains engravings and drawings of military equipment, uniforms, and flags.

Over the years changes occurred in the personnel who worked on the *Official Records* and in the bureaucratic structure by which the project was administered. Exhausted and overworked, Scott died in 1887 and was succeeded by Lieutenant Colonel H. M. Lazelle of the 23d Infantry. In 1889

Congress created a three-man Board of Publication, composed of an army officer and two "civilian experts," to oversee preparation of the *Official Records*. In 1898 the Board was dissolved, and the work was put under the supervision of an officer appointed by the secretary of war. Two years later the War Records Office was merged with the War Department's Records and Pension Office. Through all the changes, the volumes continued to appear at more or less regular intervals.

While work on the armies' records was going forward, a similar project got underway for the navies. On 7 July 1884 Congress authorized preparation of the official naval records. The Office of Naval War Records was created, and James R. Soley, librarian of the Navy Department, was named its superintendent. First under Soley's direction, and then under the leadership of others, the project moved ahead, encountering many of the same problems faced by the men who were compiling the records of the armies. In 1894 Congress began to appropriate funds for the publication of the naval records, and the first volume appeared that year. The title was *Official Records of the Union and Confederate Navies in the War of the Rebellion*.

The naval volumes were arranged in three series. The first series (twenty-seven volumes) included reports, orders, and correspondence relating to naval operations. The documents were arranged chronologically by commands. For example, the eighteenth volume includes information on the operations of the West Gulf Blockading Squadron from 21 February to 14 July 1862. The second series (three volumes) covers the construction of naval vessels and statistical data on ships, captured property, and naval prisoners. The third series was intended for material that did not fit into the first and second series. The third series was never published. Some of the material that would have gone into it, especially Confederate diplomatic correspondence, was included in the third volume of series two. Publication of the naval records concluded with an index volume issued in 1927.

The editors of the naval volumes profited from the experiences of those who had worked with the army records. The naval volumes are, therefore, generally better than are those for the armies, as the later army volumes are generally better than the earlier ones. The naval volumes also contain illustrations, maps (some multicolor), and cutaway drawings of ships.

Congress originally provided for the publication of ten thousand copies of each set of official records. Later the number was increased to over twelve thousand. By law each member of Congress was authorized to send a specified number of sets to organizations and individuals in his state or district. The intent was to place the records in libraries, historical societies, and other depositories where they would be readily accessible to individuals. Volumes not so distributed were sold to the public at cost plus ten percent.

Users have both praised and damned the *Official Records*. The publications have been called "the most valuable of all the works relating to the Civil War," "the bible of Civil War history," and "a landmark of achievement in historical publishing." The compilations have also been branded as prejudiced, inaccurate, and incomplete. A true evaluation of their significance lies between the extremes of praise and condemnation—but much closer to the former than to the latter.

There is no evidence of any official intention on the part of government authorities to be anything but fair and impartial in compiling the *Official Records*. It is possible, however, that some individuals who worked on or cooperated with the projects used the opportunity to try to enhance their reputations or to besmirch those of their personal enemies. This possibility is especially strong for the former Confederates who were in position to withhold unfavorable documents or to invent false records. One historian has gone so far as to accuse Confederate General Joseph E. Johnston of altering what was supposed to be an 1864 journal of operations kept by a staff officer so that its contents would reflect favorably upon himself.

Other historians have faulted the editors for putting too great an emphasis on combat operations to the neglect of logistics and other subjects. In fact, the documents in the *Official Records*, especially the correspondence sections, are full of information on most of these subjects as they related to the individual field armies and naval commands. Most of the more general information, however, has to be traced through the voluminous unpublished records of the quartermaster general, adjutant general, surgeon general, bureau of navigation, and other officials and organizations. Many of these documents are now in the National Archives.

The editors of the army volumes have also been criticized for omitting information on many engagements and for confusing some of the information they did include. By one count there is no information in the army *Official Records* on some forty percent of the land battles. Almost all of these omissions, however, were minor engagements. Many of the lesser battles listed in the "Summary of Events" sections are erroneously identified. In many cases, however, there were no official reports of the lesser engagements owing to casualties among commanding officers and to the necessity of pressing operations against the enemy. It is unfair to blame the editors for not publishing reports that were not submitted.

The editors have been justly faulted for uncritically accepting some information from unreliable secondhand sources. An 1867 "battle list" was used to compile the "Summary of Events" sections, and many errors from that list were incorporated into the army *Official Records*. For example, the editors listed three engagements as having occurred on 5 July 1863 as the Confederate army was retreating from Gettysburg. One supposedly took place at Cunningham's Cross Roads, Pennsylvania; one at Greencastle, Pennsylvania; and the other at Mercersburg, Pennsylvania. In fact, there was only one clash, and it took place at Cunningham's Cross Roads, Maryland. Most such errors seem to have resulted from the employment of poorly trained clerks.

Some researchers have been critical of the way in which the editors arranged the *Official Records*, especially those of the armies. No one, however, has proposed a better organization. In truth, Scott's system was far superior to the earlier plans for publishing the documents in chronological order without regard to their subject matter. Like all such arrangements, the system used in the *Official Records* requires some study before the researcher can become accustomed to it. Once learned, however, the system is simple, logical, and at least as useful as any other arrangement that could have been devised.

Most of the problems that have arisen in using the *Official Records* have stemmed from the nature of the documents and from the laziness of the users. Many historians have not bothered to learn basic military organization and terminology. Many others have failed to realize that official reports are not necessarily accurate reports.

When an officer composed his official report—often months after the events on which he was reporting—he was aware that he was writing for posterity. This fact, combined with hindsight, the natural human reluctance to admit mistakes, and the tendency to "remember" events that did not happen, make many reports less than trustworthy. One historian has observed that the after-action reports "more often than not become ra-

tionales—so much so that in the case of some battles the victorious side is difficult to discern from the *Official Records* alone."

The trustworthiness and usefulness of official reports were sometimes affected by other factors. Both governments often published the reports of their officers in the newspapers where the documents would be read by generals on the other side. This fact led Confederate General Thomas J. "Stonewall" Jackson to edit out of his reports information on why he had made certain decisions. Jackson did this, he said, because he did not want the Federals to "learn . . . [my] mode of doing" and thereby gain an insight into his character that would be of value in anticipating his decisions in future campaigns.

Other reports are not completely trustworthy for other reasons. There is strong evidence that reports by Rebel generals John C. Pemberton (for the Vicksburg Campaign of 1863) and John Bell Hood (for the Georgia Campaign of 1864) were deliberately altered at the request of government officials to embarrass General Joseph E. Johnston, a leading critic of the government. Sometimes, as was the case with Union General Philip H. Sheridan's criticisms of General Gouverneur K. Warren, an officer used his official report to heap unjustified blame upon a colleague with whom he had personal or professional differences. In Warren's case, it took almost fifteen years before a court of inquiry exonerated him from the criticisms expressed in Sheridan's official report of the 1865 battle of Five Forks.

The virtues of the *Official Records* far outweigh the faults. The compilations made readily available most of the basic raw material needed to study almost any military campaign or naval operation of the war. The *Atlas* and the other maps and sketches provide the only mid-nineteenth-century maps for many areas of the United States. Although the indexes contain mainly the names of individuals, commands, ships, and battles, the documents themselves are full of the raw material for social, cultural, diplomatic, medical, technological, and even sports history. Federal General John M. Corse once issued an order for his men to build gymnasiums where they could exercise to "add strength to the body, activity to the limbs, and grace to the motion" and thereby counteract "the debasing influences of camp vices." Because the editors took so broad a view of their task, they included much information on matters that were only peripherally related to the North-South struggle. There are, for example, several volumes containing records dealing with Indian skirmishes and other events in the Western territories.

The men who compiled and edited the *Official Records* were not professional historians. Indeed, there were few such professionals in the country until after the projects were well underway. Rather, the men who planned and supervised the *Official Records* were professional military and naval men. The volumes they produced were intended for use by the writers of the narrative histories that were popular at the time and for veterans who wanted to read about the exploits of their units and the battles in which they had fought. There were few precedents to guide the editors, and it is little wonder that they produced a work that does not measure up to the exacting editorial standards of the late twentieth century.

For all the drawbacks, the *Official Records* remain essential. If the modern historian bears in mind the nature of the documents, especially the after-action reports and the questionable nature of some of the Confederate material, he can safely use the *Official Records* as the starting point for research into Civil War topics. Only in rare cases when the exact wording of a document or the exact strength/casualty figures are important is it necessary to go beyond a document published in the *Official Records* to the original manuscript.It should be noted, however, that some of the original documents contain information that does not appear in the published *Records*—a marginal notation of the time a dispatch was received, for example.

The *Official Records*, as one distinguished historian has noted, are "not perfect . . . [but they are] a monumental achievement of enduring value, a work that is central to all serious study of the war." No scholar concerned with the history of the nation's most important conflict can afford to neglect them.

References:

Alan Conrad Aimone, "The Official Records of the Civil War: A Researcher's Guide," *United States Military Academy Library Bulletin*, no. 11A (1977);

Stetson Conn, *Historical Work in the United States Army, 1862-1954* (Washington, D.C.: United States Army Center of Military History, 1980);

Dallas Irvine, comp., *Military Operations of the Civil War: A Guide-Index to the Official Records of the Union and Confederate Armies, 1861-1865*, 5 volumes (Washington, D.C.: Government Printing Office, 1968-1980);

Irvine, "Rootstock of Error," *Prologue: The Journal of the National Archives*, 2 (Spring 1970): 10-14;

Harold E. Mahan, "The Arsenal of History: The Official Records of the War of the Rebellion," *Civil War History*, 29 (March 1983): 5-27;

Richard M. McMurry, "The Mackall Journal and Its Antecedents," *Civil War History*, 20 (December 1974), 311-328.

Battles and Leaders of the Civil War

Stephen Davis and J. Tracy Power

Battles and Leaders of the Civil War, Being for the Most Part Contributions by Union and Confederate Officers. Based upon "The Century War Series." Edited by Robert Underwood Johnson and Clarence Clough Buel, of the Editorial Staff of "The Century Magazine," 4 volumes (New York: Century, 1888).

One of the most prominent titles in Civil War historiography, *Battles and Leaders of the Civil War,* was originally published as a series of articles in *Century* magazine from November 1884 to November 1887. Most of the important Union and Confederate generals then living contributed to the series. The editors insured both accuracy and readability of the writing; fine illustrations accompanied the articles and increased their appeal. The public responded so enthusiastically that the Battles and Leaders series was expanded to a four-volume work, which appeared in 1888. The People's Pictorial Edition, with each page featuring two or three illustrations, was published in 1894. Three subsequent editions have appeared, two in 1956 and one, titled *The Century War Book,* in 1978. As the most comprehensive single collection of writings by leading participants in the Civil War, *Battles and Leaders* is both extremely valuable to historians and highly entertaining to general readers. Few historiographical landmarks have proven so versatile.

The series was conceived by Clarence Clough Buel, assistant editor for *Century* magazine. In early 1883 Buel thought of pairing an article on John Brown's raid at Harpers Ferry, written by a Virginian, with a "Comment by a Radical Abolitionist." The pieces, published that June, aroused considerable interest. Soon Buel outlined a more ambitious project using the same format: a series of eight or ten articles on decisive battles of the Civil War, written by the generals who had commanded the opposing armies. Buel proposed his idea to the associate editor, Robert Underwood Johnson. Both Johnson and the *Century* editor-in-chief, Richard Watson Gilder, liked the plan. Gilder put Johnson in charge of it, with Buel assisting.

The most important task, the lining up of contributors, was begun in the spring of 1884. In the early days of "general catching" (Gilder's phrase), the editors met with setbacks. Ulysses S. Grant, the first officer to be contacted, declined to write because his biographer, Adam Badeau, had said it all; William T. Sherman said the proposed series would fail; P. G. T. Beauregard said he was too busy. Some officers refused because they would have to criticize their dead comrades; others held back because of the living (Johnson termed this dilemma "Scylla and Charybdis"). But the editors worked their prospects energetically. They persuaded Beauregard by using as intermediary his friend George Washington Cable, whose fiction Gilder had published. Grant, attracted by the editors' promise of $500 per article, consented after his banking house had failed, and he in turn helped convince Sherman to write an essay. Eventually Joseph E. Johnston, David D. Porter, James Longstreet, and many other important military leaders agreed to help.

Despite their lustrous array of contributors, the editors regretted the refusal of some notables to cooperate. Johnson could not persuade generals Winfield S. Hancock, Nathaniel P. Banks, Simon B. Buckner, or Benjamin F. Butler to participate in the series. Philip H. Sheridan wanted to save his comments for a book; Jubal A. Early claimed that he opposed writing history for money. Neither Robert E. Lee's son, George Washington Custis Lee, nor Lee's chief-of-staff, Colonel Charles Marshall, could be induced to contribute a piece on the great Virginian.

With these exceptions, though, most of the war's major figures participated, and the series progressed. From the start, the editors emphasized an interesting, colorful format. Johnson admonished his contributors to avoid the style of official reports and tell of their battles as they would in an after-dinner chat. Plentiful illustrations, prepared by staff artists, would accompany the articles. To balance the generals' factual narratives, lighter pieces were also commissioned, such as reminiscences by private soldiers and civilians. Gilder himself demanded this miscellany, instructing Johnson in July

1884 that "it is particularly necessary that we should have interest and variety outside of our war material" and reminding him how Ralph Waldo Emerson had termed the details of battle "tedious and revolting."

With plans set, the editors chose a title for the series. After considering "Men and Events," Buel proposed "Leaders and Battles." Gilder liked the dramatic emphasis on fighting, as opposed to political events during the war, and approved Buel's suggestion in August 1884. By the time the war series was announced in the October issue of *Century*, the title had become *Battles and Leaders of the Civil War*.

The editors determined that factual accuracy would be an important aspect of the series. They checked manuscripts against the *Official Records*, which the government had begun to publish in 1881. Colonel Robert N. Scott, director of the War Records Office in Washington, helped by furnishing advance proofs for unpublished volumes of the *OR*. Scott's assistants also aided in verifying details, as did other officers and veterans whom Johnson paid with complimentary subscriptions to *Century*. Buel worked on maps. The contributors helped with pictorial material. Confederate General Joseph E. Johnston labored painstakingly on a map of the battle at Seven Pines; Union Admiral David D. Porter examined sketches of the naval fight below New Orleans and vouched for their accuracy.

One of the strongest features of the *Battles and Leaders* series was artwork. To accompany the articles, Alexander W. Drake, art superintendent for *Century*, oversaw the collection of more than 1500 combat sketches, maps, portraits, and battlefield scenes. Eyewitness drawings by wartime artists such as Theodore Davis, Edwin Forbes, Frank Schell, and Alfred and William Waud were a major source of material. Photographs were reproduced as well, including images from Mathew Brady's and Alexander Gardner's collections. Drake himself toured the major battlefields to photograph them as they appeared nearly twenty years after the war. But most of the pictorial material came from the staff artists who worked for *Century* and the other illustrated magazines of the day. Harry Fenn, Edwin J. Meeker, Walton Taber, and Allen C. Redwood (himself a Confederate veteran) were particularly adept at rendering fine illustrations from wartime photographs, lithographs, or sketches.

The work took several years, as *Battles and Leaders* continued to grow in the course of its magazine publication. Arranging their material in chronological order, the editors began the series in the *Century* of November 1884 with Beauregard's piece on First Manassas. Thereafter each issue carried at least one or two articles by famous officers. Public response was immediately favorable. Circulation of the magazine rose dramatically; the November issue sold "beyond anything hitherto known to us," Gilder proudly noted. Letters from readers, commenting on various topics in the series, so overwhelmed the editors that they created a special column, "Memoranda of the Civil War," to print some of them. Unsolicited manuscripts and illustrations also poured in, and generals heretofore reluctant to contribute now readily agreed. In April 1885 Johnson and Buel acknowledged this impressive reaction. "We had anticipated a cordial interest," they wrote, "but we were hardly prepared for the almost unbroken response of welcome which has greeted the enterprise, whether in the generous notice of the press, or in the large number of encouraging and helpful letters that have come to us from all sections of the country, or, last and most practical of all, in the extraordinary increase of the circulation of the magazine."

On the strength of this good showing, *Battles and Leaders of the Civil War*, which had originally been forecast to run for a year, was extended. But after November 1885—when circulation figures for *Century* peaked at 225,000, up from 127,000 just a year before—the editors began to sense a cooling of readers' interest. Johnson had to decide when to terminate the series. The unexpected abundance of manuscripts resulted in a hefty pile of unpublished work even after the final piece in *Battles and Leaders* appeared in November 1887. To use the remaining materials and to capitalize on the success of the magazine series, Johnson and Buel planned an elaborate four-volume publication which would serve as a complete documentary history of the war.

Preparations for the work they called "the War book" started even while *Battles and Leaders of the Civil War* ran in the magazine. The ninety-nine feature articles in the series provided the basis. "Memoranda of the Civil War" added several short, controversial pieces. A handful of articles, especially the lighter ones, were deleted for the bound volumes. In order to cover events not treated originally, Johnson and Buel collected much additional material. Officers' writings in memoirs or in other magazines were republished to supply over two dozen pieces. Nearly seventy more entries, mostly lists of statistics on the opposing forces, were obtained from the *Official Records*. In some cases the editors composed their own accounts of notable actions, such as the Fort Pillow Massacre. They also tried to enlist new contributors. Jefferson Davis was asked to write a reply to Beauregard's and Joseph E. Johnston's criticisms of him, but the ex-president declined when Johnson and Buel refused to grant him total freedom from editorial control.

From the point of view of literary history, the four-volume *Battles and Leaders of the Civil War* is notable as the preeminent anthology of narratives written by the principal military leaders of both sides. When Daniel Harvey Hill wrote of the battle of Malvern Hill, "it was not war—it was murder," that phrase was not a historian's comment but the recollection of a general who commanded five Confederate brigades and watched their futile advance. The authors of *Battle and Leaders*, with few exceptions, were not simply witnesses to the combat they described; in many instances they made battlefield decisions which won, lost, or changed the course of those battles. Though many generals had already written or would write their memoirs, others, such as Ambrose E. Burnside, John Pope, Daniel Harvey Hill, and Evander M. Law, never produced such works. Their contributions to the *Battles and Leaders* were their major literary efforts.

One feature of the series and of the subsequent volumes, more important to contemporaries than to later scholars, was that the pieces provided a forum for numerous controversies between and among officers who had served together during the war. In many instances the battles fought on paper among supposed partisans were as bitter as the earlier ones on the field had been. Generals who would cheerfully greet former enemies as "the gallant foe" despised former comrades and refused to appear with them in public. Confederate leaders were particularly prominent in such literary debates, for many of them were eager to take credit for Southern successes and place the blame for Southern defeats, and indeed the loss of the war, on others' shoulders. Union leaders squabbled less, and they were not as acrimonious with their disputes. Johnson and Buel understood the value of controversy to their project and in some cases cultivated it. Spectacular debates created widespread interest in the new books. Though many of the disputes aired in *Battles and Leaders of the Civil War* are tedious and trivial, several long articles and shorter pieces on Shiloh and Gettysburg, the most controversial battles in the western and eastern theaters of the war, are genuinely interesting and have some lasting merit.

The articles on Shiloh, for both sides, were written by or on behalf of the most prominent officers in command on the field. Grant and Don Carlos Buell argued over whether the Federals were surprised by the Confederate attack on the first day and whether Buell's reinforcements had saved Grant's army from disaster. Grant's article as originally submitted was simply a restatement of his official report. Johnson persuaded the general to write more informally and to address some of the criticisms against him; the rewritten article appeared a few months before Grant's death.

On the Confederate side the articles were prepared on behalf of rather than by the leaders themselves and had appeared elsewhere. William P. Johnston's article on his father, Albert Sidney Johnston, was excerpted from his 1878 biography. Beauregard commissioned Albert Roman, with whom he had worked on the *Military Operations of General Beauregard* (1884), to ghostwrite a reply to Johnston which was first published in the *North American Review.* Johnston and Beauregard/Roman concerned themselves with the successful attack on the first day under Albert Sidney Johnston and with the reasons for the subsequent defeat of the Southerners, commanded by Beauregard after Johnston's death at the height of the battle.

Nearly two hundred pages of the third volume of *Battles and Leaders of the Civil War* is devoted to Gettysburg, which more received extensive coverage than any other battle or campaign; by the 1880s it had already captured the imagination of the public to a degree unmatched by any other battle in American history. An outstanding account of the encounter, which is judicious and thorough, is the *Battles and Leaders* overview by Henry J. Hunt, Federal artillery commander at Gettysburg, of each of the campaign's three days. Subjects covered in detail range from the Confederate cavalry's role to the placement of the 146th New York Regiment at Little Round Top, from the artillery duel preceding Pickett's Charge to a Federal prisoner's march to Virginia.

Some of the most controversial writing to appear in the series was in James Longstreet's two articles on Gettysburg. Admirers of Lee, eager to place the blame for Gettysburg elsewhere, attacked Longstreet. His postwar conversion to the Republicans and his criticism of Lee's generalship antagonized many in the South. Pieces by Longstreet on the Seven Days, Second Bull Run, Antietam, and Fredericksburg had already appeared in *Century* and had been sharply criticized by his foes. "Lee's Invasion of Pennsylvania" and "Lee's Right Wing at Gettysburg" were more restrained than Longstreet's earlier articles and did not attempt to answer his critics at length. These pieces did, however, criticize Lee for rejecting Longstreet's tactical proposals for the campaign and on the battlefield. Col. William Allan, one of Longstreet's critics, immediately wrote "A Reply to General Longstreet," which restated old charges that Longstreet was slow at attack the Federals on the second day at Gettysburg and that his further reluctance to support Pickett's Charge insured the bloody repulse of that assault.

There were other controversies surrounding Gettysburg, on both sides. George G. Meade was defended against previous charges of slowness in pursuing Lee after the battle by Hunt and by others. *Battles and Leaders* republished a letter written by Meade in 1870 which charged that Daniel E. Sickles, by placing his corps in an exposed position on the second day of the battle, had endangered the Federal army. Johnson and Buel gave Sickles the opportunity to respond, and he did so energetically, charging that Meade was surprised by a Confederate attack and that Sickles's action had saved the army, the battle, and the Union. Confederate partisan John S. Mosby, defending J. E. B. Stuart's actions during the campaign, provoked a reply from Beverley H. Robertson denying that Robertson had disobeyed orders.

Many of the best articles in *Battles and Leaders* were neither controversial nor written by the famous generals. Such vignettes as W. T. Robins's "Stuart's Ride Around McClellan" and Daniel Oakey's "Marching Through Georgia and the Carolinas" are examples of short and lively pieces which might be overlooked in favor of those by more prominent authors. Contributions on relatively little-known actions, such as Roanoke Island, Valverde, Chickasaw Bluffs, and Olustee, also add value. Though the overall quality of the articles varies greatly, all of them are of some interest and several of them are essential.

In the end, 226 writers contributed almost 400 articles to form the four volumes of *Battles and*

Leaders of the Civil War. Like contributions to the magazine, the writings were carefully edited and accompanied by eye-catching pictures. The books sold well, too—some 75,000 sets were purchased before publication of the pictorial edition in 1894.

Battles and Leaders of the Civil War—the magazine series, the books, and their subsequent editions—can be judged a remarkable enterprise in several ways. The pictorial accompaniment was exceptionally rich, reflecting both Richard Watson Gilder's demand for fine artwork and the talents of some gifted postwar illustrators. Especially gratifying to the editors was the astounding commercial success of *Battles and Leaders*. Recognized early by Gilder as "a flank march on our rivals," the magazine series nearly doubled the circulation of *Century*, allowing it to surpass *Harper's*, the top-selling magazine in the United States. The whole project netted, in Johnson's estimation, a million dollars for the Century Company. But as the largest and most scrupulously edited compilation of war-related articles by major military figures of the Civil War, the greatest contribution of *Battles and Leaders of the Civil War* has been as an indispensable source of information, for historians and general readers alike.

References:

Stephen Davis, " 'A Matter of Sensational Interest': The *Century* 'Battles and Leaders' Series," *Civil War History*, 27 (December 1981): 338-349;

Robert Underwood Johnson, *Remembered Yesterdays* (Boston: Little, Brown, 1923);

Stephen W. Sears, ed., *The American Heritage Century Collection of Civil War Art* (New York: American Heritage, 1974);

L. Frank Tooker, *The Joys and Tribulations of an Editor* (New York: Century, 1923).

Papers:

Robert Underwood Johnson Papers, New York Public Library.

Supplementary Reading List

Bassett, John Spencer. *The Middle Group of American Historians.* New York: Macmillan, 1917.

Bellot, Hugh Hale. *American History and American Historians.* Norman: University of Oklahoma Press, 1952.

Bloch, Marc. *The Historian's Craft.* New York: Vintage, 1964.

Butterfield, Herbert. *Man on His Past. The Study of the History of Historical Scholarship.* Boston: Beacon, 1960.

Butterfield. *The Whig Interpretation of History.* London: Bell, 1931.

Carr, E. H. *What is History?* New York: Knopf, 1962.

Collingwood, R. G. *The Idea of History.* Oxford: Clarendon Press, 1946.

Cunliffe, Marcus, and Robin W. Winks, eds. *Pastmasters. Some Essays on American Historians.* New York: Harper & Row, 1969.

Curti, Merle. *The Growth of American Thought.* New York & London: Harper, 1943; revised, 1951, 1964.

Daniels, Robert V. *Studying History. How and Why.* Englewood Cliffs, N.J.: Prentice-Hall, 1966.

Davis, Allen F., and Harold D. Woodman, eds. *Conflict or Consensus in American History?* Boston: D.C. Heath, 1966.

Donnan, Elizabeth, and Leo F. Stock, eds. *An Historian's World: Selections from Correspondence of John Franklin Jameson.* Philadelphia: American Philosophical Society, 1956.

Elton, G. R. *The Practice of History.* New York: Crowell, 1968.

François, Michel, Boyd C. Shafer, and others. *Historical Study in the West.* New York: Appleton-Century-Crofts, 1968.

Freeman, Edward A. *The Methods of Historical Study.* London: Macmillan, 1886.

Garraty, John A. *The Nature of Biography.* New York: Knopf, 1957.

Grob, Gerald N., and George A. Billias. *Interpretations of American History: Patterns and Perspectives.* New York: Free Press, 1967.

Handlin, Oscar, and others, eds. *Harvard Guide to American History.* Cambridge, Mass.: Belknap Press, 1954, and later editions.

Hays, Samuel P. *The Response to Industrialism: 1885-1914.* Chicago: University of Chicago Press, 1957.

Higham, John. *History: Professional Scholarship in America.* New York: Harper & Row, 1973.

Holt, W. Stull, ed. *Historical Scholarship in the United States, 1876-1901: As Revealed in the Correspondence of Herbert B. Adams.* Baltimore: Johns Hopkins Press, 1938.

Hutchinson, William T., ed. *The Marcus W. Jernegan Essays in American Historiography*. Chicago: University of Chicago Press, 1937.

Iggers, George G. "The Image of Ranke in American and German Historical Thought." *History and Theory*, 2 (1962): 17-40.

Jameson, J. Franklin. *The History of Historical Writing in America*. Boston & New York: Houghton Mifflin, 1891.

Kraus, Michael. *The Writing of American History*. Norman: University of Oklahoma Press, 1953.

Loewenberg, Bert James. *American History in American Thought: Christopher Columbus to Henry Adams*. New York: Simon & Schuster, 1972.

Lukacs, John. *Historical Consciousness, or the Remembered Past*. New York: Harper & Row, 1968; republished, New York: Schocken Books, 1985.

Marwick, Arthur. *The Nature of History*. New York: Knopf, 1971.

Morison, Samuel Eliot. *Vistas of History*. New York: Knopf, 1964.

Nevins, Allan. *The Gateway to History*. Boston: D. C. Heath, 1938.

Nichols, Roy F. *The Historical Study of Anglo-American Democracy*. Cambridge: Cambridge University Press, 1949.

Noble, David W. *Historians Against History*. Minneapolis: University of Minnesota Press, 1965.

Odum, Howard W., ed. *American Masters of Social Science*. New York: Holt, 1927.

O'Neill, Edward H. *A History of American Biography, 1800-1935*. Philadelphia: University of Pennsylvania Press, 1935.

Perkins, Dexter, and others. *The Education of Historians in the United States*. New York: McGraw-Hill, 1962.

Robinson, James Harvey. *The New History: Essays Illustrating the Modern Historical Outlook*. New York: Macmillan, 1912.

Saveth, Edward N., ed. *American History and the Social Sciences*. New York: Free Press of Glencoe, 1964.

Schlesinger, Arthur M. *New Viewpoints in American History*. New York: Macmillan, 1922.

Skotheim, Robert Allen. *American Intellectual Histories and Historians*. Princeton: Princeton University Press, 1966.

Social Science Research Council Committee on Historiography. *Theory and Practice in Historical Study: A Report of the Committee on Historiography*. New York: Social Science Research Council, 1946.

Stephenson, Wendell Holmes. *Southern History in the Making: Pioneer Historians of the South*. Baton Rouge: Louisiana State University Press, 1964.

Stern, Fritz. *The Varieties of History, From Voltaire to the Present.* New York: Meridian, 1956.

Stone, Lawrence. *The Past and the Present.* Boston & London: Routledge & Kegan Paul, 1981.

Strayer, Joseph R., ed. *The Interpretation of History.* Princeton: Princeton University Press, 1943.

Szasz, Ferenc M. "The Many Meanings of History." *History Teacher,* 7 (August 1974): 552-563; 8 (November 1974): 54-63, 208-227.

Thomson, David. *The Aims of History: Values of the Historical Attitude.* London: Thames & Hudson, 1969.

Trent, William P. and others, eds. *The Cambridge History of American Literature.* 4 vols. New York: Putnam's, 1917-1921, and later editions.

Van Tassel, David D. *Recording America's Past: An Interpretation of the Development of Historical Studies in America, 1607-1884.* Chicago: University of Chicago Press, 1960.

Vitzthum, Richard C. *The American Compromise: Theme and Method in the Histories of Bancroft, Parkman, and Adams.* Norman: University of Oklahoma Press, 1974.

Weisberger, Bernard A. *The New Industrial Society, 1848-1900.* New York: Wiley, 1969.

White, Morton. *Foundations of Historical Knowledge.* New York: Harper & Row, 1965.

Wiebe, Robert H. *The Search for Order, 1877-1920.* New York: Hill & Wang, 1967.

Wish, Harvey. *The American Historian: A Social-Intellectual History of the Writing of the American Past.* New York: Oxford University Press, 1960.

Contributors

Murray Arndt...*University of North Carolina at Greensboro*
Barry W. Bienstock ....*Maplewood, New Jersey*
John Braeman...*University of Nebraska at Lincoln*
Peter A. Coclanis..*University of North Carolina at Chapel Hill*
J. W. Cooke ....*Tennessee State University*
Raymond J. Cunningham ....*Fordham University*
Stephen Davis...*Atlanta, Georgia*
Joseph G. Dawson III ....*Texas A&M University*
Gordon B. Dodds...*Portland State University*
Charles J. Fleener..*Saint Louis University*
Steven P. Gietschier............................*South Carolina Department of Archives and History*
Daniel R. Gilbert ....*Moravian College*
E. Stanly Godbold, Jr. ....*Mississippi State University*
Donald E. Green ....*Central Oklahoma State University*
Damon D. Hickey.. *Guilford College*
E. Christian Kopff...*University of Colorado*
David Alan Lincove.. *Ohio State University*
William A. Link...............................*University of North Carolina at Greensboro*
Robert McColley ....*University of Illinois at Urbana-Champaign*
Gary W. McDonogh ....*New College of the University of South Florida*
Linda O. McMurry...*North Carolina State University*
Richard M. McMurry..*North Carolina State University*
John C. Meleney.. *University of South Carolina*
Alexander Moore .... *University of South Carolina*
William J. Murnane...*University of Chicago*
Mark E. Neely, Jr. .... *Louis A. Warren Lincoln Library and Museum*
Michael O'Brien .... *University of Arkansas*
Robert B. Patterson... *University of South Carolina*
J. Tracy Power .... *Columbia, South Carolina*
John C. Roberson .... *University of South Carolina*
Robert Seager II.. *University of Kentucky*
L. Moody Simms, Jr. ....*Illinois State University*
Michael E. Stevens............................*South Carolina Department of Archives and History*
Marcia G. Synnott .... *University of South Carolina*
Mary E. Tomkins .... *Michigan State University*
Sally N. Vaughn .... *University of Houston*
Robert M. Weir .... *University of South Carolina*
William C. Widenor .... *University of Illinois at Urbana-Champaign*
Clyde N. Wilson .... *University of South Carolina*
John J. Winberry.. *University of South Carolina*

Cumulative Index

Dictionary of Literary Biography, Volumes 1-47
Dictionary of Literary Biography Yearbook, 1980-1984
Dictionary of Literary Biography Documentary Series, Volumes 1-4

Cumulative Index

DLB before number: *Dictionary of Literary Biography*, Volumes 1-47
Y before number: *Dictionary of Literary Biography Yearbook*, 1980-1984
DS before number: *Dictionary of Literary Biography Documentary Series*, Volumes 1-4

A

B

D

E

G

I

J

K

L

M

N

O

U

V

Y

Z